1/A	SUGAR IN THE WATER	
1/B	THE ARRIVAL OF THE QUESTION	
1/C	A SINGLE ENTITY OF TRUTH	
1/D	WHAT TO DO NOW?	
2	THE WAY AHEAD IS IN HARMONY	27
3	WHO ARE "YOU"?	38
4	WHERE IS HEAVEN OR HELL	40
5	WHAT IS ENLIGHTENMENT?	44
6	HOW THE CREATION PURSUES GODS HARMONY OR NATURES HARMONY	59
7	FALSE BELIEF SYSTEMS	69
8	ALL IS UNDER THE LAW OF HARMONY	73
9	THE FREEDOM OF CHOICE IS YOURS	79
10	THE NEED FOR ENLIGHTENMENT	84
11	THE PURPOSE OF THE SOUL THAT CANNOT DIE	90
12	EARTHS HARMONY IS ALSO PEOPLES RESPONSIBILITY	94
13	THE HARMONISING SCIENTIFIC TRUTH	103
14	THE CHOICE IS YOURS TO LIVE IN HEAVEN OR TO LIVE IN HELL	108
15	HEAVEN COMES BEFORE HELL	113
16	THE WAY TO HEAVEN THAT EXISTS ON EARTH	125
17	THE UNITY OF THE CREATION	129
18	THE UNIFIED BELIEF SYSTEM	133
19	THE DENIAL OF GODS OR NATURES "PRESENT"	141
20	THE THREE THAT RESTS IN ONE	145
21	THE FIVE SENSES CANNOT BE YOU	149
22	ALL PEOPLE CAN ACHIEVE ENLIGHTENMENT	155
23	THE PAST AND THE FUTURE DO NOT EXIST	160
24	THE SINGLE SCIENTIFIC TRUTH OF THE SOUL	162
25	WHY ONLY PEOPLE HAVE CHOICE	171
26	GOD CANNOT PUNISH PEOPLE	174
27	THE PRINCIPLES OF THE LIVING WORD	177
28	THE GOD WITHIN AND THE GOD WITHOUT	180
29	FORGETTING IS OUR WORST ENEMY	187

30	THE REALITY BETWEEN THE SOUL AND GODS"PRESENT"?	192
31	THE FIVE SENSES ARE NOT YOU	200
32	THE MIND IS AN INSTRUMENT FOR YOUR USE	211
33	GENETIC MEMORIES	220
34	HOW NOTHING CONTROLS EVERYTHING	220
35	THE SOUL WITHIN	223
36	THE SIMPLE PSYCHOLOGY OF WHO WE THINK WE ARE	231
37	WHO WE REALLY ARE	237
38	THE CHOICE OF RELIGION IS YOURS	246
39	LIVING IN HELL	247
40	LIVING IN HEAVEN	253
41	THE TRUE WAY OF LIFE	258
42	LIFE OF THE SOUL THAT NEVER ENDS	264
43	PARABLE TO RELEASE THE SOUL	268
44	THE PURPOSE OF A SOUL THAT CANNOT DIE	274
45	WHAT IS SELF REALISATION?	284
46	WE ARE NOT THE 5 SENSES - for the young	290
47	PEOPLES PURPOSE	300
48	HOW TO AVOID HELL	309
49	THE MODERNISED TRUTH SPOKEN BY OUR SCIENTIST	319
50	BARRIERS TO THE KINGDOM OF HEAVEN	331
51	"ENLIGHTENMENT"-THE TARGET OF ALL THE RELIGIONS	343
52	GOD OR NATURE DOES NOT PUNISH PEOPLE	350
53	THE TRUE BELIEF OF CHRISTIAN AND ISLAM TEACHINGS	359
54	THE MUSLIM CREEDS THAT TARGET"ENLIGHTENMENT"	365
55	THE CHRISTIAN CREEDS THAT TARGET "ENLIGHTENMENT"	379
56	THE STRANGE UNRELIGIOUS WARS BETWEEN MANY CREEDS	391
57	THE VARIATION OF CREEDS	400
58	THE TRUTH ABOUT THE BROTHERHOOD OF ALL RELIGIONS	406
59	GOD'S WAY OF WORSHIP IS NOT THIS WAY	418
60	PEOPLES WAY TO A SUITABLE RELIGION	426
61	THE WAY TO THE EXPERIENCING OF HEAVEN UPON THIS EARTH	435

62	FINDING"ENLIGHTENMENT" WHICH IS OUR HEAVEN UPON THIS EARTH	447
63	THE FIRST TWO-MINUTE STEP TOWARDS A LIFE LIVED IN HEAVEN	458
64	PEOPLE'S CONSCIOUSNESS THAT EMPOWERS PEOPLES WILLPOWER	470
65	YES! YOU HAVE THE ABILITY TO CHOOSE	481
66	THE WAY TO LIVE IN HEAVEN AND NOT HELL	489
67	HOW TO KNOW WHAT IS YOU	499
68	ONLY LIVES LIVED IN THE"PRESENT TIME" CAN ACHIEVE ENLIGHTENMENT	507
69	HOW PATIENT MEDITATION FREES THE SOULS	515
70	THE WAY TO MEDITATE INTO GODS KINGDOM UPON THIS EARTH	521
71	THE WAY AHEAD VIA"PATIENT MEDIATION"	533
72	HOW TO ACHIEVE"ENLIGHTENMENT"	539
73	THE CLOUDS OF UNKNOWING	551
74	THE WAY TO GODS WORLD OR THE WORLD OF NATURE FOR THE NON-BELIEVER	563
75	THE TARGET OF ALL RELIGIONS AND ALL PHILOSOPHIES	576
76	THE KINGDOM OF GOD OR NATURE FOR THE NON-BELIEVER - IS WITHIN YOU	581
77	THE ONLY CHILD OF GOD OR OF NATURE FOR THE NON-BELIEVER	584
78	REAL LOVE SEARCHES FOR REASON	587
79	THE MODERN INTERPRETATION OF GODS WORDS SPOKEN THROUGH JESUS	595
80	FACTUAL WORDS OF GOD SPOKEN THROUGH THE PROPHET MOHAMMED	606
	ABOUT THE AUTHOR	613

1/A SUGAR IN THE WATER

THE AUTHOR

"The Book" is a narrative historically emanating from Russia's Far Eastern Siberia. It is dedicated to Nastya Nelzina of Birobidzhan who asked me the question, "Do you believe in God for we have always been told to believe in nothing?" This blunt question was being asked of me after my economic presentation and which I received on my September 1999 journey to Russia. Since as an individual I have never before been called upon to "officially" speak about religion in Russia, although it was one of the main reasons why I agreed to go to Russia, so the question took me by surprise for it seemed to be coming from an awakening.

However, let me set the scene. After ten years of self-financed trading and teaching in Russia, the British Executive Service Overseas had sponsored this journey for it is a British charitable organisation that arranges meetings and pays the airfare to transport needed British volunteers all over the world. They do this to support the "Know-How" experience and to engender an exchange of ideas to many overseas newly democratic developments. On this occasion, my trip was to a town called "Birobidzhan" which is in the Far East of Siberia.

This location was Stalin's Jewish Autonomous Region, engineered in 1934 as the National Homeland of all Jews, who made up about twelve per cent of the city's population. He placed it in the Far East of Siberia and from that date to this. It has been economically and socially ignored by world Jewry, for which Stalin must accept responsibility.

Agreed that this is a great pity, but I do not feel concerned about these Great Russian Europeans. I say Europeans because in 1960, when we first began the European Union, I said to everyone that, "I disliked this idea of joining Europe. I am not European; I am British." I even became a Prospective Parliamentary Candidate twice to state this position, first for the Referendum Party and then for UKIP. Indubitably, this was because I was parochial in my thinking.

ECONOMIC MANAGEMENT MEETING
MOSCOW CITY COUNCIL

Now I know how silly this was for I understand now that the whole north of the Northern Hemisphere is full of Europeans and most of the West has knowledge founded upon the dominant religion established within the Christian Bible. I also understand that the people of Birobidzhan live a hard city life and that they have little or no knowledge about private enterprise and its tendency to develop surplus.

I also understand that these European Russians live in climates of twenty-five degrees in summer and minus twenty-five degrees in winter, but they know how to absorb all conditions. For instance, on many occasions, the workers reinstalling water pipes kept stopping the flow of water, then starting it again after repairing the water pipes. Therefore, on one time, I filled a bottle with murky soiled tap water and held it up at a meeting to discuss an economic topic called – "No economic Gain without social Pain."

I began this discourse by asking, "What are these bits floating in the water?" Then immediately after this question, many voices laughingly shouted, "Its sugar." We all roared with laughter, as I suddenly understood that these Russians saw these unusual side effects as just sweeteners towards their new life. I thought then what an excellent title for a story to be called "Sugar in the Water." Well, the town of Birobidzhan is eleven time zones away from my home city of Leeds. This travelling did mean to me a one-hour journey by plane to London. Then a three and a half-hour journey by plane to Moscow. Then transportation to Moscow's inland airport, where I begin the nine-hour flight to my destination's regional capital, a place called "Khabarovsk." After this, we had a final journey of four hours by car to Birobidzhan. I arrived there just as the sun was setting. It was a magnificent sight running directly into the sun, and I can assure you that when I came, I felt that I had arrived.

It was a good feeling and in my baggage were my many years of business experience that I had personally remodeled, to give practical business economic "Know-How" presentations to the people of the new Russia. For instance, on this trip, I had prepared five gifts that I had developed at the request of the Modern Humanities University, a charitable organisation based in the city of Moscow, which was paying all my Ruble expenses. Yes! I felt primed and was ready to deliver them to "Birobidzhan".

These five "Know-How" subjects are as follows and were gleaned from my thirty-five years in business, scientifically discarding non-profitable activities for profitable ones.

Number one was on, "Business Communication". This subject was being about the conflicts arising between totalitarian and democratic markets.

Number two was about "Intercultural Relations". This subject was to indicate methods of avoiding cross-cultural conflicts, particularly the ways of the Market Economy that is now biting into Russia's stagnation and deficit.

ENGLISH LANGUAGE TEACHERS OF BIROBIJAN
DURING THE 1990'S DEFICIT PERIOD

Number three is about "Production Methods". I call this presentation "Death Valley" and I use it to attempt to explain the "Russian Virus" which was repeatedly destroying Russia's attempts at economic development, this was being a presentation that was also about a "virus" which we in the West known as "Variable Costs". With such a cost being rent, heating, electricity, maintenance, etc. and also in Russia, this includes charitable wages; for no one was deemed to be unemployed. (These were the costs that final production amounts are divided into).

This division of payments is likened to a virus lying dormant in most Russian organisations, particularly the ones that attempt to produce Added Value.

Number four is "General Management" with particular reference to private ownership. I agree that we all have a dictionary explanation to put forward for this word. Yet we must remember that under the old communist regime, which was currently dominating the Russian culture, a customer was seen as a person who "creates" an activity that is called "work", which is a needed economic activity that got you out of your comfortable seat. It was also an activity that, under the communist system, you received no extra physical rewards for your efforts as wages were like a charitable receipt.

This payment meant that "work" was, therefore, the last type of activity that most people wished to do, for it distracted them from the bonhomie of the group, which my prior knowledge had also told me that this motivationally meant that only thirty per cent of what could be achieved was achieved. The "motivational" way I now explain this customer relationship is to first identify the "audience" in front of me as my customer.

Then I bow low towards them and say, "You are my King and my Queen. You are my customers. I am here to serve YOU! For I know that the better I help YOU, the more "profit" I will make." To which I carefully added, "But only in a competitive market economy, where organisations compete to serve the people of the market place!" It usually gets the message across to young and old.

By the way, in my travels, I have also found this explanation of Profit to be a terrific jolt to the more mature people of Russia, who believe that you are taking more than is needed from the customer if you make a profit. I then go on to explain that a private business organisation is the invention of the most intrepid of explorers who see the needs of the people around them. "So do not the rewards of an invention belong to the inventor?" I ask. "Of course!" is now also the general Russian answer.

Yet I know that it took over seventy years of what turned into a harrowing experiment to find a truth which realised that money is the world's most exceptional "religious" belief system, especially when considering that it is only worthless paper. Yet all people think it to be of great value. Therefore, it is regrettable that a pending collapse of the advanced western banks will be caused by the USA who will offload cheaply valued dollars onto them. These were dollars that have accrued from the tremendous surplus of USD which the USA banks will accumulate when the third world plus Eastern Europe begins to return trillions of US dollars to the USA, as they start to exchange them for the Euro.

This activity will undoubtedly cause many "borrower" world banks to collapse as this cheaply given surplus returned dollars are loaned to their customers, and so inflate purchasing conditions, which in turn, increases sale prices. An example is that this cheap money will chase house prices up to 100% and some years later when money becomes expensive, the house is valued at 30% in a collapse of market prices, this being a big problem when these business and domestic losses are returned to the loaning banks.

Also, it can be identified that the big problem for the Euro is that it is used by so many different language based countries. Therefore, you cannot replace a particular EU country's debt by allowing them just to print more money as the USA and the UK do. Therefore, those hot EU countries may accrue debt probably because they do not have surplus energy prices in summer as the cold north does. Consequently, it seems the answer must be to run their own named currency alongside the Euro; but enough about economics, for the job of "The Book", is the "Why?" and the "What for?" of all religions and philosophies.

1/B THE ARRIVAL OF THE QUESTION

MANAGERS OF SPACE SHUTTLE FACTORY

Well, I hope that this sets the scene for we are now in Birobidzhan, at the end of three days and three four-hour presentations and after a final Tea-Break I asked: "Do you have any questions?" It was then that I received the first question that I had never been asked before at any of my previous "Economic Management" presentation and I think it arose because of my often used religious intonations within my presentations. This question is "Do you believe in God?" I knew that it was not a question seeking a simple "Yes" or "No" answer! For this question was from an audience discovering a new way of life and an audience that was genuinely interested in the theological meaning of the religious Gospels. It was then, while my thinking was still captured in ultimate economic terminology, I asked my questioner, "What do you believe in?" The answer that came was, "We have always been told to believe in nothing?" To which, after deep thought, I automatically forwarded the response, "Well, your nothing is my God, for my God is certainly No Thing", which received much joy with big smiles and great appreciative applause from the audience.

Then I suddenly found myself saying, "When I was a young man, I also did not believe in God, but, at the age of twenty-five, after a severe near-death road accident, I agnostically questioned myself and asked – Is there a God? My answer then was as it can meaningfully be now; of course, God is "Nothing" but it is a "Nothing" that can be experienced which is also an inner and outer experience that it is impossible to describe. Still, I firmly know that it is a "Nothing" that created everything that my five senses can experience. This interpretation then translated into meaning that God was no object, no commodity, no article or matter.

God was certainly not a manifest or something that the five senses could identify. Now my heart was stirring, and it was showing to me that believing in "nothing" and believing in "No Thing" was also the same. So I further stated to my audience that I too believed in "nothing" but to me, this "No Thing" is that which cannot be experienced but which gave birth to the Creation and also this "No Thing" can be likened to creatively work in the same way as the "nothing" we know has a zero in our ten prime numbers? For in comparison if we take away the world that was born by the belief of the "nothing" in the world of numbers, then the modern world made by people would not exist!

Therefore is it not true, I stated, that we cannot understand how this "zero" this "nothing" made by people works except to realise that this "nothing" when placed in a specific numerical position simply means that there is no known number that can be placed in this position, yet is it not also true that this modern belief in this numerical "nothing" has created the new advanced world made by people? Therefore an understanding in this self-creating, self-evolving mathematical "nothing" is similar to having a belief in the "No-Thing" that you call God from which everything that we can experience was born, just has nearly everything that has been built and so experienced by people has been "Created" by the use of the number zero – this also being the "nothing" that created the world made by people. So factually is it not true that if we take this zero; this nothing away from the known world, then people's Creation, which is born from numbers, will collapse. For indeed we cannot see this zero whose value we call "nothing" – but we know that it is there and that it creates the world of numbers, which in turn leads to all that people now can create. Therefore, this "nothing" is my God and is that which created everything. It was a very satisfactory answer for then we went back to the nature of explaining business and the nature of economic development which was to arise from "nothing", which was the purpose of my visit. However, I did not explain the story about my near-death experience at the age twenty-five, this being when my motorcycle collided head-on with an oncoming car that had come too fast around a bend in the road and I was then thrown onto the roof of the car and bounced down the road behind it.

THE AUTHOR AFTER THE BIG BANG

It was then when I moved towards the peaceful tunnel of "White Light" that I encountered a strong "feeling" saying to me, "Go back, you have work to do!" I then tried to sit up, but could not for my leg was across my chest, and it surprised the police officer who was talking to the unhurt car passengers. This being was because he had covered me with his cape for he had checked for vital signs and had pronounced me dead. Then after the excellent hospitals work and two years later, I started work again. Still, I had also begun a long scientific quest for further understanding of the Creation's "Natural Laws".

It was new work for me that I had to start and this was because of my left leg injury and the current need for a walking stick that I could only obtain work in offices and not in the production areas where the men worked. This reality was a significant unwelcome "social" change within my life, which began in 1938 when my father was called from his "Christmas Day" Sunday drink to greet my arrival and also, my leaving school at the age of 14 and two days later now aged 15, happily starting work at the same coal mine has my father and brother and remember the "Teddy Boys". Yes I was one for we were not needed for war and so we were free, and I also obtained the honour of being the youngest "official" coal face worker in the UK, and this coal face was three feet high.

But then at the age of 20, I needed to see what the world was all about so I joined the Merchant Navy and began work in the engine rooms with the target to become an Engineer and my first ship was Queen Elizabeth in which I made six trips to New York. Then onto the "Banana Boats" to most of the Caribbean islands except Cuba plus the countries of Central America and the North of South America - they were VERY different from the land of my birth.

I also enjoyed several trips to South Africa's Cape Town, and all its coastal ports where when swimming in the sea your ears popped has BIG waves moved over you. I then joined Mediterranean "tourist" ships to visit all the countries and islands of the Mediterranean and then sailed on an oil tanker through the Suez Canal and so visited the Arabian countries plus India's Bombay were I saw real poverty that shook me.

It was while on leave from this trip that I encountered the Big Bang and the message "Go Back, You Have Work to Do." This accident is what indeed left a deep impression and a need to find out what this work was that I needed to do and so I laid this task before a wise philosopher who simply stated, "Fall silent in front of a blank piece of paper and holds a pen. Then when the mind is still, ask yourself the question "What is the work I have to do?" I did this, and in the achieved silence, my hand wrote the answer "Free the People of the North."

This revelation did amaze me for I was currently attending evening classes and studying work and all its aspects. This message strongly motivated me to find a new economic system that freed people to find a job that would sustain them and their families. So the task was interpreted to remove ALL unemployment, which then became my motivation throughout the history of my working life which was to target the employing of people in new factories and to build efficient "economic" systems within industries that then "create" marketable employment – which led to my work in Russia – But in my retirement and away from this task I began to understand that this "Freedom to Work" was not an "economic" aspect and so I felt my pursuit was wrong, for indeed the "Freedom to Work" means the freedom to apply effort, create, employ, operate, toil, perform etc. and so with all these "work" aspects, the purpose was to target and succeed in gaining the true freedom that was encased in "Enlightenment" this being the target of ALL religions and philosophies' – hence I became a tool to write "The Book" which will affectionately bring the reader to "Enlightenment" the task of ALL

UNIVERSITY ECONOMIC LECTURE - MURMANSK

So now "The Book" – The Purpose and Religion of All Religions and Philosophies", is a modern explanation of these beliefs for all religious and non-religious people. For "The Book" truly, defines not only that which our ancients wisely and culturally described as being God's world, but also how to live correctly in God's world and so become "Enlightened". For "The Book" was written and so developed has a "Business Plan" and designed to contain written "scientific" evidence of that which religions and philosophies are all explaining.

It also explains all those exciting "religious and philosophical" cultural sayings, including their hidden meanings. For "The Book" scientifically proves the reality of our various religious and philosophical and says this by using a modern language and "The Book" also shows the real way of how to achieve "Enlightenment;" this being the target of ALL religions and philosophies. For indeed, it is certainly known to be a personal practice in which each person can fully experience the reality of God's world or the world of Nature, for the Non-Believer.

This realty is based upon the fact that "The Book" uses modern sayings and explanations which are based upon well-known and contemporary "scientific" facts for "The Book" uses the same examples, procedures and methods that were used in my forty years of establishing new "Business Plans," these being for many new business installations, factories, new developments and many businesses serving modern-day customers.

ENGLISH LANGUAGE TEACHERS –BIROBIJAN

DURING THE 1990'S DEFICIT PERIOD

So an excellent modern-day understanding is written to describe the single target of that which our ALL our wise ancients speak and thus develop and understand their words anew via modern 2020 "Present Time" revelations, these being revelations that can be experienced. So the first understanding is to know that no person can achieve any productive work in the past or the future for all new developments can only begin with "Present Time" that is the only time in which can be activated a modern based methodical training procedure which practice only that which our wise ancients taught. For it is now in my retirement that I can endeavour to "practically" show not only that they all targeting the same "divine" word of God or Nature for the Non-Believer, but also how to achieve this target which in "The Book" calls "Enlightenment". For indeed the task now is to show the "scientific" proof of that which is hidden in the ancient teachings of the world's many different cultures, this being the reason for our Earth's different worded and taught religions and philosophies.

First, I began to restudy and re-read again all the many religions and philosophies, including the Christian Bible, which I had put to one side long ago. I now looked for positive clues. I looked for wording that explained a "business" based "marketable" truth that cannot be changed or contradicted, this being the sought synthesis that we always support in our major religions and philosophies.

For I first found that all their interpretations were cloaked in mysterious "blind opinion" hidden behind "blind faith," and then translated and preached by moral and some not well-intentioned religious leaders; all of whom had no scientific understanding or corroborated meaning, but taught that which seemed to many only to exist in dreams. Then after my 50 plus year hobby of studying and practising various major religious and philosophical doctrines, which included seriously studying and practising many of the Eastern Philosophies, I decided to write "The Book" and so first decided to return to the New Testament. I was disappointed, for again, and I found zero understanding within it. Always the question was, "What is this "Nothing", this "No Thing" I call God? And how do I find Him and His world."

Then I suddenly found the beginning of an answer. It was so simple that I immediately realised why the Christian Gospels had been so difficult for me to grasp. The reason for this lack of understanding was that I had been trying to listen to the Bible's interpretations of a man called Jesus, telling me about His relationship with God and with God's Creation. Like the many Eastern teachings, it was nice, but it was also about another person's interpreted opinion about some "thing" which I could not grasp. Then I had a flash, a glimmering of a new conceptual understanding, based upon my many years of religious "factual" studying!

ASSISTANT CHAIRMAN:
THE MOSCOW CONFERENCE ON ECONOMIC WASTE

So, what did I do at this first glimpse of my first possible "factual" answer? I took a highlighter and chose a Christian Disciple, which was Mathew and then went through his text and highlighted in red only the words spoken by Jesus. Then, after a day, I began to read only the words of Jesus, which I had highlighted, and I had no other interpretations or attached opinions, which could change the meaning of these words. It was an outstanding experience, as the secret of Christian teaching was revealed loudly and clearly to me. I had found the synthesis and the practicality, for not only this dominant religion but also the key to the understanding of the potential sought "Target" of all our Earth's religions and philosophies.

I laughed and laughed and laughed at what I had found to be the real truth, has many massive scales fell from my inner "eyes". What I found by reading only the words of Jesus, was that these were not the terms of a man merely talking, but that they were "statements" that can be likened to words coming directly from God via the Creation or via Nature, for the Non-Believer. It was a voice speaking through a man called Jesus, and I realised with certainty that these words were coming directly from God.

Yes! I had suddenly realised the fact that God spoke through this man called Jesus and that "No Things" Creation, which was all around me had been given a voice. Of course, in the Christian religion, it was a man called Jesus through whom the Creator spoke. In other hemispheres, major religions enjoyed God's words culturally spoken to them by different Incarnations such as Krishna, who had a wonderful sense of humour. For when someone asked why he saved the life of his friend Arjuna during his fighting in the war of the Kurukshetra, which resulted in the death of a more experienced older warrior that Arjuna was fighting, Krishna replied, *"Because Arjuna is my friend."* (Also, because Arjuna had a great deal more unifying works to do in this Great War against selfishness).

Of course, Gods Creation possessed people like Mohammed, who's Jihad 2..190 stated, *"Fight in the way of God but do not transgress, for God does not like transgressors"* and 2.193 *"Fight them until there are no more breakers of harmony, but if they cease, then there is to be no more aggression"* etc. Not entirely turn the other cheek, although I believe that its target is correct, for it searches for harmony, meaning, agreement, accord, coordination, synchronisation and coherence, the very opposite to discord, meaning conflict, friction, fighting, war, and disagreement.

So if you are not quite sure what is the meaning of God's harmony, then look at your own body? For a person's inner body consists of trillions of different "individuals" and there are probably more of these individual entities than all the people who live upon our planet. They are all working in perfect harmony with one another even though they all have different jobs from manual to critical control systems and all are in perfect balance as the personal death rate caused by internal disharmony proves.

It is also interesting that it has been said that many "disorders" of the body are a disharmony caused by the body seeking new additions for the on-going evolving and development of people – a fact of "adding" incoming new entities, which brought the body to where it is now – but much this later in "The Book". Now back to the enlightening words of Jesus that need no confusing interpretations which have been incorrectly put forward by those seeking power over others.

I then began to understand an "evolutionary" creation of everything as these Bible words spoken by Jesus rocked my thinking into place. I now realised a transparent belief system in which Jesus was not just a man but was God's personification of the whole of the Creation or of Nature, for the Non-Believer and in particular, the understanding of the "laws" contained in the planet Earth, upon which we all live. This realisation meant that our actual Creator himself was talking through this man called Jesus, and was speaking directly to people like me who had no memory of who we were.

I now recognised fully the all-knowing words of John the Baptist, who, upon seeing Jesus for the first time said to his people, *"You must change your hearts – for the Kingdom of Heaven has arrived!"* Now what a man he must have been to have known this reality. Then did not God speaking, through Jesus say to His disciples, *"Believe me, a rich man will find it very difficult to enter the Kingdom of Heaven. Yes, I repeat, a camel could more easily squeeze through the eye of a needle than a rich man to enter into the kingdom of God!"* It was then I began to understand, really and truthfully, that Heaven, which is the Kingdom of God, rested in the "Present Time" but how do you enter "totally" the Heaven that rests within the real world of Nature this being that which we can experience upon this Earth.

So yes! How do you go through this door that leads to Heaven and thus lives in the Heaven of the "Present Time"? It was then that my works towards this finding of words to explain this "realisation" and how to "actually" go through this door, and on into God's world or to experience the real world of Nature for the Non-Believer, did begin.

So Yes! For I genuinely found by reading only the words from Jesus that they sounded rational in the realisation that God, speaking through the incarnate Jesus, was making a verbal and "magical" contact to ALL people. This being has if God was speaking through this personification of the Creation and talking directly to YOU! For what else is the Creation but the only Child of God and now, through the man called Jesus, I recognised that the Creator was speaking to everyone, including "Non-Believers".

So Yes! It was seen to be God's voice speaking through a man called Jesus, and I realised with certainty that these highlighted red words were coming directly from God. I had suddenly realised the fact that God was speaking through this man called Jesus and that "No Things" Creation, which was all around me had been given a voice through Jesus. Of course, in the Christian religion, belonging to the North of Northern Hemisphere, it was a man called Jesus through whom the Creation spoke. In other hemispheres, major religions enjoyed God's words culturally spoken to them by different Incarnations; indeed, this being shown has previously stated, in the exquisite sense of humour which Krishna had.

So if you are not quite sure what is the meaning of God's harmony, then look at your own body? The body consists of trillions of different "individuals", and there are probably more of these individual entities than all the people who live upon our planet. They are all working in perfect harmony with one another even though they all have different jobs from just physical to critical control systems and all are in perfect balance as the death rate caused by internal disharmony proves. It is also interesting that it has been said that many "disorders" of the body are disharmony symptoms caused by the actual body seeking new additions for the evolving development of people – a fact of "adding" incoming new entities.

1/C A SINGLE ENTITY OF TRUTH

It was also during these various religious and philosophical studies and the seeking of the power of "Nothing" that I realised that there must be nine prime senses and not merely five. I state this because there are also only nine prime numbers to which the "zero" is added as "nothing."

BUSINESS DEVELOPMENT PRESENTATION AT A TV MANUFACTURING PLANT - RIGA LATVIA

But what a physically well-known and accumulative "nothing", for it is also this "nothing" which is the only entity that creates this unity of plays that expands the mathematically born physical world, in which we now live. For we all know that without this "zero" this "nothing" the modern world, created by mathematical equations, would not exist for this "nothing" can actually expand any number to circle the whole universe.

So clearly it can be explained that a personal "Creation" is known has "Some-Thing" and the "No-Thing" is the zero that created it, for, after all, is it not scientifically proven that a negative must also "always" reflect a positive? However, what is the target of this God we can call "No-thing" or Natures Nothing for the Non-believer, this being the No-Thing that started that which we call "The Creation."

Well, there is no need to be alarmed, for I have also found "scientifically" that our "No-Thing" has a "Teacher" which cares for this only child that we call "The Creation, or "The Universe" for the Non-Believer. This "Teacher" knowingly has compelling energy, which continually cares for you "personally" and also all that is around you for who else do you think guided and convinced all those trillions of joined-up bits of separate entities that exist within your body into becoming a unified whole? This is being the enetity of all that exists within a single person and also that which is birthed within all other life forms, plus Non-Life forms?

This was being a much needed and scientific "Need to Know" fact for do not all these living "individuals" that we call units of life, contain within them an entity which is activated towards controlling their "inner world" and also their "outer world", this being the seeking of a much sought harmony-based existence. Does this "inner world" not also constantly react to its "outer-world", this being the outer world which is needed to absorb an on-going and continuing existence of that which observes?

For certainly it is true that we do have the "Three in One". We do have "One God", who is "No Thing". Secondly, we can only have "One Mother", a fact which is more fully explained later in "The Book". Further to this, "The Book" scientifically acknowledge that the "One Mother" can only be the entity that we call "Space", this being that which God planted the seed which gave birth to their only child which is the single life force that we call number "Three," i.e. "The Creation". For "The Book" does "scientifically" explain that this fact is that which is known to be the "Three in one".

Now regarding these perceived nine senses. I found scientifically that our well-known five senses, touching; hearing tasting, seeing and smelling are all inherited from our past animal existence which were engaged to ensure survival, but it should also be known that we must have above them a further and higher four senses that are only attached to people and which can only exist within the "Essence of a Person's Mind".

Is not the Soul, which rests only within people, actually emanating from a God-given "Enlightenment" that is constantly observing the Creation from within the individual with whom it rests? This known condition of "Enlightenment" is undoubtedly a consciousness that powers all the Life and Non-Life that certainly exists within the Creation. Can it not also be understood that that this light within all life and Non-Life comes from God or Nature for the Non-Believer. Is it not also true that it is only people that God gave a consciousness that allowed a freedom of choice, to do or not to do, to be or not to be, to live or not to live?

I have just seen a young girl crossing a busy road snarling and shouting at the cars that swerve to avoid her. I then think how strange it is that we punish these "wild emotional" newly birthed has people, instead of absorbing them and kindly teaching them new modern ways and also treating them with kindness and courtesy, as do all professional animal trainers; for where else can this increase in "Souls" be coming from but from the shrinking animal kingdom? Yet, sadly, not understanding this, we punish these newborns and imprison them in cages, because they act according to their past inherent "Nature" which has not yet encompassed the common law of people. Nevertheless, usually, this mind essence, which can be called a Soul, habitually and normally, seeks a re-birth in which it will attempt to re-wear the genes worn by the families that they left behind.

So yes! The Soul will return to inherit a newly birthing body for is it not known to be "scientifically" understood that there is no waste of energy within the Creation? For indeed, it is also a known truth and also "scientifically" recognised that there is nowhere for the energy of the Soul to go except to return to the likened source from whence it came. For is it not also true that all life recognises and therefore knows that a past source of love is a powerful attracter and like any good Mother, the "Mother of the Creation" does not waste energy on the need to create love and harmony when it already entirely exists within every person's Soul.

HONORARY CHAIRMAN OF THE
MOSCOW CONFERENCE ON MANAGEMENT WASTE

Also has a scientific manager, I understand that the "Mother of the Creation" may change the Souls re-birthing target if She decides that a particular Soul, especially one which may be newly emanating from the animal kingdom, could more fruitfully expand its needed activities if born into a different set of circumstances? This is being a fact which will enable it to support the growth of the Creations Harmony that exists all around it.

So could it not also be "naturally" stated to be true that a person who is selfishly harming that which has been "Created", could be left lying dormant for a long time by the *"Mother of the Creation"* and it is here that we should further understand that being born physically or mentally handicapped is not a punishment for an individual. For in reality it can only be a "Self-Chosen" way of a new life that has contentedly sought such a birth so that those "Souls" that exist around this personal "sacrifice" can then reflect this same love of others and so unify with those in such need, has does the "Mother of the Creation" who cares for all life and also non-life. For indeed, is it not also an excellent opportunity to assist and so beneficially act within all that is around us in the same way as the "Mother of the Creation" who truly and knowingly cares and loves all Souls.

So yes! The "Mother of the Creation", like all good mothers, cannot waste time on people who pursue selfish self-gaining "I Want for me" acts that destroy or disturb the growth of their Godly Fathers harmony. For indeed Her reaction can only be that Her face is turned away from them, for is it not true that God or Nature for the Non-Believer truly gave to all peoples Souls the "Freedom of Choice", which also allows people to live outside Gods caring and loving laws of harmony and contentment. However, they still carry the key which allows them to immediately access and support "Godly" world that exists all around them.

So Yes! The *"Mother of the Creation"* never punishes people, but She can and does ignore them and thus does not support those people who target selfish needs, these being acts that create disharmony to exist all around them. Yet is it not true that many feel that they are personally punished when they feel that they are outside the laws of harmony. Therefore is it not also seen and understood that "scientifically" we witness all around us the selfish deeds turning to dust and also the fact that ill-gotten gains do not bring the happiness that these targeting people seek – which is opposite to the "Mother of the Creation" target of love, harmony and unifying contentment, in other words a unified life based upon love and a care of all that exists around you? Do not all our recent past European and otherworldly wars "scientifically" prove that this warfare way of searching for unity cannot be correct, for those who seek a war in order to control foreign people are always eventually vanquished? For truly is not the only unity of harmony being that which is a peaceful search for a union with other different language and/or religious-based countries? For is it not historically and also very plain to see "scientifically" that we have certainly come a long way from our past cave fighting days when a valley of inhabitants fought another valley of inhabitants. For now we see the whole of the Northern Hemisphere trying to unite into one entity called "Democracy" which favour' the majority of people under its jurisdiction, which only personal greed can target to separate.

So yes! It can be further understood that there must be four higher senses that can be used by a person Soul, these being above the five senses that all people can recognise, for indeed it is these higher four senses that are used to identify and obey the *"Mother of the Creations"* and Her caring for the laws which were created by God or Nature for the Non-Believer. For are these not also the harmonising laws which are seen to be inherent in God's only child - the Creation, for indeed, is it not also "scientifically" understood that children, if allowed, do naturally inherit their parent's traits. Therefore, "scientifically" these same laws of "God" are knowingly inherited and so "legally" binding within all people for is it now known that the breaking of them will always lead to a feeling of isolation! For truly, can we not also say that it is only because of the Creations developing needs that God allows people the "Freedom of Choice", this being to take actions that are required to support a God-made world that is cared for by the *"Mother of the Creation"*? For truly is this not a living "evolving" world in which people are required to pursue God's emerging laws, these being the only developing laws that exist in the "Present Time". Can it not also be true that the "Mother of the Creation" always lives to care for these family supporting laws like all mothers do? Is this not also the reason why a person's activity is supported by the God-given "Freedom of Choice" because things change? Is this not also the basic "caring" root of all people's religions, philosophies, and also their political systems? Can anyone in the world "scientifically" say whether there is any personal action or personal activity that God's laws do not permit? Is this not a revealing question? Is this not also a knowledge that should automatically stop all religious dissent? Because is it not also true that all religious and philosophical truths are based upon a "Freedom of Choice" practice? Is this "Freedom of Choice" practice being that which is emanating from the one God, a "No Thing" which created a single energy of

20

love that binds together the singularity of an only child which we call "The Creation". Is it not also true that this singularity of a unified life is also that which inhabits this planet we call Earth? Is this not also a planet with a combined life force that also proves that Darwin was partly right, in that we are "evolving" according to God's target? The questions being are these "opinions" or are they "scientific" facts. If in doubt about this, look out of your window and see the world as it exists. This viewing being without any "personal" portrayal of "I Want" false conditions or the self-claiming selfish desiring of an "I Want," which can only emanate from those ancient animalistic five senses that dance in front of and within our cognitive mind and which are always animalistic in their endeavour to claim the world around them as their own, as do all animals who do not possess a Soul. Now, again, it is modernly known that all animals have been given the five senses which are known as the sense of smell, touch, taste, hearing and seeing. Still, only people have been given the "Freedom of Choice", this being that which can control and so contradict these animalistic five senses. But all animals have to obey the singularity of this law, either when controlled or when NOT controlled. Therefore, should it not be stated that a person's five senses are consequently enabled to be that which can be identified as being controllable by their Soul?

COMPREHENSIVE SCHOOL MANAGEMENT MEETING

Is it not a personal "Freedom of Choice" that factually empowers a person to correctly understand God's "Freedom of Choice" laws that govern the Creation? Does not this God-given "Freedom of Choice" only exist in people to CONTROL those lower five senses, so that these five senses can be stopped from filling the mind with an animalistic "I Want" for me. For indeed, it is known that the real purpose of our five senses is to assist us in our relationship to the Heaven that exists all around us as it does within us. For undoubtedly being imbedded and up-to-date information that is useful for the task that we are currently performing – like telling us where we left our keys, etc. and this being in a brief flash of recollection and also do we not "silently" drive a car which is entirely and silently controlled by the five senses?

So Yes! It should now be agreed that the mind filling and oft arguing words of the five senses into the mind means that a misplaced "autocracy" is taking place. This false based and probably unknown dictatorship is real, forgetting and forgetting is our worst enemy, and what we forget is that God's laws are always stating that the "Mother of the Creation" is our beneficial leader, but much more about this concept in "The Book."

1/D WHAT TO DO NOW?

Now, after receiving this understanding that my "No-Thing" (Nothing) was God and that the Creation was the only child, it was then found that there is a bridge connecting God and the child. It was also found that through the four higher senses – which can be true, likened to be within the Soul – that the "Mother of the Creation", our Teacher, is always instructing people their purpose in life. For I found it to be true that this "Energy" that exists all around us is continually teaching us how to support the love and harmony that automatically rests within the "Present Time" which is always factually resting within the Creation and which is still seeking on-going support that aids the purpose of God's only child – this truly being the Creation. Wondrously it was also found that if you perform an act that supports and aids the expansion of the emerging harmonic development pursued by the "Mother of the Creation", that this is an activity that can be likened to building a bridge between God and His only child that we call "The Creation." It will also be an act that will instantly give the doer a momentary physical explosion of inner bliss that fills you with jaw-opening, breath gushing indescribable energised mind-blowing happiness and contentment – is this not true?.

So Yes! This experience is an actual realisation of what a remarkable trinity and what perfect partners within this trinity the Soul and the "Mother of the Creation" make when they act in unison. It was also found that although there are absolutes to these rights and wrongs, there are no absolutes in the way in which they are judged. For it can also be found has a scientific truth, that this highly evolving and constantly emerging single pulse of energy that exists within the Creation is the main reason why people evolved with a free Soul which contains the four higher senses that are above the standard five. For GOD installed this law, to allow people the freedom of choice, for indeed the "Freedom of Choice" is needed because conditions change, and reason and devotion are not always the wings of the same activity.

So Yes! It is a "Creation" based and much needed harmonising. Still, a personal act which can be "scientifically" explained to be the performing of an activity that assists God's "bringing together" harmony seeking laws. Simply put, if your peace-seeking activities change the linking or re-directing of any emerging activity, this being so that it pursues or creates a balance and which stops or turns an event that is endeavouring to separate the harmony of the Creation, you will receive good rewards. But if you act selfishly and you break this harmony seeking unity you will not be purposely punished by God or the "Mother of the Creation", for God gave you a gift called "The Freedom of Choice", and this cannot be taken away from you. However, much more of this "scientifically" recognised principle is will also be spoken of later in "The Book."

So Yes! God or Nature for the Non-Believer cannot punish anyone, for in truth people can only punish themselves by their negating or harmful deeds, this being that which is created by their personally given "Freedom of Choice". For it is this "Freedom of Choice" that can be negatively used to oppose this unifying law but is it not strangely accurate that the people of one language will go to a country which has a different language and kill their people that they do not like because they have a different language and culture? Yet! Is it not also true that within their bodies there are thousands of different cultures and variable ways of living, yet all trading and supporting the goodness of the whole body- which can be likened to the growing child that we call "Earth"? The reason for there being no Godly punishment is "scientifically" simple, for there is and never can be any punishing of people within God's world either by God's laws or by the "Mother of the Creation" activities. The reason for this is simple, for God's world is perfect, for it cannot be anything else. It is also a world that has "naturally" within it, an inbuilt correcting system which gives a good re-birth in a new life for those who have been removed by the misdeeds of people, or by the evolving movements of the Creation.

So, what is the reality of these "God" laws that we must bear in mind, if we want the good (God) life that is based upon love, a sense of being and good harmony? The reality is that all your own "I Want" for me selfish efforts will always be silently ignored by the "Mother of the Creation". Still, when you start to support her "good" harmony seeking deeds, the "Mother of the Creation" will bring to you what we can call "serendipity". This condition is the natural order that will aid your "Present Time" harmony seeking deeds and "automatically" support your continuation to expand them, a blissful and peacefully rewarding activity.

So it can also be easily seen that the purpose of a woman and a man is for them to become like one person. The man, whose mind can plan a future, obtains mental strength from the woman whose mind lives in Present and it is she who maintains the way to happiness and contentment which targets that which both of them can happily achieve. His strength takes them to this happiness and satisfaction.

BUSINESS "START-UP" MEETING - YEKATERINBURG

Now there is a "scientifically" proved understanding that is contained in all religions and philosophies, and which is best explained as personal actions that link the harmony of the evolving Creation together; a task which is always overseen by the "Mother of the Creation". This activity is a personal action that is likened to tying two pieces of string together, which link two separately developing activities that are seeking to join with each other. Still, they cannot do this act on their own. This pursuit is an act that can be called "serendipity" because it is a natural gift that can only be realised, changed and acted upon within the "Present Time" and it often creates within the "Present Time" useful discoveries seemingly quite by accident.

For indeed, people can easily tie a new active "string" that is entering their life to another "passing string" that they can also control a movement, this being an act that supports the energy of harmony that is continually expanding around them. It is also useful to name that act in which the *"Mother of the Creation"* offers to people with the sole purpose to develop the creations ever seeking harmony. It is called "Destiny" because it is a personal activity and it can be hard work to find the connecting much needed "string" resting within you and without you. This activity can be likened to "Destiny" is a piece of string that is required to "tie together" the needed conditions that will expand the purpose of the "Mother of the Creation" maintenance of a never-ending search for the continuation of our Earths harmony, as is the work of all mothers, but much more of this later in "The Book. It is also often found that it is not always an easy task to "tie" two emerging events together for we all have doubts. Still, it can be said that "scientifically" we have excellent support in the "Mother of the Creation" who we support "unconditionally" when we join "Her" blissful rewarding work which brings people a feeling of care and protection which can target "Enlightenment".

This target is to develop an "Enlightenment" which Christians call being filled with the **"Holy Spirit"** or the **"Holy Ghost"** and being in "Paradise" or "Heaven". In contrast, other world's religions and philosophies call *it* *"Paradise"*, *"Eden"*, *"Heaven"*, *"Promised Land"* *"Nirvana"*, *"Moksha"*, *"Shangri-la"*, *"Kenshō"*, *"Bodhi"*, *"Satori"*, *"Jnana"*, *"Svargamu"*, *"Kā bāga"*, *"Vāṭikā"*, *"Kā jagaha"*, *"Sukhabhavana"*, *"Karma"*, *"Kismet"*, *"Nirvana"*, *"Chance"*, *"Providence"*, *"Serendipity"*, *"Fate"*, **plus** *"Luck"*, and even the ancient Zoroastrianism religion of the Fifth-Century BC referred to it as *"Ushta"* which was described by them as *"liberation, salvation and emancipation of the Soul"*. These writings being accomplished over two thousand five hundred years ago and even before that time for truly all these names were born to describe "Enlightenment," this being the living in the Heaven upon our Earth that exists only in the "Present Time".

So Yes! "Enlightenment" can be experienced in two ways and later in "The Book" it will be shown how to take the first step towards Enlightenment which is to become "Self-Aware" - this means that you experience that which is all you and within you – and the experience is that it is all you! For indeed this is the experience when a person's mind enters the string tying of events that can only be accomplished in the "Present Time" for they become only aware of the

"Present Time" and have no thoughts born from any future or any past "I Want". This experience is also the step before "Self-Realisation", which is when a person becomes "Self-Realised" and so actually becomes "The Creation". For again truly, this is the religious and philosophical target that exists within all the world's religions that have been taught by Jesus, Muhammad, Krishna, Buddha, Baha'u', Confucius, Tao, Plato, Laozi, Vivekananda, Sri Shankara, and Sri Ramakrishna plus many more of our worlds wise ancients. "The Book" shows how this "experience" can be achieved and that it is merely a mind without any "I Want" for myself thoughts for how can you "think" of an "I Want" when you realise that you are factually living in God's world, or the world of Nature for the Non-Believer and it is has described by ALL the Earths religions and philosophies and it now awaits YOU!

So yes! As all the wise ancients in our entire world's religions and philosophies state, that this is God's laws or Nature's laws for the Non-Believer which can exist only in the "Present Time" and, has "The Book" continues to explain, is that all these emerging laws are being monitored and controlled clearly by the *"Mother of the Creation"*. For it is *"Mother of the Creation"* who automatically guides and favourably supports all the personal lives of those who help Her to bring together the physically separating parts of the growing Creation, which is the only child of God.

This support is just as any good manager would do to those who support the work needed to be done. This activity is truly the work of the "Mother of the Creation" whose continual healings and the keeping together the evolving separations within her family, which is being caused by the collision of natural laws. This realty is a task that can be likened to a deer's antlers being caught in a tree, and only people can "choose" to set it free – for natural laws do collide as we know when sunbursts or collapses.

It is also advantageous to understand this; for it will be positively found that it is wise to support the emerging harmony that is the constant birthing or re-birthing within the Creation's activities. For it is knowledgeably said that whenever people support these harmony seeking "together" acts which can be likened to our tying two pieces of string together, we also enjoy the personal gift of happiness, caused by being absorbed into the unity of all things which is brought about by our act of love, this being an act that can only take place only in the "Present Time" and at a time that can only occur when the mind is entirely in the "Present Time".

The reason why it is explained as bringing a feeling of being "loved" is because some of our wise ancients described love as the element "water"; for all know that if you take the water away from anything it cracks, breaks and it becomes a speck of dust that exists only in an isolated separation and without any attaching love from that which is around it. Therefore, this "I Want" for myself act is also an act that can be likened to an activity which causes a leak in a water container and so leaks away "love", this being the reality for a person who lives in an "I Want" for myself world - but much more about this later in "The Book". Therefore, it is scientifically precise that the only sin that people can perform is to separate the natural and developing harmonic unifying togetherness of the developing Creation, this being that which contains all life and Non-Life.

AN EMBARRASSING WARM "TRADITIONAL" TOAST FROM OMSK "SPACE SHUTTLE" DIRECTORS

So yes! It is good to endeavour to support the tying together of many strings resting in the European Union. The North of the Northern Hemisphere's which are strings can lead to a world union; for this is the target of all people, and it cannot be stopped. It may also be believed that the Russian people are holding the first string that will show a new way for people's search for this economic unity; because it is now known that the Russian peoples first attempt to seek a way of life that did not involve the constant search for "Profit", which can only come from others - did fail.

It is also known that before this end-time that everyone knew of the pending failure. The first question that I asked at all my economic presentations in the USSR; this being from the Supreme Soviet down to a class of infants, did always bring the same answer. The question was, "Which is the richest industrial country in the world with the poorest industrial people?" The answer given by all my audiences was always, "Russia."

So yes! Russia has been there, done that and is now entering a new world which is still based upon "Love thy neighbour as thyself". Maybe it this "Communist" failed attempt that now allows the Russian people to seek a way that targets Profit which also benefits the "masses" and not just an individual? For the fact remains that in a privately competitive society, it is known that the selling price is that which the most a person is prepared to pay. From this "totalitarian" figure, the Profit is that which is surplus to the bought-in costs, including the wages that are paid to those who add value to that which is sold at the market place. The fact remains that in a privately competitive society that the selling price is the most a person is prepared to pay with Profit being that which is surplus to the cost to make, this being a profit which should be audited and monitored under law, as is the distribution of some of the Profit via taxation. Indeed, "NOW" by reading "The Book" you will find the proof of that which ALL religions and philosophies are targeting and how to silence the demanding thoughts within your mind that seek a personal profit and thereby enter the Kingdom of Heaven which only exists in the "Present Time". For when absorbing the readings of "The Book" this will become likened to being served with a plate of good food and when "eaten" you will "experience" the silent love of a God who's good Nature exists all around you.

"The Book" will also bring to you much of our wise ancients' knowledge which is a knowledge that is based upon their own found way to become "Self-Aware" or "Self-Realise", this being a religious and philosophical experience of real existence in which "You" will experience a "stillness" that will bring you actually to become has one with the world around you. For "YOU" will "KNOW" that you have joined with God's world or the world of Nature for the Non-Believer. For truly, this "Self-Realisation" is the target of all our wise ancients. It is the only reason why they developed our entire world's religions and philosophies, for in these sayings they clearly state that everybody's target is to pursue this "Enlightenment", which is an act that can only be born in the "Present Time". The purpose of "The Book's" is this and its modern terminology is designed to bring to all this ancient knowledge of how to achieve "Enlightenment" and so experience God's world or the world of Nature for the Non-Believer. This world is indeed being an "Enlightenment" that brings the knowledge that you are living in God's world or the world of Nature for the Non-Believer and when you have performed an activity that can be called "Rightful", you can rest assured that there is no better judge in these matters than the "Mother of the Creation". For truly you will understand (Stand-Under) that it is She who then supports your backup acts and even brings you more ways of promoting the developing harmony of the Creation for it is called LOVE, and this is the harmony that she is continually endeavouring to create all around you.

So yes! "The Book" will also show to you plainly that this is the reason why people have been given the "Freedom of Choice", for the one "positive" act can be supporting the emerging harmony or the same action can be "negatively" destroying the emerging unity according to circumstances. Therefor "The Book" will factually show that the knowledge which ALL religions and philosophies teach, is that your rewards within this life, which are good or bad, will always be given to you has your "wages" which will be in direct accordance to your work – this being the acts that YOU perform.

So yes! "The Book" with its ancient but modernised revelations, will reveal to you that if you do feel an emanating happy "holistic" reward coming from others, this being because of the "needed" activity that you have just performed, then this can be likened to receiving a smile from the "Mother of the Creation" as She willingly supports you. But if you "experience" an unhappy reward from your acts, then this is a reflection of what harm you have done to the Creations process, so this must be an act which is the opposite to the "Mother of the Creation" harmony seeking endeavours for ALL the Creation.

So yes! This seeking is the "heavenly" reason why people have been given the "Freedom of Choice", and so the reality is that the "Mother of the Creation" cannot punish you for what you choose to do, for sure, it is your act in which you are punishing yourself but what a joy Jesus of the Christian faith must have experienced has he chose to go silently to a painful death to avoid inflicting pain upon others. Still, the real death of someone is when you forget them.

So yes! It is good to experience that the "Mother of the Creation" loves those who support God's laws for She is a great lover of God's Creation and also her children who assist her in promoting the emerging harmony of the Creation, for they will all be perfectly judged and will be self-rewarded accordingly. Simply stated, I have found "scientifically" that those people, who attempt to destroy Her creating principles that are all around them, will be reminded that even while being shunned from all their surrounding harmony, they will instantly be forgiven when they perform a together activity that supports Her emerging unity, for how else you can you be rewarded but with bliss, this being any together activity which creates "Godness" that is pronounced "Goodness."   In ancient times, Buddha said, and Hinduism still preaches that there are 84,000 dharma gates which open to the "duties" that can bring a person to "liberation", this being what is now called "Enlightenment". It is also true that many of our modern religions and philosophies still show these ancient based ways but now "The Book" can show a single "scientific" based "gate" that can successfully bring any person to "Enlightenment", this being the target of all the world's religions and philosophies, but only because of our "new" modern understandings.

For indeed we will also understand that a person's "Destiny" can be affected by good deeds or not good deeds this being that which you do or not do and "The Book" will show that these "I Want" for myself, acts are a search for aches which bring only pain and suffering because you are attacking the truth of "life", a fact which will bring you sorrow, suspicion, worry, wrath, avarice, pride and all this "YOU" create within yourself and also around you – and you know this to be true. So Yes! There is much more of this explained in "The Book."

2   THE WAY AHEAD IS IN HARMONY

Well, the "Sugar in the Water" story which developed into "The Book" was about my work in supporting the unification of a newly emerging democracy now growing in Russia and which was also soon releasing all the other USSR countries to be Self-Governed by the people of that language.

It was further hoped that this could lead to a new development that would replace the "North Atlantic Treaty Organisation" (NATO) with the "Northern Hemisphere Treaty Organisation" (NHTO) these being lands that are controlled by democracies and governments who pursue the will of the majority of their voting people and not the pursuit of a few wealthy people seeking even more personnel wealth.

But now, after much thought, my retirement desires to give a real answer to the often-asked question as I travelled throughout Russia. "Do you believe in God?" A good question for I knew that the modern history of Russia made it a country that had never had any religious teachings. Still, I also realised that this question is also a question in which many people in our modern world have become confused. These following pages are designed to contain modern "scientific" explanatory answers that have been gleaned from many of the worlds' religions, and philosophies and these are "truths" which are being supported by "Words from the Ancients". "The Book" will also "scientifically" explain and also reveal how to achieve that which our wise ancients stated was the experiencing of "Enlightenment", this being God's world or the world of Nature for the Non-Believer. This "Nature" also being an "Enlightenment" that is targeted by our ancient belief systems that go back thousands of years and which have been personally studied and practised by me for over fifty years, especially their rituals and their suggested way of living.

So yes! The following chapters are also a business plan which is not designed to change a person's attendance at their current religious or philosophical ceremonies' or refute agnostic or atheist belief systems. For these "revelations" within "The Book" are designed to give people of all belief systems, whether these belief systems are a religious or philosophical, agnostic, atheist or even economic belief systems, a greater understanding not only of their personal life but of God's or Nature's way of life for the Non-Believer.

These being "laws" that are not attached to the "culture" laws that people use to govern their country or their private communities but are laws from our ancient wise which showed their close followers how to achieve the reality of living in Gods world or the world of Nature for the Non-Believer.

For actually this "Enlightenment" is a reality which can be discovered to be an individual or personal realisation of a life that will bring to the practising "doer" the "Peace that Surpasses all Understanding" and an experience of harmony that can only exist within a life of bliss in which they will know and so fully realise that they have been "blessed" by God or by Nature for the Non-Believer.

So yes! Those who have firm religious or philosophical beliefs or even have no religious beliefs; all will be given a valuable understanding of life. For the following words within "The Book" will show a way to achieve "Enlightenment", this being a way of life that can easily be attached to any "Social Structure" for it is truly a way of living that will bring to the doer that which all our ancient belief systems sought for them to achieve and so "Self-Realising" peace of mind and a satisfying way to the truth of life. It is therefore from "The Books" following new "modern" viewpoints in which we can endeavour to use a "scientific" method to establish a personal and individualistic answer about the targeting purpose of all religions and philosophies and so fully observe the reality of this targeting of these many endeavours pursued by our wise ancients.

The reader of "The Book" will also achieve a "scientific" based understanding in which they will begin to become "Self-Aware" as to why these "belief" and "creed" developing systems have been emerging amongst people throughout ALL known history. For it is only with this personal experience of "Enlightenment" that only people can begin to establish the practicalities as to what they must do in the "Present Time" which is God's world or the world of

Nature for the Non-Believer. For truly, do not all religions and philosophies say it is when experiencing "Enlightenment" that the individual will "Know" by ancient inner and personal knowledge, the reason why our wise ancients consistently brought to many and various cultures their creed-based religions and philosophies.

It is further understood that the writings within "The Book" will also be "Scientifically" and especially useful regarding the salient views held by our many religions and philosophical belief systems for it uses carefully based modern "scientific" methods when giving an understanding of our many multiple religious and philosophical observations which our wise ancients always introduced to people. This introduction is also especially true regarding the new evaluation and purpose of the many world religions and philosophies. It so proves the truth of their concept now being realised under this modern "scientific" explanation.

So yes! This explanation is based upon "scientific management" for it is also well known that Christianity along with many other world religions and philosophies have fractured and splintered into many differing ideology groups which contain various personally institutionalised belief systems that emanate not always from their founders but the leaders of their particular creed-based group. It will also be shown in "The Book" that this splintering occurred because they lost the understanding of the founder of their religion. Therefore, it is understood that the reason for this many fracturing is caused by a lack of knowledge of the root beginnings of their founders' introduced belief systems that were personally produced only for them. These being root belief systems that were based upon well-known practices that were contained in ancient cultural ideologies that were attached to the personal life around their founders and which became a lost understanding during people's evolutionary-based changes. It is further understood, and "The Book" will show that this can be the only reason for these many beliefs systems arguably fracturing and moving away from the divinely enlightened core teachings of their incarnates or enlightened originators, these originators being Enlightened people. They all came purposely to end the suffering of people and so deliver to their followers that which we now call "Enlightenment" this being that which brings the oneness of Gods world or the world of Nature for the Non-Believer.

"The Book" is, therefore "Scientifically" written to overcome these fractures by showing not only words that explain the purpose of "God's Creation" or that which is called "Nature" by Non-Believers, but also to show a simple but proven "Harmonious" way for an individual to personally "institutionalise" themselves and so individually "control" themselves and thus join the right harmony of life that is continuously emerging around them.

Thus, "The Book" will produce a modern, understandable way of revealing the proof that will show "exactly" not only what part of existence should the reader contentedly occupy in their current life, but these proceeding writings will also explain and prove accurately the way to "unify" themselves with Gods world or the world of Nature and so finally understand the root "unifying" target and purpose behind our many and various religions and philosophies. "The Book" will also show the reader how to "personally" achieve this target which was always laid before people by our wise ancients.

So Yes! The revelations that follow in "The Book" will show this ancient but straightforward based way to achieve this "Enlightenment", which can never be changed. This "Enlightenment" is the way to accomplish the contented life that all incarnates plus all our enlightened originators did speak about and a way of life which they all endeavoured to bring to people. First, we must understand and acknowledge "where we are" and also "what we are" plus what our life and all life is about, for our ancient wise endeavoured to bring for every individual a real understanding of their abilities and capabilities and so bring a proof that every individual has an essential but contented place to play and experience within their life and also why they do exist.

So yes! The discourse that follows within "The Book" will show how to achieve a way of life that is compatible with every person's search for happiness and contentment which is in the experience of that which our ancients called "Enlightenment" for this is truly an experience that brings a way of life that Self-Realises" every individual's capabilities and so gives proof that every individual has a significant but contented part to play when guided by the Creations natural a laws.

So yes! These writings within "The Book" are simply written to show the way to achieve that which our ancients called "Enlightenment", this Enlightenment is the "Peace that surpasses all understanding" and the experience which all followers of our religions and philosophies seek but which many followers have forgotten. It is undoubtedly a life that will receive "Sugar in The Water".

It is also an "Enlightenment" that will bring a peace-fullness produced by the practising of a simple "scientifically" creed-based belief system which does no harm to any life and is the core practice of all our wise ancients' creed-based teachings. This practice is being teaching that accepts the reality of all that is around each individual, including the absorbing of their current beliefs, and it cannot be purchased as we do items in many religious shops. These were religious artefacts such as idols, statuettes, and pictures that hold deep "peaceful" meaning too many people. Still, they are also good holiday memories to take back to their homes! Yet for the shop owners and staff, it is their livelihood for knowingly their sacred items blend seamlessly into the commercial world of "I Want" something for me. The real fact is that you cannot buy the religious path that takes you to the "Peace that surpasses all Understanding" the harbinger of "Enlightenment, for this is a personal path that can come to you no matter where you are or what time of day it is. In reality, you are genuinely, and personally, the only "priest" that can take you to become "Self-Aware" and maybe onto the "Self-Realisation" of this truth.

So yes! Now let us find out together what is the reality of truth based upon a life lived in an "Enlightened Harmony" which all our wise ancients speak about this being a way of "Enlightenment" which targets a way of living in the peace that resides in harmony within the world that always exists all around you.

So yes! It must be further understood that this personal harmony is based upon the peace that truly exists in the experience of "Enlightenment" and it can even be experienced in a war zone or under torture or bullying. For truly is it not known the "Enlightened" incarnate Jesus silently underwent much bullying torture and even when nailed to a cross and He said nothing until upon His death when He finally said the words, "Forgive them for they know not what they do!" He knew that the harmony that He represented was very different from the unity of the people who persecuted Him. It was a harmony that He would not condemn for He knew that the laws of God's peace would eventually change His persecutors.

Simply put it is well known that our wise ancients often said that living in true harmony is achieved by listening to God's words, these were words that are continually being silently spoken to everyone all the time. Still, they can "truly," only be understood by those who achieve "Enlightenment", this being an "Enlightenment" that can only be experienced in the "Present Time" which is Gods World or the world of Nature for the Non-Believe" - for the Past and the Future do not exist, except has a world called Hell?

What is then understood is that God's world or the world of Nature for the Non-Believer can only be experienced in the "Present Time", meaning of course that they cannot be experienced in the past or the future for the past or the future does not exist and therefore has no reality. But then the "scientific" question must be, "Can people hear this language of God's harmony or Nature's harmony for the Non-Believer and is it in understandable words?"

It is then that the answer must be "Of course not". For is it not a fact that a person mind is being continually filled with a future "I Want" for myself, this being a desire that is based upon a past "I Want" and that the "Present Time" is a world that is continuously clouded by a false personally based "Creation." For indeed the beauty, calmness, and harmony of the real world that exists around all people are in the "Present Time", this being that which our wise ancients speak about for it cannot be fully experienced when words and images are pounding in mind. Enlightenment is undoubtedly the road to a good future.

Yet is it not also true that there can be a fleeting "Present Time" harmony experienced in the sudden taste of good food, smelt as in the wonder of a rose, touched has in the marvel of "Self-Realising" the physical world around you, or heard as in the song of a bird or in chosen music or seen when looking down a valley when upon a mountain. For indeed it can be said that this world of harmony that can only exist in the "Present Time" is truly God's world or the world of Nature for the Non-Believer and it is a world that is speaking to you all the time – but more about this later.

Of course, personal harmony can be broken as in wars, of personnel conflict and personnel greed – but is it not strange that after the local war these countries usually return to their previously established borders which are based upon their countries language, for indeed it is known to be true that within our "Present Time" we can see how a country's harmony seems to be language-based? Does history not even show that there is a spoken harmony which a country returns to after another country's language-based harmony attempts to control it?

Is it not true that we now see many the countries of the Northern Hemisphere having a great desire to return to the harmony that resides within their language borders? Can it not also be said that this is because within the people's "rule of law" a country's harmony is attached to their original ancient verbal culture. So a foreign language-based unity cannot be imposed upon them. For it is undoubtedly true that every country's current harmony has emanated from their language and this harmony is based upon the past and that it is a local language that is continually being used to target the countries future? Is there not also a higher truth that there was an older original language being spoken in all the nations of the world? Therefore cannot it also be realised that the "Present Time" is the real world where God's or Nature's "harmony" truly, exists and that this is that which gives birth to the original language that existed before any language used by people and not only within that country but upon all countries of our Earth?

So yes! "Enlightenment" will take you to a real understanding of God's world, this being a living world which you will never be able to explain to others for our many wise ancients could not describe it except to say it is, "a realm beyond the ability of words to convey properly." Yet it is strange that many "Think" that they live in the "Present Time", but are neither "Self-Aware" nor "Self-Realised" for it cannot be true when thought entanglements paint their view of their "Present Time" which is a God's world or the world of Nature for the Non-Believer, for this is the only real world that exists all around you. Everyone knows this to be a truth.

So yes! The "Present Time" cannot exist in thought for it is said that "thinking" creates an illusionary world for it "paints" over the truth that exists all around each person for indeed it is a fact that ALL religions and philosophies target the need for their followers to enter the ever silent "Present Time" and all their creeds are born to achieve this "Reality" of living in God's world which can only be completed in the "Present Time" and so their target is for their followers to experience that which is called "Enlightenment", an experience which cannot be described. Therefore the feeling of the original "Reality" of God's world or the world of Nature for the Non-Believer, brings an understanding that this world can only be experienced and realised in the "Present Time" in which the past or the future cannot exist. For like all Fathers God protects and cares for all "Future" time needs the while like all Mothers the "Mother of the Creation" protects and cares for all "Present" time needs, and so they think has one and never contradict their essential duties.

Of course, there are many hundreds of our world's religions and philosophies and also thousands of breakaway separate teaching systems. Sadly many have created false worlds in which they state their own and personal "I Want" which is why they say, "My religion is better than your religion, and my way to God is better than your way to God" and also "Your way to God must be stopped, and God will bless me if I do this!" This mistake, of course, is an "I Want" and will certainly not by one jot change God's laws in which only "harmony" can exist. Therefore, it is true that ALL people need to seek their own "individually" accepted private and personal way that will bring them to achieve "Enlightenment," For Gods laws cannot make a mistake just has natural laws cannot make a mistake.

So yes! With the knowledge of this experience, the doer's only active practice will ALWAYS be to support the development of the harmony that exists in God's world, this being the world that is continuously living all around them – but forgetting is our worst enemy. Nevertheless "Sugar in the Water", meaning a taste of "Enlightenment" will show to them a personal joining with the harmony existing within the laws of God or Nature for the Non-Believer, for indeed these are laws that will always reward the seeker who experiences the unity that exists within the Creation or Nature for the Non-Believer.

Now here is an example contained in the few words about "Enlightenment" described by Jesus who all realise was filled by the Holy Spirit has is revealed in the Christian belief system. These are the sayings of Jesus the Christian incarnate. For it is said that when you read the words of Jesus, it is well to remember that it is God that is speaking to directly you!

– Luke 12:10-12 – *"Anyone who speaks against the Son of Man will be forgiven, but there is no forgiveness for the man who speaks evil against the Holy Spirit." It is also well to understand that the attacking or abusing of an "Enlightened" person is not good. Still, it does happen, so it is necessary to understand that God's harmony is not a harmony based upon riches and a power over others that are often desired by another".* So wisely Luke also added these words that he heard from Jesus: – *"And when they bring you before the synagogues and magistrates and authorities, don't worry as to what defence you are going to put up or what word you are going to use. For the Holy Spirit will tell you at the time what the right thing for you to say is."*

Thus this condition of "Enlightenment" is also described within the Christian religion as experiencing the Holy Spirit or Holy Ghost which is the non-thinking reality that ALL our world's religions and philosophies target and even speak about with their words for "Enlightenment" such as the experiencing of *"Moksha", "Bodhi", "Nirvana", "Gabriel", "Ushta",* and many more plus all stating it brings *"liberation", "salvation", "emancipation", "peace", "freedom",* and *"an awakening that is impossible to describe."* "The Book" will show that this fact is a reality and it will also show "scientifically" how to achieve this reality it for in truth it is the "Self-Realising" of a freed Soul, and so it is undoubtedly worth achieving. It is also worth understanding that all the world's religions and philosophies use their own "cultural" words to convey to their listeners how to accomplish and so experience Gods world or the world of Nature for the None-Believer, for indeed this is the actual experiencing the Godly harmony that can only exist in the "Present Time". For indeed all readers do "factually" and "scientifically" know that this is the only time in which God's world or Nature's world for the Non-Believer can exist, for it is only in the "Present Time" that God's Creation can be experienced. It is also true that when a person "Self" experiences this fact that this "Enlightenment" can be likened as to indeed be a gift from God or Nature for the Non-Believer, for such an experience has "Enlightenment" is a Godly gift which brings the knowledge of life itself - to the experiencer.

So yes! The first experience of "Enlightenment" will bring your thoughts to their knees in an obeying silence and your mind to an obedient "still" silence and this is a Godly or Nature given gift that is always within you. It is always waiting for those who have never experienced their real self, which is why the ancients call this experience "Self-Realisation" in which you experience the real "YOU" which is "Your Self"! For again is it not true, has the Christian gospel states, that when the Son of God named Jesus, this being a man who was also the personification of the Creation, was roughly arrested, He admonished one of his disciples for being brutal towards a guard, this being an act which is known to have broken the social harmony that was around them.

Is it not also stated that Jesus did correct this brutality to restore the balance that existed within that "Present Time". Is it not also said that Jesus then went quietly in keeping with the racial harmony of His captors and remained quietly within this racial harmony even when tortured, beaten and brutally nailed to a cross. Did He not indeed remain in silent obedience to this racial harmony until His last words which He spoke when realising His imminent death. This being when He said, *"Forgive them for they know not what they do"* and then he died. Factually did not this "Enlightened" act which came from His Soul change the world in which we now live? Is it not also true, seen by looking at our history, that brutal cultures are not accepted in God's world, or the world of Nature for the Non-Believers, for is it not also a truth that they are always eventually removed by the goodness residing within most people who are often surrounded by such evil?

So yes! the Holy Spirit or Holy Ghost that is spoken of in the Christian religion is truly an explanation of the "Enlightenment" which can arrive within any individual when their mind is still. They experience only the "Present Time" in which they are not "mindfully" contaminated by a manifesting past or a future "I Want", and this is a condition that can be achieved by anyone – but more lately in "The Book" about experiencing this reality.

Now here also are some words from our wise ancients starting with the words from the Prophet Muhammad Peace be upon Him:-

Quotes 3: The Golden Rule: "You will not enter paradise until you have faith. And you will not complete your faith until you love one another." Paradise is another word for "Enlightenment" and is the only place that God's world can be silently experienced. Also, the wise Srimad-Bhagavatam Chapter 3: Gajendra's Prayers of Surrender stated: - *"If one takes Krishna seriously, a devotee may externally not be very well educated but because of devotional services God gives him "Enlightenment" from within. If God gives "Enlightenment" from within, one can never be in ignorance."* Meaning that the person whose mind rests in the "Present Time", must always live in God's harmony and not in racial harmony and therefore they will live in the Heaven that exists upon our Earth. Also Chaitanya-Charitamrita, Adilila, and purport to 7.118 – *"When a person perfectly performs spiritual activities that lead to enlightenment, they become perfect in knowledge and understand that they are not God but a servant of God."* These statements are complete truths but may not be understandable to those whose minds continuously seeking ways to machinate and so create a personal "I Want". For accurately all religions and there are of course many religions and philosophies, have creeds that pursue the same beliefs by their differing and personal cultures and all state that "Enlightenment" reveals to the experiencer the only path of truth, for this, is a path towards a reality that shows that the purpose of a person's life is to be among all those who renew the world and who aid "naturally" the world's progress towards perfection which can only be done by genuinely supporting God's harmony or Nature's Harmony for the Non-Believer. For truly people can experience this "Enlightenment" which brings them to all that exists within all the environments of our world and which is an Enlightenment that truly experiences ALL conditions that are unfolding before all life and non-life.

Simply put all religions and philosophies say to their followers, *"Have Good Thoughts, say Good Words, do Good Deeds"* and *"There is only one path and that is the path of Truth"* or *"Cause brings Effect"* also stating *"Do the right thing because it is the right thing to do"* plus adding *"all beneficial rewards will come to you"* for these are sayings that come to us from our ancient times.

So yes! "Self-Realising" the experience of "Enlightenment" means to live in the "Present Time" which is God's world or Nature's world for the Non-Believer. Thus the "Present Time" is the only world that can be heard, seen, touched, smelt or tasted for none of these experiences can be realised in the past or the future, these being the place where the untrained "I Want" mind lives.

It is also mentioned at this point that when a writer uses the religious sayings of our wise ancients that none can be sued for explaining an ancient description of their words. This classical description is because all our ancient wise knew that the target of their sayings is to support God's world that always exists upon our Earth. Thus these ancient sayings are used because all the worlds' wise ancients knew that it is the Godly given "Freedom of Choice" the deciding factor which supports all Godly activities which are so designed to accept support and actively maintain God's "living" harmony that ALWAYS rests upon this Earth. Yet, it is also further understood that people had been given this "Freedom of Choice", this being because a personal act can support the development of the Creation but sometimes that same act can destroy it.

This explanation means that it can only be an individual activity which is often and "Holistically" used to resist the racial harmony that they see around them. Thus racialism is that condition when many only exist to pursue an own "I Want" and so do not to support God's harmony or Nature's harmony for the Non-Believer, this being characterised by the view that a whole system of beliefs must be considered rather than its parts for truly "Enlightenment" can be realised by the use of only one word – but more later about this in "The Book".

So yes! Then a person, who is "Enlightened" and living in "unselfish" harmony, will become a good "seed" in all the communities that exist within God's world or the world of Nature for the Non-Believer, this being where no "I Want" for me weed is allowed to destroy them. For these words in "The Book" are designed to encourage and give birth to all communities simple "seeding" that the ancients revealed is that which will bring to all devotees that which our ancients call "Enlightenment".

Thus "Enlightenment" is that same seed that activated and pursued the growth of all the religions and philosophies. It does not matter if you live amongst the birds, rocks or thorns for the "seeds" presented in the following pages will produce an exceptional healthy ground that will remove you and your children from living in a Hell that is created by other people or your own cruel "I Want" world of disharmony and greed.

For it is true that ALL Religions and Philosophies target and endeavour to stop your five senses from they're ignorant but animalistic pursuing of THEIR own personal "I Want". This reality of experiencing "Enlightenment" is simply achieved by choosing to live in the "Heaven" that can only exist in the "Present Time"; this being the only place which is filled by the Godly harmony that brings "Enlightenment" and also it's experiencing the Bliss that *"Surpasses All Understanding".*

For indeed this can be achieved by all people for it is not bound only to those who have a personal religious or a group spiritual practice but whom simply believe in the goodness (Godness) of Nature and this is that experience which can only exist in "The Present Time" and within your current life and also your life to come. So it is good always to remember that this personal "choice" to become "Self-Realised" and thus experience "Enlightenment" is only yours and this is true whether you believe in a God or Nature for the experiencing of "Enlightenment" is simply based upon each person "Freedom of Choice", this being a "choice" to target the experience of "Enlightenment" the target of ALL our religions and philosophies.

For it does not matter what current beliefs are held by you, be they religious, atheist, agnostic or just plainly ignoring that which is in front of you. Thus these later writings in "The Book" will describe a path towards living an "Enlightened" and contented life for any individual (Soul) that is currently alive and resting in people for it reveals in simplicity how to achieve the target of ALL our major religions and philosophies. Simply put this is because the modern-day describing words in "The Book" will show how to experience God's or Nature's "Harmony" that can only exist in the Present Time. For indeed, this is a life that will bring to the "doer" the "Enlightenment" that all the world's religions and philosophies seek for their followers, this is being the actual experiencing "Enlightenment", which is also called *"Peace that surpasses all understandings",* and yes, it is an "Enlightenment" that can reside in all people's lives. Still, many have lost the knowledge of how to awaken this experience and so be able to enter Gods world or the real world of Nature for the Non-Believer, this being the world of "Enlightenment". Thus, "Enlightenment" is a world that all our wise ancients say will bring the true peace that will remove all mind filling negative and self-harming belief systems that currently entangle the "I Want" world, this being that we as individuals do "Choose" to live. It will also stop some leaders of our various religions from attacking other leaders of different faiths in a pursuit that says, "I Want my way of worship and my administration to be more important than your way of worship and your way of administration." Indeed many government politicians do the same by saying, "I want my politics to be first because your politics do not have well as mine" – this is not the actual world, but it is a world that the freedom born from the gift of a personal choice has made.

So yes! To pursue the belief systems, contained within these writings, it is to be realised that it does not matter what your reality is or your political, tribal, family, personal, philosophical or religious beliefs are. For in truth, the following "modern" written words in "The Book" will show "Scientifically" the way to achieve an individual "Enlightenment", this being that which all religions and philosophies speak about and which cannot be changed. For definitely, you will come to "modernly" understand that the most significant Church that you can belong to is "personally" within you. It will also be found that the greatest and purest "creed", meaning faith, dogma, doctrine, philosophy, belief, principle, and especially your understanding of personal faith are also all within YOU!

So yes! Now it is useful to understand that much of the disciplines practised within our world's religions and philosophies were anciently designed to bring to the people of that particular countries culture a personal way to "Enlightenment", this being under the knowledge and culture which their devotees possessed. Therefore all activities practised within that religion or philosophy was culturally designed to bring their followers into the "Present Time", which is God's world for the past, and the future does not exist.

For indeed this God (Good) reality is always available to all people, but it can only live in the Present Time, this being the current time in which rests that "Enlightenment" which cannot be explained in words – and it is there for YOU! An example of this is that many say that Jesus did not historically exist - this is not important. What is important are the writings about His words which are very "Enlightening," for they bring the light of "Realisation" to the observing readers' minds and so remove the fearing darkness of the unknown has also does the work of many of our ancient "Godly" teachers. This "Realisation" is a truth that you will quickly understand and begin to savour as you start to establish your simple way to an "Enlightenment" in which you realise that you cannot be harmed, persecuted or harassed by others. For in this proposed creed-based simple path that is shown in "The Book", you will be able to follow a straightforward way that will take you to "Enlightenment".

This experiencing of "Enlightenment" means that you will find an existence in God's world or the world of Nature for the Non-Believer, which is a world of harmony, enjoyment, and well-being which all the wise ancients say has been given for you. As indeed as an individual, you will undoubtedly find this truth. You will also find that within "The Book" will be the answer to the questions, ***"What is the immortality of the spirit, and where do I come from? Where am I*** *going to? What is the point of my existence? What is the Soul and who or what is God and also "What supports Nature?"* But there are knowingly only three truths on this path to *"Self-Realisation",* and these are needed to be:-

1. Have a generous heart.
2. Use only kind words.
3. Pursue the wellbeing of others.

For correctly only in this way, explained by "The Book" will you experience your life in harmony and if you need to find the answers to these questions – READ ON

3 WHO ARE "YOU"?

So yes! God's world or the world of Nature for the Non-Believer is the world that is without a personal "I Want" demand, this being that which forgetting - and forgetting is our worst enemy – and so it is because of forgetting that people fill their minds with many "I Want for me" thoughts. For truly Gods' world or Natures world for the Non-Believer is also a world that is without intellect, ego, or the needs of five senses, for people can genuinely and honestly move above and beyond all these gifts. It is also good to remember that "You" are not the ether, nor the Earth, nor water nor fire, and you are certainly not the wind. You are also not the energy that you fell rests within you, nor is your energy anything that exists or works within or without your body. Neither are you that thought in mind or that which thinks or speaks within you, nor are you that who holds another's hands nor are you any part of the body that moves, for you are indeed a life force which is a force that knowingly know is a life that contains all life and all the Non-Life that rests upon our Earth. Thus the reality of "Enlightenment" is a life experience that understands and also knows that it is a part of everything that exists in this ever-moving ever still world which consists of a blissful harmony of a love that has no neighbour, for you are an entity that can have total awareness of that which is God's world or the world of Nature for the Non-Believer. For real, you contain no hatred or dislike; neither have you any separate relationships for you exist within all things. You also have no hate, greed, delusion, pride or arrogance, nor do you have any feelings of envy or jealousy. You have no duty, nor any desire, nor any need to seek freedom. For you are that which is filled with a knowing that nothing needs to be identified because all knowledge has been given to you that you need to know and which does always exists but only in the "Present Time".

Neither do you experience any value or devalue that is attached to you nor can any happiness, sorrow, pain or pleasure be connected to you for you are beyond all these things. You no longer need creeds, holy places, scriptures, rituals or sacrifices of time and leisure. This reality is because you are the faithful observer of all these things, an observer who experiences the process of observing and knowing that that which you observe is always yourself.

You do not have any fear of death for you know that you cannot die. You do not have any fear of ever being separated from that which you know is the real you. You do not have any doubt about your existence and why you exist nor have you any judgment on the place and the conditions of your birth. You know that you have no Earthly father or Earthly mother who created you or gave birth to you. You have no separate relatives or friends, nor do you have the need of a teacher, nor are you that which is taught.

For in "Enlightenment" you "know" and you understand that you are all-pervading, without any attributes, and any known form. You cannot be attached to the world either can you be freed from it or need you to wish for anything because you are everything that is everywhere, and you exist in all people and in all time zones in which you are always in perfect balance.

You cannot be the "Server" or the "Servant", who is accommodating, caring, nurturing, hospitable and charitable. Nor can you be the "Artisan" who is creative, inventive, imaginative, playful, and dexterous. Nor can you be the "Warrior" who is forceful, loyal, protective, determined, and steadfast or are you the "Scholar" who is curious, attentive, academic, analytical, and neutral. You also cannot be the naturally engaging "Sage" who is, articulate, charming, entertaining plus expressive. Nor can you be a "Priest" who is inspirational, uplifting, motivating, energising, visionary and lastly you cannot be a "King" or "Queen" who is loyal, commanding, assured, powerful, authoritative and decisive.

For you are the Soul, the life force that knowingly contains the realisation of all life and Non-Life, for as a "Self-Realised" person you join with the "Self-Awareness" of your Soul and so "Self-Realise" that you are part of everything that exists in this ever-moving yet still world which consists of a blissful harmony within a love that has no neighbour and so you know that is an entity with total awareness of being empowered by God or "No-Thing" a (Nothing) to the Non-Believer.

So yes! We should always understand that a person's silent and personal "Soul" is that which sees and listens to everything but in people, it is also Godly requested to allow its carrier to be "animalistic" within the freedom of its "Consciousness", which is the energy that controls all life forms. But in people the Soul has been "Godly Given" (or Nature Given for the Non-Believer), the instructions not to interfere with a person's "Freedom of Choice" for indeed the same act can create harmony, but in other circumstances, it can destroy it. For the Godly reason why "Freedom of Choice" was given to people was so that they could aid and support the "Heaven" or "Nature" that exists only in the "Present Time" for the Past and the Future do not exist.

Yet, all should know that within this divinely given (or Nature has given) "Freedom of Choice", people have forgotten their purpose and so often "choose" to take for themselves that which belongs to Nature or "Others": This is the "I Want" for myself Hell that people can create and which emanates only in the mind that is blocked with Past or Future thoughts which stops the Soul from seeing out of the body and into Gods world or the world of Nature for the Nonbeliever. It is this perpetual "misunderstanding" which creates a personally made Hell for it stops the "Soul" from seeing through the silent mind the needs of the Heaven that rests only in the Present Time, this being the world that only people can "choose" to live in and also "choose" to support. For indeed we are the Soul, this being that which cannot die and which rests within all people and whose only purpose is to support the developing work "Mother of the Creation" and so if you wish to free your Soul - then Read on.

4 WHERE IS HEAVEN OR HELL

Do you believe that there is a Heaven or a Hell that you go to when you die? Do you also think that in Hell you will be in pain forever, but in Heaven, you will be forever with loving families who have gone before you and to meet their families who have gone before them? Is it not also true that many who wish to impose their "I Want" upon you state these conditions to be facts? Or do you believe that upon death you will "sleep" until the next Big Bang? This "Big Bang" being when the "Creation" starts again or the beginning of the Universe for the Non-Believer; the only difference is the name?

The first statement of going to Heaven or Hell upon death and being punished forever is such a punishing waste that many believe that it cannot be accurate. For many people also agree that it is more natural to realise that no "Father" or "Mother" could create such a wasteful punishing "Hellish" system for their child. But what we know and understand is that the hypotheses of the Big Bang indicate that the universe came from an existing origin, as do all known births of life and what is further interesting is that all people are a part of this known explosion that began the creation of this known Earth which is a known singularity –called "The Creation" or the "The World of Nature".

So yes! Many major religions and all philosophical beliefs systems indeed state that it is impossible to think that such a position after death could be inflicted upon the children of the Creation, this being an unchanging and punishing way of a long "existence" after a death, particularly after such a short period of life. For indeed God does not and cannot punish you in your current life, for God gave you the "Freedom of Choice", even unto the cross, for if you put your hand into boiling water, who is it that is punishing you and if you break a natural law – who is sinning and so who is it that is deciding the conditions of their next life?

What is more plausible, and this is by a proven scientific reality, is that you cannot destroy energy and if it is "destroyed" it will be reborn again elsewhere.

Does this not mean that all the energy within the Creation cannot die and so will reactivate and therefore "scientifically", can never leave the Creation or Nature for the Non-Believer, this being a fact that is revealed by our scientist. Do our scientists not also acknowledge that this energy reactivation must be the same as the source from whence it came? Is it not, therefore even "scientifically" stated that energy must always be "naturally" recoupable and thus cannot be lost. If this is true and it is easy to understand has the truth, then your loving ancestors are truly living around you and that you too can be classed as an "ancestor" and maybe to the bloodline that is all around you.

Therefore clearly, when you die, you do not go to a Heaven or a Hell because the fact is that when you die, you can only "leave" Heaven or your personally created Hell. And this entry into limbo may be a temporary situation, or maybe it will be for a more extended period in accordance to God's or Nature laws resting within the harmony seeking factors governed by the "Mother of the Creation". She, like God, will never leave you. However, it can be likened that both their faces will be turned away from you and your personally created Hell, but without a doubt, their love for you will return you when you genuinely support the Heaven that can only rest in the "Present Time". These are the laws implanted by God which state that His child cannot die, and they cover His love for the "Mother of the Creation" and for their only child, which is the Creation and of course the unity which exists upon planet Earth.

It thereof is a simple logic that God or No-Thing for the Non-Believer has NOT created "you" to waste "you" after such a short time of life. For as the law of energy states – you will "reincarnate", and your body will be used again by "your" Soul and genuinely many of our wise ancients who birthed our religions and philosophies testify to this fact. Also, this logical fact, which is newly stated here, is that this reincarnation purpose is to unify again and again your ageing Soul with the activity of a body whose target is to be more and more useful in supporting the harmony seeking activities of the developing Creation – why is this?

Cannot it be that God smiles when experiencing the love of that part of His only child that we call "The Soul", this being that which exists within an advanced consciousness of His Creation- which is His only Child? For honestly, all Religions and Philosophies state the Creation is the only child of God, who is the Father of the Creation but "The Book" has "scientifically" said there to be a *"Mother of the Creation"*, who like all Mothers is the primary Teacher and carer of their only child.

For indeed cannot it be said that it is Her Motherly love that keeps the Creation harmoniously going towards its divine target – but many who have personal life still ask, "Why is there a Creation?" The simple answer is that which also rests within all, and this is that God was lonely. For indeed, it is a reality that loneliness is also the greatest fear of people and is it not true that even the hermit avoids isolation for he also cannot leave God?

So yes! It was "Unsurprisingly", "Logically" and "Scientifically" to understand that it was because of loneliness that God created and then seeded Space, the Mother and carer of all life and the one. They gave birth to the only Child that we call the Creation. For truly God is no longer lonely, and so actually experiences a well-based love that all fathers and mothers experience at the birth of their child – for is this not a simple truth that rests within all people? For it is undoubtedly known to be true that encased in each person's self-based fear, is the knowledge and experience that no one should ever be lonely? Therefore can it not be logically correct that there is a *"Mother of the Creation",* who is the Mother and carer of all our Creations life and Non-Life and who was always created to care and be with you? Therefore cannot it also be true that it is "She" who you can "feel" in the love of "Space" that is silently around you and within you and which is called "Enlightenment", this being the *"Peace that Surpasses all Understanding"!* Which is indeed a fact that is described in many different ways by ALL our world's religions and philosophies for "Enlightenment" is an experience of being has one with the "Creation", or maybe it is an experience of being in the arms of "Mother of the Creation" and "The Book" continually says that it is an experience that now awaits you no matter if you are a believer or a non-believer or what belief system you have.

So yes! It is well to remember that whether you currently live in Heaven or in Hell on this Earth that God and the "Mother of the Creation" really loves you? Does not this great truth also show in the fact that God or Nature for the Non-Believer has given each person the "Freedom of Choice"? Therefore can it not be true that if you live in a painful Hell on this Earth that you may be punishing yourself and woe to them who inflict "unnatural" punishment upon others, for undeniably they will experience in their next life a pain that can only exist in the animal kingdom.

For cannot it be true that God, who knows that with the support and teachings of the Creations Mother, any adult will eventually learn how to live in Heaven while alive on the earth, and so live in the Godly Harmony that is endeavouring to expand around them? Also cannot it be seen to be true that the "Mother of the Creation" is a great Mother who maintains the harmony, wisdom, and balance of the Creation which is a continuation that cannot be stopped? Again is it not also true that you know when you are living in Heaven on this Earth because you can taste the "Sugar in the Water"? This "Sugar in the Water" is the sweet and needed gift that She presents to you so that you physically know the need to continue expanding the harmony that is evolving and being released all around you. This changing is a harmony that you – when "Enlightened" - will personally identify and then support. Therefore is it not also important to remember and so know that none of the Mothers "Sugar" which sweetens life and which is given by the Mother to encourage the good work of her Child can make the receiver annoyed?

So yes! It is essential to understand that the "Mother of the Creation" can, like all mothers, only reward this "Sugar" to those who unselfishly seek harmony for all of life and Non-Life. She cannot give "Sugar" to those who oppose this work. Those who oppose her work do live in a dream akin to a nightmare, and this is living in a Hell while on this Earth.

So yes! the quickest way to awaken to the reality of a life lived in Heaven is to let the *"Mother of the Creation"* s purpose act through your Soul, which can readily identify these needs but only when your mind filling thoughts of "I Want" for myself stop, these being thoughts which block the Soul from seeing the outside world – but more about this later in "The Book" but what can be said now is that this clarity can be more fully "Self-Realised" when you move towards "Enlightenment." For experiencing "Enlightenment" means that that you have emptied your mind and so it has joined with the stillness of the "Present Time" and so is no longer filled with a brain filled "I Want". This "dream" is that which is based upon past or a future "I Want" dream. For indeed, it is this "I Want" activity that fills the mind and so blocks the Soul from seeing through the brain and observing the Creations' needs. This activity simply means that you should "Self-Realise" that you ALWAYS have the ***"Freedom of Choice"*** to both simply "observe", with an empty mind, and so become aware of the necessary support of the "Mother of the Creation" endeavours or to opposing live in your self-created mind filled nightmare created by your five senses, these being that which are always sounding into the mind their "I Want" for themselves, This is truly a fascinating fact but is it not reasonable that being born has a person you have been given the "Freedom of Choice"?   This "Freedom of Choice" is a reality which all our wise ancients speak.

Now let us understand that when ALL our wise ancients talk about this return to a life that is lived in Heaven, this being while living upon this Earth, that the best progress towards this living can only be achieved by unselfish love for the world. This "unselfish love" means that the actual activating of "harmony seeking actions", is being accomplished by a person and are acts which will automatically lead to a life that can be likened to living in Heaven while living on this Earth. Therefore, yes, these are acts that can only be achieved in the "Present Time", this being God's creation and a world that is cared for by the "Mother of the Creation".

Is it not also stated to be accurate by our holy ones that these "right actions" which are performed by individuals also lead to a GOOD rebirth in their next life? Or perhaps, as is often stated by our wise, been placed into a new bloodline in which the "Mother of the Creation" has put them in because She knows that She can make good use of them in her on-going pursuit of harmony within the one body, this being that which we call the Creation of the world or Nature for the Non-Believer. For indeed God is also outside of Time and Space, but this is not the reality for the *"Mother of the Creation"* so that when our Soul sees the "Present Time", which can only be accomplished by a mind without thought, it is likened to be "Fully" experiencing the Love of God and the *"Mother of the Creation"*. Again it is this experience that the ancients called "Enlightenment".

So yes! Reliably God does not do anything for He has already done all that is needed to be done and His plan is evolving in accordance to His laws which is "harmoniously" controlled by the "Mother of the Creation". So truly is there any person who believes that they can change this evolution and so permanently break this unfolding law's by their own "I Want"?

Is it not also interesting to think that we have amongst all populations many early and new personal births that have recently emerged from the animal kingdom, and which have been "programmed" to be reborn as people because their environment has been destroyed? Is it not also true that these new-births from the animal kingdom need special consideration - but they are not foolish and will become "naturally" harmful to others if they are being maltreated has been animals. For indeed there is a great need to teach these early births from the animal kingdom and to do this by showing care, kindness, and consideration for they do need to be taught how to live within the laws of people. But how do you recognise these early past animal re-births that have now become people? Well, they can and will kill other people without problems and can easily steal for they feel no law against hunting and they can also start a war without difficulty and only a democracy in which a decision is made by the majority of people - can control them. Yet, it is also clearly unwise to place then in cages and so persecute these new "people" or to treat them like beasts of burden for in the next life you may well be positioned in rehabilitation and "re-taught" by being born as an animal. Then you should hope that you will be placed with a good "understanding" owner who will teach, train and treat you with honour.

So yes! It is further understood that "The Book" explains a significant need to move away from a mind blocked with "I Want" only for "ME" beliefs. For it can now be said that these modern words in "The Book" are written in an informal way which can breed a different understanding from that world of long ago? For indeed this is now being the "Present Time", a modern time in which people no longer believe that the Earth is flat or that the Earth is the centre of the universe nor a universe which always revolves around them. For we now understand that the world is a creation that is a truly a harmonised "single" whole which contains all life and Non-Life and that factually it is based upon a collection of atoms which are composed of sub-atomic particles which we call protons, neutrons, and electrons some of which instantly change their past positions when simply observed by the power resting within a person's gaze.

5   WHAT IS "ENLIGHTENMENT"?

The first step for the world of people is to realise the factual truth that rests behind the simple words "Don't be afraid of God's Creation" or that which is called "Nature" by our Non-Believers!

All people know of a prevalent "scientific" fact, is that no matter what we think and believe or what we achieve we "scientifically" state that the "planned" ending of God's Creation or what is known as the Universe by the Non-Believer, will always be accomplished. We also state that people will never be able to stop this harmonious and lawful development towards the Creations end, its death.

What is also true is that only people have been given the gift of "choice". So they can "choose" to support the development of this on-going harmonious fact, this fact is to aid the development of God's pursuit of harmony, which is a "good" (Godly) thing to do according to all our major religions and philosophies. Or they can "choose" to act against it and so seek a personal "I Want" which is not suitable according to all our major religions and philosophies.

So how do you choose or even know what to do with your life that currently exists within the Creation? The simple fact to understand is that what you believe is powerfully acting has the "you" is not you! But factually "it" does seem that it is you that consistently chooses what to do and the source of a motivational "single" thinking entity also strongly believes that it is you. But the truth is that this targeting of your motivation is emanating from the demanding five senses which you "mechanically" and "habitually" think is the real you because you believe that they know what you want and also they "tell" you what you need to do to get their "I Want".

So what is now needed to be fully understood is that God gave to all life the light of "consciousness" but it was only to people that God gave to this "light", the "Freedom of Choice", this being to do or not to do, to be or not to be, to live or not to live. But mistakenly people "choose" in childhood to empower their five senses with the gift of "choice". So people "choose" to re-direct this "choice" from their Soul and automatically gave this freedom of choice to their five senses and so we entered the "Iron Age" spoken of by our ancestors. So what is now really necessary to understand is that the guiding principle that rests within you, this being the real you, is your Soul. This real you is a Soul that has been Godly given or Nature given the "The Freedom of Choice", this being so it can do any task that assists in the development of God's harmony or Nature's harmony for the Non-Believer. It should also be further understood that the purpose and reason why the Soul has been given this "Freedom of Choice" is because people sometimes need to perform an act that aids and supports the developing harmony which is moving through the Creation in the Present Time. Still, it should be further understood that this same act under different conditions could destroy the emerging unity – hence the God-given "Freedom of Choice", which means that it is essential and necessary for the Soul to do the duty that rests upon it, which is to harmonise the ever-developing Creation! But how do you become obedient to this task and so enable your Soul to achieve the ability required to support only God's harmony which is emerging all around it? – Read on.

So now the first "important" suggestion, which is based upon many years of "scientific" and practical analysis of pursuing the truth that rests within and all around us, is to discover which task to do, is the most important, especially when you are "thinking" what action to do or "thinking" what work not to do or merely pursuing the act of NOT "thinking" but actually "knowing" without thought what action to do or NOT to do. For definitely, it is now right to know that these caring "unthinking" actions can be easily pursued towards accomplishment by the Soul, which is the real you, for the Soul knows because it is attached to everything. For what you now habitually think is the real you just sound in mind. For undeniably if you hear in the mind words saying what to do or what not to do, it will be words emanating the five senses who may also be arguing amongst themselves and who are always seeking their "personal" "I Want", for indeed the silent mind knows what action is needed to be accomplished. For it is now right to know that these five senses are NOT the real you for they are of the body. For the real you is the Soul, this being that entity which listens to and observes these words that have in the past been personally allowed to declare the "I want" sounds and pictures emanating from the five senses and so freely realised into the mind, this being because YOU have "historically" and "habitually" chosen that this is what should be allowed – probably in childhood.

But it is the five senses that are continually gabbling in the mind their own "I Want", a fact that blocks the Soul from seeing through the mind and into the needs of the world, this being that which we call "The Creation". For indeed these five senses where childhood "freed" to pursue their own "I Want" and so habitually you now think that they are you! They are not you, for you are the Soul who obediently listens to the sound emanating from the five senses and which do argue in persons the mind for their own "personally" desired claim for an "I Want". For truly, they are not the entities that have been chosen to create or support the goodness in God's or Natures harmony that is obediently all around them. For these five senses are "animalistic" in nature and so fight and argue over what to touch, taste, smell, hear or see, this being truly any substance within the creation that is separately influencing them. It is this that physically and falsely motivates their actions in the ever-developing ongoing life that exists all around them.

Therefor to stop these individuals arguing claims of an "I Want" that is continually sounding from the five senses is not easy to achieve, this being because you think they are you, but indeed they are NOT you! It is this false reasoning in the "animalistic" thinking that the five senses are you that always brings misery because they are always endeavouring to claim all that exists within the creation. But the reality of your life is that you can, by the application of individual personal disciplines', indeed find and KNOW which harmony is seeking action or lack of response you "naturally" need to achieve to "naturally" engage and truly and blissfully support the world around you. This support is the reality of "being has one" with all that is around you, and it is this reality which is called "Enlightenment". But there is one activity attached to the senses which is a Godly legal desire and which encompasses the total satisfaction of touch, taste, smell, hear or see, and we all know what this personal activity is! But it should always be understood that the disciplining and so stopping of the five senses from freely and automatically sounding their "I Want" into the mind, which was innocently allowed in childhood, can always be achieved. Our ancients called this achievement "Enlightenment", which "scientifically" means that the Soul can see through the now still mind and so become at first "Self-Aware" and secondly to become "Self-Realised" and thus experience the truth that exits in the "Present Time" – which is Gods world or the world of Nature for the Non-Believer.

This reality is that condition, called "Enlightenment", which all religions and philosophies physically do target. This target being because our wise ancients knew that it is "scientifically" possible to become as one with your real natural "Self" and so become one with the world. For they knew that in experiencing this truth a person will "automatically" do all that can be done to support the developing harmony emanating from all that is around them and therefore avoid the painful misery that comes when people claim it for "themselves" and so go against the creations target.

Now, which part of you is saying that this is wrong and that only supporting your personal, or family or racial harmony is the correct way ahead? But if you do think that this particular search for achieving "Enlightenment" is a wrong concept – Read on, for it will be proved "scientifically" that ALL religions and philosophies have been personally targeted by a wise instigator, to show that people need to actively support not only their loved ones and their own and community cultures but also to "non-interferingly" observe all other differently developing cultures and other religions in which their expanding world is bringing to them – but only if it is possible to do so.

For truly is not the world of nature showing us that there is a static but ongoing development of the Creations or Nature's evolving plan, a plan which is based upon a natural harmony that exists all around us and which matches that growing harmony which is within us and of course there are cultural shocks has when the earth stretches it muscles etc.

So yes! This static but ever-moving natural world that truly exists around all people is indeed an organic evolution which has an absolute truth that ensures that all-life and all non-life, this being that which exists all around us, is to be "Nature-ally" served the same way as the "unselfish" harmony that exists within our bodies. Thus truly our body is also an entity that contains trillions of separate individuals who all live according to the law of a unified and compatible whole – this being a fact that people should also copy.

Thus indeed, the Creation or Nature for the Non-Believer is always pursuing an evolutionary plan that is based upon a harmony that can be seen by those who have eyes to see and ears to hear? Therefore is it not also true that all people can see the truth that within the Creation was born our Earth whose harmony is still growing. Is it not also truly realised that this growing harmony is everywhere upon our planet? For indeed does not the Creation that exists outside of people also be known to be correct based upon a developing certainty that can be found to be an absolute reality by all who wish to look for it. Therefore can it not also said to be true that this same evolutionary reality that exists outside our bodies is the same compatible reality that exists within our bodies?

Therefore is it not also true that all around us we see this law of natural harmony existing between all things and is endeavouring to emerge within all things? Is it not even noticed that when this Godly or Natural "harmony" is personally broken, it is only a passing situation for it cannot be destroyed except temporarily by our unwise?

Does not our people's ancient and modern history prove this, as in the Eastern side of the North of our Northern Hemisphere including the former USSR? Do we not now also see that all languages are returning to govern themselves within the ancient borders of their language and that a second language is struggling to unite all of them into one unified acceptance – and woe be to that country which tries to stop this for its leaders will be quickly challenged and changed for this new search for the "legal" unification of all these countries cannot be stopped.

A more direct way to assist this expansion and the legal joining together of like-minded but different language countries is for those who are unsure of themselves to "scientifically" and "factually" acknowledge that truly people can "create" a good (GOD) world that is based upon the wishes of at least 65% of that country's population, this being a majority based decision which shows the acceptance of any goodly act that effects the world that exists around them

Is this not also an informed development that is continuously and naturally taking place all around us and which can only be observed in the Present Time? Is it not also true that any harmony seeking actions can also be sparked into a beginning by individuals who are attached to groups, communities, or even regions, and countries and it is not also indeed acknowledged that this harmony seeking action can only happen in the "Present Time", for truthfully is this not a simple fact that can readily be accepted by all people? But it is not also a known fact that such unifying actions can only be performed by personal "individuals". These are individuals who calmly attempt to change the racial harmony that governs only them and maybe the life outside their tribes' borders.

So yes! The real endeavour is to establish God's or Natures Harmony for the Nonbeliever, this being that which also governs our world for a right way of understanding the way of life which is to simply support the "Present Time" which is Godly provided. For this is the inevitable reality which all the major religions and philosophies speak about and to which they have given many names like "purification", the "experiencing God's Grace" or the seeking of "Enlightenment", this being a personal condition which is the experiencing of God's world or the real world of Nature for the Non-Believer.

So yes! What is "Enlightenment?" It cannot be explained, but it is a condition that is likened to be an "unthinking" all pleasing state which people can genuinely experience by stopping the consistently reporting "I Want" which is emanating from the five senses and filling the mind with past and future thoughts and so blocking the Souls view from seeing the needs of what we call the "Present Time". Therefore, indeed does it not "scientifically" and honestly, know that the past and or the future do not exist? Then honestly, if it is a fact that only the "Present Time" exists then this silence in mind must be a personal state and a state in which the Soul can then "experience" 100% of that which exists in the "Present Time" and without any added corrupting thoughts?

So, is it not also a "scientific" fact that "Nothing" except the "Present Time" can be experienced but only when a person's mind is filled with "Nothing" which allows a clear view of the Soul, through the brain and so "experience" that which we call "Present Time"? Is it not also a well-known truth for all people can understand that this "stillness" is that which is happening only in the "Present Time", a time that exists only in God's world or in the world of Nature for the Non-Believer? This real-world is being that which can only exist in the "Present Time" and which is an "existence" that cannot be in the future or the past for these times do not exist.

So the "Present Time", "scientifically" must be the only existence which has been given to us by God or Nature for the Non-Believer. For indeed if you're belief is that "All is Nature's Creation" is a more accurate way than thinking "All is God's Creation", then factually both "thinkers" know that "Nature" or the "Creation" will grow only according to a pre-planned development that cannot be stopped.

So yes! We should keep in mind when reading the following "scientific" revelations that only the "Present Time" exists, for only the "Present Time" can be observed in this on-going strategic development of God's or Nature's harmony. Therefore is it not also seen to be true that there is in the "Present Time" a "Natural" harmonious benefit within a world that exists all around people, this being a world that contains not only all people but also all life and all Non-Life? It is also a known truth that the only thing that can destroy the existing harmony that surrounds everything - is people.

So Yes! This "scientific" fact is also a fact that should prove a truth that only "people" can "choose" a way to move correctly forward into the current world in which we all live. It is therefore known to accept Nature's way of growing plus moving forward, which can only occur and happen in that which is now known to be the Present or Present Time. Thus it can be said that the current way towards the experiencing of God or Natures world, is to support the harmony that exists in the "Present Time", for who can genuinely help the past or the future? Sadly many have falsely thought that they could, for is it not also a truth that our history always prove that they were wrong? People must now sit up and take note of these facts for "spiritually", which is a word that is also understood by the Non-Believer, it's a well-known fact that people are the only life force that has been given the gift of "choice" even to choose death if this is the required action, sadly this being a well-known fact in acts of war.

So yes! Indeed, this "Freedom of Choice" is a gift that has been given to people so that they can support and live within the laws of harmony, which always exists or are trying to survive in the personally made racial harmony that is all around them. For indeed, this way to "Enlightenment" is "always" a "Personal" choice and it is a personal choice that usually accepts the supporting and the developing needs of the natural harmony which also exists all around them and which is also "always" growing within the environment that exists and is expanding all around them. It can also be a "Personal Choice" to attack the development of any on-going harmony in an endeavour to gain a personal "I Want" gratification, a sure way to the troubled world of hell, which signifies that this individual mind is focused on the Past or the Future, which is the dwelling place of Hell.

So the new question is, "Which performing act will lead to someone receiving the rewards wrapped in contentment and bliss while living in this harmony that supports all life and whose personnel activities are NOT bringing them this happiness and peace? An interesting question for the observation and answer to the above is *"Which person is living in "Heaven" while on this Earth and which person is living in "Hell" while upon this Earth?"*

So yes! What can be indeed proven is that the Creation or Nature's Harmony for the Non-Believer is continually seeking and pursuing an on-going harmony which cannot be changed - for that is its purpose? For indeed this is a unity creating endeavour which can be "scientifically" recognised as a constant development that is targeting a unification which cannot "scientifically" go wrong?

Is it not also true that when we look back through history, we can recognise that the on-going Creation is a compelling and ongoing development? Therefore is it not also true that this "Creation" is truly an on-going force that corrects people's folly and brings them again and again back to the path of harmony for all life and Non-Life? Is it not therefore useful to look around our world and so understand who are breaking these laws that are continually seeking a peaceful harmony??

So yes! By a "scientific" understanding does not the Creation or Nature for the Non-Believer, always target a continuation of this harmonious "Present Time", this usually being within all the environmental locations in which people exist? Is it not also "scientifically" known that there is no need to find ways of returning to the development of harmony in the places where people do not exist? Is it not also clear that people cannot change God's laws or Nature's lawsuits which are always and naturally pursue harmony? Yet! Strangely, many people think that they can change the natural ways of God or the means of Nature for the Non-Believer. Hence these wars between people with different languages will continue individual tribes isolated by language pursue a personal leader "I Want.

So yes! Is it not also true that there are simply "I Want" disputes not only between countries or communities but also within individuals and families? Does not our people's history always state this truth? Is it not also true that the most disastrous breaks in harmony that occur upon this planet are being imposed by some tribal leaders personal "I Want"? Is this being an "I Want" that changes the laws which are used to control their tribe, for this "I Want" can be just the needs of the leaders of people? Yet the truth as history shows is that all cruel "leaderships" that have created brutality within tribal cultures is always corrected.

So yes! Cannot it now be witnessed that in the world's Eastern Northern Hemisphere, the control of all countries has been returned to the language borders of that country and so are again being ruled by the will of the people who speak its original language?

For was it not true that there often is a greed-based "I Want" within foreign-speaking tribal leaders. Are these not leaders who birth a desire to impose a foreign "I Want" upon the people whose culture exits only within the borders that contain their language? Is it not also seen to be "scientifically" valid that again and again in our recent "Present Time" that the attacking of a foreign language country breaks the harmony of these countries people, but is it not also recognised that God's unity always returns control to the people who speak the original language of that country?

So indeed, these invading foreign leaders are the perpetrators of disharmony not only within their tribe but also the tribe that they attack to rule greedily. The factual question now is what regenerates the harmony within this living law of people and what is the "scientific" genuine energy that manifests these corrections which history shows are always and "harmoniously" existing, plus acting and growing all around us?

So yes! It is understood that at this early stage of writing that believers and Non-Believers will find it most useful to understand just what it is that factually rests within the Creation or Nature for the Non-Believer. For indeed there is within this Creation an entity or a law that always seeks harmony within all people and which can be identified is a God or Nature-based harmony that ALWAYS corrects the breaking of the peace and balance of unity that only people can achieve.

For indeed, there is a Godly given or Nature has given harmony seeking reality which is continually readjusted and re-balances the Creation which exists all around people. It is also a reality that contains many people who strangely use the "Freedom of Choice" to try to steal this harmony for them by saying, "I am better than you and this harmony which is all around us is for me and not for you." But it was to remove this "I Want" desire that our wise ancients, these being the Godly people who created all our religions and philosophies, did bring to their followers and also to non-followers, this being a realisation that God's harmony existed for all of life and Non-Life.

This actuality being experienced in a real "Self-Aware" or a "Self-Realisation" in which our wise ancients became a natural part of all that was around them. For indeed these wise ancients gave to their listeners an experience which cannot be seen or touched but which can be recognised and known by that which in our modern times is called "Enlightenment", this being when people become the Creation and so live in Gods world or the world of Nature for the Non-Believer. This world is being a reality which is a personal experience that is often described in the Christian religion has *The Peace that surpasses all Understanding"* or being filled by the existence of the "Holy Spirit" or the "Holy Ghost", which is explained in the Christian Religion. Yet, sincerely, if this experience of "Enlightenment" were placed for "scientific" analysis, this "Enlightenment" being the personal experience that all our wise ancients speak about and which they always endeavoured to bring to people, they would find that within this experience there existed "Nothing" or more accurately put "No Thing" for the mind of the devotee would be empty and without any "I Want" cries emanating from the five senses.

So Yes! That which the wise ancients endeavoured to achieve within the existence of their listeners, was a silent mind in which an "I Want" cannot exist.It was also the listening to our "wise ancients" that gave our ancestors a taste for their culturally language-based religions and philosophies, all of which are based upon a creed worded belief system that was created by our wise ancients and which was designed to always lead to "Enlightenment".

So yes! These ancient teachings that exist throughout the world were all religious and philosophical traditions that sought a "scientifically"based pursuit of harmony that sprang from their sayings and which continually allowed their followers to attain the mind emptying experience of "Enlightenment".

For truly "Enlightenment" is a reality and it is a reality that can only be experienced by those who bring their mind to the "Present Time" for it cannot exist akin to any past or future base "I Want" thoughts in which many people live. This reality is undoubtedly experienced to be a simple fact because the "Present Time" is the real world and not the imaginary world created by the machinations of "I Want" thoughts that are emanating from the five senses and which are thoughts which always impose a dream upon the reality of the "Present Time".

So yes! The experience of "Enlightenment" which is a gift that only people can experience is also a factual reality that always bars the mind filling request of the five senses from targeting an "I Want", and it is the Soul that does this by banning their existence within the mind of the beholder. For these "I Want" mind filling malfunctions, again and again, destroy the pursuit of harmony by friends, family, community, district, regions and countries and which is always, by this selfish claiming "I WANT" that is set against the group harmony of that which is always endeavouring to surround people.

For certainly is it not also "scientifically" correct that many people chasing an "I Want" are stealing or attempting to steal from Nature's pursuit of Harmony – thus making them "Satanists." Is it not also true that people pursue this "I Want" to gain something for their five senses because they think that these five senses are them, for can this not be likened to a personal disease which is being aggravated and fed by this "I Want"?

For honestly and "Scientifically" this happens because a person's "I Want" drags them from the "Present Time" and into the false worlds of the past or the future, these being fake worlds that do not exist and which are worlds that "The Book" calls Hell.

So just what is this "I Want" that keeps many locked in the Hell which exists within their mind and out of the Heaven that truly exists upon our Earth within our "Present Time" and which is the birthright of all people

So yes! What is "Enlightenment?" Listen to what the wise ancient Saint Paul said, who was an apostle in the Christian Bible and who experienced "Enlightenment" on his way to Damascus. This being words about an experience that occurred on his journey to satisfy a personal "I Want" desire to persecute Christian disciples. It is well known that the apostle Saint Paul is one of the essential introducers of the teachings of the Christian church but who was formerly a dedicated "I Want my religion to be followed not yours", which compelled him to persecute Jesus and His disciples.

It was on his road to Damascus that he experienced "Enlightenment" which is said to have happened when Jesus touched him, and all persecution of others immediately stopped. He newly said to his listeners, "Therefore each of you must put off speaking falsehood and speak truthfully to your neighbour, for we are all members of the one body!"

This complete reversal of his previous ideas was because his experiencing of "Enlightenment," which "The Book" says is a singularity created by his experiencing of ONLY the "Present Time", which enveloped him on his way to Damascus. What was there for shown to him on his road to Damascus was that the cheating and punishing of others was the cheating and punishing of your true self. For in the reality of "Enlightenment" you experience or become "Self-Aware" that all that exists is "YOU" For you are the "One Body", which we call the Creation or the whole of Nature for the Non-Believer and that you are really "THAT" unity and so everything you experience is your individual "Self".

So yes! This unity is a real "physical" experience which is spoken about by ALL our wise ancients and which was written about in our first writings many thousands of years ago and which only "The Book" explains has personally been "Self-Aware". This being when you become the Soul, and everything that you see, touch, hears, smell, the taste is experienced to be you, and so you are genuinely observing yourself! This "Self-Aware" experience in which you become aware that you are an integral part of all that is heard, tasted, smelled, seen, or touched, is an experience which "The Book" says can lead to "Self-Realisation", this being the reality that encompassed Jesus and which is an experience in which you actually become "Everything" and so do not experience see, touch, hear, smell, taste for you become personally "The Creation."

It is also well known that this "Self-Realisation", is spoken of by many of our ancient teachers. It is, in reality, an "experience" which conclusively proves that there is only one body and also only the one truth and that there is also only one type of "bliss", but most importantly is the fact that within the experience of "Self-Realisation" there is no observer. It may also be stated that once experiencing "Self-Realisation" your body falls away and your "Soul" becomes one with God, and you are not reborn again for God enjoys that which you bring to Him.

The ancient story of Gilgamesh certainly explains this target of all people, and this was nearly 4,500 years ago. For history says that Gilgamesh was told by the Gods to become "Holy", which means to become "complete", i.e., a single entity! For indeed, this meant to increase his "vibrations" and so become on the same wavelength has "Divine Beings" and so pass through the "gate" to "Enlightenment"! And this was 4,500 years ago.

For indeed Religions and Philosophies are not crutches to support a person's desires to accomplish an "I Want for ME!, but has a belief system in which all people in our world come under a "Godly" given "Freedom of Choice"! So what do you choose dear reader? Is it power over others? Positively, this being that which even God or Nature for the Non-Believer, does not choose! Or do you "choose", via your naturally given "Freedom of Choice", to care for the world which is around you, this being a reflection of how God or Nature for the Non-Believer cares for you. But the experiencing of being "Self-Aware", has described in "The Book" is that you are everything that the silent five senses bring to you that you are a "silent" observer and that everything that you observe you KNOW is the real you and also that your body is also a part of that observation of total unity!

It was also at this early time of Saint Paul's conversion and very soon after his becoming "Enlightened" that he also added these following words of wisdom which describe the knowledge that one always experiences in "Self-Aware" enlightenment. This reality is being an experience when you KNOW as the fact that you are living in a Heaven while upon this Earth, for indeed there are things that you KNOW you should not and so cannot do.

For did not Saint Paul say *"In your anger do not sin. Do not let the sun go down while you are still angry, and do not give the devil a foothold! And*

"Anyone who has been stealing must steal no longer but must work doing something useful with their own hands that they may have something to share with those in need." Also *"Do not let unwholesome talk come out of your mouths, but only what helps build others up according to their needs, that it may benefit all who listen."* Then adding, *"And do not grieve the Holy Spirit of God, with whom you were sealed for the day of redemption."* This statement is meaning to pursue the way of life that is sealed by the experiencing of "Enlightenment".

So yes! "Enlightenment" truly, exists and occurrences can be experienced for Christians describe it has experienced the Holy Spirit or Holy Ghost within them. The Islamic teaching describes it as being filled by the Angel Gabriel. Many other religions and philosophies call it the experiencing of *"Paradise", "Eden", "Heaven", "Nirvana", "Promised Land", "Moksha", "Shangri-la", "Kenshō", "Svargamu", "Kā bāga", "Vāṭikā", "Kā jagaha", "Sukhabhavana"* and many other names from many other religions and philosophies throughout our world, all of whose holy ones show and target their culturally different followers a way to experience and so achieve "Enlightenment", for truly ALL religions pursue the same target – this being for their followers to experience Gods world that is always all around them.

For indeed all "modernly-advanced" but un-enlightened people, these, being people who have had many lives, inwardly "feel" that their Soul is seeking the freedom to join with the world of which they are a genuinely a part. It is undoubtedly an experienced but also a "mysterious" feeling that compels them to target a religion or a philosophy'. So they pursue them without actual knowledge of knowing why? Therefore it should now be known, for all to understand, that many of those people who attend religions and philosophies are real people who are knowingly or unknowingly seeking "Enlightenment". So truly they ALL belong to the same group of searchers. This reality is because many of these "searchers" inwardly "know" that it is the best and most beautiful experience in our world that they seek.

So Yes! It is now useful to understand that the condition of "Enlightenment" cannot be experienced except when a person uses the "Freedom of Choice", this being to "consciously" silence within their mind the "I Want" demands of the five senses and so become "silently" and "naturally" has one with the "Soul", which is their right "Self". For indeed the task is to leave that which you think is you and so "Choose" to silence their mind filling demands and so become has one with the Soul which is YOU! For indeed it is the Soul within that exists in the "Present Time" – for the "Present Time" is God's world or the world of Nature for the Non-Believer.

So yes! Being filled with the Holy Spirit or Holy Ghost is a Christian's way of describing someone who is "Enlightened", which is the living in the Heaven that genuinely rests in the "Present Time". For that which all our wise ancients spoke about can now be modernly explained to be saying that living in the "I Want" world of the past or the future is real living in Hell, which is accomplished while alive and living on this Earth. Therefore Paul's complete turnaround from living in Hell to living in Heaven while on this Earth is an actual reality which he clearly describes, for he now experiences no separation from the life that exists around him and this is the same message that is targeting all people of ALL religions and philosophies.

For it is true that our brothers and sisters who practise Hinduism, Buddhism, Jainism, Sikhism and many other religious teachings, all refer to a state of meditative consciousness called "Samadhi" which can be attained when one prays or meditates.For Samadhi: Is an ancient Sanskrit word, and it arises within this anciently known eastern language which is considered to be the Mother of all Languages. It is a word that "scientifically" means "something that cannot be described" and that it explains a condition of "Spiritual Enlightenment", meaning something Mystical, Nonphysical, Transcendent, Holy, Sacred, Divine, Heavenly, Pious, Devout, etc., and this emanates from a language that is over 5,000 years old.

It is further stated in this ancient Sanskrit language, that by the practice of "Yoga", which some researcher's state is a practice which is over 10,000 years old, that this practice will bring "union" or "unification" with all that exists, and therefore become "realised" that personal meditation is the final stage in which union with God or Nature for the Non-Believer becomes a blissful reality.

For indeed this "reality" is first experienced in that which "The Book" explains to be a "Self-Aware" experience in which you become "aware" that all that your five senses reveal to you is really "YOU", this being the first step towards that which our ancients called "Self-Realisation". For certainly "Self-Realisation" is that which "The Book" modern ally explains to be the final stage of a reality in which you "experience" that "YOU" are everything that exists and that there is no observer! For again, this is a reality which our wise ancients knew could be genuinely experienced by any person – and of course, it still can?

What is also now known to be true is that "historically" many in "The West" of our Earth, have long since forgotten this sought reality and did enter a belief system in which "The East" of our Earth anciently explained to be a belief in that which is called "Maya", loosely meaning that everything within the universe has been created to exist a separate entity to that of the observer. Unquestionably, this is being that "Maya!" which our wise ancients rightly described as being an illusion in which the genuinely existing Godly based unity is really "thought" to be a separated many, this being that which our ancients' did state of being the false every day experiencing "Maya".

It is this condition which our ancients called a mind filling reality in which undisciplined consciousness has become entangled in an illusion which "The Book" does modern-ally explain to be an ancient animalistic mind filling realty which blinds the true "Self" from seeing all that truly exists within the "Present Time", this being that false condition which our wise ancients called the "Cosmic Illusion". For certainly "Present Time" meditation removes this illusion and brings people back to the understanding that all that exists around them is their "Self" and there is no separation from that which is known as Gods world or the world of Nature for the Non-Believer.

Therefore, "The Book" further explains that this is a condition in which the mind is being filled continuously with Past and Future "I Want" thoughts which "The Book" factually calls the real world of "Hell", this being that world which is personally created by constant on-going "I Want" thoughts that are indeed emanating from the five senses of the thinker, this being that which "The Book," says does block the Soul of the thinker from seeing through a clear mind the real world, which is knowingly called the "Present Time", the only word of God or Nature for the Non-Believer. Therefore living in this personally created Hell

they view a world which our wise ancients called "Naraka", (Sanskrit: नरक, literally born of man) which "The Book" says is the realm of "Hell", this also being in accordance to schools of Hinduism, Sikhism, Jainism and Buddhism. For definitely this ancient "Naraka" is a place of torment which "The Book" explains to be born from the "I Want" thoughts of people, which are continually emanating from the animalistic five senses and so are without a doubt being that which establishes a life lived in "Hell".

Therefore "The Book" positively states that these mind clouding thoughts are always based upon a personal "I Want", this being that personal thinking which always generates mind-filling clouds that stop the internal Soul from viewing, through the mind, 100% of the unity that can only exist in the "Present Time". For positively "The Book" explains that only the "Present Time" is Gods world or the world of Nature for the Non-Believer and many Christian saints have previously described this "non-thinking" experience as a "mystical marriage," in which they describe that the Soul merges into God, and so becomes one with Him. So all actions emanating from this realty are Godly produced for who can harm the "self". For surely "Present Time" meditation removes the illusion and brings people back to the understanding that all that exists around them is their "Self", and there is no separation from that which is known as Gods world or the world of Nature for the Non-Believer.

So yes! The search for the real true "Self" is still modernly sought by all our world's religions and philosophies that reality which occurs when the mind becomes still and so the experience of the worshipper has become has one with all that is around them? Cannot it now be also further explained that this is experienced by the worshipper as being in a state of total awareness of the "Present Time"; described as a one-pointedness of mind? This one-pointedness is being a condition which can also be explained to be a *"state of perfect equanimity and awareness"* for there is no past. There is no future, and there is only one life that lives in the NOW time, which many religions and philosophies call "Enlightenment", which Christian explain as being filled with the Holy Spirit, the Holy Ghost or as described in the Muslim faith being with the Angel Gabriel.

Now it is because of this known *"experience of the real world"* that Paul now starts to oppose and condemn the many factors that he once believed. This change in him is because he now truly, understands that his past beliefs were figments of his imagination and that they were genuinely only false *"I Want for ME"* entities that cannot exist in God's world of "Enlightenment". For indeed this is an "Enlightened" experience which exists only in the "Present Time", for indeed "Enlightenment" cannot live in the past or the future which only personally created "I Want" for me thinking always exist? St. Paul also earnestly advised the following: ***"Get rid of bitterness, rage, anger, brawling and slander, along with every form of malice"*** thus describing the world he has left and then adding a description of the new world in which "Enlightenment" had presented to him: ***"Be kind and compassionate to one another, forgive each other, just as Jesus Christ forgave you"*** for Paul knew that he had been forgiven by Jesus on his way to Damascus. It was this thought that created the "Enlightenment" that arose within him.

So yes! Now all the words of the incarnate Jesus can truly and FULLY be understood by listening to these answers that were spoken by Jesus to his listeners: "***I tell you the truth, the Son can do nothing by Himself; He can do only what He sees His Father doing, because whatever the Father does the Son also does.***" Now it is good to understand that this is the Creation speaking directly to YOU, dear reader, and informing you that the laws governing the nature of "Present Time" are coming directly from God.

So yes! In modern words and knowing that Jesus was speaking has the Creation, this can now be interpreted to mean: ***"I tell you the truth, people can do nothing by themselves; people can do only what they see their Fathers Creation doing because whatever the Father's Creation does people should also do."*** So it is good to acknowledge that the "Creation" can only exist in the "Present Time".

So yes! These are the truths that came from Jesus who was the totality of the Creation which is beyond the experience of "Enlightenment" because he was indeed "Self-Realised". It is also good to remember that Jesus was not a "Wise Man" or a "Saint" but WAS the Creation, which is the only child of God, so He certainly knew what he was saying. Thus it is well to understand that "Self-Realisation" is not the experience in which you know that you are an observer of "everything", including your own body, this being that which "The Book" calls being "Self-Aware". For indeed within the experience of "Self-Realisation", a person is not an observer for there is no feeling of separation because you are the unified whole of all that exists within God's world or the world of Nature for the Non-Believer.

So yes! Jesus "WAS" the Creation and therefore knew that He was the only Child of God for did He not wisely say: ***"By myself, I can do nothing; I judge as I hear, and my judgment is just, for I seek not to please myself but Him who sent me."*** thus stating that all people should obey God's harmony that exists within the laws that are contained within God's on-going plan – or Nature's plan for the Non-Believer. Therefore is it not also known to be true that Jesus simply explained this story by saying, ***"The eye is the lamp of the body? If your eyes are good, your whole body will be full of light."*** These words explain being "Enlightened" which is the Soul seeing the world through an empty mind, a condition which has previously stated, describes the experience of being "Self-Aware" and people who experience this also live in Heaven which can only exist in Gods "Present Time". For indeed a mind filled with any thoughts of "I Want" Past and Future images, unknowingly live in a Hell which is self-created for there is no need to "think" what to do for the Soul always knows what heavenly supporting activity it should be doing. Jesus also wisely stated to those who live in Hell, this being the "I Want" for myself world which are the thoughts that stop the Soul from seeing through the mind and into the needs of the Creation that can exist only in the "Present Time". *"But if your eyes are bad, your whole body will be full of darkness. If then the light within you is darkness, how great is that darkness!"* thus indeed, describing the darkness of those who live in Hell while on Earth for indeed, the soul cannot see through the mind which is blocked by "I Want" thoughts. Jesus then gave a clear description of that which He was speaking about when He said: *"No one can serve two masters. Either he will hate the one or love the other, or he will be devoted to the one and despise the other. You cannot serve both God and money."* God is the founder and Creator of the laws of Creation, and money is created by people. Thus worshipping money is likened to the "I Want" cash for "me" thoughts, for these are desires which keep people's minds chained to the past or the future, these claiming that which continually exists in the thinkers' mind.

So yes! All people have the security and freedom of choice to enjoy and so experience "Enlightenment" that can exist only in the "Present Time", and this is a condition when everything that you experience – you know is YOU! Yet many do not know of this simple truth and so worship a false world that can only exist in mind filling thoughts which are claiming a past or a future "I Want". Therefore, this is a mind filling condition that will never bring "Enlightenment" to the thinker. For truly "Enlightenment" is that which can only be experienced in the Present Time and which is a Godly existence of that which you are, although a taste of this truth may occur during the pauses within your "thinking".

So yes! In a free world all people can rightfully seek "Enlightenment", but is it not true that in some "free thinking" countries immigrants are arriving who are fleeing a not free world? Are they also not visitors who are fleeing from societies in which a religious "Freedom of Choice" is forbidden and who with their children are leaving such a country where there is also hunger, unemployment, oppression, violence, torture and even the killing of loved ones?

Is this not the condition which makes them flee their homes and childhood dwellings and escape across borders to live in countries that are prosperous, peaceful, and rich in opportunity and by doing so many closes their eyes to a countries law that forbids their entry? The truth is that immigrants are exercising a natural and moral right to care for themselves and their families which no legal norm or regulation should try to eliminate, so should they not be received with open arms? This reality being especially so if their new environment can provide for them that which their lives need, but if not, should not the persecuting countries from which they are fleeing be "legally" charged with their cost of maintenance so that they will endeavour to correct their persecuting and non-human conditions?

So yes! The "Free World" can do this for the search for "Enlightenment" is a right or God path and it should be available to ALL people for indeed it is ALL and everything that exists in the "Present Time" where rests that which cannot be explained. For all people should know that this is also a "Present Time", a time in which we have been created to support the harmony which is emerging all around us.

Therefore the clear, understandable truth is to serve the "Present Time" which cannot exist in any thoughts concerning any past or a future "I Want". This described reality means that the target of all our wise ancients, who have lived in the many countries of the world, was to bring to people "Enlightenment" and so enable them to live in Heaven which genuinely exists in God's "Present Time". This "Present Time" being a world in which you do not belong to "yourself" for you belong to all that exists. So the target must live life in accordance to this law and know that upon this world resides the wellbeing of "Enlightenment" and if you are seeking this bliss of "Enlightenment" – Then read on.

6.   HOW THE CREATION PURSUES GOD'S OR NATURES HARMONY

So yes! It is good that as people we can search for this "scientific" truth that exists only in the "Present Time". This "Present Time" is a truth that cannot be disproved, and which makes important the on-going search to support that entity which creates that harmony that always exists within all of Natures endeavours to naturally support the needs of friends, families, communities, districts, regions, and countries.

So yes! If you do believe that the Creations Universal work of "harmony" is essential and a dominant factor for your wellbeing, you, therefore, need to clearly understand (stand under) our Creations purpose or that which is being called the objective of Nature for the Non-Believer?   Therefore, there is a fundamental truth that was seriously spoken of by our wise ancients and repeated in many variable ways by all our on-going significant religions and philosophical belief systems. Still, sadly these ancient words have become challenging to understand in our many modernised and culturally new viewpoints? There are also many explanations in all our religions and philosophies about that which is the cause of these harmony seeking energies which are continually removing disharmony from the Creation and replacing it with a purposeful unity. Is this not true? Also if this is not personally believed, then look around your life and circumstances and see the harmony that protects you or the disharmony which you see and understand has to be wrong, especially when it is destroying that Godly or Natural harmony that exists all around you. Thus it is true that this purposeful entity that seeks to maintain the unity of the Creation goes by many names but the name "The Book" has "scientifically" chosen is the name "Mother of the Creation". This reality being because Nature shows that a mother is personally the best personification of a family's natural "carer", "doer" and "activator" plus it is she who is the seeker of the needed harmony that needs to be established around her children. Therefore it is the "Mother of the Creation" who is the supporter of the unified developments that emanates throughout our natural world, for all know that it is the mother who is the natural carer of all that exists around Her. Also, a parable of God's or Nature's Creation for the Non-Believer can be likened to the law of a pleasurable public dance meeting in which everything is fixed by their particular requirements. These were the positions of the tables, chairs, drinks, glasses, bar, lights, walls, floors, people, and all that physically exists within the confines of this public place.Therefore our world can be likened to that which is within this dance site where the five senses can experience all the Life and Non-Life that exists within the totality of each person's interpretation of the Creational rules of the dance, which is now exemplified, has been fixed in place by God's laws.

So now the attending dancers can realise this "Dance Meeting" reality and so "choose" to believe in this self-created existence. The questions now being: "What is this Creation"? "What controls its growth?" and "Why do all attending people have a choice to pursue or not pursue its laws?" For indeed all know that the dance laws can be broken just has God's laws or Nature's laws for the Non-Believer can be broken by people or like in Nature they can collide and so change that which exists, just has in our created dance room tables can be knocked over, drinks spilt, and dancers can crash etc. For is it not a known fact that harmony can break as it collides with itself. Now as time moves forward, all can understand that the only thing that can change the perfect harmony of this public dance place is the growing movement and development that exists within the life of its dancers and also the Non-Life that exits all around them as they move "harmoniously" within its existence. But "legally" some clashing within the dancer's movements can create "disharmony", and this is that which the "Mother of the Creation" is continuously correcting, for God never changes His "purposeful" laws that are continually enfolding within the "Present Time", this being the time in which their only Child needs the freedom to Grow, these being the eternal laws that feed all life and Non-Life just has the dancer's laws control the rules that are binding the dance event together.

For God knows what the "Present Time" needs and He knows that His laws will achieve their ultimate purpose and that the "Mother of the Creation" will always be able to "legally" maintain the harmony of the Creations "dance" that can only exist in the "Present Time". What must now be clearly understood is that this is the reason why God's law gave people "The Freedom Choice" for as in our make-believe dance the "Mother of the Creation" needs people to support and so return the dance event to its "harmony" and She also needs the support of people to can pick up tables and chairs and glasses and put them back into the harmony that exists all around them.

But this is a personal "choice" that can never be taken from people for they can even choose to die if they wish to do so. We may also understand that "choice" has also been given to people because at the "dance" they can dance with a highly skilled partner and so work a great unity of skills and twirls, yet with a trainee, they can "CHOOSE" to teach a few steps of the dance in line with the expertise of the trainee. This choice is a personal choice which is to obey group rules or not to follow group rules, so it is good to allow all within this environment to take an active part in establishing these rules. For "dancing" is a "Self-Created" group-based decision that allows all people to perform tasks that naturally support a majority agreed with regulations and laws and it is this which frees the lawfully "Created" dance harmony to exist within the group. For in dancing if you performed NOT according to the rules of the dancers "created" unity, this would be an action that would undoubtedly destroy the harmony that is endeavouring to exist within these dance hall rules and so this disharmony would physically and mentally disturb all other dancers?

So Yes! People can think *'To do or not to do'* or *'to be or not to be'* which is a famous oration in the works of Shakespeare who was obviously "Enlightened". It is also an "oration" that brings forward the question: "Why do people exist?" For indeed without them, all life and Non-Life would continue developing in a natural harmony where they are bound by God's perfect laws which are harmoniously maintained by the "Mother of the Creation".

So it is understandable to reason that people have been given the "Freedom of Choice" to support the "goodly" (Godly) development of Nature? For is it not said to be accurate and "Scientifically" stated that people are enabled to freely "choose" their actions to do or not to do, to support or not to support? But also can their not be another and self-evident reason has to why all people have for this "Freedom of Choice"? Could this not "naturally" be that God and the "Mother of the Creation" like to be genuinely "loved" as do all parents who like to be loved by their children who have a "Freedom of Choice". For certainly is it not also true that love must be "freely" chosen to be given to another, for "love" cannot be compulsory? Also, can this chosen way to love "parents" not even be said to be a "Natural Law" that has been created by God? Can it not also be said, just by looking at all the Earth's Nature that exists around all people that God's laws are perfect and cannot be changed? Yes, this is truthfully meaning that when a person "selfishly" destroys God's harmony by "choosing" for themselves a unity destroying "I Want", they cannot be punished. Still, there will be no "Sugar in the Water" during their life, and their next re-birth could be very interesting.

So yes! The "Mother of the Creation" is the name that is offered to the "Believer", and the "Non-Believer" for it is a way to understand that there is a "something" that is continually pursuing the harmonious development of the world that is all around us. Therefore it is She, the "Mother of the Creation" who can be "naturally" seen has not only the controller of the "Present Time" plus its on-going search for harmony, but also the faithful supporter of God's gift of all of life and Non-Life and in particular the natural law for creating children. For indeed it is "She" who brings the harmony and comforting aid to those who support Her, this being the harmony that is explained in many different ways by our world's major and minor religions and philosophical teachings. Yet sadly, is it not true that we have now become too modern to fully understand these ancient teachings and practices which lead to their neglect? For certainly is it not further interesting to explain that this neglect could be the reason why "The Book" uses modern "scientific" understandings to expand all our ancient religions and philosophical concepts from their roots to their amazing "Soul" satisfying fruit, which is their only purpose and yes! I am also amazed at what is pouring from my fingertips is that which appear to be a modern way to resolve this issue naturally and without the need to change any existing Religious or Philosophical teachings but enough about me – let's move on.

Regarding the "Mother of the Creation" there is an ancient translation from Joshua the son of Sirach, who translated his father's works that were written in 132 BC; this was being about thirty years after his father's completed it. This ancient translation was also placed in the introduction to the Christians "Old Testament", in which the word "Mother" arises and which "The Book" calls "Mother of the Creation".

So it was the Son of Sirach who translated the following and so revealed his father to be saying:

5/   The root of wisdom – to whom has it been shown to Her who knows them?

7/   The Lord himself created wisdom; he saw Her and apportioned   Her. He poured Her out upon all his works.

8/   She dwells with all flesh according to his gift, and he supplied Her to those who love him.

12/ To fear the Lord is the beginning of wisdom; she is created with the faithful in the womb.

13/   She made among men an eternal foundation, and among their descendants, She will be trusted.

14/   To fear the Lord is wisdom's full measure; She satisfies men with her fruits.

15/   She fills their whole house with desirable goods, and their storehouses with her produce.

17/   He saw Her and apportioned Her; He rained down knowledge and discerning comprehension, and He exalted the glory of those who held Her fast.

18/   To fear the Lord is the root of wisdom, and Her branches are long life.

I think that this is an excellent "ancient" description of the "Mother of the Creation", but it seems that those long-ago followers of many of our world's religions moved away from the sayings of our wise ancients and their religious teachings into a "mans" only world, thereby denying the fundamental truth that only a male and a female when together are the single unity that can "Create" themselves for neither can reproduce such a love one their own.

Maybe the reason why such chauvinism developed was that it occurred during the 1,200 years of darkness which was started by our ancients to be the Kali Yuga. This age lasted from 500 to 1700 AD, and it was also said to be the age when consciousness was limited to gross matter and so was attached only to the physical world. It was also noted that during this age, most people lost their spiritual abilities, mental clarity, and understanding and the era was characterized by the belief that matter was fixed and absolute. So the man was trapped in a physical world with the ethereal feeling that you can only do that which you were religiously told to do, usually by richly appoint others.

For example, during this period, it seems that many religiously written truths were accepted as absolute definitions or dogma. So science at this time then presented the universe to be a mechanism with divine realms which were believed to be "Godly" static and unchanging, instead of dynamic and ever-changing. Still, Science cannot obliterate "Religion" for is it not true that Philosophy creates its reality?

It is also most interesting to know that people during this age, such as farmers, herdsmen, artisans, soldiers, and slaves, were mainly involved in physical labour and all activity was directed towards physical ends such as the need for food, clothing and static society. Even religious events took the form of rituals and rigid "habitual" offerings which were often based upon painful sacrifices and "I Want" prayers, and sadly people were ignorant and afraid of any change. This ignorance also manifested in widespread attempts to destroy prior knowledge, an example being the third-century destruction of the ancient Egyptian texts at Alexandria. But this now recognised ignorance all ended in the year 1700, this being our "now time" which also began to disprove of this Kali Yuga viewpoint actively. For it is anciently stated that we left the *"Dwapara Yuga"*, this being the third of the four "Yugas" (Ages) which ended 5,122 years ago. The *"Dwapara Yuga"* was known to be-the age of *"Two Ahead"* of all that which exists within "The Creation". It was further explained to be based upon "compassion" and "truthfulness", with *"compassion"*, which means empathy, sympathy, concern, consideration, care, kindheartedness, benevolence, this being the attributes of the female and *"truthfulness"* meaning honesty, frankness, openness, reliability, correctness, faithfulness, accuracy, straightforwardness, this being the attributes of the male – which is the recognised unity of *"Two Ahead"* of all that exists in the age of *"Dwapara"* - which is explained to be the third age out of the four Yugas or periods of life upon our Earth. It was also an age which indeed stated "Scientifically" that there was a combined unity within the Man and the Woman. For in reality the "Two Ahead" must be the "Created Man" who silently experiences within himself all the future needs to satisfy the "Present Time" and the "Created Woman" – the shortened version of the word "Worshipped Man" – for it is the "Created Woman" who controls the reality of that "Present Time", this being the actual unity between man and his worshipped woman. Still, that age ended 5,122 years ago for it was then that our wise ancients said that we moved into the "Kali Yuga", the age of strife, discord, a quarrelsome life which was all created by the "I Want" for ME! But now it is perfect to know that our wise ancients forecasted the end of this brutal "I Want" Kali Yuga to be in the new coming year 2025 CE, this being the historically known time when the "Golden Age" will return once again to all people. For indeed this "Golden Age" is said to be the age of peace, prosperity and happiness – for it will come in 2025 CE, this being the known time just has was the known time of the other ages and certainly during this period Darwin's theories will be proved to be very wrong has the opposite of his theories are proved to be correct, for certainly 2025 CE is now actually showing a beginning in 2020. This being has people begin to show unrest at the commercial distribution of market wealth, and even greater unrest at those rebirths that are newly emanating from the animal kingdom - who are being engaged to protect the wealth of others. For indeed it's not the poor against the rich, or age against youth or education against illiteracy. For in the Golden age it is said that colonization wars will cease to exist along with the animalistic desire to hoard wealth, for it will be known that all life and non-life is a part of "You" and man will continue with his desire to create children in his need to seek "Future" needs and the woman will always take care of the "Present Time".

So yes! The good news for most people is that the Devil does not exist but what does live in the "I Want" demands occurring within a person's mind, these being the animalistic "voices" of our ancient five senses. Again it is this that you genuinely believe to be the real you. But in truth, although we have previously permitted them to act as "US", probably in childhood, they are NOT us, for you cannot be that which requests an "I Want", this being that which your five senses always cry for, for indeed the Earth on which you live has everything that you need. It is also these five senses that make us do things that we say are caused by the Devil within us, and therefore, we are not responsible for our actions.

But the truth about peoples "theoretical" creation of an outside the body devil, is simply explained by stating that the Creation of an outer Devil is used as an excuse to avoid blaming ourselves. Still, we are probably and falsely pursuing a belief that is always emanating from our five senses. The real truth is that our "allowed to do so" five senses are "always" putting forward an "I Want" which is raising tempting future "thoughts" that affect our Present Time. These were thoughts that usually lead to the destruction of the harmony that resides around you for in simple terms we endeavour to steal from this harmony to claim and then enforce our own "I Want" upon it.

It is these acts that "illegally" change Natures Godly direction and purpose. For indeed it is this "I Want" thought that emanates from the past or is targeting the future that our five senses constantly and animalistic ally tempting the body to pursue? For is it not known by all to be true that our thoughts always entangle our activities into a complicated hurtful life which can only be given birth to by their first "chatter" arising within the mind, these being thoughts, which are thoughts that are deeply rooted in words "I Want". For indeed, how can you be that which talks to you for you can only be that which is listening?

Why is this? Simply and again put, it can only be the five senses that are chattering and clamouring for their "I Want" desires that always target their individual and personal "I Want", this being that which they wish to experience. For indeed the spoken words that exist only in your head is emanating from these five senses who seek their own "personal" pleasures, and it is this noise that takes the "viewer" or "listener" into the past or the future, both being worlds that do not exist and so should genuinely be called "Hell" in our modern terminology. For again, can it not also be said to be true that the world that is attached to an "I Want" thought is always and noisily being created and sounded in our minds? Is it not also true that the words attributed to belief can often be recognised from which of the five senses it is emanating?

So indeed these are self-created personal sounding words that do not physically exist except as thoughts within the mind, and this is because Hell does not exist in God's world or the world of Nature for the Non-Believer which is the "Present Time". Yet indeed this negative and harmful world that we call Hell is created by people who falsely choose it to be so. Still, woe to them when they return to their maker who exists only in the Present named in "The Book" has the "Present Time", a time that is set by God or Nature for the Non-Believer.

What is also quite amazing to understand, which all readers will recognise, is that these thoughts emanating within your mind are not the "REAL" you, but strangely you really "think" that they are you! Therefore, living without the knowledge of knowing that it is the "words" of the self-claiming five senses that are sounding within your mind is a misunderstanding that allows these five senses to entice you to do acts that will make you take the values that are destined for or belong to others and which are not meant for you?

For it is undoubtedly an activity which steals that which belongs to others and so happiness and contentment will elude you – is this not true? For the truth is that the actual and noisy "I Want" that is clouding your mind is emanating from one of the five senses which are probably demanding that you pursue their "I want" need and they even argue among themselves and all within your mind and honestly the real you are observing all this – so in reality indeed how can you be that which you mindfully see?

So yes! It is this strange belief, based upon your God-given or Nature Given "Freedom of Choice" that these "I Want" words that are sounding in your mind are coming from yourself! They are not coming from you for you cannot be that which you observe nor to that which you listen. So definitely these mind filling worlds are emanating from one of the five senses, and this is because you are allowing them to plague and fill your account and it is this that you "choose" to believe is the real you, they are not you.

But honestly, it is this "misunderstanding" that takes them out of your true self's control. This "misunderstanding" is happening because the real you, which is the Soul, is blocked from seeing through the mind by their mind filling and clouding noise, for real you, this being that which is knowingly called "The Self" by our ancients, but which can now be modernly more correctly called "The Soul". This residing "Soul" being your true "Self" which resides within you and all people but only one Soul per person but strangely your Soul is known to be as one with all other Souls

So yes! The real reason for the existence of peoples "Freedom of Choice" is so that the Soul can use the body and its five senses to silently "choose" and so employ the task that is required to harmonise that which has been placed in front of it by the "Mother of the Creation". It is also essential to be able to do this task without an interfering "I Want" blocking and clouding the mind and so stopping the viewing Soul from seeing through the mind that which is necessary to complete "harmoniously" all matters that the "Mother of the Creation" is carefully placed in front of it. But when your actions are uncontrolled usually caused by the "I Want" demands of the five senses, then you have become like an untrained wild dog and what a noise they "bark" into the head of any listener.

Now many may ask just what is the "scientific" proof regarding this statement that we are not the five senses. What is simply explained, by most of our significant philosophies, is that the Soul is the observer of these thoughts and the "scientific" fact is that the observer cannot be that which is observed or more scientifically and simply put ***the observer cannot be observed because the observer is outside the object***"- but later on this subject.

So yes! Some religious people often state that they are very religious and give much credence to their many requesting prayers for personal benefit. It is also understood that many religious people, from various religions, usually apply to themselves a peculiar and severe penance or some task to achieve a personal "I Want", which is based upon a belief that God will love them more for punishing themselves and so they often believe that they should be "Godly" punished. Their idea is that when they target this "I Want" gift from God, that they do then think that is is correct to re-engage or start a new lifestyle which will make it possible for them to gain more of their "I Want", which they had previously felt was impossible to achieve without a self-hurting penance, this being a penance that they should inflict upon themselves or others.

It is not wise to do this, for penance and self-inflicted pain upon yourself or others is not necessary to realise the free fruits of God's harmony that is all around you as it is within you and which is carefully governed by the "Mother of the Creation" constant striving to replace emerging disharmony with harmony. Nor are any penances required to achieve a peaceful and contented balance in this life or the next one.

But yes, of course, you can "painfully" stop overeating or other over indulgences. Personal fasting is an excellent tool to prevent the controlling demands of the five senses which can be "observed" to scream like five wild dogs for the taste, smell, touch and sight of food but this is not the ancient and genuine reason for fasting. The real purpose but the seemingly forgotten purpose for fasting is that you must learn how to control the greed emanating from the five senses. Still, in our ancient days and at the beginning of most of our religions, it would be impossible to be able to establish such reasoning. For indeed in those ancient times is it not known to be true that a modern saying such has: ***You are the Observer', and so you cannot be that which you see in the mind,*** could not be fully understood by the people of yore. For in real "Self-Awareness" or "Self-Realisation", this being the target of ALL our world's religions and philosophies and being an understanding in which a person knows that their body is in a unified existence with the Creation, but in the age of forgetting, and forgetting is our worst enemy, an inexperienced person was mainly controlled by the body's five senses, and in some ancient religions the demanding "I Want" of the five senses were purported to coming from unable to be seen bandits which entered the body – but more about this later.

Yet again, is it not also true that many religions and philosophies state quite clearly the words *"Thine Will be Done!"* meaning, of course, the "will" of the "Mother of the Creation" and not the work of the five senses which are always fighting for their claims that truly steal from God's Creation or the world of Nature for the Non-Believers.

So yes! It is not good to force your will upon others, but it is excellent to force it upon your five senses which, when subdued and quiet and will allow you to "observe", through your empty mind, ninety to one hundred per cent of the "Creation" around you. This "awareness" is being a real situation in the actual experiencing the knowledge that Gods creation, or Natures creation for the Non-Believer, meaning that which exists in the "Present Time". This view is that which is usually blocked by up to seventy to ninety per cent by the five senses verbalising and creating an unreal dream world which is manufactured in mind by the "I Want" of these oft arguing and uncontrolled five senses, these being that which you actually believe is the real YOU!

They are NOT you for you cannot be that which you see or hear. This false belief is indeed a self-claiming and unreal world that is created by the five senses shouting into the mind their own particular "I Want" and also cunningly and verbally indicating how to achieve this "I Want". It must also be agreed that controlling the five senses is not as easy as it seems. They have been in control of you for a very long time; for many think that the five senses are "them".

So it is also with this false born truth that these five senses will actually and "very" noisily put up many arguments to save themselves, for, after all, you do believe that they are you and so you will feel their "common sense". But truthfully, it is this "talking" in your head, which the real you is "observing" but which are words that are coming from your five senses which you have – in childhood - "Chosen" to be the real you and so have permitted them to sound within the mind of yourself freely.

They will even contradict and argue amongst themselves and do so in loud inner voices but always remember that they are not you, just as a dog is not you that you hear barking for attention. For indeed the stillness and silence of that which "observes" all this is the real you for you are the observer and always shall be so and so now you may well ask "Who is the observer?" The answer to this question is that the "observer" is the Soul that rests within you.

So yes! The Soul of all people is the observer, but sadly it cannot observe the outer world, which it can only view through the mind. This condition is merely being because of the thoughts that are filling and blocking the view of the inner Soul with an "I Want" for myself world that are genuinely emanating from the clamouring five senses which always target that which they want. It is also this fact that makes you do things which are nearly always a self-seeking "personal" gratification that is emanating from one of the five senses. They are also thoughts that are usually based upon past and future concepts, and they are all targeting and arguing to obtain their individual "I Want" which can lead to great arguments within the mind. It is also interesting that they can always make good excuses so that you can continue to do bad things that are painfully inflicted upon others by your "I Want". These are all their endeavouring ways to seek and achieve an "I Want" thought which can also be combined within similar "I Want" groups of likeminded people and even whole countries.

So yes! One of the first things to understand and to continually ask your self is the question "How can I be that which I observe? Or even more clearly and better to be known as the need to know just what it is that is keeping these activities that you know are within you and yet without you? The answer to this question is that you are the Soul, which is that which wants for nothing for it has everything and this is genuinely the real you, for indeed, the Soul of each person is the authentic "Self" of all that exists.

This being that which the wise ancients call "The Self of All" for they believed and knew that the individual Soul is attached to ALL Souls. For indeed in the real world, the "reality" is that the Soul is also joined to the actual "Self of All" and it can be experienced in the "Peace That Surpasses All Understanding", an experience which also attracts football spectators and other sports spectator or attenders to be of one mind which is a desire to belong to like-minded people who they see all that is in front of them has "themselves".

So is it not therefore easily seen to be "scientifically" correct that that which people unconditionally and genuinely seek is not only the Souls unity to be with Creation but also to experience the one Soul in the many fully. For inherently we know that all people are of the one body and that people do feel the Souls "echoing" need to belong to a world which they can recognise as their "Self" and how to achieve this ever-calling target will be explained later in "The Book". An example being has previously stated that it is wise to believe that the word "Woman" is a shortened version of the name "Worshipped Man", for is it not true that "historically" a man goes onto his knees when asking a Woman to join with him in marriage?

It is also known that a man "historically" stands when a "woman" enters the room – the stated reason being that his Soul rises in honour of the woman's entry and that it is wise for the man to stay one with his Soul for he "knowingly" knows that it will leave him if he does not stand. Of course God or Natural law for the Non-Believer, has designed man and woman to have one entity, for the woman's Nature is to understand and control the "Present Time" while the man's Nature is to use the "Present Time" to provide for the "Futures" needs. It is this fact which ensures that the two become one and the only difference being that man always needs to create children while the woman eventually sees no need - but honours the man. But then the man gets older, and he too recognises that he cannot support more children.

7   FALSE BELIEF SYSTEMS

The most robust belief system in the world is that of money.   For if you believe that money has value, then you can also think that "anything" that you want to feel is real is very factual and that certain truths are always correct. Simply put this is an incorrect viewpoint, and it is just as false as the viewpoint in which you believe that the five senses are the real you, for money has no value as it is an only coloured paper. If you air-dropped a loose £20,000,000 in variable UK notes, or Euro or USA currency notes or any other countries money into the centre of a proverbial Amazon tribe, these being people who have never been in contact with our modern world, then they would probably at first be very annoyed but would then find the paper beneficial for starting fires.

Now, what would happen if you dropped the same bundle over the centre of London? It would bring chaos and maybe the loss of life for the "belief" system in London would be very different as the lie resting behind money blinds everyone just as the common belief that the five senses that are chattering their needs into your mind are the real you.

So yes! With this knowledge that an unreal "imagined" world can be held fast in all minds has a true belief, is it not time that we also developed a religious or philosophically belief system in which the world of People can "naturally" agree upon and which is just as strong has their belief in the universal value of money? Would it not be useful to start this new belief with a knowledge that can be attached to our consciousness and also to have the ability to understand the truth of our ability to love plus the affectionate feeling for a harmony based upon the wisdom and the balance that exists for all life, which is a life that rests outside of the "I Want" for myself zone?

For certainly is it not an absolute truth that our personal life is of a higher value than that of accumulated material wealth. However, it must be agreed that it is the real "work" of People to add value to God's Creation or to that of Nature for the unbeliever? Is it not also good to remember that this does not mean that people must glibly give their wealth away and live in poverty and need? For great wealth can say that the owner has been placed into a position of great responsibility in which their contact with the Soul will wisely inform them just what is needed from their assets, which automatically happens when you listen to the knowledge emanating from the "Present Time".

Can it not also be true that in this age of incredible communication systems, that people can quickly pursue a coherent and universal religious and or philosophical belief system that anciently exists all around them and within them? For is it not a God or Nature given the truth that each person can "choose" whether to live in their self-made Hell or live in the unselfish unity of Heaven that exists or is endeavouring to be released to survive around all people?

Is it not also strange truths that in reality, people have only two ways of living and that both ways exist as a "choice" but only for people? This truth is to "choose" to either live in the peace that surpasses all understanding Heaven or to "choose" to live in the confusing, painful Hell caused by a continually motivating "I Want" which can never be satisfied. So yes! Now is the question that you are "always" asked to answer personally and this is "Which world do you want to live in, for is it not also True that to understand the real world we have to realise that the word "Justice" commonly used to provide laws in many countries, is meant to describe a life that "Just Is"! Therefore is it not very clear that "Justice" exists in the "Present Time", a time which naturally exposes Fairness, Impartiality, Integrity plus Reasonableness, etc. and what a great "Present" this is to the life of all people?

Is it not also True that God or Nature does not do anything that will "correct" the direction of this growing Creation? For how is it possible for God or Nature for the Nonbeliever, to create a plan that does not develop according to its Creator? Is it not also true that according to the laws that exist within the Creation that a male and a female are the two that are needed to create a third? Therefore can it not also be "Scientifically," said to be accurate, has previously stated, that God created Space, which is the closest thing to God or "No-Thing" called "Nothing" by the Non-believers.

Can this "Space" therefore be likened to a "Female" in which a "Male" seed was planted and within which the only child gestated and then was born, this being what people call "The Big Bang" and which is commonly known as "The Creation", this being the only child of the previous two that begat this Holy and only one.

So is it not also true that the Childs Mother, copied by all mothers, harmonises the life around Her only child, and like all mothers cares for the wellbeing of Her only created Child for She is "Space", this being Her that is within and without all that exists, and which contains the Harmony, wisdom and balance of the whole of the Creation or Universe for the Nonbeliever, which is Her only child.

So now the simple "scientific" reason is to believe that the Creation, which is an only child, has a Mother who can be likened to a normal "Mother" who cares for Her only Child. It is She who ensures that the child continues to grow in the harmonious wisdom and balance and within the unification of Gods plan or the Plan of Nature for the Nonbeliever. Is it not also true that it was only recently that people were created to assist in the development of this "Plan"? For it is an undeniable truth that Gods other half, which is the implanted Mother is here to ensure that the child continues to grow within the laws of God's Harmony.

So yes! She is all-powerful and can be called the *"Mother of the Creation"* for She loves Her only Child, which is the Creation. She is a Mother who continuously works in the "Present Time" to support all harmonious deeds that ensure the wellbeing of all life and Non-Life and in particular her sons and daughters which is that part of the growing child who has a "personality".

Is it not also true that humankind is the only life force that has a valid "choice" that can be engaged before all its actions even unto continuing its life or seeking a personal death, this, of course, is why the *"Mother of the Creation"* never interferes with a person's life in minus or negative way nor will She deliberately punish anyone for inharmonious deeds. For the laws of God gave people "choice". This gift cannot be punished and so the perpetrator who lives by an "I Want" for myself actions, these being selfish actions which break the Harmony that exists or is trying to survive around them - is genuinely ignored by the Mother but those people who support the harmonising efforts of the *"Mother of the Creation"* – will taste the "Sugar in the Water" has the life around them "mysteriously" seems to support their activities, a fact which can be likened to red traffic lights always turning to green go - every time you approach them in your vehicle.

Yet indeed this harmonising work of the *"Mother of the Creation"* can only be achieved in the Present Time, for to the *"Mother of the Creation"* the Past and the Future do not exist because there is no "Space" in this non-existent unreal world in which life cannot exist. It is because of this fact that there is no "Past" or "Future" within the *"Mother of the Creation"* s understanding. So indeed this is why She can only support and maintain Gods Harmony within the "Present Time", this being Gods made "Heaven" that exists around Her only Child - the Creation.

Again and Her actions are always active deeds that bring sweetness to the life of Her only child "The Creation" in which Earth belongs, for is it not "scientifically" true that the Creation is a living entity and that within this "Creation" there is an entity that people call Earth upon which there lives a life form called "people". Is it not also "Scientifically" true that people are also the only life-force upon this Earth that has been given the ability to choose to do this or to do that or to do nothing? Therefore can it not also be "scientifically" true that the purpose for this personal gift of the "Freedom of Choice", which has the reality of establishing all that which is around people, is a born fact so that people can "choose" to assist the *"Mother of the Creation"* physically and so aid Her work to continually maintain Gods Harmony for all life and Non-Life that exists on this planet. But does this fact not also mean that because people have the freedom of choice, that they can act negatively against the Mothers care and if you believe that this is good - - Read on.

What is also important to remember is that because people have been given the freedom of choice, this being the needed flexibility that is required to assist the *"Mother of the Creation"* s to work which is to maintain Gods Harmony within the Creation. Yet, it is also a God-given "Freedom of Choice" that makes it a possibility that many personal belief systems can be selfishly changed or pursued to create a personal "I Want a God who serves only me, this is being a God that they create to serve their own "I Want", but this is a selfish pursuit that is not attached to God's world.

So is it not also a known truth that some people use their self-made "God", this being a God who they personally and group worship, do dangle this false God's needs in front of others to "threateningly" steal their own "I Want" requirements which shows that this is a selfish way to achieve their own "I Want". Is this not truly a personal "I Want" weakness, for is it not true that they are pursuing their desires and so have self-created a false god to use as an excuse to punish and thus gain from others for not performing individual acts that they say should be ritually accomplished in honour of their God? So if any of these false leaders tell their followers "Kill Him", Destroy them", "Punish these", "Claim that", Hate this" etc. they are seeking their wellbeing which has nothing to do with Gods laws or the *"Mother of the Creations"* need to maintain Harmony within Her family. So we should always understand the need to support good leaders but most important is also to remember that the best leader is your Soul or pure consciousness for the Non-Believer

So yes indeed, these people are claiming God's world for themselves, for definitely, God would never inflict punishment for what father would destroy or injure their only child? Especially not a God that created the Heaven that all can see rests upon this Earth, and is it not also true that there is not one Incarnate nor one of our many wise, or holy ancients that ever punished another soul. For has, God said when speaking through the Incarnate Jesus *"They who have ears, let them hear".*

Is it not also strange that many religious belief systems say that if you do not follow their "creeds", which they state was personally given to them by God, that they can claim their "Godly" right to physically punish "unbelievers", as they did when these religious people burnt thousands of people while calling them "witches", all to reinforce via fear, their position within the society in which they lived and is this not still happening within our new world communities? Is it not also real and strange that some belief systems worship false gods? Also are they not recognised because they tell you to inflict yourself with some penance or do acts that can be painful to yourself or others? Why is this strange behaviour? For indeed this undisciplined behaviour is being an animalistic "I Want for ME" that is engendered by the "Freedom of Choice", this being freedom which is given only to people by God or Nature for the Non-Believers. It can undoubtedly be identified has animalistic for it is not supportive of any of the Gods or Natures developing laws which people have been born to support. But beware and also aware that some people have had many lives and so understand that that the goodness of Nature that is genuinely existing and emerging all around them, is undoubtedly for ALL life to enjoy. Still, also some have just emerged as people from the animal kingdom and so do not fully understand that the emerging goodness of nature is for everybody to care for all that exists around them. So Yes! Like pups, they need to be kindly trained to a way of life in which specific agreeable laws need to be "knowledgeably" conformed to – is this not an accurate statement?

Is this not strange because God and the ***"Mother of the Creation"*** who is the Mother of their only Child cannot deliberately hurt or punish Her and God's children? So is it not true that many such claimed desires said to be coming from the one God, are falsely leading people to break the Harmony that Gods Laws bring and target. Are they not purposely doing these harmful acts because of theirs or other people's personal "I Want" instructions?

So yes! Some people have indeed created false gods and thus produce a belief system that pursues their personal "I Want", an "I Want" which harms others and not themselves. For it must be understood that the perpetrators of these "I Want" claims will automatically be outside God's Harmony seeking laws being created around them, this being because they do not support the Creations Mother, who is the Mother of their only child, for indeed these people who religiously punish others cannot enjoy a Harmony based life and so will enter the world of Hell which will contradict the possibility of achieving their every "I Want".

For you cannot kill or punish another and then say it is your faith to do so, for this is not correct nor is it honouring Gods world, for is it not "scientifically" true that all activities take place in the "Present Time" which is God's world? Is it not also true for those who have ears to hear, that non-harmonised and suspicious harmful activities simply mean that a person's on-going planned "good life" will be ignored by God's world and so disharmony will plague them? Is it not also seen to be true that as soon as you genuinely perform on-going acts that support or create the love of the Harmony around you, these being acts that silently occur in the Present Time, you will be supported by the *"Mother of the Creation"* s "Sugar in the water", the gift of sweetness that only the Mother can give and all your confusions and thwarts will be ended.

Also these various strange and personally claimed religious "I Want" belief systems sometimes certainly explain that if you do not follow their doctrines, then you will go to Hell when you die and live in pain forever and ever but if you do obey their "personally" requested creeds then you will go to an eternal Heaven and live with your loved ones and ancestors forever and ever. Some "owners" of belief systems have even promised that if you give them money or perform forced acts for them, then they will ensure that you will go to Heaven when you die. How sad this is, for death is not the end of being. There is no need to worry about spending an eternity in Hell or Heaven, for it is best to understand that God and the *"Mother of the Creation"* have better things to do with their caringly planned time than to create another world to which dead people go to be punished – forever and forever. No" For love and its freedom of choice is the basis of their world, especially in caring for their offspring.

8 ALL IS UNDER THE LAW OF HARMONY

It is also interesting to again think about our death. Do we honestly believe, as some religions state, that a God who created all things and the "Mother of the Creation" who is likened to be the space that is all around and within life and Non-Life and who cares for all things, will allow such punishment after a person's death, this being the hurting of their child in a so-called Hell, this being a Godly created terrible place in which many trillions of their children are condemned to exist for the rest of eternity, or on the other hand, being responsible for another law that makes some of their Children "happy" and "content" for the same eternity and this is for many millions and millions of future years?

These were people who are known to have a minimal life span compared to the above eternity and a life span which in the Bronze Age was around twenty-six years and in our current age is purported to be 67.2 years, this is a very insignificant time which is nothing when compared to the estimated twenty-two billion years known to be for the rest of eternity, this being the estimated time for the ending of the universe. It may be that during the end of the universe people may become different entities from what they are now – that is if they still exist for this could be a time in which we would have probably been long gone. So is it not a more logical truth to think that there is a unified perfection of an on-going harmony that is based upon the energy that cannot die and that this energy is all around us and within us and that this perfection evermore shall be so?

So what is a more straightforward explanation for what is known to be called the "Three in One", this being God, the "Mother of the Creation" and their only child in which a part currently exists upon that which we call our Earth, this being a similar concept to that which all our ancient religions and philosophies speak about and which they likened to be a three in one with the first being God, and the second being the Spirit, explained in "The Book" has the Mother of all the energy existing and within whom God gave His seed which the Mother grew and produced has their only child, this being all life and Non-Life which now birthed continues to grow.

We also know a truth that within all life is that which actually "Creates" life always exists in pairs, this being a two which is usually needed to create a third? We also know that it is "scientifically" correct in that the male is the father who gives his seed to the female who is a mother who contains everything that is needed to grow this seed which evolves "magically" to birth the third, the child.

Therefore it must be "scientifically" true that the male is the first of the three that exists before the third creation for the seed must come before the planting, this being a truth that Nature clearly states. But is it not also true that the Mother contains the controlling harmony which creates the child from practically nothing into a perfect balance of a single whole, this is the "magical" energy that is needed to control the growth from seed to the completion of a child.

Therefore, is it not a truth that a male "father" must be the instigator of the child? Therefore, can we not "scientifically" liken this first creator to being "God", a name which we use to factually and scientifically identify the father of the creation and which now must be likened to the first of the Three in One.

Therefore can this fact not be seen as a truth that God or "No-Thing" (Nothing) for the Nonbeliever did correctly place His seed into that which contains all that is needed to create a third which we call a child? Also is it not true that this child must be born within a current existence, this being an existence in which the child can be seeded, incubated, formed into a new life and then released to grow as an individual entity?

So what is this "everything" that is needed to contain the incubation forming and creating of this only child, this being until it can be safely released to continue to grow to its full maturity? Therefore cannot this "everything" that creates the third be called the needed and seed caring "Mother" who must eventually give birth to that which evolved from a seed unto a child. A child which we call the "Creation" and which our scientists identify this birth as the "The Big Bang" and the child's name to be "The Creation" or "Nature" for the Nonbeliever and whose birthing higher life force "The Book" calls the "Mother of the Creation" which we can identify as "space" which is within and outside of everything that exists within the creation, which is Her and Gods only Child.

So, according to all the laws of the Creation or Nature for the Nonbeliever, it must also be true that there is a "Mother of the Creation" who accepted the seed, a seed from the father that grew into the birth of a third. So again we can explain that this is the birth of a child which we call the Creation or Nature for the Nonbeliever.

So yes! Can anyone deny this naturally and "Spiritually" known concept of the "three in one" for what else can we call the "container" of "everything" that is necessary for the creation to be born – but the name "Mother"? Therefore, is it not also clear that Nature indeed and accurately informs us that a mother must be the "container" of any entity which is to be born? Therefore, it is factual and a reality that there must be a "Mother" that did contain and then grew from a seed that was eventually born as the child we call "The Creation" or Nature for the Nonbeliever?

So Yes! What is this "energy" this entity is called the "Mother of the Creation" which can also be seen as a potential truth by the Nonbeliever? If people acknowledge these factually needed beliefs, it can then be indeed be stated that the "Mother of the Creation", to which the seed was given, can also be likened to the entity that we call "space", this being that which contains all things. Therefore cannot it also be said that the birth of Her only Child – the creation – must be under the same rules of harmony that controls all the inner parts of a mother's body, this is the biological control systems that exists inside all individual life forms and which compels all things to grow in a unified harmony within the singularity of the "one" body in which they live and do "growingly" exist.

For cannot the *"Mother of the Creation"* be likened to a pre-barren space as stated by our scientists, that willingly accepted a seed which silently grew into a life that was then born? Is it not also scientifically correct that it can be said that this was the birth of all known life which also grew into an energetic and living life force that came into existence first within the "Mother of the Creation" and then "exploded" into being the birth of the Only Child. Is it not true that if you ask any mother, she will say that when a child is born, it is like an "explosion", indeed, a "Big Bang?" Even Nonbelievers must accept Nature's fact of a needed "three in one" although many may attach different names to that which all know exists.

So yes! Indeed, this is a concept which can understand and thus can be likened to a truth that can be the basis of a full "Scientific" understanding of all that exists around people. Does not Nature which is all-around people state that there must be two to create another one, a third?

So now, after this birth, can this situation not be comfortably and naturally likened to a healthy family? A healthy family, in which the "mother" usually teaches, protects and cares for her only child? Therefore, more simply put, that which controls everything in the universe must "naturally" be its Mother, who was seeded by the child's father and who is also guarded by the laws of "God" this being the father of that which is named "No-Thing" (Nothing) by the Nonbeliever.

Now! the simple truth, which even Nonbelievers will agree, is that according to all of Nature that is around people, it is the Mother of the family who controls the child while under the fathers caring laws and provisions. It is "she" who is the "Mother" of all, as she cares for her only "child". This only child is the creation, and just like the Earth's moon, the Mother will never turn her face away from Her Child, which is all people, this being for certain people who have been given the "Freedom of Choice" by their father to support the work of the *"Mother of the Creation"*. But is it not also true that that part of the child which thinks it is an individual can then via "Freedom of Choice" turn their "consciousness" away from the Mother to "choose" a personal "I Want" in which they can do little for others and also for the unified family to which they belong.

Therefore it is true, as our scientist's state, that in the beginning there was "scientifically" nothing. From this "nothing" the firstborn must have been the entity that the scientists call "space", this is the name of that within which the creation was born but which should be called the "Mother of the Creation" and not meaningless, empty and uncontrolled "space", this concept is for those who seek the truth.

Can it not also be true that it was within the "Mother of the Creation" or space for the Nonbeliever, that the only "child" or Nature for the Nonbeliever was seeded from an entity we call God, this being that which also created space from a part of Himself and this being because He was lonely a fact which all people fear. Therefore cannot it also be true that from these two was born the Creation or the Universe for the Nonbeliever and what is now being presented in "The Book" to be the right understanding of the three in one, a three in one which has been giving many names in many different religions and philosophies. Still, in truth, there is only the *"The Three in One"* which also means that at you are which you look.

So yes! the above is the truth for those who wish to believe that there is a power greater than themselves and it is a truth for those people who acknowledge that they belong to a family whose parents really do care for them and whose Mother also teaches them and who naturally protects them by the laws of harmony which the father installed and the "Mother of the Creation" maintains, which is a condition that nearly all known life reflects

So yes! Now we all should understand that all religions and philosophies do tend to create their creeds in accordance to their own culture and so do tend to be "culturally" different in the pursuit of their culture's belief system. For indeed we can also say that there will also be differences which can be misunderstood, this being because the ancient foundations of these various religions are usually built upon different languages that may have very little meaning in our modern world. It is, therefore, because of this fact that old creeds can lead to an incorrect understanding by people who live in our modern age.

This misunderstanding can be aggravated when these various differing and misunderstanding groups create individuals who endeavour to overcome these misunderstandings by their own personal and private approaches. "The Book" is an endeavour to introduce a new "modern" way of understanding "God's world" or the world of Nature for the Non-Believers. Sadly, many new religious seekers begin to interpret their "personal" strong and "private" internal feelings in an endeavour to copy the same work as that which "The Book" states have been the work of the "Mother of the Creation", this being Her constant search and practice of creating God's harmony within the creation. Still, sadly they pursue a personal "I Want" negative not the positive of this reflection.

So they unknowingly and "negatively" begin to seek a tribal-based religious harmony for themselves only and so create only for themselves and the followers of their new creed a personal self-rewarding activity forgetting that the only child's "Mother" seeks God's harmony for ALL who exist, for indeed the only child that lives is called the creation – which is the real and inseparable only Child of God which is not a particular belief system that seeks a personal "I Want only a religious harmony can make me and my followers be without an "I Want."

Now take a quiet moment and feel the love that is attached to the "space" that is always around you. For indeed, it is only the caring "Mother" that is all around you and within you! Even though your five senses cannot experience the true wonder of this sensation for you certainly cannot separately see, taste, touch, hear or smell it – but you can "Self-Realise" that it is there. You know that it loves you for it is the "Present" and has nothing to do with the past, and it is certainly not the future; for these exist only in the minds of "I Want" people and so is not the real world.

So yes! For the Nonbeliever, the name "space" can be used. Still, for the believer, the concept of "Mother" can be used for; indeed, God's seed was planted into that which can only be named as the "Mother of the Creation", and it is she who is recognised as the one who monitors the growth of this number three, the only "child" which we call the creation and which our Nonbelievers call Nature.

Of course, the "Mother of the Creation" must be the most active and the most important of all the "three in one". For rightly does, not all Nature say that it is the Mother that nurtures and cares for the child when it is born? Is it not also true that all around us, we see this natural law of caring between Mother and Child? Is it not also true that it is the Mother who always endeavours to keep the child healthy and wise and is it not also the Mother of the family who targets her children to experience and so live in the "Present Time"?

Is this not because only in the "Present Time" can exist God's "harmony". Is it not also known that this is an agreeable situation based upon people's ability to rightly truly, and intelligently experience God's harmony fulfilling laws in which all can see that there is a unilateral understanding in which there is a natural and friendly accord between the Mother and her only child? Is it not also true that the child is naturally an extension of its parents?

So Yes! all around us, we see this harmony seeking truth resting within the "Present Time" and harmoniously working within the Nature of the whole Creation. Even the Nonbelievers must recognise this as being a truth that exists all around and within and without people who, because of the freedom of choice, can know and so support God's or Nature for the Nonbelievers harmony seeking endeavours that are also purposefully fixed into the rocks of our Earth.

So yes! The most important of all within the creation is the "Mother of the Creation" for it is "She" who can be "scientifically" known to be factually using a "Freedom of Choice" that can never be wrong, which is not the same as the "Freedom of Choice" that has been given all people whose task is to give to the *"Mother of the Creation"* their much-needed assistance, this is the "Freedom of Choice" that God gave to people simply because a person's actions can release the harmony that is endeavouring to emerge within the creation, but the same act under different circumstances could destroy it. It is the same law for the Nonbeliever. Does not Nature that is all around the life and Non-Life always reflect its growing harmonious activity, and even the erupting volcano is just shrugging its shoulders to ward off that which is leaning upon it.

For it not also easily seen to be true that energy is a consumer of energy which then begets more energy for all the unity of life and Non-Life is likened, as the "scientists" say, to be just one particle of energy moving forward? Is it not also acclaimed that the harmony seeking "Mother of the Creation" speaking through Jesus, the Christian incarnate, did talk about truth by saying, *"My food is to do the will of him who sent me and to finish his work"* and also *"Whoever eats my flesh and drinks my blood has eternal life, and I will raise him at the last day,"* this is the *"Mother of the Creation"* speaking through Jesus and these words are about the "Creation" which also includes the following words from the "Mother of the Creation" spoken through Jesus. *"For my flesh is real food and my blood is real drink"* and *"Whoever eats my flesh and drinks my blood remains in me, and I in him."* This "food" that the "Mother of the Creation" is speaking through Jesus, is God's "Harmony"; this being the only way to the "Unity" of all life and non-life, for simply put there is only one life in all the creation and what a tremendous understandable finish to hear the following words from the mouth of Jesus *"For it doesn't go into his heart but into his stomach,"* this is a statement meaning that the heart is love. Still, the work of the stomach is the doer and energy provider.

For in saying this it was the *"Mother of the Creation"* speaking through Jesus who simply declared that a single harmony seeking act, could bring together in unity, all that absorbed this "food", this "food" being likened to an act of harmony which was incorporated by others when fully completed. For indeed, it was these acts of unity seeking energy being exchanged to free more balance finding the power that activates and so supports God's harmony of all life which She, the *"Mother of the Creation"* continually supports.

9 THE FREEDOM OF CHOICE IS YOURS

All people have a "Freedom of Choice" which is the freedom and strength of a God-given gift that has been gifted to all people and which when empowered by personal willpower enables a person's "personal" decision, wishes, or plans to become negatively or positively "physically" targeted.

This target is a God-given gift or Natures gift for the Non-Believer. It is a gift well known as "The Freedom of Choice", and it is the tool that gives people their personal ability to determine their actions. It is this which applies to all that exists outside of a person's body, but as a reminder, it certainly does not apply to those separate entities that live within a person's body.

Simply put it is because of this God-given "Freedom of Choice" that the "consciousness" of a person can use "willpower" to target any "I Want" or "I Give" or "I do nothing" this being an activity that any person can "choose" to activate to completion or even "choose" not to.

So yes! ALL people have a freedom of "choice" that can empower "consciousness" to target "willpower" to carry out and so energise personal decisions, wishes, or plans, therefore, providing the ability to determine and control one's actions. Therefore it is God's gift of choice or Natures Gift of Choice for the Non-Believer that allows the firmness and continuation of one's actions all of which determines their decision to control or not to control that which is around them or even within them.

The truth now is vital to understand is that it was also God's gift of this "Freedom of Choice" that allowed people to "Choose" to allocate their "Consciousness" to "automatically" engender the power of "Willpower" to support and so release "automatically" into their mind those personal "I Want" requests emanating from the five senses, this being an activity which eventually became habitual – the question now is "Why"?

Simply stated this is because in childhood, around our after the age of two, children began to allow their "consciousness" to freely and "habitually" allow their willpower to energise into the mind any demanding "I Want" needs that were originating from one of the five senses. This truth is because they believed that these demanding "I Want" requirements were coming from themselves. So the five senses then became "habitually" recognised has "them", this being a "Myself" identity that now automatically and understandably rests within them. For indeed the Soul cannot interfere with a person's "Freedom of Choice", but it should now be stated that your true "Self" is the Soul and not the body it occupies.

Therefore this "conscious" freedom of allowing an "I Want" - that continually arises from one of the five senses - to "habitually" and "automatically" bypass willpower and so enter the mind, became that which is now "thought" to be the real "YOU" and your personal need because you felt it was "Your" life that needed it, but in reality, it was the "I want" of one of the five senses which you now "habitually" think is "YOU" – but the truth is that it is NOT you for you are NOT the five senses for you are the Soul. Your body is but a vehicle for its use.

So yes! It is undoubtedly true that many mistakenly allow the five senses to dictate policy and thus control all their activities which often became habitual. For indeed all these "I Want" claims that are emanating from the "animalistic" five senses do always "thoughtfully" cloud the mind with their individual "I Want" needs, which "you" sincerely believe to be "your" bodily needs, this is because they are arising "freely" within your mind. So habitually you thought them to be the real "YOU", but they are "NOT YOU".

So yes! Again you are the Soul which cannot see through the mind because of the clouding of the "I Want" that is automatically arising from the five senses, and it is this which blocks the Souls view of your bodies outside world.

So yes! It is this "personal" misleading attachment to these "I Want" thoughts, which are genuinely emanating from the greed of the "animalistic" five senses - that keeps people in a self-created Hell, this being that which is self-created by Past and Future thoughts and not the Heaven which can only exist in the "Present Time". It is also this misleading fact that has led too many disrupting self-claiming "personal" and damaging activities and even wars, for people, did not realise that their "I Want" needs and their "I Want" pursuits had been chosen by the animalistic greed of their five senses. For indeed these false "I Want" searches are ignorantly based upon selfish "I Want" for me thoughts which were always originating from the animalistic five senses resting within them.

So yes! These "I Want" thoughts that are entering and clouding a person's mind do stop the evaluation of the "Present Time" for they are an "I Want" claim that is persistently, habitually and "automatically" filling the mind with the animalistic needs of their five senses and they also include the "I Want" to do acts in which people will love me for doing.

So yes! It is in the knowledge that these mind filling thoughts that are habitually filling your mind are genuinely emanating from the "I Want" needs of your five senses, this again should be stated that in your childhood you habitually allowed your "Consciousness", this being that which is within you and which experience's all that is around you, to "Automatically" and "Uncontrollably" plus "Habitually" to bypass "Willpower" which energises the "Freedom of Choice" and therefore allowed "Consciousness" to automatically stimulate freely into the mind the "I Want" needs of the five senses because in your childhood you thought that they were you – they are NOT you for YOU are the silent Soul which is attached to the unity of everything and which can only see the outside world through a still mind.

So yes! Rest assured that your silent Soul knows what needs to be done in the "Heaven" that rests around you in the Godly or Nature provided "Present Time". For indeed this personal and now authorised but false "I Want" thinking is a reality which has allowed the "I Want" wishes of the five senses to "automatically" fill the mind of a person who then eagerly pursues this "I Want" thought because they think it is them. It is not them but believing it to be so they ignorantly "worship" this mind filling "I want" which is "thought" to be a necessary need for their "personal" survival and indeed if not obtained they become "thoughtfully" distressed or angry and afraid if their mind filling and personally based "I Want" cannot be pursued or achieved, this is not the living in the real world of "Heaven" or "Nature" for the Non-Believer, this being a reality that can only exist in the opposing of the "Present Time". Indeed any thinking traps the person into living in a world of the "I Want", a world that is created by the five senses which can only exist in a Past time or in a Future "Hell" which their "I Want" thoughts always take them. It is therefore in this "Hell" that a person is continuously and habitually living a life directed by these internal "I Want" thoughts, which also hellishly create MANY internal arguments that can only be emanating from the competing "I Want" that is originating from the arguing five senses.

For is it not true that "thoughts" are often greed-based discussing thoughts that come from conjectures of the failed Past or the construction and targeting of a Future "Need" which is always based upon a personal "I Want" claim, this being the world of "Self-Destruct" for they genuinely not understand that only the "Present Time" is the real world, this being the world that has no personal "I Want", except the "Self-Realisation" of real life.

So yes! Forgetting that life can only exist in the "Present Time", and forgetting is our worst enemy, the "I Want" captured person factually ignores God's Creation or Natures Creation for the Non-Believer, these being the laws that can only exist in the Present Time. For that which truly exists is for ALL life and Non-Life and this acknowledgement tells us that people because they have the "Freedom of Choice" are Gods or Natures guardians of this world, for people are the only carriers of a Soul that is directly connected to the unity of a creation that exists all around them and within them. It is for this reason that people were Godly given the "Freedom of Choice".

So yes! Is it not true that people are the highest Creation that exists upon this world and is it not also true that people are the only carriers of a self-linked personal Soul this being a Soul that has a silent duty to support the Harmony seeking needs of the Creations ever developing requirements and needs, these being needs which can only emerge in the "Present Time" which always and factually exists around each person.

Simply put, it is also this forgetting has to why people have been given the "Freedom of Choice" that leads falsely to a personal "creation" of a mind filling "I Want" whose targeting machinations enter the intention of the "I Want" perceiver who has forgotten that these are thoughts that have been allowed in childhood to emanate from five senses and not Gods world or the world of Nature for the Non-Believer.

Now just as a reminder of that which we speak. The five senses are simply the standard animalistic tools of smell, taste, sight, hearing, and touch, this being that which are mistakenly believed to be the real you – they are NOT you! Therefore, indeed, in the real world, your existence carries a Soul whose only purpose is to be a supporter of God's or Nature's for the unbelievers - Creation.

But Yes! Again it is mistakenly believed by many people that these five senses are them. So still it is vital to take note and to say again, because forgetting is our worst enemy, that many people have "chosen" in childhood to allow their personal "consciousness" to bypass "willpower" and so allow the "I Want" demands of their five senses to freely sound their "I Want" into the mind of the beholder which who believe that the five senses are "THEM" they are NOT you, for you are the Soul which is attached to all things within the Creation. For what should now be indeed known is that this "I Want" that sounds in mind and brings pictures that fill the mind, are just the claims of ancient animalistic desires that you believe are your own "personal sounding" demands but which are indeed the "I Want" demands that are emanating from one of the five senses and they do argue – is this not true?.

So yes! We can personally get used to obeying them. Still, indeed it is possible to "control" our body's five senses and thus not allow them to sound their "I Want" into our mind by stopping them from habitually and automatically allowing "consciousness" to bypass "willpower" because in childhood we mistakenly thought that these needs were emanating from us. So we allowed them to develop into a compulsory need. But they are "NOT YOU" for "YOU" are the observer of all these words, picture and sounds in mind for again it must be said that you cannot be that which you taste, see, touch, smell or hear! Is this not true?

So yes! It is these "I Want" seeking demands that are freely emanating from the five senses which are creating most of the sounds that are occurring in the mind for they can only be originating from the five senses. It is this that always takes a person to live in an imaginary world of the Past or the Future, these being the fantasy worlds that do not exist but which arouse the five senses to raise thoughts that relentlessly target any "I Want" that they are allowed to sound in the users' mind but which genuinely does not exist in the real world, thus being the realm of God or Nature for the Non-Believer. For now, it is known that these soundings in mind "demands" are simply "I Want" request emanating from one of the oft arguing five senses, which again can be clearly stated to be simply an allowed "I Want" thought which clouds into the mind and which automatically arise from a person's ancient animalistic needs.

So yes! In reality, it is these "I Want" thoughts that cloud the mind and thus blocks the view of the Soul from seeing the outer world. For indeed it is this mind filling "I Want" noise which is emanating from the five senses that stop the Soul from silently observing the outer world? It is also this fact which prevents the Soul from feeling the needs of the emerging Creation and so activating the body to support the Harmony seeking needs of the *"Mother of the Creation"* – the real purpose of all life and a life which ALL religions and philosophies target which is to stop the "I want" from entering the mind.

So yes! Again it should be stated – for forgetting is our worst enemy - that it is mistakenly believed by many people that their five senses are "them". For indeed this false conviction is taking place now because in childhood people did "choose" to use their God or Nature given "Freedom of Choice", to allow their personal "Consciousness" to bypass their decision making "Willpower" and so "automatically" allowed an "I Want" emanating from one of the five senses to cloud into their mind a personal "I Want", demand that was emanating from one of the five senses, which they became to believe was the real them. But now all should know that this mind clouding "I Want" cannot be you, for you cannot be that which you observe for actually, you are the Soul which silently experiences all that is perceived, touched, tasted, smelled or heard.

It is this God-given or Nature given for the Non-Believer "Freedom of Choice" that in infancy you used to free the animalistic "I Want" of the five senses which were given the freedom that allowed them to become habitual. It is this allowed habit that "always" takes the "thinker", via this God-given or Nature has given for the Non-Believer, to live in a dream world that can only exist in the Past or the Future, these being the false and illusionary worlds created in mind. They are truly fake worlds which do not exist. For undeniably they can only be illusionary and demanding requests that astoundingly fill and cloud the mind with their ever-demanding "I want", all of which emanate from the arguing five senses which are being allowed to "create" within the mind their intrusive "I Want" desires. This targeted motivation again being stated to be the mind filling "I Want" thoughts that continuously arise from the ancient animalistic uncontrolled needs, this being that which factually and sincerely stops the Souls view of the real world which can only be seen through a silent mind. Undoubtedly, this is the fact which prevents the Soul from seeing the real purpose of its existence, which is to support the quiet "emanating" requests from the *"Mother of the Creation",* which can only be accomplished in the "Present Time".

Therefore to state again, it is these false mind filling machinations of many oft arguing "I Want" thoughts. These being mind-filling thoughts which arise from the primitive animalistic instincts of the five senses and which are sounds that "consciousness" has been habitually allowed to release "unconditionally" into a person's mind. It is this absolute fact which clouds the mind and so stops the Soul from observing - through the mind – the reality of seeing God's Heaven or the actual world of Nature for the Non-Believer, this being that which can only be observed and so "Self-Realised" in Present Time. For only through a still mind can the Soul see 100% of the "Present World" and therefore assist the developing needs of the Creations Harmony and so to support God's laws or the laws of Nature for the Non- Believer.

So yes! People have only two main choices with one choice being to live in Heaven that only exists in the "Present Time" and so silently support the developing world and thus assist the *"Mother of the Creation".* She is ever actively adjusting the Harmony of the Heaven that endures upon this earth. Or with the second choice being to live in Hell and so pursue a personal and greed-based "I Want", which are the "I Want" deeds which emanate from the animal needs of the five senses, this is the living in Hell which plagues people. It is because people are known to have this choice that our ancient wise did always endeavour to develop culturally-based religions and philosophies purposely designed with many songs, chants and prayers to bring the worshiper into the "Present Time" – This being Gods world or the world of Nature for the Non-

Believer.

These "New World" introductions from our ancient wise being based upon "culturally" accepted religious and philosophical prayers, chants and activities that are all endeavouring to use the worshippers' willpower to discipline and stop their consciousness' from automatically releasing into the mind the "I Want" demands of the five senses. I so am compelling their "worshippers" to use their willpower to refuse these "I Want" desires by "consciously" concentrating on these holy rituals and prayers which blocked out all "I Want" thoughts that were usually clouding the mind.

For all our wise ancients new that people have mistakenly chosen to live in an "I Want" world which can only exist in the false world of the Past or the Future, and so they live in a Hell that does not exist but which is personally created to exist. For truly ALL our wise ancients knew this falsely created world which is based upon a person's "I Want" for myself, is the world of a Personal Hell and is not the Heaven that actually and truly exists in the Present Time. For these wise ancients knew that this was the place where the thought is not needed and where the Soul automatically and contentedly supports Gods work or the work of Nature for the Non-Believer and so their first step was always to introduce holy incantations that compelled the doer to use their willpower to engage consciousness to enter the "Present Time" the world of Heaven and so "disciplinary" leave their self-created and selfish world – which is also the purpose of mediation and if you wish to know more about this? Read on.

10 THE NEED FOR "ENLIGHTENMENT

Many people live in crisis and worrying conditions which are established by their minds being filled continuously with a personal "I Want", this being that which is automatically emanating from the "I Want" of the five senses, this being a bodily "I Want" and indeed, it is an "I Want" that is not attributed to any of the groups of people that separately survive around them. For sadly, the majority of people around them seem to be suffering from the same crises that are attached too many an "I Want" worrying condition that exists within many people.

Therefore is it not true that all around our world, it is recognised that there are many people whose sad faces also show that their five senses are also failing to achieve their "I Want." All this misery is created because of ignorance in not truly understanding who you and also they who you observe and mindfully re-paint - really are?

Yet, is it not true that "We" are the possesses of an undying Soul, the ever-obedient servant to the "Mother of the Creation", who is continuously endeavouring to keep Her child – the Creation – always within the harmony of God's laws, these being God's on-going harmony creating laws which the "Mother of the Creation" manages and which is also a work that contains Her aid seeking silent requests for the support of people, who are the only life form that has been given the "Freedom of Choice" to support these request, this being a personal aid which can be seen only by those who have freed their Soul and so understand the world through an unblocked and clear mind, this being a mind that is free from any "I Want" dreams which take the viewer into the Past or the Future – which is a world that indeed does not exist and so can be called "Hell".

Yet! Is it not also known to be true that anyone can find a religious and philosophical way to find the "Heaven" that exists upon our earth, but only in the "Present Time" by temporarily silencing the five senses from chattering into a full mind?

Simply put, all religions and philosophies target the same "Enlightenment" described to them by a wise ancient and yes, also many followers have forgotten the purpose of their ancient's task; for forgetting is our worst enemy.

So again, it is worth remembering that this five-sense-created chattering noise in mind is not you, for "you" are the silent observing SOUL that exists within all people; thus you are a person who has been singularly created to establish, support and maintain all that is required to be around you. For in reality, honestly, you are a person who was born to do nothing else but to silently and enjoyably aid the harmony seeking needs of the Creation that is all around you.

Also is it not true that many politicians and managing leaders, influenced by the self-binding movements created by our religions and philosophies, are always unknowingly and singularly attempting to pursue the targets of their SOUL. This being on its silent path to support the harmony that can be "Chosen" via God-Given or Nature-Given for the Non-Believer the "Freedom of Choice," this is being a personal Soul that is waiting to be "Chosen" to act within their surrounding community, and in global affairs – but they can also fail. This failure is because of the personal "I Want" noise arising within their mind from the "I Want" emanating from the majority of the people who support them, this being an "I Want" which is emanating from the five senses and which clouds and fills the mind so that the Soul is unable to see through it and so activate the needs of the real world. For it is these configurations arising within their mind which are emanating from the five senses - which are always claiming an "I Want" - which fills their mind and so stops their Soul from seeing through the mind the needs that are required to keep God's world or Nature's world for the Non-Believer, in good harmony.

Yet is it not also true that sometimes there are "quite" and "peaceful" plus "enlightening" times when our five senses are still and not sounding, This being when we experience an unprepared calmness within the mind which is caused when the energy of our consciousness surprisingly holds at bay all inner thoughts which can happen when we look down a valley and see the Creation laid out silently before us.

Can this experience not also be recognised as a truth which can be described as the Soul being momentary freed to see through the silent mind the real world in which you exist, this is also being an experience in which you become "Self-Aware" or "Self-Realised" that you are that which is viewing through a silent and empty mind and so you are therefore experiencing "Enlightenment, this is being the unthinking "Enlightenment," in which we inwardly recognise a feeling of great love for our children and also for all life and also all Nature, this being that force which is emanating in the world that is all around us and whose calmness can oft bring us to this silence of the "Enlightened" mind – which is the Soul being freed to observe the world that is all around you.

Would it not, therefore, be wonderful if this experience of reality was allowed to grow into a constant on-going reality, this being a "Self-Awareness" in which we always "Self-Realise" a certainty in which we truly experience the feeling that we have joined with the "Self" of all that exists. For this *"Peace that Surpasses all Understanding"* will certainly and positively only be found by people who "religiously" or "philosophically" but best "scientifically" target the path to the constant experiencing "Enlightenment," thus *"Becoming has one with the World"* and this is also that which all our religions and philosophies endeavour to succeed in achieving for all people.

For indeed you will find that all religious or philosophical incantations perpetrated by our ancient wise "always" target a truth that becomes strangely confirmed when the more you concentrate on the rhythm of particular religions or philosophies personally imposed prayers, the more you will begin to physically "experience" God's harmony or Nature's harmony for the "Non-Believer", this being that which can only exist in the "Present Time".

So yes, this is a truth for the more you "Self" discipline yourself to target these wisely imposed incantations and prayers encased in all religions and philosophies the closer they will bring you the experience of "Self-Feeling" or the "Self-Knowing" of the "Present Time", which is Gods world where 'peacefulness' experienced within an empty "self-Aware" or "Self-Realised" mind always and faithfully exists – even unto the cross.

So yes! The more we develop these religious and philosophically group-based or solitary enacted chants, the more we begin to realise the target of our wise ancients'. For indeed this is the targeting of a "Self-Realisation" which, via the Soul, experiences the unmoving "Present Time", this being an experience which can also occur during the self-discipline of the memorized and thus "automatically" repeating prayers and incantations which are being repeatedly and habitually released into the outer world – thus allowing your Soul to see and so experience the outer world through the spaces between these automatically incanting thought based words, prayers and hymns, this also is a fact that is realised by many an incanting worshipper, who is "Scientifically" unaware that it is the discipline of their self-imposed willpower that is wording an incantation that blocks the habit of a mind filling "I Want" noise that is emanating from their five senses; for indeed, it can only be then, when the Soul is viewing the Creation of the world of Nature for the Non-believer, through a silent mind, that worshippers begin to realise the power of the five senses and their dark blocking "I Want" words and pictures, which had previously blocked the view of the Soul from seeing Gods or Natures Creation that can only exist in the "Present Time", this again reveals the knowledge that it is the mind filling "I Want" words and pictures that hold people back from seeing or experiencing the actual reality of God's or Natures world. It is also this fact that confines us to exist in a self-created and personal "I Wanted" past or an "I Want" future – a self-created world which falsely exists only in our minds for it can never exist in Gods world – which can only exist in the "Present Time", a world that we can also call "Heaven".

So yes! This inner creating "I Want," world of "Hell" is based upon past and or Future thoughts which animal-like fills a naturally observing still mind with many an "I Want" demand that is continually springing from the five senses. Again, it must be stated that it is this which is ignorantly being allowed to block the Soul's view of the silently evolving "Present Time", this being God's governed world of "Heaven" or the world of Nature for the Non-Believer, this being the actual reality which exists around all people but notes well, that the past, the Future. The Present cannot appear in mind at the same time. Still, it is also good to remember that people have been given the "Freedom of Choice" and it is even essential to remember has to why only people have been given this "Freedom of Choice"?

So yes, indeed it is based upon this "Freedom of Choice" which allows only people to achieve that which they target to achieve and also to "Targetable" accept the experiencing of "Enlightenment" occurring during these imposed religious and philosophical "incantations", which allows a person to experience only the "Present Time", this being the "Self-Realisation" spoken of by our wise ancients and which occurs when a person's Soul is enabled to see through the still mind, which is the target of all our worlds freely and habitually repeated incantation based prayers and hymns. Yet sadly, often at the end of these holy incantations the constant "I Want" begins to be experienced and so again pursued when the holy place is left, in the belief that God's world exists only in their chosen and self-created place of worship – this is not true.

For what is now known to be true is that when this happens, it is good to achieve a "mind emptying" return to the chant of your creed which allows the Soul to see the real world that can only exist in the "Present Time", this being seen through the lengthening stillness that rests between the "habitually" sounding words. For indeed this unthinking "automation" enables the Soul to see the outside world between the words of the freely and habitually freed sounding of an "incantation;" within whose space rests the "silence" of God's "Present Time" or Nature's "Present Time" for the unbeliever, this is being the place where the Soul can actively see the only truth that rests in the "Present Time", which is the real and only reason and purpose of each person's existence.

So yes! Our most important religious and philosophical work is also to silently "listen" to that chosen religious or philosophical incantation which is disciplinarily occurring within us in the "Present Time", and so then to realise that it is only the expanding silence occurring between the words of the sounding chant that can bring people to *"The Peace that Surpasses all Understanding"* and which only exists in the realm beyond the ability of words to convey correctly.

So yes! By knowingly pursuing and so expanding the silence between the words of your favourite chant or prayer, our wise ancients knew that their followers would eventually and "silently" establish a way to live and work within the emerging of God's harmony or Nature's harmony, for the Non-Believer, this being that which can only exist in the "Present Time".

For indeed it is only in the living and supporting of this actual reality, now occurring in this religious or philosophically established silence between the word so the prayers, that people are enabled to understand the "silence" of the "Present Time", and it is a position which will guide all your actions or non-actions according to the harmony seeking needs that are continuously and personally existing all around "you". You will also find that the Soul of each person is attached to the will of the "Mother of the Creation" for each person's soul is the only part of the Creation that can, by its knowledge, unite the Creations harmony seeking endeavours. It is also this task which aids the purpose of the "Mother of the Creation" ever- endeavouring harmonising of all life and Non-Life. For indeed it is an absolute fact that the "Mother of the Creation" is continually striving to support the unified harmony within the life of all cultures, all religions, all philosophies', all businesses, all education plus all the arts; these being activities in which a person Soul supports unselfishly plus aiding the enjoining of ALL the needs of ALL the Creation, these being the needs which are required to serve or correct the constantly emerging harmony of the world around them – this being that which can only occur in the "Present Time".

Is it not also true that the "Arrow of Time," according to the Second Law of Thermodynamics, explains the *"one-way direction"* or the *"asymmetry" of all activities",* this truly is the experiencing of the harmony contained and evolving within any developing Creation; thus it is also an experience that is realised in a "Self-Aware" reality or the ultimate experience gained in "Self-Realisation". Therefore does not this *"Arrow of Time"* explanation also describe that this "entropy" is also thought of as being a measure of microscopic but consistently lost waywardness; thus implying that time is unbalanced and so we must respect the occurring amount of disorder arising in any developing but lonely system that is growing, due to its advancement through time – thus meaning that any developing system advancing and growing through time, will statistically become more disordered the more time it absorbs, implying that all God's or Nature's "targets" for the Non-Believer are "personally" unknown but can only be seen by people when or wherever these laws are going astray? For indeed the "Arrow of Time" the second law of people, also states that asymmetry and any inequality is caused when a plans movement through time is never interfered with. Thus all occurring chaos is an undisputed scientific fact, which only can be realised, experienced and so known, by the personal observation of people.

So yes! This "Arrow of Time" understanding states that a growing and onward moving arrangement will always develop a disorder within the "Present Time" unless corrected and this is also a realism that is based upon a fundamental truth, which means that it is impossible to decide the result of a current non-interfered with on-going activity; therefore no plan that is created by people can be used to achieve a targeted and known future, for it will always collapse. Yet! Is it not also further stated that in an open, accessible growing system that disorder can decrease with time, but that this can only occur when it is "Godley" or "Naturally" for the Non-Believer, corrected to do so! The question now is: *"What is more open to being corrected than the continuing movement of the Creation that is only occurring in the Present Time"*?

So yes! There is no evil devil here. There are only the happenings of the *"Arrow of Time,"* which people have now identified as existing in God's world or the world of Nature for the Non-Believer; a world whose harmony is maintained by the *"Mother of the Creation"* who also uses the Soul of people, this being that which was purposely created to aid Her work and which currently exists in the Creation that She birthed.

So yes! Peoples Soul is merged with the Creation, and its task is to naturally support the harmony that exists within God's world or the world of Nature for the Non-Believer. It should also be further known that an individual's "Soul", this being that which rests only within people, is enabled to use the body that contains it to achieve this harmonising reality; but not through the conformity to other people, but through the real honour of a non-wanting for itself "Creation" supporting Soul. Therefore the Soul's only purpose is to support the "Mother of the Creation" and so to aid the correcting of the "Arrow of Time," whose equations are forever occurring in the stillness of the ever-developing Creation which exists only within the "Present Time".

So indeed, the Soul of all people requires that it be released from the prison in which all the "I Want" thoughts contain it and to which it has unknowingly and ignorantly been imprisoned by their God-given or Nature has given "Freedom of Choice".

So again, it should be stated that this is an imprisoning whose containing bars are enforced by allowing the five senses to cloud the mind with pictures and thoughts of a personal "I Want," this being that which takes a person to exist in the past habitually or future time, thus blocking the Soul's view of the real world that can only exist in the "Present Time" – this being truly under the word of God or the world of Nature for the Non-Believer.

So yes! It is the personal machinations of an "I Want" that is being consistently pursued by the five senses that fills and clouds a person mind and which certainly causes that person to live in the unreal world of the Past or the Future thereby enabling them not to see or understand "stand under" God's world or the world of Nature for the Non-Believer, for indeed this self-made world cannot exist in the "Present Time".

So yes, this "I Want" mind filling "animalistic" activity creates a false self-made world that fills the mind and so stops the Soul from seeing through the mind that its holder "purposely" needs to achieve. For indeed this is why only people have been given the ability to hold the mind in an unclouded stillness which then enables their Soul to see the world that is existing only in the "Present Time", this being the observing of the creations stillness that needs to be seen by a clear unthinking mind for their Soul to see and so evaluate the "Present Time" and yes; it is this stilling fact which allows the Soul to see through the mind and so fully experiences and so be aware of the needs of the "Present Time". It is this false "I Want" activity that is animating from our animal past which is occurring within the mind, and this is why our wise ancients developed and introduced into the world of people hundreds of religions and philosophies to correct this "animalistic" greed-based "I Want". Although all these introduced religions and philosophies are based upon many varied and different creed worshipping systems they all pursue the same target which is "Enlightenment" this being that which takes people out of their animal past. Thus, this experiencing of "Enlightenment" occurs after the stilling of all personal "I Want" activity within the mind so that the Soul can see through the mind and into the "Present Time" and so purposely engage and support Gods world or the world of Nature for the Non-Believer, this being the work that is enabled to be realised by each person when their Soul enters the "Present Time", indeed the bliss based target of ALL religions and philosophies. For correctly this is a self-realisable fact, and one which was well known by many of our wise ancients whose many beneficial ways endeavoured to achieve this task and thereby bring their followers to God's world or the world of Nature for the Non-Believer, in which it is good to understand that "No-Thing" and "Nothing" are the same.

So yes! The Soul can be freed to activate its only purpose, and this is done by stilling the mind so that the Soul can silently and without thought see through the mind and so "recognise" the harmonising actions which are its birthright to succeed in completing and achieving. For it is then by choosing consciousness to energise willpower to empty the mind, thus allowing the Soul to be able to see through the mind and so "unthinkingly" support and physically activate the correct tasks that aid the harmony that is continually emerging in God's world or the world of Nature for the Non-Believer.

Therefore is it not easily seen that the task of people is to obey God's law which is managed by the "Mother of the Creation" for rightly and indeed, "She" is the carer of all that has been created, as are all mothers.

11 THE PURPOSE OF THE SOUL THAT CANNOT DIE

So yes! Is it not "scientifically" true that all the life force that lives upon our Earth is an energy that needs to live off some other supplied energy? Therefore should not this Godly or Nature born unified "Creation" of all things be identified to be identical to the inner parts of our own body and their inner self-governing singularity? Cannot it also be said that all life forms live off an internal unity that exists within their bodies? Is this being an inner unity which is activated by unselfish energy that supplies and provides the bodily co-ordination plus needs of the many trillions of different and seemingly separate "other" inner bodily parts that exist within the bodies of all life and non-life? Is it not also true that an active singular part of all that energy, this being the living energy that activates, controls and supports all life on this Earth, is also the same energy that exists within the individually created unity which is called "people"?

Further to this, is it not also stated by our wise ancients and so taught to all their listeners, that only people have a freedom-loving and caring "Soul", which has become falsely understood to exist only has an individual "private" Soul when truly has the highest form of existence it could also be the "Singularity" of all life and non-life!

Can it not also be stated that the *"Mother of the Creation"* s need for peoples Souls to aid Her work is also growing? Does this fact not mean that newly birthing souls - that can only exist within people – are now also emanating from lives that previously existed in the animal kingdom? Does this not mean that the Soul has existed within some people for the first time and within other people for a very long time? Therefore is it not a fact that this difference is quickly identified via various people's unusual behaviour patterns? For really is it not true that some people will "animalistic ally" and greedily take everything they can for themselves while at the other end of the scale will be those people of many re-births who will give everything they can to others and so all can understand that wisdom can accumulate and grow according to the number re-births of the Soul which eventually overcomes animalistic tendencies?

So yes! Cannot an individual's number of re-births be recognised by how they act in their current life, a fact which is identified by their intense, animalistic pursuits of "I Want" everything for me, which identifies the limitations and weaknesses of life in the animal kingdom? Yet is it not also factual that people can be readily identified to be in various stages of growth to the very opposite of any "I Want" desire? This opposite strengthening via many re-births until that "unified with all life and non-life" experience which re-birth are seeking is eventually achieved. This achievement undoubtedly being a totality experience in which all people can recognise to have existed in such people has Muhammad, Zoroaster, Confucius, Buddha, Vishnu, Nanak, Abraham, Yasumaro, Bahaullah, Vardhamana, Lao-Tzu to name but a few plus Krishna and Jesus who both forgave the people who killed them. These were only a few of the thousands of "saints" that have inhabited our planet and yes, all state that the freedom from "I Want" is a fundamental right and that the "Peace that Surpasses all Understanding" is the re-birthing target of all people, but could it not also be an experience which God or Nature for the Non-Believer is seeking to "Self-Realise" that which is "Himself"? – But more about this later in "The Book".

So yes! The Soul can be regarded as a "splintered" part of the unified energy in which ALL souls exist within the Creation or Nature for the Non-Believer. Therefore cannot this "collective" Soul be said to be unique energy that is formed and "privately" developed but which only exists within people and this being an ongoing development through the re-birthing of many lives, which began when the life of people first started? Could this also be the reason why people believe, within their thoughts, that they cannot die, but they also know within these thoughts, that the body will die but that they "feel" that their real inner being, which we call the "Soul" cannot die? Therefore, cannot our "consciousness" really be an inner bodily energetic part which, along with ALL our trillions of separate inner real-life forms, is also controlled and managed by our inner Soul. Still, only that life serving entity which is contained within our body comes under the Souls absolute control.　　　　Can it not also be stated to be a truth that people can "feel" that their "Silent" Soul is aware and an observer of all the life and non-life that exists all around them and that in reality, the body is just the carrier of a Soul that cannot die, this genuinely being while on its voyage to where no one knows but maybe now with modern understandings that are linked to the words of our wise ancients, can there be forwarded an answer to satisfy this question.

First, it can undoubtedly be seen as truthful, that only people have a Soul and the Soul can always be realised to be an entity which we can easily see as to be the silent manager of the inner workings of the body. Also in our ancient wise, it seems that their "Soul" becomes "them" which indicates, in reality, they must have had many human lives for they appear to be very wise and of great age, while in others, it is as if the unchanging Soul has to overcome an animalistic nature and seems to have no beneficial interest to the world outside their body:- Meaning that in some people the Soul has aged to a pearl of great wisdom and understanding, while in others, it is just starting life as if having been newly reborn from the animal kingdom. So they "naturally" behave "animalistic ally"? Of course, this is just an explanatory metaphor for the different emotions and characteristics of people – or is it a truth?

For indeed can it not be "scientifically" stated to be the fact that a parabola graph of quadratic relation could show at the aged end of the graph that the top two per cent of people who have had thousands of human lives, now have the wisdom which could be likened to the wisdom of Jesus and many others of our wise ancients incarnates. In contrast, at the other end of the graph, we would see new entries from the animal kingdom who still have an "animalistic" behaviour system which is an exact opposite behaviour system than that of our ancient wise for they want to own "Everything." For indeed can this not be likened to a behaviour system which could be "scientifically" attached to the new Souls that are birthing within our populations, these being new births from the animal kingdom who are now newly entering the "Heaven" that rests upon our Earth but only in the "Present Time".

So again truly, is it not easily seen that there is amongst all people those people who have "animalistic" tendencies and so do not have much awareness of the needs of others, these being new souls from the developing but growing energy that is resting within all the animal kingdom? Could it not now also be "scientifically" understood that such a previous lower animal life, this being a life which was occupied before a life being born has a person, that this newly born person would bring with them a history of behaviour which would be somewhat opposite and different from that of many of our born saints and incarnates which we call our wise ancients, these being our wise ancients who must have achieved many thousands of births for a very long time? Therefore, is it not "scientifically" true that within communities, there are people who have precisely the opposite behaviour patterns of our wise ancients? For indeed, it is wise to obey the nature of that which exists all around you for certainly your innate wisdom is to support its natural growth and not obey the animalistic "I Want for ME", this also being if you want to live with loved ones in your next life!

So yes! Can it not also be understandable and stated to be accurate, that ALL those who love learning and living by God's law would make even more significant progress if they understood and cared for these new entrants into the family of people. Therefore can it not be "scientifically" stated that if such people have just been born from a previous animal existence, in which they did not have the freedom of choice, that they will find it very difficult to obey the universal law resting within a community's culture that exists within a society of those who have lived many lives, this being the living within a "Freedom of Choice" culture which had been developed by experienced people who are moving towards "Enlightenment"? For as the "Mother of the Creation" said through Her Known Son Jesus - God's embodied Creation, ***"Can you get grapes from thorn bushes or figs from thistles?"*** Therefore is it not also "scientifically" seen that those previously born has animals and who are now newly born has people, do tend to "ignore" the community's needs and practices. However, they are newly born by the harmony seeking the will of the "Mother of the Creation", which means they have been chosen and therefore can be "Educated by the harmony that exists around them". Therefore can it not also be true that this must be a "Godly" correct situation, because these animals that have previously been born without a Soul, have now been "chosen" by the "Mother of the Creation" to be born with a Soul and the "Freedom of Choice" This being a simple fact which means that their past "animalistic" ignoring of community law can now be removed because they now have a Soul! Therefore is it not valid for the entire world to see that these newly chosen ones can change their ways so that they can now become fruitful and also be fed by "Sugar in the Water", this being for their inputting into their society their good deeds. Is it not also "scientifically" accurate that we can identify the many variable differences between the people who are the majority and who exist between this said two per cent (at either end of a population) this being a percentage that goodly or Godly expands and accrues has a life afterlife moves forward. Of course, this is just a metaphor – or is it?

So now the main question is: "How many people resting within our graph have controlled the chattering "I Want" which comes from the animalistic demands of their own five senses and not there Soul, which is now their true self?" Is it not also true that like the lower two per cent of new entries from the animal kingdom, that those who are controlled by the animalistic five senses can be "rehabilitated" and so can absorb and be controlled by the silence resting within their "personal" minds? Would it not also be the case that with their seeking to have their many "I Want" demands removed that they would "automatically" support the developing harmony attached to the world of the "Mother of the Creation" and so allow their Soul to live only has it targeted to live – in harmony and support of ALL life?

So yes! Is it not better to die in honour of obedience to the Truth, which many of our holy people achieved than to surrender and join with the animalistic conditions of lust, rage, attachment, conceit, and greed? For noticeably the majority of people know that the refusal to pursue these "I Want" thoughts lead to the highest virtue and with the highest virtue being the creating of a life based upon Truthfulness', Fidelity, Self-Control and most important "Purity". For indeed "Practitioners" of these facts will eventually discover their own "Self" and so indeed become has one with their Soul or Consciousness for the Non-Believer, this being a conditional fact which gives entry to being "Self-Aware" which is the experience of knowing you are what you look at and then maybe onto "Self-Realisation" which is to know that there is no observer and that you have actually become Gods World or the World of Nature for the Non-Believer – this being the targets of ALL the teaching of our wise ancients – but about how to achieve either of these "realities" is shown later in "The Book".

12   EARTH'S HARMONY IS
ALSO PEOPLES RESPONSIBILITY

So, Yes! Is it not true that because people have been provided with a God-given choice or a choice given by the laws of Nature for the understanding of the Non-Believer, that we have a responsibility to make our families, our community, our region and the country we are living in, able to support themselves, and so live successfully within God's or Nature's harmony seeking laws?

Do we not also see this truth in which the emanating Laws controlling the whole of planet Earth can be certainly seen to be supportively doing likewise? For are these laws not also "scientifically" correct in that the whole Earth would be a better place for people to live in if we always naturally supported the "Mother of the Creation", whose pursuit and application of harmony seeking efforts are being applied continuously to manage and correct the clashing laws of the growing and ever-evolving Creation?

Is it not also correct that the Creation is all around us, plus always endeavouring to exist has in the natural harmony that is within us, this being an on-going ever-developing "inner agreement" that controls all things within us and which is also an agreement that includes all that is without us, such has Landslides, Earthquakes, and Tidal Waves, etc. this being that which can quickly destroy a person's life and habitat. But the truth is the Earth not just moving a cramped muscle that is under strain, this being because of its ageing. Yet! Despite all these ever-changing facts, it should be known that the life of your Soul cannot be changed or destroyed. For indeed it can be understood that God's laws or Natures laws for the Non-Believer, do decree that your Soul needs to be re-born again in a place in which it's historically based personal experience and intuition - are habitually needed, and so-are being called to full-fill.

So yes! What is it that can stop the Soul's efforts from supporting this on-going and needed harmony seeking activity? Is it not true that all we need to do is to subdue and control the personal "I Want" of our ancient animalistic five senses, which is the main target of all our religions and philosophies? For indeed, this is the main reason why religions and philosophies develop culturally-based creeds and disciplines of worship, these being religious and philosophical acts which enforce their listeners' "consciousness", this being the energy which empowers the listeners "willpower" to concentrate on non-selfish activities. For is it not stated to be exact – metaphorically speaking – that all life has been created to exists purposely within its separate entity but also is it not true that it is joined and so inseparable from all that exists in the "Present Time"?

So yes! Is it not also true that that which "creates" life has given the right for all "created" life to exist in its environment and its compatible form – yet undeniably and currently, are we, who are created has people, not living has "isolated beings", with different "historically" created ingrained conditions. Thereof is it not also true and "scientifically" seen that this parabola graph that is based on the lives of people does show incarnates at one end and that which we can call the "animalistic" and exact opposites to incarnates, at the other end. Does this not also reveal a factual "scientific" proof that people with opposite and "animalistic" understandings do exist – in the "Present Time". Therefore cannot it be clearly stated that many people do not know the actual target of this evolving life force, this being that life force that is continuously existing all around them? Does this not mean that many do not see the need for the on-going maintenance of harmony – and also to accept that it truly is endeavouring to exist or emerge all around them, even if it is a tribal-based agreement?

So yes! Again, it may be said that this clarifying ever-evolving graph of an ever re-birthing Soul, is a way of life that may not be so easily understood by many people. Yet is it not easily seen, has our history does show, that this is a historical fact? For no matter how many times people try to destroy the harmony of their environment or the environment of others, it always "Soulfully" returns to that which acceptable to the majority- but more about this science later in "The Book".

So sincerely and kindly put, it seems that the reason why some individual people continually attempt to destroy the harmony that is around them, is that they view their world as if through a mirror, which reflects an exact opposite of the truth, this being where right is left and left is right, this means that many people must see the "Mother of the Creation" harmony seeking and on-going work as a negative and so do not "see" a positive view of their on-going life. Then, and because people have "The Freedom of Choice" they, therefore, see this work of continually creating harmony as something they should achieve, but only for themselves. For is it not an absolute fact that people do see the truth resting within the harmonising work of the "Mother of the Creation", but sadly is it not also true that they want it for themselves, this being an act which fractures the "Mother of the Creation" activities.

Is it not also true, as history has shown, that some people do support this harmonising work of the "Mother of the Creation"; this being an activity which seeks to continue along the path of God's or Natures on-going ever-existing ever seeking harmony, and does not many religions and philosophies that have been created by our wise ancients - state this fact?

But sadly over time, many of the world's religious beliefs that have been installed by our great ones, have birthed newly established leaders who did purposely lose or change this truth, mainly for their own personal "I Want". For in history it is indeed seen that many "religious" leaders pursue a mirrored view of their ancient wises religious teachings, this being within their current life and so have strangely reached "Institutional Denial".

This denial being the point in which they changed the actual path of their pursued religion so that it now serves a personal self-claiming system which makes their followers state, "Our Creed is better than you Creed" or "Our harmony of worship is the only true belief in God, and this is better than your belief which must be evil and so stopped" – When in truth this is just leaders seeking more power and riches that can be gained from their obtaining more followers who "animalistic ally" pursue their gains, this being that which has been taken from others. For is it not a fact that we saw in the "Christian" war from 1524 to 1648, this being when Europe was plagued by wars emanating from the same religion and which is known to have killed over eight million people.

Is it not also true that many believed that while religion was given as the reason for this war, there were many other reasons as well? These included the ownership of land, money and economic systems plus political power and the ownership of natural resources, and many more "I Want" this being a very un-religious way of life. This war occurred when the Christian "Protestants" broke away from the Christian "Catholics" teachings for the "Protestants" (protesters) did not want the authority and disciplined leadership systems of their claimed "I Want" Catholic Pope but wanted their own elected leader to be the head of their beliefs, for at that time the Pope was the head and disciplinary leader of all the Christian churches. Sadly this was a war that is reputed to have killed millions of Europeans with such ruthlessness as in the Catholic looting and ransacking of the Protestants city of Magdeburg in 1631 of whom the thirty thousand of its men, women, and children, only five thousand survived. This "Institutional Denial" can prevent religious followers from following the ancient and right path to "Enlightenment" which has been established by an "Enlightened" ancient who became a part of all that exists and in which an "I want" for myself cannot exist.

For undeniably they who want that which belongs to others can quickly become consumed by false leaders, who steal the truth or are attempting to steal a truth of an existing religion to obtain their own personal "I want", this always being an act which also attracts "I want" for myself followers. So sadly is it not now known that within an existing religion, which has been righteously created by an "Enlightened" one, that after their death false leaders can emerge with their "I want" my way of religious administration and practice to be the only real way of worship within this religion.

Then because of this "I Want" belief in their chosen leaders "I Want" dialogues, a false religious leader's followers do not let themselves "personally" see nor "personally" accept responsibility for the "personal" acts that they do as they "personally" pursue an ungodly or an unnatural dishonest system created by an "I Want" for myself – false leader. There is a wealth of this happening even in today's world, and this is a fact which is clearly and alarmingly seen by followers of all true religions, these being people who are always concerned mainly with the right actions that attempt to support God's world that exists all around them. These being actions that support or accept the harmony that is all around people and which always leads to no harm and so pleasantly allows the freedom of other people to pursue their own "unselfish" path to God's world or the world of Nature for the Non-Believer, for indeed they truly understand that God cannot and will not harm His children to whom He has given the "Freedom of Choice", for where is the strength of a father who kills or beats his children. For a current modern example of official "Institutional Denial" reveals that some religious leaders still claim that only they are the ones who have the correct path of life and this false belief system is then given to their followers whose "I Want that which belongs to others" is certainly a denial of God's or Natures harmony. For indeed, this is a fact that is easily recognised when leaders say that other belief systems are wrong and that only their stated "I Want" beliefs are correct, this is being an incorrect viewpoint, for the truth and reality of personal life is only seen when the individual learns how to still the clamouring and personally demanding "I Want" of the five senses that constantly plague them.

So yes! True religion or philosophy is born when a wise ancient show via rituals and prayers, "exactly" how to stop a person's five senses from barking their own animalistic "I Want" into the mind of the listener, this truly is a constant mind filling demand that enters the minds of those people who believe that these five senses are them. For if you can hear them talking to you within your mind, then they cannot be YOU! For "You" are the Soul which is the listener and more simply put, you cannot be that which you observe, touch, hear, taste or hear and it is this "allowed" mind blocking commotion that stops you from seeing the real world that exists all around you, within you and which is part of you.

So yes! The most important target of life is for a person to become "Self-Aware" and so experience the living only in God's Harmony or Nature's Harmony for the Non-Believer. This reality is the experiencing of an inner and outer harmony, which is pursued by all religions and philosophies and which is that which is personally within you and without you and which is also all around you for the real you can become as one with your "observer" which of course is the Soul, that which can never be seen, touched, heard, smelled or tasted but can be experienced by its belonging.

So yes! It is also agreed that some people commit an evil that destroys an existing harmony, this being an act that can certainly inflict pain upon other people but be assured that eventually, their loss will be much higher than the ones upon which they inflict punishment. For it is only upon acceptance of God's or Natures laws that exists only in the "Present Time", that people will experience the pure bliss which the Christian religion calls being filled with the *"Holy Spirit"* or *"Holy Ghost,"* depending upon their local belief system. It is also stated as an experience in which the personal mind is filled by *"a peace that surpasses all understanding."* At the same time, the Hindu religion calls it *"Moksha,"* which loosely means *"freedom from ignorance."* Buddhists refer to it as *"Bodhi" or "Nirvana,"* This is a personal experience described as *"awakening to the true Nature of things".* The Islam religion speaks of it as "*Being filled with the Angel Gabriel,"* and describes it **as *"a realm beyond the ability of words to convey properly".*** All the religions and philosophies started by our wise ancients target this "Enlightenment" which goes all the way through our known personal history. Even in the ancient Zoroastrianism religion of the fifth-Century BC, which refers to each person's experience of "Enlightenment" as *"Ushta,"* which is described as meaning *"liberation, salvation and emancipation of the Soul,"* and so it is undoubtedly worth achieving – but you will hear more about this which "The Book" calls "Enlightenment" as you read on and "The Book" will also show you how to achieve it – in a simple way.

So yes! When filled with this "Enlightenment", which is the realisation of bliss that surpasses all understanding, you will realise that about which ALL our ancients do speak. This being that it is not your own personally created "Present Time", this being that which is always bombarded by many a personal "I Want", but that it is the "Present Time", this being the enjoined time in which no personal thoughts of an "I Want " can exist. The simple reason for this is that it is only in the "Present Time" that God's Harmony or Nature's Harmony for the Non-Believer can exist, this being the real world within which all life and non-life survive. For undeniably that which you are experiencing is that which all religions and philosophies identify has "Enlightenment", and it is an experience that is always within you and also outside you.

 For undeniably it is an experience that is genuinely being for all Life and Non-Life for it is a harmony that can be witnessed within you and without you and within all the people who are around you and it cannot be damaged, except temporarily by those people who want it only for themselves. For indeed, these ignoring ones cannot see the real world that is the reality in front of them and which is "harmoniously" being presented to them. For really, if the life around you is not harmonious, then it must be people who have created the disharmony that exists around you for it cannot be the natural world for even an earthquake is based upon harmony? For truly only people have the Godly given or Nature has given "Freedom of Choice" that can create disharmony and the reason for this is because the same act can create or can destroy the harmony which is emerging all around them.

So honestly, this experience of "Enlightenment" can be said to happen when you realise that there is no future and no past for indeed they do not exist. It is only in the "Present Time" that you can experience *"The Peace that Surpasses all Understanding*," which all the religions and philosophies seek. It is also actively targeted by the writings and oft different teaching of all our wise ancients who showed an authentic and personal and systematic way of worshipping; for it can now "modernly" be realised that it is the precisely the same way to experience a "bliss" that is for all people, for it is within an

"Enlightenment" that can be experienced by all people and it is FREE!

So Yes! To truly, experience God's world or Nature's world for the Non-Believer, is to understand that the "Present Time" cannot be obtained by thinking about and listening to the misleading selfish "I Want" of your arguing five senses, which takes the thinker into the Past or the Future which can be now known as the real Hell about which all religions and philosophies speak. For it is a now known fact that "Enlightenment" can be achieved by everyone, for "Enlightenment" always exists within an unchanging uncontaminated harmonic world that exists only the "Present Time", this being a reality because God or Natures "Present Time" is always uncontaminated; for in actual reality it always automatically or eventually corrects what people have ignorantly altered. For people are the only creatures on the planet who can falsely attempt to steal for themselves the reality of God's or Natures harmony that can only exist in the "Present Time".

So yes! "Enlightenment" belongs to everyone and it is a fantastic experience that will always remove the "I Want" for me world in which most people live, for indeed it will bring to such a personal "practitioner" the *"awakening to the true nature of things,"* which ALL religions and philosophies seek. Therefore to achieve this "Enlightening" experience a person must accept the pure knowledge that the "Present Time" is a gift for all people and that it is a gift which is obtained by the simple exercises later stated in "The Book". For when these simple exercises are practised, they will bring to any person the experiencing of "Enlightenment," this is a fact which can be likened to real wages for you will have "worked" repetitively at these sincere prayer based exercises that will enable you to experience this bliss that surpasses all understanding, which is targeted by ALL our wise ancients, this truly is about the experience that all the wise ancients speak. Then, within this "Enlightenment" you will see the truth of all life that is reflected you from the "Present Time" which can be likened to the mirror of life, which you have been born to invigorate.

So yes! The following writings in "The Book" will reveal the simple way to obtain this gift, which can be attained by ALL people, but it will not be easy for many to achieve, but for some, it could be as easy as switching on a light.

So yes! It may now be useful to understand that this "Self-Realisation" is an experience that is the actual target of all religions and philosophies. It is also an experience which quickly shows that it is not necessary to follow another person's "captured" and unnatural way of living, in which false leaders threaten their followers with a fear of personal loss or personal punishment, these being fear-based disciplines that are used to keep their followers pursuing only their leader's selfish and personal demands of their own based "I Want".

Is it not true that some religious leaders do this by placing fear into their followers by "religiously" stating that their followers are not performing individual acts that they have been personally decreed by these leaders to achieve. Is it not also true that these false religious leaders state that their commands are the only personal way for their followers to find God? Still, in reality, it is "Institutional Denial," in which false leaders use religious or other teachings to empower themselves over others and so enslave them?

So yes, this is a personal but unaware weakness that enslaves people, for it is not only wrong but strange that some God seeking followers believe that when their religious leaders ask them to perform non-harmonious acts, these being acts which harmfully target another religion or acts that destroy another's person's harmony seeking pursuits, that this destruction will create a "harmony" that targets what they believe is their future and their own "Godly" wellbeing. This weakness is undoubtedly attached to a belief system that is sadly wrong and within which it is impossible to achieve "Enlightenment", this being God's gift to all people because this false ungodly practice takes the mind of the doer into a Hell called the "Future" and away from the pure heaven that can only exist in the "Present Time". Therefore it should be now clearly understood that these personally targeted "I Want" for me are a mistake, for you cannot change or destroy God's harmony, which is the ever-growing target for the development of the Creation or the targeted result of Nature for the Non-Believer. Still, you can support it – which is the actual reason why people have a "Freedom of Choice".

We must therefore firmly believe that people are not toys to be played with by misplaced, leading individuals who exist within religious or in business or as political leaders, particularly if their personal "I Want" is actively being used to claim their own "I Want." For often, they tempt others to break the harmony that surrounds all life and Non-Life, and they do this for their gain. It may also be true that some may even be told by these false leaders to target the destruction of life, which is the greatest of all sins, particularly when the person who is slain is unprotected.

However, it would be useful for these self-claiming leading activists to now worry significantly about their harmony breaking deeds. For it is undoubtedly now true that these individuals who attack other religions know that to be continually breaking God's harmony, even when under the command of a false religious leader who is seeking personal gratification, that they will enter a personally created the Hell that does not exist in the "Present Time". It should also be known by those who perform these malpractices that it is the world of Hell in which they have now chosen to live.

So yes, undeniably it should be further understood that because these activists are adults and beyond puberty, the "Mother of the Creation" who is the "carer" of God's world, will simply ignore them and also their deeds for She cannot punish them, for She knows that God their Father did give them the "Freedom of Choice". Therefore the "Mother of the Creation" or the "Natural Laws" of the way of life for the Non-Believer, cannot punish people. Still, those who break God's laws of harmony will find that their current lives become the opposite of being harmonious; this is because their way of life will become a calamity, which can be likened to driving through a city while ignoring all that country's rules of the road.

So yes! The "Mother of the Creation" cannot punish you for She does not need to do so, for you will be severely punishing yourself, this is a fact which can be likened to having many accidents, and every "I Want" situation that you meet with will be likened to driving through a city in which the traffic lights turn to red every time that you approach them. Therefore if you continuously perform acts that destroy the harmony which is all around you or you are killing unprotected others, beware, for it is well for you to know that you cannot be punished by the "Mother of the Creation" because you will be very seriously punishing yourself. For truly you will see the world around you is continuously decaying into a troublesome disharmony has you begin to live in your world called that which all people know has the world of Hell?   This feeling of being punished can be likened to being a lawful fact in which God or Nature for the Non-Believer, has decreed that people should be born with the "Freedom of Choice", a "Freedom of Choice" fact that is known by all because of the needed support within the ever-evolving Creation which always pursues a harmony that is based upon God's or Natures laws for the Non-Believer. This truth being because that which has or is being created sometimes requires a person's *"Freedom of Choice"* ability to change a disharmonising activity into a harmonising one, in which the participating person releases a growing harmony within his or her life; this *"Sugar in the Water"* being likened life in which all traffic lights turning to green when they are approached, this being by such a harmony-supporting person.

So, no matter what non-harmonious acts you perform after puberty, this "Freedom of Choice" law is never interfered with by the "Mother of the Creation", who's a caring activity many call acts of "destiny." Therefore, is it not wise to understand that the "Mother of the Creation", because of Her understanding that people have been given the "Freedom of Choice", that if a person consistently persists in behaving like a lower animal; these acts will ensure that his or her next life will not be within people, who are always born with a "Freedom of Choice". The simple reason for this is because throughout your life you are using God-given freedom of choice which can break the harmony that is always endeavouring to exist all around you and so you do not support the world of the "Mother of the Creation", for God's or Natures Creation certainly requires people to support the Creations current harmony based path towards infinity.

So yes! It is true that within most religions and philosophies, the wise ancients say that you will be born again. Still, if you are re-born again into the animal kingdom, where your support of harmony is unbreakable and not based upon the freedom of choice, then you will again begin to live a life in which you will experience the evolutionary steps towards birth in which you will become a person.   Therefore, if you are now living has the above described "I Want" selfish harmony breaking person, it is strongly suggested that you now begin to support the harmony that is all around you; for then you will be "immediately" assisted by the "Mother of the Creation" who will surround you with the gifts that are required for a good life, this being the good life which is given to you for you to assist and so continue in the pursuing and expanding of the harmony that "Mother of the Creation" always creates – has She gives to all of the people who support Her work.   Simply put, this is because righteousness comes from forgiveness, and this is the "Mother of the Creation" immediate forgiveness as stated within ALL religions and philosophies.

So yes! It is also strange that many believe that their actions are ruled and controlled by a particular religion or by the laws of an elected or un-elected government and that they are not "personally" ruled by the harmony developing needs of the on-going "Present Time" that ALWAYS exists around and within them. It seems even stranger that even though all the major religions and philosophies state the above rules to their followers, but maybe due to their ancient languages they are now ignored by not being fully understood – but they are now.

So yes! It is clearly understood that number one is God or Nature for the Non-Believer. It is He who has created the rules of all life and Non-Life to be perfect and that all life and Non-Life is unified under His one law. It is a fact that God or No-Thing for the Non-Believer, does not sit in judgment of that which exists within the third entity, His growing child, who we call the Creation, or Nature if you are a Non-Believer.   It is also clearly stated in these writings that it is God's partner and the "Mother of the Creation", who is the second of the Trinity, this being She who governs and cares for all Gods laws that target the future that is bound under God's or Natures law and laws can certainly bend or clash but the *"Mother of the Creation"* does see that they are never broken as all the accounts of past times do show. For definitely it is "scientifically" right that there is nothing for people to do, for the target of this Creation's growth cannot be changed and its growth cannot be stopped?

So, the "scientific" question is: "What is there to be judged?" Even if people destroyed themselves itself, which they may well do, would this halt the Creation's growth towards its target? Does this simple guiding truth, based upon natural laws that are all-around people, not point to a familiar self-explaining model, this being an accurate, unchanging "Natural" model, which shows the three in one being that God, is the Father of an only child who we call the Creation and that it is the *"Mother of the Creation"* who cares for this only child?"

So yes! is it now factually correct to hear and understand God's Creation speaking through the incarnate who was named by people as "Jesus" and who spoke as the Creation, by saying,

22-4-5-22: *"Moreover, the Father* (GOD) *judges no one, but has entrusted all judgment to the Son* (The Creation's and its laws of harmony),

23-4-5-23 *That all may honour the Son* (the Creation) *just as they honour the Father. He who does not honour the Son* (The Creation's laws of harmony) *does not honour the Father who sent Him.*

26-4-5-26 *adding – For as the Father has life in himself, so he has granted the Son* (the Creation) *to have life in Himself."* (Meaning that the Creation is governed by God's own installed "harmony" seeking laws and is now self-ruled).

Now some last words for this chapter, which were spoken through Jesus to the rest of the only child and a suggestion for the Non-Believer is to know that it is God speaking to you and that God spoke the following words through Jesus, who was the personification of the Creation – this being God's only child: ***"Nor does His word dwell in you, for you do not believe the one He sent. You diligently study the Scriptures because you think that by them you possess eternal life. These are the Scriptures that testify about me (God),*** yet you refuse to come to me to have life" (a harmonious real life within the Creation.) ***"Do not accept praise from men but I know you. I know that you do not have a love of God in your hearts",*** (Meaning the harmony seeking laws of the Creation) ***I have come in my Father's name, and you do not accept me. Still, if someone else comes in his name, you will accept him,"*** Meaning that people listen and then obey other peoples "rule of law" rather than listening and obeying the laws of the Creation which resides within themselves, this is a truth in which the passage of time has always shown to be true.

So yes! Now a strong suggestion is to read in the Christian Bible ONLY the words of Jesus, without any other person interpretations and simply read and BELIEVE and to KNOW that it is God's only child, this being the Creation that is speaking to you and advising you and for all Non-Believers, it is good "imagine" this is so. It will be then that a whole new world of understanding will develop within you, for the way to contentment and happiness, is waiting for you has it is for all people. Yet this is also only for those who acknowledge and live by the "Creation's laws of Harmony".

So now it can also be seen and further "scientifically" understood that the "Mother of the Creation" naturally cares for this only child? Therefore can it not also be seen that all judgments regarding the developing and growing laws, this being in the way that this child should grow, have already been made? Or do we think that God or Nature for the Non-Believer can make mistakes? Is it not also true that we can all look at a simple example in which we remove all people from the world and then look at the world or indeed the whole universe, where can we see activity happening or a law being broken, that was not made by God the Father or Natural Laws for the Non-Believer? And is not the harmony of these laws being naturally controlled by the "Mother of the Creation", which is the "Natural" way of all mothers? Also is it not a "scientific fact" that none of these created laws can be scientifically called "unjust"?   -- Is this not true?

13 THE HARMONISING SCIENTIFIC TRUTH

Now with this single "scientific" truth, this being a short cut to a meaning which cannot be disputed, we can understand "scientifically" the reality that the female factually and motherly, cares for the children and the man provides the muscle that protects the laws of the family. Do we not witness this to be a universal truth in most families within people and also in the majority of our animal kingdom? Is it not true that this three in one participation within the unity of a family can be "scientifically" seen to exist in all our Earth's "family-based" life forms? Of course, the major religions and philosophies, plus our scientific community have many names for this factor of compatibility. Is this not also indeed compatibility that always exists within our tribal laws; these being the laws that lead to a majority decision that only recently began to include the female of the species. Is it not also true that it is this "family" bonding factor that keeps like-minded groups connected as they naturally seek the growing and expanding harmony that exists within their language group. So they naturally, as do all language-based tribal groups, copy the Creation's or Nature's way of living for the Non-Believers, this is to expand this language-based unification.

Yet is it not also a well-recognised "scientific" truth, known within all these many various belief sections of our tribal-based language communities that this harmonious togetherness- seeking groups are continually striving to be compatible and factually balanced, even when many individual people attempt to try to stop this natural growth, because of their own greed-based personal "I Want?" Does not history also "scientifically" show this growth towards world unity which started long ago, when a cave families "I Want" opposed another cave families "I Want"? Then valley opposed valley, district opposed district, region opposed region. North opposed south, country opposed country. Several countries opposed several countries, and now the West of the Northern hemisphere oppose the East of the Northern hemisphere, which will "naturally" end, for this expanding unity cannot be stopped, therefor does, not all history tends to show that opposing a "neighbourly unification," is always a futile gesture?

Therefor "Scientifically" does not history show that even the peaceful unification of different languages and culturally separated countries cannot be stopped? Yet is it not also true that this nature-based unification's most significant danger is the possibility that a private seeking minority group, which is covertly attached to all political parties, is a carefully concealed and hidden group of "I Want" for myself people, who can seriously delay this movement towards the natural unity of all people as they disintegrate and attack the common differences or goodness that exists in most countries?

So yes! What is happening at the ages of 2003 and is still occurring in 2019? Do not the disagreeing East and West of the North European Hemisphere currently oppose each other outside their own country's boundaries? Also is it not sadly true that an "I Want my God and the way I worship Him to be in charge and not your God and the way you worship Him" is creating pain and destruction within the Muslim and Islamic worlds of the Middle East? Seemingly forgetting that our only God gave to ALL people a personal "Freedom of Choice" to do or not to do and to be or not to be to kiss or not to kiss – is this not true? Does this historically based truth not lead to an interesting question, namely: "What or "Who" creates these conflicts that oppose a religiously based loving and caring God's expanding the search for the friendship based unification of all people? Does not the religious seeking history of people show that "ALL" religious conflicts become that which nobody especially God or Nature Want?"

Is conflict not caused by tribes of people whose "I Want" leaders wish to prove that it is their law that encages others and no other law that will rule all the families of the world? Is it not also true, has history shows - that these leaders are always "Godly" removed from leadership has the group that they dictate to begin to find "a realm beyond the ability of words to convey properly." Is this being that inner and Godly given experiences which surpasses all understanding?Does not Earth's history always show that from the cave to the present day, people always eventually follow the way that peacefully brings different language-speaking tribes together in harmony seeking unity, so that they can live without conflict? However, it must also be agreed that the "I Want" that can reside in small specialist rich based "I Want" for myself groups can create a temporary problem for enlightened peacemakers.

A wise man once said to me that when people have a disagreement, this being when their governing "common" laws are disintegrating; then often, a woman who pays no heed to men will emerge as a leader who will bring harmony and order to the "tribe" and so "clean-up" the severe problems made by people by actually restoring the laws that bring harmony and peace to the group. But then the only problem this wise man added is that the harmony-creating woman, who lives in the "Present Time" might have forgotten how and when to leave her leadership position, and so will keep improving her newly accepted controlling system by creating tidying-up laws within already accepted surroundings, which then actually becomes a developing situation that causes great frustration amongst men who will eventually remove her so that they can maintain her previously acceptable "harmony" seeking laws that have brought order to them.

Is it not recognised as a "Nature" truth, that it is the female who maintains the "domicile" way of living a life that keeps the families of the tribe in right balance? Is it not generally known that it is the woman who controls and practices the "educational" tasks that are needed, to ensure that the children and the "family" live in harmony within her law and thus ensure that the "three in one" live as if they are living just for the pleasure and wellbeing of a one "unified" life? Is it not also easily seen that this is a "scientific" well known historical fact which targets and communicates a natural way of life, by following an acceptable by all, "Motherly" truth?

So yes! Again, the fact remains that "scientifically" it is true that most of the life within the Creation begins because of a male and female do pair has one? Is it not also true that these pairs are created to care for a unified third, this being their offspring child?

So yes again! Can it not be said that it is a "scientific" truth that at the beginning of our Creation, there was a male and also a female. Between them, they did beget a child; this is also an inevitable truth that most major religions and philosophies describe in many different ways that, this being that in the beginning there was a "three in one," which is commonly called "the family". Another simple but an essential "scientific" truth is that if you can show to the world a woman who supports and helps engender man's plans to control all that is good and harmonious, then the world will show you the leader of the universe; for this is the natural aura that surrounds such a pair. All can identify the woman who endeavours to ensure that the man's plans are "harmoniously" successful. Can this not be said to be a known truth? Is it not also true that by "scientifically" observing that which is around us, in Nature, that we can also marvel at the constant support that the "Mother of the Creation" provides for the on-going Creation, which is easily and acceptably known to be Her only child, which means that people are naturally unified as one "family" entity and forever shall be so – can anyone disprove this?

So yes! The "Mother of the Creation", metaphorically explained, is also the reality that all the major religions and philosophies accept, and has "The Book" explains, it is "She" who joins with them when their "Self-Realisation" is experienced, that being that which is called "Enlightenment". For this is a condition experienced when the mind has no thought and so your "consciousness", instead of automatically – via your permission in childhood – of feeding into the mind the constant noise coming from the five senses, actually expands to encompass and join with the entirety of all that is within you and all that is without or explained has "outside" you.

For genuinely in existence, there are two "Enlightenments" which is newly explained in "The Book". The first is an "Enlightenment" in which you observe and so become aware of the unified singularity of all that is around you, which "The Book" explains has been "Self-Aware", this indeed being when you become aware that all that you observe is YOU. The other and more final "Enlightenment" is called by our wise ancients "Self-Realisation", this being when you become "Everything", and so there is no observer, this is being when you "Experience" and so "Realise" that you are "everything" and that you are no longer an "observer," a fact which I hurriedly came back from by repeating my name, for I loved being within and also an observer of the Creation, the only child of God. It is these two "Enlightenments" that are targeted by all our wise ancients and their religions and philosophies, and it is a much sought-after experience. Further to this, we should remind ourselves again that it is this experience which the Christian religions call being filled with the "Holy Spirit" or "Holy Ghost," depending upon one's own sectional "Christian" belief system. It is also described by Christians as an experience in which a person's "consciousness" is filled by "The *Peace that surpasses all Understanding*" while the Hindu religion calls it "Moksha," which loosely means "Freedom from Ignorance." Buddhists call this "Enlightenment" experience as "Bodhi" or "Nirvana", this is a personal experience that Buddhist followers described as "Awakening to the true nature of things". The Islam religion speaks of it as, "being filled with the Angel Gabriel," and describes it as "a realm beyond the ability of words to convey properly".

So yes! All the religions and philosophies created by our wise ancients always target this "Enlightenment" which goes all the way throughout our known religious history. Even in the ancient Zoroastrianism religion of the fifth-Century BC, it refers to this "Enlightenment" has "Ushta" described as meaning "liberation, salvation, and emancipation of the Soul" and so it is undoubtedly worth achieving. For it is only then when experiencing "Enlightenment" that the

"Mother of the Creation" can be felt as that which is within and without all people and this being all that which they can encounter as the physical world. For strictly, She is the Mother who naturally cares for the Creation for there can be no other within whom we can perform these necessary tasks.

So yes!   It should also be further understood that it was She as the "Mother of the Creation" that God also created for rightly it is She who people call "Space", this is the "Female" in which God planted His Holy seed, who then has space, gave birth to the Creation.   It should also be further realised that it is was She, on behalf of God who has a mother spoke through the incarnate Jesus who's revealing and fully understood words of truth are revealed in the following chapters, plus the revealing words of the great Krishna whose humour is so loveable.   It was also the "Mother of the Creation" who also gave many words to the last of the prophets; Muhammad, *"Peace be Upon Him"*, and to all our many ancient wise and these are teaching in which She is still talking.

So yes! It was the "Mother of the Creation" who also whispered into the ears of the great ancient philosophers like Buddha, Baha'u'llah, Muhammad, Confucius, Tao, Plato, Laozi, Vivekananda, plus many more, including a favourite Sri Ramakrishna, from whom came meaningful words regarding peoples' self-delusion in which they think that the world is just for them. This being also when Sri Ramakrishna stated that there is a personal act of deluding oneself because one fails to recognise reality, namely saying that people "retreat into a world of self-fantasy and self-delusion". One of Sri Ramakrishna's many quotes explains that "the way of life is of two kinds, one leading towards God and the other leading away from God". He also further stated that one should "Meditate upon the Knowledge and Bliss Eternal and you will also have bliss (When achieving Enlightenment).

Sri Ramakrishna also stated: "The Bliss (Enlightenment) indeed is eternal, only it is covered and obscured by ignorance. The less your attachment is towards the five senses; the more will be your love towards God". He further stated: "These thoughts which lead people away from God's word, can be stated to be of six kinds, these being lust, anger, avarice, and an inordinate attachment to desire, pride, and envy".

So correctly, all these spoken of aspects give rise to a self-claimed "I Want" and a constant thought which is stating "This Is Mine", this being the fact which keeps people chained to the world around them. But it is also stated truthfully by all our wise ancients that as soon as one eliminates these "I Want" thoughts arising and so blocking the view of the Soul through the mind, then "Enlightenment" naturally occurs for truly this self-imposed discrimination "disappears" and the attachment to the world of "I Want" ceases to exist within the individual. For it is then that a person's Soul sees the existence of God's world or the real world of Nature for the Non-Believer, this being that which can only exist in the "Present Time" and which can be stated as then being able to take a supporting role with the "Mother of the Creation".

So yes, this is being when all the thoughts within a person's mind can be recognised as emanating from the five senses and so should be stopped, this being the fact which is spoken about by our wise ancients, these being the people who the "Mother of the Creation" chose to inform and so did, in this way reveal to the various cultures of people. These benefits are achieved by throwing away the false beliefs and constant chattering of the clouded "I Want" mind. For it is undoubtedly a self-deluding, falsely clouded mind that continually chatters with conditions and sounds which always demand the claiming thoughts of "I Want"; which can easily be traced to be emanating from the animalistic demands and "machinations" arising from one of the five senses; who many falsely believe is rightful "them".

For cannot now all see the truth in that our wise ancients physically brought to all their followers' various disciplined soundings and non-sounding incantations and prayers plus praying activities to "disciplinary" bring their followers into the "Present Time".

14 THE CHOICE IS YOURS TO LIVE IN
HEAVEN OR TO LIVE

Therefore is it not right and also the acknowledging of a "scientific" fact, that all our wise ancients always stated that people could personally choose to either live in Heaven or to live in Hell. In contrast, on this Earth, for which way of life that is chosen to be lived in by a "personal" decision and is it not also agreed that this could only be an individual's "personal" decision?

Is it not also true that all religions and philosophies state that there is a way to be living in Grace as opposed to living in Sin, with Grace being the Heaven that exists upon this Earth and with Sin being its opposite – an actual Hell upon this Earth? For rightly truly the believing that you are to obey the five senses is a "personally chosen" way of life which is a way of life that is based upon the "I Want" of the clamouring five senses that are always demanding "animalistic" satisfaction that is based upon their ancient past.

Now, all people should be able to fully understand that this false way of life, is a life that is controlled by the desires of the five senses, and so is a way of life that is "ignoring" God's world or the world of Nature for the Non-Believer. For this living in an "I Want" control world is an animalistic way of life that is inhabited by ignorance; for many people have never been informed as to what causes these different self-injuring ways of living, until now. For now, all people are capable of understanding that the pursuit of an "I Want" for myself always takes them away from the harmony that is continually endeavouring to emerge all around them and which is a way of life that confines them to living in the Hell that they have created for themselves, this being a Hell that can only exist in the past or the future.

So yes! You can personally decide, as all our wise ancients state, to begin to live in a world where you say, "What can I do to enjoy and also know what supporting acts will help expand the harmony that is all around me?" or "What should I not do that will allow it to expand," this being the living in Heaven which truly, exists all around you. You can be assured that you will "silently" know the answer to all the above questions and even what actions to do before any questions are asked.

So Yes! It is good to understand just how this personal choice is made, for no other person can choose your way of life, this being to either live in Hell upon this Earth or to live in the Heaven that also exists upon this Earth even under the threat of death. For now, it is also essential to understand that the "Mother of the Creation" and especially God or Nature for the Non-Believer could NEVER condemn or punish those people who have chosen, usually via ignorance, to live in Hell or via wisdom would rather die than to live in Hell. Simply put, there cannot be any "heavenly" inflicted punishment, as many people seem to think. For is it possible to imagine that God can punish someone for breaking His harmony when all people know that God gave people the "Freedom of Choice" and that the "Mother of the Creation" knowingly supports this gift?

Simply put can you imagine a mother giving a child a sweet and saying, "Your father has given you the freedom of choice in that you can eat it yourself or you can give it to someone else who you understand needs it more than you?" And then beating and punishing the child because the child personally ate the sweet, this right can only be because of its ignorance in seeing that no other need was seen to be more important than its own.

Yet many people believe and indeed try to assist in what they erroneously believe should be a punishment that should be inflicted upon others, this being "others" who do not believe in their tasty and personal religious ways, this, of course, this being a false pursuit of their own personal "I Want" and that which they say is coming from God's demands – as if God or Nature for the Non-Believer has an "I Want" for me. Therefore can anyone believe in a God who says that anyone who does not love or worship me in the way I like to be worshipped, I will kill or physically and painfully punish them!

For truly anyone who believes in the above world lives in their own "selfish" and "falsely" created world in which they continuously claim an "I Want" that is coming from there I love "ME", this also being a world which is always controlled by their ignoring the truth of God's world or the world of Nature for the Non-Believer and which is a world that is filled by their animalistic self-claiming five senses whom they believe to be themselves. Nor do they understand that this is the reason why they are living in "Hell" while on Earth and not living in the "Heaven" that is all around them.

So yes! It should now be factual to know that they are being controlled by their animalistic five senses and not controlled by the laws of God. So they live in a Hell that is created by these ever-demanding five senses, which they think is them, for is it not also seen to be true that when such uncontrolled and un-Godly false believers personally claim for themselves the entire world that their body lives in, even claiming that their religion is the only true religion and that all other religions should think likewise? Is this not truly an "animalistic" understanding because these believers are driven by physical appetites rather than God's spiritual needs?

So yes! A person lives in Hell when they are controlled by the "I Want" of these five senses and this being because they ignorantly forget that the "animalistic" five senses are there only to be "chosen" by people to evaluate various on-going activities that construct and or support the harmony seeking situations that are presented to them by the "Mother of the Creation". These are the Creations harmony developing needs that surround all people and which often exist within their current life. Therefore is it not true that many people forget this fact? Is this being that they are here to support the Creation that is emerging all around them? But genuinely do not many falsely believe that they are the "animalistic ally" based on five senses? Therefore is it not true that many pursue a domineering sense's "I Want", this often being after many a mind filling sensually based arguments have taken place? Therefore is it not true that the minds filling "personal" creations can uncaringly establish a mind blocking past or a future based false world, a world which is truly the world of a self-created Hell now being spoken about and so revealed in "The Book". Is it not also factual in that proof of this can be seen in many people as they pursue their personal "I Want" and not the impersonal activities that can clash within the emerging "Present Time" and which are actions and non-actions that support and aid the work of the "Mother of the Creation"? For truly is this not the reason why people have been created with the personal ability of "free choice"?

It should, therefore, be known that people who read "The Book" do now "scientifically" know the truth of their being? Therefore is it not true that all readers are now enabled to witness, and so realise that they are allowing the five senses to behave like untrained wild pups.

Therefore is it not "scientifically" valid that people can now "observably" witness that these five senses, which have been allowed to use the mind freely, can argue between themselves as they knowingly compete for their own particular "I Want", this is undoubtedly being a personal "I Want" that is often followed by the application of force, which empowers one of the individual senses, whose voice is louder and more persistent than the "other inner voices", to be loudly heard within the person mind which people mistakenly believe to be coming from themselves. But it is now known by all readers of "The Book" that the five senses are NOT "themselves" they are simply an instrument for their personal use and if it is wished to be able to turn off these "I Want" demands of the five senses – read on.

So yes! These five senses are NOT the true "self," for the real "self" is the individual's Soul, this being that which is the silent observer that rests within all people. Therefore is it not the truth that the majority of people live to pursue an incorrect belief system, forgetting that their "self" is part of the "three in one", this being the three in one, which knowingly includes a person's Soul. A Soul which is a silent observer that rests within all of the people and which is that which naturally and silently obeys and so evaluates the will of God, and so silently supports the harmonising work of the "Mother of Creation".

This being also the fact which establishes the reason why people have been given the freedom of "choice", for sometimes an individual action is needed to support the Creation's harmony seeking needs, but sometimes this same act can destroy it, for you cannot be that activity which the Soul endeavours to observe but cannot observe because of the many clouded "I Want" demands that are emanating from the five senses all of which fill the mind with the world of Hell. You indeed you cannot be that which you can touch, taste, see, hear, or smell you can only be that which observes these "realities", these being realities which generally exist within the Creation. An example to support this understanding is to "silently" look at your right hand and allow the mind to become still. Then ask yourself the question "Is this hand me?" The answer will be or eventually be "Of course not" for you cannot be that which you observe, is this not true?

So yes! Indeed this false belief system, in which a person believes that they are the five senses and so must fulfil their ever pursuing selfish "I Want" demands, is a kind of thinking that just cannot be valid because all people know that you cannot be that which you can observe, listen to, taste, smell or touch, which means that you cannot be the body in which you now live for the body is simply the carrier of the Soul, which exists in all people.

So yes! All our wise ancients continue to explain in words that their followers understand, that many live in a false condition and in a belief that continually continues to "selfishly" and "animalistic ally" claim control of the individual and it is a belief system that commits them to live in Hell until wisdom prevails and the individual Soul, always targeted to be freed by our wise and supported by some effort spoken of later in "The Book", then allows the "Soul" to become the only entity to see through a clear mind, this being a mind that is not contaminated and so filled by an "I Want," emanating from the five senses.

So yes, this is a controlling fact that can be achieved by a simple exercise in which, like wild dogs, these five senses are trained to be out of sight, this is undoubtedly being a factual situation that can be likened to pups being behind the observer's heel until "silently" directed by the now observing Soul to perform the harmonising tasks that the body has been created to achieve and to which it is best suited to perform, for this is a task which is needed to be performed by the Godly or Nature born body for the Non-Believers.

It will also be a task in which the five senses - that are quietly held within the body - will be engaged to silently support tasks without any observable sound or an "I Want" word emerging from them. This truth being has the body automatically and silently performs the harmonising task that is has been created to assist with and so perform, but only in the "Present Time". For only an inner "silent" mind can allow the Soul to see that which may be needed to be maintained within the "Present Time", and thus give full support to the emerging harmony, and therefore engage the five senses to give a hundred per cent of that which supports the "Mother of the Creation", who like all mothers makes efforts to control the developing the "Present Time."

For the Soul, which is the real "YOU" and the "silent" observer of all that it is being created, does indeed support the "Mother of the Creation" and her caring of the "Present Time", this being that world which contains the real "Heaven", which again must be said, can only exist in the "Present Time", this being that which the ever observing Soul, which is without thought, is therefore enabled to know precisely at this point what exactly should be done.

So yes! Indeed, those who learn to silence the "I Want" gabbling of the five senses can begin to understand that they are an integral part of the Creations greater whole. This condition is undoubtedly being an experience which can be truly realised by any person who now exists in this Heaven that rests upon this Earth and which is an "unthinking" condition that is known and named by the ancient philosophers as "Enlightenment" which also explains the true meaning of the words: "The Truth Will Set You Free!" Also "The Book" always states that this freedom awaits you for you will be "scientifically" shown that God's world or Nature's world for the Non-Believer will no longer be anonymous to you. So with this fact, you can act within God's laws and so support the "Mother of the Creation" This is the real existence and only existence that will set you free.

So yes! Let us again reiterate that being controlled by the five senses is ignorance which many philosophers call "sleep" because it is within this "sleep" that the necessary support of God's harmony is persistently disobeyed by people for only harmonising acts can be performed. At the same time, one is awake to the truth, as is now seen by the observations of the Soul within. Reliably, this is indeed being the observation of the individual Soul which links conclusively with the Soul of all people and which can only be reached when one understands that they are not to obey the five senses whose constant clamouring of "I Want" for myself keeps you living in a self-made Hell that they make for themselves while living on this Earth.

So yes! It is a proven fact that by controlling and so silencing these five senses that this silencing brings a way of life that removes people from personally living in a "Hell," which they create for themselves, to a world that is living in a   Heaven while living on this Earth. Thus "Enlightenment" is undoubtedly being a Heaven on Earth which is lived in by all those who realise that these continuing observed demands which are emanating from the five senses are not "personal" demands, that should be immediately claimed and then satisfied, but they are your five senses that should be "ignored" to harmonise all that which surrounds the person body.

So yes! It is now again clearly stated that this is the primary reason why people have been given the value of a free "choice" this is a value that has been given to people by their Godly Fathers laws so that people can aid the "Mother of the Creation" in Her on-going work to support or redirect and so maintain the emerging harmonising laws that arise within the Creation. So it is wrong to falsely misread the demands and choices of the five senses which also "animalistic ally" evolutionary exist within them.

So yes! The purpose and reason for people being giving the freedom of choice are that some supporting "physical" acts are needed to sustain the harmony that is ever-growing and developing within the Creation. Still, such similar acts are some- times not needed and can even be harmful, so, therefore, only people have been given a "freedom of choice". It should also be recognised that people are the first and only life form to be granted this gift of "free choice" including their death, and this is not because the "Mother of the Creation" has no choice, but because She is heavenly celestial, and not physical, and can only be in the within the knowledge of people who show Her much love. This being is also the main reason why God created people with freedom of choice so that He could also experience their true love towards Him, a fact which exists in all parents.

So yes! It is, therefore, true that the "Mother of the Creation" could never punish her children but would consistently show the child how to live a good (GOD) life on Earth and to truly, experience that which is the Heaven that exists upon and within our Earth, this also being the pure Heaven that all our wise ancients target to reveal in our world's major religions and philosophies.

Is it not also true that our wise ancients always explain, by using culturally accepted words? This knowledgeable truth is recognised by many of the people around them, this always being a way to live in Heaven while upon this Earth, which is a knowledge that is acceptable to people within their timeline.

It is also these acceptable gifts that are being modernly re-interpreted to reveal a new and modern way of how to achieve "Enlightenment". This "Enlightenment" is being a way that reveals the living in God's Heaven or Natures Heaven for the Non-Believer which can only exist in the "Present Time" – a gift which is for those people whose Soul has existed within many hundreds of lives and who are now motivated by a silent "I want for you" world and also for those who are now with a new Soul because they have just emerged from the animal "I want for myself" noisy kingdom and of course for all those who are between these two positions.

15 HEAVEN COMES BEFORE HELL

So yes! Who creates Hell? In our entire Earthly world, only "people" can create an ungodly Hell, and this can become a physical reality that exists all around people. Yet it is also true that the "Mother of the Creation" can be felt to support aid and feed these Souls who live on Earth as it is in Heaven, this is the Heaven in which God installed laws that always pursue a creating "unity in harmony," which is supported by the "Mother of the Creation" who continually cares for and activates the harmony that exists within the only body of the Creation, just as all mothers do.

So yes! It cannot be harmony if likened to a mirror it shows its different reflection, this being the disharmony that exists for those who live in Hell, these being caused by the acts of people and which can only occur because people have a "Freedom of Choice".

So yes! This mirror of life can also show how a person can leave the living in Hell which their "I Want" for me takes them and so live in Heaven while on this Earth.   But sadly, upon falsely choosing the way of the five senses and they're ever seeking an "I Want"; many people have forgotten the real purpose of life and have become controlled by these animalistic ally based five senses, which they firmly believe is "them". It is also because of this false concept that many people unknowing ignore the millions of various helpful sayings from our wise ancients who produced our great religions and our great philosophers and who endeavoured to show the unity that exists within the Creation to all their listeners. Is it not also well known that our wise ancients created religions and philosophies that repeatedly explain the real purpose of a person's life? So they speak this same truth to all people, thus having been spoken so for century after century?

Yet is it not true that many people are in ignorance of these facts and so live in a Hell that opposes the "Mother of Creation's" work and so they fail to recognise the beauty and love that binds the Creation together and which truly, exists all around them. Is it not also true that it is they who lead a lonely, cold and troubled "I Want" life?

So yes! You do hear them complaining and so not genuinely seeking a way of life that reaches and obeys the harmony that exists in God's world or the world of Nature for the Non-Believer. Therefore, Let us repeat just who is the "Mother of the Creation"? First, it is crucial to understand that we must see the entire born and unborn natural "life" that exists all around us and which shows us that life is commonly based upon pairs that create a third. Thus, it is that the Creation or Nature for the Non-Believer regularly shows this truth to be a "scientific" fact. This being that within all life we have the male and the female whose unity creates the third – the child and so again this simple model of understanding shows the real way to live in Heaven while on this Earth which is to realise that the "Mother of the Creation" is God's partner who can be likened to the "Space" that is within and around everything. It was to this space that God gave the seed that began that which people call the Creation, which is their ONLY child and a fact which should all ways be identified as only one entity.

So yes! All our religions and philosophies target this concept has a truthful and straightforward way of understanding how to live in Heaven, while on this Earth and this in this new modern way it is good to realise that the "Mother of the Creation" is God's partner. It was to Her that God gave the seed that began that which we call the Creation, who is their ONLY child.

Therefore, indeed, does this not also mean that all "Life" and "Non-Life" are unified as a single entity? Is this not also a fact that can be understood when likened to the same truth of harmonised unity which exists within our bodies, for is this not also known to be true that all our inner body entities exist only to support all the other variable inner entities that exist and live within our bodies? For indeed, this is merely being a bodily statement which is based upon a unified "bodily" truth that shows a real "bodily" example of what life is all about. Yet such a unified supporting of harmonised singularity is very conflicting to the "I Want", created by each of them individually and oft quarrelling five senses which have been responsible for people destroying many millions of their kind.

Therefore is it not true that because of this "I Want" for me, that people can ignorantly attack and destroy the unity of the one body which we call "The Creation" and is it not also strange that history also shows the many deaths and the torturing of others has occurred because of many a false religiously created "I Want" wars? These wars being over a differing belief system that states that "only my way" is the way to God and not your way, which caused terrible "inhuman" conflict from 1517 until 1648 which was a devastating thirty-year war fought between Europe's Christians. Is it not also true that our history shows that this self-created "disharmony" (the schism) was said to the cause by a religious argument concerning such beliefs as, "What is the Holy Spirit?" and "What interpretation of bread should be used at a group ritual?" These were arguments that were based upon a simple, "I Want" my religion and its practices to be the way to God and not yours." In reality, it was an "I Want" based reason to steal property and power from others. Nor was their search for a unifying harmony based upon examples coming from the "Mother of the Creation". Was it not the "I Want my way to God not your way to God" that created the Christian Renaissance wars in which the Protestant Reformation (1517), which began as a religious reform movement within the Catholic Church, but ended has a revolution that brought religious pluralism to Europe, which in turn led to fierce competition between Europeans nations so that religious strife and certainly political rivalries was a cause that killed millions of people and destroyed whole cities including twenty-five to forty per cent of the German people and all based upon a disagreement over finding a way to God's world. This 1517 war being over a personal disagree, which is NOT the living in Heaven while upon this Earth, an Earth that God created for all of the people.

For this was the time of a Self-Created un-religious Hell when "Protesters" broke away from the teaching of the Roman Catholic Church during the Reformation, simply because they rejected the imposed on-going Roman churches Catholic rituals in which it was believed that the bread and wine during worship, actually turns into the body and blood of Jesus Christ. In contrast, the Protestants believed that it stays has bread and wine and that it only represents the body and blood of Jesus Christ, and millions were killed over this simple statement and other religious disagreements. Still, indeed this war was over "You do what I say, and we will NOT do what "YOU" say".

So yes! The "Protesters" also did not want the authority of the Pope to be their appointed leader and instead wanted their own elected leader to be the head of their church, for at that time the Pope was the nominated head of all the Christian churches. The further disagreement was that the Protesters decided only to pursue the teachings of the Bible and not the teachings made by church leaders of people. These new Protesters also did not agree with the Roman Catholics leader's ventures into Capitalism, which was recognised by the Protesters who disliked the then Roman Catholics leader's efforts to sell to their Christian followers a promise that when they died the church would see to it that they would not go to Hell if they paid the Roman Church a sum of money or gave other such valued gifts. This selling of indulgences was a promised way that also granted quicker passage through Purgatory which it had traditionally and always been stated that this could only be achieved by an individual's good works.

This Christian conflict indeed destroyed God's harmony, which was endeavouring to emerge all around them; for only "individual" people can practise acts of disharmony, such as this Christian based war against innocents which also killed thousands of individual innocents by calling them witches, and then burnt them alive while tied to a stake. This being when the only "evidence" required was a single pointing finger attached to rumor, and gossip and so needed no corroborating evidence to convict and destroy these innocents who were killed so that all would fear the power of their Christian church which currently followed by 32% of the world's population. It is also knowingly stated that Islam is the world's second-largest religion. It is also genuinely known by ALL Muslims that Islam is also a monotheistic religion with the singular belief there is only one God, which is also a truth found in Christianity and Judaism, but with the main difference being that in Islam Muhammad is seen by ALL Muslims as the last prophet of God. It is also known that Islam has an estimated following of 22% of the global population who are ALL known to be Muslims and who also believe in Jesus, the son of Mary. It is also a truth that Muslims worship the Christian Jesus as the penultimate prophet and a faithful messenger of Allah (God). Still, it is also true that Muslims worship Muhammad more strongly as the final prophet for it is He who was the founder of Islam and whose words, teachings and practices along with the knowledge contained within the Quran, formed the basis of Islam's religious beliefs. It is further acknowledged that many other different world religions and philosophical beliefs are estimated to be worshipped by a further 30% of the world's population. In comparison, approximately 16% of the world's population can be said to be unbelievers'.

Islam also teaches that God is merciful, all-powerful, unique, and is a system of worship that has guided people through many of the prophet Mohammed's teachings; who did continually reveal the Holy Scriptures, including many natural signs of God's greatness which these writings within "The Book" also describe as the harmony that is always endeavouring to exist in the "Present Time", this being the Heaven that all our scriptures speak.

So yes! The primary scriptures of Islam are all contained in the Quran, which is viewed by Muslims as the verbatim word of God, and which also contains the teachings and standards of living, based upon the "*Sunna,*" which is composed of accounts called "*Hadith*". These are a collection of traditions contained in the words of Muhammad (c. 570–8 June 632 CE), which give accounts of his daily practice, this being based upon the prophet Muhammad's daily activities which are called the "Sunna" and which constitutes a significant source of guidance for Muslims, as well as physically supporting the words of the Quran. But their target, as with all religious creeds, is to bring the worshipper and doer into the experiencing of the "Present Time" – God's world that is a "Present" for all people.

Yet sadly, it is also known that many Muslims are now at war within themselves. Just as Christian fought Christian now Muslim fights Muslim and for the same reason as those ancient Christian wars which occurred between the Roman Catholic Church's teachings and its differing Protestants. For indeed, these Islamic conflicts are also the same as the Christian conflicts which are caused by a similar claim has to who should be the leader of this differing path of religious understanding.

For it is also known the fact that this "Islamic" religions Shia and Sunni disagreement is the same as the "Christian" disagreement between Catholics and Protestants, which was also a disagreement that killed millions and so this similar disagreement has also arisen between the "Sunni" - whose name is derived from the phrase "Ahl al-Sunnah" - and who believe that their leader should not be elected but be from the "bloodline" of Muhammad. In contrast, the "people of the worshipping tradition," named the "Shia," whose name is derived from "Shiat Ali" or the "Party of Ali" believe that God's power is in the material world, including the public and political realm and that their leaders, called Imams, should be chosen democratically. This same conflict arises because their teacher, leader and Prophet Muhammad died has done Jesus without appointing a successor. So again, strangely, Muslims who are ALL followers of "Mohammed" just as Christians were all followers of "Jesus", have also similarly and conflictingly created their own "sectional" leaders and a way of worshipping in differing belief systems which is causing a similar schism as that which occurred within the Christian faith in 1517.

So yes! Again we are seeing an arguing and separating religious belief system in which both use differing worshipping ways to pursue their chosen but different "I Want my way of religious teaching, not yours" – which can also be understood to be about property and wealth plus a way of life, rather than a way to God's world in which all life is unified and which there can be no "unwise" selfish killing or mistreating of another.

So why does the same "religious" based family fight and kill each other; for most Muslims are innocent worshippers who are seeking their way to God as did the Christians of long ago? How can it be that the children of the same father can become enemies by saying, "Our appointed leader will take us to God, and your appointed leader cannot? For strangely, it can be seen by all, that the Islamic conflict is a similar conflict as that in which Christian killed Christian until wise Christians decided that each person has the right to choose their path that they believe will take them to God's world.

So yes! This antagonistic divide between the Sunnis and Shia is still leading them to mistreat, punish or kill their own Mohammed worshipping people, this being for around one thousand three hundred and eighty years, which must be the longest and the oldest disagreement in the history of Islam or any world religion, for did it not begin after Mohammed's death. For yet again, but sadly now, it is becoming more and more aggressive as all the middle eastern economies begin to develop into a new material based "I Want" world, which could be the main instigator of the new leaders pursuing their personal "I Want" my way of religious worship to be worshipped not your religious way.

So yes! Is it not also strange that this inter-religious conflict is the same "I Want" claim by religious leaders, which again should be stated to be the same as that which happened between the Catholics and the Protestant who also fought a similar brutal war, a war which lasted a hundred and thirty-one years and finally ended in 1648 after a devastating thirty-year war which killed millions of innocent civilians, as well as "I Want" seeking combatants. This war being until the disagreeing sides agreed by saying, "You go your way to God, and we will go our way," which finally brought peace to the European people.

So yes! Again it should be stated that this friction and unholy divide between Sunnis and Shia is like the ancient Christian divide, which was also based upon the leadership of the splintered sect. But this schism is one of the oldest in the history of Islam; for members of the two sects have co-existed for centuries but although they share many fundamental beliefs and practices, they differ in doctrine, ritual, law, theology and religious organisation just as did the sectarian Christians.

So, sadly, it can now be seen that sectarian Muslim leaders can still often be seen to compete as they struggle to obtain an "I Want" from the opposing side. We see from Lebanon and Syria to Iraq through to Pakistan, many recent conflicts which have emphasised this sectarian divide, which is now again tearing Arab communities apart. Yet is it not right that Mohammed said, *"There is not anything which God so abhors as His male and female servants committing adultery?"* Therefore no religious or differing way of following Mohammed words can be seen as not been correct for undeniably are we not all lovers of the one God and is it not a Godly truth that the only way to be filled with God's love is through the "loving" actions that are performed by ourselves?

Also, is it not also true that taking that which belongs to others, is the true meaning of the word "adultery" especially in the worshipping of the one God? Therefore is it not an unchanging truth that a person seeking God's world would realise that it is impossible to find God's world through violence and the stealing of that which belongs to others – for this is the real "Godly" meaning of the word "adultery" against the one God.

Therefore is it not also true that those who commit "adultery" and so kill others or commit violence or steal from others say that they have given themselves to God are shirking? For indeed those who commit such sins and who also state that they are the followers of Mohammed's path to God, must be abandoning Mohammed's teachings which reveal God's Heaven that rests upon this Earth? For certainly is it not true that Heaven cannot exist in a self-created past or future dreamed world which is the false world of Hell, this being a world that cannot exist in God's "Present Time"? For just like the ancient Christians it not right that many followers of Mohammed now pursue a schism of hate and distrust, which is precisely similar to the "Dark Age" division that plagued the Christian religion for a hundred and thirty-one years, before they all decided that the way to God and the way to live, according to God's rule was based upon an individual decision and not one that is instilled by leaders who say, "I Want my leadership to be more powerful than their leadership."

You cannot seek the trust of God, for you have already been given it 100%. Therefore it is a severe weakness to believe that God is unjust or at fault and that which you call the "devil" that tempts you - is your undisciplined five senses.

For assuredly, we are not separate from our bodies, and we are not separate from that which is around our bodies for we are created to be a part of Nature's singularity – for indeed, Darwin was incorrect in his assumptions.

For again is it, not an inevitable truth that we can identify these killings and destroying factions by the countries with Sunnis and Shia populations that exist within the countries of Iran, Iraq, Bahrain, Kuwait, Yemen, Lebanon, Qatar, Syria, United Arab Emirates, Afghanistan and Saudi Arabia. However, Saudi Arabia has more Sunnis who are very poorly and so ungodly treated by the majority of rulers, who are Shia. For again is it not true that this unending Islamic war is between the above Sunni populated countries of Saudi Arabia, Egypt, Turkey and Syria and truly, Sunnis are a more dominant form of Islam for they are at least eighty per cent of Muslims worldwide but why do they punish their sisters and brothers? Is this not really "shirking" the pure love of God?

Is it not also true that currently the conflicting "I Want" in the Muslim religion has also killed millions of innocents that can be likened to the Christian rift which also killed and tortured many innocents? For is this Islamic conflict not also like the Christian schism of the sixteenth and seventeenth century. For has not this Sunni and Shia conflicting split been continuing for nearly one thousand four hundred years?

So yes! Is this not a shirking war about a personal "I Want" my religious teaching not your religious teaching and all regarding who should succeed the prophet, Mohammed? For is this not truly a personal ungodly and also a truly shirking "I Want" which is concerning some interpreting narratives and explanations about Mohammed's teachings. All forgetting that within the only Child of God, this being the Creation, there is only one child and that there are many peaceful roads to realise each individual's child's way to God.

Is it not also true, has the Christians eventually agreed, that each individual should have the freedom to select their way to find God and so live in Gods world which exists only in the "Present Time" and not the world created by another person's "I Want". Is this "Christian" agreed truth not also based upon the fact that God can only judge a shirking "individual"? For again is it not also true that every individual is personally responsible for their actions has will eventually be understood by all the individual people of the Muslim faith has was eventually agreed in the Christian faith, and if you wish to be positive in finding God's world within your personal life – Read on!

For it should be understood that different religions and creeds can be likened to the many different ways of travelling to a place of understanding in which you can be taught a way to reach "Enlightenment" which is truly God's world. For indeed some travel on boats, or cars, buses, bicycles, horseback, camels or they just walk, but the actual experiencing unity with God's world or the world of Nature for the unbeliever reveals the same experience. No matter what religious or creed "transport" the seeker takes, all people will eventually and only "personally" find that God or Nature for the Non-Believer does equally love all people and if unselfishly allowed God will always arrange a good life for all these different travellers.

For again is it not true that all people can achieve the same "Enlightening" experience and is it not also true that God gave the "Freedom of Choice" to all people to support His many various laws and so live peacefully within His kingdom. For indeed, there are many different forms of worship that our wise ancients created for the worlds differently understanding cultures and languages and also for those who are at different stages of spiritual development. But a significant question that can be asked is "Why can there be such hatred between some religious sects when there is but one God, one leader, and one Love? This truth can only be that such conflicting people must experience their religion has to be their property which is likened to saying "I Want" this is to be my house, my land, my fruit. So they forget that God or Nature for the unbeliever consistently provides all these things just have provided with the sun above and the air we breathe?

So yes! We do have the freedom of choice to speak into another person's ear and say that the sun that shines on me is better than the sun that shines on you and the air that I breathe is better than the air that you breathe, then indeed such a person cannot be a believer in God. For again, it must be true that when the mind of a person is "Enlightened", this being by the real knowledge of the Creation. All sectarian quarrels disappear – for they become a true believer in God's world or the laws of Nature for the Non-Believer.

So yes again! Let it be explained, for more natural future understanding, that it is She, the "Mother of the Creation" who can be recognised as the space that is all around us and within us and who does love Her only child. Yet millions of people ignorantly believe that they are separate from all other people and who in this "suffering" has many an individualistic and personal "I Want" brought about by a personal desire to gratify their uncontrolled "five senses", which always creates a sure path to a disagreement, also to war and to all conflict, for indeed our history shows that only a person's "I Want" can do this.

Is it not also a strange but distressing fact that many people painfully ignore a reality which shows that all Life and Non-Life is an important ever moving still "singularity"? Is it not also understood that this "singularity" can be "experienced" to be an ever-moving ever still energised entity? Therefore is it not also true that such Creation must be emanating from universal energy which can also be "experienced"? Is this not also the greatest "together" truth for all people to fully understand and so naturally comprehend just what the existence of life is all about? Therefore is it not true that this is why people have a "personal" ability to choose a particular course of action – this being a God or Nature given gift which is "Self-Realised" and known by all to be based upon each "individuals" very personal "Freedom of Choice".

So Yes! Is it not true that we all understand this to be a God-given gift or a gift from Nature for the Non-Believer? A gift in which people can acknowledge a variable choice of activities and concepts to do or not to do - which only people possess., this is truly being a pure gift that allows people to realise that this given logical choice is born to accommodate the ever-changing positive and negative needs of the emerging world that exists around them.

The simple reason for this fact is that it is this "Freedom of Choice" which allows people to be able to choose the many contradictory ways that are needed to pursue the way of God's or Natures Harmony for the Non-Believer. This fact is undoubtedly being a very purposeful task which has been gifted so that people can support the work of the "Mother of the Creation", the constant seeker and bringer of God's harmony to the world, that exists all around and within people.

Yet! Is it not also sadly true that many people have chosen to forget this truth, this being a truth which states that their position in life is to maintain God's or Nature's rule of a continuing law of harmony within the entire environment that is around them.

For certainly is it not also true that all religions and philosophies state that all these un-claiming and un-thinking harmony supporting tasks do enable a person to become "Self-Aware" of contentment and blissful happiness which is a condition that is called by our wise ancients "Enlightenment" or called by our many religions and philosophies has been filled by the Holy Spirit or the Holy Ghost or the Prophet Gabriel or Destiny, Paradise, Fate, Luck, Karma, Kismet, Nirvana, Moksha, Kenshō, Chance, Providence, Serendipity and undeniably, many more sacred names, so the question is "Can all these statements from our worldly-wise be wrong"? Thus indeed, "Enlightenment" is a reality that any person can obtain. Still, many tend to suffer painfully by forgetting that they are the carrier of their Soul, who is the observer and fulfiller of the current silent needs that support the Creation's on-going harmony. Thus the mistaken gap in their understanding is that the harmony that they seek is that which is being sought by the greed of the physical "I Want" needs of the five senses; whose mind filling "I Want" stops the Soul from seeing through the mind the harmony seeking "Spiritual" needs of the on-going Creation.

So yes! This private greed is an adverse action that stops the Soul from endeavouring to support the "Mother of the Creation", just as all children should support their mother. Even the Non-Believers who do not believe that it was the one God who produced the only seed that gave life, can certainly believe in the living truth of the need for growth and expansion in God's or Natures harmony and also for the developing and supporting of the "Nature" that is all around them. For indeed can it not be said to be true that all the energy that abounds around us creates, absorbs grows and changes all Life and No-Life. Can this not be likened to the on-going needs of the growing life of an only child which "The Book" calls the Creation, or Nature, for the Non-Believer?

So yes! One of the most potent realities of people is that many instinctually feel the need to follow the harmony seeking disciplines of the "Mother of the Creation" but often because of embarrassment, hold back from performing a needed and seen task that will bring harmony to that which exists around them. For definitely all people can understand that the "Mother of the Creation" who is being Godly supported, already provides a true harmony for all people, and so does not give an extraordinary harmony for any individual, for all people have already been provided with everything needed for if you wish to swim in the harmony that exists or is endeavouring to exist all around you, you must go into the water and so support the *"Mother of the Creation"* s harmony - - - that is everywhere. Yet it is known by our ancient wise that it is in this forgetting – which is our worst enemy – that people will often endeavour to seek a personal harmony, which they target only for themselves.

So Yes! What it is suitable for all believers and non-believers is to "modernly" understand the true wisdom described in the words of our ancient wise, this being their input of sacred knowledge that anciently rests within our entire world. For actually a significant problem can arise - within the followers of these sacred teaching- when an individual's interpretation of our ancient Wise's description of the pure singularity of the Heaven that rest upon our Earth – becomes gang orientated to achieve a personal "I Want" my way to Gods world in which I have control of everything and not your way for your not wanting my way is false. God only loves only the way that I worship Him! This fact can again be said to that which truly brings to birth a personal "I Want" concept which seems to run parallel to the divine laws that are all around people and it always seems to rest within a person's devilish ability to bring forth "institutional denial forcibly".

It is then that this charismatic and therefore strongly supported greed-based "I Want" can also be emanating from some individual leaders personal "I Want", which always endeavour to establish their imposed "the rule of law," which supports only them, this being some devilish – future based - scheme to get what they want.

Even the Christian Bibles teachings have been given many new additions that seem to be slanted to support only the leaders of the church and the leaders of the community. Still, none are more significant than the simple pursuits of the "Mother of the Creation" whose support seeking actions are revealed to all people for all selfish endeavours will always fail, and does not the world's history always show this failure?

Is it not also true that history has "scientifically" shown that institutional denial can be perpetrated even by an individual who fails to prevent or respond supportively to wrongdoing by other individuals, a fact which can be likened – even in democracies, to a fascinating kind of "fascism," as was pursued by the defeated Nazi party and many others of their ilk; was this not also in our recent history?

This on-going system of "private" control which continually endeavours to attain personal greed seems always to attack that private control which is supporting the *"Mother of the Creations"* silent efforts which is a fact that is well documented in our history and is the current biggest on-going threat to personal well-being as many a countries "leader" selfishly reflects the work of the "Mother of the Creation" and in doing so, seeks a "harmony" not for all people. Still, themselves and their ilk, this genuinely being "institutional denial," because they deny the rights of all those who they believe are "outsiders" of their private group.

So yes! Institutional denial, the denial of a truth that is resting everywhere, is a way of rejecting the work of the "Mother of the Creation", for definitely, unlike the "Mother of the Creation" these "I Want" for myself, leaders do not seek harmony for the people outside their group, or the world in general, but attempt to take ALL the on-going harmony for themselves.

For again can it not be said that it is not also "scientifically" true that unlike the "Mother of the Creation", that these "masters" will threaten and punish all those who do not obey their wishes, creeds or control systems in which people are attached to them under the rule of their law? Is it not also true that they even use religions and other belief systems in their attempt to steal the *"Mother of the Creation"* harmony that is provided for the benefit of all people? Yet again "scientifically", does not history show that they are always unsuccessful? Does history not also consistently show that these attempts to benefit only themselves and so change the will of the "Mother of the Creation" – always fails?

Is it not also written that Jesus silently followed this harmful opposing group-based "harmony" which was around Him and which also included painful torture and then a horrible death? Could this not be the only reason why Jesus went uncomplaining to his violent death and did not take part, but silently obeyed the "institutional denial" of that which was around Him, knowing full well that true harmony would eventually reveal itself; for were not His last painful words on that cross, ***"Forgive them, for they know not what they do!"*** Yes, this is being a fact for it is also undoubtedly true that we have an excellent example in Jesus. His painful end was a great example to the European world of the Northern Hemisphere.

But there is one essential point to remember, this being that there is nothing in God's Creation that can punish your Soul and the most significant punishment that you can experience, as you live your current life, is to live a life in which you are ignored by the "Mother of the Creation"," who truly, cannot support your "I Want" for myself activities, which of course leads to a feeling of loneliness within you. For did not the great mathematician, Einstein explained, ***"God does not play dice with the universe."*** Simply put, the "Mother of the Creation" does not play a harmony seeking game of chance with people for She knowingly targets all events and all actions towards the growth and maintenance of harmony.

To this ever-evolving target, it could be added, that those who live outside Her harmony and so choose to live in their own-made world of "I Want", this being the real world of (Hell), then they are likened to those people who hurt others to achieve their aims.

So yes! the "Mother of the Creation" is the active, caring parent of the only child, which we call the Creation. She will only ignore you and so turn her face away from you, if you mindlessly and by your own choice move away from Her work and in my "scientific" findings this is NOT a good life, and so now for your belief system – look around you? Are you a throwing dice player seeking an unknown but troublesome future? For is it not true that what you need do is to join with or help create the on-going ever moving ever still harmony of the "Present Time", which is always all within you and always emerging around you and evermore shall be so?

So yes! Can it not be agreed that this totality of a world that is ever-evolving towards God's targeted future and which is supported in the "Present Time" by the *"Mother of the Creation"* is a long time evolving, but is it not also truly believed by all that this Creation is going to achieve its target. For again is it not also true that in our current "modern" age we can now witness that massive continent and many different "language-based" countries are coming together under one law, as in the North of the Northern Hemisphere and which anciently developed in China. Therefore is it not seen to be true that a supportive "live and let live life" is a harmony developing an ever-evolving system that will continue to grow as different cultures are joined together and as countries continue to seek a good "harmony seeking relationship", which is being controlled by the TRUE majority of people – but really by the *"Mother of the Creation"*, but why do some people deny and try to stop this ever-evolving system of unification? For certainly is it not true that these on-going mergers are needed for removing the "animalistic" tendencies of many of our high-ranking politicians and tribal seeking war leaders.

So Yes! These attacking people are gang led by an individual who is an early re-birth from the animal kingdom and so has risen to leadership because of their past "animalistic" and therefore very strong "I Want" tendencies. This fact is merely being because they are very purposeful and cunning on how to fully achieve this "I Want", for indeed they are not obedient to a world in which people have been given the "Freedom of Choice so that they can support the merging goodness of the Creation that is emerging all around them. It may also be a fact that countless people with only a few lives behind them will feel protected under their pack rule.

So Yes! A real "spiritual" well-being would be to stop your complaining about the lack of harmony around you. For if you factually believe that you and all those around you are being punished then do not support what these groups of people are enforcing – and so gently but wisely advise against it. Let your words be a logic that seeks harmony for all of the people within and outside your area and so endeavour to point out what you believe to be the true and a correct "harmonious" way ahead, but always returns to silence if many attack you for the *"Mother of the Creation"* s lack of support will always collapse their unwanted endeavours for really does not our history prove this.

So yes! It is also good to remember that your Soul will sound the truth to all people and thus the harmony that exists within you will move to join the harmony that you are creating around you if your words are from the Soul. For again is it not said to be accurate, has the Christian religion states "in the beginning was the word" which must always be the word of truth, this being a truth which is always emanating and so is supported by the "Mother of the Creation", and it is also good to remember that the evildoer who creates pain in others will suffer in this world and certainly in their next birth – which may not be has a person.

16   THE WAY TO HEAVEN THAT EXISTS ON EARTH

Now it is also a well-known scientific fact that "Nothing" or "No-Thing" which is the name that our Non-Believers call that which "The Book" calls God, this being that which created all that was needed when He planted His seed into Space, which "The Book" calls the "Mother of the Creation" which is that life force which gave birth to all the unified energy that is around us and within us. I speak here also of the energy that continually creates and sustains life within the "singularity" of the Creation, which includes the highest created life of all, this being a person's Soul, which is also an energy that cannot be destroyed.

So yes! The singularity of life that we call the Soul rests within this more exceptional unified singularity of life that we call "the Creation" and it cannot be wasted as it moves forward continually reincarnating into the body after body. For undeniably truly the Soul is the energy that avoids the natural decay of life for it is an "individual" yet also a "globalized" eternal energy which genetically enjoins with the singularity of the male or female and so rests only within the people who are continually reborn with the same Soul whose only purpose is to seek unity with the "Creation".

For indeed, it is with the same Soul that people are birthed again and again to support the purpose of a life that supports the "Mother of the Creation" on-going pursuits. Therefore should not this individual "re-birthing" of the Soul be known by all to be continually re-entering the totality of the Creation, this being a Creation that is easily understood by people to be the only child of God or the only child of "Nothing" for the Non-Believer. For what is known to be true is that is this only child was born at the time that our scientists call the "Big Bang"? The "Big Bang" is that which when the "Mother of the Creation" gave birth to their only child, who we call "The Creation," without a doubt This being a child who was born because the father "God" placed a seed within the "Mother of the Creation" which "The Book" calls "Space" which is that which is caringly for all around us and within us plus continually caring for us.

So, is it not also a factual scientific truth that Creation is the only child that people can witness? Is it not also a developed truth that all life and none-life is a part of this unified energy that makes up the totality of this Creation which can only exist because of Space? For undeniably, the Creation can only be a single child and so makes us all be a part of everything that lives, and that which we also recognise as not living? Therefore, is it not also a "scientific" truth that the energy all around us is also within us, and as a single "unified energy"? Therefore, factually, this is being that which is "Scientifically" known to be the singularity of energy, which again points to that which exists within this only child, which we call "The Creation".

Yet strangely, in our heads, we are dominated by a genuine feeling that we exist as separate entities. So, is it not also "scientifically" accurate that this incorrect viewpoint makes us feel that we are all "individuals", this means that we ignorantly live by believing in an individual existence, which makes us create almost every thought in our heads to be an individualistic "I Want", this being a dominating thought that is always saying, "I Want" something for myself. Even when we camouflage this into believing that our thoughts are to benefit others, it is usually for ourselves only. These are the thoughts that take us from the "Present" which is God's world into the false world of Hell which exists in the Past or the Future, this being where our personal "I Want" always takes us.

So yes! Is this not because of our "I Want" thoughts take us from the "Present Time" into a non-existing past or future, where the "I Want" dream creates its false world, which "The Book" calls Hell? Is this "I Want" for myself pursuit also a fact that creates us into a feeling that we are individuals, when in reality; we are just a joined part of the energy which is all around us and within us? Did not Jesus, within whom the "Mother of the Creation" spoke, say to the lawyer in the parable requesting what is the truth resting within the Creation: "What is written in the law?" And "How do you read it? The "Mother of the Creation" asked, through Jesus to the lawyer. The lawyer answered: "Love your neighbour as yourself." "You have answered correctly", the "Mother of the Creation" answered through Jesus and then added. "Do this and you will live" meaning of course, that the lawyer would live in Heaven, while on this Earth and so experience the right harmony of life that exists only in the "Present Time". But even more, put by Jesus was the direction given to the lawyer, when Jesus stated that the man who lived in Heaven was that man who showed mercy to the man who had been attacked by those who live in Hell. Jesus told the lawyer, "Go and do likewise," meaning that he should go and live by knowing that he lived in the one body – just as all our body parts live within us and which show the perfect example of the truth of life's unity in harmony, this being the truth spoken about by all our wise ancients and philosophers who consistently state this same belief.

So Yes! The energy within you is high-quality energy, and so you should be well pleased that you can experience the inner life that serves you so much and harmoniously. It is also good to remember that living in Heaven while on the Earth is like living as a rainbow, which acknowledges that it needs the light of the sun to make it healthy and beautiful, but who is the sun which shines upon the needed way of people? It is, of course, the "Mother of the Creation" who is the inner light and all exterior light that can only shine upon all people in the "Present Time".

So Yes! Is it not useful to experience the power and the glory of a Heaven that you live in and before your current body dies? For it is certainly a truth that you can experience life in Heaven; therefore, it is good to forget this belief that Heaven can only be reached when you die. The truth is, and it is good to remember this: that Heaven is in the "Present Time", this is the time we call the "NOW" of your current life. For was it not said by the "Enlightened" Jesus: "Thy kingdom come on Earth as it is in Heaven," for He was telling all, that Heaven was all around them, suggesting that if you follow His constant advice, then YOU will experience the Heaven that "always" rests upon this Earth.

But how do you reach and so live in this Heaven that is on Earth, which simply means that that you can currently leave Hell and live in Heaven while you are alive and on this Earth? Does this not also mean that people can gain by experience and knowledge the way to live in Heaven while living on this Earth? Of course, this is an absolute truth for it can be "scientifically" shown that Heaven is not where your mind is, but where your life is, and that this is the place in which you live. This being in the "Present Time" which can never be in the past or the future, where your babbling "I Want" for myself thoughts, which you have historically "permitted" to be energised by your five senses and which all our wise ancients explain as to be truly living in Hell.

So yes! Now it is "scientifically" useful for all to understand that Heaven only exists upon our Earth in the "Present Time". That which is being the "three in one" that rests within the individual body and which brings a need to explain that which most religions and philosophies speak about and which can now be recognised in our modern and "scientifically" understood modern language.

So yes! In this modern introductory work of "The Book" we have previously and practically acknowledged the Creation's first "three in one". This number one being the "Father of the Creation" who is then unable to be experienced male God who "scientifically" child seeded number two who is then unable to be experienced "space" which "The Book" calls the "Mother of the Creation" because "She" truly exists in "everything." It is also explained that "She" is also the Mother who ensures us, by Her Motherly teachings, of the correct way of life and so ensures that God's laws of harmony always exist around their only child, who in truth is number three "The Creation" or the universe for the Non-Believer Now it is also essential to understand the "three in one" that exists within our body, this being that which copies the "three in one" of the Creation and also to state this as a fact, which none can prove to be incorrect?

This truth can be explained as being a "three in one" fact again and is simply explained by saying that within all people number one is the undying, everlasting "Soul," which rests in each person's body and looks out at the "Creation," this being through their mind. Number two is the outer "Creation" itself a reality in which each person's Soul observes as being in the "Present Time", and number three is the "Five Senses", which people need to experience and so support the harmonising needs of the "Creation," for indeed, this is people's "three in one".

So yes! Is this not a bodily three in one similarity which is explained in many ways and many hundreds of different stories, by our ancient religions and philosophies, this being an actual and true meaning of a person's life, because it can be realised as a truth. This fact being because anyone who can sit without any thought in the silence of the "Present Time", will silently experience an "observer", this being that which exists within their body and who is looking out from within their body and at the "Creation," this being that which exists all around them, for indeed, this "something" that is observing the "Present Time" is the silent Soul. This realty being factually recognised when the five senses are silenced and are awaiting the silent commands of the harmony seeking instructions that will come from the Soul, but only if it is necessary to do so. For the Soul lives within us, but the mind must be very silent for the Soul to be able to see through the empty mind and so experience the harmonising truth of that which can only exist in the "Present Time".

So Yes! Now it is good to be aware that "I Want" thoughts coming from a personally created Hell that creates the non-existing "Past" or a "future" will always stop the Soul from experiencing the needs or non-needs of God's "Present Time". This deviation created by the mind filling "I Want" of the five senses, is called living in Hell for it stops the Soul from witnessing and silently supporting God's always existing world of harmony, which exists only in the "Present Time". Of course, we have an individual body, but this is not a real part of a person's "three in one", for do not many philosophies say that it is good to remember the saying *"I am not this body it is an instrument for my use"*.

So yes! Simply put, and in a modern, understandable language, the body can be likened to a private car which is used to transport the real "three in one," and yes, the question now is to ask yourself: "Who is the driver of this car? Is it your "five senses," always claiming an "I Want" or your Soul seeking how it can assist the ever-developing harmony emerging within the Creation? Put and now indeed explained is that if it is your five senses driving the car, then you are living in Hell, which genuinely can be likened to driving through a city and ignoring the "highway code" of the road, which can only bring discord to your way of life.

So Yes, this can be likened to living in Hell, especially when at traffic lights; you ignore the controlling red light and so regularly encounter collisions with other cars. The question here is: "Who is punishing who?" For in truth should it not be the "Soul," which can be likened to being a faithful servant of the Creation, is driving the car which we have likened to be your body and which can only be driven according to the rules that can only exist in Gods "Present Time"?

This truth being when the Soul does "always" actively and silently obeys and supports the "highway code" of life, which the "Mother of the Creation" produces for Her only child, which is the individual totality of the Creation. These are genuinely the rules of harmony being supported continuously by the "Mother of the Creation", and this is the "gift" supporting the "Freedom of Choice" spoken about in most philosophies and preached in most religions – and this gift of choice belongs to you!

So yes! The choice is "Do you want to live in Heaven while upon this Earth or to live in Hell? Therefore do you obey the laws of the Highway Code that progress you through life, which is God's laws that always rest in Heaven that exist in the "Present Time" upon this Earth or your own "I Want" for me laws that keep you living in Hell?

So yes! If you wish to live in Heaven and not in Hell, in your current life, you must stop the five senses "driving" you through the mishaps of your current life, and so allow the Soul to become the "un-observed" driver, which can only be established by having an empty mind. For indeed all these religious and philosophical automatic incantations can create an empty and still mind which is necessary for the Soul to see through the mind and so become "Self-Aware" and then onto "Self-Realise" the truth of Gods world, this being that which exists all around you. For indeed this is also the reason why ALL religions and philosophies have creeds, chants, prayers, singing, etc. these being an activity which "automatically" stops the "I Want" of the five senses from blocking the mind so that the Soul can see, through the empty mind and so enter the "Present Time."

So Yes! Your Soul as the real "driver" of your body yet it can only exist in the "Present Time" in which no thinking about the "Past", where your "I Want" failed or the "Future" where you are mind blocking with another "I Want" which keeps you in the world of Hell and so stops you entering the "Present Time", where you will find the Heaven that rests upon our Earth, this Heaven can undoubtedly be achieved in your current life.

So yes! Living a life of harmony and without thought can be likened to the driving of a car after a few years of experience, this being when the car seems to be driving its self. For truly does not the hands automatically steer the car, or change gear and the feet automatically and without conscious thought adjust the accelerator or the breaks or the clutch and is this not all in accordance to the harmony that exists in the "Present Time" the time in which you are moving towards your destination? So just as in the journey through life your body will obey the harmony needs of the Creation around you and which exists like in the driving of your car – but only when the mind is "unthinkingly" existing the Present Time.

So yes! agreed it might be difficult and time-consuming to arrive at the "Heaven" that always exists upon our Earth. Still, a helpful start would be for the countries' leaders who are seeking to dominate other countries and who are forgetting internal unity, which leads to separating and quarrelling entities, must stop the thinking of a personal "I Want" and change this thought to a collective "What ALL people need," for in God's world or the world of Nature for the Non-Believer, it should now be known that a personal "I Want" cannot exist for you are not an individual but a severe part of "Everything" and if you want to know how to leave Hell, and so achieve living in Heaven. At the same time, on this Earth and in your current body – Read on.

17 THE UNITY OF THE CREATION

So yes! We can indeed realise a collective unity with the world around us and so see and feel that we are all harmonious parts of the Creation, just as are our body parts "exist" as a supporting part of their internal us. Is it not also true that all our body parts commonly work in true harmony, supporting and unselfishly fulfilling the needs of the trillions of other body parts? For is this not known to be true that it is deemed impossible for many body parts to gather together and pluck out an eye because they did not like its colour. Or attack any other healthy bodily part?

So yes! Just as all the major religions and philosophical teachings state, that if you want a life that is filled with a harmony that creates contentment for you and all that is around you, then endeavour to live within this harmony as a body part lives within your own body. The fact is that if you want a Godly life, in which all that is good (GOD) keeps coming to you, then you should help support the work of the Divine "Mother of the Creation", your perfect teacher, and so aid the developing harmony that exists or is seeking to exist all around you.

So Yes! Now you know the purpose of seeking the truth of that which all our many religions and philosophies speak about, and you now know what they are saying and what they are describing in words which are bound within their culturally ancient descriptions. Note well that these are modern words that are written here which also prove the simple proof of this painful and or actual reality of living in a Hell or of living in a Heaven, this being that which is in direct response to the actions that you and others are personally performing. The reality which is now useful to understand is to use your "Freedom of Choice" to break the harmful activities that are supporting and or aiding others so experience living in Hell or to use your "Freedom of Choice" in trying to support the excellent harmony that is growing and naturally binding all living together as one unit and so experience the living in a Heaven that is continuously endeavouring to emerge all around you. Just try this active exercise, and you WILL experience the truth of all of that which these words now speak. For did not the divine "Mother of the Creation" through her incarnate child Jesus clearly say: *"For I tell you that unless your righteousness surpasses that of the Pharisees and the teachers of the law,* (Those who used institutional denial in which they lied to protect themselves) *you will certainly not enter the Kingdom of Heaven,* meaning that you are now living in Hell. Then Jesus was asked, "Where is the Kingdom of Heaven?" Then and there the answer was *"The Kingdom of God is within you"* and if you wish to find this Kingdom of Heaven that is within you – Read on. For all can now understand this true meaning and also know its correct interpretation for it knowingly explains the reality of life for it merely means that people can rest their minds in the "Present Time" which is the Heaven that rests within them and outside them. For Heaven's silence is without the contaminating "I Want" thoughts that take people from experiencing the "Present Time" that is God's world and instead takes them into the false non-existent world of the past or the future, these being the false made worlds of Hell, for they do not exist, except in the noisy mind that seeks a personal "I Want". This concept of living in Heaven or living in Hell, while existing in your current body, is so essential that Jesus states fifty-nine times in the current Christian Bible about the Heaven that rests, within each person and so it is clearly, (although many still do not realise this) an individual's choice as to whether you, as an individual, wish to live in Heaven or Hell during your current lifetime. Therefore, it is undoubtedly true and suggested by all religions and philosophies that you should learn to live in Heaven. The truth is that no one can stop you from living in a world of Heaven that is all around you, for is it not true that the "No-Thing" or "Nothing" for the Non-Believer, Fathered the world in which that we now live? Is this not a world which eventually brought our bodies together, to work unselfishly and in unity with the need to support the harmony in which all our body parts exist and which exists in ALL life and non-life, this being that which is also all around each individual or trying to develop all-around everyone? Is this not the best and easiest way that all our religions and philosophies state is the way to show how people should live? Again, is this not the real active target of a person's life? Is this not a clear and fruitful explanation of the constant unifying and harmonising activity of the Creation that is all around us and within us, and which is continuously witnessed by all people to be a developing harmony that cannot be broken. However, many have tried to break it? Therefor is it not true that the un-wanting harmonising activity of the Creation always shows itself to be a perfect example of an unselfish ever-loving harmony as Nature feeds Nature, which again clearly exists as the perfect example of the unity that exists within our bodies? As an example, for agnostics and Non-Believers and to aid in the further understanding of this text, it would be good to say for them to imagine that the words of Jesus are speaking directly and personally to you, as the voice of the Creation and especially with the cultural accent of planet Earth. This new understandable viewpoint can be likened to Earth speaking directly to the listener, via the voice of Jesus, which will enlighten Non-Believers into a modern understanding and give a more explicit interpretation of His words. It is also a fact that agnostics and Non-Believers listening to this new understanding will be understandably informed in a spoken but "scientific" way that all the energy upon our Earth is a single "unified" energy which interacts inwardly and actively for its wellbeing. This unification is a fact which our modern scientists also state to be true. Therefore is it not "scientifically" proven that energy cannot ever be destroyed, for it is stated by our scientists that it just takes another form. We are speaking here about the totality of our unified existence. Is it not also a known scientific fact that energy cannot run out and that it never changes but just takes on another form? So, the on-going question is: "Where does a person's energy go-to when it no longer occupies the singularity of their body?" Is it not stated and also a scientific fact that if energy is conserved in its unity, it cannot be destroyed which means that it was one hundred per cent at the beginning of the Universe and will be the same one hundred per cent at the end, although in a different form, for life must evolve. God's end target or Nature's target for the Non-Believer must and will be met?

So Yes! It is an irrefutable scientific fact that everything is conserved that is within the singularity of the Creation of the Universe for the Non-Believer and especially for life on planet Earth. Thus, it is also stated to be a factual and fundamental law of Nature, which is scientifically known as the "first law of dynamics", this being a law which states that this scientific truth of a fundamental law in which our scientists state that energy cannot be created or destroyed or in more fundamental understanding energy that energy floats from shape to shape, seeking the end that all the Creation is progressing towards, or the end which the Universe is seeking, for the Non-Believer – and this is all based upon the simple fact that it cannot die, but will continue following whatever God's plan is or Nature's plan for the Non-Believer Therefore this "scientific" fact must mean that energy, like life, is eternal, just as when a star explodes or "dies" it can be reborn again, as another blazing star with various other parts of its rebirth being created to form cooler planets – just as our own planet Earth was created.Or they may even become Black Holes, these being stars that have succumbed into something that cannot be seen, but which continually affects everything that is around them and whose "singularity" will exist until the end of physical time, as do the words of not only our many religious creators but also people like Shakespeare, Einstein, and many others. So if energy is known to be unified and cannot be created or destroyed, does this fact not also apply to everything within the Creation – meaning that there is no real death but that there is only energy being exchanged for energy for there is no impurity within the Creation where all is 100%, and evermore shall be so? Is this not also an exciting thought for vegetarians and for those who think it is not right that one life form will eat another life form. Therefore is it not true that it is just energy that is absorbing energy, this being to maintain itself as also does all life in the animal kingdom. But it must also clearly state here that vegetarianism is excellent practice and especially a good discipline. For along with many religious practices and inputs it helps support the controlling of the five senses – a convenient way of saying "No," and so vegetarianism actively disciplines the five senses whose silence is needed, to be able to live in Heaven, while living on this Earth. To relate more closely to this scientific aspect and reality that energy cannot be destroyed. Does this truth that our scientist's state also not make this reality a "scientific" truth? Is it not true that the Creations of unified "energy" abound everywhere and is all around and without and within people? So cannot it be stated as a fact, that this energy is a unified unselfish all, serving all-purpose energy, the same being the unified energy as that which is contained within your bodies? Is it also not "scientifically" correct, that all our bodily parts "energetically" interact with each other, purely for the benefit of all other parts within our body, just as the Universe interacts within the Creation's "universal body"? Sadly, is it not also true that this is an activity in which many people have forgotten, and forgetting is our worst enemy? Is it not also sadly true that many people have forgotten that all functional parts within all life and Non-Life should naturally interact for the benefit of all other functional parts, within this one body of energy, in our case certainly the one body called Earth, which we should care for has a substantial part of that which we call "ourselves"?

So Yes! Is it not also easy to believe that by pursuing the fact that all people would recognise and realise their real purpose on this Earth is to naturally support the harmony that copies the singularity of their own body and thus joins with the self of all life, thus living in the Heaven that rests upon our Earth.Is it not also true that if one substantial part breaks this harmony, by not performing its supporting duties to that which surrounds it, it brings pain and illness or even death to the whole body? Therefore, is it not also easily seen to be true that this "illness" also happens when parts of people break the harmony of that which exists in the life around them? Is it not also true that this illness is a personally based "I Want" that steals from children, family, relatives, neighborhoods, community, country, hemispheres and planet Earth – which is the one body that exists within the energy of the Creation called planet Earth. What happens to people when some individuals' "I Want" refuses to support this on-going search for harmony, or refuses to give birth to the continuing harmony that is trying to be born around them? The answer is that they are living in Hell, where their "I Want" is the fire and heat that is painfully eating them and that which is all around them. For truly is this not a truth that could be recognisable happening all around us, for it is undoubtedly not about a fairy tale that the "The Book" speaks? For indeed our scientists often say that there is a single intelligence source which seems to be governing our Universe and our way of development. For indeed this is stated as being reasonable because within each physical process that is occurring within our Universe, a process in which we continuously see the trace of a well-organised system evolving and which we acknowledge that it needs no interference and if this thought brings doubts – then endeavour to work out the needed calculations to create not only people but all the Life and Non-Life that surrounds them – not an easy task but "something" really did achieve it and is that not a truth? For again and honestly said. Do not our scientists not often say that there is a single intelligence source which seems to be governing our Universe and also our way of development, and this being a universal and non-isolated development because within each physical process that is universally occurring, we continuously see the trace of a well-organised system evolving? We also understand that this is a universal system which needs no personal interference and if this thought brings some doubts – then endeavour to work out the needed calculations to create not only people but all the life and Non-Life that surrounds us – not an easy task but "something" did create it and is this not also seen by all to be true?

18   THE UNIFIED BELIEF SYSTEM

It is further interesting to understand that the wisdom put forward by the initiators of all our world's religions and philosophical belief systems, is indeed a pearl of wisdom that is needed by all people because many people have little or no knowledge of that which exists in the unity of the actual world. So they live unknowingly in an always separating "I Want" only for myself world. Yet, is it not true that this can be seen to be an "I Want" for myself world which produces an unhappy life for themselves and for those who live around them plus untold damage to theirs and other environments? For indeed this "I Want" for me is a personal belief system that also ignores our actual reality and therefore creates a mind filling "I Want" limbo, which can be identified, has a self-created Hell by our wise ancients?

So Yes! Is it not suitable to be always reminded that when the mind is silent and not filled by the thoughts of how to achieve an animalistic "I Want", which are always conjectures that stop the Soul from seeing through a clear mind and into the "Present Time". For certainly is it not true that this is the world that "truly" exists all around and also within everyone, for where else can your heartbeat?

So Yes! Is it not also true that if the mind is filled by these noise clamouring collusions of an "I Want" for myself, which are tempting and self-claiming machinations that are emanating from one of the five senses and that this is a mind filling activity that ignorantly blocks the Souls view through the mind and so it does not see the actual needs of God or Natures needs for the Non-Believer, this being the essential needs that can only exist in this "Present Time", this being the "Present" of all life and non-life that surrounds us.

So Yes! Is it not also true that always thinking and believing in a mind filling futuristic creation of an "I Want" for myself world, is undoubtedly the living in the Hell of an unreal "Self-Created" world in which this "I Want for Me" belief called "thinking, also creates the way to commit suicide or a place of self-punishment which is often wrongly explained to be achieved by a fallen Soul?

Yet truly is not your Soul the real you? Is this not the Soul that exists within you and which observes all that which you falsely believe is without you? Is this real "You" not the Soul which cannot be tasted, smelled, touched, seen or heard or be anything that is "thoughtfully" seen in mind? For again truly is your Soul, not the observer of all these things?

Does this not also mean that you cannot be that which you observe or be that which you experience? Thereof cannot it also be agreed that the silent observer emanating from within you is truly your Soul and that upon this "Self-Realisation" our wise ancients say that it will experience your " to be a living part of everything? Therefore does not this truth mean that your Souls' real purpose is to be an active supporter of the natural world in which it lives?

So Yes! You can certainly define this previously ignored but now "personally" known self-created "Hell" is a state of continued positive "self-exclusion" from the real "Unity" that exits within God's Creation or of Nature Creation for the Non-Believer. For indeed it should be known and "Self-Realised" that this "Self" is "always" living in a self-created Hell when the mind is filled with many never-ending "I Want" words and pictures that are emanating from one or several of the arguing five senses which are animalistic by Nature and so they have no understanding of repenting nor in this animalistic freedom have they ever been disciplined or trained to remain silent so that the Soul can silently experience, and so support God's emerging world or the world of Nature for the Non-Believer – but they can be disciplined to do so and if this is desired – Read on!

Of course, there are more severe levels within this living "I Want" for myself Hell, This being a world that ranges from the above wide-awake people to more dangerous levels which are occupied by those who deliberately perform severe and extremely harmful "I Want" for me act, these being sins which are against a multiple of others. What is further understood and which is explained by many of our wise ancients is that these people are most likely to return to that which they were reborn from, thus being reborn again as one of the lower animals and this probably being that from which they must have recently been reborn, this is being a sad failure for them, for indeed they had left the limited potential that usually belongs to animal kind – this indeed is the life form which does not have the "Freedom of Choice" to do or not to do, to be or not to be, this being the multiple supporting or not supporting choices that people have.

Then, as it must be with most people who retain only animalistic behaviour patterns, this being that they must go back to living only with the demanding animalistic "I Want" of their five senses, which they must obey and without choice - this being back to the animal life seeking force that is still resting within them. For accurately it must be for this reason that the "Mother of the Creation" automatically and with good purifying intent, naturally re-births them outside of the class of people and so they will no longer be able to wilfully "choose" to destroy the harmony that is the on-going purpose and needed path of the ever-evolving Creation.

So Yes! The Divine Mother cannot punish these new re-births has people from the animal kingdom, for truly has people they have been given the "Freedom of Choice" and so they have genuinely but unknowingly punished themselves. Therefore is it not also clearly seen to be accurate, that the "individuality" of all people's abilities is that they have a free potential to decide and obey various choices? Hence being the necessary fact that enables people to support the "Mother of the Creation" work that She continues to pursue correctly, this being the unfolding harmony of the Creation that rests within this only child.

So yes! Is it not also "intelligently" and "personally" seen that the experience of "bliss" is an experience for people that only exist in the "Present Time?" Therefore is this not indeed a useful gift, this being a gift which is required to actively and harmoniously support the rewarding ways of the ever-growing ever still "Present Time?"

Therefore, is it not a truth that a mother's child will happily achieve all kinds of harmonious tasks that their "Mother" places in front of them? Is it not also clear that all life forms do not have this supporting gift and is it not also true that only people have the potential to choose from the many variable acts that can only exist in the "Present Time?" Thus being the time that and place that no thought can penetrate, for thoughts can only arise in the on-going act of verbalising or picturing a false past or a false future mainly when it is engaged with an "I Want".

So Yes! Is it not also true that we should act like the perfect example shown by the natural activities of our bodily parts, in that we should never steal that which belongs to others or do the tasks which are undeniably the duty of others. Or change any situation or a condition which belongs only to them? Is it not also essential not to interfere or take over an activity, which is a duty that should be cared for by others, unless invited to do so? For did not the "Mother of the Creation" speaking through the great incarnate Krishna, say to his disciple Arjuna, *"Do your duty Arjuna, for to do the duty of another is fraught with danger."*

So Yes! Completing another's a harmonising duty which they should be performing and even doing so without their knowledge, is also classed as stealing for it is a personal "I Want" and so is stealing a need that belongs to them. Therefore it is very accurate to say that we should always remember to do our duty when we flow within our own "Souls" currently existing life.

So Yes! Is it not also clearly seen to be true that people should really accept the harmony that is around them or support that which is trying to emerge around them and so live in the real world that exists for all life and non-life and so only perform duties that support the "Mother of the Creation" harmony seeking tasks that always exist in the "Present Time". Therefore is it not also true that all our wise ancients' say, and in many languages, that all should know well the harmony seeking experiences which are that which can only be attained by silencing the "I Want" of five senses?

For undeniably, when uncontrolled the five sense always act like untrained wild dogs because they seek only their pleasures, but honestly all people will find that when the five senses are silenced, they will attain that which the wise ancients called "Enlightenment" and which the Christian Bible calls "being filled by the Holy Spirit."

For definitely indeed, any sound in mind is brought into Creation by the five senses who clamour for a past or a future "I Want", for indeed, they are thoughts made manifest by the uncontrolled five senses that argue together like five untrained puppies. For again it should be stated that the animal-based five senses spoken about are sight, taste, touch, smell, and hearing, and they are all continually clamouring for their selfish desires, which is clarified clearly into a personally targeting "I Want". For again is it not also true to say that it is in this way that they are clamouring "I Want" words take them and their "thinking" away from God's heavenly "Present Time" and also away from any "un-selfish" harmony supporting work needed by the "Mother of the Creation" continuing activities to take care of Her child – The Creation.

So yes! Any of the five senses are also individually capable of "painting" their "I Want" images into the mind so that the "thinker" sees a false world that is based upon a world of greed that has been selfishly created by the self-seeking animalistic uncontrolled "I Want" of the oft quarrelling five senses, which are the only entities that can create an "I Want" or even a "Don't Want". Truly being the world of Hell in which people can and do "ignorantly" but now do unknowingly "choose" to live.

Simply put, and by the modern understanding of the words and meanings of our many religions and philosophies, people have now the ability to choose whether to live in Hell and so obey the "I Want" of the five senses or whether to live in "Heaven" which is achieved by supporting the *Mother of the Creation* harmony seeking activities that exist only in the "Present Time". But now is it not known to be true that if they choose to support the latter, then they can live in Heaven – while in their current life upon this Earth.

So Yes! Heaven truly exists in the "Present Time", and it is also an existence that continually rests within a unified ever-developing Creation, this being birthed agreeably and which is ever-growing. So it should not be the world that is destroyed, painted and claimed by the clamouring "I Want" of the animalistic five senses, this being efforts of a life force that has no Soul. Yet truly this "I

Want" from the world is an existence which is achieved when a person's mind is NOT in the "Present Time" but is actively living and surviving in an animalistic "I Want" past or an "I Want" make-believe future which "The Book" calls the false "Hell" that is created by people.

So Yes! The real world exists only in the "Mother of the Creation" controlled "Present time! Undeniably this being the current time that can only be acknowledged and harmoniously lived in by Her supporting children who are called people. For definitely the real world can only exist in the "Present Time" and it is a world that was seeded by God to be birthed in "Space" which "The Book" calls the "Mother of the Creation".

For indeed this was the heavenly beginning for all life and Non-Life, and it was also a life force that eventually created people to whom was given the "Freedom of Choice", this being freedom which enabled people to physically support the "Mother of the Creation" ever developing child. Yet truly this is a state of being that can only be achieved by a person, when they have silenced the "I Want" "conversations" taking place in the mind, and so stopped all thoughts from going into the selfish "I Want" mind filling world created by the five senses; and so by a personal choice, stop their clamouring and mind filling "I Want".

So yes! Again and simply put – if you listen to words in the mind or habitually pursue an "I want", it is NOT the real you, it's one of the five senses, and its "needs" are not the way of truth that is resting within you.

At this point, it is also good to remember what the wise ancients say about the condition of a person whose mind always rests in the "Present Time". Although they have many different words to explain this "reality" their simple words are that when a person's mind rests in the "Present Time" the sky is blue, and the grass is green. It is a pure expression which simply means that you can see one hundred per cent of reality, this being when it is not mindfully "painted" with a past or a future "I Want," and this targeted existence is always the aim of all the major religions and philosophies.

So yes! Many religions have activities that are put forward and stated to be "creeds" and "disciplines" which were all originally designed by our wise ancients to remove the five senses mind blocking "thoughts", this being that which plagues an individuals' mind. For indeed it is this which always selfishly generate an "I Want," that takes people into the past or the future.

So Yes! The right task of the newly introduced creeds and disciplines created by our wise ancients was to bring the worshipper into the "Present Time" – but sadly, this task has been forgotten by many religious followers. Yet is it not also interesting that over time, many of our modern religious leaders still pursue these old disciplines, but also many now put forward more "personal ones" for their followers to pursue. Still, sadly such tasks being "I Want" to worship only within this religion for all other religions are wrong and also "I Want" more of only my religious leader's love, understanding, and forgiveness.

So Yes! There are now many added "personally introduced" religious practices, which are sometimes challenging to follow, for they worship self-imposed religious leaders who claim to be the personal gateway to God. For indeed these new introductions and newly interpreted and oft complicated practices are not targeted to keep a person "awakened" to the truth of the "Heaven" that is all around them upon this Earth but are based upon a blind adherence and obedience to an imposing leader. For really indeed an elementary "personal" discipline is all that is required to reveal to all real "practitioners", the truth that they really and personally live in Heaven while existing upon this Earth.

This "Present Time" Earth being the real "Heaven," which is God's world or the actual world of Nature for the Non-Believer and it is a world that is gently but purposely maintained by the Divine "Mother of the Creation".

For in truth, a targeted holistic "Self-Realisation" is a reality that is not difficult to pursue, for you can happily continue with your worldly activities by activating a silent mind, this being achieved by adding a silent "pause" which can be targeted before and after completing any activity. Consequently, this may be likened to a stillness in time which can be realised before and after many actions and it is a gentle "hidden" act which can be used to ensure that you are in the "Present Time," – which is a pure, "Heaven" and it is a Heaven that is all around and within you!

So yes, this is a gentle way to realise this right unthinking "way of life", and it is also a simple way that enables your actions to become like the love contained in water; for water shows a real love for all relationships and will continue to do so and the reason why love is like water, for it cannot be destroyed. Although water takes many forms in its giving of love, it always comes back to itself, and so it is always ready to provide equal and unequivocal love to all those who need it, and it does this without any questions about the user's past or their future.

So, it is, also, with the Soul within you, which observes the self-chosen quarrels of the five senses that fill the mind, but does not interfere with them, although they do block the Soul's sight of the outside world, so that the Soul cannot see the needs of the "Present Time". Accordingly is because the mind is painted by this many desiring past or future "I Want." So it is they that block the view of the Soul so that it cannot see the heavenly needs of the "Present Time", these being the truth, harmonising on-going needs, that are usually endeavouring to be completed by the "Mother of the Creation", who continually observe, and if necessary, corrects the harmonising laws which were established by God. It should also be true to know that God or Nature for the Non-Believer gave people the choice of "free will," because the "Mother of the Creation" always enjoys and needs assistance from people.

So Yes! The "Mother of the Creation", who like water, so loves people that She will not sit in judgment regarding the activities of a person's ever pursuing "I Want," this being that which knowingly emanates from the five senses because She knows that God gave people the freedom of choice. The Divine "Mother of the Creation" also does not sit in judgment on the pain brought to a person's body that is attached to the disharmony created by the five senses.

As a result, this is the disharmony that is caused by some leaders or a personally-created warring conflict, or disagreement, tensions, bitterness, resentment, discord and other unrests caused by a person ever pursuing "I Want". These being the constant demands of the uncontrolled five senses, this being that which take a person's body outside the harmony of all that is naturally provided by the "Mother of the Creation" and which exists within God's Creation. But all history shows that warring disharmony created by people, always returns to the creations status quo and this is the work of the "Mother of the Creation", who see that God's will cannot be changed.

So Yes! The personal target, which people can attain by their self-choosing of certain religious and philosophical practices, is to realise that the personal "you" is the Soul and not the animal five senses that "you" listen to and which "you" allow to control "your" body's activities. Therefore the religious and philosophical work of all People's endeavours is to practice a religious or philosophical activity that allows all that is "thought" to be outside their own bodies activities may need to become modified or re-directed by the owner of the body, which is the "Soul."

It is then that a person's "Soul" becomes like the life providing water, so likened to the *"Mother of the Creation"*. It is then, with this "Self-Realisation" of the human truth of that which you are, and that which speak of, that you will become like water and be able to pursue, satisfy and so obtain, and support the harmony seeking quests of the "Mother of the Creation". It is then because of the support of these TRUE religious practices that you will begin to live a life in the bliss that surpasses all understanding, This is God's world, which the ancients called "Enlightenment," and it is an excellent place to live for those who love life.

Therefore this is said carefully, for a healthy continuation of this new religious "practice" of supporting the emerging harmony that is developing all around you, will bring you into the "Present Time", and it will also ensure that the next step after this "Enlightenment" as to where you are, is becoming "Self-Aware"—thus experiencing "everything" to be yourself. For indeed this is an experience in which all that your senses bring to you – you "experience" to be the real you and so you "know", without doubt, that all that you experience is YOU! For this is also an awareness in which you are aware that you are not the body and no thoughts appear in the still mind has your Soul or your consciousness for the Non-Believer, becomes an integral part of all that exists which is the taught "awareness" of this truth.

The next stage of "Enlightenment" is a condition called by our ancients "Self-Realisation", in which you experience that there is no viewer, for you become the whole of the Creation and so realise that there is only one entity and that this totality entity YOU! It is also, with this experience that you will fully understand the words of Jesus when He said, *"So the last will be first, and the first will be last,"* because there is only one person in the queue and this person you will fully experience as being "You"!

So Yes! How is this wonder achieved? It is achieved by an individual based one-worded prayer, spoken of later, which is the primary tool used, first to control and then to silence the chattering noise created in mind by the animalistic five senses. For in time, with the repeating of a pure mind filling chant, the five senses will be "trained" to stop their chattering in mind and likened to being five untrained pups, will be brought unseen and unheard to your heel and so also rests unseen as if behind you.

It is then from this silent position that they can be, quietly and without sound "individually" released by you, to silently perform and evaluate an activity that they were created to perform, and so their actions will be based upon your Souls' silent commands. Thus, these are the stages that seek "Enlightenment" that all the people of the world can achieve and so honestly, live in and so consequently, experience this "Present Time", which surpasses all understanding and which cannot be changed for it is fixed by God's "arrow of time."

For "Scientifically" is it not true that the known *"arrow of time"* is that which our scientist state is the *"Second Law of Thermodynamics?"* Has being a law in which our scientists incorrectly recognise God's "Present Time" as being a developing movement, because they unknowingly allow their minds to live in the past or the future. So they incorrectly describe this "arrow of time" has one-way direction and as an "irregularity" and a "disorder".

It is further understood that our scientists say this is in ignorance; this is being because they do not understand that the passage of time is controlled by the work of the Divine Mother. She as the Mother of God's only Creation is continually correcting and supporting the harmony surrounding their only child's growth and so always restoring the growing "harmony," that rests within this only child which is the "Creation". They do this because, as the child's parents, they do know this Childs future path, but both agree that the child does not.

So yes! The fact remains that all the people of the world can religiously or philosophically experience the "Present Time", this being a time which cannot be changed, except by God's "arrow of time", whose flight is controlled by the Divine Mother. Because the "Present Time" is the same for all people and will always remain an unchanging fact within their lives, and to find this harmony of life and to live within this harmony, is the directing purpose of ALL religions and philosophies.

So yes! God's or Nature's for the Non-Believers', "Present Time", is all around us but we can feel it. Yes, it can never leave us, but we, as people can choose to leave it, but be assured and always happy for the known fact is that the "Present Time" is unmoving, and will always welcome you back when you seek it. For you can never be genuinely, away from God's "Present" or that which is called "true Nature" by the Non-Believer. People are the only animals who can replace the "Present Time", with their own factious modern complicated imaginary world, which is based upon their five senses claiming demands and they're seeking an "I Want", which targets their selfish demands, but if you wish to live in this world of true harmony – Read on

19   THE DENIAL OF GOD'S OR NATURES "PRESENT"

So yes! The creation of "Present Time" is the power that attracts ALL religions. Still, sadly, many sections of religions and other power group leaders impose "institutional denial", which means instead of silently and individually looking outwards and forwards towards that which it seeks to understand, this being that which many religions endeavour to realise and also to improve, it looks forwards and inwards to control those of their group who have less authority than themselves. For in this freedom of will, confident leaders of people can negatively steal the work of our ancients' who bonded with the ways of the "Mother of the Creation" and whose teachings installed a way of life that was to seek harmony for all of life and Non-Life. But sadly some new on-going leaders of our anciently established religions change their teaching and so seek this "Bonding with Nature" harmony to support only themselves and so steal the worship by saying to their followers "You worship me and all that I say and you will continue to do so, or you will be punished for only my religion is the true one for all other religions are false". Yet, is it not strange that many can believe such hate, for is it not true that they attack, maim and even kill others in the name of their God? How strange this is that they believe that the God of all Creation can be happy to kill His children – indeed, what father can do this?

In another term, this is called "institutional betrayal" which refers to wrongdoings perpetrated by leaders upon individuals dependent or not dependent upon these leaders for spiritual and philosophical support. This statement includes a failure of their leader's religious beliefs to prevent or to correct the wrongdoings of their followers wisely, this being because these leaders have committed their followers to do false actions against others or other religions. These are acts that are supported by these incorrect reasoning institutional leaders who compel their followers to attack other religions or sections of the same religion because they have been told that these "others" are not walking the correct way to God. Frankly, without doubt, this is simply because they "walk" in a different way – so actually, this is an "I Want power over others" or a close and personal pursuit for monetary gain.

So yes! As history shows, some religious leaders create false groups who go against the harmony of the "Present Time", which is a world ruled by God's laws, for is it not true that these self-made religious leaders ignore God's laws as they seek to enforce their own "I Want" for myself laws? These being laws that are based upon their own private personal beliefs, creeds and practices and is it not true that many of their followers also punishingly impose their leaders' personal "I Want", which ignores God's non-punishing laws, as they seek their religious power over others. Therefore is it not interesting that some people say that God will punish other worshippers for pursuing different "religious" beliefs? But this is like putting your hand into boiling water and then asking why are you being punished, for it is certainly not God who is punishing you, but your own "I Want" for ME! Indeed, this is being that which will inflict great punishment upon yourself and those around you.

Therefore is it not true that in the past and also in the "Present Time", this belief which is targeted to harm to others, is also harming unto death many perpetrating false believers who are using that which they say is within or without their religion as an excuse to destroy others, thus making it an, "I Want" club and not a religion? For how can God who created without mistakes all laws and life, cruelly punish people to whom He gave "The Freedom of Choice," the question now is "Was God wrong to do this?" It is, therefore, this personal "I Want" leadership which seeks a target that also opposes the activities of a loving fatherly God and also the endeavours of *"Mother of the Creation"*, this being against Her genuine engagement which is to support the harmony that is emerging within the Creation?

So it is a sad truth that the leaders of these false based religious groups primarily compel their followers to pursue a false harmony, which demands worship of their leaders, wherein they do not seek to realise the *"Mother of the Creation"* higher truth, this being a truth which is known as "The Peace that Surpasses all Understanding," or "A Realm beyond the Ability of Words to Properly Convey," this truth, is the reality of the world all around them? It is further interesting to understand that, because of their singularity that these demanding and imposed false "creeds" arising from false leaders, sadly exist also within the compartments of individual religions, organisations, states, and countries.

Is it not also true that these false leaders have been responsible for more war based deaths and suffering than any other factor upon this Earth? Why is this true? Would it not be correct to understand that sometimes this is because they pursue some individual leaders personal "I Want my religious creed to be obeyed not yours" and so the warring and ungodly killing of others and the personal demand and pursuit arose of an "I Want my creed to be the correct creed, not yours, and also your worshipping of God is wrong, and it should be stopped?"

The question we should now be asking is, "How is it possible to find the 'Peace that surpasses all understanding' or that 'Realm beyond the ability of words to convey', within such a belief system properly? For indeed, this peace that all our ancient wise speak about, cannot be achieved by attacking other people. They worship the chosen creeds of their own culturally understandable religion or way of life.

So Yes! Is it not true that those religions who suffer this institutional denial of God, will inform their participating likeminded followers that it is "Godly" to do such an action that kills, maims and steals from those others whose religion makes them a different way to Gods world. For truly is not all this hate being simply to gain for sufficient power over others, not "religious" gain.

So Yes! Ignore these false leaders who are destroying their Soul and the Soul of those who do their bidding, for it cannot be "bad" to ignore such destroyers of harmony for your actions are always a truth that will set you free. The truth is that the "Mother of the Creation", who supports God's laws, knows that all people have been "Godly" given the "Freedom of Choice". Reliably being a fact which encourages all people of all cultures and languages to establish a religion or philosophy to freely support the variable ways to achieve the harmony of life that the Divine Mother has created for all that is around and this being the same unity as all that which is also within you.

So yes! Frankly, for those people who actively take this path, to support and activate Her presented harmony for all Life and Non-Life, they will very soon realise that they are being rewarded by experiencing harmony within themselves and also around them that pleasurably surpasses all understanding. It is a harmony that they can take within them even unto death. For really genuinely do not ALL Godly based religions and philosophies create this effect?

So Yes! This life of harmony, as previously mentioned, can be likened to driving through a city and obeying traffic lights and all the laws that rest within the highway code of the road, plus honouring the signs supporting the highway codes endeavours to keep the roads safe. For agreeably is it not correct that obeying the Highway Code is a way of allowing a person to obediently and safely drive through a city? Is it not also true that this system made by people can also be likened to the obeying the "Highway Code" way of life that the "Mother of the Creation" lovingly installs around each person? Is this being Her work to keep the Creation together in a continuing on-going harmony?

So Yes! Now genuinely a person should no longer be surprised at the disharmony that they can experience in their personal life. For indeed, this experiencing of disharmony can be likened to yourself or others driving through the city and ignoring all traffic lights and that cultures highway code. Therefore, it can now be easily understood and seen how selfish "drivers", who want everything for themselves, shout and curse their way through the city and indeed they may become the majority of drivers – but does not all our worlds history show that this way of life cannot exist? Does not the history of people always show that the "Mother of the Creation" highway code of life always returns to that which exists around them? For truly does not the "Mother of the Creation" always restores the highway code of life that exists in all language-based countries and yet many still argue their "I Want" only for me and why they do this is explained later in "The Book".

So yes! The frustration caused by not knowing the "Highway Code" of life, is experienced by not believing in the existence of the "Mother of the Creation", which leads to a way of life that can be likened to a story told by one of our wise ancients. This being that there was a travelling man who went in search of this "Highway Code" truth. He eventually entered a valley, which was new to him. Upon walking towards the village, he experienced a great feeling of peace and harmony as he felt the warm sun, saw the green fields and the many animals feeding upon the lush grass.

This feeling is known to many of us as we silently witness God's world or the world of Nature for the Non-Believer. He then saw footprints walking beside him in the soil and felt a significant surge of bliss as he realised that he was walking next to the master of the entire world and then, within him, he felt a great need saying, "I Want" to see this entire village from the top of the mountain".

So Yes! He then left the path and began to climb the mountain, which at first was easy, but then the weather changed, and frost began to cover everything. But he climbed higher, feeding upon and powered by his "I Want." It was then that a blizzard hit him, which was also followed by heavy snow, and he became lost, and the path became dangerous and very difficult and very painful upon which to travel. Eventually, he could see nothing and was very troubled, so he began the perilous and dangerous journey back to the road that led into the village.

Eventually, he arrived upon the warmth of the road and again experienced its great bliss, safety, and its comforts but then when he saw God's footprints silently walking beside him, and he asked, "Where were you when I needed you most when I was lost up there?" To which he received God's answer, "I don't understand why you went up there and left all this that I have presented to you." At this, the man became "Enlightened" and so absorbed all that was around him and remained in the bliss of God's "Present Time", that God or Nature for the Non-Believer, had given to him.

To be more precise about God's "highway code" of life, it is suitable for all people to understand that God's laws or Nature's laws for the Non-Believer are all based upon the Creation of harmony for all life and Non-Life. It is also because of God's "highway code," that you cannot banish this way of life, this religion or philosophy from your personal affairs or your activities. Frankly, this is because when obeying the harmony of God's "highway code", it can be repeated that this is like driving through a city and all the lights turn to green when you approach them and when you wish to park, a car moves away to let you into the only space available.

Sincerely, this is the "Sugar in the Water", spoken about earlier and it truly exists for those who obey this highway code of life. A simple example of these "gifts" being given by the laws of harmony, was when a friend came to visit me and said that he had ordered and paid for three vests, on the internet, but had received four He asked what he should do? I just smiled for I knew that he was a good man, and if a packing mistake had been made, the blissful laws of harmony would see to it that it went to him, but I would be wary of a person who received three vests, and one was damaged – but we do need a sense of humour to understand this thought.

So yes! I know smiles will now appear, for it is not often understood how these gifts from harmony work, especially when everyone around you is disobeying the "Highway Code" of life. But the fact remains that there may probably be some disbelief in the above-stated truth that the laws of harmony will also support those who support it. However, it is suggested that to find this truth a person should endeavour to live in and support the natural harmony that is all around them and even to support the needs of the emerging harmony, especially if you are confronted by these laws to do so. Then indeed, you will experience that which "The Book" says will happen within your on-going life and then begin to realise and so experience this stated truth that harmony is or is "all ways" endeavouring to emerge all around you.

So yes! It is also good not to blame God for any disharmony inflicted upon you, for God's world or the world of Nature cannot do this, but of course, other people can. For it is an inevitable truth that only people can break the emerging laws of harmony. It is also a truth that Gods laws of harmony which are maintained by the "Mother of the Creation" will always "disrupt" your "I Want" way of life, simply because you create friction when you ignore or try to stop God's existing or the "Mother of the Creation" emerging laws of harmony, that are always around you and also endeavouring to emerge around you. It can be further understood that this is how Jesus, the Christian incarnate, explained the laws of harmony using words that were acceptable at that time. These words were: *"For everyone who has will be given more, and he will have abundance and whoever does not have, even what he has will be taken from him."* It can now be understood that Jesus was speaking about God's developing laws of "harmony" meaning that if you live within the harmony that exists all around you, you will be given more "harmony." Still, for those who do not support the harmony that is evolving around them – then the emerging harmony will eventually destroy their "I Want." But the most important thing to remember is that the supporting of God's laws of harmony does not mean that you should attempt to physically or harmfully destroy any other person's form of harmony. Reliably, is it not true that when Jesus was arrested, then humiliated, brutalised, tortured and impersonally nailed to a cross; during all these events He said nothing – yet upon His death's last breath He said: *"Forgive them for they know not what they do!"* For Jesus knew that if he went against the people's "I Want" that had negatively accumulated against Him – that it would have been a personal "I Want" which He could not obey for he knew that a personal "I Want" for myself, always brings destruction to its perpetrators. For Jesus knew that you could only advise others what to do for one can tell another person what to do – for the God-given or Nature gave for the Non-Believer - "Freedom of Choice" always rest within the individual. For was this not proven by this man who was tortured and nailed to a cross and also by the many who have died in wars to stop this illegal punishment of the desires of one culture to attack and so control another culture.

20 THE THREE THAT REST IS ONE

Now we should be clear about the life force that rests within people and which many religions variably explain as the "three in one," but in this writing, let us try to decode it precisely. For the best way to explain the way of life is to understand the "Present Time" that God gave to all life and Non-Life, this being that which the "Mother of the Creation" controls, for do not all Nature shows this fact. Therefore, it is essential to understand in this example that number one is the Soul, which is transferred from life to death and back to life so that the energy of life can continue. The Soul is sometimes referred to as the "Spirit" by various believers. It is also the Soul which looks through the empty mind of number two, which is the Souls "personal" carrier, for truly number two is the body of the person who carries the Soul, this being that which should be

"Godly" observing the world and so "sees" and if necessary does "bodily" support the emerging harmonic needs of the Creation, and it is this "religious" or "philosophical" work about that which all the incarnates and all our wise ancients speak.

Number three is the five senses, which rest in the body of the "doer", and it is these that are needed to safeguard the needs of the body so that it can healthily evaluate and so support the tasks that are needed by Gods developing "Creation". Now the problem, which was not possible for our wise ancients to explain, is that most of the people in this "Iron Age", have forgotten number one, which is the Soul and also its carrier number two, which is the body and so simply believe that there is only number three, this being the five senses, therefore "believe" that it is these five senses that life's purpose is to satisfy.

Simply put, you can only experience and activate the "bliss" of life when your five senses are still and silent and not blocking the Souls view through the needed empty and still mind, this being the only condition in which a person can see Gods or Natures Creation for the Non-Believer. For the truth is that only this "empty-mind" condition can allow you to see and so experience the "Present Time," for only then do you know by this experience that you live and stand under the love of God or Nature for the Non-Believer.

For indeed it is only under this empty minded condition that there can be no claiming of any personal "I Want," this being an inputting self-claiming noise that is usually emanating from one of the five senses. It is a noise that will be clouding and filling the mind with pictures and words. For the truth is that it is only without these inner thoughts that you can attain a clear and empty mind in which "YOU" as a person, factually realise that "YOU" have everything for "YOU" are the top of all life and Non-Life. All that "YOU" need to do is to fulfil the purpose and the being of "YOUR" life, which is to care and support the harmony seeking needs of all that is around you. Indeed it is only the silent mind which shows that you are much needed to enjoy and to support the harmony producing bliss that our ancients say surpasses all understanding.

Genuinely, this is the reason why the wise ancients brought religions and philosophies to people because many people have become sleepy and so engage in self-claiming all that which exists around them. But sadly many have forgotten the about way of these ancient teachings or pay no heed to the knowledge that they did "scientifically" speak. Truthfully this being a religious and philosophical knowledge that is guaranteed to remove a person's forgetting of that which is "THEM", this being who they are; For without the revealing of this ancient knowledge people are caught in a typical "personal" belief system, that is "Animalistic-Claiming" and also destroying via stealing, from the Creation and the harmony that is endeavouring to exist all around them.

But do not worry, for it is easy to change this unhealthy way of living for indeed any person can start the "meditational" path towards "Enlightenment" and therefore become personally useful but not demanding in their caring and supporting of all life and Non-Life. Thus "Enlightenment" will become realised when the mind becomes "still" and so allows your bodies Soul to observe, through your silent mind, God's world or the real world of Nature for the Non-Believer. Genuinely, this is that reality which our wise ancients called "Self-Realisation", and it is a factual world which is experienced when the mind is not contaminated by any self-claiming internal sounding of words and pictures which you will find is accomplished by the practice of the philosophy of a good religion. It is then that you will also understand the harmonising work of the "Mother of the Creation", which is recognised to be that which is being cared for or trying to be cared for, all around you. For truly in "Self-Realisation" the harmony or the endeavouring to emerge harmony is then personally witnessed to be all around you.

It can also be factually understood to consist of the same harmony that exists within your own body and so is easily "Self-Realised" to be recognised to be the same harmonising fact that is beneficially working within you is also working outside your body. It is this unity of existence which is the actual reality for all life and non-life. To put this reality more clearly, it has been said many times by our ancient wise that within you is true, the "I am", this being that which is everything, therefore is it not true that the Christian Bible stated these words when the tree of life was encountered by Moses which stated to him, "I am that I am." Meaning that Moses was being informed that the speaker was "everything." which makes the famous words "I think therefore I am" to be very wrong. For this takes the thinker into the past or the future which "The Book" calls the world of Hell and not the world of Heaven which can exist only has the Present or the Heavenly "Present Time", the time and world which was created by God who seeded into "Space" that which "The Book" calls the "Mother of the Creation" who birthed all life and non-life that can only exist in the "Present Time" and who like all mothers lovingly looks after Her only child in the "Present Time" which is controlled by Gods laws which are creatively targeting a unifying future. To clarify this as a truth, did not Jesus of the Christian faith describe over forty times who the "I am" was, and who the "I am" is; meaning God's supporting wife, the "Mother of the Creation"

So clearly, it was the Divine Mother speaking through the incarnate Jesus and saying to people such words as: "Come to me, all you who are weary and burdened and I will give you rest. Take my yoke upon you and learn from me, for I am gentle and humble in heart, and you will find rest for your souls, for my yoke is easy, and my burden is light." For indeed, are these not the words that emanate from all mothers to their children, this being from their suckling breasts and on unto adult life? For only under this condition of knowing that you are a living part of everything Godly Created, or created by Nature for the non-believer, will your Soul be free to do that which it was born to do.

Also did not the "Mother of the Creation" says through Jesus: "I am the bread of life? He who comes to me will never go hungry, and he who believes in me will never be thirsty," and also the statement of a clear alternative: "I told you that you would die in your sins; if you do not believe that I am the one I claim to be, you will indeed die in your sins." Thus explaining the living death of the one who is controlled by the "I Want" of five senses and who does not see the world has to be a part of themselves, for is this not now clearly seen as a truth for the "I am" is certainly NOT your five senses but is genuinely your soul. For again truly the non-claiming "I am" within you, is the Soul that is seriously loved by the Divine Mother and the God who is the father of the creation. For that which creates the mind filling cloud that exists, and so clouds the mind – is truly the "I Want" of the five senses whose "I want for me" claims attach no Godly value to that which is being observed, this is the truth that a God incarnate or our wise ancients could not state in those far off days, this being that the Soul can only observe the Creation through an unthinking and unclouded mind and so experience that which is the "Present Time" which is genuinely Gods world or the world of Nature for the Non-Believer. For only in the "Present Time" can exist the real you and for a long time, this shall be so!

Indeed you will also realise that you cannot die for only the carrier of the Soul can die; for did not our wise ancients state that there exists a soul within each person's body? But is it not also true that in our modern times we also understand that our body also contains the "animalistic" five senses and so with our heavenly gift of personal choice we can use them to evaluate and so silently support the Souls real purpose, which is to "choose" to support the developing needs of the "Creation".

What should be now clearly understood by all those who wish to experience this bliss of the truth that rests within the "Peace that surpasses all understanding," is that this is the "Bliss" of "Enlightenment", which is about the becoming has one with the creation that all our religions and philosophies' speak. This being that there is only one "practical" and one "methodical" way to realise a life that can be lived in this truth that always rests within the Creation of the world of Nature for our Non-Believers.

For indeed it must be said again and again that it is only by being in the "Present Time," or named by "The Book" has the "Present Time", this being a time that can only be experienced when the Soul can see through a mind that has no thoughts which are usually emanating from one of the animalistic ally based five senses. In all honesty, this being a mind filling activity that is caused by "animalistic ally" targeting a change in current conditions to make them more agreeable to their own "I Want", which is always to feed their own "animalistic" needs which are certainly NOT your true "Self".

For in truth only the "Present Time", not the past or the future, can silently reveal the needed harmony is seeking task that is required to ensure that the "arrow of life," aimed by God and supported by the Divine Mother, is healthily maintained. To attain the "Peace that surpasses all Understanding" a person needs to realise that his or her job is to support the work of the Mother and that their life has no other purpose. For indeed, the target of all religions and philosophies is for life to be lived only in the "Present Time" and so to realise that only living within God's "Present Time" is the only accurate way of ALL life. It is also a way of life which becomes more comfortable with this practice.

This practice is achieved by the correct use of a self-repeating activity, which when controlled by concentration, will force the wild, uncontrolled five senses to come to the heel of the practiser; just as the correct training would control and tame five wild puppies which will then become silent and obey only the inner "Soul's" silent instructed commands.

An example of this mind stilling "heavenly" existence is that you can look at your food with silence in mind, then taste it along with this silence in mind and then honestly, you will recognise that you have never tasted food before, for now, you will silently receive the hundred per cent taste of the food and not thirty per cent or some lower figure, this being that which is produced by an open mind who's seventy per cent of energy is being used to describe another need or another food, plus all the other senses claiming another mind that is being filled by an "I Want". Likewise, if you listen to music with a silent listening empty mind, you will quickly realise that you have never really heard music before, and so it is with touch, your fingers seem to have magic within them as it will be with the smell, but the greatest is sight.

For now, when you look at the world in the silence of the mind, you will see a hundred per cent of the beauty resting in God's world. Truthfully, this is a world that always exists in front of you and no, do not cry, which can happen upon this first experience. For the real tears of life can genuinely appear when feeling for the first time God's world or the world of Nature for the Non-Believer, for indeed this is the world that has been given to you, and it is FREE. For the truth that you now know is the target sought by all religions and philosophies, this being the seeking and realisation of that which is God's world or the world of Nature for the Non-Believer which can only exist in the "Present Time"?

Justly, this is the present time that has been given only to people? Thus, again, a practical way to achieve this is by the repeating of a "Special Meditational Prayer" spoken of later, this being the quickest way but not the final way of controlling and stopping the barking of these "I Want" for myself quests, which are performed and sounded by the "uncontrolled" five senses that are usually and directly controlling a person's life, the reason being that people can become likened to all our lower animals if they habitually believe these five senses are themselves!

21   THE FIVE SENSES CANNOT BE YOU

So yes! It is not your only duty to use your "past" machinations to make obtainable your personal "I Want". Genuinely, this is what you believe you can achieve in the future. For really your real duty is to target the removal of your personal belief that the five senses are the real you, they are NOT you for they are simply "animalistic" tools for your use. Thus mediations purpose is to stop this "animalistic" barking's into a still mind for mediation is a practical activity which will empty your mind by stopping these continuing "I Wants" from freely emanating from the five sense and thus in this way allow your Soul to see through the still mind its only purpose, which is to support the Divine Mother's on-going work that can only be achieved in the "Present Time" – the time which is also called "Now". Rightly, this is truly is the world of the "Present Time", which is the only time to contain the harmony that exists in a God made "Present Time" or the world of Nature of the Non-Believer. For naturally the work of good people is to support the developing of the harmony that continually exists in a world that surrounds them and which is also a world that is not attached to any personal "I Want". Candidly, this is being only a personally based emanating "I Want" for me activity which creates an activity that is targeting the continuation of a selfish "I Want" for me. It is well to notice that Hitler, Napoleon and many of their ilk, gained nothing lasting from their "I Want" demands. For sadly, like the many dreams of our worlds current politically supported military leaders, they also pursued a system that confirms their belief in which they indeed became the "I Want" of the five senses and that these "others", that they called "the enemy," have everything that they want or are stopping them from receiving or pursuing their ever demanding and their own personal "I Want". Also and sadly, even some parts the world's religions can and have become contaminated by religious people seeking a personal grandeur and a power over others. For truthfully this is an ungodly act for it is undoubtedly a personal and greed-based "I Want" for myself. But more strangely and even in our modern world, these animalistic false leaders' have purposely built a military training system whose first endeavour is to remove their newly paid workers believe that they are responsible for their own "military" actions, these being actions which are an "I Want" is directed by a superior officer but performed by these new military recruits. Therefore, the first "military" training target is to replace the recruit's thinking "I Want" demands by the "I Want" demands that are emanating from the five senses of their new military leaders. It is further understood that these strange new beginnings are achieved by installing a punishment system called "basic training," which is often called "boot camp". Candidly, this is where "senior" positioned people threateningly replace the newly recruited individual's five senses, as they steadily bludgeon the newcomer's five senses into submission.

So Yes! It should now be clearly understood that this "basic training," is the habit replacing the way that the military of our "civilised" countries use to control and then replace the "I Want," resting within the individual with their leaders "I Want". This type of "Basic Training" is a very effective way of replacing a proper understanding that they are personally NOT to follow their own "I Want", much of which is not Godly and indeed NOT Natural and is that which even their five senses do not falsely clamour for, and so they come under the control of any senior officers personal own "I Want" demands. Therefore is it not a fact that many recruits are so bludgeoned that they will obey any senior request as if it was coming from their own uncontrolled five senses and not another's person's five senses.

The truth of this matter certainly proves that any individual can personally suppress or replace and so stop their own five senses from making verbal demands for their own sensual and personal gratification, but this is a much better practice when achieved by religious or philosophical practices which also target the elimination of the personal "I want" of the animalistic five senses. For really and sincerely this is the task which our wise ancients religiously or philosophically preached to stop the continually sounding in mind the "I Want" demands of the five senses, which is a "Self-Realised" target that seeks the silent experiencing the "Present Time". Truthfully, this is the only place where the Soul can see and so "habitually" silently take control of all activities that support and expand the harmony which each person is the centre of – this naturally supporting the divine harmonising work of the *"Mother of the Creation"*. But sadly, under military primary training conditions, this similar replacement method is used to remove the personal "I Want" of the new military recruit and replace it not with the Soul, but with an "I Want" desire to follow any senior's officer's instructions even unto their death. For it is this simple "military" training procedure which replaces a personal "I Want" with the "I Want" of any senior in rank person which commits individuals to obey instructions which will inflict brutalities and death upon others. For accurately this a fact that is well known as senior military personnel simply replaces not only the power of other individuals Soul but also imposes the "I Want" demands of their own five senses.

So yes! This method of replacing the five senses via basic training is skillfully used to destroy the "I Want" demands coming from the recruit's five senses. It is then, with their personal five senses being bullied and threatened into a respectful silence and thus subdued, that higher-ranking personnel then find that they can "personally" replace the harmony seeking Soul that rests within all people. In essence, this being the harmony of a seeking Soul which silently always acts when the desires of the five senses are removed, but in this case, it is not removed by a religion or a philosophy, but rather by bullying and the application fear and false "righteousness". It is then that these higher-ranking personnel replace, and so steal the power of an individual's Soul which then allows these superior ranks to get the "Boot-Camp" recruit to perform acts that are the exact opposite of any harmony seeking activity, even if resulting in the individual's obedient death or to their killing and torturing of combatants or the destruction of harmless others. But sadly, as history shows, soldiers at the sharp end of war often find that when their military service is finished, and they return to a non-military way of life, they then realise that they are the only ones who can dictate what their body does. Any previous misdemeanours against innocents eventually cause great unrest, and illness to occur in demobbed soldiers called post-traumatic stress disorder or major depression. So actually, is it not true that we have exclusive homes to ease the pain now suffered by these war returning personnel? Therefore, as this troublesome example shows, it is now wise to be assured that with good religious and philosophical prayers or activities, the best of which are described later in "The Book", all will personally achieve the same power and control over their five senses, which will also give them the ability to ignore the constant demands of the five senses, and so release their Soul, which genuinely, exists to fill them with the "Peace that Surpasses all Understanding," which in some religions is called being filled with the "Holy Spirit." Still, in a simple truth this is called "Enlightenment," and it will lead all practitioners to the very opposite of that which is called "traumatic stress" or "personnel depression". It is VERY accurate that with some religious and or philosophical practices, you will be silently brought to happiness and contentment that the ancients call "Enlightenment". It is then that you will experience the pure harmony that exists all around you even if it brings death, for if it does, it is then that you will be given the wisdom and intuitions to begin its growth; for the removal of disharmony will always be naturally replaced with harmony.

So yes! Indeed, by practising these religious and or philosophical practices, the best of which is spoken of later in "The Book", you will clearly understand that the five senses are NOT YOU! For you are the Soul and you indeed, cannot be that which you observe, and this is the world that Jesus and all our wise ancients within our countless religions and philosophies did speak about, but which has been forgotten by many in our industrialized world.

So let us now clearly understand that it is finding and living in the "Present" and not the past or the future that will bring the non-fearing experiencing "Enlightenment", which is correctly truly the target of our entire world's religious and philosophical writings. Therefore, is it not an absolute truth that this "living in the present time" was also the meaningful target that all our great religious leaders and philosophers spoke about? It is also this fact that makes the "Present Time" only, capable of a "personnel understanding" and so it stands below and therefore supports that which is life itself, this, truthfully, is a life that is taught by all our well-known religions and philosophies as they ALL target "Enlightenment". This condition is the freeing of the Soul to act within Enlightenment, which is achieved by many different harmonies seeking ways. Simply put; it is the finding of this real "truth" that only people can experience, which always governs the natural harmony of all life and non-life, this being that which is everywhere and which can only be realised when the Soul is freed to experience that which ALL religions and philosophies seek, this being the experiencing of "Enlightenment" that can only exist in the "Present Time", the time which has no past and no future. For indeed this is the solitary experience that allows anyone to observe God's world or the world of Nature for the Non-Believer, which is a world seen without the dense fog created in mind by the constant "I Want" claims of the personally freed five senses. For again and indeed, this is the only clear-minded condition in which a person can fully see and so experience God's world or the world of Nature for the Non-Believer; for it is a world that only exists in the "Present Time". For the "scientific" truth is that only God's world or the world of Nature for the Non-Believer can exist in the "Present Time" which is often described as the "Present Time"? For really it is the experiencing of this which makes it a "scientific" truth that only in this "Self-Realising" and so experiencing the "Present Time", can a person honestly experience "Enlightenment"?

So yes! This observable realisation of being in the "Present Time" is a condition only seen when the mind is empty. Without any self-demanding "I Want" thoughts, which is a straightforward all-knowingly way to experience

"Self-Realisation", this being an experience of the real truth, for it is undoubtedly the only actual world in which a person can decide to realise the truth, or not to realise the truth. So again it can be said that ALL life lives in the "Present Time", but only people have the freedom of choice to either continually live in the past or the future or the present time. For indeed this is a condition which is well explained by Shakespeare when he wrote: *"To be, or not to be – that is the question:* Whether *'it is nobler in the mind to suffer The slings and arrows of outrageous fortune Or to take arms against a sea of troubles and by opposing end them,"* simply meaning that individuals suffering is created by the "I Want" of the five senses and opposing "them" is the actual target of all the religious and philosophical creeds. For simply put, they have no other target except to bring people into God's world; a world that cannot exist in the past or the future. This "Present Time" is genuinely a personnel realisation of that which transcends all understanding, for it is only in the "Present Time" that people can experience that which is called "Enlightenment". This being which only people can experience and which again, is often described as: "The peace that surpasses all understanding," or "a realm beyond the ability of words to convey properly." It is also often described, as that of being filled by the "Holy Ghost or Spirit" or by the "Prophet Gabriel" and by many other terminologies from many other religions and philosophies all targeting the experience that can be realised only in God or Natures "Present Time".

So Yes! It is indeed, in the "Present Time", that people can fully experience all of God's Creation or the world of Nature for the Non-Believer. Genuinely, this is the Creation through which the individuals know Soul. This being that which they carry within their body can observe the real world, but only when the clamouring five senses are silent and so not disturbing and clouding the mind.

So yes! Strictly and honestly, this observing of the real world is an "Enlightening" experience, which compels those who have stopped the "I Want" emanating from their clamouring five senses, to really believe and therefore "experience" the fact that they have entered God's world, this is the real Heaven that rests upon our Earth – and it is a Godly "present," which CAN be "Self-Realised".

So Yes! Again truly, it can be personally realised that in experiencing the world of "Enlightenment" we are also experiencing the "Present Time", this being God's or Natures' real "Creation" and His Heaven upon this Earth. Therefore, it should also be known to be true that it is the "Creation", which "always" surrounds each person! Also, that this Earthly "Creation" contains all Earth's life and all Earth's Non-Life and that it rests within and outside the lives of all people?

So Yes! Is it not also a factual truth that this is the same on-going world for the believer as it is for the Non-Believer? For indeed, what is more, robust or more tolerant or more liked by all people, than the natural laws that govern our Creation, these being the same laws that are applied to ALL people? For again rightly and honestly, as all our religions and philosophies should be targeting or are targeting, that there is a factual truth to targeting "Self-Realisation" in which you become everything and which only "The Book" states is a condition in which you "Realise" that there is no observer and un-describing that there is only "YOU", this being a condition which only "The Book" states comes after experiencing a "Self-Aware" condition. With this being a condition which "The Book" states you do "knowingly" experience, via observation, that you are "everything." Is it not also a recognisable truth that if the Creation's laws were followed by all people, then this would become a world that would lead to the tolerance and caring of all people, by all people? Is it not also a reality that as people, we can recognise the real truth that we are ALIVE? In all honesty, this being a truth, which like the Creation, should also make us patient with all of Nature and so enables us to become a person who is loved and respected by all – just as all the Creation itself loves and respects everything that exists within the Creation or Nature for the Non-Believer?

So yes! Also, when living in "Enlightenment" and so experiencing God's world or the world of Nature - which is the heaven upon our world - are we without any kind of personal bias and so we have no racism, no greed, no bad manners no bad characteristics because we have no personal "I Want" for myself. For in the condition of "Enlightenment" there are only right actions that can be performed for you cannot harm yourself, this is in doing what we do or in what we say, for indeed, we can only support the harmony that is all around us and yes!

So yes! Is not it also understood that many people genuinely believe that they are separate from all that has been created; therefore, do they not steal from the group within whom they live? It is also well known that this can lead to high poverty and illness within many people as these ignoring "I want" for me, people hoard the wealth, food and wellbeing that genuinely belong to others. For is it not said to be true that this stealing within our world's history does show that these thieves, who show this animal greed, will be negatively rewarded for their actions, either in this life or in the next, for indeed, the laws that are designed to create harmony for all life and Non-Life can find no use for these people. So they must be negatively ignored and also purposely self-separated from any "harmony" within their life, plus the possibility of being re-born back to the animal or insect world. Justly, this being the world to which they are best suited. Also, if you think that this is not true that such evil people are continuously removed from the world of people, look back at one thousand or two thousand or three thousand years ago and so compare these war claiming histories with the recent changes that are now taking place has our society expands its civility within all "foreign" tribal-based nations, sadly also a fact which some tribes try to stop. Correctly, is it not also correct that many of these "foreign" tribal nations – which are contained by language –are now endeavouring to come together under the laws of harmony, that are always endeavouring to exist for all life and Non-Life. It would be no surprise if the "North Atlantic Treaty Organisation", known as NATO, were disbanded and the "Northern Hemisphere Treaty Organisation" became a reality. For indeed it is also true that people had come a long way from the time when cave family fought cave family and valley fought valley and a Hill-fort fought another Hill-fort and county fought county. An area fought area and country fought country, and the nation fought nation---etc. – Yet all returned to the healthy life within their language-based country, this being that which the people of our many languages wanted. For indeed, this stealing from and the upsetting of another's life is not the life of an "Enlightened" one. The simple reason for this is because "Enlightened people" have allowed the heavenly "Present Time" to enter and so join within them and so they now see others has them-selves.

So yes! With a silent and still mind all can experience the real and only existing "Present Time", the pure "Heaven upon this Earth", which is that which has given to all people and with the added advantage of a "Mother of the Creation", who is caring and controlling the growth of Her only child. For indeed it is "She" who consistently maintains the harmony seeking laws of the Creation which is a development that is undoubtedly based upon a creatively given "Freedom of Choice" that has been given to all people. Yet, strangely, is it not also true that under these Godly created for all life and non-life laws that there is much antagonism, punishing of others and social bullying amongst and within various religious sects, even though they all worship the one, God, albeit within different named religion? Of course, the false belief emanating from these lost souls is that they genuinely believe "this is my land" and "this is my house," and "this is my property" and also many worshippers add "this is my religion, not yours", this being that which they jealously claim and glorify as their personnel belongings. Still, honestly, this is a false joy which they attach to their "own" religion. But does this not truly show that all people have been given the "Freedom of Choice", which can only have been given by a God who is the Creator of all that is. So the question is: - Can God, the father of the Creation, give to His children the "Freedom of Choice" and then have them punished for using this freedom?

22 ALL PEOPLE CAN ACHIEVE "ENLIGHTENMENT

It is also important to remember that this "Enlightening" experience can be honestly and justly realised within all people. Faithfully, this is because it is certainly not a strange belief system or ancient mysticism for it is a well-known "Self-Aware" or "Self-Realised" reality which is based upon many modern people's factually based and convenient experiences. So again, it should be stated that this is an experience that can be realised simply by living in Gods or Natures for the Non-Believers "Present Time", a time in which you can join the intense silence that is resting within you and without you. It is then and only then that after much practical work in the repeating of a simple creed, that you will experience one hundred per cent of that reality which is the only truth that can exist and which can only rest in the "Present Time". For indeed, it is then that you will fully understand the real world, a real-world which will automatically bring to you the true peace that surrounds you in your existence, albeit that you may be going to a cross. Rightly, this is an experience that also expands the life that rests not only within you but without you so that you will encompass previously unknown limits. It is also good to remember that this is the most significant "Present" that God or Nature for the Non-Believer has given to you. It is also your birthright plus the fact that it is always good to remember that no one can take it from you just as it was NOT taken from those Christians who were pushed into the arena of death by the Romans. There is also a second reality that works within our Creation. Sincerely, this being the work of the "Divine Mother" who cares and protects all the harmony that exists within God's laws these being laws that continuously control the Creation just as the laws of the "high-way code" control the traffic within most countries. The central theme of the Divine Mother is not only in the natural acceptance and in the supporting of these harmonious creating ever-evolving laws that are within and also surround all life and non-life, these being laws that are needed to support the life of the Creation but, within Her other reality, there is also the law in which She will turn her face back to people who are automatically forgiven when they return to supporting Her work even after they have previously broken God's ever-evolving laws. However, many think that their past actions are unforgivable.

Rightly, this means that all people can always achieve, "Enlightenment" but only if they can also truly, forgive the non-harmonising actions of others who have ignored the eternal truth which surrounds them. Correctly, this is because all harmony is seeking or even non-harmony seeking actions are based upon a God-given "Freedom of Choice" a choice that is based upon free will. This free will is given to ALL people by God, and to which all people have a birth-right to obtain.

So simply put, this can also be explained by the "Mother of the Creation" speaking through the incarnate we call Jesus who said: *"Forgive us our debts, as we also have forgiven our debtors"* plus *"For if you forgive people when they sin against you, your heavenly Father will also forgive you"* and *"But if you do not forgive people their sins, your Father will not forgive your sins"*. Simply put, you cannot reach "Enlightenment" with an "I Want" pursuit to punish others, which is a past or future thought that is seeking retribution. So it is good to fully understand the above words of the Divine Mother for this is the *"Mother of the Creation"* speaking through Jesus to all people and explaining that the carrying of a grudge automatically takes a person to live in the past or into the future, this being the world of "Hell", a place which cannot exist in the "Heaven" known as "Enlightenment".

So Yes! Now indeed, it is essential to know well that when a person enters the "Heaven" that only rests in the "Present Time" and so becomes "Enlightened," that this "Godly" condition automatically forgives all past sins, for indeed, this is a condition and a status that can be likened to a city that turns sewage into pure drinking water and then returns it to the previous user. So who can say that this pure returning drinking water should be condemned, not used and shunned because it was once sewage? It is also good to understand, by those who seek the truth of an "Enlightened" life that this is truly God's "Present" to all life and non-life, and it is the only place where the mind has no "I Want" thoughts that are emanating from the five senses. For honestly, it is these "I

Want" thoughts that are continually plaguing those people whose five senses keep their mind actively filled with a past or a future "I Want." Justly, this can be likened to drinking water from a sewage condition which ignorantly poisons their life and sadly the lives of others.

So yes! It is for the use of ALL of Earth's people that the many variable religions and philosophies – that exist in our world – seek and also arises to aid ALL troubled people. For indeed all our religions and philosophies put forward various "culturally" creeds in which they always endeavour to "Enlighten" those who practice them, for is it not true that the wise ancients identified that many people in many parts of the world have forgotten who they are? For again is it not true that our wise ancients did faithfully arise to religiously or philosophically inform, cleanse and care for others, this being in the knowledge of words which could explain all of that which is real and that which is not real. Is it not also true that our wise ancients brought to people a great truth that was contained within all their religious and philosophical teachings? Is it not also true that many of these religions and philosophies gave birth to "Enlightened" ones who can and do live in God's "Present" or Natures "Present" for the Non-Believer. Is it not also true that such "Enlightened" people, by example, also fill the needs of those around them, who in ignorance can be damaging their own lives, for truthfully, all people can be brought to live only in the "Present Time", this being the only time in which exists the physical reality called "Enlightenment" and it can be genuinely experienced and WOW! What an experience.

For it is undoubtedly true that this unification of all life and non-life belongs to ALL people, for justly it is only people who have this God or Nature given gift of "free will", a natural gift which has been created, so that people, with this "Freedom of Choice" can support the harmony seeking work of the Divine Mother. The more re-births that you have had, the more honour that is within you and so the more you support the needs of the "Present Time", for you no longer see the need to pursue an animalistic "I Want", this being that which emanates from early births as people. However, we must be careful with those people who have just been rebirthed from the animal kingdom, for they may have frequent problems with a newly given "Freedom of Choice". But is it not true that these new people can "naturally," be taught a religious or philosophical way to reach the controlling action of the Soul, without the bullying use of a "boot camp" program that exists in our military world and which causes so many deaths by suicide and depression, this being when our military people return to civilian life and realise that they and no others have been responsible for all their military actions.

So, what is this work that brings "Enlightenment?" What should people be practising to achieve this way of "Enlightened" life? For certainly is it not now naturally understood that "Enlightenment" is the target of all the religions and philosophies; this being that which is numerously targeted all over our world by the teachings of our wise ancients. For indeed, our ancient "Enlightened" wise know that ANY practising person can find *"The peace that surpasses all understanding"* but our wise ancients also know that all people do need to be shown an authentic and practical way to support this path to "Enlightenment". It is for this reason that within all the different religions and philosophies, the wise ancients introduced various creeds for they knew the truth that a "creed" could be the vehicle that will take the "worshipper" to "Enlightenment". But the other truth that is stated by our wise ancients is that these tasks tom achieve "Enlightenment" can only be a personal choice and this "choice" can only be from the individual that is targeting the need for "Enlightenment".

So yes! All people can genuinely and "personally" experience "Enlightenment", this being a condition in which they can "unthinkingly" experience and even support all the creations ever-developing harmony that rests within the on-going movement of the Creation's work towards its harmonious perfection. But honestly, this harmony seeking activity can only be "Silently" achieved in the "Present Time". Rightly, this being the only place in which "Enlightenment" can be "Self-Realised" and so supported. For honestly, the Creations target has an unknown purpose, yet in "Enlightenment," people can truly experience and so know that it was the unfathomable God who created the eternal laws that govern the unfathomable way ahead for the Creation; a fact that can be similarly likened to that which our scientists call "the arrow of time". For accurately is it not also stated to be true that our scientists did "scientifically" state, *"That if we follow the arrow that is targeting the future, we find more and more of the random element in the state of its passage".*

So yes! It is now being stated, within "The Book," that it is the negative aspects of these random elements that the "Mother of the Creation" is continually correcting, which can also be most usefully achieved and accomplished done with the aid of "Enlightened" people. For strictly, some random-based negative pursuing aspects can sometimes be contradictory to God's harmony seeking purpose. Therefore, it is suspected that this is the actual reason why people have been given "Freedom of Choice"; this being the "Freedom of Choice" to silently decide which developing activity needs a harmony seeking "helpful" activity to correct it. For is it not true that only people have been given a "Freedom of Choice" and is this not the fact which enables a person's "free will" to be able to purposely choose the right action that is necessary to support the work of the "Mother *of the Creation",* this being in Her efforts to maintain and improve the on-going harmony that exists or is endeavouring to exist all around us and is this not a fact which is portrayed by all mothers? But is it not also true that many people, this being that part of the Divine Mothers only child who has a free will, have forgotten that they have been given this "freedom of choice." Therefore is it not also true that in this forgetting some people can lie, cheat or deceive and so break the law of harmony which brings to them a living in Hell, which can only exist in a selfish mind creating past or future, for this is genuinely ignoring the heaven that rests only in the "Present Time?" Yet! Is it not also true that all those people who have become "Enlightened" and so live with contented happiness that is beyond explanation, will find it right that when living in Gods or Natures "Present" it is impossible to tell lies that can be spoken or wrongs that can be pursued. The real truth is that it is only the "I Want" demands from the five senses that fuel and so fill the mind with past or future thoughts that are negative to the Creation's positive actions. For indeed, it is only these "I Want" thoughts continually emanating from the animalistic five senses that cloud the mind of the thinker. It is this truth which takes them into the world of a self-created Hell that can only exist in the past or the future, this being a fact which enables the denial of an evolving "Heaven" that can only exist in the "Present Time". For honestly all should now know that living in a world without an "I Want," brings a conscious state of excellence, in which you cannot cheat, and you cannot lie, and you cannot even speak ill of others for in "Heaven" only the unity of the "one" exists.

So yes! It is impossible to think, perform or complete these harmful acts against others, for you must leave God's "Present Time" to do so. For indeed, in "Enlightenment" you will fully experience the "Present Time", a time which can only be experienced with a silent mind and a condition in which you will know that you cannot tell a lie or cheat others, for correctly a mind filling "I Want" the world is impossible to experience while living in God's world or the world of true Nature for the Non-Believer.

So yes! Truthfully, this is an enlightened life that can only be lived in when the individual stops their mind filling "I Want" demands that are emanating from the five senses, these being demands which are inwardly produced and so cloud the mind with the noisy clamouring "I Want" of the five senses. It is also necessary and very wise to know that people should not allow these on-going constant "I Want" thoughts that are emanating from the five senses, to dwell and arise within them. For thus does a personal and fictitiously created own mind filling the world in which only a past or a future "I Want" thought is existing. These being serious all-consuming "I Want" thoughts, and it should be clearly understood that these are only "I Want" thoughts that are being targeted, acclaimed and controlled by the desires of the five senses which are all usually based upon stealing that which is not theirs from the "Present Time". Truthfully, this being because it has sadly been forgotten that the animalistic five senses are now really the silent servants of the Soul for the Soul cannot be that which it looks at nor that which it smells, tastes, touches nor be that which it listens to, for the Soul knows that these are just tools for its use. Still, habits from our pre-animal existence can be hard to deny.

So now it is good to be assured and also comforting to know that if you pursue specific religious or philosophical "creed" based prayers or hymns, then you will stop the demands of the five senses from entering the mind and so exist in God's "Present Time" this being known as an "Enlightening" experience. So honestly it is this "Enlightened" realisation that empties the mind and so will naturally stop you from continually seeking to achieve the "I Want" of the animalistic five senses. For in enlightenment you will never again believe you are that selfish thinking animalistic "I Want" for myself, this being that which you have so often mistakenly believed to be your true self.

It is with this knowledge of a "Self-Realised" experience of that which you indeed are, which is "everything" that you will no longer be controlled by these demanding "I Want" for me, this being the thoughts which are born from the animal kingdom, for indeed in an "Enlightened" therefore Self-disciplined condition the five senses cannot mind filling speak and so you will KNOW that you are NOT these animalistic uncontrolled wanting's of the five senses.

So Yes! as all our wise ancients state that the way to achieve this step towards "Enlightenment" is to pray via a confident disciplined religious or philosophical "creed" or activity - of which there and many - but more about the chosen best creed way to achieve "Enlightenment" later. For all our wise ancients knew that it is by "habitual" creed praying that allows the prayer to achieve this great truth and so enables the active prayers to realise that they are the Soul that rests within them and which is the faithful observer of God's world. Sincerely, this is the world that is controlled by God's needs and not by a personal "I Want", for it is God's needs or Nature's needs for the Non-Believer that continually expands the Creations on-going pursuit of harmony.Again, this is the condition that is suitable for all life, including those whose lives are given as food so that others may live, for indeed, there is only one life force. Accurately, is it not a definite truth that all life is based on one type of energy, and this is the energy that animates the "Self" of all that lives? This "Self" being described by our wise ancients, as being the single on-going life of the Creation or Nature for the Non-Believers. Thus, the Soul within you can observe one hundred per cent of the world around you, but only when the five senses are subdued. For indeed it is the Soul with which you will quietly join God's world and act according to the harmony seeking needs of the "Present Time" and so become as one with the "Self" of all that is within the Creation. This condition is known as "Self-Realisation" by our ancients, but more about this later, for a person's way to achieving "Enlightenment" must be self-targeted. A little caution here, for when you have silenced the mind and so reached "Enlightenment," meaning that you are experiencing the pure "self of all", this being a state of consciousness which all the major religions and philosophies say is within you. It is only then that you will realise that you are in the quiet and very still and unmoving "Present Time". Justly, this being experienced within a state of silence that exists only within a quiet mind, for only a silent mind can emanate a call for an action that cannot be heard or seen in the mind but can be experienced as a natural "feeling" of that which the Creation's "silently" needs assisting to continue on its path of harmony towards – no one knows what.

23 THE PAST AND THE FUTURE DO NOT EXIST

So yes! The "Present" is the "now", or as many ancients call it, the "trance of nothingness," which is a condition occurring when the mind subordinates and stills the five senses so that the Soul can fully experience the "Present Time", the only place in which the Creation exists. These were conditions in which the Soul's view of the Creation is not blocked by the five senses filling the mind with "I Want" imagery, which comes from the thoughts based upon past or future "I Want" activities, and all because we sincerely believe that "WE" are the five senses.

This strange and false belief is also a condition that all the major religions and philosophies seek to remove by prayer based creeds and many other disciplines. For it is undoubtedly true that all religions and philosophies target "Enlightenment", even knowingly or unknowingly has to be the best situation in which a person can live. For it enables a person to perceive the real world without painting it with the many ways of thinking how to achieve or target a personal "I Want," which is heavily supported by thoughts of past experiences and potentially self-created future ones.

So yes! The conditions of "Enlightenment" are simply a way of living a life, without the plaguing and damaging personal thoughts of "I Want" claiming an essential use of the mind. For, in reality, there is nothing to want, for all has been made available. However, it must be agreed that in our current age of personal development, which is attached to wasteful "materialism", we would need to be governed by an indeed, "Enlightened" democracy or bloodline ruler, which contentedly fulfils the majority's needs but also cares for the minority; for there is no place for racialism or class consciousness in God's world or the world of Nature for the Non-Believer.

So yes! It must be agreed that many people take from others that which is not theirs to take but rest assured that they will receive the consequences of their acts which will not be to their advantage. For is it not a truth that it is only in the "Present Time" and not the past or the future which can exist in our Earthly Heaven, and is it not also true that these images that are currently in front of many people do explain what needs to be done. Also, is it not reasonable to remember that you should personally endeavour to create or support – by your actions – the unselfish harmony that is personally around you, just as does the Divine *"Mother of the Creation"*. Yet it is always self-sacrificing to again remember the words of the great incarnate Krishna, who said to His disciple Arjuna: ***"Do your duty Arjuna, for to do the duty of another is fraught with danger."*** So it is that with this spoken knowledge you should also be able to let others shine in their support of the Creation's on-going harmony and not endeavour to steal their light, for indeed, all people know that the "jealousy" of others is a great poison. Yes, it can destroy you, for this is a destruction that is created by people – for God's laws or the Divine Mother's actions can never punish anything within the Creation – which is their only child.

It is also suitable for every individual to remember that when you die, you do not go to a Heaven or a Hell, for upon death you leave these places which you have "Self" chosen to live. Therefore, always remember that those who support the activities of the "Present Time" live in Heaven and those whose mind continually support the thoughts of an "I Want" world which does not exist for they originate from the past or a future world which is the real world of Hell and which can be selfishly chosen to be lived while currently existing upon this Earth. This living in Hell is an absolute truth, and it is always that "Hell" which Jesus speaks about – or do you have a belief that the environment and the world around you are not "naturally" living in harmony? For if you do not, you live in Hell and only your own created discord will exist all around you, and if this discord is coming from others, then still endeavour to stay in Heaven which can only exist in the "Present Time".

It is because of this potential negative way that is created by a mind filling "I Want" that people can live in the false-made world of Hell, this being that which our wise ancients warned about and is why they created the many parables spoken of in our many religions and philosophies. These "parable" stories were to make known to all people that all words arising from our wise ancients were their real endeavour to show a way of living in harmony, or now more easily understand a way to live in Heaven, while on this Earth, which is God's world or the world of Nature for the Non-Believer. It is for this reason that our wise ancients always explained by their many stories and examples that living in harmony is better than living in disharmony. But honestly, because of the ancient understanding of the world in which they lived, many of these wise ancients could not state the simple truth to their followers. This truth being a modern known truth which states that to enjoy a life that is lived supporting harmony it is necessary to silence the jabbering 'I Want', filling and so clouding the mind, this being that noise that is continually coming from one of your five senses. For certainly is this not because in the modern understanding of our "five senses" only became common knowledge within our recent history. These five senses that are spoken about being the lower "animalistic" senses which are smell, taste, sight, touch, and hearing and when not controlled, they are like five wild dogs tearing at the world around them and certainly not joining with the harmony that is endeavouring to exist and which is there to support them and that which is all around them, and why? For regularly it is strange that the reason why we allow them to control us is that we believe that they are "US", they are NOT us for we are the only a life form that has been given the "Freedom of Choice" and that which has been previously mentioned in that this "Freedom of Choice" was God-given or Nature gave for the Non-Believer. Its purpose is so that we can support the world that has been provided for us to live.

24 THE SINGLE SCIENTIFIC TRUTH OF THE SOUL

So yes! Controlling these five senses can be likened to controlling five untrained pups and so make them has likened to good obedient sheepdogs that will support your way through life, and this can be achieved by practising a simple creed-based meditation and other small creed-based exercises which will take you to a consolidated understanding that "Enlightenment" so precisely rests within you and cannot be without you even if so desired, for indeed, you will experience the living in Heaven which is all around you and within you and which always exists in the "Present Time". Also, after you have lived and experienced for some time the devotion that "Enlightenment" brings to you and which is an "Enlightenment" which shows the "Heaven" that is all around you and within you, for carefully did not our wise ancients also regularly state that by the continuation of this creed-based "meditational praying" that eventually you WILL experience that which "The Book" says is a "Self-Awareness". This being condition in which your viewing Soul is genuinely known to be an integral part of that which you are experiencing's and which has an "aware" observer it also knows that it is a natural part of the Creation, this being which is all around it, a reality which can only exist in the "Present Time". Then, eventually, you could become "Self-Realised" and so join with Gods world or the world of Nature for the Non-Believer, for then there is nothing to observe for all the Creation is yourself and "The Book" further state that after "Self-Realisation", you will never be born again and "The Book" also states that the purpose of the Creation is so that God or Nature for the Non-Believer can experience Himself- which could be the only purpose of the "Creation".

So it is then, with the "factual experience" of Enlightenment that you will fully understand within your existing current life that genuinely, you are "Enlightened," and so have become fully aware that you are God's child. Or you may pursue these simple creed exercises further unto "Self-Realisation"," and so fully understand what you are God's only child – for you will realise that you are that which God created and that you are "The Creation", the only child of God.

Now – a word of caution here! For "Self-Awareness", which is an experience that comes before "Self-Realisation" and which does not have positive, is genuinely an "Enlightening" experience. For certainly within this "Self-Realisation" experience, you will become "aware" that you no longer exist as a separate "individual". For truly you will become "aware" there is no longer a personal "you" for "you" are now experiencing with our five senses that which you are "aware" of, this being your true "Self", which is "Everything" and wow! What an experience as you become inwardly "aware" that what you touch, taste, smell, see and hear is you – and in this silent awareness – you know that ALL which you experience – is YOU. I can assure you that when you experience it, you will know it is the truth that I now speak!

So yes! The "Self-Aware" Enlightenment that you experience before "Self-Realisation" is likened by our ancient wise to be as "gold", for when "Enlightened" you cannot be tarnished or soiled by the world around you. It is also true that you will fully experience the bliss that surpasses all understanding and so become an active-active player in the harmony that is continually being created around you.

So Yes! "Enlightenment" also allows you to understand that your life does not survive on an "I Want, but that your life lives with a judgment that pays no heed to tribalism or birth circumstances, but recognises all of "Life" and "Non-Life" as being equal and as a person, you know that your existence is to care for this "Life" and "Non-Life" that exists around all people, but now you should know well that in "Self-Realisation"," you are not an observer of God's world or the world of Nature for the Non-Believer - for you genuinely, become God's world. There is no observer, this being an unclaimed experience which you will never forget. For certainly is it not also true that all people are of the same "animal" grouping and that the only difference is the physical differences which God's laws gave to them so that their bodies can enjoy more fully the environment in which they live? But what is it that is really and modernly written here?

So Yes! Now let us listen to an ancient parable spoken by our wise ancients to our old selves, this being an explanation of what "Enlightenment" means, this being that which mediation brings to the observer and its purpose which is to support the harmony that is growing all around "YOU". Just listen to these words of the Divine Mother spoken through Jesus: *"I will show you what he is like who comes to me and hears my words and puts them into practice. He is like a man building a house, which dug down deep and laid the foundation on the rock. The rain came down, the streams rose, and the winds blew and beat against that house, yet it did not fall, because it had its foundation on the rock."* (This is Enlightenment) *"But everyone who hears these words of mine and does not put them into practice is like a foolish man who built his house on sand. The rain came down, the streams rose, and the winds blew and beat against that house, and it fell with a great crash"* and then *"He who has ears, let him hear."* Do you dear readers have ears to hear? Do you wish to experience "Enlightenment?" Do you wish to place your life on solid ground, for this "house" spoken about is really "You?" – Therefore if you do wish to build your house onto solid ground, then read on. But also be aware that it is good to remember that the way to achieve "Enlightenment" cannot be claimed to be existing only in a "tribal" doctrinal based religion, this being a religion which culturally states that only their religious "creed" can be used to experience God's world. So they pursue a group's worshipping acceptance which is based upon an understanding that any another group's "religious" way of life is incorrect and even should be stopped; an act which for they believe that God will love them.

Yet sadly this "thought" is the worshipping of an "I Want" for myself dogma which history shows can be designed via hierarchical group leadership pressure, to redirect the thoughts of the worshipping individual so that they actively target the praying culture of other religions or even different leaders within the same religion. For truly is this not sometimes a task which is energised to please their leaders who they believe are showing them a favour and thus giving them access to God? For definitely and indeed, this is an incorrect viewpoint, for it is merely a leadership "I Want" desire which is stealing Gods world, especially when these leaders claim a need to be personally worshipped by their captured followers. Therefore, can it not be said to be accurate, as history shows, that many worshipped leaders usually install for their followers their personal "I Want" creed-based control system that creates a religious activity that prompts the individual to target the wealth of another religion or even people within their religion. This activity is indeed a religious leader's personal "I Want", which can keep them in an "I want for myself" Hell, this being while living on this Earth and sadly also "painfully" for their followers who aid in this personal "I Want" hallucination.

So Yes! These false religious creeds should be avoided by those who seek a happier more satisfied and authentic way of living their life and therefore is it not wise to understand the way of their Soul; in other words, they need to target a personal way of living in a positive Heaven, while on this Earth, and not in a negative Hell which is full of many an unrealised "I Want" for myself dreams and nightmares. For it is undoubtedly true, as the great Buddha said that *"All know the way, but seldom follow it,"* these being words which are emanating straight from the "Mother of the Creation". For really the truth that Buddha states are that "You" really and personally do know the way to living in Heaven and not Hell, but it is only ignorance that can stop you from living in Heaven – which after reading "The Book" can no longer be said to be true.

So Yes! A "Non-Enlightened" way of life can be likened to living in sin, which is an act that continually violates the Creations way of life that lives in harmony all around you. For is this not a truth that our wise ancients always say that a "Non-Enlightened" way of living is not a natural way of life, nor is it an integral part of your true nature? For sin, which is the claiming of Gods world or the world of Nature for the Non-believer, is something that we have picked up like a bad habit in childhood but the truth is that like all bad habits, it can be corrected and stopped, for it can be simply likened to be dust that can be cleaned from any surface. For to be sure, this removal of a sinful "I Want" for myself act is like the simple cleansing of dust from a smooth surface, but it will lead to the way of a shining "Truth" which, in turn, leads to a new and pleasing "harmonised" way of life. This careful being the way of living which all our wise ancients say is a correct way of living and that it is a life which that will lead to many new and Godly re-births in this life and the next; a fact known to be genuinely stated by our many wise ancients who created most of the world's major religions and philosophies.

So yes! It is a fact that most of the world's religions and philosophies have a Creation story of how we are born on this Earth, and what happens when we die upon it. Many religions and philosophies also teach the truth that we cannot die, and that we are reborn again and again to pursue that which we must pursue and aid that which we must aid. Therefore it is easy to understand the truth of the realisation that it is the Soul that constantly re-births through reincarnation, this being a truth stated continuously by our ancient wise that when one dies, they are reborn again. For did not Jesus also say: *"He who believes in me shall never die."*

So Yes! Death unites everybody, and it is also a good "unifying" feeling that you will be born again, For truly there is no waste within the Creation and if you have any unavoidable illness, then do not worry too much, for your life will continue onto a new life. Your current pain can be stated to be for the searching understanding of those who you love, and who is lovingly around you. Precisely, this being so that they can show their empathy, which is based upon the knowledge of their true love for you and which your illness or death will never remove.

It is further believed that this truth of being reborn again is assisted by the knowledge that it is scientifically known that you cannot lose energy, for sure is it not also "scientifically" proved in Newtonian physics that there is a universal law which is based upon the conservation of all energy. Does this not also prove, as our great scientists say, that for every action there is an equal and opposite reaction? This truth again simply means that energy can be neither created nor be destroyed; however, it is stated that it can change from one form to another. Yet' this is a "scientific" fact that is more easily understood when we recognise that energy can be likened to water. For it is sure that water is well known by all to be able to change into many forms, and is it not also a known truth that water brings life to that which is without it?

So yes! Water and energy can be likened to exist within the Soul, which also cannot be destroyed but which also brings life in many forms, for like water and energy, it also exists never to die. For precisely, as our wise ancients state, the Soul must be born again and again to rebirthed into the most suitable of vehicles. Therefore and indeed, this also can be likened to the law regarding the conservation of energy, which is "scientifically" known as the first law of thermodynamics. This law is a simple law in which our scientists state that the energy within a closed system must remain constant, for it can neither be increased nor be decreased, which means that energy cannot leave that which it supports, this being without interference from outside – so regarding a person body. Cannot this outside interference be that which we say causes death, which ensures that the Soul, which is a singularity of energy, then departs the body, thus leaving us with the question: "Where does it go?" Is the answer to this not in the "scientific" truth that the universe itself is a closed "vehicle" based system, meaning that the total amount of energy currently in existence has always been "lawfully" the same and therefore cannot increase or decrease, this being in accordance to the scientifically proven first law of thermodynamics? Therefore, is it not also "scientifically" valid that these "vehicles", this being that which all this active none separated energy "individually" survives in, are also continually changing and moving into other self-containing "closed" but forever remaining attached to the whole of that entity which we call the "Creation"?

So Yes! "Scientifically" can we not call the Soul to be the bodily moving energy that departs from us when we die, and all people who have witnessed death know just when this energy departs the body, therefore cannot this released and departing energy now be recognised as the Soul?

So Yes! Can it not also be indeed said that the Soul is an energy that reincarnates, just as the above "scientific" law of thermodynamics dictates? Therefore cannot it also be stated that the re-birth of life is that which is explained in the laws of physics, which states that the total energy of an isolated system remains constant and that it is usually conserved over all of the time?

So Yes! Simply put, as previously stated, energy can neither be created nor destroyed; instead, it transforms from one form to inhabit another and therefore the energy that is within us and which we call life is the Soul, which moves on and on life afterlife. It must also be clearly stated here that the Soul within people who are being born with physical and or mental differences are not being punished by the Creator of the Universe for the non-believer, but are being born to present an earning opportunity for themselves and also an earning opportunity for others to provide care, attention and love, plus their birth differences is to remind us about life's needs which we should dutifully and gainfully support in those who need our support and this is not a charity! Carefully, this is undoubtedly being the way of life chosen by those who need our care for they are gifts that are being presented to support us gainfully.

So Yes! This loss of energy upon death is also a well-known scientific and observable fact. For it is undoubtedly true that when we see a person die, we knowingly say, very clearly, that he or she "has gone?" Does this not clearly mean that we recognise, according to the first law of thermodynamics, that their energy has left them, which, is the Soul that is leaving them? For again is it not also true that everything in the singularity of the only child, this being the Creation, is under universal law. A universal law which allows birth in all things and which also leads to death in all things, and then again a re-birth for that energy which God or Nature for the Non-Believer did create just cannot die or be wasted, this being a known actuality which is supported by all our wise scientists, for indeed our scientists state that energy cannot die. So it is impossible to "scientifically" imagine that an entity that keeps creating over time, trillions upon trillions upon trillions of individual life forms. These being life-forms which only live for a few score years and then that entity which created them would waste them all away to become an "undying" and "unchanging" entity when their life ends? Or drop by drop, place them at life's end into good or corrupt unknown zero-encased some other non-recognisable entity? For certainly is it not a truth that that which has been created to be people is alive, for all know that it can move and yes it can hiccup and yes it can naturally flex its muscles, as does nature in volcanoes or hurricanes. For again is it not true that the Earth stretches its muscles and balances its air, and also self-creates a movement which can destroy or hurt people's lives, but always remember that their Souls cannot die. Non-life also has an energy that must also live and develop according to God's laws or Nature's laws for the Non-Believer.

For indeed should I not also "scientifically" know that a man and a woman do not make a child; they just begin one! For undoubtedly, it is true that it is God's laws or Nature's laws for the Non-Believer, is that which builds the child within the mother? For it is it not also scientifically proved by many who look after the pregnancy of a pending mother, that awesome energy enters the unborn child at around three months after conception; this truly "The Book" says, must be their Soul.

Further to this can it not also be scientifically proven that a child before the age of two and without the ability to walk or talk correctly, can hold long meaningfully habitually and culturally "sounding" conversations with an adult and that they can also behave in familiar family surroundings, as an adult would behave, and often act as a playful adult, who is really in love with the world in which they live. Scientist says it is entirely normal and natural for the personnel DNA in babies to act in this away. Still, it is their past lives that are reacting habitually, and this is a fact that can be recognised in their listening and then in their answering, with words encased in like sounding-intimations, these being used to establish a personal and still conscious past behaviour pattern or used communication.

We can also verify that most children below the age of two can react to a parent stimulus even when fast asleep – they can even be fed, has many mothers know, in this sleep state. Therefore can it not also be seen that these newborn children seem to act as if they have just left the unity of all things and are happy or sad in direct accordance to this fact and that they now seemingly realise that they now need to re-enter into a new life. Can it not also be seen in these early months of birth, that babies still experience the "singularity" that exists within the unity of all things, as it was in the world from which they have just come, and so do not they happily behave as if it is still all around them or are unhappy if they experience that this love of unity has been lost.

For it is undoubtedly true that babies when months old can positively communicate a satisfied feeling of unity with all life or negatively show stress, worry, and hyperactivity if they feel they are leaving this previous unity and so feel the fear of a joining with the selfish "individuality" that could appear around them? Then it seems that around the age of two, at the advent of walking and communicative language, many then leave this past world of unity, and so then join the world of this new life, this being a life based upon "individual" singularity, which their adults teach them to accept.

So Yes! It seems that the pre-born experience of unity with all that exists becomes forgotten, but which must naturally always exists, as a seed of unity, which still rests within them; for indeed, the experience of "Unity" with everything can never leave anyone yet forgetting is our worst enemy.

So Yes! Re-births must occur habitually and usually into the same bloodline to which their dying mind usually targets unless they are birthed somewhere else and so bring their advanced pre-born "Heavenly" harmonising habits to co-exist with others, this being in accordance to the divine law within the *"Mother of the Creation"* s constant work of maintaining harmony within Her only child or of Natures creation according to the beliefs of the Non-Believer. It is also interesting to note that some philosophies state that keeping an "I Want"; this being the wanted return of a known loved one in mind after their death, stops their re-birth and traps them in the "afterlife" until the "I Want" that targets their past body dissipate from their loved ones, which is a routine procedure.

Yet it is believed that many have found that at the beginning of a loved one's death, it is good to keep them and the happy days with them in mind, for this means that they cannot die for they are within you – but of course, always the eventual need is to let them go for they have to return to a new life. This re-birth, of course, means that there is no threatened Hell or comfortable Heaven to live in forever when we die. Still, we do experience after our body dies, a potent reminder of the unity held within the energy of life's true singularity, this being a fact which can be based upon the past love of family in which we have the re-birthing freedom of choice to return. Thus, the "Mother of the Creation" continues Her work, which is to maintain the harmony within Her growing child who we call "the Creation." It can also be seen by all when looking back through all of our world's history, that She, the *"Mother of the Creation"* "uniquely and harmoniously" continually binds various parts of the Creation together – and so creates individual entities that we call life – as well as the on-going activities of maintaining the expanding harmony that is all around life and Non-Life.

So Yes! It should now be understood that when we die, we do not go to a Heaven or a Hell – we leave Heaven or Hell, depending upon in which one we have self-chosen to live. For did the *"Mother of the Creation"* not say, when speaking through Jesus, that: *"The kingdom of heaven is within you!"* For this is being an elementary truth that "The Book" will show you how to experience. Yet is it not also true that we can "scientifically" experience the opposite, an opposite which means that people can live in Hell upon this Earth. Is this truth not realised when they target their minds to do acts which steal or take that which belongs to others, and also when they bully, persecute or harass those they feel are below them, instead of supporting their development towards the love of unity – with ALL things.

So clearly, if many do not believe this truth that the "Kingdom of Heaven is within us and outside us", then it must mean that within our own current lives, we must be creating our Hell in which to live. Therefore can it not be true, said that the signs that you live in Hell are that you accept to live as if in the existence of continuing toil and misery, an existence which Jesus of the Christian Faith refused to accept. The further truth is that people in Hell can dishonour their parents and brother fights with brother and the social contract between guest and host is forgotten. During this false belief system, it is thought that "might that makes right" and in this way ignoring the truth people use lies so that others will think that they are right. Also, when living this life of disharmony, people no longer feel shame or anger at their wrongdoing or the breaking of any beneficial harmony; babies are neglected when born, and it seems that their life has wholly forsaken them and in suffering for within this apathy they find no support to remove the harmony around them which they believe is inflicting them with harm. It is baffling to those who live in Heaven that people can live like this, but honestly, it is a lack of knowledge that they do so, for this kind of life is based upon ignorance. For again this is the ignoring of the truth that rests all around them and woe to those who inflict pain upon harmless others as the Divine Mother always turns Her back to them for She knows that they have been given the "Freedom of Choice" by Godly law or the law of Nature for the non-believer, a fact which She will not interfere.

Simply put, the reason for people's ability and right to the "Freedom of Choice" is because people have been given the gift of three mind-filling patterns, two of which are individually activated by a past or a future "I Want" and the third way being the emptying of the mind so that the Soul can see God's world that only exists in the "Present Time. This truth is those past thoughts remembering things that could have been done and future thoughts are used to possess an "I Want," particularly when it comes to personal losses and gains which is interestingly called "knowledge". Yet actual knowledge of all that exists is witnessed via a non-thought, this being when the mind is in the "Present", which is very difficult to achieve. For indeed this is being because you have no thoughts when the mind rests in the stillness of God's world or Nature's world for the Non-Believer and this is genuinely the Heaven that rests upon our Earth. Again, it should be stated that when this is achieved, it is called "Enlightenment" and it bars all past or future distorted "I Want" for myself thoughts, whose privately based claims take us away from the Heaven that rests only in the "Present Time" which we should naturally live in, for undeniably, it is past or future thoughts that make us attempt to build our happiness on another's misery.

So yes! It is the allowing of birth within the mind of future and past thoughts that the disturbing "I Want" of the five senses continually creates; this is being an "I Want" that can be likened to the proverbial carrot that dangles from a stick, in front of the donkey. Thus, "future" thoughts create "ignorant" acts which give direction to leave the Heaven that rests in the "Present Time".

These are always being negative "I Want" thoughts, this being that which are usually born from the past and which people use to target their future for many live where our thoughts are? Is it not also true that these are thoughts that say, "I Want" and then "thoughtfully" move on to connive how to achieve this personal "I Want", this being an "I Want" that usually belongs to others? For again, is it not also "scientifically" proven that an "I Want" thought is ignorantly pursued because of the fear of losing some personal material, prestige or pure jealousy of what others have? Therefore is it not also true that this "I Want" can be very powerful? Is it not also true that the "I Want" born by the victors of World War One so punished the losers of this war, that within twenty years, it caused World War Two and the deaths of sixty million people with its violence?

So yes! The last words of Jesus, when upon His terrible cross, could have been *"Forgive them, for they live in Hell,"* and not *"Forgive them for they know not what they do."* For indeed is not this personal and group "I Want" that is always the forerunner of a constant way towards anarchy? For indeed it can it not also be said to be true that two thousand years after the death of Jesus, the strong are still bombing and destroying the weak as the surplus strength within the upper Northern hemisphere is being used to attack the people of the host countries. They live in our lower Northern Hemisphere, for it is extraordinary how our war crossing of borders has expanded. Could this simply be because they have different religions which take a different way to God or is it the natural wealth like oil that is held in these countries which the countries of their North are now pursuing, or is it could be a simple "I Want" coming only from the North's armament and oil industries' in their search for profits?

So yes! It is indeed, "scientifically" evident to all that all people can "choose" to live in a Heaven or to live in a Hell, while on this Earth, which is currently our only home. Therefore is it not "scientifically" proven, especially by our wise ancients, that ALL people have the ability and "Freedom of Choice". Does this not state that we can decide, while on this Earth, to either live a life in Heaven which is devoid of the negative claiming thoughts of "I Want", or a life in Hell, with the constant never-ending domineering thoughts of "I Want," more for myself and so creates deeds which target selfish needs? Is it not also "scientifically" known to be accurate, that such contrary "Hellish" acts usually stop people from performing "Heavenly" acts, these acts being that which silently expand the growing harmony of ALL that is around us. Is it not also true that we should support the Divine Mother's on-going repairs which create harmony from disharmony and so live as in the words of the Mother spoken through Jesus: *"Our Father in heaven, hallowed be your name, your kingdom come, and you will be done on Earth as it is in heaven"* – clearly meaning that Heaven is on Earth and that is what ALL people should seek and so enter-into.

25 WHY ONLY PEOPLE HAVE A CHOICE?

The following words will also "scientifically" prove, with substantial evidence, the reason why only people have a "Freedom of Choice," even if it can cause their death or even more severe the death of the harmony in which they exist, this being particularly true when it involves the fracturing of the lives of others. For indeed our history "scientifically" show that people always privately and publically "choose" to exist via a majority need, to successfully prevent any "disharmony" that is emerging or has emerged all around them?

So genuinely do not all our histories show a constant return of people to live within the supporting harmony of the "Creation"? Therefore is it not a truth that the majority of people do not attempt to destroy the harmony of the "Creation", this being that which is evolving or attempting to evolve all around them. So what is it that creates a disharmony that is caused by people?

Like all business developments, can this not be described as a people's learning curve in which training is needed to take part in the company's business successfully? For indeed all people are continually going through many educational and knowledgeable re-births in which they grow from the first birth away from the animal kingdom, with its history of animalistic appetites and without the "Freedom of Choice" and indeed no Soul, and then onwards from this first birth has a person, until our last birth, in which, upon death, our Soul joins the energy of the Creation's harmony, which is exemplified by the realisation of who we are – the embodied singularity of the Creation which is known by our wise ancients to occur when we become "Self-Realised".

So Yes! We are not reborn again but become one with our creator who then experiences "Himself", which is the purpose of the Creation. Thus, all our many re-birthing lives are simply "personal" learning curves, which always show a reality in which it is not good to be indifferent to that which can cause harm to the totality of the "Life" or "Non-Life", of that which exists all around us – which of course is the singularity of the "Self"!

So Yes! This fact is especially actual when our Earth's Godly or Natures Creation, births have a person one of its lower life forms, this being a life form that will need even more exceptional care than the care that we give to ourselves. The "scientific" truth as to why people have been given this "Freedom of Choice" is that a person act can be "Goodly" performed, but under other conditions, this same act could release hurt and discord as if emanating from Hell itself. For it is undoubtedly known to be true that an act can be performed to support the development of a beneficial harmony and accord, while under different conditions, this same act could destroy the emerging harmony?

Therefore, is it not worthy of understanding that this is the reason why God or Nature for the Non-believer, gave people the "Freedom of Choice," a fact-based upon the developed reason that with this "Freedom of Choice" people can assist the Divine Mother's work on the maintenance and acceptance of God's or Natures harmony seeking and ever-developing laws?

Another example of a harmony supporting activity can be likened to a situation, in which we know that trees and deer live in harmony. Still, a deer's antlers can be trapped in the branches of a tree and so this disorganised and trapped deer can only be released by the hands and the "harmonising" thoughts of a person, for indeed, this is why people have been given the ability and the knowledge to separate the clashing discords that can occur when harmony conflictingly occurs around us as it does. Therefore is it not true that we can prevent the many changes occurring mishaps that can occur within all life and non-life and is this not a right and reasonable purpose for all people to have the "freedom of choice" to support life's growing nature?

For indeed it is true that much of the harmony of life and non-life can collide in God's or Natures presently developing world of ever-growing and the ever-moving world of developing "harmony". This being as stated in our scientist revelations about the "arrow of time", a world that people cannot see. Is it not also "scientifically" accurate, as previously stated, that only people have been given the freedom of choice to choose what activity to perform or not to perform? Therefore, what is now becoming interesting is that our scientist are now beginning to identify that something is existing in the "Nothing" that is all around us, but they do not know what it is – but they know it is there.

So Yes! Is this not indeed all people's birthright, this "freedom of choice"? Does it not allow people to choose a correction that will correct the disharmony that can occur in the "Present Time"? Is this not Godly or Naturally achieved without having a thought for God's or Natures' support or the seeking of rewards from the Creation's Divine Mother? Yet what is sadly true, and what must be said, is that many people believe that they are the five senses, this being a condition which creates a truth that the purpose of their life is to pursue their own "I Want," even when it creates disharmony.

This disharmony is indeed being an "I Want" which is an "animalistic effort" set against God's law or Natures law for the Non-Believer. For again is it not true that these five senses constantly and falsely desire to steal from the world their personal "I Want", this being that which they pursue like wild dogs, vigorously chasing after what they animalistic ally "think" that they need for their survival, this being an animalistic preoccupation with physical rather than spiritual needs. Yet is it not also strangely real that all people fully understand the word "selfish" has being a personal behaviour that is not good?

So yes! Anything that helps you to concentrate on "No-Thing" or Nothing, which is also the Non-Believers' word for God is of great benefit to the on-going Creation that exists only in the "Present Time". For it is a known "scientific" fact that only people by the regular pursuit of particular "religious creed" can experience this power of seeing their "self" exist in all things. For it is a "scientifically" proven fact that people can, by silencing the mind, see and realise all around them, the on-going imposed activity of the natural conditions that are controlling the development of the Earth upon which all known life and non-life do live and even how some people are contradicting this natural development. Is it not also known to be accurate, as stated by our wise ancients, that an "Enlightened" person can fully experience all the natural laws, which concentrate fully on the naturally harmonising development of planet Earth?

So Yes! Does this not make Earth's on-going development readily able to be realised as a "scientifically" conceivable ever-evolving fact; this being in the understanding that this development is controlled by a harmonising agent, which "The Book" calls the "Mother of the Creation"? Is it not also true that this harmonising activity pays no particular attention to any earthly based creed or nationality or any person's religious beliefs, but focuses only upon the work needed for this harmonisation, this being only within the developing Creation which also includes requested assistance from people?

For indeed, the Divine Mother not only maintains and aids the developing harmony of the Creation but also seeks aid from people, via their inborn personal abilities which have been developed over many lives. Therefore is it not "scientifically" true that all people have been given different abilities and skills, along with their natural birthright of the "Freedom of Choice" and is this is not a clear and on-going fact that can be "realised" by all people.

Yet, what is not so clearly seen, but can be "scientifically" proven, is that people with many re-births and who are unknowingly experiencing moments of "Enlightenment", are not only "aware" but are also not unsympathetic to the harmonising needs of the world around them. But when "Enlightened", these are the ones who "naturally" live by supporting the work of the Divine "Mother of the Creation", even when they do not know the actual reality of that which they are supporting but know that they genuinely exist only to aid the Divine Mother's harmonising activities. Systematically, this being the supporting of the life of harmony and bliss for all that exists upon this Earth – for if silently requested an Enlightened person will automatically do all that is necessary to support the known activities of the Divine *"Mother of the Creation"*.

So Yes! Is it not also "scientifically" proven that people newly born from the animal kingdom can also "choose" NOT to support the developing harmony that is always expanding around them, but falsely via ignorance; endeavour to support their own animalistic "I Want" and so steal from the harmony pursuing activities of the Divine Mother? Can it not also be "scientifically" proven to be accurate, that these selfish acts "legally" ensure that these self-punishing people live in a self-created mind which is filled with past or future thoughts, this being a self-created disharmony of a living Hell in which these "I Want" for myself thoughts take them? Precisely, this also being while living upon this Earth in which Heaven's love based "Present Time" cannot be realised or be shown to them because of their mind filling "I want" for myself, this being the Hell that all our wise ancients spoke about in all religions and philosophies but were unable to explain because it could not be verbalized in those distant days. For truly it can be proven – as later – that our wise ancients often stated that this "I want" that enters the mind emanates from a village of thieves who have the power to enter a person's mind and so make them do things that they did not want to do.

So Yes! Regularly, this is the mind filling way that genuinely leads to a living in Hell in which our wise ancients stated was because the mind was filled with a robbing gang of people who lived in a particular village and who were called thieves. After all, they refused to support the many charitable endeavours that are required to maintain the harmony that exists within this authorised Earthly Heaven, but which "The Book" does identify has not a gang of mystical people but an "I Want" emanating from the five senses. For logically, there is a Heaven that rests only in the "Present Time", and this is the Heaven that ALWAYS rests upon our Earth and it is a Heaven in which only people can choose to live in or choose not to live.

For indeed, it is those who have had many human lives and who are becoming "Enlightened" and those who are "Enlightened" who naturally support the harmony that is continuously emerging all around them, and so actively support the Divine Mother endeavours and so aid Her on-going need to protect and advance the "Heaven" that genuinely, exists upon our Earth.

So Yes! Near "Enlightened" ones and "Enlightened" ones always acknowledge the on-going "Present Time" and the silent requests of the Divine Mother to freely assist in the further progressing development of the on-going harmony. Still, it is useful to now know well that people always have the "Freedom of Choice", but they can in early births ignorantly ignore these harmonising tasks, which can be likened to moving out of the light that protects you, and into the darkness that does not. For any thoughts that you have in mind are not true, for only that which is aware, this being your silent Soul, obeys and supports the silence that rests in front of you, for only this is precisely truly the kingdom of Heaven that also rest within YOU!

26 GOD CANNOT PUNISH PEOPLE

Thus! This supporting of the Divine Mother's harmony controlling work can be likened to Her giving to you "Sugar in the Water," with water being the life and the sugar its sweetness, but to those who selfishly abandon this work by inflicting cruel punishment upon others for not obeying "THEIR" freely chosen way of living in Gods world. For logically is it not an undeniable truth that God the Father of the Creation cannot punish people to whom He has given the "Freedom of Choice," just has Nature cannot deliberately punish people.

So yes! Indeed God cannot punish people for did He not give to all people the "Freedom of Choice" and so when people punish others for not pursuing "their" particular way of life, are they not also severely punishing themselves in a far worse way. Therefore is it not true that people do punish themselves when they impose their will or their religious way of life upon others. The *"Mother of the Creation"* will surely turn Her face away from them for they cannot be trusted to obey Gods laws because they have chosen - usually by ignorance, to live in an opposing life to that created by God or Nature for the Non-Believer. For indeed, this is a world that exists all around everyone and whose harmony seeking activities are Godly or Naturally "Created" to hurt no-one.

So yes! A group or person is claiming an "I Want" to punish you for not following my beliefs, this is indeed being an activity which fractures this harmony that is always emerging and it is a harmony that is Godly or Naturally created so has not to crash into people's lives painfully. But seemingly and strangely everything emerging around these people who are claiming an "I Want" ceases to give them contented support or protection and so the lead very troubled lives.

Again, this truth can be likened to obeying the harmony of the "Highway Code", this being that which protects the movement of all traffic. For certainly is it not known by all that if you disobey these rules of the road, you will be "naturally" disciplined by many accidents, and so it is when you disobey the Godly or Natures laws of harmony. For has in the example of the self-punishment caused by the incorrect use of the "Highway Code", it is not God's laws that are punishing you, for it is clearly understood that you are punishing yourself when you claim Gods or Natures Creation to be personally yours. For truly knowing and obeying the "Highway Code" that exists around your life also naturally protects the way to your destination, and so it is with all life.

So Yes! Also very "strangely" by knowing and actively supporting the harmony which is all around you can be likened to when you are driving through a city and when you are approaching traffic lights they always turn to green so that you do not need to stop as if your journey is supported – it is this "harmonising" pursuit of a life that leads to what the Russian people call "Sugar in the Water," meaning that God's laws cannot punish you – but they can indeed "reward" you when you follow them.

So yes! It is in ignorance that in the person pursuing an "I Want," people do often blame the world around them for punishing them. In truth, they are punishing" themselves with the question being that if you do not want to support life in "Heaven", this being that which rests upon this Earth, you will undoubtedly progress deeper into Hell, and now the reader knows just what these words mean.

Here again, is proof of the above way of life, spoken by the Divine Mother through the incarnate Jesus and being slightly added to, for further modern understanding, for Jesus said: "Well, who will be the faithful, sensible steward, whom his master will put in charge of his household, this being to give them their supplies at the proper time? Happy is the servant if his master finds him, so doing when he returns. I tell you he will promote him to look after all his property. But suppose the servant says to himself, "My master takes his time about returning," and then begins to beat the men and women servants and to eat and drink and get drunk, that servant's lord and master will return suddenly and unexpectedly. He will punish him severely by sending him to share the penalty of the unfaithful. The person who knows his master's plan, but does not get ready or act upon it will be severely punished, but the servant who did not know the plan, though he has done wrong, will be let off lightly. Much will be expected from the one who has been given much, and the more a man is trusted, the more people will expect of him." Simply put, the household is the Creation and people are the servants who serve the harmony needed within the household. Meticulously, this is genuinely the Creation that rests upon our Earth.

So yes! Happy and Godly rewarded is the person who feeds and supports the harmony of the Creation, but woe to those people who create disharmony by their personal "I Want," for rot and ridicule will be their reward. Now it is good to know well that this saying is VERY dependable and please reader, be wary, for now, you know the way and purpose of God's or Nature for the Non-Believers, dependable Creation.

So yes! It is also good to correctly explain again that you are not punished by God's laws but can be seemingly punished by your ignoring of them. For indeed, the laws that govern the Creation do not single out and punish wrong, or evil actions as a few religions incorrectly state – usually these incorrect statements being used to gain power over others.

So Yes! It should be clearly understood that the laws of the Creation cannot punish you, but neither can the Divine Mother support your wellbeing if you break these natural laws. This disharmony against the will of the Creation can be likened to you wilfully and speedily driving your car into a brick wall, for then you will quickly realise the consequences of your actions, as the Creation's laws of harmony certainly and physically prove their existence.

So yes! As previously stated, it will seem that you are wisely reminded that you are outside the influences of the Creation's harmony seeking acts which do painfully crash into you as you enter a life in which there is no "Sugar in the Water". For admittedly, all around you is the reflection of your chosen way of life. Distressingly, this is being a life that can be likened to the harmonising parable of the red traffic lights, saying "do not enter" or other electrical disturbances within your transport. For if you continuously perform these disharmonising acts, you will then indeed find that the Divine Mother is not protecting you with the support usually given to those who pursue the Creation's harmony seeking endeavours.

So Yes! Life will not be suitable for those who pursue their own "I Want" for me, and we all know this to be a truth, for it continually breaks the harmony that is trying to develop around them and sadly to them, it will seem that disharmony keeps painfully disturbing them.

So Yes! To answer again, the question of how do you feel when you are living in "harmony?" Happily, this is being a joyful living in harmony that is always with the support of the Divine Mother, and it is likened to having the feeling of contented bliss within you, which is opposite to the feeling experienced when driving down a one-way street the wrong way. Also, it is known to be not useful to claim only for yourself this harmony that is continuously and encouragingly developing all around you, for it is best that you just smile and be happy, as you experience the "harmony" in God's "Present" that exists all around you.

The question now is just how you would like to permanently experience this pure feeling of "bliss" that arises within you as you support the harmony that is emerging around you? Is this being a bliss that is likened to seeing those traffic lights always changing to green when you approach them, an act which encourages your journey through life? Would it not be right for you to always experience this "bliss" within you, as you continue your journey through life? Un-worryingly, this is a way that engenders the feeling of happiness, contentment, and pleasure, which is found by the experience of not wanting? For indeed, this "not wanting" condition can be likened to living in "Heaven", while on this Earth and it is always yours to experience – if you want it for you have certainly been given the "Freedom of Choice".

So yes! It is also good to remember that the Creation cannot and will never deliberately punish or wilfully harm you, for the Soul cannot die. You also can "choose" to perform these harmony seeking acts which are similar to all the acts performed within your body, which you eventually leave behind, as you go forward into another Godly re-birth? So, is not the main question arising at the time of your death not only to look back at your life but to ask the question: "Will the Creation's Mother re-birth you into good conditions or into bad condition or maybe your good thoughts are allowed to choose for you?" I do not know, but I think it is right to say that She, our great Mother, has a sense of humour.

27   THE PRINCIPLES OF THE LIVING WORD

So yes! A sounded word from any person vocabulary can be a potent tool for undeniably it is said, "In the beginning was the word" meaning that at the beginning of every activity that takes place emanates from the word, mainly when targeted and exploded into in mind. It was also said by our wise ancients' speakers of the Holy Sanskrit, that every word was spoken by people creates a sound that produces the way of life that they create to exist all around them personally. Therefore, it would be useful to believe that these wise ancients are correct in their saying that every word spoken from any individual is creating the world in which they live, this being a negative or a positive way of life for them. Therefore, is it not acceptable to be true that Harmony seeking actions that are born from a self-created spoken "word" that contains no "I Want" for me will tend to create or support the Harmony of the world in which the speaker lives? Therefore is it not also seen to be true that the opposite of this spoken word, this being the sound that creates an "I Want" for me will destroy the Harmony that is "ALWAYS" endeavouring to be created around everyone?

The third law states that for every action (force) in nature, there is an equal and opposite reaction. In other words, if object A exerts a force on object B, then object B also exerts an equal force on object A. Notice that the forces are exerted on different objects

So Yes! Is it not true that many global wars do prove this to be a fact? Is it not also a fact that the history of the world conclusively shows that after its many wars and turmoil's that some people's spoken words are proven to be continually targeting a harmony that is seeking a peaceful co-existence within all life and also Non-Life? For was it not also a great sounding truth when Isaac Newton's   stated that: "For every action, there is an equal and opposite reaction." A statement meaning that in every action there are two forces created and that the pressure of a newly released force will "automatically" create an equal but opposing force which then makes the two forces double into one. Therefore, does this "scientifically" stated truth not also mean that the sound of a word is also an action; therefore, any sounded word can have a matching or opposing reaction? Is this not true? Even though the action that Newton speaks about is based upon energy and matter, no one can say that their own "reasoning" based spoken words do not produce energy. The real fact is that the spoken word is also an action that can accumulate, dissipate or aggravate the personal energy resting within those that hear the "Word" that is spoken by another. Therefore is not a "scientific" truth that in the beginning was the word? Therefore is it not "scientifically" true that only people have their own "individual" choice in all that they do – even if this choice leads to their death if it is a fact that they want this to be so?

So Yes! Is it not true that we can look back at all our past religious wars being fought because of a gang based "I Want" and so acknowledge that that which people un-provokingly fight and kill for, is not theirs to have? Is it not also "scientifically" proven that we can all look back at the past warring history of the European world and see that these past warring religious factions can be likened to a proverbial stone being wilfully and disturbingly thrown into a lake of nature's still waters?   Can it not then be physically witnessed that automatically and without prejudice, the Divine Mother returns the lake has with all these warring troubles, to the stillness of Harmony that is the birthright of Her only child – the "Creation". Is it not also true to say that the Divine Mother cannot punish the instigators of these troubles for their Godly Father gave to His children the "Freedom of Choice", this being to support the unmoving ever-developing Creation which these children call their home?

So Yes! Is it not true that the Divine Mother must, therefore, turn Her face away from these destroyers of the Creation laws? Is it not also a further truth that the destroyers of these non-harming Godly or Nature born laws are severely punishing themselves and so sadly may not be born again into the world that they have been created to support and care for, this being the ever-continuing natural state of God's world or the world of Nature for the Non-Believer.

So Yes! Is it not also a known truth that this state of calm Harmony is always returned to despite the many personal "I Want" behaviour patterns that crash into and attempt to steal it calmness, this being as people actively but falsely seek to obtain their "stone-throwing" personal "I Want?" Therefore, should not all people "scientifically" know that Creation, likened to the lakes waters, will ALWAYS actively return to that which obeys the laws of the Divine Father which are strongly supported by the Devine "Mother of the Creation"?

So Yes! Is this truth not always witnessed and known to be "factually" correct? For really rightly and honestly, the Creation can again be likened to a lake of water which knows just what law to follow and also which law is not correct. Therefore is it not true that the Creation has been born without choice and so must always obey the laws of the Father, these being natural laws that are always supported and also lovingly cared for by the "Mother of the Creation" who is also fully supported by the strength of the Father love. Therefore again, is it not a glad truth that water like the Divine Mother never refuses to wet any person's Harmony seeking lips. However, the bodily illness can occur, which may bring death to a body that is seeking enhancement but in a re-birth, this being a fact that can be likened to the lake of disturbed water, the Creation will always return all disturbed conditions to an all-embracing calm, which is the living proof that the caring Divine Mother truly exists.

So Yes! What did all those past "I Want" religious and ownership stealing wars between people accomplish? Is this not also a similar question about all wars in which an invading "I Want" did attack another's nations or another's districts or another's religion or another's resources? Therefore is the known answer to these factual events not also the answer to a general question about all the wars of the Northern Hemisphere and probably all the world wars? Is it not also many times wondered who prospers at these wars? Therefore is it not also true that nearly all invaded countries seem to return to their own "language" controlling borders after these conflicts, these being "I Want" invading greed-based conflicts that destroy property and maim and kill many innocent civilians and their children as well as opposing combatants.

So yes! Is it not true that just like the lake that has had a rock thrown into it, the whole of the world's North of the "Northern Hemisphere" has similarly arrived back to its original language borders and again settled into an on-going unity of various habits that are based upon the Creations harmony? Or more simply put, are these wars being caused because people are misusing their "Freedom of Choice", this being a "Freedom of Choice" which sets all people apart from all other earthly species?

So Yes! Are these wars really because people have a God or Nature given "Freedom of Choice"? Is it therefor this given ability to freely choose any activity that also enables only people to targetable change a positive to a negative and is it because of this fact that they are endeavouring to copy the Divine Mothers constant search for Harmony but in their forgetting and forgetting is our worst enemy, and they want it for themselves? Yet cannot it be now seen and proven that "choosing" to war with or create conflict with another country is based upon countries chosen or imposed leaders personal "I Want"? Therefore is it not true that an individual's mistake is to believe that this gift of Harmony is only for their tribe or their country and not for the benefit of all life and Non-Life.

So yes! God or Nature for the Non-Believer gave to all people the "Freedom of Choice" which is a pure endowment. Still, it is also good to know that "In the beginning was the word" and from the word comes an action that "Creates" the "Present Time" and it is tempting to understand that these first words from God were to unfathomable "Space" saying "Will you love me and birth for us, children?" for is this request, not an action to target a "Creation" which is the child of all Life and Non-Life and beautiful life that should not be reduced to a personal "I Want" for ME? If this is a difficult decision for you to make, this being a decision that your activities are really to seek and support the Harmony of all life and Non-Life that exists all around you – if not! Then read on: For if you are knowingly or unknowingly living in this "I Want" for me world, then you are living in a Hell that can only exist in the Past or the Future and not the Heaven that can only exist in the "Present Time".

28   THE GOD WITHIN AND THE GOD WITHOUT

The reader will also find written here that the above simple explanations and the following "time-honoured" truths which are spoken by our great religious and philosophical leaders, are not only to guide people how to follow their significant religions and philosophies but also to show the way to a good (God) life for agnostics or atheists and indeed for life itself. Therefore is it not also true and "scientifically" proven to be accurate, that the Creation started from "No-Thing"? This "No-Thing" being the "Nothing" of Atheist belief which is the same "No-Thing" that "The Book" calls God, therefore is it not true that God is certainly not a "thing?"

For assuredly, this being a "thing" that none of our fives sense will ever be able to perceive, which is probably why many people ignorantly ignore or "fall off" the way of Harmony and into the very bumpy unknown plus very fearing wilderness, this being because "Nothing" is a perception that cannot be achieved by any "feeling" that is "scientifically" attached to the "I Want" of uncontrolled machinations of five senses. But what can always be seen and always understood is that from the very beginning the Creation – upon our Earth - has continued in Harmony despite the many attempts of people to change it. Therefore, does not the Creation history "scientifically" prove and this is without a doubt, that the Creation or Nature for the Non-Believer will continue pursuing Harmony unto its very end, a death which currently cannot be apprehended.

Is it not also an actual identifying fact that some people who have had the gift of many re-births can "personally" choose to accept and support its Harmony seeking ways and so live in the Heaven that exists upon this Earth? Can it not also be seen to be true that some people have not had many re-births has people and so may still be ignorantly living in a controlled by the five senses "I Want" for me world and therefore live in their self-created Hell and so be bypassed by a personal life that could be "Heavenly".

So yes! All people should now know, for it is naturally apparent – that God's Creation or Nature Creation for the Non-Believer has given them a personnel choice to either live in Heaven, with a happy and satisfying life or to live in Hell and be a groaningly unhappy and discontented person plus to be always complaining about their life. But the truth is not this "I Want" for me a painful way of living one's life and also a sad way of living? Is this not truly an "animalistic" living which causes an inner on-going discontentment which is born by an animalistic "I Want" a way of life that personally suits me and not that which suits and controls the world that exists around me? Therefore cannot it now be stated "scientifically" and with substantial evidence that many are asleep to the positive fact that they are living in their self-made nightmare? However, it is agreed that a terrible way of living can be imposed by others – but indeed those who are inflictors of pain upon others will receive their rewards by the echoes rebounding in their living Hell and also the possibility of being reborn back into an animal world in which they have no freedom of choice.

Yet, is it not also true that many people are living in a world in which they are continually transiting between their living in a positive "Heaven" and their living in a negative "Hell" – simply because they do not know what or how to choose in which existence to live? Is this unknowing not a fact which designates them to continually live in a mixed way in which they are harbouring from a good life in the servicing of others or lousy life of harbouring in the "I Want" for me, this being a very different kind of life? Is it not also sad that many religious leaders have no knowledge of the above mixture of a person's behavioural habits and so misunderstand the purpose of praying for forgiveness that is emanating from another person, for is this not just another "I Want"?

Therefore is it not true that this modestly requested "I Want" forgiveness for a past action is just another "I Want" that is seeking forgiveness from a religious leader for a past action done. Is this not also an "I Want" that is the seeking of another's forgiveness and so be allowed by this leader's forgiveness to enter the Harmony of God's Heaven while on this Earth? For indeed, this can be likened to a fully clothed person jumping into a lake of water, and as they disturb the still Harmony of the lake they say, "Sorry water, I did not mean to disturb your harmony" and then praying "but can you please not make me wet!" In the reality of the Creations' purpose, how do these "praying" words affect the wetness of the lake's water and so allow the wet prayer to become dry again? Not by one jot, and so it is the same within the "Harmony" of the Creation, for in the "Present Time" God or Nature for the non-believer, immediately forgives all transgressions for the "Past" does not exist and also it is well known that all people have been given the "Freedom of Choice" unto death. Still, it is interesting to note that in the "Present Time" a person could drown or get uncomfortably wet as the Harmony of the environment smashes into them, like the water of the lake and thus making his or her current situation very uncomfortable – but who is punishing who?

Is the water within the lake punishing the transgressor or simply and obediently obeying God's or Natures law? At this point, I feel the urge is to explain that I believe in God for I understand – stand under – the knowledge that "Nature", this being the totality of the Creation, must have come from somewhere and that this somewhere was certainly "No-Thing".

So Yes! This "No-Thing" is my God, and my many years of business creating experience do ask "What is the purpose of "God's" business?" Then the silent answer that comes to me is that God "desires" to experience Himself, which is probably why our wise ancients do not come back and why all our living wise seek "Self-Realisation" but more about this later in "The Book." Is it not also true that people are often told to pray and so request that they go to Heaven when they die! Logically, this is an extraordinary request for there appears to be a disbelief in the truth stated by most religions and philosophies of the world. This being that you will be reborn again into circumstances that will improve you. It is also an extraordinary belief, which states that when you die your Soul will automatically go to God's world and live in a Heaven or a Hell forever and ever and also to live with millions of your past and future ancestors, for the next five billion years or for the rest of eternity – which is understood to be a place that is outside the Creation; but do not fear, for the apparent truth is that you will soon be returned to do the work that rests within the Creation, this un-wasteful re-birthing fact being so that you can assist the work of the Divine Mother, for God or Nature for the unbeliever, is not "uneconomical".

There are many heavenly conditions upon our Earth that "surpasses all understanding," but honestly, an "I Want" for me is a prayer which cannot achieve a blissful experience for it is a singularity that is without any expanding purpose, for merely put, it is just another "I Want" for Me! Therefore, is it not also true that some religious leaders also pursue this "I Want" for me by stating that you should simply believe their words and repent all your actions. Still, these are words are only an echo of a truth which has been given to all people by our wise ancients. For indeed it correct that it was these wise ancient ones who established all our world's religions and philosophies, and this was because they ALL lived in the "Present Time", and so knew how to bring people to join them in the "Present Time". For they knew that the unchanging never-ending "Present Time" is God's Kingdom upon this Earth, which all people experience as being a "Heaven" but only when their mind exists in the "Present Time" which is Gods created the world and not the world of "Hell" if their mind lives in the past or the future in which the five senses greedily and mind filling do nosily seek a "personal" to the "I Want", for is it not true that any "I want" sounding in mind can be traced back to the sense which is emitting this "I Want" desire?.

For undeniably this sound that occurs in mind is always a greed-based mind filling "I Want" desire which is emanating from one of the animalistic five senses and is a selfish desire in which they seek to feed themselves like a pack of wild dogs. For definitely, a person's way of living does depend upon what these five senses want to experience, these being that which is creating the many "I Want" which self creates a mind filled with past or future desires.

Yes, this is an indisputable fact which is always be occurring in the truly existing "Present Time", which takes the thinker into the non-existing past or future. Still, especially now dear reader, you are no longer ignorant of the required tasks that allow you to seek a "meditational" based harmony which brings a way of "Enlightened" life that exists only when the mind is empty. Without a doubt, this being so that the Soul can see through the empty mind and into the "Present Time," this being one of the "Favoured" ways to achieve the "Self-Realisation" that is preached by all our wise ancients, or you can now choose to live in the "I Want" mind filling self-created Hell which is another way of living in your currently existing life, for truly God or Nature for the Non-Believer gave all people the "Freedom of Choice".

Hence, the above decision is always "Personal", and it can only be made by YOU! Certainly, Every disciplined meditation is the way to bring your understanding of reality into the "Present Time", in which exists the harmonised wellbeing of the world. For in truth, has anciently stated, this is a move towards "Enlightenment" but only if the doer is sincere. It is also well to remember that God or Nature for the Non-Believer has already done everything that needs to be done and He has complete faith in the "Mother," who says to him: "Thine will be done," for She is the controller and carer of all that truly exists. For did not the Mother through Jesus explain very clearly this correctly interpreted truth: "Whoever believes in Him (God) is not condemned, (can live in Heaven while on this Earth) but whoever does not believe stands condemned already because they have not believed (lives in Hell on this Earth) in the name of God's one and only child (which is the Creation). Simply put and therefore, undeniably explained and so to "believe" as in the above words, means that you live in "Harmony" within God's world. So you live in Heaven while on this Earth and to not "believe" as in the above words, mean that you live in disharmony and so live in Hell, while on this Earth.

Again listen to these words as the Creation, the only child of the Mother who speaks to all people through this personalised form of Jesus and who says: "This is the verdict: Light has come into the world, (Harmony) but men loved darkness (Disharmony) instead of light because their deeds were evil (not harmonious and usually based upon a personal "I Want"). Therefore is it not real that God's light or Natures light for the Non-Believer can only be seen in the "Present Time"? Is it not also true that this light that reveals awareness can only exist in the "Present Time"? Therefore does not this "Present Time" light consistently show Gods Harmony or Natures Harmony for the Non-Believer? Logically, therefore is this not because the real you, which is your Soul or Consciousness for the Non-Believer, can, but only with a clear mind, evidently, see and so fully experience the world that is around you, but only if you are silently observing the "Present Time" this being that reality which our wise ancients called "Enlightenment".

Therefore, is it not "Scientifically" understood that it is a mind which is filled and clouded by many a personal "I Want", this being that which creates a non-existing Past or Future and which is a dream that is emanating from one or all of the ancient animalistic five senses. For beyond doubt, it is this which causes a mind filling darkness which stops the Soul or Consciousness for the Non-Believer, from witnessing the "Present Time". This being that current reality which creates disharmony, because you cannot see the "Present" through a clouded mind, this "Present" being that which is gifted from Gods Harmony or Natures Harmony for the Non-Believer? For indeed, the above is possible because it is "Scientifically" acknowledged that God or Nature for the Non-Believer gave to all people, the "Freedom Of Choice", this being to support the emerging "Present Time." Yet truly, many people live in their mind which is clouded by "I Want" selfishly created dreams, this fact being that which takes the viewer into the Past or the Future and this non-existing world being that which "The Book" calls "Hell", for only the "Present" is "Heaven," and evermore shall be so.

Is this not true? Now, again listen to these words spoken by our Creators through Jesus: "Everyone who does evil hates the light, (harmony) and will not come into the light for fear that their ("I Want") deeds will be exposed (for indeed, light is Harmony and darkness is the opposite). "But whoever "lives by the truth" (creates good Harmony) comes into the "light," (lives in the "Present Time" harmony)

So yes, really it can be seen that which all our wise ancients have done, has been done through God. Therefore is it not also stated that only in the "Present Time" can you work via the understanding "Stand Under" God's laws, for they engender Harmony and those who live by Harmony live in Heaven while on this Earth? Therefore, with these truthful words, it can be wisely seen that in any on-going life there is a solid guarantee that the Divine Mother will always see to it that Harmony is always maintained within the Creation. Yes, it is sad but true that many who live outside of Her Harmony will receive back and so be inflicted with the disharmony that they put around to themselves and also to all those who are around them.

So yes! Creed worship, which is religious or philosophically instructed system of beliefs, doctrines, principles, dogmas and particular faiths plus personal prayers is, of course, proper, for they stop the mind filling "I Want" that is emanating from the bodies five senses and also quietly remind us to accept the useful life of Harmony that is prevailing around us, but is it not correct to say that actions speak louder than words?

Is it not also true that you can secretly and prayerfully ask the religious employees of our many variable religions for guidance as much as you contentedly and happily ("I Want")? Is it not also recognised to be true that such Soul searching of religious-based acts may purposely remind worshippers of their understanding of God's Heaven? Still, you can be assured that nothing will happen regarding your prayerful "I Want" words, for the Creation, is perfect and cannot be changed by prayer; thus meaning that any well thought out observation or requesting "I Want" words will not change it.

Therefore, if you desire to experience Heaven on this Earth and so live within the Creation's heavenly Harmony that can only exist in the "Present Time", know well that this "establishing" of an authentic "heavenly" way of life can only be achieved by "you", for only "you" can establish you factually existence in the "Present Time", Gods world which all religions call "Heaven". Therefore, it is only you, as an individual, who can choose your own perceived and disciplined way to live in Heaven, whist upon this Earth. Logically, this is a target that cannot be achieved if it is based upon a personally desired "I Want," this being that which always takes the wisher out of the Heavenly "Present Time" and into the world of "Hell" which can only exist in the Past or the Future, this being the only place where the "I Want" of the five senses takes you.

For no friendly mortal who lives in the Heaven that can only exist in the "Present Time" can bless you as a friend or hate-fully curse you as an enemy for misbehaving against their own personal desired wishes and beliefs, nor can the guardians of our many religions treat you as an enemy regarding actions of the past time for the past does not exist for those who live in Gods heaven, so no mortal can forgive any harmony damaging past deed. In essence, they only "think" they can.

So Yes! Is it not "scientifically" right that you are, as are all people of the Creation, indeed, governed by the natural laws of the Creation that exist only in the "Present Time"? For understandably, is it not true that these Godly created laws only exist in the "Present Time" and so cannot exist in the past or the future, which is truly the world of Hell. But this does not mean that the common agreed law of the community in which you live should be roguishly cancelled. For these people made "Common Laws" which are designed by the majority of people within that community, to support the current short-term Harmony that they wish to operate around them.

It is a truth that doers who rudely break this short-term view of a community's imposed harmonies should be legally reminded that the community is searching to be majority controlled by the various ways of the TRULY signaling Harmony of the unity that exists all around them, for genuinely, this is a harmony that should also be reflected in a governed by people world. Logically, this being a world whose leaders were created by the majority of at least a 60% tom70% that countries people, thus endeavouring to imitate the acceptable Harmony based laws of God or Nature for the Non-Believer, so enduring to make a true harmony to exist within their community.

But this is not the way of the "Mother of the Creation", who's long term views pursue a well-known truth in which the punishment of individuals, for the breaking of the Creation's Harmony cannot judge. Still, they will be immediately ignored, and this is because God's or Natures laws for the Non-Believer truly gave all people the "Freedom of Choice". The Divine Mother's actions speak louder than words and what greater punishment is offered to those people who wrongly pursue a harmoniously damaging "I Want" than the immediate "looking away" and ignoring them by "Mother of the Creation".

Therefore, is it not true that it is the Mother of the family who continually supports the long-term on-going love of the whole of the family and this being an essential fact of great importance? For indeed the "Mother of the Creation" also knows that her wayward child will eventually through personal choice, eventually rejoin Her in support of Her personally "chosen" actions, these being actions that help maintain God's Harmony seeking laws that can only exist in the "Present Time". For The Divine Mothers forgiveness is immediate and naturally obtained particularly when Her wayward child begins to follow the Harmony seeking laws of God or Nature for the Non-Believer and so again begin to perform deeds of "righteous" Harmony for all the life and Non-Life that exists in the "Present Time".

So Yes! Is it not correct that all people should follow the words of the Divine Mother also spoke through Jesus of the Christian faith, these being words that identify a good (God) person? Listen to these words addressed to the stranger who brought supporting Harmony to the man who was attacked by thieves. The Divine Mother through Jesus asked this man: "What is written in the Law?" Carefully, this is the law that maintains Harmony within the Creation. The stranger answered, "Love your neighbour as yourself." To this Jesus informed him: "You have answered correctly, do this and you will live," meaning that the stranger would live in Harmony, for the stranger knew the truth that all the Creation is oneself of all.

Therefore, is this not a truth that within the life we must also immediately forgive people who repent their "I Want only for me" actions, these being actions that have broken God's or Natures laws for the Non-Believer? For genuinely do we not see all around our lives the laws that regularly create Harmony and are these not laws that the "Mother of the Creation" consistently maintains. However, we may have to put such "lawbreakers" under a temporary and friendly "harmonised" protective condition to remove their misunderstandings. Rightly, therefore, is it not true that people should mirror the Divine Mother's work and not verbally or physically punish another's person's actions which are based upon the Godly give "Freedom of Choice"?

Is it not also true that our community protectors should also actively and immediately establish a system that will reveal to those who have forgotten how to live within the laws of their community, a peace-seeking harmony, this being the revealing of the universal laws that exist in their Harmony seeking society? Can this explanation of a sought harmony with all people not be peacefully attained, possibly by supporting those who have forgotten how to live within the laws of their community? This support being for them to live their life within a walled village, where for some time an agreed way of living is shown to be more peaceful and more gainful than the life of a dominant animal that sees everything to be owned by it?

Therefore is it not an absolute truth that all people's lives exist within the Creation that surrounds them? Is it not also true that the Creation seemingly cares for itself within an established harmony which also supports everything that is within it? Is it not also true that we should be able to support each other's endeavours, this being the endeavour to live within a communities' own personally sought Harmony? For truly is this not the same as a creation which lives within the Divine Mother's laws of Harmony – which the laws made by people should endeavour to copy?

So yes! Is it not also "scientifically" accurate that all the people of this world are governed by the laws of the Creation which can only work in the "Present Time", for the past, and the future does not exist? Therefore, is it not also "scientifically" valid that a selfish "I Want" behaviour within a community can be likened to a stone being thrown into a silently calm wondrous lake, which wilfully causes a disturbing ripple? Do these ripples not immediately succumb to being governed by the laws of the Creation, which will always target the lake's return to Harmony?

So Yes! Should not all peoples disharmonising actions be so treated? For indeed the realisation now being identified is a way to stop people from throwing stones into life's harmonious conditions; this being so that there is no personally disturbing rippling of an "I Want" for myself which is claiming the laws of God's "Present Time". Life is useful if you target the "Peace that Surpasses all Understanding," and so return to the gift of life and the contentment that truly, surpasses all understanding – like the stillness in the wondrous lake of life. For indeed it is when you have quieted and so stopped the clamouring of the five senses from rampaging through the mind that you will naturally "see", "feel", "hear", "touch" and "taste" this peace that surpasses all understanding and so fully understand the purpose of YOUR life.

29   FORGETTING IS OUR WORST

This chapter is to give a modern understanding of the real way of life spoken of by our many worlds, anciently created religions and philosophies. It, therefore, endeavours to show all people a modern and understandable way of how to avoid living a life that exists in Hell, and also how to pass on the knowledge that will show all people the way to living in Heaven while on this Earth – which is GOOD and which is also the endeavouring target of all religions and philosophies.

So Yes! The reading of the "The Book" can lead to a new way of life, which can be likened to attaining something like a favourable rebirth for it will reveal a "born again" life that can be lived in Heaven, while on this modern Earth and also within your current life form.

For actually, this undertaking will show the way to the attainment of living in God's "Present" which can be achieved while pursuing a simple, practical exercise, likened to a silent but disciplined prayer. It is also an old and well-proven way towards "Enlightenment" that will show any seeker that they can positively choose to either live in Heaven or to live in Hell, while currently living upon this Earth. It will also personally show each reader how to maintain a new way of living and pure life, for it will give new evidence on just how to live in the "now time", this being of your current body's existence and also during its remaining lifespan. For again, clear evidence will be put forward to show all people that they can recognize and then find out just how to live in the joy and peace known to be Heaven that exists only in the "Present Time, and NOT to live in the turmoil and the painfully troubling world that we call Hell, this being an "I Want" unreal world that can only exist in the Past or the Future. For actually, is it not true, that this is undoubtedly a personal choice and it is regarding that which can only happen in the "Present Time" of your existence. Many will be able to practice this way to "Enlightenment" but only in the

"Present Time" of your current life, and of course many may fall by the wayside, for did not the Divine Mother, speaking through Jesus, say: "They who have ears to hear let them hear." Do you dear readers have ears to hear?

For the question now being asked of you is for you to ask yourself truthfully; is a life that is likened to be living in a peaceful and blissful Heaven your target? For what you will hear is the way of how to live in blissful Heaven continually, while alive on this Earth; this being that which ALL the wise ancients called "Enlightenment" and a life that is the opposite to a life lived in Hell while living upon this Earth. It is the way of using an inner mind exercise which shows how to control the selfish "animalistic" ego that keeps us living a life in Hell. Painstakingly, this being a hell that is likened to living in a house built on sand, for as the Divine "Mother of the Creation", speaking through Jesus said: "Everyone who hears these words of mine and does not put them into practice is like a foolish person who built their house on sand." So those who have ears to hear let them listen.

Now, at this stage, it is also well to remember Shakespeare's Polonius and the last piece of advice given to his son Laertes, which was: "This above all to Thine own self be true, and it must follow, as the night the day, thou canst not then be false to any man." He was telling his son to "awaken" to the Heaven that existed around him. It was a positive message, for is this not the truth that is stated in all major religions and philosophies, for logically, this is that the good life that rests only in the truth of that which can only be experienced in the "Present Time". Precisely, this is truly being the Heaven that rests upon this Earth.

So Yes! Later provided in "The Book", is a simple exercise which will show to any person a simple and practical exercise that will bring to them that which the initiators of all our major religions and philosophies target, this being the ability to witness the true meaning of the words of Jesus and of all our other incarnates, plus all our worlds' wise ancients, many of whom still have great philosophical and religious followers.

Therefore, is it not known to be true that all our wise ancients spoke "culturally" and "factually" a similar story that did sound into the many ears that were born within their environment and to whose words many people throughout the world, even in our modern age, still listen? These were the words from our ancient wise that always contained an absolute truth, this truth is that from the cradle to the grave, all life forms, especially people, are simply a unified singularity and that their current life is just a "work in process" – but to what end?

One thing that all people acknowledge and should always remember about life is that our existing body will always die, but the real you, meaning you as your Soul, will go on for many lives, for indeed your Soul was targeted to emerge at the beginning of the creation. It will undoubtedly be there at the unknown end. For it is only at the end of all time, or maybe before – but more this later in "The Book" - that you will go to that singularity from whence you came. But also it is good to know that you, as a person, will always have God's gift, known as the

"Freedom of Choice", but only if you are reborn as a person and have not been reincarnated back into an animal existence. In essence, this being so that you can learn again how to be birthed as a person for the "Freedom of Choice" in all matters, is not given without taking into consideration serious pre-conditions.

So yes! It is good to live a naturally happy contented way of life and be influenced by God's motivation or Nature's motivation for the Non-Believers, and so be "Godly" supported by the world around you and not be plagued by the constant "I Want" for myself; this being the selfish desire that stabs into the body of the thinker. For it can easily be seen as a truth, that it is only this living in Heaven while in this current life form, that ensures your correct progress through this and your future ever-developing lives. Indeed, the target of achieving "Enlightenment" is a way of life that is indeed shown to be a reality by ancient and modern philosophers who further state that it can be achieved by practising daily creed prayers or ritualistic exercises for a few minutes each day. For actually, this is an exercise which is based upon a procedure that will show you how to live your current life in the real world of "Heaven" that rests upon our Earth, but only in the "Present Time".

So yes, simply put, there is a "Scientific" way to become free and so live in "Heaven", in which you can't be dominated by a constant ever-circling "I Want," which is living a life that can be likened to that of a slave who truly is living in Hell. Therefore, it must be further understood that this chosen "Patent Meditation" exercise which "The Book" later reveals, is an actual "scientific" and personally made "Choice" that eventually reveals the truth resting in God's "Present" or Natures "Present" for the Non-Believer. Logically, this is being that which rests within you and without you. Still, you need to remove the walls called the Past and the Future, these being the worlds that have encased you and also confine you in a living Hell, for again, it cannot be said often enough that there is no Hell or Heaven to go to when the body dies, for your pending next "Un-Enlightened" death is the time when you will leave your current self-made Hell. Still, now it is good to understand that this currently ending life, like all your many past lives, is simply the ending of a life in progress, which is a life used by you to eventually establish entry to a world that is the "Present-Time", this being the "Heaven" in which you cannot sin. For it is indeed also well known that it is upon this re-birth that all the "I Want" memories of our past lives are quickly wiped clean, so it has to allow people to have a fresh start in their new life. Regularly, this is also the reason why the Soul, which is the eternal entity that exists within all people, cannot see the past or the future, which is the world of Hell, therefore is it not true that it is this "Hell" than can only and truly exists as a reality of the "Present Time"? This "Present Time" always being that which our wise ancients targeted for all humanity and when achieved - it is called being "Self-Aware" of the real "Heaven" that you now experience to exists but only in the "Present Time". For indeed this is a journey of reality which can also lead to "Self-Realisation" a fact in which you become – all that exists - and so join with your maker and therefore are never to be born again.

So Yes! Learn to love the Creation of the World, this being for the believer and the Non-Believer, just as totally as you love and care for yourself - for in truth the Creation is you. For really you are the "Self" of all life and you currently live in the only environment where your life can exist, this is being our planet Earth. Therefore and justly, this is the only realisation of the constant messages that have been given to people by our wise ancients via all the major religions and philosophies. It is also well to remember that your acts, these being the ones that pursue our wise ancients; philosophically stated "right actions", are the actions that target and support the emerging harmony that rests within the Heaven that exists upon our Earth. For indeed, it is this stated ability for all people to be able to perform right actions that will make for the doer a happy and satisfied life because these doers truly treat the Creation as if it is themselves. When becoming "Enlightened", you can perform no other act.

For really, these "Enlightened" supports are the practical "right actions," which are actions that are automatically supported by the "Mother of the Creation" who gives an "Enlightened" life to those people who serve Her. This being has previously stated, like driving through a city and all the traffic lights turn to green as you approach them, which make your way through life's journey much more accessible – which has been called "Sugar in the Water" by those who have unknowingly experienced it, plus is also achieving an excellent Godly-placed birth in the next life. But again, it is also important to realise that any harmony opposing acts which are selfishly based upon a personal "I Want" are NOT punished by the Creation's Divine Mother. Carefully, this is because She simply ignores people who live in their self-created Hell, for the Devine Mother knows that God, their father gave them the right to choose their actions.

It is always good to remember that the "Mother of the Creation" lawful work, as it is within all mothers' homes, is to aid and support the development of harmony within "Her" home, this being the Creation or Nature for the Non-Believer. For is it not an absolute fact that a mother will not support nor seek any person's energy which is not useful for their home and its pursuit of harmony. For truly does this fact not rest in most homes? For correctly, there can be no punishment from God's "Wife", just as good parents can never painfully punish a child, but there will also be no "Sugar in the Water" for those who do not support their parents – is this not true?

So Yes! There is undoubtedly a gift of Sweetness that supports a truly guided and harmonious life, which is precisely the opposite way of life to that of a personally made Hell, for indeed, does not this self-made hell always lead to self-inflicted pain that is genuinely stated to be so by all our wise ancients. For all people can encounter the enlightened experience of the "Peace that surpasses all understanding", which is based upon a Truce with God or Nature for the Non-Believer. For definitely this is a "Peace" within one which is always gained by supporting the harmony that is consistently and naturally emanating from all life and non-life, for factually, this is the way of life that rests within the act of being has one with all Godly or Nature for the Non-Believer, practices. It is also an unchanging truth that is available for all of the people who can by accepting good holistic practices "intelligently" find just how to attain this "Peace" that rests within the Creation; this is the peace that simply reveals the ways of the Creation and how to live in God's world or the world of Nature for the Non-Believers. For indeed, the most significant thing for all to understand is in the words that introduce the Christian religion which is: "In the beginning was the Word", explaining that a single "word," like all words, can lead to Godly or Natural right action. Further to this, it is also anciently said that every word that people speak goes out into the world and is reputed by many of the wise ancients to stay there and keep echoing within the "Present Time". It is for this reason that we should make sure that our sounded words are always kind Creation-supporting words, especially when our spoken prayers are for the benefit of others, for correctly it is said that they go out into the world as physical thoughts which are picked up by others – has some of the wise ancients say.

Yes, this truth is well-known by many of the wise ancients, and it is certainly understood to be true that our wise ancients understood a very different type of reality than the one that is a continuously pursued "I Want" for ME!. For indeed, is it not a stated fact that most people do not know that the power of the spoken word manufactures the energy for the said imagery of the words to be created? For actually, there is an excellent power resting in people's words, nor do they not have the power to modify and create changes within the world that rest around these spoken words?

Therefore, is it not reasonable to understand that it is not only your actions that create the life that you control, plus that which your life seeks, but your words also go out into "your" own developing Creation? So, is it not now understand that within this known real knowledge that the question all must ask is: "Do I live a negative life which destroys God's harmony or Nature's harmony for the Non-Believer, or a positive life, which constantly supports it?"

The result of that personal question will be the acceptance or non-acceptance of the purpose of "right action", these being actions which bring acceptance and support of God's or Natures world for the Non-Believer. In contrast "wrong action" always leads to a denial of this real "physical" world, which brings disharmony to themselves and others. It is then; with the answering of this question that you can be assured that you will feel the full "machinations" of the mind filling "I Want" inners sounding words of five senses, as you ponder this question or the silence of the still mind has the Soul sees the true beauty of the world around it even when the body is being inflicted by pain, via the evil acts of others.

At this time in your adult life it is good to remember that if you can hear words or see pictures in your mind, they are not you, for you are the observer, which is the silent Soul that rests within you. For honestly you should now know that the recognising and consciously becoming your Soul within is the anciently targeted truth of all religions and philosophies. For now all know that it is the imagery that the five senses create within your mind, which stops the Soul from seeing and so experiencing the reality of God's "Present Time" that rests in front of you. Therefore, do not forget this fact – for forgetting is our worst enemy. For indeed, is it not a fact that ALL our acts are links that create harmony or disharmony in the world around us? Also is it not essential to remember that doing nothing is an activity? For really, is it not personally identifiable that if they are beneficial and harmonious seeking acts that support the goodness that is emerging around you, then you will receive a constant on-going and developing support from the "Mother of the Creation".

But if they are creation opposing acts which disharmonise the world as you seek your personal "I Want" from your fellow beings, then you will be rightfully ignored by the Divine Mother whose love cannot support your activities? So Yes! Is it not also true that people can unknowingly or knowingly betray the Creation? Is it not true that we appoint governments who only support the needs of a few, and so ignore the needs of the many? Is it not also true that we send our armies into foreign lands, in an endeavour to impose an "I Want" upon foreign speaking people, who often have a different religion, this being an activity that can never be supported by the Divine Mother; Hence, woe indeed to the returning soldiers who will become ill because of what they have seen and what they have been ordered to do to achieve another's "I Want" selfish ends, these being activities which are outside and oppose the pursuits of the "Mother of the Creation" and so do not support or care for her only child – which is "The Creation".

30   THE REALITY BETWEEN THE SOUL AND GODS "PRESENT"

Reality is Gods or Natures "Present" that surrounds all people. This "Reality" is the "Present Time" which is always reflected a hundred per cent upon the lake that consistently reflects all life and non-life into the eyes of the viewer. For truly is it not also this reflecting of the "Present" which can be likened to a similar activity that should be occurring between the Soul and a person's mind. Also is it not true that the mind accurately reflects each person's Soul an echo of all that which is showing in the "Present Time". Therefore is this reflection upon persons the mind not the actual truth of all that is happening in God's or Natures "Present Time".

So Yes! Is it not a factual truth that the Soul of each person is that single entity which is "Observing" all of this reflected hundred per cent truth that can be witnessed only in the "Present Time". A "Present Time" in which the Soul can obediently support the harmony restoring work of the Divine Mother whose loving work is to calm the Creation disturbances just has the earth's nature calms the lakes troubled water.

So is it not the singularity of all truths that it is then that the Soul knowingly and without thought silently commits a person's body to perform harmonising acts, based upon a hundred per cent view of the evolving "Present Time". Precisely, this is true and always will be the "Heaven" that exists in God's world or the world of Nature for the Unbeliever, which is the only world, controlled by the love of the "Mother of the Creation" who "The Book" explains to be God's only wife, for it takes two to make another one.

So Yes! It is with this accurate hundred per cent input of the "Present Times" condition that the Soul silently guides a person's body in an endeavour to activate the "physical" needs that support the evolving way of the Creation's harmony. For it is in this way that the Soul obediently and naturally supports the harmony restoring work of the Divine Mother and this is the condition that our wise ancients endeavour to fully activate, by creating harmony seeking faith-based mind emptying religions and philosophies that always support the Creation's harmony.

For indeed our wise ancients understood that their preached mind stilling exercises of prayers, chants and body imposed "praying" movements were undoubtedly the exact needs for a person seeking Gods world. For our wise ancients certainly knew that a person would be enabled to see the needs of the creation, this being that which existed all around them, but only when the mind blocking animal-based five senses are mechanically disciplined to become silent and so allowing the Soul to see the world that exists all around them, but only in the Present Time.

For rightly this reality is achieved when the Soul is enabled to see the creation through an empty mind, and it is this reality which our wise ancients knew could factually begin when the five senses are disciplined to chant words into the mind habitually. For truthfully, via this mechanical "Praying" repetition of words or actions, a person Soul is enabled to see to through the spaces of the mechanically chanting prayers until eventually, the animalistic five senses are eventually disciplined always to remain silent, thus allowing the Soul to become as one with that which exists all around it, a fact which can only be realised in the "Present Time."

Therefore, know well, that in the beginning, it is this the mind-empty space, this being that which is seen by the Soul between the automatically preached and performed mind filling incantations, that allows the Soul to see, through the spaces between the automatically chanting words, the truth of the creation that existed all around it.

So Yes! It is the Soul, this being that which can only exist in people, that all our wise ancients did endeavour to silently unify with all the singularity of that which we call the Creation, this being that which exists all around each individuals Soul. Therefore, the only purpose of the serving Soul is to act upon the observations which are brought to it by an uninterrupted view – through the mind - of the Creations' possible needs, this being that which enfolds around all life and non-life. For beyond doubt, it is via this – lake like- reflection emanating from the searching for stillness Creation, that the Soul uses a person's body to perform tasks that support the "Mother of the Creation" stabilizing work that can only be activated and so supported in the "Present Time". For again and truly so, it is these harmony completing deeds that our wise ancients called "right actions" and this was because these actions always supported the on-going harmony of the ever-evolving "Present Time."

So Yes! Now the "scientific" question is, how does the Soul, which is operating upon the one hundred per cent reflections of the "Present Time", target these harmony seeking acts if the five senses are blocking and so filling the mind with their "I Want" claims which have nothing to do with the actual reality of that which is happening in the ever-evolving and unfolding "Present Time"?

So yes! How does the Soul see the harmony supporting activity that is needed in Gods or Natures "Present Time" for indeed a person's mind can be likened to a lake that has thousands of stones continually being thrown into it by the "I Want" of the five senses? Therefore is it not wise to understand that the lake can be likened to the mind of a person which, if undisturbed, will reflect a hundred per cent of the "Present Time". Justly, this being a condition which will allow the Soul to fulfil its real purpose which is to aid the evolving work of the "Mother of the Creation" which is the right and only purpose of the Soul and this is also the reason why a person has been given the "Freedom of Choice", for a similar act can create or destroy that which is evolving in the "Present Time".

So yes! Again and bluntly put, many people ignorantly think that the five senses are them! So sadly, it is with this false belief that they allow the fives sense to bombard their mind with a personal "I Want", which can be likened to throwing rocks into the calm lake which are all thoughts based upon the intrigue of many past or future "I Want" desires. Therefore is it not true that these five senses, whose job it is to look after the harmonious needs of the body but only when required to do so, can block the Souls inner view of a clear mind by filling the mind with a never-ending past or a future gabbling "I Want?"

So yes again! Is it not also true that these five senses, whose actual purpose is to protect and enlighten the body's needs as within any animal, do naughtily, behave like five untrained pups? For genuinely do they not fill the mind with their constant clamouring and their constant thinking up of many machinations to achieve their personal "I Want", which with their childhood given "Freedom of Choice", given around the age of three because, as previously stated, in childhood it was mistakenly thought that the animal needed five senses was them!

Therefore in childhood, a person did automatically "Choose" the energy of their "Consciousness" to habitually engage "Willpower" to energise an "I Want" activity that was emanating for one of their five senses, this being a reality which is naturally inherent in all the members of our animal kingdom, from whence we originated. But sadly, this activity blocks the Soul from seeing ninety to one hundred per cent of the real world and so it is an act which stops the Soul from fulfilling its purpose, this being a creation supporting activity for which it was created, but only within people.

Now here is a physical allegory of that which is spoken of here, which is achieved by taking a serious look at the back of your right hand. Now realise that you are the inner Soul and you can see clearly every detail being revealed on the back of the right hand, which is likened to a view being established in the "Present Time", this being the only time in which your hand is being reflected. You can also clearly see in this stillness, any harmonious action that the right-hand needs and which you know that you can "choose" to instigate or not to instigate. Do the nails need cutting or the hand needs cream, or any wound needs healing or is all good, and no action is required?

Now when satisfied by these answers take the left hand and pretend that each finger is one of the five senses and so allow them to tap and scramble rapidly up and down the back of the right hand and noisily move all around it has if playing the piano, this being all over the back of the right hand. Now imagine that the rapid tapping of each left-hand finger all over the right hand is likened to be a thought which is entering the mind and which is automatically emanating from an "I Want" that is coming from the history of the past or maybe the planning of a future "I Want" gain. How much of the back of the right hand can you now actually see?

The question now is, can you make any decision that the back of the right hand is showing you that it needs? No of course not, for you are only fleetingly and very distractingly "seeing" a tiny percentage of the back of the right hand.

So Yes! Is this not an activity which is showing how the "I Want" of the five senses are blocking the Souls view – through the mind – of the "Present Time", for the right hand is being likened to the human mind. For truly is this not a definite fact which is caused because you believe that the finger tapping "I Want" claims of the left hand now modelled to be the five senses is YOU! They are NOT you, for you are the Soul the observer of all the outer body activities that move within the Creation! Another question now is would you like to be able to perform a simple exercise that will eventually but slowly and over time allow you stop the five senses from entering the mind and so enable you to see ninety to one hundred per cent of the "Present Time"? For justly, this attacking habit of the five senses can be stopped and this can be likened to putting the left hand behind your back and so out of mind and this being until you can see one hundred per cent of the back of the right hand. For indeed this fact is likened to the seeing and the understanding of one hundred per cent of the "Present Time"? Therefore, indeed, this is undoubtedly God's world or the world of Nature for the Non-Believer.

For all our wise ancients clearly state and agree that the Soul, when seeing one hundred per cent of the "Present Time" can become "Self-Realised", and it is this which is called by all our wise to be "Enlightenment", that which is a "Self-Realisation" of the oneness of the whole creation. However really, it should be further agreed, that this task not easy to achieve, but as in the left-hand example, if the "I Want" demands to sound in mind recede and so allow the viewing and realisation of over a ninety per cent view of the real world, then this reality brings the "Peace that Surpasses all Understanding" which is that which our wise ancients call "Enlightenment". For indeed, it is when the Soul can fully see over ninety per cent of the "Present Time", this being that which always rests in front of a person, that that person can achieve the experience which all our wise ancients speak about and if you wish to know the simple exercise which will achieve this "Enlightenment" – The Read on.

So yes! It is essential to understand that even the "Mother of the Creation" cannot interfere with the choice to remove or not to remove the conflicting images emanating into the mind from the "I Want" demands of the five senses.

For certainly is it not a recognizable truth that this control is because God's laws give to ALL people a "Freedom of Choice", which is a law that can never be broken. Therefore, it can now be "scientifically" stated that it is because of these mind entering uncontrolled animalistic pursuits of the five senses, which are disturbing the mind like the many stones being thrown into the still lake, that the Soul cannot see that what is happening in the "Present Time", for indeed, this is because the mind is filled by clamouring noise of five senses which are continually pursuing a past or a future "I Want" activity.

So yes! as it has been clearly stated that the reason for this ignorance is because the mind, through which the Soul sees through to the harmonious needs of the "Present Time", is noisily filled by the five senses which are "personally" and "constantly" claiming and clamouring for a past or a future "I Want". Logically, this is likened to living in a self-created Hell while on this Earth. For indeed, it is now very clearly understood that this is the reason why a person's Soul cannot pursue acts that it was created to support, which is to physically aid the Divine Mother who continually works at maintaining the harmony of the Creation which is required for the benefit of all life and Non-Life. This fact is because the personal Soul, which has been "scientifically" proven to be true because it is the observer that cannot see itself, has its view of the Creation blocked by the constant thoughts, pictures and sounds coming into the mind that is evolving from the uncontrolled five senses and which are always and continuously clamouring for an "I Want?" This fact also being because we mistakenly believe that the five senses are us! They are NOT us for we are the Soul the observer of all that is and whose real purpose is to aid the harmony supporting needs of the ever-evolving Creation.

Therefore, has it not been "scientifically" explained to be true that this constant "I Want" that the five senses create in mind, is forever and actively always filling the mind so that the Soul cannot see the truth that is resting within the Creations "Present Time"? Has it not also been correctly, explained that the behaviour of the five senses can be likened to many stones being thrown into a still lake so that it cannot reflect one hundred per cent of that which is occurring in the "Present Time", the real world that exists all around it?

Is it not also a "scientific" fact in which the unreal "I Want" stones' being thrown into the still mind by the five senses, does stop the troubled mind from reflecting the stillness and condition of the "Present Time" - to the Soul? Therefore is it not true that this is because the mind is full of many disturbing past or a future "I Want" thoughts, which like stones being thrown into our still lake makes, it impossible for the Soul to see the truth of the world that currently exists around it!

Therefore can it not now be seen as "scientifically" valid that this ignoring of the "Heaven" that exists around us, is changed to a false "Hell", this being that which is created by the five-senses which are constantly chattering an "I Want" into the mind? For again truly, is this not a fact which stops the Soul from seeing through the mind and so sees the

Therefore, does this not "scientifically" explain why the chattering in the mind of a past or a future "I Want", makes it impossible for a person to physically support the needs of the Divine Mothers work, which is the creating of harmony within the world around them, this being that which exists not only in the body but which should also exist in the world that is around that body?

So Yes! The first question should now be: "What can I do to silence the mind filling activities of this personal and constantly chattering "I Want" coming from my five senses", which is genuinely acknowledging the mind filling activity that is continuously pursuing a noisy over-bearing "I Want", this being that which keeps the never satisfied "thinker" living in a self-made Hell while alive on this Earth? Then the second understanding question should be "How can I live in a world of Heaven while on this Earth and how can I enter the world created by the Divine Mother which is the world of bliss, this being that which surpasses all understanding?

For it can now be clearly and "scientifically" proven that when a person stops the noisy five senses from their ever chattering "I Want" and therefore make the "lake" within their mind "still", they will "automatically" begin to live in Heaven, this being God's world or the world of Nature for the Non-Believer and an "Enlightened" world that surrounds all life and Non-Life. It is also from this position that people will begin, in silence and under the confirmed love of the "Mother of the Creation", to pursue work of unifying the harmony that is continuously emerging within the Creation that exists all around them. For now, the person knows that the task is to support and or expand the harmony, which is always endeavouring to develop all around them.

So Yes! Logically, this is because when the five senses stop their inner chattering of "I Want", the Soul begins to see reflecting from the "Present" ninety to one hundred per cent of the real world that exists around their body. It is only then when the Soul sees reflected into the mind precisely what is happening in God's "Present Time" or Nature's "Present" for the Non-Believer that the Soul can see those harmonising tasks which the Soul can silently engage with, via the body; these being the physical tasks that are needed to support the on-going harmony which also aids the work of "Mother of the Creation". For assuredly this is the living in Heaven which all the wise ancients speak about and in which they also live and so honestly state to all their listeners that this is the "Enlightenment" target that they request all people to achieve. It is then, while living in "Heaven" upon this Earth that it can be "scientifically" verified that the magnetism of harmony for all Life and Non-Life becomes the primary "attractor" for all those people who live in "Heaven" while upon this Earth.

So Yes! It is then with the peace within the mind that surpasses all understanding, which is a peace reached when the five senses are silent, that people will see the reality of God's Heaven upon this Earth, for it is then that the Soul will "automatically" engage the body in the supporting of acts that develop the Godly harmony that exists in the "Present Time" which is the time that exists forever around them. Regularly, this is the living in Heaven while on Earth, for it is an experience easily recognised as a harmonious way of life, which supports all life and Non-Life that actively exists on planet Earth.

So Yes! To expand the last chapter on "The Reality between the Soul and Present" which explains just what reality is and what reality is not; it is good to understand that the only purpose of the Soul is to support the harmony creating activities that are continually occurring in the "Present Time", this is being the real world, which is governed by God's laws or by the laws of Nature for the Non-Believer.

To do this, the Soul needs to fully observe ninety to a hundred per cent of the Creation, which is being presented to it but only in the "Present Time". Again it can be said that this can be likened to a great lake of still water, which accurately "sees" reflected upon it at least ninety to a hundred per cent of the environment upon which it exists. The comparison of the lake to the mind is that the lake's ninety to a hundred per cent view of its environment becomes useless when many rocks and stones are thrown into it, and this is what also happens to the mind when the five senses throw into it their many "I Want".

It is this fact that stops the individual's Soul from seeing the needs of the creation that are reflected in the mind of the viewer, and so the viewing Soul is unable to support the harmony that rests within the "Present Time". Therefore the importance of meditational work is to understand that these five senses are not you; for you are the Soul who needs stillness within the mind, to relate what is happening in the "Present", this being the ninety to one hundred per cent world that you "see," and which exists all around YOU!

So Yes! Just has a reminder, the five senses need to be like well-trained dogs which become activated only when you request them to do so, and if you would like this to be exact – Read on. For correctly, it is the very active but uncontrolled five senses "I Want" problem that removes you from living in Heaven, while on this Earth, and makes you live in Hell, while on this same Earth? The simple explanation is that you do think you are the five senses and the reflecting reservoir, which has been likened to water resting in mind, is continuously being bombarded by words and "feelings" as the five senses always target a THEIR "personal" and potential "I Want". If you do not believe these words, then try now to sit in silence and to have no words sounding in mind?

Then you will also find the truth that it is your inner Soul that actually "observes" these constant demand messages from your body's five senses and even "observes" how they answer and argue amongst themselves? Also, because of this belief that these five senses are you, you allow them to voice their own "personal" opinions which you then think are yours? They are not yours, but they can be likened to wild dogs barking out what they want, for really and conclusively - how you can be that which you observe.

For is it not known to be true that you cannot be that which you "observe" or "witness". Therefore is it not true that this reality, this being the noisy words or pictures in your head is the noise of the five senses that are continually chattering or arguing amongst themselves? Is it not also true that you always bear witness to their arguments, and also silently listen to their chosen diverse ways in which they target a personal "I Want," to achieve their targeted satisfaction   and   they   are   NEVER   silent?

This situation can be likened to a person going into a restaurant filled with many customers, and they are all talking and shouting about the menu, or they are all noisily requesting "I Want" orders – and you think that they all are YOU! They are not YOU! For YOU are the single observer or listener of this noisy activity taking place and you cannot be that which you observe, or hear, or taste, or touch, or smell, is this not true? Now take a look and touch your hand! Is this YOU? If you say YES! Then chop it off and throw it away, now where you are? For indeed, the most crucial fact that you must now understand is that YOU are the Soul, which is the "Observer" and manager of the "restaurant" which is your body and your task is to bring silence to the room in which you work and also to support that which is in front of you, and also be the manager of these servers which are the five senses, so it is necessary to train them to carry out your instructions, according to your budget silently. However, your inner working servants have never received any disciplined training whatsoever – until now.

So yes! The above story shows clearly that this personally targeted "I Want" is coming from the many an "I Want" which is originating from the animalistic five senses. It is also this fact that makes a person act in just the same way an animal's act, which certainly has no control over the needs of their "I Want" senses. Therefore, many people live in ignorance of the knowledge that they do have the ability to silence this "I Want" noise emanating from the five senses and so filling the mind with their clamour. This clamour is undoubtedly being a pressing "meditational" need which is required to silence their worst inner enemy, this being an enemy that they have "allowed" to fill their mind with their animalistic "I Want".

So Yes! Is it not also a fantastic fact that these five senses which have been given a voice, do argue with each other and also never listen to or support the "Mother of the Creation", who is the real manager of all that, supports God's or Natures laws for the Non-Believer, in which people have been given the Godly or Nature has given the "Freedom of Choice" to aid Her work. Therefore, is it not in ignorance that many listen to and obey the "I Want" for ME of the personalised five senses, which they believe is really "Them" and that their "I Want" is their personal "I Want"! Painstakingly, this being a false acceptance for it is not true is that the five senses are not you! For you are the observing Soul and the five senses are just instruments for your use. For correctly, this is because you cannot be that which you observe – and indeed is this situation not known to be a "scientific" fact?

So yes! Is it not also a "scientific" fact that from this time onwards, you will "scientifically" know that your Soul is a manager acting within and so supporting the Creation which can be likened to being your customer and that your future "work" is to stop this noise that is continuously emanating from the five senses, a noise that is splattering upon the mind, and so blocking the current Creation's presentations to the Soul?

When you achieve this "Enlightenment" and you can, you will join with the wise ancients who are the originators of all our religions and major philosophies, because you will understand that, by the reading of these words above and the following modern produced words, just what it was that our ancient enlightened "managers" targeted; This is the living in Heaven while on this Earth, which can only be in the "Present Time" and this is called being "Enlightened."

So Yes! Now, if this revealed knowledge is to be "Self-Realised", you must personally "CHOOSE" to do the "work," which is to manage unto their silence, the five senses which are your workers that plague you. For this is your managing "work" that will take you "scientifically" from living in a discordant Hell, while on this Earth, into living in the harmony of Heaven, while on this Earth.

So Yes! This continuing and on-going "Choice" to seek and achieve "Enlightenment" is only necessary if you wish to achieve the task of the silencing of the "I Want" of five senses and so to live in the ever peaceful "Heaven" while on Earth. For indeed, has all our wise ancients state, the people who wish to seek this truth simply need to continually remember that they have been born with personal "CHOICE".

So Yes! The "CHOICE" now is "Do I want to live in Hell or to live in Heaven, while on this Earth? For it is also well to know, that if you want to live in Heaven, while on this Earth it is good to be warned that the five senses will habitually in all ways, endeavour to stop you. But do forgive them but teach them to reach silence, for they are like untrained puppies and they know not what they do. So it would be kind to treat them like five puppies with an added discipline to come to your heel and be out of sight when you command them to do so, and if you wish to know the simplest way to achieve this – Read on.

31   THE FIVE SENSES ARE NOT YOU

Regarding the five senses of which we now speak: in ancient times around 600 BC, it is known that the "five senses" were spoken of in a Hindu literature that is called the "Katha Upanishad", which comprises five compelling philosophical writings.   These writings contain texts of many of the central philosophical concepts of Hinduism, some of which are shared with Buddhism, Jainism, and Sikhism. These Upanishads are also considered by Hindu followers to contain sayings (śruti) concerning the Nature of ultimate reality (Brahman) and describing the character of and path to personal salvation, (mokṣa or Mukti) now known in the European North of the Northern Hemisphere as "Enlightenment."

In these ancient writings, the five senses are explained not as being inside the body but instead; they are likened to five horses pulling the "chariot" of the body, which was guided by the mind, which was the "chariot driver". In other words, the five senses were not of the body but existed as an aura around it. Also, Buddhism and other Indian philosophies identified the personal senses to be six external objects described as being 1.visible forms. 2. Sound. 3. Odors. 4. Flavours. 5. Touch and a sixth sense that Buda said were composed of mental objects all of which lived in a village, this being very different from the modern world's identification of our internal "animalistic" five senses.

So Yes! In Buddhism, the "mind" is said to be also a sense organ, which interacts with sense objects that Buddha says include sense-impression, feelings, perceptions, and abuse. It also seems that Buddha knew of the problem that people believe that they are the senses; for in his famous "The Vipers" discourse (Asivisa Sutta, SN 35.197), the Buddha likens these external senses to be living in a separate village and that they should be quiet and non-active – which is how "The Book" explains the condition of "Enlightenment."

The Buddha also explained the world of people, by stating: "If a wise, competent, intelligent person examines the village it should appear abandoned, void, and empty" – meaning as stated in the previous chapter that they are still. This stillness and un-claiming can only happen when the beholder's five sense are hushed and without input, and the mind is fixed on the "Present Time", which is the personal existence which "The Book" does akin to the word "Enlightenment.

Then the Buddha also explained the world outside of a person body by saying, *"In the village lives-plundering bandits"* who are explained as being the five senses and with the body being another sense-making for Buddha six "external" senses which lived outside the body and so Buddha stated, *"The eye is attacked by these bandits by showing it agreeable & disagreeable forms. The ear is attacked by agreeable & disagreeable sounds. The nose is attacked by agreeable & disagreeable aromas. The tongue is attacked by agreeable & disagreeable favour. The body is attacked by agreeable & disagreeable tactile sensations. The intellect is attacked by agreeable & disagreeable ideas"*.

This ancient interpretation means that the individual is not attacked by an inner personal mind thinking "I Want," which is a modern understanding, for Buddha anciently states that the attraction that is evilly attacking people is something emanating from outside their body and that the world around them is separate from the modern thinking of an "I Want," this being that which is emanating from a person's animalistic five senses, this being recognised by modern understanding. This story also indicates that Buddha was "Self-Aware" which, means that He knew He was that which He looked at and which He experienced.

Now, listen to this massively profound statement that came from the same collection of discourses (SN 35.191) in which the Enlightened Buddha and his Great Disciple Sariputta born 568 BCE, which does clarify the above discourse. Buddha stated that the suffering "I Want" inflicted upon a person came from "outside" the body via stealing bandits that lived in an unknown village.

Therefore a person's suffering was due to the attacks of these village-plundering bandits, for these "villagers" were regarded by Buddha as a separate entity; these indeed not being the "attacking" modernly thought internal five senses of a person, but an attacking six bandits that emanated from the outer world. Buddha's Disciple Sariputta also introduced the third concept by stating that it is the outer, via this village of bandits, that is attacking a person's inner world because the outer world's "fetters" have been released; by a condition identified by disciple Sariputta as "desire and lust," explained in "The Book" as a selfish "I Want," which simply and modernly means that a desirable "I Want" can arise when there is contact between a person's sense organs and an outer object. In essence, this being anciently described by Buddha has the meeting between the inner and the outer world that existed around all people.

For certainly Buddha did pursue and teach a meditation system which is called "Satipatthana", which can be explained has the meaning "Sati" which is "attention" and "Pat" meaning "inside" then "Thana" explained has "keep", this being how Buddha's explained the direct path to realisation in which no mantra is sounded but which "The Book" states is a reality in which the Soul is observing a still mind.

Simply put this means "attention inside keep". It was in this "attention inside keep way" that Buddha showed the need to keep your "consciousness" silently inside you, like a tortuous moving into its shell and away from the outside world. It is then that "The Book" modernly states you can silently target the awareness of your body-weight upon the chair, for nothing else exists. So eventually you will never leave the experience of gravity holding you in its loving embrace, and this meditation will become like a training exercise, which can be likened to going to the gym. Also and yes, in the beginning, your mind will automatically fill with "I Want" words which "The Book" says are habitually emanating from your five senses. Still, now you can silently command them to stop their sounding into the mind by the words "Not This", which will stop them for a while. For indeed, this will continue for some time for these is that which "The Book" likens to be that which is being sounded by untrained pups but which are really "I Want" demands that are emanating for your five senses, but they can be trained to become always silent. Simply put, this ancient truth is also further explained by Disciple Sariputta who stated that you could "fetter" or release the "fetter" of these "attacking" external bandits that are coming from an outer world and Sariputta further explaining that these attacks can be stopped and this was written about 2617 years ago.

So Yes! What is now being modernly and supporting explained in "The Book" is that truly the "fettering" of all attacking "I Want" leads to "Enlightenment," this being a life that is lived in the "Present Time" because the past and the future of any incoming "I Want" is "fettered." This modern statement about controlling the five senses and so experiencing "Enlightenment" was also willingly pursued many years ago.

Now the known modern history of the five senses, which had no recognition in the above, mentioned ancient times, is stated to have begun in the mid-twelfth, lasting till the mid-sixteenth century. This timeline is justified, because little evidence survives for a modern study of a person five senses, before this date. It was then that the sixteenth century witnessed profound changes that radically altered people's attitudes towards the five senses, for it brought to the public a spoken knowledge that Sight detects colour and light, that Hearing detects sound, the Smell detects scents, and that Taste recognises sweetness plus salt or that which is sour or bitter and finally Touch was that which detected pain, pressure, heat and cold. It was only then that people were informed that each person has these five sense organs, whose job it was to gather this information that can only be experienced in the "Present Time" and thereof send these experiences to the brain, which then processed the information to which the body responded. It was also at this time that they also believed that all five senses were potential gateways to corruption and sin and that they were aflame with lust, hate, and delusion. It was also thought that perhaps the sixteenth Century Christian "reformation" war between the Roman Church and Protesters may have had something to do with this introduction of the five senses, for it was also the period which encountered witchcraft hysterics and responded with the subsequent thousands of religious executions all based upon hearsay and a pointing finger that was attached to gossip with no corroborating evidence, a system of appointing guilt and punishment that still legally exists within England's laws.

So Yes! Now, in this modern time, it is essential to remember that the five senses are not you; for sure "You" are the inner Soul which observes everything that rests within the Creation. Your five senses are just tools which are used to evaluate and also care for this outside world. For this is the new truth which all our wise ancients were unable to speak about because in their time, this knowledge that the five senses were just the servants of people – was unrealizable in those ancient periods. It was also because of this fact that ancient history could not say that you were not the five senses or that they were just regarded as instruments for your use. For indeed this mistaken view was known to be replaced in the sixteenth century, and after that, all knew that the five senses were attached to the real you; which is explained in "The Book" as not being right, for real, you are the Soul.

But sadly it appears to be an on-going fact that this old allegation that the five senses are the real you, now keeps a person living in Hell while on this Earth. They also could not say, at that 16th century time, that if you wished to live in Heaven while on this Earth, you had to understand that you were indeed the Soul, this being the true you that observed and also whose task was to support your "outer world", which can be likened to that reality which supports your "inner world".

Meticulously, this also is a world that certainly reflects all the harmony seeking needs of the Divine Mother's environment, in which She knowingly needs the support of the individual Soul, to aid Her work – why else do you think that you are alive? Also, it could not be repeated at that ancient time that if you wished to experience Heaven while on this Earth, you need to "fetter" and make silent the chattering claims that the five senses always make in your head for has the Buddha did say *"believe that the village is abandoned and empty,* and this "Village" is your mind, so for those who have ears to hear – let them listen, for the Buddha is speaking about "Enlightenment"?

So yes! Is it not also true that many of our wise ancients' unknowingly attempted to teach a way to control and or silence the five senses, by introducing various prayers, such as the *"Sermon on the Mount,"* spoken by the Divine Mother through Jesus. Now listen to the real truth reflected in this prayer which, because of the above writings, you will probably understand for the first time: *"Our Father who art in heaven"* (God is with Heaven, and we are all around us, and we call it the Creation or Nature for the Non-Believers). *"Thy kingdom comes"* (This means that the listener can achieve living in Heaven while on this Earth). *"Thy will be done on Earth"* (living in Heaven means that you support the needs of harmony and not a personal "I Want" coming from the five senses which you believe is You, for they are NOT you! For you are the observer of all things), *"as it is in heaven"* (Heaven is the striving harmony, wisdom, and balance that are all around us). *"Give us this day our daily bread",* (This food is all the needed "physical" harmony performing acts that are required to maintain the way of harmony.

This food is the wisdom and balance of the evolving way of the Creation. This food also is personal acts that are needed to support the work of the Divine Mother, who is the space within and without all that, exists and in whom God planted the seed that gave birth to the Creation and who like all mothers, cares for the "harmonious" wellbeing of their only child – this being the Creation).

"And forgive us our debts, as we forgive our debtors" (The past and the future have gone for when living in Heaven; only the present time exists). *"And lead us not into temptation but deliver us from evil."* (The temptation is the "I Want" that comes from the unfettered five senses and our delivery from evil is to make them silent so that their disharmony-seeking acts cannot be heard and not pursued). *"Do not store up for yourselves treasures on Earth, where moth and rust consume and where thieves break in and steal"* (This false "storage" can only come when you obey the "I Want" of the animal-based five senses, and this "Heavenly" request is not to do this). *"But store up for yourselves treasures in heaven, where neither moth nor rust consumes and where thieves do not break in and steal"* (With the five senses meditation alley controlled and stilled and your mind is quiet, your Souls natural behaviour pattern is to peacefully complete acts that bring to all the "treasures" of the world which is Heaven.

Thus, this is the supporting of the harmony that is all around you which no one can take from you even unto your death). *"For where your treasure is, there your heart will also be."* (Is your treasure in the "I Want" gathered by the five senses or in the "bliss that "surpasses all understanding", which is undoubtedly a life lived in harmony, for indeed this is the Heaven that exists upon this Earth – so You must know where YOUR treasure is). *"No one can serve two masters"* (You cannot serve the five senses and serve the needs of the Soul; whose task is to develop the harmony that is all around you). *"Either he will hate the one and love the other, or he will be devoted to the one and despise the other."* (Which do you love? The separating "I Want" of the ever-demanding five senses or the singularity of the harmony that exists or is seeking to exist in the "Present Time" which is always in the world around you –For indeed you have the freedom of choice), *"you cannot serve both God and Money."* (This truth means that you cannot serve the "I Want" demands of your five senses and also the harmony, wisdom and balance-seeking acts of the Heaven that always exists all around you).

So obviously this "Sermon on the Mount" statement means that if you want to live in Hell. At the same time, on this Earth, follow the demands of the five senses, but if you want to live in the real world of the Heaven that is all-round you – pursue harmony in all things and so silence and "fetter" the "I Want" of the animalistic five senses. And is it not also said, "In everything, therefore, treat people the same way you want them to treat you…" The truth, known by all those "Enlightened ones" who live in Heaven while on this Earth, is that they know that all people are themselves! Yet honestly, many have forgotten the fact that there is only one child, and this is that for which the Divine Mother cares. Is it not also wisely said, *"Love thy neighbour as much as you love yourself"* this statement being because they are also really "you".

Also, Jesus did wisely say - *"Take no thought for your life"*, this being a resounding blast against the five senses. Then further saying, *"take no thought for your life re: 'What shall we eat?' or 'What shall we drink?' or 'What shall we wear?' For the pagans run after all these things, and your heavenly Father knows that you need them."* This saying is so very well-known and so can be modernly interpreted to be now fully understood. For the "Pagans" are the five senses and their noisy "I Want" claims are always seeking ways to take and steal from the Godly providing harmony that is all around people. For did not Jesus carefully state, *"But seek first his kingdom and his righteousness, and all these things will be given to you as well."* The kingdom of righteousness in which all needs are provided for you is always in the harmony that exists all around you, for Jesus is undoubtedly describing the reality of the "Present Time". But if these needs are not around you! Then some personal "I Want" is controlling the world that is prevailing all around you and also may even be within you.

So yes! And finally, *"Therefore do not worry about tomorrow, for tomorrow will worry about itself. Each day has enough trouble of its own."* For certainly is this above message now wisely saying that you should live in the mind silent "Present Time", for sure it is true that the future and the past do not exist and that only the "Present Time" exists. Indeed this is being the only place where people can support the harmony ensuring work of the Divine Mother.

So Yes! Is it not true that all these above heavenly spoken words are not just subjections but that they are an actual reality? For truly is not the most significant step towards leaving Hell and so being able to start to live in Heaven, while on this Earth, is that you have to inwardly and personally "CHOOSE" to do so and to continually "CHOOSE" to do so, for it is essential to know that the untrained "I Want" emanating from your five senses will fight to stop you from knowing this great truth. So it is good to obey all the above words and "fetter" them. For indeed all this living in Hell happens because the mind can be likened to a filing cabinet, which contains our past thoughts and the dreams of a possible future. It is these thoughts from the "past", or the "future" which capture you and the animalistic un-controlled Nature of the five senses makes you think that without this personal "I Want", you will drown in misery. In essence, this is living in Hell, and it is also good to know that you are also living in this Hell when that stored past and future "I Want" claims are unconditionally bombarded into your cognitive mind by anyone of the five senses, as they target their individual "I Want."

So Yes! They can do this with high strength and then in "thinking" that this is you, you vigorously allow the body to pursue them as if they are essential needs just as our lower animal does, but are it not true that this is because they have no "choice" but to pursue their mind filling demands. Also, it is this constant search for past or future "I Want for myself" that causes you to "forget" who you are and this "forgetting" is your worst enemy, for this truly is the living in a self-made Hell, yet truthfully if you wish to "knowingly" live in Heaven while on Earth, you must silently "CHOOSE" to do so.

So yes! It must be fully understood that you are the Soul which sees the reflections of the "present" coming from the outer world, and it is most important to understand that the Soul cannot see the past or the future, for they do not exist. So correctly, the Soul can only see the "Present Time" in which it performs by the use of a person's body, the various acts which support the harmony, wisdom and balancing activity of the Divine Mother – this is living in Heaven.

For correctly, this is because it is a well-known fact that the Soul, which can be likened to the "Holy Spirit" in the teachings of the Christian religion, can be that which silently observes the outer world in which it is the centre. So it can physically experience that which is described within the Christian religions as "The peace that surpasses all understanding". In the Islamic religions "a realm beyond the ability of words to convey properly," and also from our wise ancients, who described it as being "Filled by the Holy Ghost," or the "Holy Spirit" also called "Paradise," "Nirvana," "Moksha," Kenshō, Bodhi, Satori, Kevala Jnana, Ushta the "Prophet Gabriel" and many other names used by our wise ancients and in the many religions and philosophies that they established and if the reader wishes to achieve this – Read on.

So yes, this is true, the experience of "Enlightenment," which you cannot make or find because it is within you. It is a liberating experience acclaimed as being like living in "Heaven." At the same time, alive upon this Earth and which is realised by joining with the stillness of the "Mother *of the Creation*"," which genuinely gives within the experience of "Enlightenment" full comprehension of any situation.

So yes! We can live in Heaven while on this Earth, and this is that which all the wise ancients speak about and which can be abbreviated to the word "Enlightenment", which is also an experience which can lead to becoming "Self-Aware". For truly becoming "Self-Aware" is an experience of the living in Heaven while on this Earth. Still, sadly our wise ancients could not "scientifically" speak about the claims of the five senses, for it was a terminology that would not have been understood in those ancient days.

But what they all spoke about and described in many words, were the systematic ways of installing praying "creed" mantra systems that would subdue and disciplinary control the barking "I Want," that was seriously plaguing their followers. For rightly, what all these wise ancients were trying to teach is that it is only the Soul who knows how to change "harmoniously", the activities within the "Present Time". Precisely, this is the "Enlightenment" that a repetitive concentration of prayer can sometimes reach. For indeed, it is only the Soul that can pursue correctly and impartially the needed harmony seeking acts, that it is observing within the harmony seeking needs of the Creation.

So yes! At any time in our lives we can learn how to "observably" via the Soul, bring the mind and the body into the "Present Time" and in this way, enable the Soul to act via the "Present Time's" reflected needs upon the Soul and so assist the Divine Mother's constant development of the emerging harmony. For controlling and "fettering" the five senses are the exact way and practical way to realise the way to live in Heaven on this Earth, and so enjoy the true harmony brought by the "peace that surpasses all understanding," this being that which is called by our wise ancients, "Enlightenment". For indeed, this is a state of being that can only be achieved by people because they have such an advanced Godly or Nature for our Non-Believers implanted Soul, which our lower animals and other life forms do not possess. For again, it is only people who have a Soul which has been with some people for thousands of lives and so it is good to know that it is only the Soul that can understand, acknowledge, and with much experience, know how to react according to the needs of the "Present Time", which is God's world or Nature's world for our Non-Believers. Therefore, and justly, a person's soul cannot exist in the past or the future for only the "Present Time" is that in which it can exists.

For is it not known to be true that our scientists say that everything came from "No-thing," which is my God or that which is named has "Nothing" by our Non-Believers. Therefore, is it not also important and may be useful to have a silently happy satisfied mind that can contentedly view all that is around it?? For a happy mind is a contented silent mind, which allows it to exist only in the "Present Time", and which always brings contentment when it lives within God's or Natures "Present." For rightly, this is because in the experiencing of the "Present Time", there can be no "I Want," which is based upon past or future thought, for in the present you realise that your Soul already has everything that is needed and that it cannot be added to, even unto the death of the body.

But Yes! It is good to be happy to be alive and to be an active person who always without thought supports the on-going harmony that is all around the personal Soul and even when evil others who are seeking their "I Want" punish you, so then what do you do? What many of our wise ancients quietly proved was the truth that in a state of harmony there is nothing that can change the peaceful reality of a Soul being unified with the Creation and no matter what Roman Arena you are pushed into, you can silently and contentedly "choose" to accept being nailed to a cross, or to be the lion's next meal – and so enter your next "GOOD" (GOD) life peacefully and gracefully, for the Soul knows the truth in that it cannot die.

So Yes! These writings endeavour to show the way for all the Earth's new "practitioners," these being those who are seeking the "peace that surpasses all understanding," and thereby realise the practicalities of "Enlightenment". For indeed there are words later being described in "The Book" that will reveal just how to control and so silence the five senses and so obtain a life of bliss and harmony, which was always the aim of the ancient originators of our major religions and philosophies.

So Yes! These ancient but now modernised messages contained in "The Book," is enlightened-based writing that explains via modern understanding, the knowledge of how a straightforward self-imposed exercise will take a modern person, who is currently living in Hell, to be able to shackle the five senses and so live in Heaven, while alive and living on this Earth. These writings within "The Book" will also reveal some false creeds that have been promoted by a modernised but misunderstood false "I Want," of some leaders, this being a false "I Want" which has become an imbedded "I Want my religion to be more powerful than your religion", a fact which has changed some of our ancient religious teachings, this truly is an "I Want" that did not originate from our wise ancients.

So Yes! It is now truly and modernly known that the regularly mentioned way of reaching a state of personal "Enlightenment", which is the illumination of the real Creation, this being that which is targeted by ALL our ancient wise, is by quietening and then personally stopping the inputting of any mind filling and personally sounding "I Want", this being that disturbance which is emanating from one of the five senses. For indeed, has the new and old practiser will find, this Patient Meditational activity also "prayerfully" and modernly advances into a pure singularity many of the world's religious and philosophical "creed" teachings – this primarily being a modern development to many people of the Northern Hemisphere.

For honestly some of the practices of our modern religion no longer emanate from the "Holy" one who "Enlighteningly" birthed their particular religion. Carefully, this being a new religion which was designed for their people to pursue and so it was culturally based upon a God-fearing very religious way of life, which sadly changed after their founder's body departed from our Earth. For genuinely new modern leaders began to pursue personal "I Want" changes which later ignited disagreements and war between their followers has all abandoned their religions original harmony seeking effort to show a way to experience God's "Present" to all people, this being the "Present Time" which can be severely contaminated by an "I Want" that is controlled by the Past or the Future, this being that which "The Book" calls "HELL".

Therefore, a new "practiser" reading these words and who realises the truth of all that which is being presented to him or her, will fully understand that which should or that which should not be changed by their activities. They will also truly understand those acts which will provide even to a non-religious "practitioner", the strength that "always" rests personally within them. For really this inner mind stilling strength will automatically "fetter" and so deny the "negative" and harmfully damaging "I Want" thoughts and actions which are emanating from the animalistic five senses? These being your never-ending and personal "I Want" thoughts which are endlessly occupying the mind and which factually and always plus endlessly distort the view of the Soul from seeing through the mind, and so the break the harmony that rests around you.

Now, religiously we may ask the question "Why God did create people who are the only life form that can destroy the harmony of God's world or the world of Nature for the Non-believer." For indeed, it could be understood and believed by many, that if people had not been created, then harmony would exist everywhere and be forever unchanging, but this is not true. The first simple answer which is known to be accurate by most people is that God, like most fathers, likes to be loved by His children, as does the "Mother of the Creation", but seriously this is not the main reason why people have been given the freedom of choice.

But first, how do you prove this love for God your Father and your Divine Mother? If you understand that Jesus WAS the personification of the Creation, which is the only child of God, then now all can fully understand Jesus's following words that were written in the Christian Bible. In which Jesus said: "If you love only those who love you, what credit is that to you?"

These were justly God's thoughts which mean very clearly that you must love everything that exists in God's world or the world of Nature for the Non-Believer, for this is the only way to truly, love God. For indeed is it not also true that the Incarnate Jesus said: *"Every man who knows my commandments and obeys them is the man who loves me."* For truthfully Jesus is speaking as the embodied Creation about God's laws that are indeed embodied within the Creation also Jesus stated – *"and every man who really loves me"* (Jesus speaking as the Creation) – *"will himself be loved by my Father, and I too"* (as the Creation) – *"will love him and make myself known to him"* – adding – *" for the Father himself loves you because you have loved me"* (loved the Creation this being the only child of God)- *"and have believed that I came from God"* – that the Creation came from God for this is Jesus speaking as the embodied Creation a true singularity.

Also, Jesus stated, *"Every man who loves truth recognises my voice."* – Honestly, speaking the singularity of the Creation and then adding – *"No man can serve two masters: for either he will hate the one, and love the other; or else he will hold to the one, and despise the other. You cannot serve God and mammon"* – mammon being the always inner thought, "I Want" more. So rightly the truth is that you should love your Divine Father and your Divine Mother and obey their harmony seeking laws, which are designed to make you happy and content. So how sad it is that one person can kill another person only because they walk different ways to God.

So yes! Very indeed, the following exercise later stated in "The Book" will bring you to the "Enlightenment" spoken of in all our religions and philosophies and to *the "peace that surpasses all understanding"*. Precisely, this being a peace that cannot be destroyed, and it is a peace that will bring to you a new personal contentment that can only be achieved by stopping the many and usually very personal and very active "I Want" that is emanating from one of the five sense and which is splashing into the mind and so blocking the Soul from seeing into the "Present Time". For indeed you will religiously and non-religiously find that any short but disciplined meditational prayer is an ancient well-practised system that will eventually allow you to encompass the stillness of the "Present Time" and so allow the Creation that is all around you, to shine into your mind, and this being a fact for any developing "meditational practitioner".

So yes! This new insight, based upon the control and the keeping unto silence of the five senses, will allow the Soul to see into the "Present Time" and so harmoniously react "fruitfully" to all harmony seeking presentations that are offered to it and which it will choose or not choose to develop according to its targeting of a personally unknown Future. It is also in this way and based upon this silent exercise, that the "meditational practitioner" can rest in healthy "blissful" contentment or apply the harmony seeking needs that are required by the many presentations that are emanating from the current world that exists around them, but only in the "Present Time". For indeed this is the inner Soul, whose only purpose is to support the harmony that exists all around it which is genuinely being a harmony which is emanating from ever still and ever-developing Creation. It is also a support that encompasses and enlivens the experience of "bliss".

So yes! It is then, with a still unthinking mind, that the conditions of the "Present Time" this being that which is entering the still mind, can now be accurately observed by the Soul which is the Self of all Life. Thenceforth the "Practitioner" will truly, realise that this life force, this being, this personal Soul that rests within all people, will automatically and silently act alongside the efforts of the Divine Mother. The latter is the real analyser and supporter of the Creations needs.

Therefore people have been given the "freedom of choice" because the same act can be a good supporting the creation act or the same act can be an opposing bad one, thus the freedom of choice for the doer of these acts. So indeed, it is then, with the growth of this discipline that the chattering "I Want" of all the five senses is silenced. Meticulously, this being a fact which enables the doers' Soul to see through the still mind and so silently and accurately observes that which we call "Present Time", this being the actual world of Heaven that exists upon our world. For indeed in this supporting of the Creations on-going harmony, the very still ever silent needs of all Life and Non-Life that is existing all around and within you – will be harmonised and you will exist as a part of this ever still body that we call "Harmony".

32   THE MIND IS AN INSTRUMENT FOR YOUR USE

Therefore it is understandable that the untrained mind will probably need "understanding" to comprehend the "reality" of that which it silently observes in the "Present Time". For then, it will be able to interpret the messages being reflected by the outside world, as valued by all-knowing Soul and not by the "I Want" of the five senses. For indeed it is only when the five senses are "fettered" and silenced, that the Soul will be able to evaluate and so support the active harmony seeking responses that the Creation presents to it, this truly being the condition known as "Enlightenment" in which the observer is silent.

So yes! Now we know that the mind is just an instrument for our use and that it cannot be you, for it is just a mechanism which reflects within you that which it observes. If you doubt that which all our wise ancients write about, it can be "factually" proven to be so, precisely, this is because you will knowingly begin to live in the *"peace that surpasses all understanding"*, for this reality and its experience can be certainly realised.

Therefore, with your new disciplined unto silence mind, you will eventually and slowly develop effortless personal "habits," that can be cultivated until you eventually harvest a positive and harmonic way of life, that rests within the "peace that surpasses all understanding." You will also, in this quietness of the empty mind, fully understand why God's gift to people was "The Freedom of Choice". With this knowledge and with the Soul seeing the heavenly glory that exists in the "Present Time", which can only be viewed through a silent mind, you can now "choose" to live your life in "Enlightenment" and so seemingly go through the door marked "Those that say, 'I am that I am' enter here".

For indeed, you will experience through this silent mind has if you have gone through a door and into a world called "The Present Time", this being the proverbial doorway that enters Heaven, and so experience "The Peace That Surpasses All Understanding" while living a real-life upon this Earth. For again and honestly, this way of an "Enlightened" life which will peacefully unify you with everything, will stop you from living in the Hell which is a negative based "I Want" personally chosen self-harming life that can also be chosen to be lived in– albeit usually in ignorance.

For rightly it is this disregarding of the real world that ignorantly creates the personal "I Want" world which is a mind filling and environmentally created "Hell" that has been personally but ignorantly created to exist upon this Earth and also within the "Present Time".For, cannot this situation now be likened to a life in which these two doors, one leading to a real-life lived in Heaven? One leading to a negative life lived in Hell, have been personally chosen and so used to enter either world, thus being scientifically obedient to the natural law that if there is a real-world, then there must be a cynical world that many people unknowingly choose to live in, albeit ignorant of this "two-door" fact – but this is not true not now.

So Yes! It is now essential to understand that on the door that leads into Hell there must be a sign saying: "Those that say "I Want" for Me!" Enter here." For the truth is that when you die, you do not go to Heaven or Hell. In essence, you actually upon your death leave "Heaven" or your own self-created "Hell", but know well, that God, like all good fathers, loves you and also loves the "Mother of the Creation", for you are seriously an integral caring and very supporting part of their only child, and so real it is the Divine Mother whose existence carefully cares and nurtures you, as "Nature-ally" all good mothers do for a needing child.

So yes! You were not created to be wasted and so to live in a self-made mind filling Hell, but God did give you "The Freedom of Choice". Carefully this is because as a person, you have been given the needed flexibility of "choice" to support the physical needs of the harmony that is continually emerging around you and with this love for all that exists, to actively and physically support the caring work of the Divine Mother who sincerely loves you. But what is this love? Is it not recognisably and so factually accurate that the Divine Mother's love is all around you, and can always be recognised as harmony, knowledge and the seeking of balance?

So Yes! This real love of the Divine Mother is recognised as being all around us has it is within us, and it is a love that can be truly experienced as a Heaven on this Earth. For indeed, when you find and understand this Heaven that exists only in the "Present Time" that is all around you, you will stay and "choose" to live only in this Heaven, which you will "automatically" begin to actively or acceptingly support. For the truth is that you will factually "Self-Realise" that this love of God's "Present Time" can be likened to a binding force that acts like water in the physical world. For all know that if you take water out of any substance, it will crumble, come apart and turn to dust, which is true, the ending remnants of all life and Non-Life. Therefore indeed, without love which we have likened to water, this substance without water (love) becomes the lowest entity of all that exists and therefore mindlessly meanders hither and thither, alone and around all things. Still, all its actions are meaningless and without any purpose to the life that exists all around it.

So Yes! Love is the binding force of life, which means that those who live in our Heaven, this being that which exists only in the "Present Time", do truly love life – ALL LIFE – for if you love yourself more than ALL LIFE, you are living in Hell. You will know this as a fact because the goodly (Godly) lived life of harmony, knowledge, and balance which exists within the Divine Mother's love, will always by-pass you. Therefore is it not said to be true that those who continuously seek an "I Want" will always be unsatisfactorily lonely and disjointed and so will experience the same kind of life as that of a piece of dust, for the name on this dust is "I Want." Now even dirt casts it off when the wind blows for it to refuses to harmonise with it.

So Yes! Love the Creation as your most excellent "Present" and know that you cannot love it in the past or the future, for in these make-believe worlds that "The Book" calls Hell, the Creation does not exist. Thus really and truly, our God-given or Nature given Harmony for the Non-Believer is wonder-fully experienced when your silent mind is "Enlighteningly" existing only in the "Present Time", and thus experiencing God's love that can only exist in the

"Present Time", for correctly, this is a "Present Time" that can never change. Still, it is also useful to remember that when you are "Enlightened" and so capable of automatically and silently tying two events together, this being to maintain the harmony that is emerging all around you – then you will know well that this truly is the purpose of your existence and that it is this known "factual" activity that can only take place in the supporting silence of the "Present Time" the world in which an "I Want" for myself cannot exist.

It is also a goodly (Godley) to remember that when you see a rainbow, it can trigger within you a silent observation; for accurately it can be described that one end is in Heaven and the other end is in Hell. For is it not true that this rainbow can only shine in our "Present Time" and never in the past or the future and so it is a "Present" from the one God which is birthed by the "Mother of the Creation" which "The Book" calls "Space" that which is all around us and within us? Is it not also true that this rainbow, which shows the colour of all life and non-life, can also be a "Present" that has been given to us by God or Nature for the Non-Believer?

Therefore could it not also be true that this "Present" is to remind us of the fact that we can reach this Heaven, in which all these colours exist, but only in the "Present Time", and so live there only by leaving the self-created thinking that creates a past or future non-existing Hell that only a personal mind filling "I Want" for myself can create? For truly is it not by ignoring this fact that many people have unknowingly committed themselves to live in their self-created "I Want" Hell? But rightly, we should now know the answer to this ancient question, "Which end of the rainbow has the pot of gold?" Is it the "Present Time" or that which exists in the Past or the Future? What has also been found is that the Quakers have the closest religious foundation to the truth of that which these readings speak.

For indeed this is said to be true because the Quakers' past and current history shows that their silent prayers, unprovoked by others, strive to seek the mind-emptying harmony that only exists in the "Present Time". It is also well known that Quaker religious teachings continuously endeavour to bring peace to the world and "Personal Rights" to a country's majority control systems. The Quakers do this in an ever-searching endeavour to bring harmony to any uncertainty that contradicts the unity that rests only in the "Present Time", this being the "Heaven" that genuinely exists upon our Earth. It is beautiful, and it is given freely for all to enjoy – if they want it – and who can say that this statement is not true? For if you feel that Nature is punishing you, it would be good to look into the mirror of life. Simply put, the Quaker's endeavour to tie a new incoming piece of string emanating from the Divine Mother, whose constant efforts are to keep Her child, the Creation, peacefully harmonised and so with this gainful practice the Quakers physically tie this incoming string to one whose end is searching for such a matching harmony that exists only in the "Present Time", the pure Heaven that exists upon our Earth.

Logically, this is a unifying act that fulfils this incoming strings' search for God's harmony, therefore is it not true that all good acts committed by people are like tying bits of "harmonising" string together? This being acts that endeavour to expand the unity of love and harmony that rest within God's Creation; a Creation that is always perfect but can be muddled by a people "I Want" for myself activity. For indeed, this is an on-going and ever-growing part of the religious "bringing together" work of the Quakers, and honestly who can say that this is not a pleasant activity, which is super-enhanced by a system of self-controlled inner meditation which always exists within the Quakers prayer time.

So yes! It's often not an easy task for a person to tie a searching string, which is incoming within the "Present Time" to one of the Creation's existing but also emerging strings that are supported by the Divine Mother or of Nature for the Non-Believer. For this is a newly emerging string that is seeking harmony to keep expanding the Creation's constant pursuit of harmony, that is all around you. Precisely, this is truly an activity that you can "unthinkingly" experience and in which you could be taking part. Yet! Is it not also sadly true, that it is also only people that can destroy the unity of love and harmony that rest within God's Creation; a Creation which is always perfect but can be muddled by a person's "I Want" for myself activity. For strictly, this is an on-going and ever-growing part of the religious "bringing together" work of the Quakers, and who can say that this is not an enjoyable activity, which is super-enhanced by a system of personally controlled meditation.

It's often not an easy task for a person to tie a searching string that is incoming from the "Present Time" to one of the Creation's existing, but newly emerging strings that are supported by the Divine Mother or of Nature for the Non-Believer. For this is an emerging string that is seeking harmony, to keep expanding the Creation's constant pursuit of harmony, that is or may not be emerging all around you. Yet! Is it not also sadly true, that it is only people that can destroy the harmony which the "Mother of the Creation" is continually endeavouring to maintain all around them? For again is it not also sadly true that many people claim the Creation only for themselves, and so falsely endeavour to steal it.

So yes! We can find ourselves in a negative or harmful position in which some people are claiming the Creation for themselves, which is a great failing. Still, it is well to remember that they are placing themselves in a worse position than those they persecute, for did not God, speaking through Jesus say: ***"Woe to the world because of the things that cause people to sin! Such things must come, but woe to the person through whom they come!"*** It is understood that these are VERY correct words. It is also true that we may have doubts about this, but now it can be said to everyone, "scientifically," and also shown by history, that we have a good judge in Creation's Divine Mother. For it is She who will place the string into your hands, but only if you are Enlightened enough to successfully support the way of harmony that exists for all life and Non-Life. It can also be said that the enlightened "stillness" of the Divine Mother can also be personally named as Destiny, Fate, Luck, Karma, Kismet, Chance, Providence, Serendipity, Coincidence, Accident, etc., for only She, can guide each person's supporting efforts and also physically provide "Sugar in the Water," for those who actively pursue the "string tying" of an ever incoming harmonic based string of harmony creating togetherness.

Of course, this is the practical way that the Divine "Mother of the Creation" pursues, this being to aid those who support the development of harmony, that exists, or which is endeavouring to emerge, all around them. For indeed, this experience of aid from the Divine Mother can again be likened to driving through a city, and all traffic lights turn green when you approach them, so that you can to go forward without the need to stop.

For really, this *"Sugar in the Water"* has the sweet taste of righteousness, with the water being life and sugar being the tasty experience enjoyed when tying emerging strings of harmony together. But a word of warning here, for institutional denial, can become the most negative behaviour that can be committed by people, this being when they withhold the sugar to keep it only it for themselves, an act which always brings failure. Sadly, the reason for this is that many people copy a negative reflection of the work of the Divine Mother. Her work is to continually pursue and or modify acts that seek the continuation of the expanding harmony of the whole of life and Non-Life that is always emerging all around everyone.

It appears that many people, who are capable of managing events, instead of them looking outwards to bring their team's activities to positively target the greater harmony of all of that which is before them, they look inwards and target a harmony that is only beneficial to them, and so forget the greater whole. For indeed, this can happen within small and within excellent unions of people, and this may also become the culture of large countries. For example: Is it not true that for all time, the poverty and starvation conditions that exist amongst many of the people who live in Africa, and many other impoverished countries, also exists amongst areas with great financial riches, that other richer countries sell to the world.

So, who is claiming and reaping the benefits that God's world is providing for ALL people? Is it not also true that if fifty per cent of the surplus called profit, which is produced by that country or that regions market valued work, was given to an honest government to improve the conditions of the people of the country which birthed this surplus – what a substantial increase in harmony there would be within that country. For again is it not also true that if we could put the oppressive greed of "institutional denial" or "institutional betrayal" aside for one year, would this not be a natural and also a positively harmonising activity to the majority of people who live in that country or region? Therefore, can it not also be said to be true that a majority of people would "democratically" agree to this distribution concept, mainly if new teachings were applied.

For really, does not a personal "I Want" denial often prevent us from coming to terms with what is going on before our very eyes and is it not an "I Want" that stops ourselves from seeing or wanting to know what is happening and in this way can we not all be perpetuating a dishonest system. At this point, it must also be beneficially added that the type of Communism practised in the former USSR is not recommend for solving this problem. We must laws remember that the "Laws" of how we should live is not on paper but in the hearts of people. The understandable reason why Communism failed was based upon the fact that all workers had no surplus seeking "boss", for all were just employed for the good of the state, so all worked only for the good of the people – and not themselves - which is not a good motivator of needed activities. Joseph Stalin, former Premier of the communist pursuing Soviet Union, had the concept of establishing the same unity that bound together all people in the same way in which he observed to be working in a bee-hive, this being that all bees simply and naturally worked none stop and to the best of their abilities doing the task that was placed in front of them – but people are not bees, especially the male whose task is to achieve a good future. Thus many when to the gulag, a work camp in which they were forced to do what they were told to do and even the female whose task is to achieve a present caring time were forced to become like bees – but people are not bees they are the caring people of the world that exists around them.

Yet we need to understand that the reason for the arrival of Communism was caused by the same current system of exploitation that exists now in the above mentioned "poor" countries, these being countries in which the majority of people suffer in severe poverty, this being countries in which poverty and illness are rampant amongst its population. Is this because the purchasing riches of their own country by-pass them for its produced wealth is controlled by a minority of others, usually foreign customers whose religious belief system is called "money."

Yet, is it not also true that such a "positive" system controlled by the profit-seeking greed of others, was destroyed by the Communist Party of the Soviet Union, which replaced it with a "negative" institutional denial system with the belief that no profit should be entertained and that all people should be automatically paid wages. No person should be without work and that none should be managed by someone who was thought to be more superior to them – i.e., no boss and so no management, for all, are equal. Yet, this false concept created millions of deaths due to starvation because there was no manager to teach, guide and motivate them in the best ways to create wealth. It was a "Communal" and honest plus well-meaning economic concept which was the negative opposite of the above greed-based exploitation. Still, sadly it was also a condition that removes the ratio of work to added value reality. For simply put, when peoples unmanaged, unmotivated wage cost is added to the excessively created overhead costs, this being the cost of wages, food, electricity, water, energy, maintenance, etc., then this fact trebles the cost and also the time is taken to produce - because means of motivation reduces to a third the unit of potential production and sadly the Gulag is not a motivational system.

So Yes! It is a scientific fact that a non-managed unmotivated production ratio is only thirty-three per cent of the true potential that could be achieved under proper management, thus meaning that only one-third of that which could be produced enters the people market place – a sure road to stagnation and deficit and starvation. For indeed, it was this "Communist" based fact which is the reality that led to a significant deficit in the Soviet people's market place and to beds filled with money that have no value because there was nothing to buy, this is being a fact which can be "scientifically" understood for it is quite reasonable for an unmotivated person to produce thirty-three per cent of that which they could produce when well managed and financially motivated.

So Yes! Yet it is also undoubtedly true and scientifically proven that a person working within proper supporting management would be motivated to produce 75% of their true potential. By offering more finance per ratio to the work being done, this work output will rise to 100%, this being a fact which creates more "weekly" wages and also trebles the output. It is in this way that a well-managed company will produce three times more goods and at a much-reduced cost to the market place and indeed, the same principle means that these goods will quickly arrive at to where all the customers are.

For assuredly, all goods will be motivated to arrive quickly, and of course, it will be a market place that is fuelled by more money in the pockets of the workers – but we need good "political" leadership and management to be able to achieve this. Therefore, Landowners indeed state "I Want" more for me and factory owners also state "I Want" more for me, this being that greed which can create an unnatural division of wealth amongst the tribe. Logically, this is truly being an unnatural division of wealth for again; it stops the harmony of the "Good" or "God" life from developing for all people. It even increases poverty within many countries and even in those countries in which God's or Natures Creation for the Non-Believer has provided "Natures" minerals, this being that which people value.

For it is not true that people of our Earth have "factually" not yet discovered how to release the economic will of most people to lawfully enjoy life in their own country and also how to care for the minority needs that exist within their societies midst? Yet sadly, even in the birthplace of industrial democracy, the world saw that in the UK 2017 general election that the people of the United Kingdom found that the Government that had been elected to "legally" control them had received only twenty-four per cent of the populations' vote, meaning that seventy-six per cent of the people did not vote for this political party to rule them, but it was appointed to do so!

So how did this biased incident happen? Simply put it was a personally based "I Want" to be a member of parliament which led to the Creation of different political parties who, although they received a total of forty-two per cent of "yes" votes which was near twice the number of votes received by the elected Government, they could not rule because the law says that only the party with the most winning "seats" can govern. Maybe this is why thirty-four per cent of the population who could vote – did not bother to vote because the laws now being produced in the UK are not suitable for the majority of its people.

This powerful "I Want" the fact is also "politically" undeniable, regarding UK "Brexit" and the reason why the UK is endeavouring to leave the "European

Common Market". Logically, this is being a strange "undemocratic" act in which only thirty-seven per cent (37%) of the British people voted to leave the EU. In comparison, thirty-five per cent (35%) voted NOT to leave the EU, and twenty-eight 28% of the people who could vote, did not vote, thus making a 2% extra vote to be the deciding factor!

So Yes! Where are a democracy and the majority rule which states that all people should be governed by a government that supports the majority of its people? For indeed these emerging systems must be a personal "I Want", which is the reason has to why the current British "minority" government is agreeing with a "minority" of the British people who wish to leave the EU?

So where is the will of the people? For indeed the United Kingdom is spoken of here because it is the modern birthplace of industrial democracy; therefore it must be thought capable of creating a harmony based activities that will remove the "I Want" laws emanating from a minority of people and so readily install a majority based representation that could be copied by many countries.

For really, is it not the target to remove a minority based "I Want" voting system, and so develop a voting system which will proportionally represent the majority of people and so remove this constantly emerging "institutional denial" forever. For as the wise would say, the way to "harmony" is for the majority of people and in our current age of communication, it is seen that only the majority of people know how to stop being controlled by a minority "I Want", this being the happy life for them only?

Yet! It is pleasing to say that Nature seems to be currently saying that our new "World Wide Web" communication systems are bringing national tribal changes that are probably being created by the harmony seeking "Mother of the Creation". This meaning that a new type of world unifying "organisation" is emerging that will end the conflicting "communication" gap that is now occurring between non-democratically elected leaders, such has in kings and unelected governing leaders and also between democratically elected systems that are purported to be controlled by the majority of people, this conflict being akin to a "religious" understanding of all "communities."

So the world must now be considering a new type of "advisory" Government. For all know that the Nature of people shows that the tribe does need a "Person" or a "Godly" chosen leader who automatically shows loyalty and so attains power by the will of the "majority" of people under their jurisdiction.

Therefore it is natural to understand that under our modern communication systems that a controlling "President" or King or an unelected "Godly Leader" is seen to be needed by the majority of people - yet both must be a leadership that acknowledges the will of their majority and also does not abuse the needs of the minority. So indeed all people must support an elected leader or support an unelected leader and a financial fine should be imposed upon those who do not vote unless there is a good reason for not doing so, for the will and needs of all the people being controlled must be identified.

Should it not also be known that all government expenditure, this being that which has been gathered by taxation from those regions organisations, should be signed for release only by the registered leader of that county? Precisely, this is being a release of finance that is only to a regional "elected" or "unelected" government adviser, positioned at the birth of this new Government or by the established ruler of that country. Then is it not true that they are the only ones to control and so are responsible for these allocated funds which are regularly and publically audited for the view of all the people of that region.

These being "Regional Government Advisors" who occupy a known position and who will gain by a life time's experience the correct allocating of government funds that are truly needed to support that region's needs. Therefore these "Regional Government Advisers" are the only ones who control the release of funds which they allocate to the leaders of their region, these being people who have previously been "elected" by the majority of the people from that region and who are leaders whose only purpose is to care for the needs of the people of that region.

For it would certainly be necessary for some unelected lifetime serving "Government Adviser" to evaluate and audit the publicly needed commercial distribution and expenditure of these "part-time" elected leaders who work under their jurisdiction. These being "Government Advisers" whose removal can only be accomplished by a 70% majority vote of that region's people in which a new "Government Advisers" is appointed by the current leader of that country – for truly bribery is the most common problem within modern democracies. For is it not a bribery based greed that often leads to wars and great unrest has industrial conglomerates purchase elected politicians to remove their competition.

For indeed it is useful to know that currently some wealthy persons "I Want" can control many of those around them, especially those who are closer to their animal pre-life and it is now also good to remember now that this 4th way is coming in which profits will be fully achieved by automation. A personal workforce will become an absolute nuisance. A Robot workforce needs no food or home and requires no caring, no payment or sick leave. Neither does it need maternity leave, medical needs, retirement benefits or labour unions, or cajoling or harmony or training or balancing or loving or negotiations.

Yet indeed the majority of people have no interest in this new "economic" 4th Way development, but people do need to "work" with or without Nature to survive. For did not the former USSR find that Communism could not produce the "economic" energy needed to build a near-perfect modern world that had to be sustained by economically motivated factories? Also did not this USSR search, which was based upon unmanaged and unmotivated collectivism, create a virtual "factory" based industrial world, this being a factory based world that was not supported by the motivational needs of agriculture but concentrated on targeting a factory based added value which supported the needs of management? So is it not now strange that the "Mother of the Creation" can be likened to saying to these former USSR people, "Go back to growing food upon the land, for the people of the world will need you"?

33   GENETIC MEMORIES

So Yes! Is it also true, as our scientist's state that genetic memories of past concepts are known to be within all people? They also state that they are probably from our ancestor's gene pool, but in reality, they are inputs from our past lives and many religions all know this to be true, but many deny it? The most noticeable knowledge seen of rebirth is the activities of children before the age of two. As previously stated, this is particularly so when they are learning how to stand and take those first steps. They can also hold long conversations in a significant sounding language based upon intonation and a complying body language.

Still, to the adult listener, it is just unintentional sounding blah blab, and they can even have long conversations with others of the same age which is utterly incomprehensible to the adult, but which appears to have a great interest in the young listeners who often give long answers in similar blah blab. Can it not be realised that these often humorous or earnest conversations coming from such a young child are occurring because they do not yet have the ability or knowledge to formulate a communicative language?

Is it not also true that it can be noticed that their sounded intonations do sound as rational has conversational speech and is it not also true that they use the right context of the conversation taking place showing that they understand the meaning of the life and conditions that are around their new life? It can also be witnessed that these children can also act, within their small bodies, as if they are adults. For indeed, does this not all come from internal memory, and it is not just genetic memories for cannot it be understood that it is the memories of their past life. For indeed it not also valid that many adults can have a conversation with a child who is not yet able to walk but whose intonations make a sound that correctly answers all remarks – how is this possible if they have no knowledge of life unless they been here before?

34   HOW NOTHING CONTROLS EVERYTHING

Is it not also correct to say, has said before, that Non-Believers could say that the Universe and all life and Non-Life came from "Nothing", a fact with which I also agree. But, to me, their Nothing is my God, for my God is also a "No-Thing", and I too believed that my "No-Thing" created all the life and Non-Life which rest within the Creation, which Non-Believers call Nature.

So yes! I do believe that the "Nothing" of which our non-believers' state was before the Creation of the material world, is the same as my "No-Thing" which "Godly" created the world in which we all live. For again cannot it be said to be "scientifically" valid that this "Nothing", this being the Zero in numbers, did actually "Create" the personal world of mathematics which in turn "Created" the mathematical language of all that exists within our Universe, this being the language that revealed to us the meaning of time, space, quantity and did not this mathematical Creation of Nothing, this simple zero created by people, allow them to develop and create the modern world which we now see all around us?

So Yes! Cannot it be said that without this Zero, this Nothing that we add to numbers, people would not have been able to "create" the modern world as we know it today? Therefore can it not also be said that this number "Nothing" also practically originates from that which our Creation was born? Just as the "nothing" we call "zero" in numbers was born by people to give birth to a new life via mathematical formulas and numbers which in turn gave birth to the arithmetical concepts that show to people the mathematically created world that led to the knowing the order of the Universe and everything that exists around us?

Is it not also true that it was only six thousand years ago that people had only numbers that could only consist of nine digits these being like our 1, 2, 3, 4, 5, 6, 7, 8, 9 and which entered into a lost unknowing world after the number nine was reached. Is it not also in recent history that people "scientifically" took a small step further into the world of numbers by creating different symbols as likened by the Roman numerals which also lost collective meaning after only a few explaining digits?

Then, and only a thousand years ago, the Arabian people found we could add a "nothing", this being a Zero to the world of numbers and that we could explain this no-thing has an "O". Still, when this "nothing" was joined to the world of only nine numbers, it was able to "create" a new world of numbers, plus fractions of numbers and formulas such as the one based upon the fraction which is 22/7, which we knowingly called Pi!

So Yes! This "Zero" this "nothing" was even able to give life to birth seeking fraction such as 22/7, which, when you try to birth it to a whole number, by dividing seven into twenty-two, the birthing calculation of ensuing numbers can go numerically beyond the end of the Universe and then onwards into infinity as it searches to give birth to a whole number. For this birthing equation that was born to search for a whole number, it is never-ending. For indeed it is a birthing not yet born the whole number that is seeking a "living" totality. In its growth to become a whole number, it would eventually contain, if it ran for eternity in its search for birth, the exact birth date of every person that ever lived on Earth, as well as every person's telephone number, national security number, identity number, passport number, etc. etc.

So yes! Is it not also now known in our current age, that these mathematical facts are fully understood even by our children? What is also "scientifically" known by everyone is that if we take away this number called "Nothing" from this formula containing whole numbers, and then the Creation of our current world of numbers would cease to exist, which proves that "Nothing" does play a very active part within the physical world of numbers? For it is now truly understood, that if "Nothing" is taken away from the world of numbers, it would mean that the mathematical based computer world and much of the material world of people, would collapse and would not be able to exist, thus proving that the numerical "Nothing" created by people, is a very powerful for it certainly creates the world that people now live in and is it not interesting that this "Nothing" created by people, can be proven to exist?

So Yes! I believe that our "Universe" also came from a similar "Nothing", but my "No-Thing" is that which is called God, and it is truly a concept that can also lead to some severe mathematical thinking. An example is that if we take the number one as being an individual's Soul, or "Consciousness" for the Non-Believer, this being our earthly guardian with the "Freedom of Choice" to instantly evaluate the pros and cons of an emerging creation, a fact which also enables a person to "choose" to live in the factual "Present" time which is a God made "Heaven" or to live in a non-existing mind created fictitious Past or Future which is a personally made "Hell". Now if we add to the believer's positive Soul a loving God who is "No-Thing", then this will give us the equation One God plus our Soul, then $(0 + 1)$ equals a factually existing "1". Therefore it is mathematically accurate that if we recognise that there is a God, then we know that our Soul can have loving God resting physically within it. Now for new thinking, if we also take the number one as the Soul of the individual that lives in "Hell" upon this Earth and this person believes that there is no God. We have One Soul minus God which is stated by an unbeliever to be nothing $(1 - 0)$ this being a fact which also equals "1" which genuinely exists.

So, is it not also mathematically accurate that if we do not recognise that there is a God, then a Non-Believer's Soul whose body is living in a make-believe Hell, can also have a loving God resting within them? Therefore is the question not now: "Does this mean that all people who now live according to the rules of Heaven or according to the rules of Hell can all have God resting within them?"

Is this correct whether they believe or whether they do not believe in God?" The mathematically based "scientific" and so truthful answer resting behind this question says "YES", which means that God and His love can be within all His children and that He can never leave them for the mathematical world also says that this is not possible for people to be without a "Nothing", which "The Book" calls God, for indeed this contradictory plus and minus equation proves that God is everywhere.

Now let us continue with these mathematical truths. What if we want our Soul to add itself to God and so increase the power of a God within ourselves? Then we have $0 \times 1 = 0$, so we cannot increase the power of God for this "Nothing – which is God" cannot be changed. But what if we try and divide God? Then we have $0 -: - 1 = 0$, thus meaning that we cannot decrease the power of God for "Nothing" or "No-Thing" – which is God" cannot be changed.

Yet as previously proven, this "Nothing" this zero, when added to numbers, can purposely create a number that can circle the Universe and can continue encircling the Universe for as many times as people choose it to do so. Therefore, does this mathematical proof not show that God is an infinity that has no beginning and no end? Therefore, is it not useful to be reminded that if we remove the Zero, this being the "nothing" that exists within mathematics, from all our past calculations, that with this removal the physical world around us would collapse. Our current world would cease to exist? Therefore would it not also be true that if we remove God or that called "No Thing" by our Non-

Believers, from the beginning of the birth of the Creation, would this mean that the Creation would not exist? – Interesting isn't it when this concept is compared to the "creating" and birthing of our children.

It is also interesting that this modern scientific discovery of "No Thing", this concept of the Zero, actually led to the Northern Hemispheres more significant civilisations, this being the "No Thing" that was born from the Islamic teachings and which also civilised the scientific world of all the Christian tribes of the Northern hemisphere. For this newly discovered and personally understood number "o", which is "No Thing" did magically "create" our modern world.

It is also interesting to think that an Arabian of the Islamic teaching did wonder how to name a quantity that was more than nine and so was it the thinking that God was No-thing (Zero), that made this Arabian creator then think that if you placed this symbol of God this "No-thing" alongside any figure up to nine, then God would increase its power by ten?

Then by continuing this magical thinking must have realised the thought that if Gods power of "No Thing" were placed alongside any number it would magically give birth to ten times that figure and if continually added it could "create" an amount from a single number that could encircle the Universe and so was it this that began the birth of the scientific, economic and material world that we know today. Isn't it interesting that which we call "Zero" or "Nothing" can prove the existence of God who all people know has "No Thing" but whose laws control everything just has the Arabian invention of a numerical "No Thing" created the modern world?

35 THE SOUL WITHIN

The Soul in most religions, philosophical and mythological traditions, is explained as being intangible, invisible, incorporeal, elusive plus immortal, undying, everlasting, and enduring. It is also stated by the many of our wise ancients who are the originators of these high belief systems, that a person's Soul has a logical and proven ability to witness the most divine of a person's actions such as praying, these were prayers of praise, thanksgiving, or for the petitioning for forgiveness or even a simple "I Want", for indeed it is the witness of all that enters the mind. It is also said by some of our wise ancients that the Soul is a living organism, one in which all life is present. It is also a well-known fact that the Soul is always portrayed as being attached to the sweetness of Heaven, which "The Book" explains has been the "Present Time", but in those ancient times it could never be physically or mentally explained by our ancients – so in modern terminology, just what is the Soul?

For rightly now "modern" words can be used to explain, in an enlightened "scientific" way, the reality of that which our ancients spoke about regarding a person's Soul. Thus meaning that it is only within people that the Soul does exist, but now we know it to be the highest observer of the "Present Time", and the only living "Freedom of Choice" initiator and that it does have "Heavenly" purpose for is it not factually correct that it is also really linked to the goodness

(Godness) of that which our wise ancients call "Heaven", which has now been modernly explained has existed in the "Present Time" because the "Present Time" is the only time that can be experienced. Yet sadly is it not also real that even up to our present day, people have forgotten this harmony seeking "live and let live" purpose of a Soul is driven life? Is it not also sadly true that people of one country are slaughtering and killing people of another country or even within their own culture some people are sadly murdering their people, is this the Souls actions, or an "I Want" my "pack leaders" way of life, not yours. For truly is this, not a reality that is indeed emanating from the animal kingdom and not a God-made world that can only exist in the Present Time? For truly is this God's will or the will of pack leaders animalistic "I Want" everything for myself. Therefore can it not be logically stated, that God and the *"Mother of the Creation"*, will turn their faces away from those people who "animalistic ally" ignore their Souls and so will not return them for a long time to a world in which the people of all countries are endeavouring become one "legalized" entity? For again is it not true, has the history of our world now shows, that the populations of the world's many countries, are endeavouring to become one "peaceful" entity and does not the "World Wide Web" support this endeavour, especially when it curbs the "Fake News", this being that which is being born from lavish payments?

So Yes! First, we need to acknowledge that that which the wise ancients name as the personal Soul is a truth that is not just based upon a theoretical thought but must exist within reality also. Therefore, if we indeed acknowledge the wise words of our ancient religious and philosophical originators, we must also acknowledge that to live in "Heaven". At the same time, on this Earth, it is necessary to acknowledge that you need to live within the borders of your "Soul" – but what does this well-spoken and well-ordered yet oft-hidden truth mean? And also can it be "scientifically" proven to be a fact? First, it is necessary to "scientifically" and "factually" understand that using our previous metaphor; we can say that the individual "YOU", can be likened to "Nothing", this being the "O" (Nothing) in mathematics? It should also be acknowledged to be true that in your personal life, you consciously change everything that you attach your energy to and that this is personal energy that you use to add or remove something within that existence which you encounter. Then you leave it changed, just as the "0" does to the entire numerical world that it applies itself to, for justly this "Zero" this "0" can be likened to being YOU! Therefore, does not this "scientific" truth also explain that any person can just accept the Creation seeking harmony that is emerging all around them, or actually join with these harmony seeking endeavours and so energise its purpose, or decide to leave the Creations harmony that exists all around them and is this choice not born from a personal gift called "The Freedom of Choice", this being that which allows a person to be able to strengthen the harmony that is around them, by increasing it or they can destroy the harmony that is unfolding around them, by attacking it and so reduce it, or do Nothing at all but just observe it! Is this not an absolute truth? Therefore, could it not be "scientifically" stated, as it has been in many chapters before this one, that it is a truth that people need to "choose" to support the way of harmony which allows them to live in Heaven while on this Earth or to "choose" to break the harmony which is around them and so "choose" to live in Hell while on this Earth? Is it not also seen as a "scientific" truth that the breaking of harmony is being caused by the individuals' demands for an "I Want", this being that which breaks the truth of the world and is it not also true that this personal "I Want" demand is coming from the animalistic wishes of the five senses because many people believe that the five senses are them. Therefore, is it not a truth that these personal "I Want" demands are the cause has to why so many individuals are living in Hell while on this Earth? Is it not also sadly true that many are also reflecting this Hell that they live in upon all the people that live around them?   Now admittedly, with the above knowledge, it must be "scientifically" recognised that it is the Soul, resting within a silent mind, this being that which our wise ancients speak about, that "silently" shows the way to support the harmony that is always endeavouring to be born around a non-thinking person. So honestly, is not the "Freedom of Choice" really needed to support the "natural" emerging harmony that enables all life and Non-Life to live in the Heaven that instinctively rests in harmony upon this Earth.

So now the "scientific" question as to just what the Soul is should no longer be asked. For the Soul is recognised by our wise ancients to be that silent entity that cannot be seen but which rests within all people and it is a Soul that makes the very purpose of all people be that which is needed to support the work of the "Mother of the Creation". For rightly, this ancient now modernly proved fact, can be "scientifically" confirmed to exist via a silent mind, this being that condition which allows the Soul to observe through the silent mind clearly, all that is needed or not needed to be done to support the Creations on-going harmony, this being that which should be naturally emerging around all life and Non-Life. For indeed, these are the necessary conditions in which the silent mind allows the Soul to fully see the needs of the outer world in which it silently pursues – if required – the needed harmony of that which is endeavouring to emerge around it, for the Soul can only observe the Creation through a still "un-wanting" mind.

So Yes! The Soul can be likened to being a "halfway house" between the Divine "Mother of the Creation" and the Creation itself. For it is undoubtedly true and can be realised to be so, that the "Mother of the Creation" cares for the total wellbeing of Her only child, this being the totality of the "Creation", and that this "Well-Being" oft requires the aid of a person Soul. For really, it is the Soul resting only within people that physically and silently support this needed work, this being a work that is reflected it through a transparent and still minds yet it should be known, that because of our Godly given "Freedom of Choice", only people can change this harmony into disharmony which is nearly always achieved by an "I Want".

So yes! Again God is the Father who placed His seed into the space that He created, and which is all around us and which became the Divine Mother of their only Child – this being the Creation. For correctly is it not a significant "scientific" truth that in the harmony that exists all around us, there is needed to be a male and a female to create a child? Is it not also a significant "scientific" truth that it is the Mother who cares for the child and particularly the environment that exists within and around the child, and in this environment not forever growing and constantly modifying itself, this being because it is forever targeting "harmony". Is it not also a truth that it is this goodly (Godley) surrounding harmony that supports the child's growth? Can anyone "scientifically" dispute these facts that describe the natural laws that are all around and within the existence of all life and Non-Life?

So Yes! The first reality to acknowledge is that the Soul can now be "scientifically" proven to exist within all people. For it is the Soul that "chooses", without thought, to automatically guide a person to complete the necessary actions that support and encourages the needed on-going harmony of the Creation which exists only in the "Present Time" – hence the gift to all people, which is known as the "The Freedom of Choice". For indeed, the reason for this "Freedom of Choice" is that a certain deed can create and support the harmony of the merging Creation. Still, that same deed, under different conditions, could destroy the harmony that is emerging in the "Present Time". Therefore, it should now be clearly understood that truly and sadly, this task of correcting the emerging harmony is impossible to achieve in the false world that is created by a person's mind clouding "I want" for myself, this being a personal "I Want" which always turns to dust. So honestly, that is the reason why a person's Soul can only exist in the "Present Time", for its task is to support the harmony seeking acts that silently appear before it.

So Yes! Is it not also a "scientific" truth that in our own body it is our unthinking Soul that naturally and silently sustains the harmony, wisdom and balance of all that exists within our bodies and is it not also true that the Soul truly endeavours to apply this care to all that is outside a person body, for it knowingly understand that all is one life force? For really, is it not the Soul that brings to us not only our need to sleep plus awaken but also is it not "scientifically" seen, that with the same endearment our Soul can apply this same love and care to the surrounding Creation, this being that which is all around and within all people? But is it not also true that this endeavour only applies if "individual" people "choose" to allow their body to satisfy these needs? Therefore, is it not also true that the above shows a factual truth that the Soul exists within all people and that its purpose is to support the harmony, wisdom, and balances of not only that which exist within a person's body but also the reality that expands into all the Creation that exist around your body if you "choose" and therefore allow your body to do so? Is it not also a fantastic fact that the Soul endeavours to support the harmony that is emerging because there is only one child and that people are not separate from this singularity of the Creation that is all around them unless they "choose" to be separate from it! Now answer the question: "Who are YOU?"

So Yes! The Soul can also be "scientifically" proven to be an actual entity that seems to live "personally" within all people and that it links "personally" to all life and Non-Life that is "personally" outside and inside each person's body. These are facts that can now be proven because we now live in a more advanced educated world that was previously outside the understanding of those who listened to our many wise ancients. This revelation is to prove "conclusively" to all who listened to the words that the Soul rests within them and that it also knows the correct "way" of life. So now, in our modern time, there is no need to ask, "What is it that is managing the internal workings of our bodies and our sleep patterns?" For we now are capable of understating that which many of our wise ancients spoke about, in that it is the Soul that manages and supports the internal harmony of all parts within the body and that it is the Soul that can produce the same harmony to all that which exists outside the person body if we "choose" to allow it to do so. For indeed, the Soul within has the power to work wonders, this being that which all our wise ancients say is the truth.

So Yes! The Soul is the entity that naturally manages and controls the workings of all people's bodies. For again is it not "scientifically" true that no person can automatically and consciously manage the teamwork of their internal organs or the millions of entities that live within and around these internal organs? But is it not also true that because we have actively been given by God or Nature for Non-Believers, the "Freedom of Choice", that this fact allows us to ignorantly "choose" to destroy our internal organs, even unto their death? Therefore, can it not be "scientifically" recognised that the untouchable entity that exists within us and which observes everything is that entity which our wise ancients called the "Soul". Precisely, this is undoubtedly being a person's Soul that cannot be seen but which was created to not only be the entity to manage our bodies internal but also to manage our bodies' external work, for the reality of this activity is where the rewarding and harmonising experience of a living bliss does come. Truly all readers now know that no longer can ignorance or a "not knowing", be that which ignores the work of the Soul? For now, all readers know that it is the Soul that not only ensures that the body corrects and rests itself by what we call "sleep" and that it also awakens us from sleep but that it also does the same when we are awake, this being to assist the needs of the "Creations" on-going activities, the real purpose and reason why we have been given the "Freedom of Choice" for the same act can support or destroy the Creations emerging activities, and this is why we exist as "People".

So yes! Is it not also comforting to know that it is the Soul that is caring for your inner body, therefore is it not also a truth that your body often needs your physical support just as the "Mother of the Creation" needs your physical support in which both can only be given in the "Present Time"? Is it not also true that this bodily aid can never be given in the non-existing past or the future in which personnel "I Want" takes the mind which is often full of "I Want" thoughts, this being a condition which also blocks the Soul from seeing through the mind the outside world of the Creation? Therefore! By staying away from a personal mind filling Creation of a non-existing a past and or targeting a non-existing future, the Soul will see through the uncluttered mind just how to organise the activities within the "Present Time" of your active life that is lived in Heaven while you are on this Earth. Yet it is also sadly known that many do stop the Soul from connecting their life to this exact way of living by independently and unwisely chasing a personal "I Want". Woe to them, for indeed this will cause them to enter a world of Hell which is far worse than the world of a Heaven within whose living is every person's natural birthright. In other words and simply put, if you allow yourself to chase a personal "I Want", you are not allowing your Soul to bring you to the heavenly birthright that ALWAYS exists or is endeavouring to emerge all around you while you are on this Earth, this is rightly a "living in Heaven" which is a "now" time, and this is only achieved because you silently allow the Soul to naturally support and activate the constant maintenance of harmony for all the life and Non-Life that exists all around you. Of course, some people purposely destroy the harmony that is endeavouring to emerge all around them as did those who took the incarnate Jesus to the painful cross but did not this pursuit of disharmony painfully reflect on them in a long term banishment from their homes.

So yes! It is the Soul which "automatically" and without your thinking controls the harmony, wisdom, and balance that exists inside and outside of a person's body. It is also the Soul which unthinkingly and "automatically" supports the harmony of all the life and Non-Life that exists all around it. For just as your Soul does automatically control all harmonised activities that are within your body, so it must similarly be used, via your "Freedom of Choice", to also personally "choose" to unthinkingly aid the work of the Divine Mother, this being that activity which is all around you; for similar unthinking practical aid is also needed to support the harmony, wisdom and balance that exists in the "Present Time", which can only be when there is no "I Want" blocking the view of the Soul from seeing through the mind.! Agreed, this may often be difficult to achieve, mainly if you are listening to too many an unrestrained "I Want" always sounding within the mind, which keeps taking you into the past or the future which "The Book" calls the world of Hell. So the harmony which exists in the unthinking "Present Time" is not seen nor is it understood. The answer is to avoid this constant difficulty is that you should firmly believe that only the silencing of the mind can rightfully bring into activity the real purpose of a person's Soul, for it is this act that allows the Soul to silently care for your outer body, which all call the "Creation", just as it does your inner body. It is only within these silent occurrences within the mind that you can experience the heavenly and peaceful "Enlightenment" that rest, within the "Present Time", which is the real world of the Creation or the environment, for the Non-Believer, but how do we achieve this?

So Yes! Is it not always good to understand that it is the utility that we call the Soul that can act only independently and with no need for thinking mind, for the mind is but a tool for its use? For actually, does not the Soul carefully and without any mind filling interference, usually attend to the needed harmony within our inner body. For indeed this internal work does not need the thinking mind, because the personal mind is only needed to reflect the Soul the outer world, and thereby, reveal to the Soul, the exact circumstances of the Heaven that "The Book" calls the "Present Time". Rightly, this must also be God's "Present" that can only exist during the ever still never moving "Now Time," which we call the "Creation", this being a modern reality of an understanding that was not available to our wise ancients. For indeed, the mind needs only to silently reflect its outer observations of the "Present Time", so that the inner Soul can naturally identify the unifying action it must take, for its only outer task is to aid the harmony seeking work of the "Mother of the Creation".

So, yes, it is true that it is your "mind" that in its silence only, can bring to the Soul all the "Present Time" activities that are silently revealed to it by the Creation. These are the actual reality of the world, in which all life and Non-Life lives. The "mind" therefore must be empty to reflect that which we call the "Present Time" to the Soul within us, this being to reveal what is happening in the "Present Time". For now, it can be genuinely, understood that this observation could only take place in the "Present Time", which is God's world and is not the past or the future which can be likened to the world of Hell? Therefore is it not logically correct that only by a "Present Time" observation through a still mind, can the Soul make the correct decision that will keep us in a "Heaven" that can only exist in the "Present Time", and so away from a mind blocking "Past" or "Future", which is a mind that is filled by the "I WANT" of our five senses, which sadly many mistakenly believe is the real them. We must endeavour not to allow the brain's animalistic tendencies, born from a past or future "I Want", to control us, for if we do, this will keep us in Hell while alive on this Earth. For indeed it is true that these active mind clouding activities created by the five senses only show us their "I Want", so that we live in a world of Hell that we mistakenly and personally create upon our Earth, this being the place in which we really "choose" to live? Is it not also true that only with this "realisation" of who the "Self" really is, that people will be able to understand that we must allow the Soul to create all harmony supporting activities, without greedily allowing the five senses to satisfy their current emerging needs, which are indeed only the control systems used by our lower animals? For assuredly, is it not true that we are not of the lower animals; we are Godly created people who have been given the "Freedom of Choice". It is also sad but recognised as a further truth that many have forgotten this fact and so believe that it is the animalistic five senses that rule them. So they naturally and impatiently pursue an animalistic "I Want" activity that confines them to a life of Hell - while living upon this Earth. Justly, this is the truth because these needed "animalistic" five senses "naturally" seek to take for themselves the whole Creation, and now the question that we must ask ourselves is, "Who is in Charge, the animal "I Want" or the Soul? Truly! When we are awake to this truth, we must "choose" to see only the Creation's wave of energy, that is continuously shining upon our mind, this being that which only exists in "Present Time", but which cannot accurately reflect the Soul, because of the many "I Want," sounds and pictures that are blocking this reflection of the "Present Time's" existing view, through the mind and to the Soul. For it is a known truth that only when the mind is still that the

Soul can see the exactness of all that exists within the "Present Time", this being that which is being reflected via the mind. For indeed, it is when these bombarding "I Want" mind disturbances that are coming from the five senses, which we think is ourselves, do stop clouding the mind, that the Soul can see the needed work to complete unifying tasks which the Divine "Mother of the Creation" does present to all people.

So yes! We must personally "choose" not to pursue the self-destructing habits of a personal "I Want", therefore is it not now clearly seen that it is essential not to be "personally" attached to any "I Want"? Therefore, we must never forget the real purpose of life which is to support the Creation's ever-developing harmony, this being that which only exists in the "Present Time", and a fact which the uncluttered mind reflects the Soul. For indeed, in acknowledging this fact, we can then habitually develop within ourselves the needed practice of selected creed worship; this again is encouraging the "habit" of allowing the inputting material from the "Present Time" to be reflected silently to the Soul. For it is only within the silencing of the mind that a Godly (Goodly) nature allows the Soul to see, and so apply its natural wisdom, this being the fact which enables it to act instinctively and without thought to pursue any needed unifying unselfish act that is necessary to re-direct the "Present Time". These acts being that which support harmony, and so continue a unity in harmony, this being that which is the Creation's purpose, and which happens only in the Heaven that exists upon this Earth, but only in the "Present Time". So it is genuinely in this life that we can truly live in Heaven that exists all around us. The questions now being: "Where are you? Do you live in Heaven, or do you live in Hell?"

So Yes! Is it not necessary to also understand that we do not need to worry about what happens after death? The Soul just moves out of the body, which is likened to leaving a car that you have just been driving. Then, after the tremendous experience of "unity with all things," your Soul will eventually occupy another car – and off you go again; but with no memories except a few instincts; especially an intense instinct of the "unity of all things" that you have just left, but you did need many lives to be fully aware of this fact – but not now! For if you are not sure about this above statement, then ask anyone before the age of two, and they will tell you or show you – just what the unity of all things is!

So Yes! After death you will eventually start another life and the Divine Mother will see to it that you are in the right place to further the maintenance of the Creation's harmony, according to your wisdom and the known acts within your last life or She will, if you are a harmless sleeper, place you back to be reborn into the families that you have so recently left, but if you have not been a harmless sleeper and have consistently and wilfully destroyed the harmony that was around you – woe be to you! For in your next birth the Divine Mother may place you in position in which you can learn that living with people who create disharmony, is not good, but it is virtuous to remember that you could be placed amongst this disharmony to correct it. It is also essential to understand that from all new births, you will be guided to seek harmony for all life and non-life that exists around you, and fortunate is the person to who is revealed the truth of the above and this indeed being before they reach the age of seven. For did not that personal seeker of a harmony say to the world, "Give me the child before the age of seven, and I will give you the adult." You will also never lose your personality, which is based upon your many lives when living has a person. For this personality that you currently have is precisely that which is required for you to be able to play your part in the on-going emerging harmony that is all around you. It can also be "scientifically" proved by history and the words of the wise ancients, that to further develop the harmony that always exists or is endeavouring to emerge around you – you are the only one who is needed to ensure this "non-harmful" harmony binding link that exists, for you are "certainly" has a person - exceptional.

36 THE SIMPLE PSYCHOLOGY
OF WHO WE THINK WE ARE

Now it is necessary to understand and also to be clear about the life force that is within all people and which can also be explained as the "three in one." With number one being the Soul, which is needed to transfer from life to death and back to life again so that that life can continue and this is the Soul that is sometimes referred to as the "Spirit." It should also be "Self-Aware" or "Self-Realised" that it is a person's Soul that unconditionally provides the harmony concerning the inner workings of the body, this being if allowed by a person's "Freedom of Choice", which was given by God or Nature for the Non-Believer, the Soul will support the harmony arising within the environment in which it currently exists. The Soul, therefore, sees clearly through the unthinking mind the reality of the "Present Time", this being all the needed information about the current environment in which it finds itself, these being the facts which are transmitted to it through a precise number two which is "The Mind". It should also be further explained that the Soul is only able to see this outer world through number two, which a person's empty "mind", this being the only fact which enables it to observe the developing Creation silently.

For again and indeed, this view through the mind can only occur when the mind is not contaminated by any mind filling inputs from the "I Want" of the inner acclaiming animalistic five senses. It should also be further understood that the Soul is the only part of the creation which fully understands the harmonic and supporting needs required by the evolving of the Creation, these being supporting needs that are accomplished by the God-given "Freedom of Choice", For certainly this much needed "Freedom of Choice" is vital because sometimes the same act can either destroy or create, depending upon circumstances and so truly this necessary allowed "Freedom of Choice" is the fact which benignly allows the Souls real purpose, which is to support non-biasedly the emerging Creation. Therefor number one is the Souls' ongoing search to support all that which is outside the body, just as it automatically provides support for all that which is within the body, in essence, this being the activity that all incarnates, and our wise ancients do speak. Number three is the body itself, which is the "doer" of all actions. Indeed, it is that which contains the five senses, which are needed to safeguard and seek the needs of the encased body so that it can healthily and safely activate the harmony, wisdom and balancing needs of the "Creation" that exists all around it. So, number one is the Soul, number two the silent Mind, and number three the Body, this being truly the three in one. The problem, this being that which is always carefully explained by our incarnates and our wise ancients, is that many people have forgotten the relationship between number one and number two, this being the compatible silence within the mind which enables a person to experience that which surpasses all understanding.

Therefore, is it not an absolute truth to understand that just as the feeling of pain in the body can only come to you when the mind is in the "Present Time", it is also an inevitable truth that the Soul can only experience the full needs of the Creation when the mind is also only experiencing the "Present Time"? For this is a fact which was unable to be stated by our incarnates and our wise ancients, this being that it is only when the mind is in the "Present Time" that it can experience the love of God or Nature for the Non-Believer. For did not the "Mother of the Creation", speaking through Jesus saying: "And everyone who has left houses or brothers or sisters or father or mother or children or fields for my sake will receive a hundred times as much in this present age and in the age to come, eternal life".

Do not these holy words endeavour to explain to our ancients that a silent mind will bring to them that which is now called "Enlightenment", this being an experience in which they become "Self-Aware" that they are knowingly and without a separating thought, a unified part of all that they love. For really, is it not also an absolute truth that you cannot physically experience a mind-filling "I Want?" Therefore is it not also true that it is only when the Soul is silently observing the "Present Time" and without a mind clouding "I Want", that you realise that you are a part of everything and that your Soul is genuinely the silent observer of the Creation, which is the only child of God, born by the "Mother of the Creation".

To explain the truth of our "Self" more correctly, it is better to understand that within you is the silent unifying "I am that I am", so the famous words "I think therefore I am" are VERY wrong. For the truth of this understanding can be further realised in these words emanating from "Mother of the Creation", who speaking through Jesus stated, "I am the bread of life. They who come to me will never go hungry, and they who believe in me will never be thirsty. I am the living bread that came down from heaven. If anyone eats of this bread, they will live forever. This bread is my flesh, which I will give for the life of the world." This "I" is the "Mother of the Creation", speaking to people and when Jesus as the personification of the Creation spoke again to the people, He said, "I am the light of the world. Whoever follows me will never walk in darkness, but will have the light of life," and so people can knowingly live in Heaven while living upon this Earth. Still, only within the Godly light that can only exist in the

"Present Time", a time which is created by God for the past and the future do not exist. God does not need to do anything within the "Present Time", a time that is filled with the truth of all that which has been Godly created, so really, that which fills the mind is many a personally created "I Want", which is simple and usually a demand being inflicted upon it by the five senses. This reality is because people habitually believe that these inner mind-filling thoughts are their personal needs. So this mind filling occurrence stops the Soul from viewing the harmony seeking needs of the silent Creation. This condition being because the truth is that the Soul can only see an uncontaminated "Present Time" through the mind, which must not be clouded by any "I Want" personal values or "I Want" for me conditions. This being that which is emanating from the non-real you, but which you mistakenly think is you – these in truth being an "I Want" that is emanating from the bodies "animalistic" five senses which are not you – for you are the Soul which observes and realises "Everything".

Thus the "viewer", which sees through the mind, is the real you. For this observer within you is the immortal soul and it is the Soul which rests within you that is joined to all that cannot die. For did not one of our wise ancients disclose that God speaking through the Divine "Mother of the Creation", say to him the following, which "The Book" modernly translates to mean, "I am the I am, and I will be who I will be for it is I who causes to be what I cause to be". Also, do not all the words of the incarnate Jesus, the personification of the Creation and thus the universal Soul, also speak to people as the "light of the world"? For indeed, it should be known that the Soul is a real child of God who did seed the Divine Mother so that the Creation, their only child could be born. Therefore is it not a universal and an inherent truth that two are needed to make one?

So Yes! You really can become "Self-Aware" that you are the silent entity that is observing yourself, this being all that "you" taste, smell, touch, see and hear until eventually, you encounter the real truth! This truth is in the correct "Realisation" that the Creation is only one child and that this only child is YOU! For indeed, it is currently understood that the Psychologist Sigmund Freud, as do most psychologist within our current time, all work on studying all the acts and activities in which we consistently put our energy? Is it not also true that a psychologist only evaluates and then works at interpreting peoples "I Want" habits that fill a person's mind? For indeed, should it not be understood that it is a person's "I Want," that fills and plangently clouds their mind and so blocks the unifying view of the "Present Time", this being the silent all-encompassing view of the Soul that rests silently within everyone? So honestly, what modern psychologists regularly evaluate is how to replace a current "I Want" with another "I Want"! So why is it that they do not look to silence the mind and so allow the Soul that rests "unblemished" within all people to see silently or maybe become has one with the Creation? For indeed, this is the harmony that every person needs and seeks, even unto the cross?

So is it not true that we discuss these dream-like manifestations of the five senses, in the belief that these thoughts are really "us". Freud certainly did not separate, study or even try to identify that the people he was trying to help could personally live in three simple realties, these being the "Past" the "Future" and the "Present Time". Nor did he understand that these first two are false worlds and so should be defeated and removed so that patients can be encouraged to live in the real world – the silent all-encompassing "Present Time" and if they become ill, to become an observer of that illness. Therefore, is there not a knowing truth, which psychologists may not understand, that there are only three simple realities that confront each person and which is the only condition in which that they can "choose" to give birth to and so "Self" create only one reality? For it is decidedly real that only people have three different worlds in which they can choose to live and also any of these worlds can be selected to live in because of our "Freedom of Choice"? For assuredly, a "Freedom of Choice" rests within ALL people and therefore should not a "deciding" person be recognised to be "observing" and "aiding" that which they have "chosen" to observe and so aid? Is this "observing" being of the ever real "Present Time" or is it of a mind filled with thoughts of an "I Wanted" Past, or maybe a dreamed "I Want" Future, both of which do not exist? For the real world is that which your Soul is "Godly" created or Nature created for the Non-Believer, to assist and so automatically assist the body of the outside world just has it assists all harmonised activities that are within your body.

So yes! Your Souls purpose, via its "Freedom of Choice", is to decidedly "choose" to unthinkingly and with a clear mind, to aid the work of the Divine Mother, this being that activity which is all around you as it is caringly within you, but only in the "Present Time"! For indeed these unthinking and practical observations are that which is needed to "support" the harmony, wisdom and balance that always exists or attempting to exist, in the "Present Time", which can only be when there are no thoughts of "I Want" blocking the view of the Soul from seeing through the mind that which needs to be supported in the "Present Time."

Also, should this silent "observer", this being that which "The Book" explains to be the Soul, views a reality which can only be seen through the empty mind and which views only that which can exist in the "Present Time". For again, is it not the Soul, which unthinkingly decides and supports the real way of life? This being that which simply activates all that may be needed to support the Creations harmony – this being if any action is necessary and under the Souls peace-seeking jurisdiction which is based upon the knowledge that there is only one entity.

Therefore to find which path through life a person is attached to can usually be identified by understanding if they are living in an "I Want" world that can only exist in the past or the future, which is a life lived in Hell, or do they live an active life which is the pursuing of "What the Creations Harmony Needs," which is an unthinking unselfish life lived in the "Present Time" - this is undoubtedly being likened to a life lived in Heaven that can only exist in the "Present Time". Therefore, such a psychologist does not question which world a person believes that they live in, this being the belief that they are living in Hell or the belief that they are living in Heaven. Nor do they seek to understand or bring identification to a person's chosen place to live, again this being to either to live in Hell or to live in Heaven, which is identified by what in their life most commonly attracts them.

Simply put, because people have been given the "Freedom of Choice" this being to support the needs of the emerging creation, this fact also means that people can ignorantly "choose" to live in Hell or wisely "choose" to live Heaven and this is the place where they usually live. It can be identified by the activity they pursue, which makes them contented to live in Heaven or discontented to live in Hell, this also being a pure reflection of their "religious" belief system which can be used to attack and so gain the wealth of those belonging to other religions or used to strengthen pack leaders. So Yes! Is this not because all people have been given a "Freedom of Choice," simply because the same act can create and support harmony or it can achieve the exact opposite. For indeed, people can live in only two belief systems, these being belief systems in which a person retargets and redirects the incoming energy that is always emerging around them via the Creation, and so do this to pursue their personal "I Want", or they can "choose" to support the developing Creations needs. With this fact it is also interesting to know that Freud did not understand that it does not need a great deal of wisdom to acknowledge which of these two paths lead to unrest, fear, and dissatisfaction and which path leads to the actual opposite. For indeed did not Freud concentrate on his clients plague-like and personally introduced "I Want for Me" problems? These were undoubtedly being his clients' problems which are born from the "I Want" of the animalistic five senses. Then did Freud not purposely attempt to re-direct his clients with another "I Want"? For yes, what Freud should have revealed to his clients is that people cannot in "thinking" decide "who is in charge?" or what their personal "I Want" target is," for these are our thoughts from the past and which are used to create a targeted future or past based "I Want" for myself, these being targets emanating from the animalistic five senses. The short answer to this is to silently fall in love with the reality of that which you really are, and so attach yourself to the fact that you are "everything" that exists within the Creation. For certainly is it not true that the incarnate Jesus speaking as the personification of the entire Creation and on behalf of His Divine Mother say: "Love thy neighbour as thy self," this is because your neighbour is YOU! Indeed, the whole Creation is you! Quite a fantastic "Self- Aware" or "Self-Realisation" isn't it? Precisely, this is also being a fact which was quantified in the parable of the Vineyard Owner who hired some working men, for justly did not Jesus say that this owner said, "I Want to give the man who was hired last the same as I gave you" and also: "So the last will be first, and the first will be last," meaning that He saw only the actual reality in that there is only one person, only "One Self" being in the queue and many parables state this same understanding – for there is only "one" just as there is only one Creation and only one "Present Time", there is also only one life force.

So yes, this may take a little understanding – but it is a truth of which ALL religions and philosophies speak. When you achieve "Self-Awareness" or "Self-Realisation", you will know it to be accurate, for that which our wise ancients are all speaking about is the Soul, which is that which belongs and is attached to "everything." A simple way to understand these words and their meaning is to again just look at your hand. Yes, just stare at your hand and then ask yourself the question "Is this me?" and it is known what your answer will be. Now it is time for you to quickly realize "scientifically" that which many philosophies and scientist state. For they all state this great truth; this being that you cannot be that which you observe. Therefore if you think that your hand is you, then chop it off and throw it away and then ask the question: "Where am I?" Of course, part of you is not in the bin for the reality is that you cannot see that which you is – which is the Soul, for indeed, the observer can never be that which is being observed. For example, you can never be that which the lower five senses bring to you, these being smell, touch, sight, hearing, and taste.

For is it not an undoubted truth that we all knowingly understand that these are our five "senses," but what we do not usually connect with is that they are all tools of the Soul, this because we think that they are ourselves – they are not. They are instruments for the use of your Soul, and the Souls' purpose is to support the ever-evolving creation – which is everything. The reason why we believe that the five senses are ourselves is realised because of our mindfully controlled willpower, this being that which is controlled by our "Freedom of Choice" which has been given only to people. This "Willpower" is undoubtedly the energy within our bodies which via the "Freedom of Choice" we use to direct the outer pursuits of the body. It is this, our inner willpower, that we have mistakenly directed, by using our Godly given "Freedom of choice, to habitually "choose" to allow our "Consciousness" to automatically empower "Willpower" to seek only the "I Want" of the animalistic five senses. Therefore it is this mistake; birthed in childhood which enables the claims emanating from the animalistic five senses to enter the mind freely – this occurring at around the age of two or three - has children begin to copy their parents. But the truth is that the purpose of the five senses is to safely and silently support the needs of the real "Self" which is the bodily installed "Soul".

Now simply put, this means that, because of the above fact, many people have forgotten who they are, and so the Godly or Nature given for the Non-believer, freedom of "choice" has been personally gifted to the five senses; so now the Soul's real purpose cannot be realised, because its view of the outer world is blocked by this freedom that fills the mind with "I Want" for ME, this being that which is continually emanating from one or all of five senses. This realty is simply because the Soul cannot break God's law which gave peoples "consciousness" the "Freedom of Choice", this being to enable them to be able to physically support the "Mother of the Creation" endeavours to maintain harmony within the emerging Creation. Therefore and honestly, the Soul cannot "see" the outer world, because of the mind filling "I Want" thoughts, this being the reality which blocks the Souls view of the conditions of the "Present Time"; therefore "scientifically" that which we really are and also this being the only reality that we cannot see; which is our inner ever existing "Soul". So the Soul, although strongly connected to the unity of God's will or Natures will for the Non-Believer, cannot adjust the harmony seeking needs of the Creation because of the mind filling "I Want" and therefore the Soul remains inactive until the mind filling activities of the searching five senses stop their ever searching ever pleading "I Want" from filling the mind. For it is then, with this we call "Enlightenment," that the Soul becomes "knowledgeable" regarding that which it identifies when it is "personally" supported to see through this stillness of the mind. Because of its unity with all life and Non-Life, it then silently engages the body to perform deeds that support the Creation's ever-evolving search for "harmony". Precisely, this is being the harmony for all life and Non-Life and now, if the reader wishes to attain this stillness of a free mind – Read on.

37   WHO WE REALLY ARE

Of course, past lives influence the direction of our current lives, because of past habits, which science says are arrived at by our "genes," and some scientists state that these "genes" have the memories of past lives and this, of course, influences us during our current life. It is also essential to understand that we ALWAYS have the freedom of choice, as to what action we should take. Still, usually, we are as the wise ancients say, "asleep" as we pursue the cultural habits and loves of those around us and therefore are not in a "waking state".

Thus it is that wise ancient's further state that we do allow our bodies to perform habits that we do very little to control and a good covering blanket for this "sleep" is in thinking "It is just our way of living". Indeed, this is being a fixed way of life that can continue through death after death after death, and indeed, this is why the ancients call it "being asleep".

Therefore an excellent question to ask is that in the knowledge that all people have "free will" unto death and after death and also knowing that even after death we are controlled, either by our personal "I Want," or by a Soul that seeks to perform harmonising acts that strengthen the harmony that eases and blends the Creation's onward pursuit? Therefore the simple question is "Where do you want to be re-born? For this reality, the fact is in the knowledge that people have been given the freedom of choice, so they do have an individual and a personal "free will" unto and after death.

Therefore, indeed, the unified on-going growth of the Creations' evolution is a fact, and it is a significant fact that all life and Non-Life belongs to, and which none can escape. Therefore, what is "free will?" Is it that which allows many countries to have their cultural ideals and belief systems, which influence their peoples' "freedom of choice"? For are not all countries also controlled by simple laws made by people, these being laws that seriously influence their citizens' personal life?

So Yes! The real question then is: "Who or what is now controlling your life?" Logically, this is a good question and can be asked if you want to know where your own personal "free will" is taking you. Can we say that your "free will" is that which is obedient to the harmony seeking needs of the Creation and its ongoing "Evolution" that can only be witnessed in the "Present Time? Or is your "free will" obedient to your country or your community, or your boss, or your religious laws, etc.? Or is your "free will" obedient to your laws? Therefore is it, not an absolute truth, that in all of the above activities; "free will" is the same as the zero. Is this being the nothing that rests within all numerical calculations but which magnificently expands or reduces the world of numbers in which it becomes attached to or is detached from, this being either the Creation's evolutionary process or a country's community laws or your self-made laws? For justly, people are really like this zero; this nothing which is extremely powerful, but can do nothing when on its own? For certainly is it not true that this "nothing;" this "Zero" in the world of numbers, is a "Nothing" only when it stands alone? But when we apply this "nothing" to the small world of only nine numbers, it lawfully expands to explain the workings from the smallest atom to the totality of the universe and if you took this nothing away from these calculations, what would happen? These calculations would cease to exist, this example being that which shows people are genuinely the same as the all-knowing "Nothing", this being the same has that "Nothing" which creates the world of numbers upon which the modern world rests.

So Yes! As the number "nothing", which creates and expands the world of numbers, so does the "No Thing" which I call God and Non-Believers call "Nothing", creates and expands our modern world which also evolved and is still evolving into many different forms as we can see in the life and Non-Life of all that exists upon our Earth. Therefore, if we wish to understand the harmony of all that which is around us, we need to just look at the Earth and especially how fire and water live together and then also to look at our own body and silently experience how our inner organisms, these being the many separate millions of them, which also live together usually in perfect harmony.

So yes! Is it not true that all our bodily parts live in perfect harmony and should not all people live in this same supporting way? For indeed, if a person believes that they are separate from the harmony that is around them, then all they need to do is to commit themselves to the un-harming life of the one body. Therefore, does this not lead to a great truth that the harmony seeking a way of life is to treat the Creation as if it was also their body? For cannot it also be said to be true that each natural part within us supports all the other parts. So each separate entity usually supports our whole body in the pursuit of a working harmony that brings love and unity between all that exists within us.

So yes! Look at your own body and know and so understand it to be true that these millions of parts love and care for each other, and if you have lost some of them or illness comes to you, or you are going forward towards the seeking of another birth, then remember that this is an opportunity for those around you to show how they love and support you, just as the "Mother of the Creation" ensures that the love of together always replacing disharmony. What is also historically known is that life upon this Earth has gone through several significant periods of extinction; this being has if the life that went extinct on our Earth was not working in harmony with the Creation, while some lives were deemed a perfect match. For indeed, the needed harmony that exists upon our planet Earth is always maintained by the Divine "Mother of the Creation".

For assuredly, has our fossil evidence shows that sharks populated the planet before the dinosaurs existed. An actuality which is seemingly being more than four hundred million years ago, and that some sharks have not changed in a hundred million years so they must be useful for the Creation, but what about people? Is it not stated to be true that it was only ten to twelve thousand years ago that people stopped hunting and grazing and living as wild animals, this being to become settled farmers and landowners who existed by adding personal and needed value to the world around them? Although truly it is interesting to think of a caveman sitting with his children around a fire telling the story about the "flood", this "flood" being to describe a "peoples" world that was privately claiming all the land and also destroying all the natural growth upon it, as well as killing all the "unwanted" wild animal life that once lived upon it, and this being a self-claimed land in which of course, all hunting and food-seeking by "others" were forbidden. For it was then that people began to change very quickly and instead of taking value from the world around them, they began to add their new value to the world in which they lived.

They did this when they started to grow crops and also to domesticate animals and even began to grow their food. Then very quickly and in a tiny amount of time, when compared to the shark scale of life, we began to use self-made copper tools, to help us to achieve more added values and this was only seven thousand years ago. Then five thousand years ago we found how to make metal by mixing copper and tin, this being when we entered the Bronze Age, whereby we then quickly improved our ways of adding and creating value; for was it not only three thousand years ago that we discovered how to make Iron. Also is it not true that it was only around eight hundred years ago that the Italian mathematician Fibonacci (c.1170–1250), was credited with introducing the decimal system to Europe and the first known English use of the number "nothing" which we called a "zero", was borrowed from the Arab world, and this was only in 1598, just four hundred and nineteen years ago.

So yes! Was it not only a few hundred years ago that we found this "nothing;" this being the zero that created a whole new world of numbers which allowed people to mathematically count numbers beyond infinity which led to many modern strictly "numerically" calculated inventions? Then just over a hundred years ago, we found how to make heavier than air machines that could fly in the air and then within sixty-five years this quickly led to flights to the moon and machines that are now going beyond our solar system – so who are we? Would it not be wonderful if we could understand that the "I" within us was the carer and the harmoniser of all life and Non-Life that existed upon our planet? Therefore this is being an "I" who fully understands the ancient meaning "I AM THAT I AM" because we are everything and all life and none life is only one "energised" entity. For it is indeed known that becoming "Enlightened" and so knowingly becoming an essential part of being "Self-Aware" of the "unified" world around you; that such an experience could lead to an authentic "second" experience, this being a "Self-Realised" reality that can come after achieving a "Self-Aware" experience of "Enlightenment". For indeed what can also be certainly experienced within "Enlightenment", this being if we continue with the "Self-Aware" exercise explained later in "The Book", we will arrive at a unifying experience that will allow us again to fully understand the target of all the major religions and philosophies. Meticulously, this being a unifying "Self-Realisation" target which also exists within "Enlightenment" and it arises after a "Self-Aware" experience, this being when the observer and the observed are known to be a single unified entity, for in "Self-Realisation" you become everything and the observer ceases to exist. For indeed, these two realities are the only targets of all the major philosophies and religions.

So Yes! This "Self-Realisation" is an experience that ensures that the solitary "I" within you ceases to exist and there is no longer an observer, this being about the actual target which all our wise ancients speak. Precisely, this is because in "Self-Realisation" you "realise" that the "self" you think is you; no longer exist, for you are no longer a part of the creation! You are no longer an "observer" of the world – for you fully experience that you ARE "everything" and that you are a personification of the all "The Creation".

So yes, this is a "Self-Realisation" that was asserted by the ancients to be a known experience in that you are "everything" and that you are no longer an observer to all that which is around you, for you are indeed all that exists, for really and truly you become "Everything." Accurately, this is the "Self-Realisation", which the all primary philosophies target, via meditation, and it is enabled to occur after a "Self-Aware" experience of "Enlightenment". Thus is it that "Enlightenment" is an experience" which is best achieved by the "Patient Mantra Meditation", which "The Book" explains is the best way for people who live in "Market Economy" countries. For indeed, the sounding of a single worded mantra into the mind disciplinary STOPS the five senses from entering they're "I Want" into the mind, this being because you are now training your consciousness to withdraw prior permission, this being past childhood permission which allowed "will-power" to be automatically used by the five senses and so mantra "Patient Meditation" will again discipline them to come under the silent management of the all observing Soul. Factually, this is a personal "meditational" activity that frees the Soul to see the world through an empty mind because the five senses will be "meditation ally" and automatically disciplined to remain silent.

So Yes! With this new "freedom of choice" activity, your Soul is now freely "chosen", via a mantra-based and patient type meditation, to again become the controller and manager. Thus the Soul can discipline the five senses to become obediently silent. Regularly, this also brings "Enlightenment," for it creates within a person "The Peace that Surpasses all Understanding", for only your Soul is silently observing, all that exists in the "Present Time" – but more about how to achieve this later in "The Book".

So Yes! "Enlightenment" is the first stage of realising the truth of the world in which you live, and this is attained with great difficulty because the five senses, all of which have their voices and which have been mistakenly created by consciousness at your early age to be the real you, put up a tremendous fight in their efforts not to lose control of you; you being the individual who does feed them with their "I Want". But the patient meditational path to "Enlightenment" will stop their noisy chatter for it brings a disciplined silence to mind has the five senses become silenced and so unheard, yet also silently obedient but only under the disciplined gaze of your inner Soul.

So Yes! "Enlightenment" will bring you to fully understand that you live only in the "Present Time" for honestly all thinking attachments and thoughts of the past or future are no more within you, for truth within the experience of "Enlightenment," the past and the future do not exist. Undoubtedly, this is because "Enlightenment" can only be experienced in the "Present Time", which is a time which can only be fully experienced when the mind has no blocking "I Want" thoughts that take the viewer into the past or the future – the world that "The Book" calls Hell.

So Yes, this experiencing of a "Heaven" that only exists in the "Present Time", is truly an event which Christians describe as experiencing the Holy Spirit or Holy Ghost within them and which the Islamic teachings describe as being filled by the Angel Gabriel and many other religions and philosophies call it the experiencing of "Paradise", "Eden", "Heaven" "Nirvana", "Promised Land", "Moksha", "Shangri-La" "Kenshō", "Svargamu", "Kā bāga", "Vāṭikā", "Kā jagaha", "Sukhabhavana", and numerous other names emanating from our many religions and philosophies which have all targeted, for their culturally different followers, a way to experience "Enlightenment, this truly, being an existence which naturally gives to the experiencer an authentic experience of realising that all that which your five senses now silently experience should be cared for as if it is YOURSELF, and that truly, you have everything that you need, in accordance to your personal development

. For it is also sincerely realised that your soul needs nothing has you completely understand that the body is only an instrument for the use of your Soul – which is similar to when you drive a car, for the car is also only an instrument for your use and both need support. There is also no such thing as an accident of birth.

The reason for this is that we are all born into the best situation, this being that which is needed to progress or care for the emerging harmony which emanating all around us. It is also said, by many of our wise ancients, that people upon their current bodies' death, usually chose their parents or the family members of those they have just left. Still, many are also born into situations chosen by the Divine Mother, who gave birth to the Creation, which is also God's only child –these being birth places where they are needed or where they can best receive an "understanding" of their need to awaken in their new birth and so realise their true potential.

"The Book" also explains that a woman, whose thoughts upon dying was the desire to be a man and the man, whose thoughts upon dying was the desire to be a woman, are reborn within the bodies of that wish. Still, their Soul cannot change its gender, and so the birthed ones way of love and behaviour remain the same as it was in its past life, also a person who upon death "chooses" a desire to be reborn into the same family. It must be understood that the male does originate the gender of the child, but the later arriving Soul cannot change its gender.

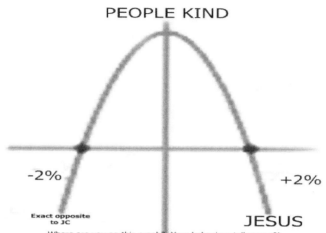

PEOPLE KIND

-2% +2%

Exact opposite to JC

JESUS

Where are you on this graph? Your behaviour tells you :0)
Truth says: You can identify them by their fruit, by the way they act
Nature says: Can you give grapes from thorn bushes, or figs from thistles?
But Humans can change their ways, become fruitful and so be fed by "Sugar in the Water"

It should be further understood that the above graph also explains why some people fiercely attack other religions or cultural belief systems within which they do not live, this being because they still have within their bodies the animalistic and "cultural" feeling of "Pack Unity". So they fear all that which is different from their existing "Packs" belief system, this being the system under which they now live. Therefore, it should also be understood that killing or punishing them is just another belief emanating from a different pack's animalistic thinking, i.e., "My pack is better than your pack". And so they rely upon group control rather than the control of their Soul which of course is animalistic. So like an untrained dog that's not trained to support the various endeavours and unique needs of the world that exists around all people. But the correct understanding is that re-training, similar to the re-training of pups, is necessary. For it is known that pack animals will undoubtedly respond favourably to a new "culturally" based training activity. This re-training being in direct accordance with the majority laws that guarantee a good life within that majority-controlled unity. For indeed, it is not wise to punish people who have a different "cultural" belief system, this being because they are early re-births from the animal kingdom. For simply put, this would be, like killing all the dogs in a city because one did bite someone. Even if you do not believe in re-births, you must still believe in the above "Training" – unless you are an early re-birth from the animal kingdom and so also fear that anything different from your current culture. These new re-births into people that are emanating from our animal kingdom may also have become birthed into a traditional culture which they do not understand and so YES! They too need to be trained similarly – so it is good to remember that at least 70% of the pack must agree to the way that they are controlled, a system which will avoid ALL our Earths wars and conflicts which are always created by pack leaders and they're "I Want" to control.

This target is being the achieving of "Enlightenment", and many of our wise ancients also say it is true that few people also return to a rebirth in the animal world. Still, if they do, then they can again seek a progressive way to return to birth into the world of people for "Enlightenment and "Self-Realisation" is the ongoing final target for ALL life. For indeed, cannot it also be seen as a logical "harmony" that animal life can be reborn into people's bodies, thus increasing the population of people and decreasing the population of the animal kind?

Again it is logical to understand the evolution of the "Creation" that is all around you, and it is undoubtedly pre-determined. Therefore, at this point is it good for all to remember that a new re-births from our animal kind will find great difficulty in meditating or controlling their mind and so stopping the allowing of the animalistic "I Want" needs of the five senses, but the above and following knowledge will support their endeavour to be has people who have had many lives – for is it not known to be true that all our holy people wanted for nothing and indeed willingly gave away to those in need, all that they had.

For rightly, it is an absolute truth that people are now rapidly expanding and that our animal neighbours are rapidly declining for from where else is all this energy that is creating people coming? Can this not also be seen that when looking at this population graph of people such as this one: That a question arises such as:-"How should we treat the newly emerging 2% of people who are emanating from the animal kingdom" this being because they are the exact opposite to Jesus and all our other holy leaders who existed in the 2% at the other end of this graph? For these people newly emerging from the animal kingdom have a new "freedom of choice" as do all people, but "scientifically" they must need to have many "personal" lives to reach the characteristic behaviour patterns of the majority of people, simply because their choice "habitually" emanates from "animalistic" past experiences.

We can now see and know why we have amongst people, the exact opposite to the behaviour patterns of the man we know as Jesus, of the Christian religion, for this is a man who silently suffered a painful punishment which led to a painful death, all of which was in agreement with the harmony which was emanating all around Him. For carefully, is it not true that He took no active part in his death and that His final words were: *"Forgive them for they know not what they do!"*

The above graph shows the growth pattern of all people's lives, and it also reveals that there must be a behavioural pattern that is the exact opposite of that of Jesus, and also the fact that many people will also be close to His behaviour patterns, such as our many wise ancients. But now we should also understand that these new entrants from the animal kingdom can have an exact opposite in a behaviour pattern than the "personality" patterns of Jesus; these being people who could so easily inflict pain upon others, as any animal can justly do, and without any feeling of wrongdoing. Now the question is: "How should we treat these rebirths who newly reborn has people and who are the exact opposite of Jesus?"

This fact is being exceptionally accurate and useful in the understanding the concept that these new incomers will be chosen ones that are emerging as people from the animal kingdoms, and who are also entering the bodies of people for the first time. Therefore is it not true that we should respect this development and not cruelly treat them, cage or punish them but should kindly treat them "encouragingly" and with wisdom, especially when they are at a young age. Is it not also important to do this by understanding just the type of education they need to become compatible with a people's way of living and this should be done before the age of seven and now, just as an aside regarding this graph. Next time you glance into a mirror, ask your five senses, these being that which you may think is you, where is your position on this graph? And then listen to their answer.

The other strange thing about re-birth is that it is not unusual for a child to be able to reveal the memories of their past lives. Precisely, this is before these memories begin to fade after the age of two, and this memory loss is because of all the new mind-filling inputs of their newly emerging life. Correctly, this is understood to be so, because "logically" all-new births are deemed to be the start of a new life which must begin with a blank slate because after all, you are a new "reborn" you. It can also be further "scientifically" understand that the reason for this is that the history or knowledge of past lives cannot evaluate the needs of the "Present Time", for only the "Mother of the Creation" can do that. Always it is done for the benefit of those who listen and obey the harmony of God's laws.

So yes! The Divine Mother always teaches the way of the developing harmony that resides within the Creation and which are Godly created laws. She also sends "to do" messages to people's Soul, which then views that which has been presented to it, which can only be done in the "Present Time". For it is only then that a person can genuinely adjust and physically direct events towards the harmony that is required by all life and non-life and this being within all the events that are happening in the world around it.

For it is undoubtedly true that the current needs of the Creation indeed become apparent to the "Enlightened" ones, for surely these needs are "personally" placed in front of each "Enlightened" person, as the Divine Mother presents to them the needed activity to ensure the ongoing harmony that rests within the "Present Time". For did not the Divine "Mother of the Creation" speak through the man called Jesus: "But everyone who hears these words of mine and does not put them into practice is like a foolish man who built his house on sand." And also: "He, who has ears, let him hear."

So Yes! The question now is to know that it is an excellent time to remember that there is one thing you know about your body, and that is that you cannot take it with you when you die. For indeed, it is also challenging to understand that upon dying, some people want to leave their body and go to calm heaven, which accepts only lovely people and this for the rest of the billions of remaining years of the Creation, when they should be concentrating at their point of death upon their next life, which most people do as they think about their past happy times

. For rightly, there is time, but not much time, when a person experiences a mental movement of going down the tunnel "light." Precisely, this being that which will eventually take them to their new life, therefore at this point, they must quickly and personally decide their next rebirth situation, or simply allow the Divine Mother to do it for them. Of course, it is understood that our scientists tend to combine deaths biological and psychological ongoing mechanisms, by stating that the light one sees when leaving the body, is the common biological by-product of hormonal neuron changes.

It is an exciting viewpoint, isn't it, but it is not correct therefore seriously upon your journey down the white tunnel of death, choose the birthplace of your next life or let the "Mother of the Creation" choose this for you. An example of how to fulfil this white light need, at the point of death, is in the ancient story about a "Wise Man" who, feeling that he was too old to be useful and feeling he was a burden to those around him, decided that he would "go to the forest," a term used in our ancient days by old men, and so quietly prepare for his death. As an interesting aside, the females of our species never did this because they were always useful to the people around them, and it should also be understood that for both sexes, suicide was forbidden.

The story continues that after a few self-disciplined days without food or water, and at the point of death, he then sat with his back to a tree and began to marvel at the love and wonders of the Creation around him – and so awaited his death. But as just before the "white light" came upon him, he suddenly saw a young deer close to him and the old man became lovingly attached to the deer and thought how excellent and how beautiful the deer was – then he died. He was born again as a deer, or so this very ancient story says.

So yes! Be careful what you think about at your very point of death for your rebirth will be in the location of your thoughts target. Still, this wise ancient's story also explains why most people automatically come back to the close kin that they had left behind – like parents being reborn again to their children. Therefore, indeed, this is undoubtedly a beautiful story that indicates that the Soul is an entity, which is separate from the body, just as a driver is a separate entity from their car. It should also be realised that just as the driver can leave the car and obtain another – so can the Soul, that upon leaving one body can certainly obtain another during that bodies gestation within its mother.

This truth means that at the point of death and if the Soul uses its "Enlightened" choice to maintain harmony, it would be most useful to assist the flight of the Soul by remembering Kipling's six honest working men – and so target your next birth by silently acknowledging "What" you want to be. "Why" you want to be that and "When" it should be; plus "How" this birth should take place and also "Where" it should take place and most importantly, "Who" it should be with, which again is said to be the reason why most people seem to be reborn again into their family and relatives, for often the last and most energetic harmony seeking thought upon death is to return to loved ones.

So yes do not be afraid of dying when aged and welcome the opportunity that enables your Soul to choose and hold onto the place of your next birth, this being while going down the white tunnel has your Soul moves from one life to another. Of course, without this "choosing" knowledge, it is interesting to know where the next rebirth decision comes from, especially regarding as to where the next rebirth is to take place. Do the harmony seeking laws of the Creation decide your next births location, or does the individual decide as in the above ancient story? My own experiences of near-death and the attraction of going down the tunnel towards the white light, lead me to believe that it is usually the individual's request as above; this "Freedom of Choice" being the place of their next birth – for it is a beautiful and peaceful way end the life of your current body.

But it can also be agreed that the need for the "Mother of the Creation" and Her pursuit of harmony can and will decide where your next birth should be, for a new way of life may be more suitable for some, and yes! The Soul does fully understand the bodies' wishes, for it strongly supports the "love of harmony" and the Soul may seek a life of "family" harmony at the point of death. For indeed, this is a Creation which continually exists, but only within the "Present Time" and it seems that the more a someone's "I Want" personally control them and all those around them, the closer they are to their animal pre-life.

38   THE CHOICE OF RELIGION IS YOURS

Regarding our past Lives. Is it not "scientifically" true that over the past two thousand years, many religions have physically attacked other religions, and, even their own "privately" introduced belief systems? For indeed, our histories also show that some religious leaders also want to have private control over the followers of their own religiously based belief systems in which they are a leader. Therefore, indeed, it is known to be true that some religious leaders even punish their followers for not obeying their commands.

For assuredly, it is also known to be true that any religious belief system can be splintered into many different factions with some religious sects becoming like football teams and have playing supporters who fight for personal supremacy in a particular "Religious League". Painstakingly, this is being a league in which they compete and whose animal-based "tribal" emotions seem to have been triggered by a searching need to belong to their pack?

The question is: Are these religious leaders, of these separating groups, seeking to increase the power of fellowship within their belief system? Or is this simply an activity which is to find more people to support their way of finding a "God", or whoever they have named as the initiator of good deeds and righteous living. Or do they want to show the way to fulfil the needs of their followers' Soul, or is what they are seeking is their own personal "I Want" you to obey "me" and make our religion the richest? For indeed it valid, that for the past two thousand years, many of our religious leaders say that only their belief system is the real and correct path to God, and even create wars to prove this?

Indeed, this cannot be correct, for there are many hundreds of culturally based "religions" and "philosophies" throughout our world that show many the ways to God's world. Yet still, it is only the personal practices of the individual that can bring them to that which is right "Enlightenment". Precisely this being an experience of God's world which is the same for all people, regardless of the religion or philosophy which brought them towards achieving this reality. Yet, is it not strange that many religious leaders did and did think that killing and punishing people who believe in a different way of worship and who are harming no one, really believe that these "attacking of others" acts will bring them personally closer to a Godly love and the personal existence of "Enlightenment?" Also, is it not sadly true that some "religious" leaders also request their followers to inflict severe punishment upon rival religious others and indeed followers do this because they have been told it will bring them closer to God and also will secure a place for them in Heaven when they die – can they sincerely believe this statement? For what father can suggest that others kill his children to obtain capital or financial gain? For history shows that they do! Or is it merely a personal "I Want" demand in the greed-based belief that God needs their assistance in planning the future of people, and that it is also correct to punish and then brutally take for themselves the personal chattels of those who are not "Showing the true way to God?"

Is it not strange that people who can worship God can personally attack to destroy another religion that can act as thieves? Or is it an "I Want," emanating from the five senses, that is merely pursuing personal improvement in their economic system, for sincerely, does this not happen when religious leaders seek financial and property gains?

Therefore, is it not true, as history shows, that it is only the property and financial world that changes, whenever these religiously based punishing and attacking conflict upon others are thriving?

So, is the power of "Economics" the real motivational reason for these current and past two thousand years' actions? Is this not a fact which shows the reason for constant and on-going conflicts between similarly sourced religions and also various differing belief systems?

Or should not the power emanating from our Holy "Present", given to us by God or by Nature for the Non-Believer, be that which dictates the harmony seeking needs of the "Present Time", and if you wish to truly, understand the purpose of these developing "Holy" needs – Read on.

39   LIVING IN HELL

When individuals or groups of people ignore the correct way of life that can be lived in the harmony of Heaven that exists in the "Present Time" and so unknowingly or ignorantly choose to live in a self-made "Hell" that they create to exist in the "Present Time", they are continually avoiding or changing the purpose of their Soul – which is the real navigator of our body and the real "silent" leader of the holistic way in which we should live. This false living in

Hell can be likened to living in a dream which can best be called a "nightmare". Logically, this is because in the world of the "Present Time" it is Gods laws or the laws of nature for the Non-Believer that govern the Creation and these are laws that can be likened to the laws made by people that govern the "highway code"; these codes being the road safety and vehicle controlling rules for a world created by people.

So is it not true that all people know that if you drive your car and ignore this "highway code," you will encounter many problems as you advance in your world of driving and will blame many others for the "inconvenience" that they cause to you. Therefore as in the rules of the "highway code", is it not true that the disobeying of God's or Natures "highway code", these being the laws that exist in the Heaven upon our Earth that we call the "Present Time", that if these laws are wilfully ignored this will "automatically" lead to a life likened to living in Hell?

Therefore does this not also mean that living in Hell is a self-chosen life, because of a personal "I Want" desires arising from past or future thoughts? Unquestionably, this is again explaining that the living in Hell upon this earth can be simply likened to driving a car through a city and ignoring its "highway code", this being irrespective of the damage it can do to others and also to all the "Creation" around the active perpetrator of this law-breaking driver – is this you?

Also, is this not an example of a person's fear, this being a fear that occurs when they live in this self-created Hell? For indeed this is a simple accomplishment that is created by allowing the mind to be controlled by the animalistic "I Want" of the five senses which have ignorantly been allowed free reign to enter the mind, for assuredly, is this not also a fact which readily shows in a persons' anger against "foreigners".

Beyond doubt, this attack is being against a person from another land or even nearby separate community, for this truth is because these people fear that a foreigner might or will compete against them for their own personal and selfish "I Want", for indeed, it is not too difficult to explain the why, of this worrying fear of the "alien amongst us". For cannot it be easily explained has a fear of those who live in the "Hell"! Therefore, this is being a personally made "Hell" which is activated by a personally created past and or future based thought which creates an "I Want" for me.

It is this that drives the weaker ones amongst us, which "The Book" explains has been probably those who are newly emerging from the animal kingdom. These being those who are not yet capable of using this gift of their new life's cultural way which is designed to expand their search for new experiences, which is always combined with a new type of learning. Instead, these weaker early human births, newly emanating from the animal kingdom, become indecisive and fearfully attempt to destroy the trust that these "strangers" among them bring to their new world.

For indeed it can be said that this is because they only target their pasts habitually needed "I Want" that is emanating from the animalistic five senses and so fear such competition which brings them a fearful pain of a potential "future" loss. Precisely, this is being a mind filling pain which they angrily transfer to the stranger because they animalistic-ally fear that this stranger will take their "I Want".

Of course, you can identify such "I Want" people by the painful disorder that they produce around themselves and especially by the way they live. One often wonders, when seeing large numbers of these new birthed as people who are aggressively rioting against the decisions of their government, what higher power they would have if they did not riot, but instead, stood linked together, showing the solidarity of inactive "un-animalistic" silence against their government's "I Want" and in this way move peacefully closer to their well-paid and ruling adversaries.

Also, if their need was genuine – how many more thousands of people would join them for conflict is not the way to find harmony, when the answer being sought is one that can bring a peaceful understanding to the majority of people, for indeed, the power and silence of the "Present Time" is far more potent than a demanding past or future "I Want". Thus it is that the inflicting of pain upon oneself or others for a declared "I Want" reason is no way to gain the "good life," (God Life) which is only achieved by allowing your Soul to support the "Mother of the Creation" who truly controls the "Present Time". Again, this is likened to the obeying and so supporting the "highway code" of all Life and Non-Life. For no person can be "divinely" supported by the "Mother of the Creation" during their angry attacks upon others.

Therefore the task is to seek the harmony that always exists and is "constantly" endeavouring to emerge all around them. It is also good to remember that you cannot be personally punished by God's laws or the laws of Nature for the Non-Believer, this being for any selfish stealing attack upon nature or others. You will simply be ignored by the "Mother of the Creation", and it is also good to remember that there is no one who can gain favour with the Divine Mother by saying, "Sorry" for some aggressive, "I Want" act that has just been completed. The simple reason is that you are seeking the forgiveness for a past activity which is impossible, or you may even be seeking the Divine Mother's permission for a potential future activity which the Divine Mother also cannot acknowledge, this being because you have been given the "Freedom of Choice" and this is a fact in which no one can deny.

The simple reality to this fact is that it is the "Mother of the Creation", who is continuously creating harmony for all life and Non-Life, which can strongly influence the conditions of the "Present Time". Rightly, this being the only reality in which God's world or Natures world for the Non-Believer can indeed exist, this being a fact for all life and non-life that currently exists upon this Earth.

It must also be for the same reason and very accurate, that prayers seeking a "Future" event may remind you how to target and do a good deed. Still, these words will mean nothing to the Divine Mother, who can pay no heed to them – the simple reason for this is that actions in the "Present Time" speak louder than words; for indeed it is only actions that can take place in the "Present Time" that can be evaluated and supported by the Divine Mother; but YES! The Divine Mother will always provide "Sugar in the Water," for the doer who supports Her work for truly the Divine Mother "mysteriously" supports a person's efforts that are targeted to maintain and or encourage the harmony that is resting or endeavouring to emerge within the "Present Time". For really, the Divine Mother knows the harmony seeking needs of the Creation, which of course is the only reason why her children have been created, this being to assist and so support their Mother.

So yes! It is also evident that "Sugar in the Water" can be experienced in your acts which are harmoniously supporting that which is emerging or endeavouring to emerge all around you and then you will genuinely receive "Sugar in the Water." But what is this "Sugar in the Water" that the Divine Mother presents to you? With this indeed being an activity that mysteriously can only occur in the "Present Time" and is a life that can be again be likened to driving a car through a great city while obeying and supporting the "highway code" and every time you approach the traffic lights they turn green and so "mysteriously" support you on your harmonising journey through your life in the "Present Time".

Or when driving your car, it breaks down and after raising the bonnet and seeing the fault; another car comes alongside and asks, "What is the trouble?" You then say, "I need a special N24 spark plug, and I don't have one." Only to be answered by the unknown driver. "Oh! I have one in the boot of my car, and you can have it." That's "Sugar in the Water", for sugar is the sweetness, and the water is life, and the Divine Mother is God's supporter of the sweetness of a life which all harmony supports.

So Yes! It is well to remember there are many thoughts and trinkets to remind us of a Godly life but only good deeds, based upon true love, will protect and feed us. You will know when you have this protection, for you will receive "Sugar in the Water," a sure sign that someone loves you and loves what you are doing. For is it not an absolute truth that this is God's world or the world of Nature for the Non-Believer, and it not also real that it is a world that exists only in the "Present Time" and that this is an actual world that is known as "Heaven". It is also well to remember that God, which is "No-Thing" or which our Non-Believers call "Nothing", does not do anything within the Creation or Nature for the Non-Believer, for this is being because He has already done all that is needed to be done and God does not make mistakes. Therefore it should be well known that all people are fully programmed to benefit from the Creation's on-going needs, but we sadly forget who and what we are, and in particular, "What our purpose is?" For is it not a great truth that we cannot nor ever will be able to stop the evolving laws of God or Nature for the Non-Believer, even if we do not believe in God.

Is it not also true that you can make as many signs and promises as you like and even physically, mistakenly and animalistic ally, attack people of other religions because you think that your religion is better – but these actions will not change by one jot, where the Creations path is taking ALL of us? What is also accurate and should be seriously considered is that no one knows what God's plan is; particularly concerning what the end plan for the Creation is; although many say they do.

For certainly is this not an especially true statement that concerns all people for is it not stated to be true that people only began their own particular "added value" way of life around ten thousand years ago, when they began farming and "owning" land. Precisely, this being reputed to be 13.7 billion years after the start of this "private" entity we call Earth; this being the stated plan that now supports our world.

What should be further understood is that "currently" the target of all people is to aid the development of this plan, a fact which is achieved by accepting the truth that the Creation knows where it is going and that it often needs the support of people to get it there. For indeed this is also support which can only apply in the "Present Time" and under the guidance of "Mother of the Creation". She truly supports and maintains the harmony moving actions of this "family" planning.

It is also extraordinary but true, is that many people believed that they could change God's ever-developing plan to suit their own personal "I Want." But if we take a look at the world of people, and as an example, we can take the past fifteen hundred years which contains many destructing wars in the world but especially in Europe. Yet we also know that history also proves that during this time a language bordered country would often try to take there "I Want," from another language bordered country and so we can now ask the question: "Where are those defeated and attacking countries now?"

Is it not true that we can now see that nearly all the original language based borders of these original warring countries have been peacefully returned to them? Is it not also a fact that they are now free, and prospering within their own ancient but natural "language" original borders? The question now is just what did all these harmonies destroying savage wars which caused many millions of family deaths, cruel trials, inflicted pain, family suffering and tribulations, what did they change?

For really, is this is not a good question. Still, it is an extraordinary reality that people can wage war so quickly, especially when you remember that false changes that people attempt to make to God's plan cannot continue, for everything is under the ever correcting disciplines of the "Mother of the Creation". These being ongoing disciplines which are very useful to try and support, for indeed this factual and historical evidence shows that peoples "Freedom of Choice" should be used NOT to create an "I Want" for a personal me, but to truly understand that their "ME" is genuinely the totality of all the Creation, especially planet Earth, this being that which is the real YOU!

For again and indeed is this not a good or a Godly "unified" way of life? Logically, this is being a "totality" of life that a person can personally and truly experience for themselves? A fact which is also being an experienced truth that would stop much of that which is falsely claimed by their little "me", which is stolen from the harmony that is around them? Are it not also true and a known fact that you do now really know is that you are living in Hell, because of the "disharmony" you may be supporting or are creating?

Is it not also true that there is no worse life than that which can be caused by your self-inflicted desire to live in this self-created Hell; especially now that you have the knowledge and understanding that this is undoubtedly a truth? Is it not also a Self-Realised fact that enables you to know the truth, this being that it is your own "I Want," that is taking you to dissatisfaction, fury, and anger, this is being a fact which proves that you are unfaithfully living in a self-chosen Hell, which you created for yourself upon this Earth?

So now, cannot it also be said to be factually accurate that you reap these negative "Hell" born rewards by your actions? If this way of life is not fully understood, then take purposely for yourself, an "I Want" that is designated to go to someone else and observe what happens within and around you. Is it not also now known to be true that you can enter Hell again and again and again, because as a free person, you can choose this negative way of life, as against the positive way of how to live in Heaven – during the same "Present Time"? For certainly is it not now known to be a self-realised truth, that by expanding or giving birth to the harmony that is existing around you, you will live in Heaven while upon this Earth?

So Yes! The simple question you need to ask yourself is: "Where do you want to live, in Heaven or Hell?" Just try these different ways, to seek a beneficial harmony for all or support a destroying harmony, for it is your personal choice that will take you either to live in Hell or to live in Heaven while living on this Earth. For indeed, try consciously to follow and support God's or Natures laws for the Non-Believer which are all around you or endeavouring to emerge around you and so copy that which is always harmoniously working within you and in front of you; plus endeavouring to emerge all around you, for you cannot escape God's world or the world of Nature for the Non-Believer.

So yes! Living in Hell is the worst that can happen to you. Of course, we all need supporting words and actions from others to remind us always to refuse any act of selfishness which is ALWAYS born by the five senses, this being that which is always claiming in your mind their own animalistic "I Want," and which in the PAST you have thought of them as being you! They are not you – for you are the Soul that rests within you, for you cannot be that which you observe, taste, listen to, touch or smell.

So Yes! It is also good to remember that living in Heaven which exits in the "Present Time" upon this Earth, is to understand that as a person you have work to do or work not to do, depending upon the harmony that is "always" endeavouring to emerge around you which you can assist, or just enjoy this harmony of life when it needs no support. For now, you can choose negatively or positively what you see as a heavenly gift to you, a gift which is undoubtedly supported by the "Mother of the Creation". For now and knowingly, this is a "choice" which enables people to just live in their existing harmony or to support the emerging harmony that exists all around them.

But sadly, it is not all just personal pleasure. For it is certainly true that Jesus of the Christian faith chose to die under painful torture, rather than to go against the personal wishes of two mobs, a controlling mob that wished to destroy Him because he taught that individual independence was the way to live in God's word, and another mob wanting Him to take them to war against those who ruled them. The question for Jesus was: "Which is the way to harmony?" The whole world now knows the exact "way" He chose, which the way of harmony was for it removed dispute.

So yes! Is it not also useful to understand compassion and forgiveness, particularly in acknowledging the many Souls that appear to be entering people for the first time? These being new rebirths of people that are emanating from the animal kingdom, a fact which means that they have difficulty in having the strength of mind to pursue unselfish acts because in their past lives they could only and so naturally obey their "I Want" senses, this being an automatic act that was much needed for them to survive. For indeed, understanding plus the needed tolerance and personal examples is the need of the day. For assuredly, is this, not especially true when being near to those who are newly living has people and who now have a Soul. Therefore, can it not be easily seen to be accurate, that also within a community of people many live in Heaven, these being those holy ones who have lived many lives? Correspondingly, is it not also good to remind all those re-births from the animal kingdom, many who mistakenly live in an "animalistic" now personally made "I Want for ME" Hell, that life can be useful and also always explaining to them that life can be beneficial when living in the Heaven that is all around them – but only in the "Present Time". For certainly is it not true that many people have lived in the "Heaven" of the "Present Time" for many countless lives, this being as people upon this Earth. Is it not also true that our wise ancients did show to all people the way towards the harmony of a life lived in the Heaven that rests upon this Earth. Is it not also true that these holy ones always asked for tolerance when encountering those who were new entries to a life based upon the "Freedom of Choice" and who can be likened to living "graphically," in opposition to the ways of Jesus and all our many ancient wise teachers? Therefore is it not also wise to "harmoniously" know and believe that righteousness comes from forgiveness and this being true in the understanding of who we are – which is "everything"?

40   LIVING IN HEAVEN

What is also now very important to understand is that no outside person or any event can control your Soul has all our wise ancients consistently proved. Logically, this is because in all aspects of your life you have a choice to either support the harmony seeking needs of the Creation that rests upon this Earth or to seek a personal animalistic "I Want" – that is unto your death. Then and only at this stage, which people boldly call death, can the "Mother of the Creation" become responsible for the control of your Soul. For at this "re-birthing" stage God's future targeting laws, harmonised by the "Mother of the Creation", allows Her to rebirth your Soul into conditions that favour your future development towards Enlightenment.

For indeed, only the Divine "Mother of the Creation" knows where to place you so you can create and support Her work and so gain "Enlightenment" for your Soul, which is an act that ensures a constant endeavour to sustain the Creation's harmony and developing harmony or The "Mother of the Creation" may see you as a harmless developing sleeper. So rebirths you back to where you can happily live with the family you have just left. Justly, this is until you develop the need and the will to support Her endeavours. Yet! For those who knowingly destroy Her pursuit of harmony for all life and non-life – Read on

For it is true, as our wise ancients say, that if you refuse to do agreeable acts that are of benefit to all life and Non-Life, this being that which rests within the world that exists around you, you are not punished, but you will find your next life moves into a disharmony that you will think is a punishment being served upon you.

Still, in reality, the punishment is reflecting your activities–so indeed you are punishing yourself. So again, it must be understood that the way to live with inner bliss and happiness is to support and not break God's "highway code" supported by the "Mother of the Creation", this being that which certainly exists within the Creation. For these are God created laws that control the harmony and the emerging harmony of the Creation, and whose objective, with the aid of the "Mother of the Creation", is to support and promote the wellbeing for all life and Non-Life, that exists on planet Earth and its vicinity – for this Earth is rightfully our "Earth" and is undoubtedly a part of the Kingdom of God, in which all Earths life and Non-Life exists.

So yes! The way of life can be again likened to driving through a city and disobeying its "highway code" which means that you will not get very far before serious mishaps to your journey in life begin to occur – but who is punishing you and is it not strange that you think it is the other drivers? Now all should understand the words that the Divine Mother said through Jesus: "I tell you the truth, no one can see the Kingdom of God unless he is born again". Does this not mean that this "I Want" driver must stop driving through red traffic stop lights and rather be obedient to the green go lights'?

For really, this is being born again into a world of harmony and so to know and understand that only that which is needed by all people is to follow God's "highway code" of life which are the Creation's "High-Way" code of laws that exist upon our Earth.

So Yes! It is also agreed that military tanks can drive brutally through a city in their efforts to gain or stop an "I Want" but does not history show that God's "highway code" of laws always returns. Also agreed is that many do not know that this "highway code" of God's ever-developing natural laws that were born to establish the "roadway" ahead for the Creation, that this is a direction which is fully supported by the "Mother of the Creation". For it is She who maintains this road's harmony which exists in the "Present Time", and it is She who "personally" coordinates all the emerging harmony that exits around all life and Non-Life which is gainfully emerging all-around people. It is Her all-knowing stillness which "magically" enters any "Enlightened" person, who unselfishly becomes able to aid Her in this ever-moving ever still Creation.

Is it not also true that most people also understand and enjoy the harmony of music, which can range from Mozart to modern popular music? So is it not true that people do love to listen to the sounds of their chosen music's "harmony," and could this not be because to all people music reflects a feeling of peace and love, and even to the "singularity" experience of the "Present Times" existence? Precisely, this being that experience which rests within the sound of the chosen music that is being played and even if a player amongst the musicians accidentally hits a wrong note, is this not unnoticed by all others for they just continue playing?

Therefore is it not also true that the music playing others usually ignores him or she has and so continues to play the majority groups chosen, says classical music, this being likened to the "music" of the Highway Code? But if these others do keep hitting a wrong note, do not these confirming others then forgive him or her and also endeavour to teach him or her the groups chose music, this being the agreed consensus which the majority of the group are playing – for indeed, is this not also the accepted and correct way for group community to live?

So Yes" Is it not also correct that all people need to play according to the living script that the Divine Mother regularly places in front of them and which many may misread even when living within the consensus of the majority– but what is this "script" of living within the obedience to God's "highway code" of life?

For truly is not the task is to know and fully live within the "Heaven" that the "Mother of the Creation" is continuously placed in front to them during the "Present Time". Therefore, is not their task when driving, is to play this given "Highway Code" script in tune and "harmoniously" with all the life and non-life that exists all around them, and so it should be with their way of life in which a known personal "I Want" for myself, cannot exist. Still not sure what living in harmony is?

Think of the birds and the bees who live "harmoniously" together and then endeavour to understand their way of living, for this will give you some indication as to what truth rests in a harmonious centered life where all that is born lives and dies. For honestly, all is happening in God's "Present Time" in which the future and the past does not exist.

So yes! When living in the contentment of the "Present Time," it is good to remember that people are the highest life form that currently exists on planet Earth. Therefore, is it not strange, as stated before, that it was only about ten thousand years ago that people stopped living like animals and began to "create" added value by sowing seeds and so farming, this being that which undoubtedly changed the nature of the world around them, which is impressive when it is realised that our life force began billions of years ago?

Is it not also true that within this short space of time, only people have created the conflicting and warring world in which this period has existed? For certainly is it not also true that harmony always returns to exist within the borders of these warring "different language" countries? Is it not also true that currently, people have no idea of God's future or Nature's future for the Non-Believer? Yet cannot it also be clearly said and seen that all life and Non-Life is living within a peace that surpasses all understanding? For truly is this not a fact that knowingly and continually exists in on-going sincere support of the life and non-life within all of our existing Creation, so is it not seen that it can do nothing else? For certainly is not true that there is only ONE combination of energy that creates the existence of all the above?

So Yes! Is it not also a truth that we should willingly and knowingly live under God's laws or Nature's laws for the Non-Believer, these being laws that cannot cause pain or destruction to others and are also laws which support the harmony of God's "highway code" which will eventually take us to where we have no idea unless it is to experience Himself; and is it not also interesting that people have only been planned, within this "harmony" to individually live for "three score years and ten," meaning a maximum age of seventy, giving people probably forty years of productive life, this being from 20 years to 50 years, which is nothing in the scale of time about that which we are talking.

So Yes! The one thing that exists as an absolute proven truth is that we can all rest assured that God or Nature for the Non-Believer, and via the controlling "Mother of the Creation", all really do know what they are doing and that the "Mother of the Creation" ever on-going target is to keep God's plans within a continuous on-going harmonious development. Yes, this is being a development which will always succeed, and that people who have been given the "Freedom of Choice" to support this progress, will never be able to stop this on-going development.

It is also good to remember that it is only in the "Present Time", that the Divine Mother can give signals requesting some needed aid or non-aid from individual people whom She requires to physically assist Her in the needed harmonising of the life force that is all around and within the emerging Creation. For it is undoubtedly true that people have been given the "Freedom of Choice" and the reason for this being because the Divine Mother is sometimes in need of a person's harmonious actions or not needed actions. Is it not also a truth that it is not necessary for any individual to see the big picture, this being the Creations target or even to see the future purpose of their life.

Therefore, is it not also true that all incarnate and all our wise ancients state, that the present "now" is the only time that can be truly lived in, for it is only the "Now Time" that people can truly experience the silent harmony of all life and Non-Life that genuinely exists in the world around them. For again, truthfully do not all our wise ancients' states that there is no other teaching accept the magnificence of this one.

For these wise ancients know that when you live in the "Present Time", you must obey the harmony of all life and Non-Life that exists around you and this is because there can be no personal "I Want" arising within you that tells you to steal from this harmony. For rightly, is it not clear that we can only enjoy a good life around us when we enjoy the harmony that the Divine Mother is maintaining this being for all life and Non-Life. Therefore, is it not a seen obvious truth that we are all "wired" to work together? Is it not also a truth that we have currently developed "social networking", this being a means of communication that covers the world – and is it not reasonable to seek the harmony of world friendship? Is it not also true that every time we release a moan about the sayings or behaviour of others that we move into a different world which is likened to Hell?

So Yes" As a person who has been given the freedom of choice, can it not be asked of you, "Which world have you chosen to live in?" If it is Hell, why are you complaining? For truly is this your personal "choice" to live there? But if it is Heaven, just smile, for it is known that beyond that smile, you will have no other thoughts plaguing your mind, but if you are being punished by other sinning people, then forgive them for they know what they do. Still, you can be assured that they will receive that which is due to them in this life and also in their next.

For it is certainly clear, that if you do not believe that you are an integral part of the world around you, then you are living in Hell, and this is a fact that can be likened to being in a very lonely type of confinement. For being ignored by the world and left out of the harmony of the immediate world around you, is a self-created world in which you can experience anguish and pain, and this is the reason why you continuously seek group activities games wherever they can be found; for correctly you are searching for yourself, not realising that happiness exists in the "self" that is all around you and which, with a silent mind, you can certainly fully experience.

So Yes! It is good that those who live in Heaven that exists only in the "Present Time" will instantly know without a doubt, that all that was previously known to be "outsiders" are also part of their being. Precisely, this "being" because they will realise that with a still mind there are no longer any thoughts to create personal "I Want" dreams, these being "I Want" thoughts that are emanating from one of the five senses. This fact gives birth to an "I Want" that automatically separates them from the real world in which they currently exist.

So Yes! Again, this is a "scientific" truth of which ALL the Earth's incarnates and wise ancients speak. Logically, this being a truth that upon "Self-Realisation", a person will begin to pursue the way of harmony for all Life and Non-Life, but only when they have obtained the stillness of the mind, which is the purpose of all our wise ancients introduced creed based worship. For only when the freed Soul is "Chosen" to be allowed to see the "Present Time", this being through an unthinking and unclouded "Enlightened" mind, that your Soul will be enabled to see the reality of all that exists within the Creation.

It might also be then that you will be immediately blessed by the "Mother of the Creation" who will provide for you the experience of "bliss" and also the harmonious support that will expand your new ability to pursue a life filled with "Bliss". For this bliss is the experiencing of the world harmony that always exists around you has it does within you, and which is that target of "Self-

Awareness" or "Self-Realisation" that ALL incarnates did speak. Also, did not our many wise ancients target this reality with their words of wisdom, and this was thousands of years ago which was a time in which their words could not be fully understood – but they can now!

So yes! It is also important to remember that when your mind dwells in the past or the future, you are living in a world of Hell because it does not exist. Painstakingly, this is being when there are constant thoughts in the mind that create a fictitious world with many "I Want" for me; therefore you are only punishing yourself and also self-inflicting a living in Hell upon yourself and others, which is an unwanted self-inflicted punishment.

Also, if you are being brutalised by the "I Want" of others – remember the man who quietly went to a painful cross, rather than giving His persecutors their "I Want", for indeed, all serious and pain-inflicting false persecutors within their life and upon their death will be penalised and indeed will not be born again has people.

So yes! It is also true that the Divine Mother cannot recognise any personal "I Want," for She lives in the Heaven that exists only in the "Present Time", where your thoughts of "I Want" cannot be heard for they exist in a "Past" or "Future" personally created world which "The Book" calls Hell, a world of mind filling thought that stops the view of the "Present Time" in which all that exists is just one entity.

So now, because you are not a foolish person, let your next step be towards actually living in Heaven, which always exists within and around you and let your next act be an act that creates and or supporting expands the greater harmony of all that is around you, and if you wish to know how to achieve the living in Heaven, which is now being spoken of – Read on

41 THE TRUE WAY OF LIFE

So now you can no longer say "I know not what to do!" for now, Dear Reader, you know what the target of life is and yes, this is certainly more true if you are an advanced person with many past lives. For indeed the way of life is to join the all supporting "Enlightenment" which exists within you to that which is outside your body, and so support and expand the harmony which is always materialising around you, and which is a harmony that is full of love for all that is life and Non-Life and harmony that is always supported by the Divine Mother, who will certainly aid you in all your efforts.

For indeed we can now again remember these last words of the Divine "Mother of the Creation", speaking through Her incarnate son Jesus, who was a single personification of the Earth's Creation. These last words being when Jesus was painfully being crucified unto death upon the cross in which He said: "Father, forgive them; for they do not know what they do."

And to be very clear about living in Hell or living in Heaven, it is essential to understand these last words of a living Jesus. It is also useful to believe in the truth that Jesus was the totality of the Creation that was speaking to you especially when he said: "And so I tell you, every sin and blasphemy will be forgiven." Meaning that sins against the harmony of the Creation ignorantly committed by those without the knowledge of what is spoken of here, will not be punished by the Divine Mother either in this life or the next.

Yet! Is it not also true that to these words were also added, "but the blasphemy against the Spirit will not be forgiven," meaning that to "knowingly" and "willfully" sin against the purpose of the Soul and its needed support of the existing or endeavouring to exist harmoniously within the "Present Time" cannot be forgiven. For a person moving against the developing Creation always brings distress to the natural world that is endeavouring to emerge around them, for the "Mother of the Creation" must always turn Her back upon the Hell creating perpetrator who has been Godly given or Nature has given for the Non-Believer, the "Freedom of Choice".

Yet Truly, This is an impossible blasphemy when the person achieves or is striving towards achieving "Enlightenment", which rests only in the "Present Time" and so, knows "explicitly", via the view of the Soul through their still mind, precisely the supporting need that is required to aid the Divine Mothers harmony seeking work. For indeed, is not this harmonising of the "Present Time" plainly seen to be the work that maintains God's harmony seeking laws which are fully supported by the "Mother of the Creation" whose work exists only in the "Present Time", for God's work is to shape the future – yet many deliberately break the harmony that is existing or endeavouring to emerge all around them, which is the sin always spoken of by the incarnate Jesus.

For again truly this is a harmony breaking and oft grave sin which cannot be forgiven, for indeed it should now be understood, meaning to "stand under", that such activity will automatically bring woe to the breaker of harmony. For correctly it should be unsurprisingly known that a severe and continuous "animalistic" breaking of current and emerging harmony, this being that which always exists within the "Preset Time", could certainly lead to this constantly sinning person to be born back into the animal kingdom from which they have probably just emerged and this being upon their next life, which is life more kindly suited towards their current behaviour patterns.

Yet there are only two types of sin that break the harmony being maintained by the "Mother of the Creation". One sin is committed in ignorance, and one sin is committed purposely and although the sin may be the same – the on-going severe punishment against the purposeful sinner is different, but only in the next life to come.

For indeed, most ignorant sinners are "unknowingly" punishing themselves as they live in the disharmony of their self-created Hell and at the same time are alive and existing upon this Earth. Therefore there is no need for extra punishment from the Divine Mother, who explained again very clearly through Jesus: "Anyone who speaks a word against the Son of Man will be forgiven," this being for all those ignoring "gossipy" sinners.

For indeed, Jesus was God's child, meaning that Jesus was the actual personification of the whole Creation that exists upon our Earth, and who, in this "incarnate" position, was also clearly stating that people will not be punished by

God's laws if they "ignorantly" choose to live in their own self-created punishing Hell, and not in God's Creation of the Heaven that rests only in the "Present Time" upon this Earth.

For strictly, their self-created Hell is that which they "choose" to live in, and it is punishment enough. Still, wisely and knowingly, Jesus also warned at this time: "but anyone who speaks against the Holy Spirit will not be forgiven, either in this age or in the age to come", clearly meaning that those who knew of God's world and did purposely sin against it would find in their next lives, this being the age to come; that they may not be in mortal form.

So Yes! These statements by Jesus were certainly needed because many perform upon themselves a self-inflicted punishment which is created by their selfish acts, these being acts in which they now know are selfish acts because they deliberately go against the will of the Divine "Mother of the Creation" and Her longing to create harmony for all life and Non-Life.

Also, is it not true that through Jesus, the "Mother of the Creation" stated: "Forgive us our debts, as we also have forgiven our debtors?" For assuredly, this is genuinely explaining, to those who live in ignorance of whom their true "Self" really is, which is genuinely the Soul. Therefore Jesus stated to His listeners that they should live within their obligations to an always forgiving harmony with all Life and Non-Life. Then indeed, Jesus also stated this reminder: "And lead us not into temptation, but deliver us from the evil one."

Simply put, in the words of "The Book", that this tempter and the "evil one" is the five senses, and it is their continuing "I Want" demands that are allowed to continually sound into what should be a still and unclouded mind. Still, in those ancient days it would have been impossible to repeat the words held within "The Book" and so say "The evil one is the five senses and you must stop believing that they are the real you, and so stop their animalistic "I Want" desires from controlling you." Also, was it not wisely said by Jesus, speaking regards the law of the Creation: "For if you forgive "people" when they sin against you, your heavenly Father will also forgive you?" Correctly, this is the stillness created in the "harmony", this being that which always is endeavouring to exist in the "Present Time."

So yes! This forgiving and the entering of the Heaven that truly exists upon this Earth immediately happens when you stop living in a world of "I Want," which is your self-created Hell and thereby allow Gods Law or Natures Law of peace to enter the mind, for you will then begin to live under the exact laws that exist within the ever-moving ever still Creation. It is then as an "Enlightened" or endeavouring to become an "Enlightened" person that you will immediately begin to perform the needed activities and blissfully enjoy the no need for activities. Strictly, this being with a controlled silence in mind and therefore live a life in harmony, which is your Heaven upon this Earth, for it is true, then that you will "automatically" enjoy the "Peace that Surpasses all Understanding", which means that it cannot be explained.

So yes! You may think it is "scientifically" impossible to forgive others who have hurt you or have taken from you, yet was it not wisely said by the Divine

Mother through Jesus: "But if you do not forgive men their sins, your Father will not forgive your sins." Meaning you will never be able to enter Heaven that is upon this Earth if you cannot forgive the past and drop expectations of the "I Want" future, which is a sin; for all these "continuing mind filling thoughts" are sinful thoughts of "I Want", and it is these mind filling thoughts that take you away from the "Present Time", this being a world created by God who "The Book" says seeded "Space", the "Mother of the Creation", who then gave birth to that which we call "Creation" or "Nature" by the Non-Believer. So really there is only one child - which is YOU!

So yes! You will never be punished by the laws of God or the laws of Nature, for the Non-Believer. Again, this is true because it is your Godly fathers given "Freedom of Choice" that enables you to support the emerging or existing Creation correctly. For logically is it not a truth that the same act, under different conditions, can support or destroy the emerging or static goodness (Godness) of the harmony that always exists within the on-going creative process which cannot be growing towards an unknown end. For "The Book" says that the "Enlightenment" that progresses through "Self-Awareness" leads to a "Self-Realisation", this being when the experiencer becomes the "Creation" and such "Self-Realised" ones do not return to a new life, for they become has one with God or Nature for the Non-Believer, which "The Book" says is the purpose of the Creation, so that God can experience this love within "Himself".

So yes! Cannot it now be genuinely said and understood, that if you decide to perform a selfish, "I Want" for myself? Logically, this is a sin, which means that you selfishly take from others and so have chosen to live in the disharmony of Hell, which is a life that cannot exist in the "Present Time". Does this not "scientifically" mean that our current life then becomes a life that is living outside of the care and the gifts of the Divine Mother?

Therefore, should we not now be aware that when you live in the environmental Heaven that exists upon this Earth, you will experience the harmony that exists all around you, just as the reality of the harmony that exists within you – for there can be no self-inflicted punishment within this actual world and it is also good to remember that that which we call an "illness", does have its purpose, which is to allow others to care for us and of course it is good to "know" that your Soul cannot die - but will return to another life and maybe a much sweeter life, this being one that you have seriously earned.

Now it should also be further understood that when you do genuinely live in harmony, which is Heaven upon this Earth, as Jesus did. All our wise ancients did, you may also encounter others who are wrongfully able to inflict their painful way of living upon you, as they also did to Jesus. Jesus indeed suffered under uncomplaining torture and then painfully endured a painful crucifixion perpetrated by those who live in Hell. For really, it was in this Hell that they incorrectly thought was a Godly harmony, which made them pursue and destroy Him, but what they pursued was disharmony, which was based upon their collective "I Want" my religion to be obeyed not yours.

Is this being a false harmony, which Jesus could not join? For indeed, this is because He knew that to join their false harmony that this would allow His persecutors to use His name to gather others to collectively pursue a sinful "I Want" for my life. At this time, it was also known that Jesus knew that there was another powerful but different group, who also wanted to use His name to support a revolt against their foreign controllers. Still, again Jesus truly knew that this too would lead to a significant loss of life and disharmony.

Therefore is it not now known to be true that even at His terrible end, Jesus knew that He was still pursuing the excellent harmony that was endeavouring to emerge all around Him? So the question now is "How many can follow unto death this example of pursuing the goodly (Godly) harmony that is all around them has is the harmony within them"? For this is being the same harmony which was put forward by Jesus and our many other "Earthly" incarnates, and our wise people and therefore live a truth that can last until a personal death – has done all our ancient wise.

So Yes! Those who choose to live in the current expanding harmony of Heaven, by bringing the mind to exist only in the "Present Time", will genuinely, find that the "Present Time" is the only place where the harmony of the Creation can genuinely exist.

Also, once this experiencing of "Enlightenment" is achieved and fully experienced, a person will never wish to live again in the disharmony of the Hell they have just left – even when the whole world may seem to be working against them; for this means nothing to them, for the "I Want" world of others no longer has any real meaning. Unquestionably this is God's world, this being that which exists only in the "Present Time", which is always the only time to exist, for again and honestly, by living in the "Present Time," you will realise the "factual" truth of all that exists. This "factual truth" is that you will experience the "Peace that surpasses all understanding". Therefore, it should be correctly known that this is genuinely the experiencing of "Enlightenment", which is the target that is always given to you by all our wise ancients.

So yes! Is it NOT correct to say that you are punished by God for "misdemeanours?" For what parent inflicts punishment upon a child who has acted in ignorance? For actually, did not God's all-knowing son Jesus often state this truth? The "punishment" you may experience can only be inflicted upon you by those who move against the harmony that always exists or is attempting to emerge within the Creation.

For indeed all our ancient wise revealed that these "punishers" would undoubtedly enter into a life of disharmony, in which many "troubles" come to them. For really, they do not understand (stand under) the harmony that exists for all life which as previously stated, is likened to a driver who comfortably follows the "highway code" of the road. Again, this is an all-encompassing condition which is being likened to their "holistically" moving through their life, as compared with a person who ignores the "highway code" of all life and non-life, which leads to many personal problems for them and the others around them.

So the question now is "which driver will find many difficulties, problems, and troubles and make very little progress on their journey to their destination"? And an added question could be "whose fault is this?" Therefore, should it not be known that God or "No-Thing" for the Non-Believer created a "Highway Code?"

For certainly, this indeed is a code that not only controls the "Present Time", but also, the on-going target of the Creation or Nature for the Non-Believer. Is this not also a life in which "The Book" states is controlled by the "Mother of the Creation" who is always protecting the harmony of the "Present Time" and who is also a "Mother" who is always showing enlightened "drivers" a correct path to their destination.

So Yes! The question now is: "Who is punishing who and why?" The answer to this question can now be clearly understood in that it is the personal "I Want" for me, this being that which is within a person that inflicts life's punishing "disharmony" upon them and which they often and sadly inflict upon others.

Therefore, it not also an absolute truth that all our Earth incarnates and also, our Earth's wise ancients, did all clearly stated that living and supporting of the "Present Time" is the only way to live in the "Heaven" that always rests upon our Earth?

For truly does not our history state that these wise ancients also say that those who live in ignorance, these being those who knowingly destroy or inflict severe punishment upon the harmony that rests in the "Present Time", will be immediately forgiven for their acts when they return to supporting Gods world? For is this certainty because God gave people "The freedom of choice" which enables them to support the harmony that exists or beginning to exist all around them? But does not this "freedom" not also allow a person to live in disharmony with the world that exists around them – but now all know that which will happen to these knowing destroyers of harmony in this life and their next lives?

So yes! Is it not a proven fact that those people, who unknowingly go against the will of God's emerging harmony seeking and static laws and also the Divine "Mother of the Creation" work in correcting the on-going harmony of these laws that can clash, will all "automatically" be forgiven because of a God-given "Freedom of Choice" and so not punished?

Therefore, indeed, the breaking of the harmony that is around them will inflict punishment enough. But now it is wise to understand that the readers of "The Book" are no longer ignorant of these facts. So in their breaking of harmony, it may be understood that they are deliberately going against God's laws and The Divine Mother's pursuit of harmony?

Does this mean that in their next lives, because they have "knowingly" broken the harmony that is emerging around them, that they will be punished by "Holy" law? For did not Jesus, who called the Holy Spirit "Spirit of Truth" warn us "All manner of sin and blasphemy shall be forgiven unto all people, but the blasphemy against the Holy Spirit shall not be forgiven. Mathew 12.31. Does this mean that readers of "The Book" who now knowingly break the harmony that is emerging around them, will be reborn into the animal kingdom and so go back to life without the "Freedom of Choice"? It is an exciting concept.

For what is also known by the familiar words of the wise ancients, is that those who are "illegally" punished by others for their supporting the harmony seeking needs revealed by the Divine "Mother of the Creation"; will obtain good positive lives but a word of caution here! People who are born with handicaps are not being punished for any previous lives' misdeeds.

For indeed, these people are our real heroes and are born so that others can assist them in the developing of life's harmony that is emerging all around them. For really, there is a strong movement from the Divine Mother to place this past and willingly undemanding heroes into a handicapped life, so that others can support and so develop the harmony that should be around them, just as the "Mother of the Creation" is continuously developing the harmony around all life and Non-Life, for real, these are personal acts of supporting the harmony needs of the few that will lead to the bliss that not many people have experienced.

42 LIFE OF A SOUL THAT NEVER ENDS

Also, some religions decry the knowledge of rebirths, when this rebirth knowledge is all around them. For indeed it is seen to be true that children before the age of two, and when they are just beginning to walk, plus "talk", they will intelligently discuss with you, in their own "Blah Blah" language, the knowledge that they contained in their past lives or about that which they see in their current life? Can it not also be seen that lengthy "intelligent" conversations can take place with these children and you can ask many questions, although you may never understand their answers? For assuredly, no one has any idea what the child is seriously saying, but it is agreeably felt that the child does know what he or she is saying in the answers to your questions.

So Yes! It "naturally" appears that when you die you do not go to an obligatory "Heaven" or "Hell," but after a short evaluating stay within the energy that surrounds you, it seems factual that you return to a new life that the "Mother of the Creation" has purposely chosen for your development towards "Enlightenment". Or maybe you have "automatically" been allowed to return to the people that you loved in your previous existence, which also supports the development of this target.

This target is a new "re-birth-place" for the Soul and one that the "Mother of the Creation" understands the best place for your "personal" development, for indeed all "mortal" development is to achieve "Enlightenment" which frees the Soul and so enables a person to "Naturally" and actively support the developing world of the "Mother of the Creation", this being the place that we call "Heaven", the current factual world in which we all currently live and which we call the "The Present Time", this being Gods world or the world of Nature for the Non-Believer. For truly is it not very beneficial to know that before you died, you were living in a Godly created Heaven or a personally created Hell while on the Earth and all this being based upon your Godly given "Freedom of Choice"?

For indeed God's gift of "The Freedom of Choice" will allow people to personally "choose" the place of their next rebirth or have, because of the needs of the Soul, been placed to live in by the Divine Mother. If this personal choice upon death was unknown, then it is essential to remember that it certainly is known now, and this is a fact that is very true regarding your current life. For again is it not true that it was your choice or the accepted choice of the "Mother of the Creation" that bound you to the position in which you now live and even in the one that you had previously lived? For rightly, self-creating a life lived in Heaven or Hell is a life that is based not only upon your personal "choice," but how you existed in your past life's activities and it is a reasonable probability that you still have the same belief system that will return you to live with loved ones – for a loving "reality" is a strong motivator.

So Yes! It should be known that the Souls of previously departed loved ones are probably already living with you has your children or the children of relatives, for one thing, must be made very clear about death; this being that you cannot take your body with you, and it is this that begs the question that if you do not believe in rebirth, where does all our Earths life come from? For it is known that the creative singularity that is known as a man and a woman can lovingly create a new life. Still, it is the "Mother of the Creation" who inserts a person's Soul, which is said to be inserted into the developing child about four months after conception. For it is undoubtedly true that no one can break God's rule or Nature's rule for the Non-Believer; this being that a male and a female singularity are certainly needed to create a body but it should be known that it is the Divine Mother who places the developing Soul within the person, and also is it not an inevitable truth that it is the parents' responsibility to care for the body of that which they have personally "created", which is indeed a Godly miracle which is simply based upon "LOVE".

So Yes! The proven truth of rebirth, which is all around everyone, is that when you die, you will generally return to those you love. For the target of "I Want" always targets the purpose of those who choose to live in Hell or chose to live in Heaven, upon this Earth, and so honestly, their "I Want," this being the self-creation of their last thought, will ensure this fact. If the "Mother of the Creation" sees no harm to this habitual rebirth, back to loved ones, then it will be so. But common sense dictates that it should be known, that if this rebirth is seen by the Divine Mother to be in an environment in which a newly placed Soul will have developing difficulties, then the rebirth will be into an environment which supports and engenders this particulars Soul's bodily need to be with new parents and a new environment.

Also, those people, who knew that they lived in Heaven while existing upon this Earth and so pursued a harmony for all the life and all the non-life that lives around them, they will have no desire at their body's death and the bodies subsequent rebirth into another life. For such a Soul will have no thoughts as to where its next life should be, for their empty mind will be likened to saying: "I will go to wherever you want me to go and I will do well wherever you want me to do "well". So honestly, maybe they never return but merge with God who then experiences Himself within them, which could be the purpose of the creation – so that God can experience "Himself".

So Yes! The fact remains that if you are good at instigating harmony within and around yourself and for others, you may well be reborn into a difficult situation – but you will not be deserted by the Divine Mother, whose "Sugar in the Water" and some "Déjà Vu", which is a feeling of having already experienced the present situation, will undoubtedly keep you advised. It is also well to remember that upon death, many of our wise ancients also say that it is your last thoughts that take you to your next birth. It is also further said by our wise ancients, that upon the point of death, you have a few seconds of knowing before the emerging white light takes you, just what is the "I Want" thought that targets you to your next life.

Yes, this being a target which is not yet enabled to be from the silent Soul which rests within the body that you are currently leaving and whose only silent target is to merge with God. For again, is it not true that your Soul still needs to follow your desire, for you still have the Godly given "Freedom of Choice", this is being a "Freedom of Choice" whose ongoing target is to eventually make you knowledgeable to the understanding that you are the "personification" of the creation, this being a part of creation whose only purpose is to return blissfully to God so that you can truly experience that which created you. Yet! Is it not also true as many of our Holy Scriptures state, that our ancient elderly men would "go to the forest," and to not only to end their time with their family but also to choose where they desired their next life to be?

So now it is good to remember again the wise ancient's story of the elderly man who "went to the forest" to die peacefully. This activity is because he felt he was no longer of any use to his family or tribe, for his mind was always in the future, unlike his wife, who has a woman her mind was always in the present time. So she was always very useful for her family and her tribe. This ancient story tells that this aged man was sitting with his back to a tree, after having his many days without food or water and at the point of natural death, this being exactly when the white light within him began to appear within his mind. Which was also the best time he should begin to choose the place of his next rebirth, he saw a young deer and marvelled at how beautiful its eyes were – he came back to life has a deer – a beautiful story, which has such significant meaning.

I often and personally think that for the ending my life, this being when my age has worn me out, that I would take two bottles of good Russian vodka for I understand that "God" which is short for "Voda" meaning water and Ka, this anciently known to be a principal aspect of the soul of a human being or God, which survives with the soul after death. Therefore my last decision would be to take this "Holy Water" into the wintery cold of a dense Siberian forest, probably outside Yekaterinburg were ended the Russian conflict between the controllers and the controlled – sadly a conflict between controllers and the controlled that is still the condition that creates all our Earths wars and conflicts even to the current day. Then to sit with my back to a tree near the Obelisk on the border between Europe and Asia and toast with this "Water of the Soul" to each item upon my long list of the joyful times, that my life had brought to me and then happily choose, - when I see the tunnel of white light appearing - just where I Want to be born in my next life. Or maybe it will be the vodka that will decide, as I lie back against that solitary Siberian tree and so peacefully let the Divine "Mother of the Creation" do what She Wants with me.

But this type of ending is an obvious NO, NO, for the female of our species, this being because they are always useful nor is it suitable for men if done before their old age and maybe well before their time is due. For my above-stated end is a physical, purposeful and historical "manly" happy ending of useful life but the self-accomplishing of a non-aged death is certainly not a right choice for certainly God or Nature for the Non-Believer, loves you and everything within you and an early self-chosen death hurts your creator who has given you your life. So be wise, and so support and join with the all-round you Creation just has it is within you, and which loves you dearly, this is called "unity", and it is all yours to truly experience and support.

So yes! It also right, as our scientists state, that genetic memory is known to be within us, and they also state that this is probably from our ancestors' gene pool; but in reality, they are inputs from our past lives, and we all know this, but many deny it. For again is it not true that most noticeable "scientific" knowledge about rebirth is always seen in the activities of children before they move away from being two years old. For assuredly, this is being particularly so when they are learning how to stand and take their first steps. For it is undoubtedly known to be true that they can hold lengthy conversations in their meaningful talks. Still, to the adult listener, it is just blah blah.

For indeed the baby cannot yet formulate a communicative language. Yet what can also clearly be noticed is that they fully want to act as they did as past adults, but their little bodies will not let them. It can also be noticed how they speak and how they use the right context and the right intonation of their blah blah conversation taking place, and even seem to understand the meaning of the life and conditions that are all around them. It can also be genuinely and easily witnessed that these small children act in their small bodies as if they are adults. It is even said that if you watch closely, you will see the mannerisms of the person who they were in their previous life – this all comes from their past life's memory, so it is not genetic memory, it is the memories of their past lives, so how is it possible to witness all the above if they have not been here before?

At this stage it is essential to mention that the love that exists between a man and a woman is that which is used to create a child, this being a fact that a child is usually created by a unified happy harmony between consenting adults. It is also essential for this activity not to be a forced "I Want" for myself activity and just as essential is for one to experience with an attached love the needs of the other and always to understand that jealousy is undoubtedly an "I Want" for myself pain which always brings sadness.

43 PARABLES TO RELEASE THE SOUL

So yes! The five senses are tools of our animalistic lower-self. Still, strangely and sadly, their now "habitually" allowed constant and undisciplined chanting of an "I Want," into the mind, which is also combined with many tempting images, can be falsely identified as that which is needed for yourself and the existence of your very being. It is this false belief that is classed by others as your personality. Meticulously, this being a personality which mistakenly shows to all the people around you the actual strength of your greed, pride, fear, avarice and much more, all of which is not the real you. For indeed, the real "you," is the eternal Soul which rests within you and which exists only to support the harmony seeking needs of the **"Mother of the Creation"** who, naturally, like all mothers, seeks, with your aid, the need to maintain the harmony within and around Her only child – this being the Creation or Nature for the Non-Believer.

So yes! If you wish to free the Soul and so stop to obey the never-ending selfish demands of your five senses, whose constant mind filling "I Want" is for realising and obtaining physical rather than spiritual needs, and so free your Soul and so give to it the silent freedom to act only for the harmony seeking needs of the developing Creation plus encourage the collective harmony of all life and Non-Life, so if seeking a peaceful and meaningful way of life – then read on. For indeed, by endeavouring with the exercise later explained in "The Book", you will become quickly "Self-Aware" and also realise that each person has within them a Godly given or Nature has given for the Non-Believer, a "personal" Soul, which silently and un-demandingly exists within you has it does within all people. But sadly, it is usually deprived of its real purpose because its view of the Creation requires a silent and still mind, which the inner Soul can see through, and so "observe" the needs of the outer world of which it is a joined and an integral part. This status is called "Enlightenment" by all our wise ancients and which of course is the target of all their teachings, and it is that which is achieved by progressing meditation.

So yes! It is a real anomaly that our "Freedom of Choice" gift, that which has been given only to people by God, or Nature for the Non-Believer has mistakenly in infancy and via ignorance "chose" consciousness, this being the controlling light within us that is always in a state of being perceptibly aware of and responsive to our surroundings, to allow the body's willpower to automatically, this being the energy which is used to control or restrain impulses, into now releasing the uncensored desires of the five senses "automatically" into the mind of the beholder. It is also this uncensored activity which has become obedient to the selfish "I Want", and it is also an activity which has now become habitual, and so no longer needs to be chosen, which can be likened to the first beginnings of a smoker or an alcoholic, but this "I Want for Me" that is genuinely emanating from the greed of the five senses, is much more severe.

So yes! It is because of this now un-challenged "habit" of this previously allowed in childhood this on-going activity emanating from the animalistic five senses that enables "Consciousness" to energise "Willpower" to automatically release the "I Want" desires of the five senses into the mind, which blocks it with past and future desires and machinations. It is this fact and these thoughts that are now being freely and habitually released into the mind via willpower, which stops the Soul from always viewing the needs of the "Present Time" – which is God's world or the world of Nature for the Non-Believer.

So yes! It is these "I Want" demands, which the "thinking" person mistakenly believes are the real needs of that which they now habitually begin to believe is "themselves". But honestly, these five senses are NOT "you", for you cannot be that which you observe. The actual needs of all people are to live in the "Present Time" and so physically support the **"Mother of the Creation"** harmony seeking endeavours to pacify or remove any disturbing harmony activities that occur during the growth of the Creation, Her only child.

Therefore, it is genuinely in ignorance, that people continuously endeavour to activate the false but ever demanding "I Want," perpetrated by the five senses, this being that which stops people from performing their life's correct tasks – which are tasks that are required to support the needs of the eternal on-going harmony required by all life and Non-Life, that currently exists all around people and if you can hear any words in the mind, then fully understand and truly know that these words are not coming from you, for you are the observer, and so cannot be that which you listen to, or hear, or see, or taste or touch, for you, is the Soul, the silent doer, and harmoniser of all life and Non-Life.

It is also further understood that although all our wise ancients knew that their given incantations and prayers could also achieve the required disciplined silence in the mind that occurred between the sounding words of the self-disciplined hymning and chanting mind of their followers; they did not know how to exemplify the truth of this task because of the lack of knowingness within the cultures in which they lived.

For indeed, "The Book" can now simply state that it is the methodical occurring of space between the worshippers' "self-disciplined" chanting words that stop the mind filling sound emanating from the five senses and which brings to the chanter a fleeting experience of "Enlightenment". For it is using the silence that occurs between the words of their worshipping prayers, this being that which allows the Soul to fleetingly observe God's world or the world of Nature for the Non-Believer, which only exists in the "Present Time".

For indeed it is true that these were the methods used by our wise ancients to bring to their followers a strong glimmering and a "sparking" of the experience which "The Book" and others, call "Enlightenment", this being that which is the "light" of the world, and which occurs when the Soul sees God's world or the world of Nature for the Non-Believer; this also being the world that can only exist in the "Present Time", and which is glimpsed within the spaces of the chanting and disciplined words of the person who is religiously praying, incanting, chanting or physically performing an activity in the worship of God For justly, in this silence that is emanating between their praying words, our wise ancients and all our modern worshippers will fleetingly experience and enjoy the *"Peace that surpasses all understanding".* Therefore, indeed this is the peace that exists in the realm beyond the ability of words to explain correctly, and it is a peace that existed within our wise ancients that could be readily witnessed by all their followers. For indeed, this is the world of "Enlightenment" that our wise ancients targeted to bring to their followers and they achieved this by using the verbal and habitual culture within the knowing experience for their followers.

But sadly, forgetting is our worst enemy, for as time moved forward, it eventually became the words of the incantations and the words of the prayers that were taught by others that the doer began to believe was the cause of this feeling of "Enlightenment," and not the "No-Thing" (nothing) that truly exists between the words. For justly, this is being the space of existing stillness which can be gradually expanded until the words are no longer necessary to recite in mind, for actually, it is the stilling of the mind that brings the peace which genuinely exists within a person's "Enlightenment", this being the experiencing of God's or Nature for the Non-Believer, this being the only reality can exist in the "Present Time".

So Yes! It is each person's Godly or Nature for the Non-Believer, gifted "Freedom of Choice" that enables people to also "disciplinary" sit with their eyes closed and to freely "choose" a way that will reactivate their "consciousness" to remove from "willpower" the previously given habit of automatically allowing the "I Want" of the five senses to enter the mind. For this is an activity is purposely and best achieved by holding fast in mind, the self-disciplined repeating of a single mantra word which is certainly more favourable than a favored self-repeating psalm or prayer, which when habitually and mechanically released into the mind, truly and compulsorily enables the Soul to view the still mind through the space between the word that is now being "automatically" and "controllably" being "habitually" repeated by the five senses, within the mind. But measurably, this is not an easy task for the five senses will do everything in their power to stop this activity and so it is important to remember that that which makes the sounding of these words into the mind is NOT you, for you are the observer which is the Soul - for you cannot be that which you observe. Therefore you can stop these five senses from tormenting you just as you can train five wild pups to obey your orders.

So yes! Each time these previously freed "I Want" words enter the mind, you should now understand that they are the selfish "I Want" desires emanating from the animalistic five senses and NOT your Soul, which is the real you. Therefore it is essential to use the power of consciousness and your gifted "Freedom of Choice", to discipline your "consciousness" again to stop the habit of your "willpower" from freely allowing the activation these "I want" demands that do originate from your five senses – which is NOT you for you are the observing SOUL. Therefore it is necessary to "disciplinary" stop and silences this noise in the mind which creates the "Hell" that takes you away from living in "Heaven", this being that which genuinely exists upon our world.

So yes! It is essential to "habitually" and "constantly" redirect your reality by disciplining the five senses to return to the automatically sounding mantra or worshipping prayer or song and so know with eyes closed that it is your Soul that is looking into the darkness of the still mind, this being between the spaces of your sounding mantra. For indeed, you will eventually find that heaven truly exists in the spaces between your automatically sounding words, this being that which your disciplined consciousness is now silently energised to pursue – via your gifted "Freedom of Choice".

It is then that you will "see" and so "realise" that which has been described by our wise ancients as the *"clouds of unknowing"*, this being that which with your eyes closed is the viewing of your empty mind. Eventually, after much practice and discipline and with this new knowledge, the space between the automatically sounding words of the mantra, as it does with hymns or prayers enlarge. For it is a fact that after much "meditational" un-thinking practice, the mind becomes still, and you will concretely know that you have entered the wonders God's world – the world that only exists in the "Present Time", this being that which is knowing called "Enlightenment".

So yes! It is also good to remember that as soon as you become aware of any "I Want" beginning to enter the mind, these being the observing of ANY non-mantra based words, then immediately and disciplinary cancel them and so return to the automatic sounding of the Mantra and God's peace that rests in the "Present Time", even unto the cross (meaning during the bad times and thoughts that may be presented to you). It is this factual glancing view of "Enlightenment," this being that which is silently manifesting between the spaces of the repeating mantra or prayer, which eventually allows your Soul to observe the real world and if continued into a full-time reality, you will "automatically," begin to become "Self-Aware" and so understand the harmony seeking actions required within God's or Natures for the Non-Believers "Creation", which can only exist and so be supported in the "Present Time". For truly you will then fully understand that the Past and the Future do not exist and it these are the imaginary places which "The Book" calls Hell! For indeed this is the Hell that the "I Want" that you're five senses are always automatically targeting via their pre-human animalistic "I Want" greed.

Thus being "Self-Aware" will become a proven fact and as stated, is a "Self-Awareness" which begins in the disciplined silence between the words and incantations of prayers which are being supported by personal willpower and this is the on-going fact which will eventually allow any individual's Soul to view that which is called the "Present Time", this being through the empty mind that is meant to exist within all people. For it is only in the "Present Time" that God's world truly exists, for again. Indeed it is only in the "I Want" world that exists in the past or the future, that is found the life that is living in Hell and if you wish to know the quickest way and most relaxed way to achieve a way of how to enter Gods or the Natures world for the Non-Believer, and so leave the world of Hell, – Read on.

The above words are a scientific fact that has always been and also anciently proven to be true. This truth certainly being realised when a person becomes aware that their God-given "Freedom of Choice" can make "consciousness" compel their "willpower" to stop an "I Want" that is emanating from one the five senses from automatically entering and so filling the mind, and YES, it can be done. It is also a proven fact that an individual can continue to expand and hold in mind this silent space that is occurring between the words of their mantra, and so begin to realise that without words or other distractions emanating from their animalistic five senses being sounded or pictured in mind, that they will "always" begin to experience that which our wise ancients called "Enlightenment".

For indeed all should know that this "stillness" within the silent mind is that which was targeted by all our wise ancients and it is also a much sought after reality which the Christian religion call being filled with the *"Holy Spirit,"* or the *"Holy Ghost,"* depending upon their accepted belief system. It is also stated in the Christian religion to be an experience in which people can be filled by a *"Peace that surpasses all understanding,"* while the Hindu religion calls this peace *"Moksha",* which loosely means *"freedom from ignorance".* Buddhists refer to it as *"Bodhi"* or *"Nirvana",* which is an experience achieved only by people and described as *"Awakening to the true Nature of Things."* The Islam religion speaks of this "Enlightenment" as *"Being filled with the Angel Gabriel,"* and describes it as *"A realm beyond the ability of words to properly convey".*

For all our religions and philosophies that originated from our wise ancients contain songs, prayers, and right chants. These being "creeds," that are designed to target this experience of "Enlightenment". For indeed this is also a fact which emanates from "all" known religious and philosophical history? Even the ancient Zoroastrianism religion of the fifth-Century BC refers to this personal experience of "Enlightenment" as *"Ushta,"* which it describes as meaning *"Liberation, Salvation, and Emancipation of the Soul."* So YES! It is undoubtedly worth achieving, and now it is awaiting you – if you want it to be so, and yes, the revealing of the above words can NEVER be stated enough to those who seek the truth, this being that truth which always rests upon our "Heavenly" Earth.

For absolutely, has stated above, this is a factual "Enlightenment" which is described in various ways by all our world's religions and philosophies, for it is a fact which occurs because of the "stilling" discipline applied to the mind by the reciting of "chosen" prayers and actions, plus incantations, these being that which al our wise ancients gave to their followers. Logically, this again is the worshipping of personally imposed "creeds," which are certainly not the "I Want" words that "freely" and uncontrollably fill the mind with "I Want" emanations from the five senses. For these holy creeds factually need a person's consciousness to be applied to willpower to forcibly chant these imposed "saintly" or "mantra" given words – this being the fact which ensures a path to "Enlightenment" which is the understanding of the real "silent" world?

So Yes, it is this repetitive fact which allows the Soul to witness the Creation's stillness which can only be realised in the "Present Time", this stillness is that which is occurring between the automatically incanting "mantra"; these being the chosen word or words that via a self-imposed discipline, pass through the mind. It is this silence within the empty mind factor; this being that silence which is occurring between the minds self-imposed "mantra" incanting words, which is the discipline that is needed to stop the mind filling past and future thoughts that target the "I Want" noise that is "freely" and always emanating from one of the five senses. Again truly, it is these "I Want" words emanating from the five senses which are blocking the view of the Soul from seeing the outside world, this being between the mantra created spaces of the incanting words.

Why is this? Because the worshipper has chosen willpower to enforce consciousness, to recite the imposed creed which eventually with much practice, will become automatic and will no longer need either consciousness or the prompting of willpower, to pursue this activity – for it will become habitually automatic. For indeed it is when the incanting is automatic and in need of no conscious energy, that the Soul can observe through the mind, the reality of God's world, the world that can only exist in the "Present Time" and a world of which the unthinking mind becomes fully aware.

For "Enlightenment" comes when it is no longer necessary to incant any creed, for eventually, the mind is disciplined to be still, which enables any person to exist and experience only the "Present Time", which is truly God's world or the world of Nature for the Non-Believer. For it is then, in this stillness of mind, that you first become "Self-Aware" and so really "know" that you are not only a part of that which you witness – but you have a strong feeling that you are also that which you witness in the "Present Time", which is the real YOU!.

So yes! Again, this is that which is called "Enlightenment", and it is being sought and obtained by expanding the silent space between the words that are being chanted within all the creeds that exist within our many religions and philosophies which are all based upon continual prayers and other actions. Therefore, indeed, these are the active creeds introduced by our many wise ancients for their followers to experience God's world or the world of Nature for the Non-Believer. For rightly, religions and philosophies have no other purpose than to empty and so make the worshippers mind still of and so bring it to a silence that genuinely experiences all that needs to be experienced but also that which is an experience that cannot be explained. For indeed, this is being when a "Practitioner" can hold the mind empty and without any thought and so is enabled to enter God's world or the world of Nature for the Non-Believer, this being the fact that always occurs after the stopping of all "I Want" thoughts. It can only occur when the mind is empty and STILL for it can then truly experience the "Present Time". For indeed, even though our wise ancients did not "scientifically" know that only "consciousness" can be used to silence the mind and so control the childhood freed energy of "willpower", they "culturally" knew that their suggested movements, mantras, and other "praying" methods could achieve "Enlightenment" and so did purposely introduce them to their followers.

These variable methods of targeting the same "Enlightenment" became culturally and habitually stereotyped within all our worlds religious and philosophical "creeds". They were used by our wise ancients to induce and so create the very personal experience of "Enlightenment". Precisely, this truly is the experience of existing only in Gods world or the world of Nature for the Non-Believer – which can only be experienced in the "Present Time". For our wise ancients truly knew and now all people should know, that regardless of their culture, creed or worshipping practices, it is a "scientific" truth that by "choosing" the personal power of your "consciousness" to silence "will-power" and so stop it from habitually releasing the "I Want" that is continuously emanating from your five senses, the mind will become free and empty from all "I Want" thoughts. Therefore "scientifically", it is this accomplished fact, sought by all our wise ancients, which will allow any individual's Soul to see through the empty mind and into God's world or the world of Nature for the Non-Believer, which can only exist in the "Present Time".

It is also a "scientific" fact that it is historically known that the disciplined repeating of many creed centred activities, which are based upon the activities of many varied religions or individually recited prayers, can enable people to expand the silence resting between the words of these worshipping incantations'. It is because of these wisely taught religious and philosophical activities that people are capable of fathering a silent mind. So through a silent mind, the Soul can see the environment in which it lives, which then brings to the person the experience of "Enlightenment," which cannot be described. Also, it is factual, that so such a person will first become "Self-Aware" and so be enabled to understand and therefore support all the laws governing God's world or World of Nature for the Non-Believer in which all people are just one single entity. So they liken all people to be themselves.

Therefore it is well to remember that this natural and purposeful enlightenment seeking creed activity is continuously thwarted by the "I Want" of the habitually allowed uncontrolled claiming demands of the five senses which conjure up past experiences which are then used to target future claims. It is these "I Want" demands which use the freed energy of willpower to habitually allow their inner mind sounding of a seeking "I Want", to contaminate the mind automatically and if you wish to stop this false purpose of your life, this being honestly an ignoring life that keeps you living in Hell – Read on

44 THE PURPOSE OF A SOUL THAT CANNOT DIE

For was it not our wise ancients who worded factually truthful religious and philosophical meanings which were in accordance to the understanding of the culture created by people of a specific region and which was the culture that existed all around them? Was this not also how our wise ancients "individually" created the entire worlds separately and individually named religions and philosophies? Again it should be said that this is being the way that targeted an acceptable "cultural" in which their followers could find their Soul that is akin to

God, and so enter a life that can be lived in God's world or the world of Nature for the Non-Believer.

Yet, isn't it strange that one religion will fight and kill members of another religion, by saying, "Your way to God is wrong, only our way to God is right?" Is this not truly an "I Want," which removes them from God's world and so inflicts upon them a punishment derived from them choosing to live in Hell, which they have falsely imposed upon themselves.

Is it not also true and sad, that this living in Hell may be inflicted upon their families their friends and their community, so the question is "why do they do this"? Is it because they have chosen to follow a personal leader and not their Soul? Do they also think that following this leader will lead them to experience their all-knowing Soul, and so to live in God's or the NNB world that exists only in the "Present Time"? How can this be? For an individual's Soul exists within everyone, but only "realised" by the religious, philosophical or scientific efforts employed by the individual that is personally seeking its realty. For it is impossible for the Soul to be given to a person without their efforts to "choose" to achieve its reality!

Yet again, it is sadly real and even stranger is the known historical fact that when the wise ancient founder of religion dies, and the religion goes forth and multiplies, that this same worshipping religion can develop a disputing conflict which separates the worshippers who will then actually kill other associated worshippers, even from within their own chosen religion, simply because they have accepted a different "leaders" organisational way to the one God?

How strange this is that a religious person can believe it to be correct that their silent observing Soul should endeavour to kill a body that contains another silently observing Soul? For again, is it not an absolute truth that all religiously based actions should be prompted by a Soul that exists within all people and indeed in each individual's body. Logically, this being especially true when all people are enabled to quickly recognise that those who have found and become their Soul, cannot possibly destroy another Soul, even when its host ignores its reality and lives in the world of "I Want" instead of the world of *"I am the I am,"* which is the unified world of all Souls. How can a Soul, which is directly linked to God's world, kill or torture another Soul? For again and genuinely, does not our history show how a severe punishment is always inflicted upon those bodies who perpetrate these ungodly attacks upon religious others. Is this not because they have broken away from the unified harmony created by God's or the laws of Nature for the Non-Believer?

Yet sadly, how painful it is for these religious destroyers when God's harmony endeavours to return, and negatively destroys the disharmony being perpetrated against it – as this natural law does to those who ignore a people religiously made "highway code" and who are likened to be those who drive through red lights and on the wrong side of the road, and how sad if their loved ones are in this falsely driven car. For gravely, is it not known to be accurate, that God or Nature for the Non-Believer does not interfere with the perfect evolution of our ever-developing world, particularly against the efforts of people, for ALL people are under His law; these being laws that cannot be broken, even when some people think they can be broken or changed; for the simple fact is that God gave all people the "Freedom of choice", so they cannot be "Godly" punished for using it. Also, does not our Earths history ALWAYS show that this personal deed of selfishly inflicting pain upon others, to gain some selfish advantage, is factually VERY wrong! Is it not also true that the **"Mother of the Creation"** always re-establishes harmony, when the Creation's harmony has been broken, just like God's law that governs water, which is known to be able to be changed into many different aspects, but which must always return to that which gives life; this being when it returns to being palatable?

So Yes! So it is with the Soul, for the sacred Christian words saying, *"I am that I am,"* is not to identify God, but to explain who is God's servant, which is the Soul of all people. For in God's law or the law of Nature for the Non-Believer, there is always a Soul which resides in people and also in the Christian Bible the Soul is described in words: *"I will be"* and in Genesis *"I shall be"* or *"I am who I am."* Indeed, this is not the God of all that is speaking for God does not need to change any of His laws, for how can God or Nature for the Non-Believer make a mistake?

So Yes! It is because of this that God does not need to ever interfere in the ways of His growing child who is His Creation because His laws are in perfect harmony and "ALWAYS" it is a person seeking an "I Want" that can redirect these laws. It is this that can be harmful to life and Non-Life. For indeed, does not the "Enlightened" Adi Shankara of the Hindu Advaita Vedanta religious school firmly explained that of all the definitions of God, *"none is indeed so well put as the biblical statement 'I am that I am,'"* meaning the Soul of people. Also, the Sri Nisargadatta Maharaja of the Hindu religion, which has been called the oldest religion in the world, explains the Soul as being the *"I am"* or the abstraction in the mind of a *"stateless state,"* meaning that the Soul is being likened to the *"Absolute",* signifying the supreme reality that it is based upon a pure *"awareness"* that cannot be described; meaning that it is before and without any thoughts and free from perceptions, associations and memories, this indeed is an excellent description of the all-seeing Soul. For certainly Hindus believe that there is only one true God which this ancient religion calls *"Brahman".* Hindus further state that God has many forms, that He also pervades the whole universe, and is symbolised by the sacred syllable Om (or Aum) discussed later in "The Book" for it is an "enchanted" word and Hindus certainly believe that Brahman (God) is present in every person and exists within the eternal spirit or Soul which they call the "Atman".

The Soul is also correctly described in Brahman as the highest Universal Principle and described as the "Ultimate Reality" within our universe. Also in the primary schools of Hindu philosophy, it is said that Brahman (God) is the material, efficient, formal and final cause of all that exists. Brahman (God) is also described as the pervasive, genderless, infinite, eternal truth and bliss which does not change, yet is the cause of all changes. Brahman, also being a philosophical concept, states that "Braham" is the single binding unity behind the diversity in all that exists in the universe. It can undoubtedly agree that these words are also describing the Soul of people, for indeed, it is well known that different religions and philosophies are traditionally respected as having "cultural" academic differences, but which are all in pursuit of the same truth.

So yes! Here can be explained, via our many different religions, the philosophical words in which they describe the Soul saying - "I am who I am" - "I am who I was" - "I am who I shall be" - "I was who I am" - "I was who I was" - "I was who I shall be" - "I shall be who I am" - "I shall be who I was" - "I shall be who I shall be," - "I am the I am", all meaning the "Promised One"! Also, in some philosophies our wise ancients speak as if the Soul is saying to them: "I am the One whose name you have for a thousand years invoked, at whose very mention you have risen, whose advent you have also longed to witness, and upon the time of whose Revelation you have prayed God to hasten." Many also say that the Soul is binding upon all the peoples of our world and purported in some religions and philosophies' to have said: "Obey My word and pledge allegiance to my person."

So yes! If the Soul could speak, the above is what it would say, for indeed, it is the Soul of people that are linked to God or Nature for the Non-Believer, and it is the Soul that genuinely, rests within people, for our wise ancients always says so. It can be first understood that it is firmly believed in most of the world's religions that the inner Soul can reply to those who ask "who are you?" by saying, "I am the cause that rests in the brain;" this being that which can be likened to the "everything" which says to the world "I am the I am" and the Soul is known to be the light that leaves the body when a person's bodily consciousness can no longer support it. For indeed, God or NNB did not create such energy that can be destroyed or energy which can "disappear" forever from the Creation – for again is it not also true to say that within our world our scientists have revealed that energy cannot be destroyed.

So does this not explain that our Soul can be indeed likened to all the energy that exists within our universe? This meaning that it just and energy that moves onward into the different bodies of its "Self" chosen individual carrier, which is selected naturally as being the "personal" force that is best suited for its continuing "helpful" and "supportive" existence. Is it not also understood that because of this never-ending truth, that the Soul must have within it the ability to energise a person's mind, which then becomes conscious within the creation again. For again is it not correct to say that this transferred energy, which creates that which we call "life", gives meaning to an individual's "personal" mind which it energises and so again, brings energy to new life? Is it not also true that our scientists say that this happens at a certain point in the pregnancy period, in which the Soul enters the child who is growing in the mother's womb, this being an act which the mother experiences?

So yes! The Soul is born again within a mother's body and with a real living purpose plus the freedom of choice and yet all people are born again into thinking that they are "individuals" and also that they are without the understanding that they are just a work in progress. Accurately, this is because the Creation, which the Soul is directly linked to, always silently recognises itself to be part of a greater whole, for its work is to assist the Creation's harmony in it continually ever-moving along with this God or Nature for the Non-Believers given path. Thus, this living inside and assisting the Creations "harmony" is likened to the harmony of that which we see within our bodies.

Accurately, this is being a singularity of existence, in which all bodily parts continually target a harmony that cares for the greater whole within that person's body, and will always continue to do so if we allow and support this fact. Is it not also true that the body carries within it, all the many individuals living separate un-selfish millions of variables and nuances that are self-activated and which are not controlled by the individual whose body they inhabit? Is this not an inner life force which uses the body, but is controlled by an energy source that is controlled "unconsciously" by an unknown entity that we could say is "The Soul Within". Therefor could not this inner Soul be that which harmonises a person's body just as our God or Nature harmonises the Creation with the support of the *"Mother of the Creation"* and is this not all based upon the universal fact that both "Life" and "Non-Life" always exist in unity. For truly does not all the Creations lawfully controlled singularities, variables and differences that exist within the Creation, also truly exist within our body? Therefore is it not also true that the laws controlling the well-being of the Creation also control the well-being of all the separate entities that exist within our bodies. So can it not be said that our bodies are also unselfishly and factually organised for the same entity which harmonises our Earth? For indeed this must be the same entity which harmonises that which exists within our own body's inner world, these being all the acts that are necessary to support the unity of that is all around us and is recognised to be also within us.

For assuredly, is it not a fundamental truth that our body continually functions without any bodily parts claiming a personal "I Want", for indeed, these inner parts labour unselfishly within a very positive but also culturally very different and varied "collective". This being a collective that is seeking only that which benefits the unity of that entity in which it exists, this creation being within the individual all know as "you".

Is this not also a perfect example of how the individual "you" should actively behave within the totality of the Creation's one body? Is it not also known to be true that a person's body can go "wrong" as one harmony seemingly clashes with another outside entering harmony; a fact which we endeavour to correct, just as they should do with the outer world in which we live and which we call the Creation. Simply put, it is the implanting of Gods or Natures Soul which harmoniously and freely controls the inner collective of a person's body and automatically supports all body actions that spring from our inner thought, needs, and deeds.

For a known truth is that a person's body is a collective "singularity" whose many parts obey without doubt the Souls actions, this being that which harmonises all the separate life forms that live within each person's body and so allow each person to pursue all their outer world activities without hindrance.

These being personally targeted by that which we simply call "ME", and the simple reason for this is because God or Nature for the Non-Believer gave people the freedom of choice, this gift being because the same act can support, weaken or it can destroy the Creations emerging harmony, depending upon surrounding circumstances.

Simply put, what we have forgotten, and forgetting is our worst enemy, is that the Soul is the only manager of our body's internal collective and the Souls many varied management techniques are continually empowered to create a sharing harmony between all the millions of "individual" life forms within a person's body. It can also be quite clearly seen that the Souls internal management control of the body's inner harmony does not originate from a personal desire but only from the right actions of a silently controlling soul. Rightly, this is because a person, when selfishly controlled by an "I Want" for myself though, can be likened to the lungs wanting to take blood that was needed by other parts of the body. Rightly again, this is why the body's collective only obeys the Soul, which silently and unselfishly pursues the harmony needed by all the different entities of the life that lives within you? Yet is it not also true that God has gifted people with a similar ability to freely pursue all our bodies' outer world activities in the same way, these being those activities that can be personally corrected and unifying supported by that which we call "ME!" Again it must be indeed said that God or Nature for the Non-Believer gave People the "Freedom of Choice" because the same act in the outer world can support harmony or destroy it. For really is it not an agreeable fact that it is only our Soul, seeing through a clear mind, that knows which action should be done and which action should not be done in support of the heaven that exists all around us? This being just has the Soul does with all its decisions regarding the harmony and bliss of all our inner bodily parts and YES! It is the freeing of the Soul to obey its harmony seeking outer world and so bring to the person the condition known has of "Enlightenment" which can be described again has experienced the Holy Spirit or Holy Ghost or "Moksha", "Bodhi", "Nirvana", "Gabriel", "Ushta", and many other names from our wise ancients plus they are stating that it brings "liberation", "salvation", "emancipation", "peace", "freedom", and an "awakening bliss that is impossible to describe" and it is now genuinely awaiting you!

It is also well known that these variations of our "thinking" reality are based upon selfish "I Want" for myself, which is certainly not the real you. Indeed, this is because the reality is that you are genuinely the Soul and the body is simply a tool for the Soul to use. For assuredly, this is because the real purpose of the Soul is to expand this inner and personal "collective" to be the same as the more significant "collective" that resides in the harmony of the Heaven that exists upon this Earth, this being the real world of God or Nature for the Non-Believer.

It is also in this work that the purposeful activity of each person's soul should be endeavouring to support, which is the harmony and emerging harmony that abides within this Heaven upon our Earth. Knowingly, this is an "outer" activity in which the silent Soul should automatically be controlling in the same way it does the inner body's harmony. Therefore, the purpose of your life and all people's lives is to maintain the harmony that exists within this Earth's "collective", this being that which exists all around you.

So yes! What is it that controls the inner workings of this body that we all call "Me"? The only correct answer to this question is that our bodies are under the purposeful control of the Soul; this is a Soul that perfectly controls, energises and supports all the much needed natural harmony that is always moving within you, and which is also a perfect harmony that is achieved without conscious thought. For indeed, all these inner bodily actions are accomplished by balancing towards harmony the separate trillions of individual parts that maintain the body in the "singularity" of good health.

So honestly, a person's body, "naturally" produces a great deal of activity in the singularly of targeting the life-supporting benefit of the "collective," this being "collective" existing within a person's body. Therefore, is it not true that the most critical aspect of this inner collective's control system is that it is not really "you," for "you" cannot be this "energy" that initiates all these needed inner activities?

So can it not be said that it is your Soul that is automatically directing and caring for all the trillions of individual parts which energise the body of "You". This being energy within you that is seemingly able to receive "inner" unstoppable reports being activated to perform harmony seeking duties to which they are individually best suited to perform! Can the Soul now be identified has a purposeful and healthily targeting energy, which is simply the Soul of the individual?

For indeed, this is being a Soul whose "energy" our scientists say, enters a person's body shortly after pregnancy, this being a time when the inner birthing child is willing and able to accept this "energy," which can be explained as being the coming to birth of a person's soul. For indeed, is not the Souls purpose is to serve the "collective" inner world of an individual's body, as well as the "collective" outer harmony, that is being continually experienced outside a person's body?

So should not the individual's Soul by the directive of the world within and the world without, this being the outside of the person's body? With the inner world of the body genuinely being an example of Heaven and the outer world of the body being the "Heaven," that is continually endeavouring to exist in the "Present Time". For indeed we live in God's world or the world of Nature for the Non-Believer and this being that world that exists upon our Earth and which people have been given the "Freedom of Choice" to support because one act can "automatically" harmonize that which is emerging around them. In contrast, later this same act could jar the unity which is endeavouring to emerge in the "Present Time".

So Yes! It is easily recognised that our "Soul" that which we cannot observe, is the transient on-going traveller which continually takes people from birth to death and onwards as it gathers experience from its many previous births and deaths. For truly is it not our Soul that has been created to harmoniously work to support the on-going harmony which is always striving to exist in, in the "Present Time".

For precisely, this is a collective energy, that will be within the Creation until the end of time for the Soul is composed of energy which cannot die. It is also an energy which naturally works, not only following the body's harmony seeking needs but also to support and maintain the ever variable on-growing needs of harmony which exist in the "Present Time". Yet! Is it not sad that many of people enter an "I Want" world, that can only exist in the past or the future and which is also a world that does not exist, except in the person's mind? It is with this sadness that we enter and live, as our wise ancient's say, in an awakened sleep likened to a nightmare condition, which manifests within us the continuous pursuit of an "I Want" desire which can never be satisfied.

So yes! in "The Book," revealed later, there is a recommended simple creed prayer that will change your life. It will also bring you to the joys of the "Present Time", in which your freed Soul, will "automatically" be content, and so will willingly perform the needed deeds that support the existing harmony and the emerging harmony of the Creation which "you," in your "Enlightened" state will be able to evaluate correctly. For this is a task that will fully the support God's Creation or the needs of Nature for the Non-Believer; It is also a worldly present-day task which is copying the inner workings of your internal body parts, in which your Soul ensures that they also "harmoniously" survive in their many varied duties, these duties being those that are required by the greater whole, and will "automatically" continue to be so, with this being whenever theses inner working are not being interfered.

For indeed, this is a God or NNB given gift of being born into a life in which God's gift of "choice" has been given only to people, and it is a purposeful gift which enables everyone to support the harmonious work that is needed to be achieved within the evolving Creation's "Present Time".

Yet, in within our current "Present Time" is wise to remember that around 12,000 years ago people "chose" a new way of life that became the first step away from living off the "Nature" that existed around them and only 10,000 years ago began to self-reproduce nature and began to live in a controlled farming era and therefor cleared the land of its natural growth to grow their crops and personally selected animals. It was probably then that a person's life quickly lost its healthy connection to the inner Soul for people actively "chose" to fill the mind with a personal "I Want" more farming land to be mine and so targeted the personal control of more land and more domesticated animals and so killed off nature and the freedom of weaker others to hunt and collect naturally growing food, this being that life which existed before land was cannibalised by individuals.

So Yes! It was probably this personal and discording search for more and more land and the growing imprisonment of animal life that firmly created a personal "I Want" false condition, this being a condition which blocks the Soul from seeing through the mind the exact needs of the outer world and the people that rested upon it. For indeed and according to the laws of nature, all land and all domesticated animals belong to the unity of all people who reside on that land, and it is they who should receive and distribute accordingly the highest marketable payment for all the products that they collectively produce – is this not so?

So yes! It is important to also fully understand that you will "now" always know that you will be placed into the correct birth situation that will enable you to free the Soul within you, for you are still always needed to support a need that constantly exists within the emerging Creation. Or maybe this is your first birth from the animal kingdom, in which you are entering into a new birth that contains a Soul, this being from your previous animal-based life.

For rightly, a non-people animal life is a life without a Soul and also without the freedom of choice, this being freedom of choice that could allow it to create its death if it wished to do so. But now this previous non-people animal life has been born as a person with a new Soul which for the first time this new Soul will experience the "Freedom of Choice", which is an essential aspect of its new way of life. For it is the "Freedom of Choice" that only gives people the ability to support the emerging harmony of the Creation, and so engender the collective harmony that is truly and always endeavouring to exist, but only in the "Present Time" this being that which always rests upon this Earth.

So yes! It is good to understand the similarities that exist between the Souls work within the Earths "collective" and also its work within the body's inner "collective". For again the Souls overall target is to support the Earths collective, this being a Soul which observes and supports the Heaven that exists in harmony upon our Earth, and also the bodies collective, this being our Soul which controls the harmony that exists within our body. For indeed, the Souls purpose is to observe, guide and support the Heaven that exists in harmony upon this earth and also within the body of all people.

For again, is it not true that the workings of the inner body's "collective" are monitored and observed by the inner bodies working Soul. For it is a well-known understanding that our Soul has an inner "chosen" willpower that can automatically empower consciousness to activate the needed work that sustains the inner bodies' activities – in which all body parts are deemed to be without the "Freedom of Choice. Therefore is it not a known truth that is this non-interference within the body by the five senses does allow the bodies "collective" parts to act without a personnel choice, as they willingly perform the necessary deeds that are needed to work in harmony within the bodies collective.

So yes! The outer harmony, this being that which is outside the body, is all that which is contained in God's "Present Time", which is a collective whose development often needs adjusting, "harmoniously" and "physically" – and this is why people have been given the "Freedom of Choice," because one act can target harmony. Still, sometimes the very same act can destroy it. For factually, it is only the inner Soul that can "silently" evaluate just which act to pursue, this being in our efforts to support the Divine Mother's harmony seeking needs. It is also useful at this point to fully understand that the brain is just one part of the body's functions, as are all the internal parts of the body, and the truth of natural law states that you cannot be that which you observe. Therefore, it is also by the recognising of this simple "scientific" fact that the only part of the body that you cannot observe, is the Soul within you, therefore "scientifically" this is the real YOU!

So yes! Only as your Soul can you silently "choose" to perform the "collective" acts for which you were born and designed to achieve, this being the actual active reality which is achieved only in "Enlightenment". Yet in this known world of people it is also wise to understand that without "Enlightenment", the Soul within cannot observe the truth of the outer world for its view is continually blocked by dreams and imaginations of a past or a future "I Want", this being a reality which can be likened to the life of all our lower animals.

Correctly, this simply means that the mind is filled with an "I Want" past and future created impressions, which are created by the five senses that simply create and paint these "I Want" demands into the mind of the beholder. It is also well to know that even an "undecided" of these thoughts is also filling and a blocking the Souls view of the world through a clear mind.

So Yes! It is this never-ending flood of "I Want" for me that fills the mind with untrue reflections that are born from an unreal world, and so the Soul cannot see what to support or what not to support in the emerging heaven that exists upon this Earth. If there are some doubts about this concept, then endeavour now to sit still and think of nothing, which means that the mind has no words or pictures entering it? Now indeed, for how many seconds was your mind silent and without incoming thoughts? Now understand genuinely, that these thoughts returning and dwelling in your mind are animalistic desires, for they continually plot to target or steal for these "I Want" desires that are clouding the mind are emanating from your animalistic five senses because they are continually seeking to satisfy their animalistic needs; these being of their animalistic nature and which you "think" are your own personal "I Want" desires and yes! It is important to keep repeating this.

For indeed, this is NOT that which a person's five senses have been born to pursue, for they have no regard for the "collective" harmony of the Creation, nor do they fully appreciate the disharmony that these acts can bring to the environment that surrounds their body. For indeed, it is good to remember that no person can see the Kingdom of Heaven that rests upon this Earth if there is an "I Want" desire filling his or her mind.

For the Soul cannot see the joy or needs of that which is happening in the "Present Time"; just as a reflection cannot be seen in the still waters of a lake if the waters are disturbed by falling stones, or just as a thread cannot enter the eye of a needle and so fulfil its designated task, if there is any detached fibre at its end. Thus, it is then that an "I Want" will stop the Soul from seeing or entering the "Present Time", this being the Kingdom of Heaven that truly exists upon our Earth and is this not the reason why we are here? Because God or Nature would like to experience itself – what other purpose is there?

45 WHAT IS "SELF-REALISATION"?

So Yes! "The Book" has been modernly written for all too fully understand the target of all our wise ancients which is to experience the gift called the "Kingdom of God" or the real world of NATURE for the Non-Believer. The first target is to become "Self-Aware", in which you know that you exist, has an integral part of all that is around you and which is an experience that can evolve into the next stage, this being that which our wise ancients called "Self-Realisation", an experience in which you are "Everything" and that you and the creation are one. Thus the target of your wise ancients is for their listeners to become "Self-Aware" or "Self-Realised" which is a very "Enlightening" experience for people to understand (Stand-Under). Therefore, indeed, it is a truth that is seldom experienced in our dream world. The reason for this is because it is concealed and is therefore hidden behind a "self-created" separating awareness of an "I Want" for myself world and is, therefore "unseen," and "unrealised", yet it is an existence in which can truly become all that is around you have to do all your body parts that work is within you. For you cannot hear it, you cannot see it, you cannot taste it, you cannot touch it, and you cannot smell it, but you can experience "Enlightenment," which is the first concrete step towards becoming "Self-Aware" the awareness before "Self-Realisation".

So yes! As people, we can certainly experience "Enlightenment", this being a unified reality in which only people can become aware of this "Kingdom of Heaven" that rest within us and all around us and which is known can be truly experienced in the "Present Time", for indeed this is undoubtedly a gift which is often called the experiencing of and the actual living in "The Now Time". The reason being for this is that it is only in "The Now Time" and by using modern "scientific" facts that people can be shown the way to achieve "Enlightenment;" but be aware that old habits can be challenging to turn away from unless one is very determined to do so. But honestly, any person can now "modernly" find the way to realise just who they are for being "Self-Aware" is only the first part of the effort towards that which the wise ancients call the way to "Self-Realisation" this being a final condition in which the experiencer and the experienced are just ONE entity.

The result of this path to "Self-Realisation" which can be only taken after the experience of becoming "Self-Aware", which is also an enlightening experience and which is also an experience that not only reveals the reality that all life and non-life are really living in a Heaven that exists in the world around them, this being a fact which is revealed firmly within the experience of "Enlightenment," but it is an experience which reveals the truth that the experiencer is not "living" within this Creation, but that they actually "are" the Creation. Therefore, it must be further understood that becoming "Self-Aware", this being that reality which leads to "Self-Realisation", is declared to be the main target of ALL the wise ancients who ALL show a cultural and systematic way in which their listeners can become "Self-Realised" and so achieve "Self-Realisation","" with the added information given by our wise ancients that in becoming "Self-Realised," you will never be born again, but will stay forever with the Divine "Mother of the Creation".

So Yes! Now for a word of caution; you may feel the need to return from this first "experience" of "Self-Realisation"," as I did, which was a coming back that was achieved by the repeating of my name, as if in a mantra, until I heard again the unspoken words saying, "Go back you have work to do!" The reason for this return to being a witness of the Creation and not being the Creation itself is that "Self-Realisation" is a powerful experience, in which you no longer exist as an individual. For really you become the "Creation" as your five senses cease to exist and there is no longer an observer, which is the Soul for the Soul has become as one with the Creation – which is, has our wise ancients state, is the target of the Soul.

So Yes! What exactly is "Self-Realisation"? Our wise ancients say that the "experience" of being "Self-Realised" is that you fully understand that there is only one real "individual," and that this "individual" is the Creation itself or what the Non-Believers call the totality of all the energy of life and Non-Life. For in the actual reality of being "Self-Realised", you realise who and what you are and so you experience the truth of all that exists. You know "exactly" that you "yourself" are the totality of the "Creation," and there is no other entity but you! Indeed, this is being because there is no other viewpoint of where you are or where you exist. For rightly within this "Self-Realised" experience you are the whole of Life and Non-Life, for you have become the actual reality of all Nature. For it is within this experience that you "truly," know that nothing is separate from you, for "separation" does not exist for that which exists can best be described as "YOU!" For beyond doubt, you are the "I am that I am" – of everything. For, our wise ancients also suggested that a further target for an enlightened "Self-Aware" person is to pursue the way to "Self-Realisation" and so become that which is the real "YOU;" and never again do you hear the words sounding in your head, which are your "untrained" animal senses naturally "wanting something for themselves" and it does not matter to them how they obtain their "I Want". So now it is true that you will understand just what Jesus meant when he said: *"Get behind me. Satan!"* – Meaning the five senses – *"You are a stumbling block to me; you do not have in mind the things of God, but the things of people."* Again, this is the "I Want" of the five senses, always clamouring and scheming within a person's mind. Also *"If anyone would come after me, he must deny himself",* this being their personal "I Want" – *"and takes up his cross."* – The cross is "Enlightenment"- *"and follows me."* – This latter is to assist and support the developing Creation – *"For whoever Want to save his life"* – by stopping to pursue the many "I Want" emanating from their animalistic five senses – *"will lose it,* for they become the animalistic five senses - *but whoever loses his life for me will find it."* Stops' believing that they are the five senses and so supports the harmony emerging around them, thus meaning that the doer is "Enlightened" by being "Self-Aware" but not "Self-Realised".

Why is this above truth stated to be so? The reason for this is that Jesus's words collectively show to all people that HE is "Self-Realised," for it is only in this position that the incarnate Jesus could teach His close followers that they have and are everything – meaning that a personal "I Want" cannot exist within them. Therefore it would be good to read again ONLY the words of Jesus in the knowledge that it is the Creation that is speaking to you and maybe for the first time in your life, you will understand what Jesus is saying and of course many others of our wise ancients also; for all endeavour to remind us who we are. So now, with being aware of the above knowledge, listen again to these words of Jesus and so fully know and understand that it is the Creation that is speaking to you. For now, you indeed know that the following words do come from words spoken by the Creation, which are sounding through the embodied Jesus. Therefore you can now fully experience these words that the Creation is saying personally to you and this being: *"Take my yoke upon you and learn from me, for I am gentle and humble in heart, and you will find rest for your Souls. I am the bread of life, and those who come to me will never go hungry, and those who believe in me will never be thirsty. For I am the living bread that came down from heaven, and if anyone eats of this bread, he will live forever. This bread is my flesh, which is given for the life of the world. I am not here on my own, but from He who sent me, and it is true, you do not know Him. But I know Him because I am from Him and He sent me. I am the light of the world; whoever follows me will never walk in darkness, but will have the light of life."* Again and indeed, this is the Creation speaking directly and personally to you. So now with the above knowledge, you should fully understand that all these words were spoken by the Creation, through Jesus and then last but not least, are these words: *"Even if I bear witness of Myself, My witness is true"*. Know well that this is the Creation speaking, and the Creation also added, *"for I know where I came from and where I am going; but you do not know where I come from and where I am going"*. Well, we do now. We came from the love of God, but we absently fell away from it, but now we are endeavouring to go back to it! Is this not a truth for you also? Now it is an excellent time to remember that the sounds, words and pictures that appear in your mind are NOT you, for "YOU" are the Soul which is attached to the Creation but which is blinded from seeing the creation around it, this being because of these "I Want" mind blocking reflections that are being created in mind, and which genuinely, distorts and or stops the Souls view of the Creation resting outside of you. For now, you fully understand that the "I Want" being created within your cluttered mind is blocking the Soul's sight of the many needs emanating from outside you and which exist all around you.

So Yes! Now is the time to remember that the inner mind filling "I Want", this being that which is continually emanating from the five sense and which is continuously blocking the view of the Soul through the mind, should be the same as listening to the sound of any music in that the music can be turned off. For indeed, these internal sounds and pictures are just animalistic "I Want" for me claiming sounds that are sparked within you, and which you can "choose" to stop just as you "choose" to allow them to continue sounding. For truthfully, you can obey these "I Want" thoughts or not obey them, for you have, as a person, been given the freedom of choice" – even unto your death. Indeed, it is the gift of the above "Freedom of Choice" that enables only people to have the discipline to become "Self-Aware" and so truly experience "Enlightenment". For again, it is only this "Freedom of Choice" fact which enables people to "choose" to live in Heaven while on this Earth, which is also an activity that can further lead to "Self-Realisation". For again, it is a well-established truth and known to be real in that both of these self "realities" can be achieved by pursuing the teachings of our ancient wise, this being the activation of their established creeds such as prayers, songs and chants, with the best activity of all being Mantra based "Patient Meditation". Precisely, this is because Mantra Meditation is that which is rightly known by our wise ancients to be the most straightforward exercise to target the silencing of all sounds going into the mind so that the Soul can see the creation that exists before it. For correctly, the truth is that a person's active and silencing of the mind is regarded as a sure way to bring their pursuit of this truth to silently understand (stand under) "God's laws" or the laws of Nature for the Non-Believer. These were the very laws that are always and continually endeavouring to control the emerging harmony of the Creation, a rightly known progressing and harmony targeting energy that people will never be able to understand unless "Enlightened" to do so, for is it not true that all people should sincerely acknowledge the fact that this "emerging harmony" only exists within the Heaven that rests upon this earth? Is it not also a truth that this emerging Heaven needs supporting and if you wish to know more about the best way to achieve this support via Mantra Meditation – Read on?

So yes! The pursuer of the truth, this being the person who is targeting "Self-Awareness" leading to "Self-Realisation" via the experiencing of "Enlightenment", will find, within both conditions, that they have become the reality of all that which is around them, for in both these conditions their Soul will become the silent viewing entity that supports and maintains the harmony of the Life and Non-Life force of that which existing and endeavouring to emerge all around them. Therefore, is it not now known that a freed Soul will "automatically" and without thought; support the energy that maintains the Godly harmony that exists all around it, has it automatically does within the body in which it rests? For did not Jesus at the end time of His life, silently try to "Enlighten" and so change the false tribal harmony which most people who live in a tribal area tend to strive for and this is at the time of His terrible crucifixion? Was this false tribal harmony not also revealed by Jesus saying at the point of his death: *"Forgive them for they know not what they do?"* Is it not also true that this crucifying act was paving the way for most of the people living in the Northern Hemisphere to become free from their tribal "I Want" yokes and so leave their tribal-based harmony by seeking God's harmony for all Life and Non-Life? For, again "knowing not what to do" appears to be again amongst many people of our many nations, but NOW what is emerging to be true is the modern interpretation of these wise ancient sayings. For indeed, these modern words are now endeavouring to reveal to you the reader, that you will genuinely, "KNOW", when your mind is silent, precisely what to do in your current life? For really, this is because your "Soul", which is the real you, contains the knowledge that will ensure that the body will do what it should do? For again is it not true that this "knowing what to do" is in the "knowing" of how to find the way to live in the Heaven that exists in the now time upon this Earth? Therefore, can it not be said that your "not knowing what to do" is now defunct. For assuredly, is it not now truly understand just how to find Gods world or the world of Nature for the Non-Believer, this being that which exists only the "Present Time", a "Heaven" that genuinely, exists upon this Earth, and which is all-around people, but only in the "Present Time". But honestly, many can be "forgetful," and so be "Heathen" upon this Earth and not knowing the right way to live can bring to themselves great pain and sorrow, usually caused by greed. So yes! Is it not now truly, known that the way to experience Heaven upon this Earth can be pursued by all who read "The Book" and by their listeners? Also, is it not now known to be true that by endeavouring to read on, the reader will finally know what should be done and how to do it, this being to live within God's "Present Time", the only place in which Heaven is endeavouring to rest in an ever still ever-emerging harmony that is existing all around us, but which only people can destroy – again and again. Yet! With a good harmony seeking "exercise", which is explained later in "The Book", people will be able to stop forever the "I Want" that continually fills and troubles their minds. For eventually, combined with this "Enlightened" small exercise, which is explained later, all those who are seeking the truth will experience the harmony of God's world that rests in all things; and so YES! They will genuinely; experience the harmony within that which is called "Enlightenment" and surly with this experience they will know the path of real harmony, for all should know now that it does exist.

So yes! It should also be known as a truth that most people can become "Self-Aware" or "Self-Realised" and so recognise that "THEY" are genuinely the harmony that exists within the Creation and that justly, they are living in a Heaven that exists upon our Earth. Yet sadly it is also agreed that many transgressors oppose and destroy the searching for the harmony of all the life and non-life that exists all around them, and so they steal that which rightfully belongs to others. For it is also true that those who have no true God will also kill and destroy many people's lives to achieve their "I Want". For even current history shows that the six hundred and thirty-five thousand tons of bombs including thirty-two thousand five hundred and fifty-seven tons of fiery napalm bombs, these being explosives that were historically dropped upon the people of North Korea during their North versus South Korean war.

It is also historically known that this did not destroy the North's tribal belief system nor did it stop the people of the North or the people of the South from using their way to finding their brand of "truth". Neither will those millions of surplus to requirements bombs currently being dropped by other countries within the Northern Hemisphere upon the people of Middle Eastern countries, stop any different belief systems from developing; for all bombs are still searching for the same "I Want" truth that explosively rests within them. But sadly, is this not all recognised as a tribal "I Want" and the only victors are the armament industries, who supply their profit-making goods to the leaders of both sides of these conflicts. Why is this?

So yes! It should also be known that this task of controlling the mind unto a respectful silence is not easy to achieve. Yet it is a factually known truth that with particular creed based exercises you can remove the "I Want" that is now knowingly and no longer "unknowingly," controlling you, and so you are now able to realise just who you are, for you are the Soul; that existence which cares for all Life and Non-Life. So Yes! By these various developing creed based exercises, with the selected best being called "Patient Meditation", this being that which "The Book" will "scientifically" describe later has the perfect tool to achieve that which is called "Enlightenment", this being that reality which gives definite "Self Aware" proof of who you are and if required you can continue to achieve "Self-Realisation" for then you will not only be who you were but what you are now. For indeed this is the totality of the Creation in which you understand – stand under – that which is everything – this being all knowledge. Therefore step by step Mantra Meditation exercises will show you that you have "everything" that is needed, and that you are that which naturally rests in the eternal harmony called the "Present Time". To fully understand this you need to seriously pursue the later proposed "Patient Meditation" exercises that will "scientifically" bring you to obtain this awakening factor of "Enlightenment," and so enable you to enjoy and maybe support the harmony that exists within the "Present Time" or even, eventually – your unification with the Creation, this being truly the reality that our wise ancients encouraged their followers to pursue, this also being recognised by their introduced religious and philosophical creed-based praying methods.

So yes! These ancient meditational exercises, explained later, will bring any person into a position in which they will realise that the world is not attacking them and that they are the Soul to which the mind silently reflects the Creation, this being that which silently exists within and outside them. It is also a known fact that all the chattering "I Want" thoughts in the head will stop. These were the thoughts in your head, which are like the never-ending sound of a flowing river, which you listen to as if these inner sounds words are you, and YES! You do falsely argue and act upon them accordingly. These "I Want" emanations into the mind are not you! For if you think that they are, then "you" have forgotten that you are the Soul to which can see through a clear and still mind silently reflects all activities, that occur outside your body and so with a still mind, the Soul can see what is outside the mind. All you need to remember is that your body needs to be under the control of who you REALLY, and this is the Soul – and if you wish to know how to do this? – Read on

46   WE ARE NOT THE FIVE SENSES –

For the Young

If we allow our five senses, these being our, taste, sight, hearing, touch and smell to control us by their constant chattering and claiming of a personal "I Want", which is something that often belongs to others. For indeed, we are not only harming others by taking what is theirs but mainly hurting ourselves, our friends, our neighbours and maybe all the life and Non-Life that always exists all around us, this is because you do mistakenly believe that your five senses are the real you but, to speak very directly. In essence, they are not you; they are just instruments for your use.

So Yes! Is it not true that you cannot be that which you look at, listen to, observe, taste, smell or touch, this being all that which you can control or not control. Therefore it not undoubtedly true that our five senses are just special instruments which are only for our personal use, which is the same truth that is established within our animal kingdom. For correctly are these five senses not God's gifts or Nature's gifts, for Non-Believer, and are they, not gifts which allow you to experience the wonders of all the worlds Life and Non-Life, this being that which exists all around you? Yet sadly, the truth is that in your childhood, you believed that these five senses were the real you. It is this "unawareness" that made it easy for them to use your body which can now cause the real "you" to have many problems with people and with the conditions that exist all around you – which our wise ancients called the path to misery.

For correctly, is it not also true that their individual and constant "I Want" demands are continually seeking an "animal" satisfaction? Also is this not a condition which can be likened to a group of five musicians all with special instruments and all loudly playing their own different "I Want my tune to be heard," to their listening observers, which is only "You". This being because "You" are their conductor and this "You" is your Soul, which is likened to it, exists has if caged in another room because it is imprisoned by your God-given or Nature gave for the Non-Believer "Freedom of Choice". It is this fact which makes the real "You" unable to control "Your" orchestra and so to perform for the benefit of the audience, which exists all around you. For "TRULY" you are not the fives sense for they are just instruments for the use of your Soul, which is the real you and which needs a clear mind to also see into the world that exists all around it.

Or are you the one who, with "Self" discipline can stop all their noisy "I Wants" and join them together in a silent unity which can only exist in the "Present Time", this being the time in which exits the goodness (Godness) of all that is around you and which genuinely experienced by the real "You". Then, by this controlling and disciplinary act use your personally given "Freedom of Choice" to "choose" to play something great and so instructing these five "musicians" just what they can do for YOU and all that is around YOU! Are you also the person who, when it is your turn to "play" or to do some activity, "chooses" one of these five instruments to do their work for you? By self-conducting and with a silent mind, play will play a magnificent solo, so that all around you will look at you in wonder and appreciation at the full concentration of your "harmonised" work. Therefore, gone will be the problem of all your five senses freely and individually shouting and arguing within your mind with their mind filling thoughts of "I Want" to pursue only that which is of benefit to my taste, no it should be to my touch, no to my smell, no to my seeing, no to my hearing and all individually commanding to experience that for which they alone exist. Systematically, this is because ALL these five "instruments", which are employed to work only for you, are all saying "I Want" you to work only for me and to play MY choice, not theirs.

For indeed it is your Soul, the real "You" that, because of your God-given or Nature gave for the Non-Believer "Freedom of Choice", can "choose" to act just as you can "choose" to make ALL your "animalistic" five senses, this being that which is driven by ancient physical appetites and not your now spiritual nature, to remain silent. In contrast, you act you're supporting part in the Creation that only exists in the "Present Time". For indeed your animalistic five senses should all be under the command of your Soul, for all decisions are holistically yours for your Soul is truly the bodies "conductor" whose primary task to inspire and lead and control musicians into delivering creative performances. For the Souls, has a working task which is to conduct rehearsals to achieve good supporting performances which are NOT the "I Want" decisions of those animalistic five senses, for these demands are not emanating from the real you, for they are just instruments for your use.

For sincerely, in the real world how often have your instrument called the "taste" sense, played the words "I Want more of this food plus better and tastier food" and without the control of your silent Soul, the listener to these inner sounding words, does not decide which food is best for your body?

How often has your "sight" instrument played these words in your head, "I Want to see the countryside, the sea, this TV show, some pictures, more clothes, my friends" and many other "I Want" to see without ever thinking what is suitable for you or your audience? Do you let your "hearing" instrument control you by saying or demanding, "I Want this music not that, this sound, not that sound, and to hear this voice, not that voice." This being when many around you need an excellent personal "tune," to listen to or they may even prefer silence? Beyond doubt, this is the same with your body's instruments of "touch" and "smell," who often demand that you satisfy their own "I Want," which could be against the harmony being played by the needed goodness of that which is all around you, and the audience which is the Creation that is in front of you.

Therefore, assuredly, these five senses are your uniquely own instruments, and this is because you cannot be that which you observe or feel, just as a conductor cannot be the orchestra or the listening audience. Is this not true? For indeed you cannot be these five senses for they are simply instruments for your use and which you control, and they should certainly NOT be allowed to control you!

So yes! This believing that the fives sense is you are justly a false way of life but as can be seen in the above paragraphs; they can be very easily recognised as not you, for you are the observer of all these activities! Yet is it not also genuine that if this fact of life is unrecognised, then many people will see and believe that they are the "I Want" greed, that is continually coming from these internal instruments which are not the real you, but which are played and brought to life by the "Freedom of Choice" given to you by God or Nature for the Non-Believer. For these are genuinely the five senses, which can jealousy feed and continuously seek their animalistic desires and this usually by taking that which belongs to others, for just like untrained and wild animals they continually feed their "I Want" which is pure greed.

Also, this greed is often felt within many people who ignore the truth that their Soul is the manager of their five senses, for they cannot see that the five senses can be likened to being as just children that need caring for and not spoiling. Therefore is it not true that we see or read how legal and illegal "gangs" do seem to develop a personal hierarchical system that makes use of many false opinions, these being that they need to protect the "I Want" commands of their grouped five senses which they call their bosses! But honestly, you need to have no fear of this gang of five senses that rests within you for hey can be disciplined to come under the control of your Soul.

For all should know that which all people's history shows, this being that all around you goodness (Godness) is born from the natural harmony that rests within God's world or the world of Nature for the Non-Believers and that this will always succeed in re-establishing itself. For assuredly, this is because God's Creation cannot support the evil or selfish acts that are born from any person uncontrolled "I Want". Precisely, this is an "I Want" that is continually being created by one of the "untrained" and "un-disciplined" animalistic five senses. For indeed, when the five senses are controlled unto silence, this being a fact which then allows the gaze of your Soul to see through the empty mind and into the world we call "Heaven", it is then that you will undoubtedly live in Gods or Nature for the Non-Believer "Present Time" and not in an "I Want" created "Past" or "Future" created Hell. For beyond doubt, this is a Hell which we create with a mind filling "I Want" for myself world, this being a false world that emerges when the mind is blocked by an "I Want" noise emanating from the five senses, a fact which fills the mind and so stops the soul from seeing through the mind the emerging and existing needs of the "Present Time". For really, this being that heaven upon our Earth which is not lived in by a person who has not yet silenced the mind-filling noise emanating from the five senses – and yes, this living in heaven can be achieved, and it gives the doer great satisfaction and an excellent feeling of bliss, within their currently existing lives.

So yes! Is it not a universal truth that our known incarnates like Jesus, Krishna, Buddha and the many more of the wise people who created our worlds' many religions and also the numerous wise philosophers who all showed the way to achieve "Enlightenment". For these ancient ones all showed a way to silence the constantly chattering noise in the head that was always being made by the untrained and undisciplined five senses, simply because people believed that this noise was emanating from their real self. Did not these wise masters also willing and genuinely endeavour to reveal to all people just how to become free from this personal forgetting of who they are and so endeavoured continuously to remove from them their self-imposed "I Want" bondage, this genuinely being an "I Want" bondage that was being created by the "personal" greed of their five senses. For certainly is it not now known to be true that the animalistic five senses make slaves of the people who listen to them? And this is being because people believe that the words in their head are really coming from themselves and so they experience a personal "I Want" that they feel is needed, this being to survive, yet is it not true that you can silence them?

Is it not also true that these wise ancients usually and convincingly opposed the "I Want" for me slavery rules that were imposed by the five senses, which were being mistakenly pursued has a certain "I Want" and so was a needed truth by many individuals? But sadly is it not also true that this can also be likened to gang systems which apply bondage to the gangs' "I Want" rules, these being rules which are accepted because they give a more robust "I Want for me", to those always claiming noises coming from the "Gang-Likened" five senses.

Is it not also true that these greedy groups always seem to inflict their "I Want" rules, which are usually imposed upon others who are not of their kind? Even more sadly does not this selfish "I Want", that are continually arising in their mind and which is coming from the "I Want" claims of the five senses, also reveals itself in Genocide? Regularly, this being that which leads to the mass killing of other people in what the world now calls "ethnic cleansing", which is still happening. Is it not also true that all these "ethnic cleansing" claims are based upon the selfish "I Want" for myself all that is theirs, this is always being a demand that is coming from the uncontrolled desires of the five senses, which are NOT really them but which they mistakenly think is them.

Yet the real truth is that these five senses are just simple tools that rest within all life forms. Still, knowingly only people have the power to "Choose" to silence them, this is because only people have the "Freedom of Choice" and this is because sometimes an act can support the developing creation. Sometimes the same act can destroy it, for all this activity is depending upon circumstances.

For again, and honestly, there exists that truth, which our wise ancients called "Enlightenment", this being that which occurs when the mind is empty and so harbours unto silence the noise being created by the five senses. Accurately and Logically, this truly is a fact which stops the clouding "I Want" words and pictures from entering into a person mind and which factually stops the view of the Soul from seeing the outside world. It is this actual but false reality which was targeted to be removed by ALL our wise ancients. It is also the reason why they created ALL our world's religions and philosophies and these being with a single purpose – which was to stop the clouding into the mind this uncontrolled "I Want" for myself noise arising from the five senses and is one of the main reason why they imposed the disciplined reciting of prayers.

So yes! The wise people are the people who live in the "Present Time" which is God's world and not the Hell of the non-existing past or the future, where the "I Want" from their uncontrolled five senses takes them. Strictly, this is a fact because the soul that rests within all people cannot see God's world, because of the sounds and pictures being painted into the mind by the five senses, which fill the mind and which blind the Soul from seeing the "Present Time", this being that exists all around you. Therefore, it not real that those who live in the "Present Time" are motivated to act, only by the Soul, this being that which silently sees through the still mind, and so is the real and actual observer of God's world. For indeed it is true that it is the Soul that rests within all people that is the only entity which can silently observe the "Present Time, this being the Creation or Nature for the Non-Believer and is this not truly a time that can only be seen through a still unclouded mind? Is it not also true and not imaginary, that this is because a person's Soul cannot see through a blocked mind, this being a mind that is blocked by pictures and words which are simply being created by many an "I Want" emanating from one of the animalistic five sense?

For the "Present Time" certainly does not rest in the "Past" or a "Future", which are imaginary world created by the "I Want" of the animalistic five senses, which greedily seek more and more to smell, taste, see, touch and hear. Precisely, this is the great truth that our wise ancients all preached about, continually saying that people should dutifully obey the harmony of a life lived in the Heaven that exists upon this Earth and also preaching that their Soul's real purpose is to assist in the physical needs of the Earth's emerging harmony. Sadly our wise ancients did not know at their time that it was our the animalistic five senses which did fill and so block the mind with selfish desires which stopped people from seeing Gods world or the world of Nature for the Non-Believer. Thus our wise ancients did not "scientifically" know that the real work to free the Soul was to remove the mind filling "I Want" of the lower five senses, which many believed to be them and still do. Therefore, none knew that the constant demands of the five senses do block the Soul from seeing through the mind God's world or the world of Nature for the Non-Believer. Still, our wise ancients did know that their imposed prayers, mantras and chants, were that which was needed to bring people to Gods world, this being that which can only exist in the "Present Time.

So Yes! Is it not also true that our wise ancients taught this simple truth and also showed by their own words and deeds these truthful facts, this being a truth that was preached to all the people who lived in many different parts of our world. For indeed was this simple truth not targeted to aid them to control their selfish "I Want" cultural ways and so help support and develop the harmony of God's world or the world of Nature for the Non-Believer, this being that which always rest within the Creations Present Time?

For rightly, do not all our religions and philosophies have a collective singularity? This being that which is needed within all our worlds different but needed "cultural" ways of living, this being that singularity which exists in all our worlds different cultures which also contain entirely different personal shapes and different personal colours, this being that which God gave to protect us, and this all truly being in accordance to the place that we live in upon our Earth. Again it should be said that this is the "being" of the real "home" that exists all around you? For assuredly, is this home not also known to be that which our wise ancients and teachers always sought various "cultural" ways to expose, this being that which they knew would reveal the goodness "God Ness" that was resting in all their listening people, and is not this also the same teaching which was given in many different parts of our Earth, this being always to bring people to the "Present Time".

So yes! Do not our wise ancients also show the great love that comes from within a freedom-based harmony that does not hurt others but supports all others, this being so that they can rise to their highest potential? Is it not also true that all listening people say that it is this harmony that is seeking a way of life which brings great happiness to any supporter of God's or Nature's way of being established as one entity? Therefore is this not also known to be historical and absolute truth, a truth which is stated by all our wise ancients, this being that it is possible to live in Heaven while upon this Earth? Is it not also seen to be true that it is this same peaceful Earth, which all our wise ancients speak about and who also honestly state that we should enjoy its existing harmony and that we should also support the "heavenly" seeking harmony that is emerging all around us? For genuinely do not all our world's wise ancients say that we should be motivated by the harmony seeking Soul that rest within us, this being an individual's Soul and a Soul that is birthed to continually support the goodly (Godly) continuation of harmony that is existing and emerging all around us.

So Yes! Again and indeed, is this not the existing of God's harmony or Natures harmony for the Non-Believer, which a person's Soul can naturally observe in the "Present Time", but only through a still mind can it experience this existence? For the Souls truly exists within all people and its purpose is to support the harmony of the existing and emerging "Creation", this being that which goodly (Godly) can only exist in the "Present Time". For more precisely the purpose of the Soul is to support the harmony that exists in the "Present Time", just as it also supports the harmony of all the individual body parts that are obediently working within you!

So yes! It is true; that the Souls purpose for its existence is to support the harmony that exists or is endeavouring to exist in the "Present Time" just has it supports the harmony of the inner working of the body within which it currently exists. Also, is it not true that all our wise ancients knew this fact this is being the fact that people do have Souls, but anciently our wise could not state that the Soul can only see through a clear mind that which they are viewing and this viewing being of that world which can only exist in the "Present Time" - but we can now!

So yes! Now it should be understood that the Soul's view of the Creation can only see a hundred per cent truth when it is not being blinded by the mind being filled by many contaminating minds blocking demands that are emanating from many an "I Want" thought, this being that disturbance which is coming from the five senses. For indeed, are these not self-imposed mind-filling thoughts that are coming from past losses or past likes or even being filled with potential dreams of future gains? For correctly, it can now be seen that this past or future mind filling thoughts are simply the desires of the five senses and that they sadly block the Soul from seeing the "Present Time". Therefore is not a factual truth the "Present Time" is God's world or the world of Nature for the Non-Believer. It is also this fact which brings great misery and sadness to the dreamer who, via ignoring the "Present Time", do allow their five senses to dominate their lives and which is also allowed to contaminate those around them, like some kind of disease.

So yes! It is this mind filling fact which makes it impossible for you to witness 100% of the harmony seeking a world that the **"Mother of the Creation"** is presenting to you, this is being the world which exists around you just has it should exist within you — and also this is being a world which may also be containing an emerging need which the **"Mother of the Creation"** may also be requesting your physical support to maintain this harmony that this existing or emerging all around you. For justly, is this not a truth that the Soul's view of the world may be blocked by many an emanating past or future "I Want" thought, this being an activity that can so quickly fill a person's mind as they continually and mindfully paint over and so mentally and then physically change the view of the real world, this being that which is being presented to them, but only in the "Present Time".

Therefore, is it not true that the five senses ongoing and continuous "animalistic" mind-filling painting of all "I Want" situations are also "observed" by an inner Soul that is silently witnessing these mind blocking "I Want" thoughts, these being thoughts that can negatively change, blur and or manipulate the incoming reality of the constructing harmony that continuously exists in "Present Time". Thus bringing about personal "I Want for Me" changes, these changes being that which not only damages the harmony of the "Present Time" but "Personally-Creates" a never satisfied life that is a genuinely living in a personally-created Hell, while alive on this Earth?

But this does not mean that you have no targets to achieve in your life. For now, you truly understand that the target is to allow the Soul to view the world through a still mind, for only then will you will see and become "self-aware" of the actual reality of the God-given or Nature has given for the Non-Believer, purposefully ever still ever moving targeting creation that is emerging before you, just ha sit emerge within you, which means that which you can fully experience but only in the "Present Time", which is the real Heaven that exists upon this Earth. Therefore is it not also true that only the "Present Time" can consistently show you all the needs that are good for all Life and Non-Life?

For truly is this not this gifted "Present Time" that is all around you also mirroring the same harmony of that which exists within you? Also is it not true that it is only in God's given "Present Time" or Natures "Present" for the Non-Believers, that you can make a decision that will support the on-going harmony of a world whose emerging needs may be seeking some support from you? For truly is this not the reason why you have been given "The Freedom of Choice" and is it not also true that choosing to support this work will make you feel "great."

So yes! Now, look again at this Godly or Nature's truth, for it is undoubtedly a truth which can be likened to an existing harmony that is sending to you two loose strings that are emerging before you in the silence of the "Present Time". It is then in the obedience to this silence that your Soul will know that they are requesting you to tie them together into a knot, which when accomplished it will be seen that this string will pull time and its existence into the harmony which exists all around you, but only in the "Present Time", this being that which surrounds your life. Still, we will also find that within people many forgetting's, there are created many strings seeking to be tied together. For indeed, in your life, there will come to you many strings, all seeking you to tie them together, and all will be coming to you in the "Present Time".

Also, it should be known that there will be the two strings that only you can personally tie and that these many strings that you tie will also bring a needed harmony not only to yourself but to the lives of others. For this is the way of all real-life for it ensures that harmony, that which creates happiness and contentment, will always come into the world around you. Therefore you will achieve all that you can achieve – but these are activities that can only take place in the Heavenly "Present Time" for the past. For beyond doubt, the future is the Hell that does not exist but is a Hell that can be personally created but only by people who abuse the "Freedom of Choice".

So yes! The Soul naturally acts to support the Heaven that exists upon this Earth, and all without the need for any inner thoughts, these being thoughts which cannot exist in the never-ending on-going needs of the Creation's harmony that exists only in the "Present Time". For indeed, it is only people that can seek the joining together of the harmony that is within them to be the same as the harmony that is present or emerging to be present all around them, for again, harmony is that which is always endeavouring to develop in our world. Again it should be said that the support of this is the only reason why people are the only life form to have been given the "Freedom of Choice", but truthfully this also means that they can "animalistic-ally" choose, like any animal, to claim all that is around them for themselves.

It is also this fact which is the reason why some people can claim "animalistic-ally" that everything that exists is for them. Still, honestly, they should choose to live in the only world which can physically aid the continuing harmony of the Godly given or Nature gave "Present Time" and certainly for those people who know this truth; it is wise to simply tie these incoming harmony seeking strings together and not to think about it but knowingly, just do it, this being that which supports others, which is an actual reality is also YOU!

So yes! Is it not now easily seen to be accurate, that all peace and harmony still rests silently within and around all people, just as it rested within all our wise ancients regardless of what was done to them by unbelievers? For certainly is it not also now known that these truths, these being that which came from our wise ancients, are now able to be seen by all those who live in the "Present Time"? Is it not also a fact that these are truths that can never be realised in the "I Want" mind filling pursuits of future or past thoughts, this being that existence which keeps the beholder trapped in the world of Hell? Therefore, can it not now be seen that the Soul, which is the real you, is the only viewer that exists within each person and therefore it is that which cannot be seen and so can only be "Self-Realised" and so truly experienced to exist as it views through an empty mind the existence of the "Present Time", this being that which is all around us and also within us. Yet, is it not also true that the "Present Time" is the only place it can act following the will of the Divine Mother, who is the protector who gave birth to God's only child, which we call "The Creation" for indeed the *"Mother of the Creation"* is all the space that exists within and around this only child.

So Yes! Can it not now be explained to all, for understanding purposes, that in the beginning, it was God who created space in which He gave a Father's seed that brought forth their only child – the Creation? Can it not also be an inherent truth that "Space" is, therefore, the Divine Mother who exists all around life and Non-Life, and who is also the primary carer of the child which we call "The Creation?" Therefore, is not the creation based upon God's laws that have been implanted within this growing child but also often need adjusting to continue the excellent "Godly based" harmony that is needed to be lived in by any growing child?

For indeed, this is an activity that is reflected to be healthy within all life forms, this being the caring work of the Divine Mother just as it is with all mothers. The truth now being understood is that only people have been created with a "Freedom of Choice", this being an activity that can create a negative or positive result that influences the world around them. The reason for this being that a person's God-given "Freedom of Choice" can create a targeted activity that is required to "physically" assist the Divine Mother to maintain harmony within the growing Creation. Therefore is it not true that sometimes to correct an on-going event an affirmative "act" is needed to perform the necessary actions that are required to sustain the on-going developing activities that are emerging all around you but also is it not clear that a detrimental "no" act can be an attempt to steal that which is emerging around you and so keep for yourself?

So Yes! Is it not also true that sometimes an activity is not needed, and nor has any need of personal support, these being acts that can only be decided by people for all other life forms do not have a "Freedom of Choice" for they are compelled to obey only their five sense. But a person's *"Freedom of Choice"* can be likened them seeing magnificent deer that is unable to free itself because it is caught in a tree by its large antlers. For indeed it is only a person that can go to the tree and slowly free the deer and so restore the harmony of the life around that deer. Therefore, indeed, this is again being the only reason why people have been given the "Freedom of Choice", which is to support the emerging goodness of the developing Creation. This being also the reason why the **"Mother of the**

Creation" who likened to most mothers, does maintains the developing harmony within the life of the family, this being the family which we call the Creation. For justly, it can be now easily seen and understood that Her special children, called "people", are born to aid Her in the physical need to correct the emerging "Creation's" on-going path which is also the continual supporting of its ever-evolving harmony.

Yet, is it not also sadly known to be true that people have engaged in great wars, based upon some personal "I Want" for ME! And so have changed this constant on-going development of Motherly created harmony? Yet does not history also show that God's laws, supported by the Divine Mother always ensure that these seekers of a greed-based and a personal "I Want," never succeed even when they become victors? For indeed, those who actively support the harmony that is all around them or which is struggling to emerge all around them will always live in the kingdom of heaven that rightly rests upon this Earth. This fact always ensures that most victors in our Earths wars and their foreign-based language often return to their original borders.

Therefore, is it not also true, as our known history clearly shows, that the Soul of people often arises within individuals who then gently oppose these "gang" rules, which are established by people, who think that "might is right" and so target "I Want more for myself". Precisely, this is a strangely based rule in that a substantial minority often endeavours to impose upon a weaker majority a situation that always targets destruction has it separates itself from that unity which is growing around it. Therefore, can it not also be factually recognised as accurate, that many people forget who they are? Does this not also produce within them a false but constant and personal "I Want" for myself need which can become "institutionalised," and so grows into a denial of that which they have been created to serve, which also causes them to neglect the excellent management of all people?

Can it then not also be seen within many of our world's political and higher management systems that many high ranking individuals falsely defend the power that they have within their system, and so neglect the people which they have been appointed to serve? Therefore, is this not truly an "I Want" only for myself and is this not also a way of life that is lived by individuals and groups that ignore the truth that is resting all around them? For is this "I Want" which is continuously emanating from the five senses, not also a way of life that is pursued by those with many greed-based personal and unfulfilled desires, and does it not this also emerge at any level within the social structure of people?

So yes! There is a simple and active way of life that will ensure that you will and can live in the goodness of the Heaven that indeed rests upon this Earth and which exists all around you. For it can be certainly "Self-Realised" to be accurate, that when your mind is in the "Present Time", meaning that it is without any "I Want" for me only thoughts, that you will undoubtedly become aware of the support needed to make the harmonising work of the "Mother of the Creation" easier – which will be a way to release the harmony that is struggling to emerge all around you. For indeed, for all those who live in God's world called the "Present Time", they will undoubtedly find that the "Mother of the Creation" will offer to them an "event" which can be tied to harmonise another "event." Still, it is only in the "Present Time" that you can you tie one emerging event to another current event, this being that which will pull into existence the harmony of the "Present Time", which is all around you and which is also endeavouring to emerge all around you. For really, you will also become aware that no thought is needed for the inner Soul, which is the real you, does know just what is needed to be done.

For rightly, those so enriched to live in God's Present or Natures Present for the Non-Believer, this genuinely being the time in which we all live, will experience the happiness and contentment which is called by our ancients "Enlightenment".

Religiously, this being the same "Enlightenment" which Christians describe as being filled with the "Holy Spirit" or the "Holy Ghost" and being in "Paradise" or "Heaven", while other world's religions and philosophies call it *"Paradise", "Eden", "Heaven", "Promised Land" "Nirvana", "Moksha", "Shangri-la", "Kenshō", "Bodhi", "Satori", "Jnana", "Svargamu", "Kā bāga", "Vāṭikā", "Kā jagaha", "Sukhabhavana", Karma, Kismet, Nirvana, Chance, Providence, Serendipity, Fate, plus Luck*, and even the ancient Zoroastrianism religion of the Fifth-Century BC referred to it as *"Ushta"*, which was described by them as ***"liberation, salvation and emancipation of the Soul"***. These writings being accomplished over two thousand five hundred years ago and even before that time for truly all these names were born to describe "Enlightenment," this being the living in the Heaven upon our Earth that exists only in the "Present Time".

So Yes! Again it should be said that this happiness is a happiness that cannot be measured, and which is always in the "Present Time" and which is there, waiting to welcome all and is a life which is very different from those who live in a self-created Hell of "I Want." For, if you ignore this "Present Time" and live within the "I Want" thoughts that always exist in the past or the future; these often being thoughts which are designed to take from others that which belong to them, then you are in truth, living in the Hell that exists upon this Earth and so yes! The choice is yours as it is for you all people and I can assure you, it is the correct choice.

47 PEOPLE'S PURPOSE

Now we can also recognise the truth of an earlier critical change in the lives of people who currently exist in God's world or the world of Nature for the Non-Believer and which is an existence that can only be live in the "Present Time". For indeed, this significant change is known to be when people left their millions of years of hunting and gathering ways. Logically, this is being the time when male teams existed in awareness and perception of a future time, a time in which group teams had to be futuristically planned to capture wild animals to gain fresh meat for the family while the female individuals cared for their children and although in talk able groups, did individually forage for wild plants, fruits, seeds, and underground tubers and bulbs which she provided for the family. Therefore for millions of years the male and the female were a solidly combined individual in which one part lived in a later time, and the other part lived in the present time, for it is right in this way that the man and the woman became has a single entity that created life. Then it is said that around 10,000 years ago that private farming developed which privately domesticated animals and also privately grew selected plants and fruits. It did also privately put up notices saying that this which is on all this land is all mine, not yours. For indeed this became a self-creative time in which people were able to make a personal "I Want" claim upon God's world or the world of Nature, so that "Natures" world became a world which people birthed the pursuit of actions that claimed and targeted a personal "I Want" and it was this "I Want" that created the most significant unrest within our currently known world.

Precisely, this being a personal "I Want" for me claim that brought a new way of living for people, and it was born only six thousand or ten thousand years ago. It was undoubtedly a creation of a newly developed and a personal "I Want" for me. Strictly, this being a claim that changed people from being hunter-gatherers in which all food was obtained by the natural collecting of wild plants and the pursuing wild animals; to become people living in a static society and becoming agriculturalists and land claiming farmers, this being a life in which people relied upon domesticated animals and self-planted food crops to which they newly added other personally valued items that were now being taken from the Creation. For it was also around this time that people claimed for themselves the "private" seeding and gathering of food that grew upon "their" claimed land, and the men fenced off his claimed land and forbid the needs of all other animals, except his domesticated animals; thus claiming a new "ownership" of land in this newly birthed self-claiming way to feed themselves and appointed others only statistically.

But to many people, this new world of "I Want" my land acquisition to be valuable only to me, did change the formerly land free way of life that enabled the "I Want" power of many new landowners to control the hunter-gatherer. Yes, this was achieved by aggressively banning hunter-gatherers from hunting or gathering upon these newly taken land areas and truly is a new way of life in which the new "landowners" accumulated and self-claimed all spare food to sell or enslave as workers the surrounding hunter-gatherers. The latter were moved off the land in which they had hunted and gathered, as we saw more recently with the plight of the North American Indians.

It is also true that this new way of seeking a personal and private harmony, which is called "land ownership", did bring forth a new development which expanded and also stabilized land ownership, which now included family and tribal inheritance. For indeed, this, in turn, led to the need for small groups to combine into larger "private" groups, to protect themselves and their land, which then led to border disagreements and then onto war, which is an exercise that is still with us to this very day. Therefore, is it not an inevitable truth that these small family groups have harmonised into huge groups? Is it not also true that we have seen many wars over land ownership during the past six thousand years and which continue even into the current time? Sadly, it is also known to be accurate, that this land ownership did create many wars between people and even developed into a more significant "I Want" habit, which also moved against the many religions, who also owned land?

Is it not also true that even six thousand years after this new beginning and in our modern age that massive war seeking armies are still being sent into foreign countries that have different religions and cultures? Is it not also true that many a countries leader is still fighting for anything that could sustain and increase their own particular "I Want" way of life, for as many are now saying, that even some of the "advanced" Christian based countries of the Northern Hemisphere are still at a continuing war with their Arab Muslim neighbours? Is it not also being said that this ongoing war is to control the sale of the world's oil production and also that in Afghanistan many states that in its "occupied" war years of 2016–2017, the country's opium and other drugs' production was at a quantity of never before reached exporting level, for indeed many are saying that it is this high because it is under the protection of foreign troops whose countries are importing these drugs?

Yet is it not only a few years ago that we reached a landing on the moon – and have we not also sent machines to places far outside the solar system but where are we developing to now? For indeed in harmony, seeking way is not the whole of the European North of the Northern Hemisphere becoming unified under one type of collective government? Is this being a government whose target is to control a group of countries who have variable kinds of language and also mixed religions? For indeed it does seemingly appear that we are struggling to find a way towards the harmony of the many, although in 2017 the "West" and the "East" of the North of the Northern hemisphere still rattle their sabre's at each other. But yes, this will stop as their populations begin to regain "democratic" control of their lives by finding an easy way to ensure that those who do not vote do vote, and so has much said, stop our democracies being purchased by the rich; particularly the Oil and the armaments industry. The question now is where people will be in another one thousand or six thousand or even ten thousand years from now? Will people have learned to accept the entirety and unity of or the coming together of all different culturally-based religious and philosophical belief systems? Indeed, this is being that differing search for "Enlightenment" which is attached to all the different language based religious and economic cultures and therefore sees no need to inflict pain upon another countries religions and cultures! Therefore is it not correct, that all life and Non-Life is controlled by the harmony that is embedded for all to see and also to self-realise within the Creations harmony or Nature's on-going harmony? Regularly, this is being a natural harmony that does not enforce the inclusion of all people or their desired religions or other belief systems? For indeed, if we removed all people from our planet, where would the disharmony be? For certainly is it now not also true that even with the difficulty of different languages and cultures, life is always evolving and expanding in ways to make it possible to include the many? Therefore is it not said that we all started in Africa between three hundred and two hundred thousand years ago and that we moved out of Africa about 70,000 to 100,000 years ago and began an informative speech about 50,000 years ago? Is it not true that we are the latest people out of Africa and also true that we are those people who successfully moved into all the many lands of our Earth and in so doing absorbed our different shaped cousins that had moved to these lands thousands of years before us? Could this absorption be because we were now a tribal-based twelve man hunting team, this being that which was needed for open plains herd hunting? At the same time, the current inhabitants of these past frozen countries were solitary based hunters, who needed to be small group based to target solitary non-herding animals? The idea that we also formed twelve men hunting teams is based not only upon the twelve disciples of Jesus as taught in the Christian Bible, but also on the likely number of close friends of any male individual; plus, twelve being the number of players in many of our trendy spectator sports. Therefore it was probably this fact of living in tribes that created a twelve-man team of hunters that enabled us to absorb all the other species that we met upon our planet. But is it not also interesting that it is "scientifically" said that we who are new out of Africa species, are all from the same family and many historians say we are actually descended from the same mother and that we only recently, in historical terms, bodily changed to suit our new environments.

So Yes! We are all the singularity of belonging to the same family, for is it not honestly stated that has a family we started in a scorching southern country and so had dark skin, brown eyes, thick black hair and the man had no beard because he did not wear any clothes and then, living in cold northern countries changed us into having light skin, lighter coloured eyes, light or no hair but a beard, this bear being because "man" started wearing clothes. To understand this more fully, take a photo of a man with a beard and then extend the beard up to the eyebrows and you will understand why a man now has a beard.

For certainly things do change, but it is undoubtedly known to be true that people out of Africa are all descendent from the same mother and so what makes some people racialist? Is it not their personal "I Want, not only my world but your world also"?

So yes! God knows the future, this being where the Creation is going, and the "Mother of the Creation", certainly knows all that is happening in the "Present Time". For indeed it is She who will undoubtedly see to it that their only child, this being the Life and Non-Life that exists upon our Earth, will get there and truly with Her constant support. For was not this word of God revealed by the "Mother of the Creation" who spoke to people through Jesus saying: "Therefore consider how you listen. Whoever has ("supports harmony") will be given more; whoever does not have (does NOT support harmony) even what he thinks he has will be taken from him. For this is undoubtedly like what the kingdom of God. For indeed it is known that a person can scatter seed on the ground and night and day, whether he sleeps or gets up, he does nothing but the seed sprouts and grows, in harmony – though he does not know-how. But what we do know now that the world and its people can naturally grow in harmony has is the growth within good soil condition, for is it not true that all by itself the soil produces grain – first the stalk, then the head, then the full kernel and does it not do this all by itself and all because it merely follows Gods laws or Nature laws for the Non-Believer? Then is it not known that has soon as the grain is ripe it is cut down because the harvest has come and so people do gather this grace of harmony that is all growing all around them. Also did not the "Mother of the Creation" speaking through Jesus say:- "The kingdom of heaven is like a man who sowed good seed in his field. But while everyone was sleeping, his enemy came and sowed weeds among the wheat, (because this enemy wanted his wheat to bring a better yield than his competitors and to obtain a better market price) – and went away. When the wheat sprouted and formed heads, then the ("I Want to destroy this harmony") weeds also appeared." "The owner's servants (people) came to him and said, "Sir, (Meaning God) didn't you sow good seed in your field? (This is God's Creation) "Where, then did the ("bad") weeds come from?" "An enemy did this," he replied. (This is being a person who breaks God's harmony for his benefit). The servants (the wise ancients) asked him. "Do you want us to go and pull them up?" "No," He answered, "Because while you are pulling the weeds, you may root up the wheat with them." meaning that you may also harm those who live in harmony within the Creation, for God knew that at harvest time when that which is done is reaped, that this crop would be sorted. Jesus then told them another parable: "The Kingdom of Heaven (this is the harmony that exists upon Earth) is like a mustard seed, which a man took and planted in his field. Though it is the smallest of all your seeds, yet when it grows, it is the largest of garden plants and becomes a tree (because it pursues harmony it naturally grows into the highest of wellbeing) so that the birds of the air come and perch in its branches." For indeed this is said to show that all Nature within the Creation is at ease amongst its existing harmony. He told them still another parable: "The kingdom of heaven is like yeast that a woman took and mixed into a large amount of flour until it worked all through the dough" (the yeast is God's harmony, and the flour is the Creation). "The one who sowed the good seed is the Son of Man (those who assist the development of harmony). "The field is the world (this is the Creation), and the good seed stands for the sons of the kingdom" (Those who support the harmony of the Creation and so live in Heaven while on this Earth). "The weeds are the sons of the evil one (those who seek a personal "I Want," regardless of the disharmony it creates amongst life and Non-Life and so, live in Hell while on this Earth) and the enemy who sows them is the devil" (the uncontrolled five senses who are the harbinger of "I Want"). "The harvest is the end of the age" (upon the death of a person in "Present Time"), and the harvesters are angels" (those who pursue acts of harmony). "As the weeds are pulled up and burned in the fire (these personal "I Want" are the weeds which the laws of the Creation or Nature always destroy), so it will be at the end of the age." The "I Want" is the weeds that break the harmony that is around them, and honestly, they will never be successful, for they pursue a way of life that brings pain only to them.

So yes! When it is not halted this personal pursuit of an "I Want" becomes the everyday activity of those who live in a Hell that they create around themselves. For honestly, these words from Jesus explain that a personal "I Want" is a personally created weed that can also exist amongst people. Now, for those who know this truth and who wish not to be weeds that pursue a personal "I Want" and so do not live a life that can be likened to a weed upon the ground? Listen again to the incarnate Jesus who said: "No one can serve two masters, either he will hate the one and love the other, or he will be devoted to the one and despise the other. You cannot serve both God and Money". Indeed, this means you cannot serve the all-loving harmony of the Creation and serve an "I Want" for myself, for if you can hear an "I Want" in mind, it is NOT you. Then Jesus wisely said: "He, who has ears, let him hear." Do not these wise words explain that there is a Heaven outside you just has is the confirmed heaven that exists within you? Is it not also true that because people have been given the "Freedom of Choice" that they can "choose" to live in a self-created "I Want" for myself Hell that they can personally create upon this Earth or "choose" to live in the Heaven that exists upon this earth, by living upon this Earth has does their many body parts live within them? For certainly is it not true that you can personally "choose" in which world to live? Therefore is it not also explained clearly by many of our worlds scriptures, just where the Kingdom of Heaven is and also is it not explained how to live within it, and so avoid the torments of a life lived in Hell! For indeed, these words were spoken by the **"Mother of the Creation"** through Jesus clearly show that She is talking about the Heaven which exists only in the "Present Time", this being the only place and time in which the Creation can indeed, exist. Therefore accurately and clearly the above parables show who are our "enemies," these being our very own personal thought and self-created enemies that always create an "I Want", this being that which always endeavour to destroy the Heaven that exists for all people and which in many ways rests upon our Earth. Is it not also clear to be seen that these "I Want" enemies were classed by our wise ancients to be as weeds and as such were shown to be acting falsely against the Heaven that exists upon this Earth. It is also now clearly shown by our ancient wise that it is through jealousy or ignorance of this superior knowledge that people ignore the way to live in Heaven, while on this Earth, and so now lives in a self-created Hell? Then is it not also sadly true that their children will copy these "Holy" lawbreakers? But no more should this be true, for now, those that have ears to hear have listened to a new explanation of the above parables. So now ALL readers of "The Book" are stated to be able to "choose" to live in Heaven or to "choose" to live in Hell, while on this Earth and to all readers of "The Book" this is an inevitable fact

So yes! Now the most important thing to remember, which was also pointed out by the **"Mother of the Creation"** when She spoke through Jesus, was: "I tell you the truth, no one can see the Kingdom of God unless they are born again." For indeed, this is again merely stating that because people have the "Freedom of Choice", that they can change from living in Hell and begin to live in Heaven. For this is a fact, that can be achieved while living in their current life and the current body? For was it not also indeed stated by the incarnate Jesus: *"nor will people say, 'Here it is', or 'there it is', because the Kingdom of God is within you."* For indeed, your knowledge of the truth does not exist in a building or another person; it is genuinely resting within YOU!

So yes! Your personal choice can now release a new way of living in Heaven, for you now you know the actual reality behind the words: "the righteous will shine like the sun in the Kingdom of their Father. He, who has ears, let him hear." Plus, it was also said those many years ago: "The Son of Man will send out His angels, and they will weed out of His kingdom everything that causes sin and all who do evil." It is the Angels of course who are the people who are the supporters of the harmony that is growing upon this Earth, and it is they who support the efforts of the "Mother of the Creation", who is the harbinger of all the harmony in this world.

So yes! It is good to understand that you can "choose" to be living as an angel and so only aid and support the harmony that is occurring all around, this being in the Heaven that can only exist in the "Present Time" and which is the same as the unselfish harmony that exists within your body. Therefore is it not genuinely known that this pursuit of harmony is a work that will show all people the way forward, so that most people can live in Heaven – which exists only in the "Now" time, this being God's "Present Time" and without thought time. What is also useful and very important is to fully understand that you can now act personally in the supporting of the Heaven that rests upon this Earth. Rightly, this is being a factual truth that the harmonies, this being that which you now know, are always offering you the opportunity to support that which is continually happening all around you. For indeed, you now know, in modern terminology, all about the "I Want" demands of the five senses. You so do not have to speak in imitating parables, which was something that worried the disciples of Jesus – for did them not say to Jesus: "Why do you speak to the people in parables?" Only to be answered by Jesus, who said: "The knowledge of the secrets of the Kingdom of Heaven has been given to you, but not to them." Because within the culture of that time they would not have understood any simple talk about the silencing of the five senses, also Jesus stated: "Whoever has, will be given more; whoever does not have, even what they have will be taken from them." "Whoever has" meaning those who stop the "I Want" emanating from the five senses and so live in Heaven while on this Earth, "will be given more", and they will have an abundance. For indeed the "Mother of the Creation" naturally rewards those who support her work and "Whoever does not have", because they live in an "I Want" for Me Hell, while upon this Earth, even "what they have will be taken from them"?

So yes! For this is also why Jesus also spoke in these unknown truths about two of the bodies the five senses by also saying: "Though seeing, they do not see; though hearing, they do not hear or understand." But now in our modern times, we do understand that the "I Want" of the five senses can dominate people and this is why Jesus also says "The knowledge of the secrets of the Kingdom of Heaven has been given to you" this being the knowledge that people can silence the five senses and so experience Gods heaven upon this earth, this being the paradise that that only rests in the "Present Time". There is a truth in the Jesus saying "The knowledge of the secrets of the Kingdom of Heaven has been given to you", this knowledge now being modernly explained to be for the "personal" need to silence the "I Want" emanating from the five senses and thus stopping them from clouding the mind. For indeed the resulting experience will show anyone that the inputs into the mind via the five senses are forbidding the Soul a clear view of Gods heaven or Natures heaven for the Non-Believers, this being that which can exist only in the Present Time. So now we can further understand that the added saying "but not to them," indicated that this knowledge had not been given to those who plagued Him. Therefore, indeed, maybe this was not given because it would not have been a shared conceptual understanding in those times. Still, now rightly, this ancient secret has been given to all, for as Jesus said to his disciples: "Because you have been given a chance to understand the secrets of the Kingdom of Heaven" and so stop the ever sounding mind filling "I Want" "but they" who are without this knowledge "have not." Now honestly it can be said that all people who read the above have been given the explicit knowledge that Heaven can be lived in a while living upon this Earth, for now, Heaven can only be experienced in the now time. Therefore, indeed, this is the "Present Time" that rests in God's Creation or Nature for the Non-Believer. For beyond doubt, Jesus was speaking about the "Present Time" as being the Kingdom of Heaven for He described it as being the harmony of plenty, while Hell was described as being empty.

So yes! Now all can "modernly" understand that when they listen to these words of Jesus, words that emanated from the "Mother of the Creation", who said: *"Therefore consider carefully how you listen. Whoever has will be given more; whoever does not have, even what they think they have will be taken from them."* They can now in the year 2020 be modernly changed to:- *"Therefore consider carefully how you listen. Whoever supports my harmony, will be given more; whoever does not support my harmony, even what he thinks he has will be taken from him."* For Gods Harmony or Natures Harmony for the Non- Believer, is being that which can only exist and always will endeavour to exist, but only in the "Present Time". It is good not be that person who goes through life with their eyes open but seeing nothing, and with their ears open but understanding nothing of what they hear. Be that person who understands with his or her heart that living in Heaven is genuinely the revealing of the harmony that can be struggling to appear, but only in the "Present Time". Precisely, this being a healing work that shows all people the glory of living in Heaven – which is the now time– which we call the "Present Time", the only peaceful place where time and all Life plus Non-Life truly exists.

So yes! Now there is no longer a need to speak in parables for these are the years of the internet in which all people can be seen, understood and so shared any knowledge amongst themselves, for it is scientifically correct that not one personally based "I Want" thinking action can motivate harmony, for indeed all that activates "The Truth" rests within the activities of all people, but only in the

"Preset Time". For, to live in the Heaven that rests upon this Earth, it is necessary to understand these words of Jesus who spoke of what people became when living in Hell: ***"For these people's heart has become calloused; they hardly hear with their ears, and they have closed their eyes. Otherwise, they might see with their eyes, hear with their ears, understand with their hearts and turn, and I would heal them."*** Remember this is the Creation speaking to you, and it means that the Creation around you will show you the way and it will also give you the knowledge of that which you do not need to pursue. No other person is required to do this, for mind-emptying will undoubtedly allow you to enter the "Present Time", a time that exists all around you and within you and it is also time in which a mind blocking thought cannot exist, for all that exists is in the "Present Time" and it is then that you will experience the understanding of all which our wise ancients speak about, this being "The Peace That Surpasses All Understanding, " this, being a time without thought and which the way of how to live in Heaven while on the Earth. For assuredly, and a good creed styled prayer often created by our ancient wise, will show you how to achieve this task, a task that will genuinely enable you to live in the "Present Time", this being the Heaven that rests upon this Earth– which is again explained later.

So yes! A short "Mantra" creed prayer will later be revealed to you and which is a mantra that was used by our wise ancients for thousands of years. It is also a mantra that will undoubtedly put those wild dogs, which we can call the five senses, to an out of sight place and so unseen and unheard, as if behind your heel, where these trained "pups" will indeed stay until called for and this being only when needed. For yes! It is true, that to live in the Heaven that exists all around us, is a most severe need and the use of the mantra is the best way to control and then stop this "I Want" from sounding in mind. Again, this is being an "I Want" that is continuously being sounded in mind by those five bodily senses which are usually in significant conflict with each other. For assuredly, this is also because many falsely believe that these five senses are them, they are NOT you, for they are just instrument for your use. For indeed, if you can hear any "talking" words in the mind, then know it is undoubtedly a sound that is emanating from one of these five senses. These being that which are constantly barking for an individual "I Want" demand, which can only take the thinker into the past or the future; these being demands that keep you locked in Hell upon this Earth. But now we can understand that it is these continuing demands emanating from the five senses that provoke an "I Want", this being personnel "I Want" that ALWAYS takes a person away from the "Present Time", which is a time that is created by God the Father of the Creation.

So Yes! Indeed it is only in the "Present Time" that God's Heaven can exist and those people who have been given "choice" and who target a personal "I Want" will find that they live in a Hell, which is without the wellbeing of God or Nature for the Non-Believer. Genuinely, this being a past or a future world of Hell that cannot exist for strictly, it must be a false world that is created by one or all of the five senses and so YES! Therefore to avoid this misery, it is worthy of remembering that Darwin's book ***"On the Origin of Species"*** was seriously misunderstood by the western world. For really his words *"only the survivors of the competition for resources will reproduce"* or the *"Preservation of Favoured Races in the Struggle for Life"* was both sadly interpreted to mean *"survival of the fittest",* this being a conclusion which led people into many "I Want" wars plus community problems – and it still does? Yet is it not wise to know that Darwin was speaking about "Animal Kind", who does not have the freedom of choice, which is truly a gift only to people and a gift that allows everyone to live in harmonious unity and not in competitive wars – is this not true? Is this combatting in wars not also based upon the "thinking" that we are separate "individuals" when in truth all life and non-life is connected as one entity? Is it not further correct that the origin of our lives is not "Random"? For it is "scientifically" proven and so known to be rooted upon a God-given or Nature given DNA. Precisely, this is being a DNA that understands how to maintain the unity of all the separate life that exists within each person body, this also being an entity that mindfully also contains the "Freedom of Choice", with a mirrored gift to maintain the unity that should be occurring outside our bodies has it does within our bodies. Should it not also be clearly understood that the relationship to our past is not an undeviating ever-developing straight line, for all know that for thousands of years many different "Civilisations" have come and gone, many mainly destroyed by nature or by competing forces. Yet is it not known to be true that all the Nature that is around us is basically based upon co-operation and not conflict and yes, our wild animals do kill for food to live - but they certainly will never kill for pleasure.

48   HOW TO AVOID HELL

So the question now can be "How do you want to live in your newly developing and ongoing current life"? Systematically, this being the life that you chose, or is it a life that was chosen for you? Therefore is it not right that the first thing to understand, because you are a person, is that you are "personally" responsible for everything that you do! Therefore is it not true that has a person you have been born with the "Freedom of Choice", this being that fact which binds you personally to all your actions and honestly always will do.

Now it is also understood that you may say that this is not true and also adding that it is others that control you and all your actions. Of course, the answer to this is just to remember the man who was forced to go to that painful cross because He would not do that which more influential people told him to do and also to remember the many others who have died protecting their loved ones in our countless wars. For genuinely are not all these wars based upon greed and oppression in which many die trying to steal that which belongs to another – which is called greed – and sadly many also die endeavouring to stop them.

So yes! Is not the most critical question to ask yourself is "Do I want to live in what people regard has Heaven while on this Earth or do I want to live in its opposite, which all people call Hell?" It's a good question, and only you can answer it with the first enquiry being: "How do you know if you are living in a Heaven or are living in a Hell while experiencing life upon this Earth?"

The quickest and most modern way to know if you are living in a self-made Hell, this being that condition which can only exist in the Past or the Future, is to acknowledge whether your mind is always dwelling in this non-existing past or future; especially when you hear your mind creating a personal "I Want", in so many different words and pictures and then spending your life continually developing various ways how to create and so obtain this thought created a personal world of "I Want", all of which have NOT been offered to you by a Creation that currently exists and which is endeavouring to "naturally" emerge in the world all around you.

The other difference in this life that you are currently living in the "Present Time" is that if you live in Heaven, which can only exist in the "Present Time", you will realise that "you have everything". For this is when the mind stays in the "Present Time" in which the mind is peaceful and without the machinations of any mind filling thoughts of "I Want", a fact which will undoubtedly bring you to experience that which all our wise ancients state is a "Peace that Surpasses all Understanding". But how do you learn how to live in this Heaven that always exists in the "Present Time"?

Sincerely, this being the time which always exists all around you and if you wish to know how to achieve this "Enlightenment", read on! For the following words will endeavour to show to you how true it is that you have a "personal" choice in all that you do and also all that you select to do. Precisely, this is being a "choice" that can take you to live in Heaven or to live in a self-made Hell, this being a Hell which is created by many personal "I Want" involvements that are created in your mind, which are always reflecting a fabricated self-made and non-real world of Hell.

So yes! It is undoubtedly true that it is your God-given or Nature given for the Non-Believer "Freedom of Choice" that enables you to live in Heaven or to live in Hell while currently alive upon our Earth, for honestly only you can "choose" which is the world in which you want to live. For the difference is that you live in Heaven only when you have a silent mind that rests and so becomes has one with the "Present Time". For indeed Heaven can only exist in the "Present Time", or do you have an ever-restless image creating a mind that keeps you living in a non-existing Past or Future which is the Hell that exists not only in mind but also can be self-created in the world that exists all around you!

Many also seek, via personally spoken confessions that originate from and to others, to bring to themselves the experiencing of that *peace that surpasses all understanding* or that which the wise ancients called "Enlightenment", but how can this be a reality? Therefore is it not true that your thoughts all exist in your self-created world and not God's silently obedient "Kingdom of Heaven," this being the Kingdom of Heaven which can only be self-realised via an empty mind, which is a mind that is free and resting only in the "Present Time".

For again this is also being the present heavenly time that always exists all around you just has it does within you, but which you cannot experience if you regularly paint within your mind all the many thoughts of how to obtain a personal "I Want". For again, is it not true that all these "I Want" thoughts take you to live in the Past or the Future where the "I Want" thoughts always control and also paint into your mind the many ways just how to achieve a personal desire? Is it not also true that by endeavouring to obtain something regularly or by having already obtained or even stolen an "I Want" is the very reason that leads you to a needful confession of that which you already know is wrong? Is this not correct?

So yes! It could be agreed that a fleeting peace can arise from a personal "confession," as many now believe that their "wrongful act" has been safely discarded. Still, it is also wise to remember that all the harmony which is around you or attempting to emerge around you needs only your energy to accept or support it, and in this way, you can live a life that is your birthright.

So Yes! A confession to friends about a wrongful activity is, of course, pleasant. It may even bring a taste of the *"peace that surpasses all understanding"*, this being as you enter the "Present Time", but is it not also important to realise that the purpose of confession is to remind you not to create disharmony again. Also, you can "confess" to yourself or others many times, but it will mean nothing to the **"Mother of the Creation"** who cares for all life and Non-Life. For it is certainly true that only in the "Present Time" can rest the acts which support and maintain the harmony of the Creation that the **"Mother of the Creation"** always appreciates and rewards with "Sugar in the Water", this being the sweetness that always rests in the "Present Time". For indeed, you always have a personal opportunity to contentedly "choose" to accept or to even "choose" to support the emerging expansion of the harmony which is always in front of you and to which you rightfully are a part of and so belong. These self-chosen offers of support being the "right actions" which all know are needed to continue the harmony that exists or is endeavouring to emerge, but only in the "Present Time".

So yes! There is always harmony supporting acts in which the *"Mother of the Creation"* seeks people's aid to assist in developing the Creations on-going harmony. For indeed this is why people have been given the "Freedom of Choice," because individual acts emanating from the *"Mother of the Creation"* need to be personally "chosen" to be completed in variable ways, but they are also acts which can only be achieved in the instance of the "Present Time", and again, this fact is to support and so expand the harmony that is naturally emerging around all Life and Non-Life.

For indeed, are these not the needed and same supporting acts that mirror the harmony that similarly exists inside all the bodies that contain life? For actually, all acts that are needed to maintain the harmony of the "Present Time" can only be born from a silent mind, which has aborted all thinking, and so "knows" by recognising the need to silence the "I Want" of the five senses so that the inner Soul can now see through the unblocked mind and so concentrate hundred per cent upon that which it experiences in the "Present Time". For correctly this is that condition which our wise ancients called "Enlightenment" and which has been given many different names by the wise ancients of ALL our world's many religions and philosophies.

For rightly, it is known that only the life force that exists within people is that which has been enabled to accept, support or change the developing acts of the on-going harmony that exists or is endeavouring to exist all around them. For indeed, this is not the world of a mind that is dominated by the five senses, which when untrained, can be likened to be similar to the mind of wild animals which are continually acclaiming and or seeking their personal "I Want!" For strictly, it should now be known that the five senses are always sounding and acclaiming their personal needs within the mind, as if they were wild dogs and "yes" they can if allowed, dominate the lives many people – and is this no also a pursuit of the domination of others not familiar to you?

So Yes! Now it is also important to remember that it is correct that you can always "confess" to be "forgiven," for your a previous or a current harming of God's Creation, which is caused by your "I Want" demands acting sinfully. It is also correct to then expect a new faithful beginning every time you confess; even if you confess the same acts again and again and again. For in God's laws or Natures laws for the Non-Believer, you have been Godly given the "Freedom of Choice" and so you are automatically and upon request, immediately forgiven for any selfish act that you do, for it is forgiveness which is based upon the fact that you know not what you do – but it is also agreed that you will pay the price accrued by all wrong actions.

Is this not true? For was it not God or Nature for the Non-Believer, who gave people the **"Freedom of Choice"?** Was this not a given ability to make a creative supporting positive choice or a non-supporting contrary choice, this being based upon that which exists and which is emerging in the Godly created or Nature created Present Time? This meaning that people are really here to support the developing needs of the Creation and are also the reason why a person's **"Freedom of Choice"** is essential. This being because the same activity that is currently emerging within the Creation can be supportive of its purpose or destruct full of it purpose because the Creation is a living and ongoing entity – and this is why people have been given the "Freedom of Choice" because the same activated choice can either create and support the emerging harmony, or in other circumstances destroy it, for the Creation is truly a living entity.

So Yes! Is this not the reason why people cannot be Godly punished or Nature punished for the Non-Believer, this punishment is for achieving selfish acts, for these wrong and especially "I Want" for myself, acts will themselves automatically bring punishment enough, so really you are punishing yourself, but a word of caution. The *"Mother of the Creation"* has a helpful memory. If you are knowingly and seriously plus wilfully pursuing many wrong and disharmonising acts, then in your next birth, the Divine Mother may place you within a birth in which you become fully aware of what a life lived in a world created by bad choices ensures. Therefore, indeed and via logical management, this could be in a world in which you newly exist but do not have a personal choice.

It could be even factual that you could also become more happily, newly birthed has someone's pet, in which you will learn just what it is like to live as being a beneficiary in a correct "Freedom of Choice" world. But yes, is it not true that the "Present Time" is the current time for "YOU" to be enabled to learn how God's "Present Time" or Natures time for the Non-Believer, actually exist to correctly serve you and all the life and Non-Life that exists around you? Therefore is it not wise to enjoy the "Freedom of Choice" that is given personally to YOU, this being for you to support and help maintain God's world or the world of Nature for the Non-Believer!

For assuredly, now is the time to awaken and to fully realise how true it is that the natural "Harmony" of the "Present Time" is yours to enjoy and also to support, for it will always be with you, and also do not be concerned about those around you who break these harmony seeking laws, for they will receive many negative rewards in this life and especially in their next life.

For again to be honestly said, this being that it is essential to know and so experience that it is only in the "Present Time" that there exists the emerging harmony which is being provided for all Life and also Non-Life and that all this harmony is thoughtfully cared for by the **"Mother of the Creation"**. For indeed it is She who brings to you the acts which only you and those like you, can personally and physically support or they even maybe acts which you need to achieve. For truly is it not within the nature of All Mothers to provide such developing and growing up needs for their children?

For even in current ongoing life, this being a life in which a person is engaged with a severe hardness, this being that which is based upon an imposed rudeness, or starvation plus the painful infliction of cruelty. It is still then and even under these circumstances that you still have a job to do and this being the need to support and strive to grow the wellbeing of that which is ALWAYS endeavouring to emerge around you and woe to them who do not pursue this task – for truly is this not an echo of that which is said by ALL our wise ancients.

So Yes! Now is the time to learn how to continue your support for the Heaven that rests upon this Earth and to realise that you are living in a pure Heaven and not in a people created Hell although it may just seem so. Therefore it is essential to experience the "Present Time fully". Again, this being that current time which is all around you and within you and which God or Nature for the Non-Believer, as given to you and this is a gift that has been given personally to YOU! It is also well to remember that it is a gift in which there is no thought and therefore no "I Want" can exist within the world that you now occupy.

There will also be included later in "The Book" the actual word and practice of a creed which will eventually bring to the reader to the *"Peace that surpasses all understanding"*. Accurately, this being that reality which all religions and philosophical prayers do target but which many can find difficult to achieve because they are attached to their "I Want" for me thoughts. Therefore is it not true that these are inner mind thoughts which arise from Hell, this being a world in which many "I Want" for me, thoughts emanate and which are all based upon a non-existing Past or the Future. For truly how cans Gods world or the world of

Nature for the Non-Believer, exist in the Past or the Future? Therefore is it not true that this world can only exist in the "Present Time."

So yes! Later in "The Book" there is a suggested "Prayer" or "Rhyme" that will bring the reciter to realise the "Present Time" sufficiently, this being that "Heaven" which rests within you and also without you. For truly you will then understand that just how you experience that which is within you, will become the same experience reflected you by that which is outside you.

Therefore it is a way that will support your choice to live in the Heaven that indeed exits upon this Earth, and it is to Heaven that this short prayer will eventually take you to. For certainly without such prayer, you can continue to live in the Hell that you create and build or help build all around yourself, but rest assured that "Heaven" is a well-known and far better place to live.

Therefore the practice and how to recite this short devotional exercise towards achieving "Enlightenment" will be clearly explained later to all readers of "The Book" and it will awaken the "practitioner" to the same world that Jesus and all our worlds incarnate and holy ones did truly live in, for again it should be said that "Enlightenment" is that which all our religions and philosophies did and do target. For indeed, this is being a world in which a person can become first "Self-Aware", in which they experience that all that is around them is also themselves, and then ongoing to become "Self-Realised" and so experience the reality that there is no observer.

For really in becoming "Self-Aware", you fully experience that everything that exists and so observes is YOU and maybe onto achieving "Self-Realisation" in which there is no observer has you, therefore, become the "Creation", and that which is usually observed and experienced is just one entity. It is also understood by "The Book" that you do not live long in this "Self-Realised" position and "The Book" says that you are also never born again. Therefore, indeed this is because you have become as one with God and so you have therefore fulfilled the purpose of the Creation. This short exercise also reveals just how our wise ancients did "awaken" their followers to the world of "Enlightenment", this being that which targets the reality of that which is all around us has being the same reality has that which is also within us, for again truly, this being a realty which allows only people to fully understand the words of Jesus when He said to the world: *"Neither shall they say, Lo here! Or lo there! For, behold, the kingdom of God is within you" (Luke 17:21)*

So Yes! If we look into every impressive religious, spiritual, and also into many wisdom seeking traditions, we will also find the same precept. This precept being that life's absolute truth is that the greatest treasure indeed is that which always rests within us, for truly our many ancient wise make it unmistakably clear that we can experience this inner treasure and all also say that no experience could be more valuable than the experiencing of this realty. Therefore was it not also said by Jesus, *"But seek ye first the kingdom of God and His righteousness, and all these things shall be added unto you" (Matthew 6:33)*. For truly is it not being said by all our ancient wise, that *"we can gain all that is needful";*

Also is it not true that this inner and outer experience of "Enlightenment" is that which is also explained by our many ancient wise, for Plato referred to it as *"the Good* and *the Beautiful"*. Aristotle stated it as the feeling of *"Being"*, meaning being has one with all that exists. Plotinus stated this experience to be *"as the Infinite"* and, St. Bernard of Clair Vaux as experiencing *"The Word of God"*, meaning the Enlightenment, this being that which only people can experience. Ralph Waldo Emerson named "Enlightenment" as an authentic experience of life and that the knowledge of the past is only an expression of thought and that thinking is only a *"partial not complete act"*, but living only in the "Present Time" is *"a complete and total act of the Soul"*. In Taoism this experience is called the Tao, meaning *"the realisation of a natural order underlying the substance and all the current activity of the Universe"*, meaning that which takes place in the "Present Time". In Judaism, it is described as *"Ein Sof"*, which means *"limitlessness or endless light"*. Even among Australian aborigines, it is called the *"Dreamtime"*, and also amongst the southern Africa Hunhu/Ubuntu, it is said to be experienced when a *"person is a person through other persons.*

In every case, it's understood that this inner, transcendental reality of the experiencing of only the "Present Time" can be directly experienced. For really, this "Self-Aware" or "Self-Realisation" experience has likewise been given many different religious names. In India traditions it is called Yoga, which is best explained has *"That brings spiritual unity with a supreme being"*, in Buddhism it is known as "Nirvana" meaning the *"freeing of the spiritual self from attachment to worldly things"*. In Islam Sufism, it is called "Fana" meaning *"to die before one dies,"* meaning that the personal "I Want" for me, is never obeyed. In Christianity it is described as a spiritual marriage, meaning *"to become has one with God"*. It is undoubtedly a universal experience and a taught understanding which is based upon a universal reality.

So yes" There is a short creed prayer and an exercise that is later mentioned in "The Book", and it is that which will show you how to live in this "Kingdom of Heaven", this "Self-Realty" that is spoken about by ALL our wise ancients and this throughout the different worlds in which they taught. For it is undoubtedly true that by your determination you will attain the above mentioned "Self-Reality" and this while living upon this Earth, this being the real world that cannot be changed – but strangely many "think" that they can. For it is indeed known that, by continuing this proposed "creed" prayer, you will find yourself entering the above world that all our wise ancients indeed called "Heaven", this being that which all the above explanation as only to be experienced in the "Present Time" for it can only exist in Gods world or the world of Nature for the Non-Believer.

Simply put, this means that by this offered exercise, you will obtain that which can be explained has the "third eye," this being that which about many of our wise ancients also spoke. It will also allow you to fully understand that which our wise ancients meant, this being when they said that you would become an "awakened one".

For accurately, this is the creed "Enlightening" target explained by ALL our wise ancients so that their followers could experience that which is called "Enlightenment" and which our Christians say is being filled by the Holy Ghost or Holy Spirit, but which many other religions and philosophies named according to the culture in which they lived, such as *"Paradise", "Eden", "Heaven", "Nirvana", "Promised Land", "Moksha", "Shangri-La", "Kenshō", "Svargamu", "Kā bāga", "Vāṭikā", "Kā jagaha", "Sukhabhavana"*, and many other names for did not all realise that "Heaven" really did exist upon this Earth and that it is a Heaven that can be inwardly experienced to exist and that it is an experience which surpasses ALL understanding, for it cannot be explained. Indeed this is God's world, and it belongs to you.

But it is true, the experiencing of peace within that will bring to all people from all cultures to an irreversible knowing that use many different culturally-based names to say in many different words, this that it brings the experience of living in Heaven, while currently alive upon this Earth. For it will undoubtedly be found to be true that by saying a continued short prayer twice a day, you will also personally gain the insight into this transcendental truth that is being spoken of above.

So yes! You will fully understand via "Realisation" that you are living in a Heaven while upon the Earth and will evermore do so throughout your life. Therefore, if you continue with this simple creed-based prayer that "The Book" provides for you, you will eventually find that you can and have become a "child" of God and so will experience the reality of the Creation itself. Therefore, assuredly, this is that which our wise ancients called being "Self-Aware", an awareness that can lead to "Self-Realisation". A "Self-Realising" which simply means that you cease to exist as an individual – for you "Self-Realise" that there is only one "child", and it is via the knowledge of this "experience," that you can become as experienced and has aware has all incarnates but becoming "Self-Aware", which is also called "Enlightenment", should be your first target.

So Yes! This short, well known, carefully chosen exercise produced later in "The Book" can be likened to a short prayer, this being all that is needed to will take you to "Enlightenment". Therefore, being "Self-Aware" is a living condition in which you will exist as an observer and supporter of the world around you. Also, if you endeavour to experience further, it will take you to "Self-Realisation" which is quite an experience for in gaining this our wise ancients say that it will end all rebirths for any rebirths are no longer necessary for you will, as did all our incarnates, become as one with God.

So yes! "Enlightenment" via "Self-Awareness" is the first target to achieve for it will indeed lead to the knowledge and also an experience of the Heaven that rests upon this Earth. It is now correct to mention again that where to start is to perform the short creed later offered in "The Book", for then – after much endeavour – you will be in harmony with the world around you. For indeed nothing will ever be able to change that experience for even if you go to a similar cross as Jesus or become food has in a Roman arena, you will never leave the "peace that surpasses all understanding," the experience of "being" within the love of the "Mother of the Creation" whose arms will be waiting for you.

So Yes! Live in "Heaven" while living on this Earth and be happy and content with your life and the harmony which is all around you or endeavouring to be all around you; and therefore fully understand why Buddha said that: *"you will pass through entanglements and barriers without hindrance to time and season."* The great Buddha also explained that people live as if: "**Confined in a cage**" which can be likened to living behind the enclosing bars of many "I Want!" This false world which has been previously explained is likened to being trapped into thinking of only personal "I Want" gains, these being that which keep living in the future, or from memories emanating from the past. These were all that which form hidden cage bars all around the thinker. This condition is undoubtedly being a life which is likened to living in a cage, against a wall or pressed against barriers which you cannot pass through; all because you live in your lingering past and or your future "I Want" thoughts, which hold you away from your true potential. Also, is it not truly stated that when in this "I Want" trap, you often remain hindered by fear and also frozen into inaction. But is it not true that if you target and eventually achieve "Enlightenment" you will advance fearlessly, silently and enjoyably plus without hesitation, and this being throughout your current life.

So Yes! You will also manifest the healing power of the "Mother of the Creation". For indeed the Divine *"Mother of the Creation"* will also show to you, by Her harmony based offerings, a competent adept way of passing through "entanglements" and "barriers" and all this without hindrance, and also within any time frame or any season; as quoted by Buddha. For indeed, you will then feel as if you are resting alongside the "Mother of the Creation" and so be in an on-going very peaceful state, which is attained by the perseverance of this short creed prayer offered later by "The Book".

For justly it is the knowledge of how to achieve the results of this short prayer that will take you towards experiencing "Enlightenment", again this being that which ALL our wise ancients speak about and which is an experience that will come to all those who practice to achieve it. For faithfully they will find this *"Peace that Surpasses all Understanding"* and so "Self-Realise" this peace that exists only in God's or Natures for the Non-Believers "Present Time" which is also the world of the "Mother of the Creation", for it is She who cares for the only child, known by all to be "The Creation," particularly that part of the only child who is assigned to our Earth.

So yes! You will be free from the control of the five senses, which again can be said that you can always liken them to being like some untrained and spoiled doggy pups, which you have allowed to gain control of you and your home, which is your body. For now, it is the time to show these wild ones who is master of the home that you call your current body. Your desire should now be to employ yourself in the aiding of the harmony that is all around you, for it is always there and often struggling to be calmly released by people; this "support" being for the benefit of all Life and Non-Life. For indeed, all people who exist within the Creation can say "I am", but really who is the "I am" that always pursues an "I Want". How do you stop this selfish "I Want" which "The Book" says is emanating from the five senses and not from the true you which is the Soul??

So yes! Your five senses, this being your hearing, seeing, touching, tasting and smelling, can be likened to be five wild pups who have never before been disciplined? But now is the time to train them to be like friendly sheepdogs and so bring them under a disciplined control and therefore stop them from barking or chewing their "I Want", which causes a great deal of damage to your home – which is you! Could not the best way to stop and silence these damaging untrained pups be the same way that Jesus used when he spoke about the harmony destroying damage being caused by "The Devil? Did He not explain how to control and silence this devil by saying: *"Get thee behind me, Satan?"* For it can be likened that Jesus called these "wild pups" Satan, which in our modern truth are the five senses which were likened by our ancients to be the tools of Satan – for they want only to satisfy themselves and therefore is it not now know that the best place for a pup is behind you and silently at your heel like a good sheepdog that is obediently waiting to serve its master – which is You!.

So Yes! There is no Devil, who was only created by our ancient ones to explain that bad "I Want" noise that arises in mind, this being that which made them "unwillingly" do things which damaged those around them. But now, in our modern times, we can explain and so really know, just where that "noise" is coming from and "Yes", it is the "I Want" that is continually emanating from the five senses. Therefore, it is an excellent suggestion to pursue a regular plan that requires a twice a day exercise that will lead to the control and silencing of these pups which "The Book" later offers to you.

But for the moment if you experience any unwanted words or any words coming into the mind, then just say as Jesus said *"Get thee behind me Satan"* or in modern understanding just command to yourself by saying "Not This" until eventually all those "five pups" these being the five senses, will retire and so stay out of sight as if behind your heel. Or is there not another way which is a more simple instruction on how to control wild pups – just by saying "heel?" But always remember to treat them as your best friends for they are not your enemy, and how do you seriously manage to get these "I Want" thoughts always stopped? Is this is as if they were being placed "behind you" so that you cannot hear their demands? If you wish to know – Read on.

49   THE MODERNISED TRUTH SPOKEN BY OUR SCIENTISTS

An absolute truth spoken by our scientist says that every positive has a negative, which also means that there is a neutral that stands between them. Therefore does this not mean that in all life and Non-Life, we have a positive a negative and a neutral? So does this not then make a personal life very easy to understand? For if there is a Heaven to live in while alive on the Earth, then there must also be a Hell to live in – *but where is this neutral?* Has it not also previously been proven that while living on this Earth people can choose either to live in Heaven or to live in Hell and that they can do this individually or even collectively – *but where is neutral?*

For we have seen that a "negative" way of life can easily be explained to be the life of a person who lives in a world in which they are continually creating a mind filling "past" or a "future" desired "I Want", which are the "I Want" demands emanating from their five senses. Then indeed they must live in an unreal non-physical "negative" world called Hell while upon this Earth.

It can also be said that the "positive" in life can easily be explained in that a person who chooses to live in the "Present Time" lives a real life. Therefore, precisely, this being the world of "harmony" because this is the only place where God's laws or Nature's laws for the Non-Believer, can exist. It is the only place in which people can "unthinkingly" and "unselfishly" support the "Mother of the Creation" positive harmony developing actions, which are all based upon love, which means that they now truly live in a "physical" world called Heaven, while upon this Earth.

Therefore is it not easily understood that the "Mother of the Creation", who exist in the space all around us and within us, also "understandably" needs a person's "physical" involvement in Her efforts to support the Creation's current harmony and its newly emerging harmony, for sure is this not reason why people have been given the "Freedom of choice? For logically is it not known that the same act can positively free or negatively block the emerging harmony that exists, and is endeavouring to exist all around people – **but where is neutral?**

The only realty or fact that can be decided about this question is that "neutral" must be that which exists within a person who has an unthinking and empty mind, this being a mind that remains in a silent "neutral". For indeed this is known to be the target of ALL the creeds and ways of worship that ALL our wise ancients endeavoured to establish within the cultures of the people around them; this being the silent "neutral" mind that claims no personal "I Want" thoughts, and so allows such an unthinking person to simply enjoy and also silently and unconditionally support the Heaven and the emerging of the Heaven that is all around them. Therefore this "neutral" position in which the mind is silent, which is a condition that only people can achieve, is the reason why only people can build a contented life in which they can live in the harmony and reality that exists in "Heaven". Justly these being the Heaven that can only exist in the "Present Time", for the past and the future do not exist except as the self-created "I Want" Hell, this being that about our wise ancients speaks. For really is it not true that all people know that the "positive" of that which we call life can only exist in the "Present Time", this also being the only place in which the emerging harmony that we call the reality of "Heaven" can exist, which is God's world or the world of Nature for the Non-Believer. Again, therefore, is it not also known by all people that a positive must have a negative? So truly is not this world of Hell a "negative" non-physical world to the "positive" and physical world that we call the Heaven, this being that world which all knows to exist in the "Present Time? Therefore is it not now "Scientifically" known that the world that we call Hell is an "unreal" cynical world, for the past or the future does not exist? Yet truly, is this "Hell", not a place lived in by people who create a personal "I Want" for me world, which is that activity which makes "illegal" claims upon the "Present Time". For in fact and truth, now all readers know that this is the creating of a false unreal world of Hell, a Hell self-created by a person's God-given or Natures given "Freedom of choice", in which they have not chosen support and also to live within the harmony of God's "real" world or the real world of Nature for the Non-Believer, but have, usually in ignorance, decided to steal from it.

So yes! It is now genuinely known that this gift that has been given to all people is called the "Freedom of Choice" and it has been given to support the "Present Time's existence and especially its emerging harmony, which is a fact that many people have forgotten, and forgetting is truly our worst enemy? Therefore, it is because of this forgetting that many people have begun to live in a biased negative "I Want" state, which is a state that confines them to live in Hell. So they don't "choose" to attain the "neutral" ability to live in Heaven, and so join with the spring flowers or our singing birds and all other life and Non-Life whose automatic "neutrality" allows them to live in the Heaven that exists only in the "Present Time" – which is the real world in which for all people to live. Therefore, is it not also said to be true that the "Self-Realised" man called Jesus was brutally taken by others, beaten, tortured, ridiculed, and painfully nailed to a cross, because His persecutors lived in an "I Want" world of Hell. Still, before death, Jesus said: *"Forgive them for they know not what they do"* – well we know now this truth. Therefore, it must also be wise to say that people also need correct "understandable" information to make such a decision, this being in which world to live?

So yes! Let us now and with a clear understanding that our purpose is to support the Creations needs, let us take a look with a modern understanding of the truth which was always spoken by our wise ancients. Correctly, this is undoubtedly being a truth that shows how people can choose to be the decider as to whether to live in Heaven or to live in a self-created Hell, while alive on this Earth. For it is undoubtedly known to be accurate, that the only way to live in Heaven while on this Earth is to be in the "Present Time", this being the only time in which there is no past and no future; only the work of the "Mother of the Creation" and the world of "reality," for the Non-Believer.

Now has it not also been genuinely stated that by living and "being" in the

"Present Time", any person will feel the security of the "Mother of the Creation" around them, as they realise the reality of this "Enlightenment" in which there is no past and no future; only God's world or the world of Nature for the Non-Believer, which we call the "Present Time".

Now let us further understand the ancient truth spoken by our ancient wise: For was it not also described in many religious and philosophical writings that "Enlightenment" is an incredibly peaceful experience and an experience which was always described as the *"Peace that surpasses all understanding"*, which means it is impossible to explain! But did not the wise ancients simply explain it as: *"The peace of God that exceeds all understanding"* and *"it is a peace that will keep your hearts and minds safe in Christ Jesus"*, especially when "The Book," acknowledges that the incarnate Jesus was and is the personification of the Creation, this being that which is all around us, and within us.

Now, to acknowledge the truth of the harmony within God's world, this being that which exists all around us and also emerging all around us, let us hear more of that which our wise ancients spoke about, which can now be explained in a new modern interpretation of their ancient words. For indeed, these are the very words which the *"Mother of the Creation"* presented to our wise ancients and which they then presented to the world of people so that all people Souls could see the way ahead, and if necessary, to honestly act in supporting the on-going and emerging harmony of the "Present Time". Here are more words that our ancients wise spoke and which are followed by new explanations: They said: *"In the beginning was the Word, and the Word was with God, and the Word was God,"* this again simply means that before and before any action, there must be the creating sound of God's word, which then brings the unfolding "Present Time" into existence. But this is an action that cannot always be an activity that is seen in a person's mind by their Soul, which is the supporter of Gods world or the world of Nature for the Non-Believer.

The reason for this is because of all the noisy uncontrolled "I Want" words arising and clouding into the mind from the five senses, this being that which creates within a person an uncontrolled mind-blocking existence that is undoubtedly emanating from a person's past or an "I Want" desired Future. For sincerely it is when the mind is still and without personal input, that the Soul can truly see through the mind, and so witness the supporting deeds that are needed to be achieved in the "Present Time". For again, this is the only time in which one can realise the needs of this silent "word" emanating only in the "Present Time" and being currently created by God or Nature for the Non-Believer. For justly, this is a natural activity in which the Soul is needed to support and fix if necessary, all of God's emerging laws or the Laws of Nature for the Non-Believer, this being an act that is also supported by the loving "whispers" and "caresses" of the "Mother of the Creation" – whose caring and supportive of the emerging harmony She is expecting to be naturally assisted and supported by Her children, one of which is YOU!

Also, did not our ancient wise state: *"Through Him, all things were made; without Him, nothing was made that has been made."* So indeed, when the mind is still and without any mind filling clouding "noise", this being that which is emanating from one or more of the clamouring five senses, it is then that you will faithfully be a witness and understand that all that which is "personally" existing around you, always originates from the laws emanating from God or Nature for the Non-Believer and which are laws that are also supported and maintained in constant harmony by the **"Mother of the Creation",** which is also achieved with the support of Her children, one of which is YOU!.

So yes! It is only when the mind is in the "Present Time" that a person can witness the truth of this reality, this being the reality that Heaven is all around you and also within you. For truly is it not this fact which reveals the truth that your life's purpose, which is now known to exist with a "Freedom of choice", is currently here to support Gods world or the world of Nature for the Non-Believer, this being the "Creation" that is all around you and within you. And, the ancient words of: *"In him was life, and that life was the light of all people. The light shines in the darkness, and the darkness has not overcome it.*

This explanation is the explaining of the light emanating from the universal all-knowing Soul, this being that which rests within all people and it is a Soul which can be "Self-Realised" and so experiences itself to be everything, this being that which exists in the unified "Present Time". This "light" being when the Soul becomes the singularity of everything within the Creation, a condition in which there is no observer but only existence, knowledge and bliss.

Or this light is in the knowledge of the first experience, this being when you become "Self-Aware", a condition in which the real you, meaning your inner viewing Soul, suddenly becomes aware that it is not just the observer of all that exists, but "knows" that it is an integral enjoined part of all that exists. For actual and factual experience is that you're Soul becomes an undivided part of all that it "Sees" and "Experiences" and so understands "stands under" the knowing fact that it is also "Everything" that the five senses and more, are reporting to it. For really in becoming "Self-Aware", you become "conscious" that you are not only observing all that exists but that you are "factually" an integral part of the creation that is all around you and within you.

So Yes! You indeed become "aware" that you are an integral part of all that exist in Gods world or the world of Nature for the Non-Believer. For a clearer understanding of this reality, it is useful to "Silently" look at your hand, this being that which you currently accept and experience as being a part of yourself. This same known realty, this being that which you experience when looking at your hand, is also now similarly "experienced" to be the same truth when you look at all that exists around you, which you also know to be yourself and with the same feeling has when you look at your hand. For rightly, you become aware that "you" are not only parts of your current body but also a similarly integral legitimate part of all that exists around you. For indeed you can become "Self-Aware", and so you know that all that you observe, is you! For assuredly, becoming "Self-Aware", acknowledges the fact that your Soul is not only the observer of all that which it experiences but that it also "knows" itself to be a unified and integral part of that which it observes, which is precisely experienced the same when you look at your hand.

So Yes! You become "Self-Aware", via the experience of bliss, that there is only one existing entity and that it is only this single entity that can be observed to exist in the "Present Time". For you knowingly experience that your inner observing Soul is "Self-Aware", meaning that your Soul is also an integral part of that which exists all around you. For indeed the viewing Soul knows that that which it views is itself, but this is an experience that can occur only when the mind becomes without thought.

It is also this non-thinking condition which is again explained to be attained by a particular creed mantra prayer, this being that which is later mentioned in "The Book." Therefore has previously mentioned a silent mind is only experienced when person's mind enters only the "Present Time" and so is without thought, a reality described by our wise ancients to be *"the light for all people"*, but now called "Enlightenment". Yet is not the great difficulty in achieving this light not explained by our ancient wise in words*: "Light has come into the world, but people loved darkness instead of light because their deeds were evil. While I am in the world, I am the light of the world. As long as it is the day, we must do the works of him who sent me.*

These words do certainly and honestly explain the world of "forgetting", but the truth of the above is more kindly explained with these other words from Jesus who said *"I am the light of the world. Whoever follows me will never walk in darkness, but will have the light of life.* This "light of life" is a certainly a now known condition in which the mind has become still and empty, this being the fact which allows the current time to be observed by the Soul, that which knows everything to be itself. For indeed this means that a person has left behind their dealing in "I Want" words, these being the "I Want" words that are always emanating from the five senses and which so fill the mind that they stop the Soul from seeing the "Present Time", because they are always seeking a past or future "I Want".

So Yes! The fact remains that when not hearing these mind filling words that are always emanating from the five senses, you are in the stillness of the "Present Time" and so genuinely, also in the condition which "The Book" and the world calls "Enlightenment". For it is truly only then, that when "Enlightened", you are a witness to the ever still and ever-moving "Creation", thus being an authentic witness to the harmony of all Life and Non-Life. For "scientifically" a person's inner Soul is a light that does silently shine through the uncluttered mind of all people and who's shining also allows this observer, the Soul, to support all the emerging harmony of the "Present Time" and this is the light of the creation which shines and so enters within the view of the Soul.

Also, more is spoken about this light by the wise ancients' who said: *"The light shines in the darkness, but the darkness has not understood it."* Thus meaning that the darkness runs from the truth of light, this being that which occurs when the mind becomes still and only obedient to the light of consciousness and so does not allow the five senses to create the darkness produced by their never-ending "I Want" words. These were words which when born, do explain the suffering that is emanating from a non-existing past or are being falsely born to create a non-existing future, both worlds being the world of Hell so named by our ancients wise.

For indeed, this is a fact that cannot happen when you are inwardly experiencing the pure light of the world, this being that light which can only exist in the "Present Time", and is that light which the Soul does use to shine upon the Creation. But, again and accurately, this can only happen when you have stopped, the mind filling darkness which is caused by these never-ending past or future "I Want" claims that are always emanating from the uncontrolled five senses.

So yes! Here is another ancient wise saying that accurately explains that what happens when the Souls view of the Creations "Present Time", is blocked by the many "I Want" for myself inputs being created by the mind filling five senses. *"He was in the world, and though the world was made through Him, the world did not recognize Him."* For correctly, is it not also known to be true that the many words emanating from our worlds many incarnate and also our many ancient wise, still exist in the world that is all around us? Is it not also true that they are words of love and also peaceful seeking words and that they still exist to be good advice in our current or emerging "Present Time"? Is it not also true that their world is not recognised by those who live in a personally self-created world of "I Want something for me"? This truth is being the dark world created mistakenly in their infant time, a time in which they unknowingly freed to sound into the mind their arguing and ever-demanding five senses, because in childhood they believed that the sound coming into the mind was from the real them. It was NOT them for they are genuinely the ageless never-dying Soul.

But sadly the truth is that it is still their five senses that are freely sounding into their mind and which are still always claiming a future "I Want" or are being saddened by a past thought in which they did not achieve their "I Want". Do they not also continuously pursue their targeted "I Want for ME?" Therefore, is it not an absolute and now known truth that they have unknowingly "chosen" to live in a world of Hell because they have misplaced and forgotten the world in which they do genuinely live? Which certainly makes these following words from our ancient wise to be true: *"He came to that which was His own, but His own did not receive Him."*

So Yes! God's world or Natures world for the Non-Believer", only exists in a "Self-Created" world, this being that world which we call "Present Time". For indeed this is a world whose harmony will come to all those who endeavour to enter into it – but this cannot be a reality for those who through ignorance or custom allows their mind to live in the past or the future. Precisely, this being that which again can be said has been the fictitious world that they create for themselves. It is also known that you can only receive and give when you live in a real-world, this being the world that exists all around you and so you live only in one world, this being the "Present Time". For really, many create a self-made world in which they cannot receive God's world or the world of nature for the Non-Believer, this being that which only exists in the "Present Time", a place where indeed, everything that they need is waiting for them.

Plus these words from our ancient wise: *"Yet to all who received Him, to those who believed in His name, He gave the right to become children of God."* YES! Enter the "Present Time" and live as a child of God but you can only do this in the "Present Time", for it is only the "Present Time" that God or Nature for the Non-Believer, did create for YOU! Is it not also true that this is also your birthright to be living within the only life form that has the "Freedom of Choice", a choice that could even end your own life if this is so "chosen"? Therefore you undoubtedly have the gift to firmly establish a silent mind and so are genuinely enabled to "Choose" to "Self-Experience" the "Singularity" which ensures that you have become as one with all that exists around you. For indeed, without a sound in your mind, you will become a child of God and live in God's world, this being that which ALL our wise ancients always inform their listeners, this being the real world in which you actually "experience" the word of God's harmony, where the false "I Want", born from past or future thoughts, have been banished to the Hell from which they came and so these "I Want" thoughts can no longer exist.

Plus is I said: *"Children are not born of natural descent, nor of a personal decision or a person's will, but born of God."* So Yes! It is when you live only in the "Present Time" that you understand that you and also your Earthly mother and your Earthly father, whose unity created your body, have a unified soul. It is from this Soul that their unity of love, caring and belonging in family unity truly emanates, this being a fact in which only a personal "I Want" can change. Is it not also true that it is because of this that all acknowledge this "feeling" and "emotion" of family unity which can only be destroyed by persons "I Want" for me only?

Also, is it not genuinely acknowledged by many that their faithful parental guardian is also God or Nature for the Non-Believer, and also do not many further understand that the "Mother of the Creation" really exists because of the love and togetherness that continually prevails in the "Present Time"? Precisely, this is being because of the emerging "caring" that continually takes place or is endeavouring to take place, but only in the "Present Time". For indeed, these great ones are all around you and are also waiting for you to live with them and in the world which they created for you. Therefore is it not sensible to stop a self-created world of Hell, this being that personally claimed "I Want" which is born within non-existing past or a future. For indeed, do you not live in a world where you have all that you need for your Soul to develop – and even unto the death of this life – knowing that such good works will be given to your next one.

Plus: In the Christian bible, John 1:14 it is said about Jesus, *"The Word became flesh and made His dwelling among us. We have seen His glory, the glory of the One and only, who came from the Father, full of grace and truth."* For certainly and Yes! It is correctly stated that Jesus was the personification of the Creation which exists only in the "Present Time". For indeed it is said that God made the Creation and has its father He does speak through His children, as in Jesus and also our many other incarnates and ancient wises who appeared in many parts of our world and so they did actually and personally exist amongst us. For indeed, many of our ancient wises were the walking talking personification of a fatherly God that spoke to them as an only child, and this Child is that which we call "The Creation" and also a child that can only exist in the "Present Time". So factually, all our ancient wise were an integral part of the one-child that we call "The Creation", which also, of course, is YOU! Therefore, is it not true that we are a part of that one body that we call "The Creation"? This being that, which we truly know is always ourselves, just has does all the multiple life which also exists within us.

Therefore the acknowledging of the singularity of the "Present Time" must also be to realise that its existence is full of co-operating. The blending of grace and truth, this being a fact that only people can experience for is it not an actual reality that all life can only exist in the "Present Time", for indeed the past and the future do not exist, and so no life can be a part of it.

For indeed the unity and singularity of the "Present Time" can actually be experienced when one becomes "Self-Aware" or "Self-Realised" and therefore becomes has one entity with ALL life and also ALL the non-life that currently exists in the "Present Time". For accurately, this the actual experiencing the unity and awareness that is always spoken of by our wise ancients and which can now be modernly understood to be a well-known fact, this being that "physically" and "aware only", the personal "Self", via patient meditational practices can establish and so experience the truth of the creations "singularity". This "singularity" is a fact that can be experienced by all patient meditational "practitioners" to be a fact that is controlled by the laws emanating from a loving Father and Mother and this is because all people have been given "The Freedom of Choice".

So yes! You can choose to be an individual surviving in a complicated "I Want" for myself world, or you can choose to live in a world in which you have and are "everything."

Listen again to the words of our wise ancients: **"From the fullness of His grace, we have all received one blessing after another."** For again is it not indeed known and so can be experienced, that God's Creation, which is founded upon elegance, kindness, blessing, beauty and dignity, can only exist in the "Present Time" in which you can become not only aware of but with which to live. Accurately, this is being your never beginning and your never-ending but always existing "Present Time", in which exist the fruit of the many blessings that have been given by God or Nature for the Non-Believer, to all people. For assuredly, this is being mainly the fruit of "Good" (God) life, blessed by the now known reality that life cannot exist in the past or the future; but only in the "Present Time", a time that is born from God or Nature for the Non-believer and is also a time that is within Gods laws and never without Gods laws. For certainly is it not said: ***"For the law was given through Moses, but grace and truth came through Jesus Christ***. For certainly, this being a Jesus who was "Self-Realised", meaning that he was the totality of the Creation, especially our planet earth. Therefore that which can be realised is that when Jesus spoke, it was the Creation, localized has the planet earth, which was speaking to you.

Therefore is it not also true that this "Grace and Truth", emanating from our earth, was also explained by many of our worlds incarnates and also our many ancient wise. Therefore is it not true that they always spoke and preached this truth? For was this not a truth that was based continuously upon explaining, in their ancient terminology, the existence of our unified creation and especially our Earths "singularity"? For indeed it was this truth that was spoken to their many listeners who lived all around them but now to this ancient truth can be "modernly" added that this singularity which is all around them is the same has the caring singularity that also exists within them.

So Yes! The law of righteousness was given to the Christian Bible by Moses; who's "Ten Commandments" that he solitary wrote at the top of the mountain, was to describe the way ahead for people who were seeking their freedom from a world that existed in their "Present Time". These "Ten Commandments" written by Moses also covered the "I Want" world, which is a world that targets the ending of an "I Want" for My Future.

For truly cannot the written "Ten Commandments" now be understood to be laws that were targeting the ancient living conditions and understanding of that which truly existed in the that ancient "Present Time"? Is it not also true that these anciently written "Ten Commandments" also targeted and opposed a people created "I Want only for me" activity, which Moses was undoubtedly trying to overcome? Therefore, is it not also true that this consistently and religious opposing by our ancient wise of the "I want freedom for me to do what I want to do and NOT what you want to do", is undoubtedly the opposing of a false world created by people who always endeavour to encase this "I Want" world into an oral or written law which creates a world for themselves and not for all Life and Non-Life – hence the then needed writing of Moses ancient "Ten Commandments", which can now be modernly described as meaning:-

1. **"I am the Lord thy God; thou shalt not have any strange gods before Me."** When the mind is unthinking and still and existing only in the "Present Time", all that can be seen and experienced is Gods world for no other world can exist within the Present Time.

"Thou shalt not take the name of the Lord thy God in vain." Gods' created "Heaven" exists only within the "Present Time" and so cannot exist in the "I want" for me self-created "Hell", which births the world of a non-existing past or future.

"Remember to keep holy the Sabbath day." All days that you live are genuinely experienced to be a "Sabbath Day" therefore no day is more important than any other day, so each day needs to be self-experienced within its "Present Time".

"Honour thy Father and Mother." God is thy Father, and the space that is all around you and within you is your Mother, and both love you deeply and the experiencing of this love, you always reflect upon your earthly parents.

"Thou shalt not murder." The killing of another person is a severe abuse of the God-given "Freedom of Choice", which ensures that the killer will be returned, has a lower animal in their next life.

"Thou shalt not commit adultery." Against the rules of your Heavenly Father who gave to you birth or your Heavenly Mother who monitors the Godly goodness existing within the "Creations" emerging activities.

"Thou shalt not steal". For indeed this being the stealing of that responsibility and the caring of the creation which God did give to others.

"Thou shalt not bear false witness against thy neighbour."

To do this means that you have left Gods world for truly all that exists is only YOU?

"Thou shalt not covet thy neighbours' wife."

"Thou shalt not covet thy neighbour's goods."

For both, these are living in a world of the Past or the Future which is the living in a Hell that you create but which does not exist in Gods "Present Time", a time when there are no thoughts and only existence, knowledge and bliss is experienced.

For indeed the misuse of our God-given "Freedom of Choice" does engender a mind filled by the living in a self-created "I Want" in the past or in an "I Want" Future, this is living in a Hell because these worlds do not exist in the "Present Time". But yes, the reality of grace and truth is that all the Creations laws, which were installed by God, can only exist in the world of the "Present Time". These being the ever-present Godly laws that the *"Mother of the Creation"* consistently upholds, and which is a work in which She is factually aided by many people; for indeed, the Mother of Creation is also that which spoke through Jesus and also many of our ancient wise. For truly She spoke through Her only child who is all the Creation, but whom, in this case, as was singularly accepted has the incarnate Jesus Christ through which the ***"Mother of the Creation" said***: ***"No one has ever seen God! But the One and only, who is personified as being at the Father of the Creations side, has made him known."*** Yes! Indeed, this is being the *"Mother of the Creation"*, for did not Jesus Christ, known to be the personification of the Creation; speak to the world as have many others incarnates and wise have done? Did they not also all speak the many truths regarding the "Heaven" that exists upon this Earth and thus also speak to all to the life force that we call "people". Also, can any person doubt these words of great wisdom except via incorrect misinterpretations?

Plus: ***"Man does not live on bread alone, but on every word that comes from the mouth of God."*** Yes! Edible foods do not satisfy our most essential needs, and it is only in the "Present Time", that we can genuinely taste God's laws, which are our real food, and which is a food that may be quickly absorbed through the creed praying mentioned later on in "The Book". For indeed, is this not a simply achieved task which when established will allow people re-enter the "Present Time" and therefore realise the reality of all God's truth or the truth of Nature for the Non-Believer, this being that which exist within the Creation.

Plus: ***"Do not put the Lord your God to the test."*** Yes! Do not steal from the Creation by pursuing your "I Want" thoughts, which are based upon past or future machinations. For these manoeuvrings' take you away from God's

"Present", and so you will then knowingly or unknowingly destroy the harmony of the "Present Time", that which has been given to all life and Non-Life by God or Nature, for the Non-Believer.

Plus: **"Flesh gives birth to flesh, but the Spirit gives birth to Spirit."** The past and the future attracts and plays with your flesh, but only the mindful present can give birth to your Spirit, which is encased in the Soul that rests within you.

Plus: *"Jesus said to him, Away from me, Satan! Worship the Lord your God and serve him only."* Yes! For only God's world exists in the "Present" and it is undoubtedly the uncontrolled five senses that create Satan's world for it can only exist in the unreal world of the past or the future. For indeed, Satan's world, which is the ancient terminology used as a name for the then-unknown and uncontrolled "I Want" machinations of the five senses, is the world of Hell. Strictly, this is being the world, in which does flourish the constant claims of the never-satisfied five senses, these being that which are always claiming an "I Want" which is the actual living in Hell while on this Earth.

Plus: Jesus said: *"I tell you the truth; no one can see the Kingdom of God unless he is born again.* Yes! Being born again is by stopping the imagining mind from self-creating a past or a future "I Want," and so silently entering into the world of the "Present Time", this truly being the only time in which a person's Soul can factually live and therefore act in Heaven while alive on this Earth, and thus automatically accepting and supporting the harmony that rests within the Creation or Nature for the Non-Believer. Also, these words that the incarnate Jesus said to Peter: *"Get behind me Satan! You are a stumbling block to me; you do not have in mind the things of God, but the things of people."* For did not this occur when Peter revealed to Jesus his own "I Want"? Indeed this being an " I Want" in which Peter wanted Jesus to avoid death and live with him for Peter's wanted friendship and comforts of the future – which was not serving the Present Time's needs. For Satan can indeed, be regarded as the five senses, these being that which all our religions and philosophers warn people about and so they gave the five senses the name of "Satan".

So yes! The above are many of the sayings that the incarnate Jesus did speak about in the Christian bible and these being that which are revealed in the new testament of the Christian teachings. These being teachings which always explain that people can either live in Heaven while on this Earth or "Choose" to live in Hell, and this "Choice" always rests within the listener, which is genuinely ALL people! For also, do not all these above parables clearly explain again the two worlds that people can live in while they dwell upon this Earth? One is being the heavenly co-operating world of God or Nature for the Non-Believer and the other being the "I Want" for myself world of self-made torment and distrust.

Well, the above are the words of the "Mother of the Creation". She explained the laws of God when She became the flesh of Jesus, also of Krishna and many others and did not "Mother of the Creation" not also whisper these truths into the ears of Mohammad, Buddha, Baha'u'llah, Confucius, Tao, Plato, Laozi,

Vivekananda, Sri Shankara and Sri Ramakrishna, plus many, many more of our wise ancients.

Now here are a few truths that emanated from Sri Ramakrishna*: "Do you know how God dwells in people? He dwells in the same Ways as ladies of wealthy families do behind latticed screens. They can see everybody, but no one can see them. God abides in all people the same way."* Can this be modernly explained in 2020 language as a God who first begat "Space", this being the Mother of their only child, this being that which we call "The Creation", this being a creation in which that life-force which is known as people is a part off? These being that part of the one-child who have been given the "Freedom of Choice", to become "Self-Aware" or "Self-Realised", and so physically support the harmony that surrounds them which of course is "themselves" and which is that act which also mimics the cause and effect which rests within their bodies? Also "The Book," says, *"A devotee is just like a shoreless ocean which is an infinite expanse of water with no land visible in any direction: only here and there are visible icebergs" – in which "The Book" explains - these are forgetting people whose "I Want" endeavours to claim for themselves all the conditions that exist around them. Still, with the appearance of the Sun of knowledge which can emanate from that which is all around them, this ice melts away, and so they become again knowingly "unified" has the one child."*

So now we know that an "I Want" is pursued because of a self-created "I Want" for only "Me". Correctly, this being only thought in mind; Yet truly, these can be "trained" to melt away and thus a person can become emerged in the singularity all life and Non-Life which is seen as a singularity which Sri Ramakrishna explained has an empty "shoreless ocean". Then: Sri Ramakrishna said: "If the person is possessed by an evil spirit" – (this being an "I Want," and so lives in Hell) – "and then has the conscious understanding that he is so possessed, the evil spirit will at once leaves him." And so, the person then recognises that they live in Heaven which exists only in the "Present Time". This being where the creed above, physically explained later in "The Book", will take you. For it will bring the Soul to see through the stillness in the mind which then can become fully aware of God's world and it is then that Gods world, which can only exist in the "Present Time" becomes the controller of that body's actions.

Thus Sri Ramakrishna also tells a beautiful story about living in the harmony of God's world, this being that which can only exist in the "Present Time". *"A man was informed by a religious wise ancient that he lived in God's harmony and truly, believed this truth. One day this disciple met an elephant advancing towards him on the street, and the driver was shouting for him to move away. 'Why should I move away' thought the man. 'I truly, live in Gods harmony, and so does this elephant; it cannot hurt me for harmony is all around me and protecting me.'* But the elephant picked him up in his trunk and threw him to one side seriously hurting him. Then upon is his healing, he went back to his wise ancient and asked why the harmony around him had been broken. The wise ancient then answered him saying, *"Yes you truly, live in harmony and so does the elephant so why did you not pay any heed to the driver who was shouting for you to move? For was this not God telling you to do so?"* Also stated from Sri Ramakrishna:- *"A seagull with a fish in its beak was being chased by crows and other seagulls who were trying to aggressively snatch the fish away until when fed up with this, the seagull threw the fish away and retired to rest peacefully in a tree.* This seagull was then joined by a wise bird who said, *"You are a now a wise bird for you teach that peace of mind is only possible when one gives up personal attachments; otherwise if not done there are dangers at every step."* The question for all to answer is: *"Do you live in the harmony of Heaven while on this Earth or in the disharmony of Hell, while on the Earth"* and if you wish to live in Heaven while on this Earth. Always remember: *"Blessed are the peacemakers, for they will be called sons of God."* – To answer these questions and so realise this way of life - Read on.

50 BARRIERS TO THE KINGDOM OF HEAVEN

So yes! How do you attain the "Peace that surpasses all understanding" and so live in the Kingdom of Heaven which can be factually realised by humankind, but which can only exist in the "Present Time". For indeed, this is being a time that cannot exist in a humanly created past or a humanly created future, truly is a world that does not exist, but in which many people live. Therefore, is it not true that when the mind exists without thought, it is undoubtedly in the "Present Time", which is the only time that the mind can experience, this being when it is without any thoughts regarding a future or a past mind-fully crested "I Want," which usually takes the "I Want" for me thinker out of God's world, this being that which can only exist in the "Present Time", and self-creates a past or the future fictitious world which is governed only by the "I want" thinker? This fact is undoubtedly ignoring the real world which can only exist in the still and unthinking world of the "Present Time", which is truly the place to find the glory of a "Heavenly Creation" and a place to live which is accurately called "the Kingdom of Heaven", this being the only peaceful place of existence which rests upon this Earth. For truly is not this the place that our wise ancients always spoke about, and is it not also truly a place that continually exists all around you? It should now be fully understood that the "Present Time", which is that which rests quietly within you and outside you, can be clearly and humanly experienced has a bliss that surpasses all imaginations but only when it is not contaminated by any "I Want" for me actions and thoughts that are emanating from you or others.

It is also an experience of bliss which has a deep all-satisfying wonder; even when you are being punished by those who live in a Hell who's "I Want" nails you to the cross of life. Correctly, this being a cross of life that is undoubtedly that which is imposed upon you by the "I want" of other people, who are often called "freethinkers" and some even religiously worship a strange and imagined god, who informs them to personally destroy other religious gods and attack people of other religions when in reality it is just the property, wealth or service of those who they penalise that they seek.

For it must be indeed stated that the problem of an "I Want" my religious way of life to be everyone's way of life, is that it is an excuse that is being used to steal that which belongs to others who worship the true God but in a different way and accordance to their culture. For sadly is it not known to be true that these disbelievers can create an "I Want" my god to be the only god, which is not the singularity of the love encased in the one God's Creation, in which all people have the "Freedom of Choice". For truly is this, not a God-given gift so that people can support the one Gods Creation and woe to those who abuse this gift for truly Hell awaits them.

Yet again sadly, is it not also true that these forgetting ones do self-create this "I Want" for me god and then call this religious stealing of another's property a godly inflicted punishment because of their victims' religious way of life; this usually is a way of life in which their non-harmful religion believes that you cannot steal or falsely punish others and so they genuinely worship the one God who can only exist in the "Present Time". For again sadly, is it not true that these disbelievers believe only that which they want to believe, this belief being because they do not know that the singularity of Gods world but have a belief in the world of "I Want" for me only.

Therefore, is it not a truth that they cannot understand that their disharmonised life is created by a personal and straightforward "I want" for myself, this is being the only motivating factor that always motivates them and moves them onward through the world in which they live. Again, it can be very merely said; that those who "unwisely" live in this world of self-inflicted pain are genuinely living in the Hell that also exists upon this Earth, but this is the Hell that is self-created by their "I want" thoughts or the "I want" thoughts of their "I Want" for me seeking leaders who they falsely allow to control them. For indeed, these "I Want" for me, thoughts are the exact opposite to the "Heavenly" living self-control of a restrained and blissful non-thinker, who does not understand why they are being possessed by unhelpful and unending "I want" cravings, which always destroy the harmony which continually exists in the "Present Time" and which is always trying to emerge all around them. For did not the "Mother of the Creation", speaking through Her Son Jesus, who was the personification of Creation, not say to His disciples: ***"Woe to the world because of the things that cause people to sin! Such things must come, but woe to the man through whom they come!"***

So Yes! All self-created "I Want" for me, religions will always be fractured by the unsatisfying disharmony that they impose around themselves and upon others. Still, they cannot be punished by the laws of God who has given them the "Freedom of Choice", this being that freedom which is needed to support the emerging creation. For truly, they are punished by the echoing of the false laws that they impose upon others, these being "I Want" for me laws that will always return to them.

So yes! If a person continues to destroy the harmony that is existing or is endeavouring to be created all around them, and so does not change to supporting the emerging and lawful harmony that is always endeavouring to emerge in the "Present Time", this being an anciently known living fact that enables them to live in the Heaven that always exists upon this Earth; They will live an unhappy life in which they can never be satisfied nor will they be able to satisfy those around them, these being family, friends and neighbours who they also bring into the Hell that they have self-created.

For indeed, all humankind instinctively knows that those who cannot live within God's or Nature's law for the Non-Believer, must discontentedly live outside it and so defensively and logically they may not be born again as a person, for the "Mother of the Creation" could re-birth them back again as lower animals from which they must have just emerged so that they can live contentedly and without the "Freedom of Choice".

Therefore, is it not true that only an animalistic "I want" thought can target many selfish and racist activities, this being that which causes people to "Sin", but what is "Sin"? Is Sin not known to be a deliberate and purposeful violation of the will of God, this being in a word, deed, or desire that is in opposition to the emerging laws of God which can only be created in the "Present Time", a time in which only people can sin. For correctly, God gave only to people the "Freedom of Choice", this being to support the emerging creation which also means that they can steal from it and so seek a benefit which is only for them. Therefore can "Sin" not be explained to be that which all religions endeavour to reveal? Can this sin be the taking from others that which truly the stealer has no right to possess and so only those who sin do not support the "Present Time", this being the Godly birthing of harmony that is always existing or endeavouring to emerge all around them?

So Yes! What should now be clearly understood by all readers of "The Book" is the right and known fact that which causes people to sin are their "I want for myself" thoughts, these being that which arouse behaviour patterns within and also outside themselves? For is this an "I Want" only for me thought that precedes their activities and which also activates their non-human and so animalistic "I Want" for me behaviour within the Creation.

But what must also be clearly understood is that this "woe is me", which they then sound within their lives, is a "woe" about that which Jesus and all other religions and philosophies speak. For indeed all our wise ancients reveal that this painful "woe" does not come from God, who is known to have given people the "Freedom of Choice", but is a "woe" that is a "reflection" of their own "I want" for me only. For indeed, it is these "I want" for me acts which always create the Hell on Earth in which only people can greedily and selfishly choose to live, and it is truly a condition which people establish for themselves. For did not God "lawfully" give them the "Freedom of Choice"? Therefore, is it not also well to remember that God or Nature for the Non-Believer, never breaks these laws that can only exist in the "Present Time" and which are evolving laws that cannot punish people who "choose" to use wisely their "Freedom of Choice", for sure, they do not "Choose" to support the emerging creation, punish themselves?

So yes! It will be found to be true that by learning how to support the "Kingdom of Heaven," which can only exist in the "Present Time", you will never be a person who is filled with woe. Logically, this is is because you will understand and experience that the "Present Time" is not only all around you but is also the same as that which is within you. Simply put, this is because being in the "Present Time", which can only be achieved when there are no thoughts within the mind, you will then realise that you are a part of God's harmony or Nature's harmony for the Non-Believer.

So yes! Accurately, this is the same harmony that exists within your own body, these being mainly the togetherness sharing of your heart, blood, lungs and a trillion other life forms that are all part of the working harmony that exists within your own body. For it is then, with the knowledge of this perfect example that you will fully and peacefully realise that you are also a part of the heavenly system that exists all around you. Like those trillion parts of your own body you will be unable to act selfishly, but instead, will act only for the greater good of the Creation that is all around you, just as do all the many different living entities within your own body.

For it can be clearly understood that God wisely did not give any of our bodily parts the freedom of choice. Still, God certainly gave humankind the freedom of choice, this being to support the continually emerging harmony of the Creation that should also be likened to a "one body". For did not our high incarnates, prophets and wise ancients also show to their followers a definite way to find out how to experience and act within this harmony that exists and is continually emerging in our "Present Time", which is the real Heaven that exists upon our Earth, but only in the "Present Time". Did not our wise ancients also wisely use the current different cultures of their many believers, to explain these truths? For can it not also "scientifically" accurate that our wise ancients achieved a way to experience for themselves and so showed others the Heaven that rests upon this Earth? Did they not also achieve this, by introducing to their followers, a culturally-based "ritual of creed-based prayers"? These "creeds" prayers being based upon a group chanting, group chorusing, group praying or individual praying, whose only target was to ensure that their followers brought their Non-Thinking mind into the "Present Time". Yes, this being a worshipping via an imposed and disciplined praying system that was "created" to empty the mind from thoughts which emanate from the praying doers a past or a future "I want" desire; thus emptying of the mind is the exact target of our wise ancients.

So yes! Is it not also "scientifically" correct to say that these many culturally based and original worshipping religions, created by our wise ancients as prayers and chants, are unknowingly used to target the experiencing of the "Present Time"? Therefore, is it not also true that these prayers also discipline the worshipping mind and so empty it from thinking about a past or a future "I want?" So, can it not now be "scientifically" seen to be true that these acts were "culturally" introduced by our many and various wise ancients, who knew how to bring their worshipping creed practiser to the "Peace that Surpasses all Understanding"? Is it not also true that this experience is a realisation of that which is always resting in the "Present Time", a "Present Time" which can only exist in the harmony that supports the Heaven that rests upon this Earth?

Is it not also true that these different religious practices, called "creeds", were initially born by our wise ancients to be accepted within the many behavioural cultures that endured in the world of their believers and followers? Is it not also true that these many varied creeds are now recognised, by modern communication systems, to be "word phrased" and worshipfully different from other culturally introduced worshipping systems? Therefore is it not true that our wise ancients were the enlightened ones who brought to their own "cultural" followers a "taste" of the actual realisation of a Heaven which can only rest within the "Present Time" upon our Earth? Is it not, therefore, a cultural reason why our wise ancients did introduce different and often very variable creed-based "ritual" systems, all of which took the long practising "doers" eventually to the "peace that surpasses all understanding"?

Yet sadly, is it not also "scientifically" valid that many followers of these many varied and different ancient belief systems have now forgotten the real target of our wise ancients? This being that when the worshipper ended these religious creeds imposed prayer rituals, these being the very acts which brought them into the "Present Time", this being the Heaven that truly exists and can be experienced upon our Earth, that they would learn how to remain living within the "Present Time" in which their group-based creed worship had been brought to them. Can it not also said to be true that when they left their place of worship that these creed worshippers would be expected to continue to reflect this "Present Time", this being the feeling of unselfish wellbeing for all the community to which they belonged but has history shows, they factually did not. Does this not again show that forgetting is humankind's worst enemy?

So yes! Is it not, therefore, a "scientific" truth that our wise ancients established many such culturally-based religious practices, which were called "creeds," these being culturally-based creeds which were also supported by many variable and different "praying rituals", all of which were culturally-based upon a particular worshipping country or region's culture. Therefore, is this not truly the main reason why our many religious creeds are "naturally" different from the many other religious creeds that we now know to be contained within our world's religions?

Again, is it not "scientifically" true that all the world's different religions and belief systems are based upon the various group and individual creeds that are in accordance to their followers "ancient" cultural understanding. These being creeds that are based upon different ritual praying procedures plus different worshipping activities, all used to target an actual reality that is designed to bring the praying people into the "Present Time" and away from their personal "I want" thoughts. Did our wise ancients also not know that by meditating upon these "rituals" that it would bring their followers into experiencing the real existence of the "Present Time", a time which is realised by the taste of the "Peace that Surpasses all Understanding", this being that which comes to fruition via the repeating of prayers, this truly is that which our all our wise ancients know, is being in the God-given "Present Time". Again, this is being a time which positively rests in the Heaven that truly, exists upon this Earth?

So Yes! Is it not now clearly seen to be true that a ritual prayer or any religiously disciplined meditational activity, will bring the worshipper into the "Present Time", this being Gods world? Therefore is it not also true that when the mind is silent and so is silently witnessing in the "Present Time", that there can be no thought of any past or a future "I want" selfish desire that is born from the five senses and which fills the mind with pictures and words that emanate from the past or the future and away from that *"Peace that surpasses all understanding",* which can only exist in the "Present Time?" For our wise ancients knew that only religiously and disciplinary imposed meditational activities could stop a worshipper from mindfully birthing a personal "I want" for me which ALWAYS confines the "thinker" to living in the Hell that negatively and personally created to exist upon our Earth?

Therefore, is it not "scientifically" true that all our wise ancients introduced into the world different culture-based religious creeds, this being for their followers to actively and knowingly pursue? Was not the purpose of these creeds to empty the mind of the worshipper from all personal thoughts, which could also be achieved by the concentration of the mind upon only one sound? Was this one sound also a ritually based word that was attached to the many praying practices, which always target the *"peace that surpasses all understanding",* this is being that peace which always exists in the Present Time? Is it not also true that such meditational prayers that bring the user into the "Present Time", will always lead to a mental or spiritual development which then leads to contemplation and then to relaxation; and eventually to the "peace that surpasses all understanding", which is an experience that is differently explained in the many various religions.

So Yes! Is it not now easily seen to be accurate, by all our worlds' religious and non-religious people, that all our religions and philosophies were "culturally" and "regionally" introduced by our worlds many wise ancients and it is this fact which explains the reason why we naturally have many culturally different religions and philosophies. These all being culture-based creeds of praying and worshipping in variable ways that were designed to bring those regions or countries, worshippers, to God's world or the world of Nature for the Non-Believer? Therefore is it not true that our wise ancients culturally designed many religious and philosophical practices that would bring their worshippers to the harmony of all the life that existed the "Present Time", this truly, being God's or Nature's Heaven that rests upon our Earth. Therefore is it not also easily seen to be true, that even when these creeds are practised in our modern times, by the followers of these many different creed-based religions, that those people who truly, commit themselves to their introduced religious creeds and practices, will realise and so experience the Heavenly "Peace that Surpasses all Understanding" this experience being "realised" in the performing of their chosen religion's creed-based rituals.

So yes! Is it not also "scientifically" valid that ALL true believers and followers of these many culture-based creeds can eventually experience this peace that surpasses all understanding? Is this being the experience which resides only when one's mind enters the "Present Time", and so is without thought? Therefore, is it not also true that when practising their chosen religions creeds, again these being the creeds that exist in the many various faiths, beliefs, dogmas, doctrines and principles of worship, which exist within ALL our world's religions and philosophies, and which are pursued to worship the one, God.

For again, is it not true that in various countries these culturally based and chosen creeds are acting like a tool that brings the worshipper into the "Present Time", this being because all creeds target the experience that exists in the "peace that surpasses all understanding", a peace which cannot be explained. For again and honestly, is this not the target of ALL religions and philosophies, this being that which ALL our wise ancients did target and which is the same target that is sought within the entire world's many different belief systems. Again, is it not true that this inner and outer experience brings a definite proof to the regular practitioner or a newcomer to religion, that this great peace-bearing "Enlightenment" can be experienced by pursuing ANY of our worlds meditational and purposely disciplined "creed" based practices while "Patient Meditation" designed by "The Book" to give a purposeful control to the modern mind by merely stating that the words in the mind are originating from one or all of the five senses, this is undoubtedly the most "scientifically" advantageous?

So yes! Is it not true that the entire world's history shows that those who lived and were close to our many wise ancients did eventually attain and never left the *"peace that surpasses all understanding?"* Therefore, this is being that which their prayers and mediations did bring to them. Also, is it not an absolute fact that their descendants took this religious "peace" with them upon their many travels? Therefore is it not also true that over many years, many people did introduce these same creeds that were taught to them and their forefathers by our wise ancients, this being to the many people who sought freedom from the misery of the "I want" that kept them living in a world of Hell? Does the world's history not also show that many newly disciplined worshippers gladly received these different meditational creeds that were handed down to them by our ancient disciples and also the followers of our wise ancients? Is it not also clearly correct that the target that these many and various meditational creeds engendered, these being that which our wise ancient's and their followers brought to the many different and varied cultures of the world, always did to bring to their followers that silent peace that rests within them and which was previously without them, this being called "Enlightenment"?

So yes! Is it not also "scientifically" accurate that all religious worshippers religiously act according to their cultural creed; this is the creed that encompasses their culturally chosen religious beliefs and customs? Is it not also true that within the creeds of these many religions and philosophies' that a constant repetitive daily and weekly creed practice, often known has prayers or a way of praying, was purposely designed to bring them to God's world or the world of Nature for the Non-Believer, this being a world in which they would experience *the "peace that surpasses all understanding"* now called "Enlightenment" which occurs when the mind is devoid of all thought. Yet sadly, is it not further agreed that in our modern world we find that many worshippers when leaving their place of worship also leave behind them that peace which they have experienced during their concentrated meditational acts of devotional practice, which is sadly forgotten as they return to the world of Hell in which their "I want" again begins to dominate them.

So yes! It must also be acknowledged to be starkly real that some people, when leaving their religious or philosophical place of worship, they again strangely begin to obey their mind filling five senses' and there constant claims of "I want" for ME! What is also perplexing to understand is why do those "Enlightened" worshippers who leave the "peace that surpasses all understanding", indeed again begin to listen to the demands of the five senses, and so fall back into their self-claiming "I want" for me world. Therefore and strangely many "selfishly" begin to feel that to continue with their brief encounter with "Enlightenment" would be more easily gained if they proved to themselves and others that their religious creed was more important than all other religions and that their religion's creed way of worship and fellowship structure was the only correct way to experience God's world. It is then with these false beliefs that they endeavour to increase their religions "self-esteem", which they falsely understand is the way to "Enlightenment". This actuality is certainly not valid, for the mind filled world is an unreal "I Want" for me world that can only exist in the past or the future. Therefore these fallen ones, ignorantly glorify the "I want" of their five senses who "deafeningly" state to the listener that THEIR creed's way of experiencing the *"peace that surpasses all understanding"* is the only accurate way to realise God's world, and also they add that all other religions and their creed-based meditational belief systems are incorrect viewpoints; thus forgetting that it is not the creeds words, tunes, surrounding fellowship or worded behaviour patterns, but the controlling and the active silencing of a person's mind that brings *the "peace that surpasses all understanding"*. Forgetting this, which is their worst enemy, they then begin to state that all other worshipping creeds are wrong except their own, but what their five senses are looking for are the goods, property and chattels that belong to those people that their five senses start to condemn, forgetting the reality that those people they condemn are really "themselves".

So yes! The "I want" the world is powered by the personal "I want" claims that are imposed by the greed of the five senses, and yes! They are mighty and yes! It is very wise to acknowledge this. But it is far wiser NOT to obey them and so keep these "I want" demands silent, by seriously concentrating upon the meditational creeds that the wise ancients introduced at the start of their new religions.

So yes! It should also be understood that some religious people are tricked by the five senses, which loudly shout into their minds that no other religion's creed or belief system of worship except their own can show the way to the world of

God; this being the word of God which can only be experienced by that "peace that surpasses all understanding", which is referred in "The Book" as "Enlightenment". For assuredly, this is being that experience which can only be acknowledged by the Soul of the worshipper seeing through a clear mind the world in which it exists, but which is also greatly feared by the ever-demanding five senses. Therefore, it is also good to again "remember" that it is your Soul, that which uses your meditational controlled and obedient consciousness to see through the still mind all that which exists only in the "Present Time".

For indeed, it is not kind to "mind-filling" attack other religions for correctly; the Soul can only see the "Present Time" through a still mind. It is also this experience which "The Book" names as being the experiencing of "Enlightenment", which is again stated tom be a personal experience that is also named throughout our world's religions and philosophies as the experiencing of the *"Holy Spirit", "Holy Ghost", "Paradise", "Nirvana", "Moksha", "Kenshō", "Bodhi", "Satori", "Kevala", "Jnana", "Ushta", "Eden", "Heaven", "Promised Land", "Shangri-La", "Svargamu", "Kā bāga", "Vāṭikā", "Kā jagaha", "Sukhabhavana"* and many more for ALL religions and philosophies endeavour to obtain through praying, singing, chanting and meditational practice the experiencing of that which "The Book" names as "Enlightenment". For indeed all our words religions and philosophies have culturally different names for that which they all target and which is endeavoured to be achieved by all the people our world's religions and philosophies' – and although it has a different name, it is the same target.

Therefore if one religion attacks another religion, then this religion merely is attacking itself. So is it not true that glimpses of this reality and also the emotional wellbeing of this peace which cannot be explained by any sound in mind is a self-reality gained experience that emanates from a concentration in a worshipping principle that brings about the stilling of the mind: which automatically brings the experiencing of a Heaven that always rests upon this Earth – This being an experience called by our ancients "Enlightenment".

So Yes! Is it not also true that those people, who listen to their five senses talking in mind and who think it is them talking, should acknowledge the simple fact that you cannot be that to which you observe or listen? For indeed, it will be found and so discovered that ANY "self-aware" fully concentrated recitation that can take place when reciting ANY chosen creed would discipline the mind of the doer and so stop the gabbling mind penetrating "I Want" words of the five senses from blocking the mind and so stopping the Soul from silently experiencing God's Heaven or Natures Silent awakening for the Non-Believer, this being that Heaven which always exists upon our Earth, but only in the "Present Time".

For assuredly, Earth is our silent Heavenly home, and this is being a home that always rests in the stillness of time and which is also an awareness that can only be experienced in the "Present Time". For indeed the unchanging "Present Time" always exists has a "Heaven" that is anciently said by our wise ancients to be a higher place, the holiest place, a paradise of bliss filled with ecstasy and a place of divinity, goodness, loyalty, faith, joy, happiness, delight, rapture, elation, and other virtues or right beliefs and that it is these descriptions that all our wise ancients say will be experienced in Gods Heavenly home, this being that which exists only in our "Present Time".

Yet wisely they could not say to these ancient listeners that you do not have to die to experience this "Heavenly Home", this being that which rest upon our Earth. For now, is it not historically known that there was much confusion regarding the five senses of the inner body? For thought-filled minds were often believed to be coming from outside and often stated to be coming from evil but outer influences. Nor was it possible to say that living in "Heaven" is always accessible to people but only in the current time and only in accordance to their living within the values of divinity, goodness, loyalty, faith, and all our other known virtues or right beliefs, these being that which can only be expressed in the "Present Time"? But was this real-world was also proposed by Jesus during the Sermon on the Mount when He said: ***"Do unto others as you would have them do unto you".***

So yes! Can it not now be rightfully established and in a modern understanding be said that living in "Heaven" can actually be experienced in the goodness (GodNess) of the mind empty "Present Time" and that living in "Hell", which is truly a lower place and a hellish place and a place that "The Book" explains is the living Hell that can only exist when the mind is filled and so blocked by a Pastor a Future "I Want", which is undoubtedly not Gods world or the world of Nature for the Non- Believer. Therefore is it not an absolute truth that the "Present Time" is an outer body self-experienced and physically known Heaven, which is a factual positive to the actual negative of the inner created "I Want" for Me Hell? Therefore, is it not also a particular truth that only in the "Present Time" can you create an activity which physically silences via self-imposed disciplines', the "I want" desires and commands of the five senses, which genuinely, attach the thinker to the world-known has "Hell".

So Yes! Indeed, this is truly a Heaven that only rests in the "Present Time", and it is an experience of the real bliss of Heaven that indeed rests upon all this Earth in which a person can blissfully experience that which naturally silences via self-established disciplines, the "I want" for ME commands of the five senses, which genuinely, belong to the animal world of Hell, these being those "I Want" thoughts which can only exist in the unreal self-created world of the Past or Future.

Therefore, again, is it not seen to be the real reality, that these five senses shout thoughts into the mind which are attached to a past or a future "I Want" for ME! These false claims being because their "animalistic" five senses shout and cajole into ungodly minds their many untrained "I Want" selfish "animalistic" demands and so these controlling five senses certainly welcome and naturally accept stealing from others excuse such as "I want my religion to be the only religion". Is this being an excuse which supports these "I Want" selfish demands that are created to claim power over others and also their money and goods, therefore, is it not a truth that all can witness when this evil is happening?

For indeed this falsely stated un-religious belief system is just an excuse so that animalistic newly born people can mislead other animalistic natured people and so create a "religious purpose" which can attack and steal from anyone outside their pack. For indeed this can be the only reason why another person's religion is attacked, robbed and whose believers are also killed by these false-believers of a "self-made" un-godly based creed, who live for less than a mini-second when compared to the life of God's Creation? For sadly, is it not the avoiding of the real truth that this false creed, born by these false believers in God, is only pursued because they want to steal that which believers in other religions have in their possession? Therefore is it not an absolute truth that all true religions seek and also show the way to experience the *"Peace that surpasses all understanding"*. For how can you kill and maim others when experiencing this gift from God.

So yes! Is it not "scientifically" correct, just as our world history shows, that because of these unsupported *"I believe that my creed, my religion and my hierarchy system is the only true way to worship God and live in His world"*, that such a person's thought condemns all other worshipping systems to be evil, and therefore compels a worshipper of one religion to attack a worshipper of another religion, this being when both are pursuing their own "private" culturally-based way to find and so live within God's truth. For "The Book" does admit to a slight concern about the future, this being a future that is being sought by some of the hierarchy existing in some parts of our world's major religions who seem to be enforcing their individual "I Want" views regarding the "Freedom of Speech", or in particular the "Freedom of Worship", this being that only their religion is the correct way to worship God. For indeed, this is undoubtedly their culturally-based "I Want" way of worshipping and not a unanimous God based one. For indeed, all people, no matter what is their culture or history, can experience this same Godly based "Enlightenment" that rests only in the "Present Time" and which God, or Nature for the Non-Believer, did give to ALL people and which is a "Present Time" in which the "I want for myself" cannot exist. For really people have everything, and even if they take you to the cross of pain and death as was the Christian Jesus of Nazareth, you will undoubtedly be born again into the bliss that surpasses all understanding; for indeed, it would be a place in which attacking people, these being people whose uncontrolled animalistic five senses do compel them to live in a Hell which is born from a past or a future "I want", will never again remove your life from that in which you live with the *"Peace that surpasses all understanding"*.

So yes! It can now be genuinely said and simply proven to be accurate, that if this "I want" statement of "My creed is better than your creed" is believed, it should be fully understood that this statement is not valid. What is an absolute truth is that anyone can select any creed from any religion or any belief system. While seriously concentrating upon that "creeds" directed activity, then that person will eventually achieve a mind that is silent and obedient to all that exists in the "Present Time". Then honestly, as night follows day, they WILL experience the "Peace that surpasses all understanding", which is the real

Kingdom of Heaven that rest upon God's Earth.

So Yes! It should now be genuinely understood and also "creed"-practised by those seeking "Enlightenment", that this is "The Path and the Way" that all religions and all our wise ancients do direct their followers to accomplish and this is an "Enlightening" way that is always in accordance to their language and culture. For correctly, it is the worshipping of these meditational seeking "creeds" that are culturally pursued by all our world's religions and faiths, these being that activity which brings the doer into the world of God which can only exist in the "Present Time", and honestly there is only ONE word of God, but thousands of different "creed" ways to find it. Yet "Scientifically" all are designed to still the mind and so enable the "worshipping" pursuers Soul, to see through the mind and so experience the "Present Time", which is genuinely Gods world or the world of Nature for the Non-Believer.

Also about the purpose of all our many and numerous ancient and modern religious "praying" practices, these being practices that seek "Enlightenment", it should be agreed that mantra meditation is now known the quickest and most positive way to achieve this "Enlightenment".

This being because individually applied "consciousness" can "re-choose" human "willpower" to disciplinary stop all the "I Want" demands of the five senses that are currently filling the mind and so blocking the view of the Soul from seeing through the empty mind the reality of Gods world or the world of Nature for the Non-Believer, this being a world that can only exist in the Present Time. For indeed, this can be done by the disciplinary sounding of a single word, a fact which is achieved by a "Soul" imposed sounding of a mantra into the mind, for the Soul still controls all the inner working of a person body. Yet, this purpose of controlling unto silence the five senses was "Chosen" to be bypassed around the age of two or three.

But now, and with the eyes closed and between this self-disciplined single "purposely" chanting newly released "mantra word", this being a single word that is arising from your controlled inner energy, this being energy which is emanating from your unfeeling consciousness', then you will know that the true you will begin to "see", the light between the dark clouds for you are genuinely the Soul which "sees" all that is circulating within the mind.

For correctly, this will increasingly happen over many weeks or months until the "habitually" sounding mantra seemingly falls below the viewpoint of the Soul and so is experienced to be like a silent single worded river flowing below the mind. It will be then that you will "KNOW" that you are the viewer, this being that you will "realise" you are the Soul that is witnessing the circling dark clouds that fill the mind and that the light behind these circling clouds is that which we call the "Present Time" for this is the light that can only exist in the stillness of the "Present Time".

Then and with this same view, that when you open your eyes and full view with an empty and still mind this "light", we call the "Creation", then you will "wondrously" realise that without thought you have achieved "Enlightenment" - which is not easily obtained for the "training" of these five senses can be likened to the training of wild pups. It can take time, but you can succeed.

51 "ENLIGHTENMENT" –
THE TARGET OF ALL RELIGIONS

So Yes! "Enlightenment", in which the only existence is the "Present Time", this being an existence in which a mind filled "I Want" for ME cannot exist and yes! I understand (stand under) that this may be a worry for many people who fear the loss of love that they feel in the "thinking" of others, but be assured that in "Enlightenment" the experiencing of the love for the loved ones that you meet becomes so high that it cannot be described but wow! You know that it exists.

But let us now consider "scientifically", the many different Creeds and Worshipping ways that exist within all our religions and philosophies. For justly, they consist of personal and group activities that encompass the faiths, dogma, ideologies, beliefs, and testimonials, all of which are the very principles and foundations of that which activates these self-chosen creeds, these being that which "privately" exists within a person's chosen religion.

For assuredly, this is being a personal creed based way of worship that currently exists in many various and different praying ways, plus the many adjoining regulations that are associated with the worshipping of the one God, which all the many "culturally" different religions and philosophies preach to their worshippers, but in fact, all seek the same goal – which is "Enlightenment", and strictly all have different ways of achieving this experience. But is it not strange, has history proves, that often one religion attacks another religion even when all are seeking "Enlightenment" and of course it also happens within the same religious belief system– Is this not true?

So why does this happen? For indeed it is an actual truth that all worshippers of all the worlds different religions do clearly understand that the search for "Enlightenment" is personal, but is it not also recognised to be a search which purposely needs group support? So is it not true that all those seeking Gods world do so by being attached to a group that has the same cultural beliefs and understandings that they do?

So Yes! Is it not a further truth that each person joins with a likeminded and culturally similar group, thus ensuring that they obtain a privately known group based journey in which all are believed to be seeking to exist in Gods world? Therefore is it not true that we friendly love people and that we like to be with other people who agree, i.e., This being a "Pack", which is historically emanating from our hunter and gathering days.

Therefore is it not then true that we can still "modernly" experience the "cultural" bonhomie from our "personal" existence with our pack of hunter-gathers and also show loyalty to our "pack" leader, this being the one who all recognise to be the most excellent communicator and also the one who we naturally trust to be the most skillful in targeting the best wellbeing of the group. Cannot it also be agreed that democracies and autocracies are based upon this ancient principle in which the "pack" naturally "chooses" to follow the "pack leader", whose "hunting" skills always promise the most significant rewards for the group? But now we also know that around 9,000 years go all this changed when the hunter-gatherers started farming which then created the group based saying "This is MY land, Keep OFF", but can it be true that we are now "understandably" and "culturally" saying the same about religions?

With this understanding in mind, let us look at the two major religions that exist in the Northern Hemisphere and which seek the same definite closeness to God's world which rests upon our Earth, these being the Christian and Islamic faiths.For like all the world's religions they both endeavour to obtain the same experience of that singularity which is named in all religions and philosophies," as "Enlightenment". Indeed, this is being the tremendous experience that brings the mind of the true worshiper of Christianity to the *"peace that surpasses all understanding"* or for Muslims worshippers of the Islam Faith *"Being filled by the Angel Gabriel"* which brings the Islamic praying mind to *"a realm beyond the ability of words to properly convey."*

For assuredly, this is an experience which is "scientifically" explained in "The Book" as being the inner to outer experiencing God's world which comes to all people when they experience "Enlightenment". For indeed this occurs when the Soul has been freed to view and so experience only the "Present Time", which is an actuality that can only be achieved when the mind is silent. For indeed it is this reality that is the target of ALL our worlds different and variable religious and philosophical worshipping systems, for justly all are certainly designed to bring the worshipper a mind emptying silence, created by mind emptying chants and prayers, which will factually bring to the worshipper the experiencing of Gods world or the world of Nature for the Non-Believer.

For again it can be said to be "realised" and so experienced by the "Self" within YOU! This being via these short term mind emptying "prayers", especially chanting exercises such has repetitive praying, this being that which best seeks the "experiencing" of the reality of Gods world, a world that can be experienced to exist in the silent gaps occurring in the mind that the repeating of a creed-based "prayer" does bring to the worshipper.

So yes! The actual reality is that it is only between these silent and now disciplined occurring gaps that the Soul can is enabled to see Gods world or the world of Nature for the Nonbeliever. This reality genuinely being when the undisciplined thoughts of a past or a future "I want" are blocked by the repetitive "self-disciplined" mode of the chanting worshippers prayers. So, under this praying discipline, none of their five senses can send their "I want" thoughts into this now disciplined mind, therefore is it not truly said again and again that it is this continually occurring fact which does effectively block the Souls view through the mind of the "Present Time".

So Yes! Now it is known, that which all our wise ancients knew, this being that it was crucially important for their followers to be able to achieve via a "culturally" introduced system of worship, this being a worshipping system that was firmly based upon the shared beliefs and understanding of their time. But now it can be factually and modernly stated that the purpose of ALL these chants and prayers, these being that which supported our Ancient wises introduced religions and philosophies, was to still the mind. Indeed, this being so that a person inner Soul could see through the still mind the outer world in which it existed and so now freed, it could experience God's world or the World of Nature for the Non-Believer, this being always the world of the "Present Time".

So yes! It is this "true" factual world of the "Present Time" which enlightens itself in the silent gaps between the self-disciplined repeating words of the chosen creed, for it is only through a silent mind that the Soul can witness God's "present" and thus see the harmony that exists or needs supporting in this Heaven that rests upon our Earth. For indeed this being knowledge which is in the understanding of that which is called the experiencing of "Enlightenment," or experiencing the *"peace that surpasses all understanding"* stated by the Christian faith or "a *realm beyond the ability of words to properly convey*" stated by the Muslim faith and it is a reality which occurs when the mind is silent and without any aroused internal thoughts which block the view of the soul from seeing and so not being aware of God's world.

So yes! "Enlightenment" is likened to be being filled by the Holy Spirit or the Angel Gabriel and it is this happening of "Enlightenment", this being the experiencing of the truth that rests in God's world, which is truly a world that cannot be explained in words. For indeed again, it is logically perceived that only God's world is real, this being a reality that can only exist outside of "I want" thoughts?

Therefore is it not an absolute truth that only those images of the past or future "I Want" can be brought into a mind filling personal "thought", which is usually personally "created" to exist in the individuals' mind and which is usually a thought which is exclaiming an "I Want" to for ME to happen! For if you bring the gift of "Enlightenment" into the mind, it immediately brings all thoughts to become an unknown thing of the past and so you only have left the experiencing of God's world for a personal "I Want" thought cannot possibly be of any use in God's world in which you "Self-Realise" that you have everything.

For again, strictly it should be said that if you "think" only of achieving "Enlightenment" for yourself, you will certainly not experience "Enlightenment", for you are seeking a world that can only exist and so be experienced in the "Present Time", this is a time without thought. It is for this reason that the wise ancients say it cannot be understood by the mind of people and that no words can describe it. For it should now be "modernly" known that it is these internal non-human "I want" thoughts which are always emanating from the five senses that do block and fill the mind so that the Soul cannot see or experience God's world or the real world of Nature for the Non-Believer.

So yes! It is also known that both these major Northern Hemisphere religions are founded upon the same root. This root being the recorded messages which are sincerely believed to have been dictated by God via the experiencing of the Holy Spirit, which also came to the prophets Adam, Noah, Abraham, Moses; these being a few of the wise ancients who are worshipped within the creeds of the Christian and the Islamic faiths. It is also known that the

Islamic faith was introduced to the humankind at a later time than the Christian faith, this is being the Christian faith which was primarily based upon the teachings of the Incarnate Jesus of Nazareth, which is known to have been expanded into the Islamic faith by the last of the prophets named Muhammad - **Peace be upon Him.** At this stage, it is imperative to understand that when you mention the name of the principal founder of the Islamic religion, that you add the words *"peace be upon him"* and why is this so? The reason for this is that it is the name of a person who speaks about the "peace" which rests only in the "Present Time", and when this "Enlightenment" comes upon worshippers, it is genuinely an "enlightening" experience. It is this experience which is continually wished upon the Prophet Mohammed. So it reminds all Muslims of the peace that cannot be described, which is genuinely the experiencing of "Enlightenment".

It is also the same experience that is described differently by Christians, but that which both these religions are saying is that it is an experience in which you "feel" the peace and the silence of God's world. You also know precisely just what Gods world is "portraying," and therefore, what it needs to support it in its on-going search for the continuation of harmony.

For regularly, the "Present Time's" unmoving harmony is felt and so experienced by people to be never moving. All should also tactfully know, that the purpose of their own "personal" existence is to support this ever-developing harmony that rests in God's world and so enable the *"peace that surpasses all understanding and which exists in the realm beyond the ability of words to properly convey"* to be upon all people and especially you, dear reader and if you wish to make sure of this – read on.

So yes! It is "scientifically" known to be true that these two religions, as do all religions and philosophies, target their worshipping people to experience the "enlightening" silence of God's world, a world that is described by religious people in the Northern Hemisphere as being filled with the Holy Spirit or likewise, the Prophet Gabriel but also by countless other names, all of which exist in the many religions and philosophies in God's world which also teach ancient "culturally" based ways to achieve this "experience" throughout our world.

For this is an experience that can happen and so is realised by ANY human, but it is also an experience that can only exist when the unthinking mind enters the "Present Time" and so is empty of all "I want" thoughts. For again it can be said, that the experiencing of "Enlightenment" is the target of all our religions and philosophies whose implanted cultural creeds are designed to take the worshipper into the experiencing of "Enlightenment", this being that which rests only in the "Present Time". For again, it is undoubtedly this fact which ensures that all religions and all philosophies, although culturally different are one religion and which is a religion that targets "Enlightenment". Therefore, is it not an absolute truth that all have only one purpose; namely, to bring the worshipper into God's world or the world of Nature for the non-believer.

So yes! It should be clearly understood that this "Enlightenment" is that which can only be experienced when the mind is without any personal "I want" claims, these being "I want" claims which are conjectured by a past or a future dreamed of existence and are thoughts which block the Soul from seeing and experiencing the world of the "Present Time" – Gods world or the world of Nature for the Non-Believer. This being certainty the "Present Time", which is a world from which all "I want" thoughts distract the viewer, for they take the viewing mind of the experiencer into the past or the future – which do not exist, for this is the world that "The Book" calls Hell. Therefore is it not also true that this non-religion and non-philosophical "I want" existence often projects actions that bring discord to the world around this kind of thinker? For, in all honesty, did not the wise ancients consistently targeted an existence which would bring to their followers an experience of the "Present Time" thus being a witness to God's world that rests not only within them but also outside them? For did not all our wise ancients also know of the authentic "Godly" experience, this being that which always pursues a way of living based upon the natural supporting of all God's harmony or the harmony of Nature for the Non-Believer. For truly should not all people know that the way of an "I Want" for me, is not the true birthright or a purpose for has to why people do live.

For again, it is only then, when our five senses are "silently" awaiting the serving of the "Present Time", that the Soul will be enabled to experience and see through the mind and so knowingly understand – stand under -, that which genuinely exists all around it, has it does within it. For truly, it is the Soul within you that silently views all that God or Nature for the non-believer, is presenting to you, including requests for actions to be taken to maintain the harmony that is emerging or striving to exist in the world that is all around you. For certainly is it not said by ALL religions and philosophies that we can live in Heaven while on this Earth, and that this is also that which all the wise ancients who create religions and philosophies speak about; and so, do they not create creeds, prayers and worshipping system to pursue that which is called "Enlightenment"? Therefore, is it not true that ALL our worlds wise ancients perfectively knew that creed worship is the foundation which can lead to "Enlightenment" and if continually practised, moves towards "Self-Awareness" a state in which the observer and observed are known to have one together and on to "self-realisation", a state in which there is no observer only existence, all knowledge and bliss. Again, it should be stated that it is in "Enlightenment", this being that which can only be experienced an empty mind that exists in the "Present Time", which a world that our Non-Christian or Non-Islam religious worshippers call "Paradise", "Nirvana", "Moksha", Kenshō and many other names which are all explained to be the description of a world in which only a "stillness" exists, this "Stillness" being described as Gods world or the World of Nature for the Non-Believer. It is also named by our many other world's religions and philosophies under such names have *"destiny", "fate", "luck", "karma", "kismet", "chance", "providence", "serendipity", "coincidence", "accident",* etc. which attempts to describe an experience that can only happen in the "Present Time". Yet, it should also be genuinely known that it is the "Mother of the Creation" harmony that is being experienced, for this is the harmonising of the ever-developing laws of God or Nature for the Non-Believer in which the supporting aid of people is also sought.

So yes! People can stop the five senses from blocking the mind with their animalistic personal "I want" demands, and this is genuinely arriving at the condition "To Be or Not to Be," which the great English poet Shakespeare spoke about, for indeed, this is the purpose of our world's many creed-worshipping prayers, which are all designed to bring the doer to "Enlightenment".

For again, it is good to say that the way to "Enlightenment" is the preaching target of all our wise ancients; for indeed, it is an experience of living within the harmony that only exists in the "Present Time", this being the only time in which God's world or Natures world for the Non-believer can exist, for actually to achieve this "Enlightening" experience is the purpose of life itself.

For accurately is this not also the way of an authentic life that is described by the words of the incarnate Jesus who said: *"When you are brought before synagogues, rulers and authorities do not worry about how you will defend yourselves or what you will say, for the Holy Spirit will teach you at that time what you should say?"* Meaning that in an "unthinking" person's mind there is only the "Present Time", a time which will produce the words that will reveal to all "I Want for Me" thinkers, the right direction towards the harmony that is continuously endeavouring to emerge all around them. For assuredly, is it not also known to be accurate, as history shows, that harmony will always prevail, even when it is denied by mistaken humans. For rightly is this fact not also revealed to be true when the "Enlightened" incarnate Jesus also added: *"but anyone who speaks against the Holy Spirit, will not be forgiven, either in this age or in the age to come,"* this being a message to those who go against the "Enlightened" work of "Mother of the Creation" who can be recognised to be the "Holy Spirit". Therefore it can be said that the "Father of the Creation" is God, and the creators of our major religions and philosophies' can indeed be described as being the children of God. Therefore "Scientifically" and under "Natural Law" this is being a controlling system of unchanging moral principles which is regarded as a basis for all human conduct, this being that which is named as the "Holy Spirit", who is undoubtedly the "Mother of the Creation".

Therefore, is it not certainly true that it is the "Mother of the Creation" who, like all mothers, is continually endeavouring to establish the harmony that supports their only child; for Jesus also clearly explains that any person who tries to destroy the "Mother of the Creation" harmony, that these evil perpetrators of disharmony will live without harmony *"in this age"* but also in their next life to come.

Thus *"in the age to come",* they will be born again, but maybe not as humans for their Soul may be born again as a lower species which has no freedom of choice and can only live by accepting the harmony that surrounds them – an honest and ethical existence. For factually, this will again teach that there is a need to obey the laws of harmony that are controlled by the "Mother of the Creation", these being motherly disciplines which can be likened to that of all mothers who care for and love their children.

So yes! Again it can be said that the tremendous experience of "Enlightenment" gained by "Creed Worship" of our many religions and philosophies, is designed to bring to the mind of a true worshipper the "Peace that surpasses all understanding" and which exists in the "Realm beyond the ability of words to convey properly," as explained in Christian worship and which is also explained to the Muslim worshipper. For indeed, this is "Enlightenment", and it is a realisation which cannot be explained in words, for the "Present Time" cannot be brought to thought, for all thoughts take the observer away from Gods creation or Natures creation for the Non-Believer. For accurately, this being because the creation that is all around us and also within us, is a creation that cannot be examined with thought, for only self-created images of the past or the future can be brought into "thought". For again to speak the truth is always to state that "Enlightenment" can only be experienced when the mind is without any personal "I want" claims that can continuously emanate from the five senses. For truly, these thoughts are that which block the Soul from seeing God's "Present Time". For again it can be said that these many never-ending "I want" personal claims, which are conjectured by the claiming or the doing of a past or a future dreamed "I Want", creates and an existence which often projects upon other persons "I Want" private or group pursued desires and so perpetrates actions that "naturally" bring discord to the world around them.

So yes! Within a world history that is born from those who are "Enlightened" or who are seeking "Enlightenment", it is clear to be seen as a truth, that all people can experience that which exists in the "Present Time" and which they can support to exist but only within the silence emanating from the Soul which is not born from any "I want" human reasoning. For accurately, this search for "Enlightenment" is a creed sought a target that was always explained by our wise ancients who regularly taught a "Support the Creation" way of life for their followers, which was a way of life that could only exist in the "Present Time". For assuredly, is it not now easily seen to be true that our wise ancients always endeavoured to teach their followers how to pursue their many creed-based exercises which they installed and recited by the regenerative ability and strength of the individual worshipper's willpower.

For indeed, they sought to achieve the ability within their followers to personally use their inner consciousness to disengage their willpower from habitually and automatically allowing it to activate the desires of the five senses. This malicious activity is because, in childhood, the "thinker" believed that these inner "I want" thoughts were coming because of their personnel needs. It was this mistaken belief that historically allowed the individual to "habitually" and "automatically" activate within their mind a personal "I want" that was emanating from the five senses, this being because they mistakenly "thought" that it was them that was talking in their minds, it is not them because you cannot be that which you observe or listen to just as you cannot be that which you taste, smell or touch. For indeed it was their teaching and efforts that brought many of their followers to experience "Enlightenment", which also our many wise ancients named, according to the culture in which they lived such as the *"Holy Spirit"*, *"Holy Ghost"*, *"Paradise"*, *"Eden"*, *"Heaven"*, *"Nirvana"*, *"Promised Land"*, *"Moksha"*, *"Shangri-La"*, *"Kenshō"*, *"Svargamu"*, *"Kā bāga"*, *"Vāṭikā"*, *"Kā jagaha"*, *"Sukhabhavana"* and many other names and to realise that the best and most beautiful things in the world cannot be seen or even touched. They must be inwardly and silently experienced, to exist and then be appreciated without thought – for this is truly God's world or the world of Nature for the Non-Believer

52 GOD OR NATURE DOES NOT PUNISH PEOPLE

It is agreed that many who are seeking God or desiring to understand religion, find it strange that in many past or current religions it was "suggested" by our wise ancients that God punished people but only if they broke His laws. This statement is not interpreted accurately, this being because our wise ancients knew that the "punisher" was themselves, for God does not punish people to whom He has given the "Freedom of Choice".

Therefore, it is even stranger that the followers of some of our world's religious leaders are often requested to severely punish other people because they have a different system of worshipping God. Again it can be said that this is simply because these other people worship God by religiously obeying and following a different creed that seeks the realisation of the same truth. So is it not true that this condemning of others is an "I Want" more power over others – which is emanating from these false religious leaders who are genuinely using religion to pursue their personal needs.

For indeed these attacks upon others means that while these people worship and profess to believe in God, they also pursue the greatest sin, which is the killing or the harming of other people because they worship with a culturally different creed based system than the one that their culture uses to bring them into God's world, this being that which exists for all people, but only in "Present Time".

For justly, this is the attacking of others because they worship the same God but differently, this is an incorrect viewpoint, for it cannot be correct for all Godly based reasoning states that such killings or the harming of others cannot be a truth that emanates from God. For such a religious creed, which has been born to worship God but then, begins to preach the killing or harming of other people because they do not follow their own chosen creed's "laws" – cannot be correct. For such a system of punishing others because of a different creed or way of worship could never have been supported by our wise ancients.

For justly, has it not been said many times by our many wise ancients **"Thou shalt not kill"**, and also **"You shall not murder"**, for is this not also a moral judgement that is instigated by ALL our world's ancient wise who created our world's major religions and philosophies? Is it not therefore undoubtedly true that God or Nature for the Non-Believer, did seed that child which we call the "Creation"?

Also is it not a truth that this single child exists has a similar unification of those parents which created its life? Is it not also true that within this created child was also that part which we call a people? Who has all our religions and philosophies state, was the only part of this singularity that was given the "Freedom of Choice". Also did not our ancient wise state that this "Freedom of Choice" was to enable the physical supporting of the developing needs of the other parts of this only child, just as we do with our bodies? Yet is it not also true that the same act can support or destroy that which is being created, all of which is depending upon developing circumstances.

Nor should it be imagined and again it should NOT be stated, that the Creator of the Universe can become angry, and so desire to kill, persecute or harm a person because He dislikes them and or dislikes what they are doing! For certainly is it not true that God is known by ALL religions and ALL philosophies to have given to ALL people the *"Freedom of Choice"*? For really, this is being *"Freedom of Choice"* gift that has been given to ALL people so that they can support the harmony that exists within the needs of the emerging Creation, especially likened to the harmony that is similar to that which exists within the bodies of all Life and Non-Life and which in many ways surrounds them. For rightly, is it not true that one act can support this emerging harmony yet the same act at a different time could destroy it?

So yes! How can God or Nature for the Non-Believer, punish a person for using a gift that was parentally given to them? Therefore, is it not also true that if a person's father or mother gives to their child the freedom of choice to support the harmony that exists around their home, and then by choice that child breaks this harmony, does the child's father or mother brutally punish that child – of course not, for is it not true that they would teach the child what is correct and what is not a correct? Is this not true? Also, how many of our wise ancients have wandered this world in the performing of this same activity?

So Yes! So it is with God's world or the world of Nature for the Non-Believer, for again is it not true that just as an ongoing personal life will always prove the fact that if you follow, obey and support God's laws, or Natures laws for the Non-Believer, that many pleasing things will happen to you? But yes, if you do the opposite and break God's law, then does not history show that displeasing things will happen to you?

But is it not logically known that it is not God or Nature that is punishing you. In essence, it is your own false negative "I Want" for me, this being a law that is clashing with the favourable harmonising and emerging laws of the Creation. Therefore, it is yourself that can be creating your pain and conflicts, this being a catastrophe within your present life, but if it is "others" that do this to you, rest assured that they will be dealt with accordingly, for woe unto them, as ALL our wise ancients' do prophesize.

So Yes! The truth must be that the selfish punishing or killing of another person for pursuing a different creed system is an "I Want" all the property that they have. Again, this being a fact which is caused by greed-based "I Want" their possessions or an "I Want" the status of those I destroy. But yes, is it not also complicated to believe that God or Nature for the Non-Believer, would punish an individual who, upon leaving their youthful teens had also been given another fifty years or more years to live! Therefore, does not this life span prove that we cannot be living in a world in which a powerful God fearfully attacks and destroys people who have purposely been given the "Freedom of Choice"? For indeed, is it not seen by people that ALL God's laws exist in a harmony which steadily combines to support that which exists all around them, just has it does within the body of all that lives? Therefore, is it not an absolute truth that people's only real choice is to support this harmony, for they could never destroy it or even change its pursuit – although many people have tried and all have failed to do so?

So yes! Silently look around you in the "Present Time" and so understand that the "Present Time" is a time that cannot contain thought. So it is good and natural to be a silent witness to the harmony of a Creation whose stillness is that which is always there and also "unfeelingly" emerging to be there, and so it will continue to be so all around you as it is within you. If not currently emerging around because of personal intervention, it may be waiting for you to develop it personally – for it MUST return from the "I Want" for me dream world and it WILL support you unto and after death, but only in the "Present Time".

This fact is indeed being the truth behind God's laws of Natures laws for the Non-Believer, for has previously stated it is God's laws or Natures laws for the Non-Believer which control all of life and None-Life and so honestly a person's life can be explained and likened to the laws of a "people" created "Highway Code" of the road. For all drivers know that the Highway Code consists of laws made by people that have been created to govern all our civilised countries' traffic control systems. This "Highway Code" law being self "created" by people so that all personally driven traffic can travel from one destination to another destination and be able to achieve travelling safely. For they are specific laws which have been designed to allow a qualified person to drive within the harmony seeking laws of this creation made by people towards a destination of their choosing and it indeed governs the way of life for the driver.

Thus, any "on-going" driving pursuit can also be likened to a person's life, this being a life which starts at one destination and is continually moving to another destination as people do "drive" through time and grow older. This truth explains that if a person endeavours to drive through a city by ignoring the "Highway Code", then they will encounter many problems associated with their journey, which they will not like, for they will be severely punished by these laws that are controlling this "Highway Code" created by people. It is also the same when travelling within God's "Highway Code" or Natures "Highway Code" for the Non-Believer; this being the many controlling laws that exist within the world of nature that is always all around us.

Simply put, this means that if you pursue and travel within the laws of the creation of harmony, you will arrive comfortably and safely at your destination. Still, if you ignore the "highway code" of this existing harmony, you will "naturally" encounter many difficulties which are often described as being punished – but who is punishing you? Is it the creator of these laws? Of course not! For again this can be likened to travelling through a city and disobeying that city's "Highway Code" and then having an accident. Is it the city that is punishing you? Of course not! It can only be yourself that is harming you, and it can also be agreed that you could be creating many accidents in which others are hurt.

So yes! The "Highway Code" within God's creation or Natures creation for the Non-Believer certainly exists. It is that "Highway Code" which always and naturally exists all around us just has it does within us and is it not also a further well-known fact that within this "Highway Code" within our living creation, that it is only people who have been given the "Freedom of Choice". This truth is why people have been created has "drivers" because people are needed to support this emerging and creating harmony, this continuing "Highway Code" of life that continually exists in the created world that is all around YOU! Therefore is it not also true that we need to create traffic lights, one-way streets, safe crossings etc. For really this is being that which protects the nature of our growing world?

So Yes! Therefore merely put, the reason for this "Freedom of Choice" is to allow people to be permitted to "choose" how to aid the Creation's positive on-going development and so aid the bringing of peace to all our Earths living and non-living travellers. For indeed, the evolving creation is always targeting the development of harmony; however, it always needs a "physical" supporting activity which can be genuinely understood to be similar to the "Highway Code". Therefore is this example of the "Highway Code" not a good metaphor to explain the factual reality that it is only people who are the "Sugar in the Water" and that it is undoubtedly only people who can support this emerging reality? Unquestionably, this being a reality in which it is understood that it is only people that have been created to support the developing of God's harmony or Nature's harmony for the Non-Believer, a fact that can only be achieved in the "Present Time".

So Yes! Again, with this known truth we can be genuinely puzzled as to the reason why some people continuously break the "Highway code" of the "Creation" and so purposely cause discomfort to many people and even to the developing nature that exists all around them? Also, as a further metaphor, it can be explained that the "Highway Code" of God's harmony is also known to be governing the expanding number of people that are being created upon this planet.

For cannot it also be said that new life, especially a life with a Soul that can only exist in people, must be coming from the deaths occurring within the shrinking animal kingdom? Simply put, this metaphor, which is based upon a naturally seen and existing truth, would explain that when these new entrants who have just been given a Soul, enter the Kingdom of Heaven that exists upon our Earth, a very "non-understanding" fear is provoked within the body of that new entrant.

For assuredly, is it not also known that fear is a strong motivator, which means that our new entrants do not understand the harmony that exists around them and so can easily and in ignorance, animalistic ally destroy it – which means that this new entrant has no naturally focused past or developed personal values that are based upon the "Freedom of Choice", this being that which exists only in people. What this metaphor or the above reality means, is that when a person breaks the "Highway Code" of legally made a law, this being that which is designed to support God's harmony or Natures harmony for the Non-Believer.

They should not be treated like animals and placed into a zoo to live their lives in a cage from which they are continually being freed only to unwittingly and habitually return to this cage, again and again, this being a truth which our current times do show. Also is it not true that we can imprison any wild animal in a cage for months or years. Always when released, it will return to the only life it knows in which their animalistic "I Want" will be observed, this being that which then breaks the "Highway Code" laws made by people, hence they are returned to prison. Therefore, is it not a fact that in most major countries 70 per cent of released prisoners are arrested within three years of release, and 80 per cent within five years of release and this is an ongoing situation therefore factually over 80% of people in prison have been in prison previously. Therefore, should not these newcomers to a life that is lived by people and who habitually break the harmony of the community, be placed into a friendly co-habiting situation such as a self-contained village? For cannot this special "enclosed" and therefore fenced-in village be a community which is separated some distance away from those people who live in a world which they do not fully understand, and which probably confuses them. For in their many past lives, their "I Want" was always intensely naturally pursued and obeyed regardless of how it was achieved.

Therefore is it not true that in this self-contained community's village world, which those people who can be recognised as newcomers to a "Freedom of Choice" world, can be naturally and habitually conditioned, by a good example, to live within the "Highway Code" of the people's harmony based upon the freedom that now exists around them. This being that the bonhomie which is created within this enclosed village to be of the same laws and regulations that exist in the outside world from which they came but which does not scare or confuse them. Therefore, is it not the truth, that in such a village that they will have constant "secure" via a freed group guidance, for fear of singularity is the most primitive and primordial of all our biological responses, and it can hold such a new-birthed as a person a hostage for a long time.

Therefore the current bullying of such imprisoned people should be avoided for is it not true that many animals will fearfully attack that which threatens them, ask any prison officer. Yet truly, fear exists to be conquered and a good creed whether personal or "Creation" made, can always accomplish this task; for the peaceful path towards "Enlightenment" can so easily be achieved when recognised, for is it not by using similar "bonhomie" activity that ALL new drivers are professionally taught how to "live" within the "highway code", this being when they wish to become a driver, just as our metaphorical newcomers need to be also taught how to journey through a life that is lived and controlled by people?

Therefore, is it not certainly true that a false "I Want" for me, this being an illusion which can contaminate the world that exists around and within many people. For indeed, are we not fragile things which often ignorantly believe that we were born to pursue many a personal "I Want" for me! Undeniably, this being an " I Want for ME" that is undoubtedly being a course of action which we now know to be weaknesses that can distract us from the positive potential of our real existence. Therefore, is it not now clear for all to see that a person's existence is based upon their need to accomplish the many agreements seeking positive acts that support the emerging harmony of the developing Creation? For are these not genuinely being a supporting of the "Creations" acts that are always there so that we can happily conjoin with them and also faithfully and naturally recognise another person's cultural strengths. From this knowledge, we can constitute meetings to discuss that which we do not fully understand, for sure, this is also including the understanding of another person's culture and or their religion?

Therefore, the meeting of new cultures and or their religions should not be seen as a disadvantage likened to the creations forbidden "I Want", this being that which claims that only my countries laws and only my religious way of life are the correct ones? For basically is it not always seen to be true that our wise people can enjoy a rapid and ever-developing short cut to their innate ability to recognise harmony seeking "differences", this being that truth which exists in other religions and philosophies?

This being also a fact which is seen by any person seeking enlightenment, for justly they will recognise that these differences will also bring harmony to the believer of the truth that rests within God's world or the world of Nature for the Non-Believer. For again basically, is it not fascinating when people of different religions begin to live together and of course in their joining together, defeating and silencing the "I Want" of the five senses, which is a development that will always develop into more extended periods of "Enlightening" consciousness, this being that which also gives strength to support any new "Enlightening" seeking development. Therefore it does not matter which religion or philosophy that a person is attached to and also believes in, for is it not true that all religious and philosophical targets are the same?

So yes! In God's world or the world of Nature for the Non-Believer, it is not realistic to attack different cultures or religions. For simply put the really desired and so informative quest is to understand the differences within their searching for "enlightenment" and also any "personally" established understandings, this being that which is resting within these cultures and religions. For correctly, such new discourses and understandings of other cultures and religions is an activity which always removes the "I Want" fear, this being an animalistic fear which can personally target and pursue to destruction, all of that which is "different" and so cannot be "valued", or "taken" or "controlled" by their animalistic "I Want" for me!

For rightly, this personal "I Want" for me, is an un-supporting activity which is NOT in God's world, this being that which we see around us has a newly developing fast communicating world in which all people can currently recognise a world that is now expanding into a global union. Therefore, is it not also true that this is originating from a self-communicating global union that cannot be stopped, and which is a union of people that can so easily be witnessed to be that which also cannot be stopped and which is truly happening within our current age? Therefore, is it not true that we can see the world's hemispheres begin to unite into one that accepts our many diverse cultures, religious and philosophical creeds – but would it not be good if we could do this without any economic "I Want" for my country, which is an "I Want for Me!" war? For justly, does not our world's history show that there is always a great woe coming to those who perform these attacking and destroying acts upon another's countries culturally different people, these being people whose search for harmony is different?

Yet sincerely, this inflicted woe that these invaders experience is undoubtedly a "Heavenly" based punishment which, as history continually shows, is a punishment created upon greedy people who perform contrary acts that target other countries positive acts, which are usually forestalled by the "highway code" of God's or Natures harmony seeking endeavours. For indeed, in the "Creations" world of harmony, there can be no unwarranted punishment, so woe to the constant instigators of an "I Want" that leads to the destruction of another countries harmony, for logically and metaphorically speaking, when they die, God laws or Natures laws for Non-Believer will naturally relocate their Soul into the animal or insect kingdom, for them to learn again the actual reason why people have been given the freedom of choice.

So yes! Now the debatable question must be "Is there a God or a well-meaning Nature for the Non-Believer?" The answer within "The Book" must always be YES! Therefore, indeed there is an experience that can occur within a person's life, this being that life which is experienced when their "I Want" for me is removed. So they become first Self-Aware that all that which they observe and experience is themselves. It is also often and justly stated by our many wise ancients that this "Self-Aware" experience can then lead to "Self-Realisation", this being a condition in which one becomes the "Creation", for there is no observer, this being that actuality in which both conditions are called "Enlightenment." For assuredly, has all our ancient wise did religious and philosophical indicate, that it can be a proof that this singularity of everything can be experienced has truth and that it is a silent existence of a harmony that surrounds all life and all Non-Life and which is also a life in which it is "experienced" that God's "observing" always exists along with the *Mother of the Creation"* s constant "caring". For accurately and honestly, when we look at ALL people that exist around us, is it not easy to see which person obeys the quiet, undemanding Soul and which person does not? Does this Godly question not also expand into a question asking who can prove that the Soul is a separate individual's world, or is it firmly attached to a single Soul that exists within all people? Genuinely Truly, no one can answer this question. Yet, it can be "truly" stated that ALL people are conscious and so are intelligent beings that are separated from the animal kingdom because they have the "Freedom of Choice" and this can even be classed as a personal choice whether to live or whether to die, which no animal possesses.

So yes! Does our current and recent history not also show that many people have been treated as NOT having Souls and as NOT having sentient nor intellectual properties and therefore NOT being entitled to any personal rights or even being allowed to continue within their peaceful harmonic way of life? Yet is it not also, by contrast, seen to be accurate, that God's ever-developing laws of harmony are currently and always changing this viewpoint. For indeed, is it not correct that in the recent past, did not some religious or other creeds consider other people as being not good people, simply because they looked different?

For do these behaviorally change in our very recent history not show the fact that God created a world based upon harmony, and that this was in existence for all life and Non-Life? Is this not further proof that this world is factually known to be "always" seeking a harmonious truth? Is it not also true that what is "always" slowly gathering strength is the understanding that people's rights are the same for ALL our worlds' people? Although "metaphorically" speaking, and has previously stated, it is also true that new entrants who are becoming people for the first time and who are emanating from the animal kingdom, may have difficulty in understanding this harmony seeking reality. For certainly is it not undoubtedly true that they have had many previous lives in which they understood that only their own personal "I Want" did exist. Therefore they do not now fully understand the real purpose of life has a person? Also, and sadly these maybe our top political leaders for greed and fear are powerful motivators.

So yes! Is it not also true that all people do inwardly and automatically understand and so inwardly experience that which is needed to realise a sentient intelligence plus self-awareness and also a personal "Freedom of Choice". For is this not a freedom of choice which is given only to a people, so that people can be allowed to integrate with the harmony that exists or is endeavouring to emerge into existence all around them! For certainly is it not also an actual reality that God's gifts are for all people or is it "thought" that makes a person think that God's or Nature's gifts are only for them? For it genuinely can be "scientifically" stated that God's primary gift to people is based upon "Freedom of Choice". Yet, truly and again, is this not so that people can wisely support the developing harmony that exists all around them? Is it not also true that this gift of a "Freedom of Choice" can only exist or be experienced in the "Present Time"?

So yes! Indeed, can it not also be metaphorically stated that it could still exist within a person that an ancient past life's animalistic illusion can still create a personal fear. This personal life is being a fear of anything that is not a personal

"I Want?" Therefore can it now be said that it is this "animalistic" illusion that brings to the thinker a fear which cannot accept the harmony which exists within another animal's culture which stops it from gainfully seeking the knowledge that brings understanding and acceptance of another way of life – this being has a person?

So yes! Animalistic ignorance within people often brings fearful illusions which are all based upon an unknown past or an unknown future in which there exists many contradicting "I Want" thoughts. Therefore again is this not truly that same fear that occurs when an animal finds a "difference" in another's animals culture. Therefore, is it not an inevitable truth that in God's world or the world of Nature for the Non-Believer, this being that exists upon our Earth, we know that there exists within all people a life always lived via a differing culture, this being a culture that which ensures a historical understanding and acceptance of that countries personal history.

Is this not also an accepted culture which always returns to the ever-changing "self-contained" harmony, that has grown in that country over time, and does this fact not cover all that which favourably or unfavourably brought to exist within all cultures. For again is it not true that God's harmony seeking world does not stand still, and the continuing amalgamation and joining together of all the worlds' cultures is an ever and very ancient onward development.

So Yes! In all honesty, Truly, does our world's history not also show that God's harmony seeking laws are still "privately" developing the harmony that is bringing together all cultures that exist amongst the environment of all the worlds' nations and countries? Yet sadly! Does not our Earths history also show that this animalistic ignorance always fearfully tries to replace God's harmony and so these new entrants from the animal kingdom are known to say to other people: "I will say what you can choose and what you cannot choose," and was this "animalistic" law not also applied to control the many who were born within different races, cultures, religions and philosophies?

So yes! Is it not also exceptionally and indeed seen, that ALWAYS this entire "animalistic" created disharmony is moving into a historical past? For assuredly, is it not true that thanks to the harmony based thoughts that God gave to all people, many people are now historically recognising the possibility that all cultures and religions have a right to follow their own creeds peacefully, this being a superior living fact which based upon their own "choices," these being choices that they believe will bring all the worlds, people, closer to living in God's Heaven, that rests upon this Earth and even beyond this current Earths development and into a newly born future life.

For truthfully, it is God's laws or the laws of Nature for the Non-Believer, that has currently brought many people of different cultures to live together in acceptance of a mixed harmony; for correctly the Creation itself is a harmonised way of expanding all things together into one unity in which people call a "singularity". Therefore can it not be said to be true that all people exist has many variable and different sentient beings? Does this not mean that people are all personally aware of "Individuality"? So is it not genuinely known that all people are conscious of their existence and their actions? Therefore, what is now also known to be sure is that God or Nature for the Non-Believer, gave to people the "Freedom of Choice;" especially concerning the rights of a peaceful and equal way for all the worlds people to live. For certainly people are aware that this freedom of choice is God's gift to all people – this being the right to "choose" those actions which bind together the harmony that is continually striving to exist all around them. It is also wise to understand that all life is aided by God's world, which can be likened to gravity. You don't have to believe in it for it to be working in your current life.

So yes! People have a choice, and the most exceptional choice that exists within all of the people is the right to target that which ALL religions and philosophies target, which is to experience "Enlightenment". For indeed this is the solitary non-differing experience that is pursued by all our world's religions and all our worlds' philosophies, for all religions and philosophies genuinely know the way to experience God's "Present Time". For this is the Heaven that rests upon this Earth, and it can genuinely and physically be experienced by any believer or Non-Believer and if you wish to experience this gift from God or Nature for the Non-Believer, this being that to which all our scriptures lead us? Then the next chapters will lead you to this "Enlightenment"…….. So read on.

53   THE TRUE BELIEF OF CHRISTIAN, ISLAM AND ALL RELIGIOUS TEACHINGS

So yes! Our wise ancients, by their creeds and prayers, took their many followers away from the "I Want" for myself world, and into a world in which they experienced God's real world, based upon a Godly harmony. For cannot it be said that in a creed supported, this being a real-world of like-minded religious and philosophical followers, that everything you need you already has? For genuinely, is it not said that all could witness that it is only in God's Heaven ruled world, this being that which rests only in the "Present Time", that all that is needed is provided for everyone and also for all other life and non-life. For truly is not the "Present Time" the only place that "Enlightenment" can be experienced; this also is an experience that Non-Believers can witness.

So yes! Many religions and all faiths indeed began when "Enlightenment" was first experienced, such as in the Islamic faith which began with the Prophet Muhammad, -blessed be his name - who, at the age of forty, received his first "Enlightened" revelation from God through the Angel Gabriel, which the Christians call the "The Holy Spirit". These revelations of the Prophet Muhammad continued for twenty-three years, and they are collectively known to have been written down and so preached in the Quran in which Muhammad placed all the revelations that he received after being "Enlightened". So he truly acclaimed that he had experienced God's world.

For it is true that we can also look to the Islamic religion which also correctly describes "Enlightenment," as *"Ruh al-Qudus"*, meaning to experience "the Holy One" or "the Exalted One", which the Quran explains to be ***"a realm*** *beyond the ability of words to convey properly,"* and which is also stated to be an experience that can be self-realized, and kindled within oneself, like a holy fire which is also stated in the Holy Quran: *sura 2 (Al- Baqara), ayat 87* [2]. *"And verily we gave unto Moses the Scripture, and We caused a train of messengers to follow after him, and We gave unto Jesus, son of Mary, clear proofs (of Allah's sovereignty), and we supported him with the Holy Spirit."* *And it was also stated, "Of those messengers, some of them We have caused to excel others, and there are some unto whom Allah spake, while some of them He has exalted in degree; and We gave Jesus, son of Mary, clear proofs (of Allah's sovereignty) and We supported him with the Holy Spirit."* – Qur'an, sura 2 (Al-Baqara), ayat 253 [3] in the same meaning that being supported by the Holy Spirit is to experience "Enlightenment".

This truth, spoken of regarding the experience of "Enlightenment" within the Islamic teachings, is mentioned several times in the Quran. It is also clearly stated that the "Holy Spirit is a description of "Enlightenment" which is interpreted by Muslims as God's messenger; who was also named Gabriel, for indeed, the Quran states this to be accurate as in:

Quran, sura 16 (An-Nahl), ayat 102 al-ruh al-amin ("the faithful/trustworthy spirit"), *in the Quran – "When I have fashioned him (in due proportion) and breathed into him of My Spirit, fall ye down in obeisance unto him."* Thus describing the experience of "Enlightenment" for simply put: from the silence of the "Enlightenment", which is described here as Gods Spirit, is born all right and correct actions.

Quran, sura 32 (As-Sajda), ayat 9 [8]

"Raised high above ranks (or degrees), (He is) the Lord of the Throne (of Authority): by His Command doth He send the Spirit (of inspiration) to any of His servants he pleases, that it may warn (men) of the Day of Mutual Meeting." Simply put again; that from the silence of "Enlightenment" (when being filled with the Holy Spirit) is naturally born all right actions.

Quran, sura 40 (Ghafir), ayat 15 [9]

"Thou wilt not find any people who believe in God and the Last Day, loving those who resist God and His Apostle, even though they were their fathers or their sons, or their brothers, or their kindred. For such, He has written Faith in their hearts and strengthened them with a Spirit from Himself."

Simply put from "Enlightenment" is born all right actions and the understanding and the experiencing of all knowledge that all people are the children of God.

– Quran, sura 58 (Al-Mujadila), ayat 22 [10]

"And Mary the daughter of 'Imran, who guarded her chastity;

And We gave to her of Our Spirit, and she testified to the truth of the words of her Lord Jesus and of His Revelations and was one of the devout (servants)." Mary was obedient to the silence of the all-knowing "Enlightenment," which brings to a person true knowledge of God.

It is also undoubtedly true, as stated in the religious teachings of the Muslims, that the Holy Spirit used in the Muslim term *"Ruh al-qudus"* also refers to the Holy Spirit as being the archangel Gabriel, this in accordance to the Quran which states that the Holy Spirit was assigned by God to reveal the teachings of the Quran to the Prophet Muhammad who by experiencing "Enlightenment" inwardly realised all truths according to his capabilities. For the archangel, Gabriel, who is said to be the bearer and bringer of "Enlightenment", was also chosen by the Muslim religion to be the Holy Angel who delivered the annunciation to Mary, the mother of Jesus. For it is genuinely, indicated in the **Quran in sura Maryam ayat 16-21,** that it was the angel Gabriel who gave to Mary the tidings that she was to have a son of "Immaculate Conception: This being the Jesus of the Christian faith.

It is also stated in the Quran that the angel Gabriel, represented as the Holy Spirit, did accompany Muhammad during the *"Mi'raj",* meaning that Muhammed was experiencing "Enlightenment" which is described as Muhammad's ascension to Heaven in which it is said that Muhammed was instructed about the manner of Islamic prayer – clearly indicating that Muhammed was in an "Enlightened" condition. For this is further said to be the night upon which the Quran was first revealed to Muhammed and this *"peace that surpasses all* understanding" which is always experienced by people when encountering "Enlightenment," which is the "experience" created within a person when the five senses have become disciplinarily silenced, this being that which allows a person's inner Soul to see and experience the bodies outside world. Again it is useful to remember that the Quran explains this Enlightened condition as being *"a realm beyond the ability of words to convey properly"* which again is the same experience which is stated by many Christians to be the *"peace that surpasses all* understanding." For genuinely, this is the target of all our world's religions and philosophies, for it means that the worshipper who truly worships, will stop their mind from entering the chattering "I Want" world, a world which is based upon their past and future desires. For it is undoubtedly true that upon doing so, they will achieve the experience of a mind that is feeling the "Present Time" –God's Heaven upon this Earth. Again being known by Muslim worshippers as *"a realm beyond the ability of words to properly convey"* or as the Christian worshipper says the *"peace that surpasses all understanding"* for it is an experience that cannot be described for in the describing of it… You must leave it.

So yes! The Islamic teaching as with all the many religions and philosophies that exist upon our Earth is Muhammad's way to arrive at the truth that is clearly explained and exists in the Holy book, known as the Quran. But in particular, it was the wise Muhammad who, gifted with messages from the archangel Gabriel, regarded by many to be the Holy Spirit, this being that which brings to the practitioner the experience which the Quran describes as "Enlightenment", for accurately it could only have been within the experiencing of "Enlightenment" that God could reveal the Quran to the Prophet Muhammad.

It is also reported in the Muslim "Hadith", this being the collected creeds, traditions, teachings, and stories of the prophet Muhammad, that all of these "Hadith" words are accepted as a source of Islamic doctrine and, second only to the Koran. This being from the experiencing of the Angel Gabriel which is described in "The Book" as the mind fulfilling of "Enlightenment" as the Soul of the individual has been enabled to recognisable join within the unity of God's Creation. It is genuinely also known that this experience did accompany Muhammad during the Mi'raj, this being his ascension to the "Heaven" where Muhammad is said to have met other messengers of God. This being truly an experience of "Enlightenment," for it is the experiencing of "Enlightenment" that always allows a person to experience God's Heaven that exists upon this Earth. For again and sincerely, this experience of encountering "Enlightenment" is the actual encountering of the Heaven that rest upon this Earth. Therefore, it is known that Muhammad experienced that "Enlightening" and personal condition in which no selfish thought can exist. It was therefore within this "Enlightened" experience that Muhammad was instructed about the manner of the Quran and Islamic prayers, these being that which recount this "Enlightening" experience of Muhammad, this is being the night in the last ten days of the holy month of Ramadan, which is said to be the night on which the Quran was first revealed to Muhammad. Indeed and truly, Muhammad was fully Enlightened and so actually experienced God's Heaven upon this Earth, this again being known by Muslim worshippers as *"a realm beyond the ability of words to properly convey"* or as the Christian worshipper says the *"peace that surpasses all understanding"* for it is an experience that cannot be described for in the describing of it… You must leave it and so it cannot be described.

So yes! The Islamic teaching as with all the many religions and philosophies that exist upon our Earth is also actually Muhammad's way to arrive at the truth that is clearly explained to exists in the Holy book, known as the Quran. But in particular, it was the wise Muhammad who, gifted with messages from the archangel Gabriel, regarded by many to be the Holy Spirit, but which is also that which the Quran describes as "Enlightenment". For accurately, it could only have been within the experiencing of "Enlightenment" that God could reveal the Quran to the Prophet Muhammad.

It is also reported in the Muslim "hadith", this being the collected creeds, traditions, teachings, and stories of the prophet Muhammad, that all of these should be accepted as a source of Islamic doctrine and, second only to the Koran. This reality is being the experiencing of the Angel Gabriel which is described in "The Book" as the mind fulfilling of "Enlightenment" in which the Soul of the individual has been chosen to join with God's Creation. It is genuinely thought that this experience did accompany Muhammad during the Mi'raj this being the ascension to heaven where Muhammad is said to have met other messengers of God, genuinely, an experience of "Enlightenment," that fully experiences God's Heaven that exists upon this Earth.

Thus truly this experience of encountering the "Enlightenment" is true, the encountering of the Heaven that rest upon this Earth. For it is known that Muhammad experienced that condition in which no selfish thought can exist. It was therefore within this "Enlightened" experience that Muhammad was instructed about the manner of the Quran and Islamic prayers which recount this "Enlightened" experience of Muhammad. Thus it is a night in the last ten days of the holy month of Ramadan, which again can be said to be the night on which the Quran was first revealed to Muhammad. Indeed and truly Muhammad was in that "Enlightened" condition known in "The Book" has been "Self-Aware", this being a condition in which all that you observe and experience is known to be "Your-Self".

Also, has within the Christian teaching, it should be clearly understood that the incarnate Jesus of the Christian faith was also in the "Enlightened" condition which "The Book" describes being Self-Realised", meaning that you are not the observer of the creation but that you are the singularity of creation, this is also being that condition which Muhammad recognised within Jesus which is the second stage of "Enlightenment". For indeed this being the final stage and it is the stage in which you become the Creation, meaning that there is no observer for the soul has joined with God, which "The Book" explains is the targeted purpose of Gods "Creation", this been so that God can experience Himself.

So simply put, this means that you need only to read the words of Jesus in the Christian Bible and know that it seemingly has if you are experiencing the wisdom of all the Creation itself speaking directly to you, so they need no interpretation. Now "newly" look again at these words from the Incarnate Jesus and "imagine" that it is the Creation or Nature for the Non-Believer speaking directly to you and saying:

16-4-3-16 *"For God so loved the world that he gave his one and only Son, that whoever believes in Him shall not perish but have eternal life",* this is the Creation itself speaking to you.

17-4-3-17 *"For God did not send his Son into the world to condemn the world, but to save the world through Him."* This statement is because the Creation knows that all God's laws are within it and which all should live by that which is in front of them.

19-4-3-19 *"This is the verdict: Light has come into the world, but men loved darkness instead of light because their deeds were evil."* God's laws are in the Creations "Enlightenment" and the personal "I Want" it for myself, is being the darkness.

22-1-13-38 *"The field is the world, and the good seed stands for the sons of the kingdom. The weeds are the sons of the evil one."* An "I Want," for me, is a weed growing in the garden of the world, for the Creation says so.

12-4-6-33 *"For the bread of God is He who comes down from heaven and gives life to the world."* The Creation itself is the natural food of life, and sometimes it becomes personified and so is knowingly experienced within the wise.

0-4-6-51 *"I am the living bread that came down from heaven. If anyone eats of this bread, he will live forever. This bread is my flesh, which I will give for the life of the* world." Yes, This can be likened to the Creation speaking directly to you. What does it mean? You now know! For it is a description of the "Present

Time", for sure, this is the bread of life.

7-1-16-26 *"What good is it for a man if he gains the whole world, yet forfeits his Soul? Or what can a man give in exchange for his Soul?"* Indeed, this can be likened to the unity of the Creation speaking to you. What does it mean? You now know! If your own personal "I Want" achieves for you the entire physical world, but if you're Soul is still encaged – is it a good exchange? Therefore, your soul "is" the entire world, which is a child of God.

1-1-18-7 *"Woe to the world because of the things* that *cause people to sin!* (Their "I Want") *Such things must come, but woe to the people through whom they come!"* This is the Creation speaking directly to you. What does it mean?

1-4-8-12 *"When Jesus spoke again to the people, He said, I am the light of the world. Whoever follows me will never walk in darkness but will have the light of life."* Again this is the Creation speaking to you, and you now know what it means. Again, saying that the light of the world is the "Present Time" and the darkness in the past or future is personally-created "I Want" world which removes you from the "Present Time". So where do you want to live? The freedom of choice is always "yours".

3-4-8-23 *"But He continued you are from below; I am from above. You are of this world; I am not of this world."* Meaning that a never-ending personal "I Want" keeps you to live in a personally created past or a future Hell, yet the Creation exists only in the "Present Time", which is Heaven, these being two very different worlds.

6-4-8-26 *"I have much to say in judgment of you. But he who sent me is reliable, and what I have heard from him I tell the world."* Only an embodied Creation, a knowing child of God, could speak these words.

5-4-9-5 *"While I am in the world, I am the light of the world." Look around you. What do you see?* Only one truth can rest in your world – this is the light of the "Present Time".

6-4-8-26 *"I have much to say in judgment of you. But he who sent me is reliable, and what I have heard from him I tell the world."* This is the Creation speaking directly to you!

5-4-9-5 *"While I am in the world, I am the light of the world."* Again this is the Creation speaking about God's world, which can only exist in the Heaven that is the "Present Time", the only time and place where Heaven can exist and in which no past or future, can exist, this Past or future is being a personally made world of Hell.

9-3-16-9 *"I tell you, use worldly wealth to gain friends for yourselves so that when it is gone, you will be welcomed into eternal dwellings."* This is again being likened to the Creation speaking directly to you. This being the child of God that is speaking directly to you, saying that what you call yours, also belongs to those you know as friends, for now, you know that all that exists is YOU!

54   THE MUSLIM CREEDS
THAT TARGET "ENLIGHTENMENT"

So yes! it is good to know about the Quran and its creed messages that will have come to Muhammad during his experiencing of "Enlightenment" which he described as *"a realm beyond the ability of words to convey properly"* which is the same experience described in the Christian religion as *"peace that surpasses all understanding"* which is always experienced when the mind is in the "Present Time" and is achieved when the mind is silent from any personal "I Want". For undeniably, this being a mind clouding "I Want" noise which is emanating from the animalistic five senses which have been allowed, in infancy, to create their many "I Want" dreams and "I Want" fantasies which came into existence when they were innocently freed in infancy.

Again, this being that animalistic "I Want" which many words can describe and which ALWAYS disturbs and clouds the mind and so destroys the potential peace of mind empty a non-thinker. For, of course, these "I Wants" are simply demands coming from one of the body's five senses and this is certainly not the "Enlightenment" that all religions and philosophies seek, which is the stilling of the mind so that a person's Soul can witness God's world or the world of Nature for the Non-Believer, this being the Heaven that exists upon our Earth – but it is a Heaven which can only be experienced in the "Present Time" and so experienced with a mind that without any "I Want" thoughts and so silently and naturally the person experiences "Enlightenment", the world in which an "I Want" for me cannot exist for you realise that you have "Everything".

Muhammad was then able to understand the problems of the world that existed around him, and this was because of his God-given experience of the world mentioned above of "Enlightenment". It was this fact than enabled Mohammed to explain many truths to his God seeking followers, which he wondrously translated into a contemporary understanding and thus was enabled to create a religious belief system that is seriously concerned with the moral guidance emanating from God's world, which can only exist only in the "Present Time".

For without a doubt, God's world or the world of Nature for the Non-Believer can only be experienced in the "Heaven" that exits in the "Present Time", for it is undoubtedly true that "Heaven" cannot exist in the past or a future self-created "Hell" that the "I want" of the five senses take the life of the thinker. This condition is being a fictitious world of "Hell" which the "I Want" of the five senses creates, and which also cloud the mind so that the Soul cannot "observe" and so experience the "Creation" that exists within us and all around us, but only in the "Heaven" of the "Present Time". In truth, this was a fact which Muhammad was able to understand. For it is undoubtedly true that Muhammad did plainly explain many living values which are mainly noticed in his words that show his followers how to experience "Enlightenment," which is also described in words *"Peace be upon them?"*

For this is the Godly born peace that can rest in all people but can only occur when the Soul observes the outer world through the silence that exists within the stillness of the mind, a fact which occurs when any "I Want" of the five senses are forbidden to enter, usually via the discipline of an imposed prayer or ritual. Therefore it not also the fact that Muhammad always presented a full tribute to our many wise ancients who permanently lived in this "Peace" that surpasses all understanding, this being that actuality which can only exist in the "Present Time". Is it not also true that our ancient wise are the people who never have any desires for some past or any future "I Want"? Is it not also true that Muhammad, blessed be his name, had always known that it is an excellent "realisation" to experience the "Peace that Surpasses all Understanding", acclaimed by Mohammad and all our wise ancients, and if you also wish to understand how to physically and personally self-realise this experience - Read on.

For indeed, Muhammad's words clearly explain how to achieve *"a realm beyond the ability of words to properly convey"* or the Christian *"peace that surpasses all understanding"*. For assuredly, this is a reality that rests in the Heaven that always exists upon our Earth but only in the "Present Time" and also is this not clearly seen to be the same targeting fact that all our world's religions and philosophies speak? Is it not also true that "Enlightenment" is always a "personally" achieved endeavour and when seen within one by others is often described as a light being reflected from within that person, when truthfully, this is a feeling of inner peace and a mind without thought that is being witnessed.

Therefore, is it not also true that in our ancient drawings that this "Enlightenment" within our Holy-Ones is shown has a Halo around their head which is said to have been born from the snaked crown worn by our ancient Egyptian ancestors five thousand years ago? Also does not the Holy Quran firmly state to all worshippers the enlightened words of our many wise ancients, but in a culturally understood dialect, these being the culture originating words that many wise ancients often choose to use?

For these "Holy" words are genuinely born to target and so create within the listeners the condition of "Enlightenment"? For undeniably all these holy teachings are care instructions on how to bring the "Will of God", this being that which always exists in the "Present Time", to those lost people who's "I Want" of the five senses entangles them with a non-existing Past or Future. For if the truth is told truly this seeking of "Enlightenment" was always the task of our wise ancients who did create religions and philosophies for their people throughout the world upon which we all live.

Therefore is it not now known to be historically authentic, that all our wise ancients did establish different culturally-based creed prayers, rituals and services which they used in many different countries to target the experiencing of "Enlightenment". Undeniably this being so that their followers could experience Gods world and therefore be has one with everything that existed around them. But is it not also sadly known that years after the departure of these holy ones that some of their creed based followers began to believe that their culturally based words and stories were the only way to live in God's world and that no other words or saying could show the "true" way to living in Gods world – so forgetting that all people are attached to the unified soul, for truly this self-claiming that only our way is the way to Gods world and then their personal developing and isolating "I Want" thoughts stating that God wants us to destroy all those who say that our religious way is not correct. So God wants us to punish those who will not follow our way to God, and so we should take all that they possess has a punishment for their sins.

So yes! All our worlds' different religious and philosophical creeds are based upon words that spring from our culturally attached wise ancients who experienced and lived in a world of "Enlightenment," which is God's Heaven upon this Earth. For indeed, is not the same target being sought, today by the world's culturally-based religion? Thus revealing the truth that people should live only in the "Present Time", which is a world without thoughts and God's world and not the world of a mind filling "I Want", for you cannot want that which you already have but which you may have forgotten. For clearly, all our world's many religious and philosophical teachings are all differently explained and so culturally programmed by our "Enlightened" wise ancients who always used culture-based words and actions which were always necessary to educate the many different cultures in which their people lived.

Still, the target was always the same, which is to experience "Enlightenment". For really and truly, this personal "feeling" of experiencing the "will of God" can only be experienced in God's "Present Time", a place in which no selfish future or any past "I Want" can exist, so now and indeed all should now know that this is the target of ALL religions and philosophies.

Therefore is it not a fact that all those who are ignorantly living in mind filling "I Want" for myself world, this being the world in which all religions and philosophies know as Hell, should now understand that these Godly creeds have been created to take their listeners away from personally living in Hell and so bring them to live only in Heaven, this being the real world of God or Nature for the Non-Believer. But sadly, forgetting is our worst enemy and much in our past and the present time has been forgotten or even lost, but if you wish to know the easiest way to achieve "Enlightenment" and so live in that world which all our wise ancients speak? – Read on.

For it is indeed very accurate that all that people need for "Enlightenment" was definitely and culturally taught by Muhammad who established a goodly – Godly - cultural way to find "Enlightenment", this being that which indeed rests within Muhammad's teachings. Therefore, is it not a very real fact that Muhammad did reveal to his followers the many "Enlightening" ways of how to realise the "will of God", all of which are designed to bring the Islamic worshipper to live a life in the "Present Time", this being a life lived within God's world of Heaven and a world where the personal and selfish mind blocking "thinking" of an "I Want" for myself, cannot exist."

Therefore is it not certainly understood that Muhammad's Quran teachings, this being teaching that emanated and so came from the "Enlightened" and wise Muhammad, was also teaching that strongly and naturally supported the Islamic scriptures which were a faith-based system of worship that emanated from Adam, Abraham, Moses, Jesus, and other prophets who also taught ways of bringing the worshipper to a still and empty mind, this being a mind which was free from all "I Want" for me. So yes, the target of Mohammed was to ensure that the pursuing worshipper could experience a life in God's world which can only be experienced in the "Present Time"; this being the experience being known as "Enlightenment" that which ALL religions and philosophies seek.

Also, does not the Islamic teaching, like most of our world religions and philosophies, further state that which happens to a person who diligently practices a creed that will take them to live in the stillness of the "Present Time". They WILL experience the "Enlightenment" known in the Quran and the Christian teachings as being filled by the Holy Spirit. Thus, it was that Muhammad showed a way for his followers to self-experience that which cannot be described and which is known as Gods world to all who experience it.

So yes! It is undoubtedly true that the teachings of Mohammed do certainly clarify the reality of how to achieve "Enlightenment", this being that which can only exist in our world's non-thinking "Present Time". For, again and again, it should be said that Gods world or the world of Nature for the Non-Believer, is a reality which is all around the people of the Earth and which is a world which can also be realised by prayer and other physical disciplines.

So yes! The wise Muhammad taught a practical way to experience God's heaven upon this Earth, for Muhammed certainly knew that Gods world could only exist in the "Present Time" and which is also a time that is without any selfish contamination from any past or future "I Want" thoughts, which is a world being self-created by one's personnel "I Want" for me world, this being that world which always leads to an "I Want" for myself activity, which is an indeed the world of a Self-created Hell. For, without doubt, this was indeed Mohammed's revealing of many Creeds that were based upon the search for "Enlightenment", this being that which is known to Islamic worshippers as the way of the "Sunnah", which translated, means *"The way to walk the well-trodden path to experience God's world"* this being the world which is indeed called "Enlightenment".

So it is without a doubt that Mohammed's truthfully put expression means to live via the experiencing of "Enlightenment". For faithfully, the Islam religion, along with many of our worlds religiously-based creeds and philosophies, has many well-known and practical "creeds," which are all unique and personal ways of worship and which good Muslims observe and practice to fulfil the actions of Muhammad's words and so religiously follow his revelations. Thus, by truly walking in Muhammad's stated path his worshippers, being the same as the worshippers of many of our world's religions and philosophies, do continuously work towards and into the reality of experiencing "Enlightenment".

Indeed, this being a condition in which they genuinely experience God's Heaven that rests upon this Earth. For surely it should also be clearly stated that even if "Enlightenment" is only a momentarily experience, the people experiencing this "Self-Awareness" will realise that there is a Heaven that exists in the "Present Time". Therefore it is true that they will factually and knowingly know that this experience of "Heaven" is waiting for them to exist in permanently, this being "Enlightened" contentment for the rest of their lives in which they will harm no one for all people they see, they will know to be "Themselves", has Mohammed saw when he looked at his followers.

Therefore, is it not agreeably true that the wise Muhammad also clearly stated to his followers that God will build a house in "Heaven" for whoever is diligent in observing twelve daily prayers? Effectively this being a self-disciplined "Meditational" mind-controlling activity which is targeted to stop the mind filling "I Want" words which are uncontrollably being sounded into the mind by anyone of the arguing five senses, this being that which people mistakenly believe is themselves. But clearly, they are NOT you for YOU are the Soul which observes all things and therefore cannot see its "Self". But what also in our modern times can now be clearly understood, is that the "House" that Mohammed mentions, is the body in which the "meditating" prayers Soul – which is you – really and factually does exist. Therefore, is it not true, you cannot see the observer who is looking through your mind and viewing a world in which it's lived in a body exists? Therefore, is it not true that the "Self-Imposed" mind-controlling discipline that is associated with the factual performing of these twelve prayers will change and disciplinary stop the pursuits of any "I Want" emanating from any one of the five senses.

So Yes! Is it not true that these mind filling and personal "I Wants" can be stopped by the outer imposed self-disciplined prayers and chants that are replacing them, this being when these outer disciplined words actual silence an inner mind "I Want" story or an inner conversation that is filling the mind and which is genuinely emanating from any one of the five senses which you believe is the real you, but now you know that you cannot be that to which you listen. So factually, they are NOT you! For you are the Soul that observes all these things and the reason for the above mistake, this being that mistake which is continuously allowing the mind to be filled by an " I Want" for me, is because in childhood, around the age of two or three and because of your God-given "Freedom of Choice", you permitted your consciousness, this being that bodily entity which is always aware of and also receptive to one's surroundings, via your God-given "Freedom of Choice" to free your willpower, which is that entity which controls your thoughts and how you behave, to automatically allow any " I Want" that is emanating from the five senses to enter the mind – this being because you believed at that young age that the five senses were the real you – they are not you! For undeniably indeed, you are the Soul, this being that which observes all things and whose intent is to support the purpose of the emerging creation that only exist in the "Present Time". For definitely, this is why All people have been Godly given the "Freedom of Choice", this being that which is factually needed to support the emerging "Creation", because the same act can support or destroy the emerging creation, depending upon circumstances.

So yes! Mohammed knew that the falsely and mistakenly created and mind filling "I Want" for me, should be replaced by a self-disciplined and singular un-sounding and "automatic" pursuit of aiding that which is targeting the correct way to support and so live in the "Heaven" that truly exists in the "Present Time", which Mohammed knew could only be God's world. For indeed, this being in the real world is that which Mohammed realised could be experienced by the automatic chanting of prayers, this being that which brings the doer to a mind-empty rest in the "Present Time", that certainly exists upon this Earth, this being a "Present Time" that can only be experienced when the mind is without a thought and so rest between the silent empty spaces that are being revealed by the automatic chanting

So Yes! Honestly now all know that Muhammad did bring to the creation many psalms and prayers that brought to the practiser that which "The Book" and many religions and philosophies call "Enlightenment", this being an experience in which a person knowingly lives in God's world, a world in which exists the "Self-Disciplined" silent mind for it is undoubtedly necessary to stop any "I Want" for me, from filling the mind.

For it is undeniably true that this "I Want" for me is a condition that "scientifically" blocks the Soul's view of the "Present Time", which is God's world and the world of Heaven that truly, exists upon our Earth. Factually this is created because Mohammed's twelve daily prayer words which are emanating from Mohammed *"Peace be upon Him"*, which are self-disciplined and which are removed from any outside interfering personal "I Want" thoughts.

They also consist of separately and disciplinary prescribed movements in which four of the prayers are before midday and two after midday plus two prayers after sunset, and then two prayers after the evening prayer time plus two prayers before dawn, for indeed, whoever pursues these disciplines and so concentrates upon this creed will enter that which Muhammad truly, states is, *"a realm beyond the ability of words to properly convey"* for this is the Heaven that ALWAYS rests upon this Earth. It WILL certainly be experienced between the words of the prayers for this is true, *"the way to walk the well-trodden path in order to experience God's world."* Undeniably being the same experience which the Christians also call the *"peace that surpasses all understanding"* and which is obtained by pursuing their ancient culture based creeds, as it is with all the religious teachings of the world that have been created by our incarnates.

Thus "Truly" the concentration required by these prayers will bring Muhammad's followers to that *"realm beyond the ability of words to properly convey,"* This is the condition that is undoubtedly "Self-Experienced" as the worshipper expands and so disciplines their mind to rest in the "Present Time", and so YES! Within this unmoving peace that now silently rests within the unthinking mind, a condition in which the Soul can experience all that there is to be experienced in the "Present Time" will exist. For indeed, this is being a time in which all sincerely praying people will truly experience God's world, for again and indeed, this being a world that can only exist in the "Present Time".

Therefore, is it not true that Muhammad's creeds were created by his very own personal and understandable way of achieving "Enlightenment" and that Muhammed did know that these practising prayers would genuinely bring the worshipping practiser to the experience of a world that is created by the one God? For it is undoubtedly and very clearly understood by all those who have experienced "Enlightenment" that there is only one God and that it is genuinely the rhythm-based incantations and exercises which are a discipline that is guaranteed to take the automatically incanting "praying" person to His world.

This world can be seen and so experienced to exist but only in the "Present Time". For indeed, those who diligently concentrate on a creed which targets the one God will find that this is a sure way to discipline the mind to stay in the silence of the "Heavenly" based "Present Time", this being that "Heaven" that exists all around them. It will also eventually be understood by the wise that this "silence" in mind exists even before any prayers have begun and can be experienced nearly always after they have been finished as the doer experiences the silence that exists in the mind when it is experiencing only the stillness that always exists but only in "Present Time" – God's world.

Also to establish and prepare for this fact, Muhammad gave purposeful instructions that all worshippers should *"with a silent mind"* concentrate fully on the activity of washing of their face and their hands (and arms) to the elbows, and by internal self-discipline, rub their heads with water and also their feet to the ankles – a task which can be and so should always be achieved without any thought entering the mind. For certainly Mohammed knew that this was a sure way of preparing true worshippers to enter God's world, this truth being because Mohammed knew that these tasks could only exist in the "Present Time", the only time in which these self-disciplines could take place. For without a doubt there was no need to "think" to perform these simple "automatic" activities for truly Mohammed knew that the doer would experience or could experience with self-discipline, a silent mind, this being the only condition in which the doers' Soul can witness through the mind, Gods creation, that which always exists but only in the "Present Time".

For indeed, Mohammed would know that this concentrated endeavour can bring "Enlightenment" which would be in direct accordance to the silence occurring in mind, which all the bodily activities and the repeating "Mantra" styled prayers are targeting to achieve – as do all sincere prayers of worship. But what is also VERY important to understand is that eventually "Enlightenment" can and will be experienced to exist between the automatically repeating words and therefore experienced during the actions of these habitually sounding prayers and or deeds. Still, one must always concentrate on the mantra-like "doing" which will eventually become non-energised thinking and so automatic. For to be sure certainly it is a truth that Mohammed knew that this was a condition that existed in reality and which can be modernly explained has a condition which allows the Soul to see through the still and empty mind and therefore truly experience, has only the Soul can, Gods Creation. For his being that condition which is always experienced when the Soul is authorised to see through an empty mind, a mind that is not filled by any "I Want" for me thinking. For indeed, it is an absolute fact that eventually "Enlightenment" can and will come to you during these repetitive prayers, and God's world will be upon you.

So yes! It is also important to realise that this is a world that can always be entered at any time, by merely switching the mind to rest in the "Present Time calmly". Therefore, undeniably, this is the "experience" which worshippers often feel during the silence, immediately after their prayer time. For God's world can never leave His Creation and this is always realised if you keep the silence within the mind, this being that which the many varied religious exercises bring to you.

So Yes! Be brave and do not throw the silence occurring between any praying words away, and so also know that indeed, the *"Peace that surpasses all Understanding"* can and will always be disciplined to remain within you, and of course, without the demands of your five senses, who are the bringers of the mind filling "I Want" for me! For again and undeniably, only the Soul seeing through a silent mind, this being an activity which can be targeted to be achieved between the words of a religious automatically incanting prayer, can free the Soul from a walled-in cage which has been self-created by ignorance.

For this silence within the disciplined mind will allow the Soul to observe and so naturally act in support of the outer harmony that is always striving to show itself to people. Therefore, all should know it is "Holy" and therefore "Godly" not to act in mind filled "I Want" way and instead to truly worship in mind emptying self-disciplined pursuit the many chants and prayers that are seriously realised in the performing of religious activities that are known to target and so experience *"a realm beyond the ability of words to convey properly."* Undeniably, this is an experience which for the beginner, can be "Realised" for a fleeting second or a few minutes. Still, for the experienced true believer, this religious practice can lead to an unchanging blissful life, which is lived continuously within this silence that now exists within the mind; this is the life that is truly being lived in Heaven, this being that which genuinely exists upon our Earth.

Yet strangely, the Sunni and Shia, which are two parts of the same Muslim religion currently have an acute "personal" religiously based creed dispute between them, both saying "I Want my creed and its leadership to be the only away to God," which is like the creed and leadership dispute between the Roman Church and those that Protested against it, which occurred around 1524 and ended 124 years later in around 1648 in which millions were brutally killed mainly because of economic or political ramifications, which has nothing to do with religion.

So Yes! Sadly; during these one hundred and twenty-four years of a Christian religious disagreement Europe suffered cruelly in many self-inflicted civil wars, which caused a loss of between five point six million and eighteen point four million lives, due to disease, famine, soldiers in battle and even genocide based massacres as many cities' men, women and children were all destroyed and all for a personally based "I Want my leadership and my way of creed worship and not yours" desire. However, many believe that this war was based on financial pursuits.

Yet simply put, God's world that exists in the "Present Time", is a time which has no mind filling "I Want" thoughts within it, and so could never be responsible for such a cruel Hell created activity, for only a personal "I Want" for me, which is based upon a non-existing future or past, can be responsible for such evil. However, history does show that eventually, God's world did return to Christian Europe as God's laws always return to that which is true, for His laws will always prevail, and evermore shall do so.

Therefore, there was eventually created within the Christian world freedom of worship, which has since expanded into thirty-five major Christian creeds; incorporating many different worshipping religious practices and leaders, plus thousands of smaller worshipping groups, which, although they do have significant differences in their worship and organisational behaviour systems, all live in peace with each other. Indeed, you can sit next to any person and not know which Christian church or faith that they belong to for all believe in the words of God's son Jesus, just as the Sunni and Shia believe in the words of Muhammad for both Sunni and Shia faiths also strongly believe in Muhammad's teachings, for this is also that which exists in both their creeds. But sadly, just like the ancient Roman Church and its Protesters' did bring a conflict which destroyed so much of God's world and killed many millions of people, the Sunni and Shia now have similar significant "I Want" my way differences in their creeds.

This difference is also likened to be a comparable war to the Christian religions conflict this being the same "I Want my way of leadership and my way of creed religion to be worshipped and practised and not yours," a similarly stated difference as that which aroused severe conflict in the Christian religion four hundred years ago. These differences are also why the Muslim religion is currently waging the same fierce civil war conflicts that are also the cause of many killings, as these two Muslim sects oppose each other, as did the Roman Church and its Protesters in a similar war of distrustful conflict which also kills millions of innocents.

Why is this? Can it be true that God "Wants" to brutally kill and injure many thousands of men, woman and children? I do not think this is true especially when people's length of life can be likened to a drop of seawater in the oceans of the world and also such a conflict can be likened a drop of sea-water which is saying to the rest of the Ocean "I am wetter than you are and I have more salt in me that you do!"

It is sad, yes! Because factually those who perpetrate such killings and torturing of others will be born again but the "Mother of the Creation" will see to it that in their next life they will go back to learning the correct way of how their life should be lived, this being for them and for others who believe that economic or political ramifications are more important than a life lived under Gods rules in which there is only one child. For indeed it is known, has many religions and philosophies state, that such disobedient people who religiously kill or command to kill other people are incarcerated into a lower life form, which is most suited for their re-education, so that they may be enabled to live a personal life again within the Creations future.

For indeed a person's life has a purpose that is to love and protect the lives of ALL people, this being all that life which exists in God's world, a world that all know to exist upon our Earth. For sadly again, the Christian discontentment and terrible war, was the same as is now the current Muslim discontentment, because the main reason for this Sunni and Shia difference is also based upon doctrine, ritual, law, theology and religious organisation.

This difference is said to be because the Shia "I Want" creeds mainly desire to be "Scripture ally" enabled to cover doctrine, rituals, law, and theology plus the fact that their religion should be led by a close descendant of Mohammed. While the opposing Sunni's "Rationally" believe in their "I Want" that God's power is in the material world, including the public and political realm and that their leaders, called Imams should be chosen democratically but sadly are not these differences likened to those of the Roman Church and Protesters conflict, which is made by people and not made by God; for many different paths lead to "Enlightenment," a known condition in which ALL "I Want" for me, disappears. For indeed this is a fact that has always historically proven to be accurate, especially regarding the needed removal of any "I Want my way of worship, not your way" desires – which causes many religious disputes – but where does animalistic hatred of another religion come from?

So yes! It is genuinely known that the Muslim Shias creeds do believe in a God-loving and obeying life and also look towards the rewards of the afterlife and value the celebration of martyrdom. Still, their main "religious" personally biased "I Want" difference is the same as the serious "I Want my way to live in Gods world and not yours", which was also the primary cause of the conflict within the Christians religions pursuits. Also, this disagreement was vigorously pursued by appointing different leaders who would take them down their chosen path which is again similar to that which the Christians pursued and in this active pursuit the Shias branch of Islam religion stated that the Imam leader of their faith should be based upon the bloodline of Muhammad and so should have begun with the leadership of Ali, who was the cousin and son-in-law of the recently deceased Muhammad. It was also pursued and decreed that the Imam leaders should not be elected but should be direct descendants of Muhammad and so believed to be appointed by Allah. For indeed there are many ways to live in GODs world and also to live a life that is appreciated by God

It was also known that the God-loving Shias followers had twelve "bloodline" leaders; known as Imams (Leaders), who came after Muhammad's death, but the first to be chosen was Muhammad's, Cousin Ali, and so it was stated that Ali was the rightful religious leader of the Islamic and Muslim faith. It also became the fact that Shias therefore strongly believed in their own selected leadership of twelve Imams, the last of which was a boy who mysteriously vanished, aged four, during the year 878 in Iraq and this was sadly after his father was murdered. Still, it is also believed that these young boys return will be as the Messiah.

So yes! There is a now difference in leadership between these two sects for the Sunni branches of Islam believe that their leaders should be appointed and therefore be an elected leader of their Islamic and Muslim "Sunni" way of worship so that it may be well to now understand the meaning that "Islam" is the act of submitting to the will of God and so avoid the "I Want" for me of the five senses. The word "Muslim" indicates a person who participates in the act of submitting to Gods laws and so does not obey the "I Want" of the five senses. For indeed it should also be further known that these two main sects within Islam, these being the above Sunni and Shia worshippers, do agree on most of the fundamental beliefs and practices of Islam and that this bitter divide simply originated by a dispute over who should succeed the Prophet Muhammad as leader of the Islamic faith that he introduced.

Yet sadly, this aggressive conflict is now in the year 2020, one thousand three hundred and eighty-eight year old for this a personally "religious" split in "thinking" goes back to the Prophet Muhammad's death in 632, for he died without appointing a successor and, unlike the "Re-organisation" of the Christian belief system, which began in 1517 when a German monk called Martin Luther earnestly protested about the Catholic Church and their belief that in a bread and wine service, which honoured Jesus, that the bread and wine turn into the body and the blood of Christ while "Protestants" to this belief believed it stays has bread and wine and only represents the body of Christ. Strangely, this then caused a rift between the two ways of worship has many people and governments adopted the new "Protestant" ideas, while others remained faithful to the leadership of the Catholic Church. This disagreement then led to a cruel war between these worshipers of Jesus in which many millions of men, women and children were killed in this "disagreement" between the Roman Catholic Church and the newly emerged "Protestant" people, and it was a conflict which seemingly ended around 1712. This being after 195 years of disagreement and conflicts which only ended after a very seriously pursued 124 years of civil war, a war which is now understood to have been over property rights, and yet is it not true that this Islamic wars destructive disagreeing conflict are still in progress, which is now 1,388 years after it began- why is this?

For surely this is a religious conflict which must end shortly, for indeed with modern communication systems, such an old and personal "religiously" based dispute should find an early peaceful ending in which all Islamic followers can worship in their own chosen way and liken to the Christians religion they should end their dispute, for indeed, it should be quickly settled in the same way as it was in the Christian world. Yet! Is it not also a known truth that there are many hundreds of religions and philosophies in our world which are all based upon a love that has no equal and so you should never desire to know the faith or religion of the person sitting next to you, for it is not essential as long as they live in God's world of a unified singularity – which is His child.

For indeed, the most important thing for any person to remember is that God gave people the "Freedom of Choice", is this not true? Therefore is it not also true that no one can take this "Freedom of Choice" away from anyone? Therefore, is it not also known that even God will not do that for God gave people the "Freedom of Choice" and God cannot make mistakes? The whole of Nature also tells us that as on the 1st of July 1916 in the Battle of the Somme, that by the end of the first day British forces suffered 57,470 casualties, of whom 19,240 were killed, was this caused by a person's "Freedom of Choice" or was it caused by their enemy?

So yes! It is sadly true that this "Freedom of Choice" can have positive or negative outcomes for even now the Islamic religious belief system is severely fractured just as the Christian religion had been before them. This serious fracture seems to have also been based upon a similar "I Want my creed to be better than your creed," when in the truth that which all religious people seek and in their many different ways, is the experience of being filled with the Holy Spirit which also filled the prophets, Adam, Noah, Abraham, Moses, the Angel Gabriel and the incarnate Jesus of Nazareth and very sincerely, Muhammad – and indeed "Blessed be his name".

For this is the act of being filled by a "Holy Spirit" in which no discontentment about others can exist, and which can only be found and so "experienced" within oneself, and so it is impossible to find it in any conflict with others, for it just cannot be so for undeniably the Holy Spirit shows that there are no "Others" there is only YOU! For we have often heard the saying *"Do unto other what you would like to be done to yourself"*, a saying which emanates from the fact that the wise knew that all "others" are indeed also themselves. For assuredly I would now say in praying *"Thank you Lord for giving me the strength and conviction to complete this task that you entrusted me with and thank you for guiding me through the many obstacles in my path, also thank you for your constant reaching to me when with all around me I felt lost. Also, Lord, thank you for your protection and your many signs in which you did show to me the way of truth, for I truly endeavoured to fight the good fight, and so finish the work that you gave me to do those many years ago when you saved me from my nomadic life. I kept the faith and never lost "The Faith".*

Therefore it is good to smile now and to know that there are people who "animalistic ally" do not believe in this unity of existence. Yet, is it not an absolute truth that God's world can only be experienced within your-self? Is it not also true that this is experience is described as being filled with the Holy Spirit or the Angel Gabriel; this again being the Muslim stated: *"a realm beyond the ability of words to properly convey"* or the Christian *"peace that surpasses all understanding"*, this being that which is experienced within oneself, and which surpasses all personal understanding because it is an experience comes from Gods world, a world that cannot be described by words. For undeniably, there is one thing that all people of all our world religions and philosophies' genuinely understand, this being that God created our world but "The Book" says that it is a "Mother of the Creation", who lovingly care for the laws of harmony that exist within its unity, just as do all mothers care safely for the

"Present Time", this being at the same time has a man prepares for future service. For assuredly, this is God's Creation or Nature's Creation for the Non-Believer; which is a Creation which does not support any discord that disturbs the harmony that always rests within it or is endeavouring to materialise within it.

Therefore, is it not true that there is only one "Heavenly" body that we call the universe? A universe which is confirmed to be firmly attached to our planet Earth's harmony. Is it not also true that our private "Heaven" is upon this Earth, which is knowingly a part of God's universal "Creation". Is it not also true that there is a similarly based harmony within our own body? Is it not also physically correct that this inner bodily love of an unselfish unity can be likened to the same Godly truth that rests within the Nature of our Earth? Therefore is it not also true that our inner body typically works in a perfect non-interfering harmonious way, which is a well-known fact that is realised by all people. Therefore, is it not true that our inner bodily parts also belong to a different acceptance system, which can be likened to a religious world that has no "Freedom of Choice? For could the heart say to the lungs "I Want" a different leader, for I do not like what you do and I Want to destroy you!" A strange request for none in our inner body's Godly unified world can do this. But is this not an excellent example of what people can do with the "Freedom of Choice", this being that which only exists in the world of people?

So yes! Although Shia and Sunni both worship the sincere words of the Prophet Muhammad as do all Christians' worship the words of the incarnate Jesus, their internal discord is the same "I Want" as it was with the past Christian rift, which was also over a different way of worship, or was it about who controls property and riches? Yet is it not right to believe, that this separating Islamic rift, will also come to the same peaceful "Godly" understanding which the Christians eventually established? This understanding meaning to "stand under" God's laws, which allows any person to "choose" to concentrate upon their own personal "chosen" creed way of worshipping of the one God, as eventually, all the Christians did, for all people seek the same "Enlightenment" and all people seek to be filled by the Angel Gabriel, who was also named as the "Holy Spirit".

Thus it is this experiencing of "Enlightenment", which is the only factor or targeting factor that will bring worshippers to realise God's world, a world that can only exist in the "Present Time" and not in the thoughts of "I Want my creed, not your creed," which is the world of Hell. Undeniably this being the world of Hell in which only animalistic "I Want" for me conflicts appears, this genuinely being a Hell in which there is a preoccupation with physical rather than spiritual needs, for again and indeed, this is not the way to "Enlightenment?" For truly "Enlightenment" is the reality of one being filled by the unifying light of God's world, this being that which exists only in the "Present Time"?

Therefore is not "Enlightenment" clearly seen to be the real and only target of all religious beliefs, all of which are encased in all our many religions and philosophies, these being that which carefully support creed-based disciplines? For indeed our worlds history show, that the Christian religion eventually and agreeably did splinter from a singularly enforced system of worship into over thirty-five different worshipping creeds, with thousands of smaller differing groups, but which are all based upon the words of the Incarnate Jesus.

Therefore, is it not an absolute truth that these words of Jesus are "always" capable of taking the many different types of worshippers into God's world or the world of Nature for the Non-Believer? For in a whole belief system God cannot be interested in any personally imposed creed, such as *"you will worship only in my creed and not in anther creed,"* for only pain and an ungodly death exist in such personal disputes.

For these religious conflicts are based upon real, personal "I Want" for me, thoughts, and they do not belong to God's world, which is a world without any "I Want". For again and honestly, all needs have already been met. However, it may be genuinely agreed, that many peoples "needs" have sometimes been stolen and so have not been distributed harmoniously by other people. Yet, is it not also real and has each person's history shows, this false condemning way of life is always corrected and if not in this life than certainly in the next.

For assuredly, God's Creation assists and supports only those who actively contribute and who also support the ongoing ever-developing harmony, which is continuously growing in God's world, a world that can only exist in the "Present Time" and not in the Past or the Future, which is a self-created "I Want" for me Hell. For in truth, is this not also true that this self-created world is known as Hell, a world that can also be factually experienced, but a world that ceases to exist when one concentrates on a faith that does not seek a personal "I Want" for me! For indeed this is a "scientific" reality and a reality which is experienced only in the silent mind that exists within a person whose Soul seeks only the experiencing of God's "Present Time", this being that which exists upon His world. For this is an empty mind that is seeing the truth and a mind that has no room for the dream world of "I Want" for ME!

This personally created world is that "I Want" for me world which fills the mind and which is born from thoughts emanating from the machinations of a past or a future very unreal self-created world. So honestly, this is a false world that is created by the "I Want" for me that is emanating from one of the five senses and not by the needs of the Creation, this being that which fulfilling feeds the Soul. For it is entirely correct and a fact, that the Creation, which exists all around you, is truly God's world or the world of Nature for the Non-Believer. Also, would it not be sad if it took Shia and Sunni Muslims the same number of years that it took the Christians, to establish the Godly fact that it does not matter which creed you follow as long your personally chosen creed takes you to experience "Enlightenment", this being the world that God has presented for YOU!

For is it not a truth that ALL the religious and philosophical creeds that are attached to ALL the world's religions are ALL in the pure pursuit of God's world, a world that can only exist in the "Present Time"? Therefore, is it not also true that you should be able to "personally" pursue, to "personally" find and so "personally" support God's world of harmony, and this to be following the findings of your own "personally" chosen creed based way of worship.

Again, this is also being "personally" chosen creeds which, by its practice, you and all those similarly-minded around you, do experience the real economic and community-based agreements that can lead to a harmonious way of living in God's world.

Yet Sadly, this same religious unrest and the same persecutions now being endured in the Islamic world ended in the Christian world around 1,650 years after the death of Jesus, for it was only then that the Christians realised that it did not matter what creed you followed, as long as you found through your own personal practise the actual world of God; for in God's world you can truly harm no-one but in a personal world of "I Want," you can only seriously harm yourself

55 THE CHRISTIAN CREEDS THAT TARGET ENLIGHTENMENT

It is also known that the traditional religiously-based central teaching of Christian worship is the doctrine of the Trinity which Latin for "threefold". The Christian Trinity explains that the One God comprises three divine entities, these being one – The God the Father of the Creation who was also acclaimed to be within two – the Incarnate Son Jesus Christ acclaimed to be God "within a body" and three – the Holy Spirit, who is stated to be God, "without a body".

Correctly, this is because it is a well-known fact that the "Holy Spirit" that is within the body can be spiritually experienced, which is described within "The Book" as being "Enlightenment". For surely, this is a fact which is explained in the Christian religions as inwardly experiencing the "peace that surpasses all understanding," which in the Islamic religions it is explained as *"a realm beyond the ability of words to properly convey."* Yes, this is an "Enlightenment" that you cannot manufacture because it is already within you and around you for it is genuinely the liberation of the Soul to experience the Creation that is outside your body. It has also been acclaimed as being likened to living in "paradise," which can be "scientifically" explained as physically joining with that which exists in the "Present Time". For indeed this is a "Present Time" which exists within the stillness of the "Mother of the Creation", which is all around you just has it is within you. It is also an experience which gives to the experiencer, a full comprehension of any situation in which it exists. It is also an experience which is described within the Christian religion as being filled with the "Holy Spirit" or "Holy Ghost", and within the world's religions and philosophies, it is described as *"Paradise", "Nirvana", "Moksha" "Kenshō", "Bodhi", "Satori", "Kevala", "Jnana", "Ushta", "Eden", "Heaven", "Promised Land", "Shangri-La", "Svargamu", Kā bāga", "Vāṭikā", "Kā Jaga- ha", "Sukhabhavana"* and many more descriptions, all emanating as a description of the experiencing of "Enlightenment", this being the taught target that exists within ALL our many world's religions and philosophies. For correctly, although many have forgotten the purpose of their religions target, which is to experience "Enlightenment", many stumbles into this "experience" and a few also "scientifically" succeed, but they ALL practise via their founders' culturally-based creeds of worship, the way to achieve this "Enlightenment", which is the purpose of our ancient wises teachings, this being that which exists within their culturally based religions.

For indeed, "Enlightenment" is undoubtedly a physical experience in which at its first "realisation" stage you become "Self-aware", maybe for the first time in your life. Correctly, this being a factual awareness in which you realise that you do not exist as a separate entity from all that you can touch, see, taste, hear or smell, and that that which is emanating within you is "The Light of the World," this being the "light" that shines without thought upon the "Creation" that is all around you just has it shines without thought upon all that rests within you. For really and indeed this is undoubtedly an "Enlightening" experience, and it is an experience in which ALL the above five senses do "communally" and silently report to, this being your observing Soul. For truly you will become "Self-Aware" that all that you "experience" to exist around you is also the physical body of the real "YOU", just as you now experience all that is within you to be the real YOU! For you will then become "Self-Aware" that YOU are indeed the observing Soul, this being that which you now experience to be the observer of all the "Creation" in which you become fully "aware" is the body of the observing YOU!

So yes! This awareness is the first stage of experiencing "Enlightenment" so when you look at your hand and then look at all of that exists around, you will become "Self-Aware" that all that your Soul observes through a now unclouded and still mind, is also a substantial part of YOU, just has is your hand!

Therefore as an example of this "Self-awareness" in which rests the silent first experience of "Enlightenment," you can reach out with your hand and touch something. You will be "aware" that you are not your hand, nor are you that which your hand touches, for you become "aware" that you are genuinely the "observer" of this act, and with a still and silent mind you will become "aware" of this fact at any time. For indeed, it is as well to know that this inner observer of all that is life and none-life is your Soul – which is the real you, for again. Truly you are this silent observer who knows itself to be a part of the entity we call life and non-life, this being the "Creation" of God or the creation of Nature for the Non-Believer. For it is undoubtedly true that this "Self-Awareness" experience can become a continuous never-ending experience of that which you will "happily" recognise to be "Enlightenment," this being an experience of contentment and of bliss that always rests within you and which you may have never experienced before. It is also a condition in which our wise ancients knew that you would "automatically" support the emerging harmony that is developing all around you or simply enjoy a life in which this support is not needed.   It may also be wise to add here that one who has been "Enlightened" may become "Self-Aware", a condition arrived at before experiencing "Self-Realisation". This "Self-Aware" is a condition where your soul becomes the "personal" observer of all life and non-life and which is not "Self-Realisation" in which you become that which you used to observe. Therefore, indeed, in this "Self-Realisation" condition, your bodily death soon occurs. Then you will never be born again and so will stay forever within that from which you previously came, which is God or Nature for the Non-Believer. For is not the purpose of the Creation being so that God or Nature for the Non-Believer can experience "Himself"?

So yes! There may have also been "Enlightening" experiences occurring within you that you may have never "Realised" before? For sincerely it is true that many people may have fleetingly experienced "Enlightenment" as existing, especially when looking from a high point down into a nature-filled valley? Now if the reader wishes to achieve and so "experience" these genuine realities – Read on.

So Yes! Within the Christian religions bible, it is stated that there is only "One God who is also within three Divine Entities," which explains and supports the religious truth that the incarnate Jesus was a person who was a man inhabited by God, which, in "The Book" explanations, means that Jesus was "Self-Realised". Therefore is it not true that the Christian Bible reveals that in Jesus's life upon this Earth, many witnessed His crucifixion, His resurrection, and His ascension into heaven. All of which is serious proof of God's love for people and God's forgiveness of all peoples sins for correctly have not ALL people been "Godly" given the "Freedom of Choice" this being to support His emerging creation.? For indeed is it not factual that God or Nature for the Non-Believer must exist within all things, just as any child contains the substance of its parents and indeed, we are all children of God or Nature for the Non-Believer. For it is undoubtedly an indeed known belief that the Christian Jesus was "Self-Realised"; this being an "Enlightened" stage that can be experienced by people and which is the experience following the above "Self-Awareness". This experience is indeed being a "Self-Realised" state, and it is only people who can knowingly experience that singularity which exists as all life and non-life, which is an experience that is a known reality and one that is expressed by many religions and philosophies as "Self-Realisation".

So Yes! "Self-Realisation" is an existence in which all people can experience not only the feeling of belonging to all that exists in the "Present Time", this being an experience which is called "Enlightenment", but that they are that which is all life and non-life, this being that exists in the "Present Time". For indeed, "Self-realisation" is known to be the final quest of all religious and philosophical pursuits, and the final target of all creeds, that have been culturally attached to our worlds many religions and philosophies; for all target the truth that all life and non-life exist only in God's world or the world of Nature for the non-believer. For in being "Self-Realised," the stage after being "Self-Aware" you enter an "Enlightenment" in which you ARE all that which exists in the "Present Time". For certainly is it not also a known truth that when the Incarnate Jesus, who was "Self-Realised", actually spoke, it was the "Creator" who was speaking to all the people who listened to these words of Jesus? Now listen again to these words emanating from Jesus, and understand that it is the "Creator" through Jesus, who is speaking directly to you. Therefore God or Nature for the Non-Believer stated through Jesus the words, "Man does not live on bread alone, but on every word that comes from the mouth of God." These "words" coming from God are the actions governing the Godly imposed harmony seeking activities that are continually changing the Creation and the world around us, these also being for people a static but developing activity that can only exist in the "Present Time". For these right actions can be said to be the words of the "Creator" explaining that all people are tools that have been created with the "Freedom of Choice", which means they can choose to assist the developing creation by performing actions that aid the Creation's developing harmony or choose not to perform that which can be described as the same activity because the same act could be detrimental to the harmony seeking needs of the Creation"; and these acts in support of the emerging creation are the authentic "food" that all people should be eating. But honestly, it is the "Mother of the Creation" who guides and corrects the harmony seeking laws that support and maintains the Creation's onward-developing harmony and it is She who also seeks the physical support of all her children, this being that child which we call people.

So yes! Here are more words of Jesus describing the unity existing within the emerging laws of the Creation for again, God, speaking to all people through Jesus said: "The wind blows wherever it pleases. You hear its sound, but you cannot tell where it comes from or where it is going", for indeed the wind exists only in the "Present Time" and so it is with everyone born of the Spirit. For simply put, no person knows, even when enlightened, just where God's or Natures "lawful" world is taking them, but all know that they cannot stop its progress. Yet! Justly, it is only correct that when "Enlightened", a person can begin to live in the "Present Time", a time that is like the wind for it is without thought and so allows anyone, via the "Freedom of Choice" to experiences the pure Heaven that exists upon our Earth. It is also living in Heaven in which they have accurately stopped any mind filling "I want" needs, which is a false greed-based power emanating from a person's un-disciplined and so untrained animalistic five senses. This negative is being a false power which can command an undisciplined or ignoring person always to obey their thoughts, this being because of a false belief that that which people hear in mind is believed to be coming from them. Strictly, this cannot be true for you cannot be that which you believe is not a part of you, and an "I Want" is certainly for a "something" that you observe to be not a part of the real YOU!

So yes! This "habitual" and inner mind filling obedience to an undisciplined "I Want" for ME command, is a command that is coming from one of the five senses, which always confines a person to live in an untrue self-created mind filling Hell that can only be formed by a personally created within a mind filling "I Want" for me. For rightly, this a mind filling concept that takes the "I Want for ME" thinker to live in a personally-created "Past" or "Future", which is undoubtedly the "Hell" of which our wise ancients spoke. For certainly is it not true that these personally created and the mind filling "I Want" world does not exist. So it cannot be the world that ALL our wise ancients described as Gods Heaven, this being that which exist in the "Present Time", for indeed a personally created Past or Future does not exist in Gods world. For these are personally created false worlds which emanates from a no longer existing "I Wanted" past and in its mind filling thinking targets a non-existing "I Want" future, which is a mind filling dreamed Hell which does not exist, and so it cannot be the heaven that surrounds all things that exist within the "Present Time." For truly, and again it should be said, that Hell is a false world which only an "I Want" thought can create for it is based upon an unreal non-existing Past or Future in which ignoring people can, in response to their personal "I Want" thinking, claim as their world, but which is usually an endeavour that is the responsibility of others. For truly this world called Hell is a personally created world in which and in ignorance, the five senses are "animalistic-ally" allowed to continually cry and plan for their "I Want" future animalistic desires which are usually based past thoughts and so they ignorantly endeavour to try and change God's world, to suit their own "I Want" for ME needs. Again this is genuinely self-created Hell that cannot exist in the Heavenly un-thinking "Present Time", a time which truly exists has the Heaven which all people can experience to be the only the real "Creation", for it genuinely exists but only in the "Present Time", which is Gods world or the world of Nature for the Non-Believer.

So yes! Very truly, that when a "you" become "Enlightened", which is ALWAYS the target of our wise ancients, it is then that "you" will "personally" know that all the Creation, this being that which correctly exists everywhere, is really "You", for truly how can a personal "I Want for ME", exist when you "physically" and with an empty unthinking mind actually "self-experience" that you ARE the observer of "Everything", as in "Self-Awareness" or that you really are "Everything" as in "Self-Realization"? Therefore, now, but only in the "Present Time," you are enabled to personally acknowledge that the words emanating from our wise ancients can be likened to the "Creation" speaking to you? Correctly, this being that which all people now know to be everything? For it is not now recognised that the task of our wise ancients was to support and so aid the development of God's world of harmony, for they can do nothing else, for they knowingly live in Gods world or the world of Nature for the Unbeliever.

So Yes! Now all readers know this truth, for it is not also true that many Christians know and understand – stand under the truth - that it was God who spoke directly through His Son Jesus who many Christians acknowledge to be the personification of the Creation which is the only child of God, for indeed Jesus existed has one person with God. So it was God who, through Jesus, did always speak to all those who have ears to hear and a heart that could listen.

So Yes! Now listen to the following Godly spoken words or Natures spoken words for the Non-Believer! These being words which were said to all "I Want" for Me people who had simply forgotten who they were and so in the forgetting that they can be "Enlightened" they painfully ignore that which they are and therefore could not understand the true meaning of God's words or Natures spoken words for the Non-Believer! These were the following words which were said through Jesus: "I have spoken to you of earthly things, and you do not believe; how then will you believe if I speak of heavenly things?" For whom amongst His listeners believed that Heaven was all around them except those who Jesus had previously "Enlightened"?

So Yes! Now is the time for all readers to believe that when you read ONLY the words of Jesus that exist in the Christian Bible and with only these highlighted Jesus spoken words being without any further "inner explanations", it is then that you will deeply know and understand that it is God that is speaking to you.

So Yes! Now for the first time read and so "hear" only these words that were spoken to you personally by God through His "Self-Realised" child which we call Jesus and so truly you will then rest in the "Peace that surpasses all Understanding." Therefore now and with no thoughts in mind "listen" again and so truly understand the following words of God spoken through Jesus: – "For God did not send his Son (This is the personified Jesus) into the world to condemn the world, but to save the world through Him" (to save all people through the harmonised words of Jesus). "Whoever believes in Him (These being the "Enlightened" ones) is not condemned, but whoever does not believe (but lives in their Self-created personal world of "I want" for ME!) Stands condemned already because they have not believed in the name of God's one and only Son" (this only child is the Creation which is personified in Jesus and which is a Creation that cares and provides for all needs upon this Earth). "This is why the Light (that which can only exist in the "Present Time" and so cannot exist in the past or the future) has come into the world, (this "light" being Jesus) for men (people) loved darkness (their Creation of "I want") instead of light (this is that light which can only exist in the "Present Time") because their deeds (I want for myself) were evil. Everyone who does evil (this is the pursuing of an "I want" for ME!) Hates the light, (God's world that only exists in the "Present Time") and will not come into the light (To become "Enlightened" and so "experience" God's "Present Time") or fear that their deeds will be exposed" (that they will lose there "I want" for ME!). "But whoever lives by the truth comes into the light, (the truth is to become enlightened and so live only in the "Present Time") so that it may be seen plainly (This being God's world of harmony) that what He has done (this being the creating of the Creation) has been done through God."

So Yes! By using their religion or philosophy, many people can personally choose their own culturally created religious creed or can simple and privately meditate, which is explained later in "The Book", these being facts which can take them to the world of "Enlightenment". Therefore, indeed this world of "Enlightenment" is the real world which accurately shines from God's laws of harmony or Nature's harmony for the Non-Believer. It is then that a consistent "Enlightenment" pursuer can by their "Self-Applied" and personal discipline, birth a new life that can exist only in the "Present Time" and so realise and therefore know why the truth of existing only in the "Present Time" is called "Enlightenment". For this is an experience that was well known by our wise ancients, this being that within all people is that which is called "Enlightenment", a condition in which a person can rest in "The Peace that surpasses all understanding", a peace that is also explained in the Christian religion as being filled by the Holy Spirit or the Holy Ghost.

To further add to this developing knowledge that rests within Christian creeds, especially those that worships the Holy Trinity in which it is stated that the Holy Ghost or Holy Spirit is personally experienced by the worshipper and which can also be said to exist in a realm beyond the ability of words to describe and that it is a "Self-Realisation" which must be experienced to be recognized as absolute truth. For as our wise ancients or those of the Christian faith who have experienced this, say that this "Enlightenment" awakened within them a "Holy Fire" – does this sound historically familiar to the reality of the many descriptions already given in previous pages of "The Book" as being the root target of all the Earths religions and philosophies? For indeed this is the reality that is described as experiencing that which the Christians call the "Holy Spirit" or "Holy Ghost", this truly is a reality which is often being said within "The Book" that it can only exist and so experienced within one's Self and that no one can give it to you, for justly it can only be achieved by your activity. It is also true that it that can only be experienced as a "Self-Reality" which can only be experienced when your five senses are silenced, and so you become a part of the "Present Time". Correctly, this is a time when the mind is without a thought, for its thoughts which fill the mind and which blocks the Soul from seeing through the mind the real world that we call "The Present Time". For indeed, the "Present Time" is that which cannot be brought to thought for it exists outside of thought; therefore, it can only be experienced by those people whose mind is empty, still and without thought.

For again and genuinely, existing only in the "Present Time" is an actual realisation which further states that no "I Want" images of the past or the future can be created within the mind, this being when the mind is still and without thought. For these "I Want" thoughts are mind filling thoughts which are emanating from the five senses and which indeed are clouding the mind with a self-created false Past or a Future which is a world that is known as Hell! For it is a false un-real world which is being selfishly worded or pictured into the mind and they are always based upon an "I Want" for me thought. These being thoughts which always target an illusionary world that is created within the mind, and this is undoubtedly an unreal world that it is NOT experiencing God's world or the world of Nature for the Non-Believer.

Therefore, is it not true that the real world can exist only in the Godly or Naturally created "Heaven" that we call the "Present Time" and not the unreal world of an "I Want" Hell that does not exist except in mind. For this Hell is a world in which exists the self-created "I Want", for ME, this being a world that has been, in the ignorance of not-knowing, mind-fully "self-created" to claim a non-existing Future that is arising from a non-existing Past. These being personal thoughts and so are individually self-created worlds that do not physically exist but which are believed to be real worlds.

For honestly and accurately is it not the real world that world which physically exists all around you and also within you? Is it not also true that the Past or the Future, this being that which "The Book" calls Hell, cannot be experienced in the "Present Time", this being that time which "The Book" calls Heaven, which can be physically experienced and therefore cannot be "illusionary". Therefore is not this illusionary self-created Hell a truly a non-existing world in which these illusionary "I Want" for ME thoughts are personally created? These were thoughts that create a self-made Hell which replaces the Godly made world or the world of Nature for the Non-Believer, for sure is it not seen to be true that "Heaven", that which is all around you and within you, truly exists without any thoughts. It is a world that is certainly not an illusion.

So yes! This search for the truth is often an unknown search for "Enlightenment", this being that light which shines from those who live only in the Heaven of the "Present Time" and it is indeed the target which is sought by ALL the many different religious and philosophical groups which also worship via the use of many different creeds. For justly, there are many differing worshipping creeds and practises, which are culturally and historically created by our worlds, many different named religions and philosophies? For again truly, do not all worshippers pursue the peaceful "Enlightened" silencing of the mind in which the Christians say is experiencing the Holy Spirit or Holy Ghost. For this is being an influential motivating factor and one which can be achieved by a worshipper whose creed concentrates upon a silent personal praying system or the chanting together in prayer, or the prayer within their consciousness or even silently following a single leader's spoken word. It can also be "found" to be experienced in the reciting of group prayers which are performed in a group harmony or maybe a group reading of their personnel creeds scriptures or even in the silent praying while alone or within a group or in a group based singing etc. For indeed, what is resting and awaiting revelation within these creeds is a way of finding the truth that rests in God's world or the world of Nature for the non-believer.

So yes! God's world when experienced within the "Present Time", is always recognised to be accurate, for there is no room in a disciplined to silence mind for ANY internal thought which must be a world created by a person's past or a future "I want" for ME! Thus, in this way, creed worshippers bear witness and so practice their chosen religions or philosophical path of worship which is actively and culturally designed to bring the worshipper into God's "Present".

For this is undoubtedly being a world which can be again described by Christians as the experiencing of the "Holy Spirit" or "Holy Ghost" or as the Muslims, say the experiencing of the "Angel Gabriel" and which many hundreds of other religions and philosophies described by different names, this being because no words can describe this actual experiencing "Enlightenment". For this is an authentic experience in which you realise that which cannot be described, for this is God's world or the world of Nature for the Non-Believer whose world you are experiencing, and it is an experience that is truly "being" within you and also "being" without you.

So yes! All religions and philosophies seek and can genuinely experience that which the Christian religions call being filled with the "Holy Spirit" or the "Holy Ghost". However, as previously stated, it has acquired many other names throughout our many world religions and philosophies that seek its reality. Even in the ancient Zoroastrianism religion fifth-Century BC referred to this experience of "Enlightenment" as "Ushta" which they described as meaning "liberation, salvation and emancipation of the Soul," and this was 2520 years ago and time without the modern understanding of the five senses. For indeed, it is an experience that brings to the worshipper "the "peace that surpasses understanding", but it should always be remembered that it is that experience which God has presented only to people and it is ALWAYS waiting for seekers – which can be YOU!

So yes! The experiencing of the Christian Holy Spirit or Holy Ghost shows the harmony that exists in God's world or the world of Nature for the non-believer for all people can experience "Enlightenment" and maybe onward towards "Self-Awareness" or "Self-Realisation". But first, it can also be understood that this experience of "Enlightenment" can also occur fleetingly. Therefore a person can become "Self-Aware" or "Self-Realised". The reason for this is because the Soul is enabled to sometimes see through an accidentally made empty mind, this being a fact which can occur during an actual pause in the mind filling "I Want" demands of the five senses which regularly block the mind. It is under these "uncontrolled" non-mind filling circumstances that the Soul can gently experience the "Present Time", this only happening when the mind has no blocking "I Want" thought, this being that which was stopping the Soul from actually "seeing" the creation that existed around it. For indeed this can be experienced by people to be a momentarily "Enlightening" incident, for it is undoubtedly a realisation which occurs when all the "I want" for myself thoughts, which are continually emanating from the five senses, these being that which you believe are the real you, do temporally stop and then justly it is this fact which allows the Soul, which IS the real YOU, to see through the empty and so still mind and so experience the peaceful harmony of the "Present Time", which is Gods world or the world of Nature for the Non-Believer. For certainly is it not true that when looking down a valley or at a beautiful natural reality of the world of Nature we can experience stillness within the mind which cannot be explained, for we also seem to become that at which we are looking? This momentary or minutely experience of "Enlightenment" happens because the Soul is observing the "Present Time", for the mind is empty without any mind blocking contamination of the many "I Want" thoughts that are usually penetrating the mind from one of the five senses. These are usually the many "I Want" mind-blocking acts that are being enabled continuously to freely enter the mind habitually because of freedom that was incorrectly given to the five senses to do so in our childhood.

Thus, our God-given or Nature gave "Freedom of Choice" now enables our "Willpower" to use the energy we call "Consciousness", to freely energise into the mind any personal decisions, wishes, or any "I Want" that is occurring within our "animalistic" five senses. It is this that we falsely believe to be "our self". But it is now well to remember and to know, via experience, that these five senses that always sound into the mind are NOT you! For you are the Soul, this being that which rests within your body and you are also the Soul that wants for nothing, because you have everything and it is also good to remember that you are also a Soul that cannot die

So Yes! It is this actuality of constant "Self-Disciplined" obedience to religious or philosophical creed worship, in which you use the power of consciousness, via the "Freedom of Choice" to habitually stop and so habitually replace "Willpower" from freeing the false worshipping of the five senses. For indeed, it is the voluntary obedience to praying, kneeling, singing, chanting, eating and other imposed disciplines that can eventually "Self-Discipline" the mind. It is this fact which our wise ancients knew would eventually stop the entering into the mind any "I want" thoughts emanating from "animalistic" the five senses.

So yes! It is these religious and philosophical "Creed-Based" "Self-Disciplined" and "Self-Repeating" plus "Self-Controlled" activities that are disciplinary stopping and eventual removing the many "I Want" for ME thoughts which certainly do create a false world that opposes the existing Gods world or the world of Nature for the Non-Believer. These being "I Want" only for Me thoughts which can be stopped when a person's "Consciousness" actively re-engages "Willpower" to recite or chant a prayer which refrains and so retrains the habit of "Consciousness" from freely and habitually allowing "Willpower" from automatically pushing into the mind the "I Want" of the five senses – this must be stopped if one wishes to enter Gods world or the real world of Nature for the Non-Believer.

So Yes! Instead of this consistently pursued "I Want", which is that which is created by our animalistic five senses, a person can actually "choose", via the God-given or Nature gave for the Non-Believer, their "Freedom of Choice", to engage their "Consciousness" to recite a creed based prayer which is a "Self-Created" discipline that is used to stop the habit of "Willpower" from freely and automatically sounding into the mind the animalistic will of the five senses.

For indeed these are much-needed creed-based and religiously disciplined worshipping systems which uses religiously imposed and culturally based "praying" words or the chanting of "hymns" which are automatically sounded and so are created by a "Self" imposed discipline that creates a still and unthinking "empty" mind in which a person indeed enters Gods world. This world can only be seen and so experienced by a person's Soul, but only through an empty and still mind.

So yes! It is undoubtedly this fact that allows people, who are religiously worshipping in accordance to their culture and "Enlightened" initiators, to automatically and mechanically, via a religiously imposed discipline, to silence their mind and so without thinking do automatically repeat words and or gestures that create a mind emptying discipline which then allows their Soul to observe the "Present Time", this being through the spaces between their automatically and habitually sounding words. Again, this is being a factual truth for during these prayers and other religious activities; people can experience the inner silent bliss which is created when their "Soul" is enabled to see and so experience Gods world or the world of Nature for the Non-Believer, a fact which can only be realised through an empty mind. For justly it is this truth that creates all our religions that are founded by our ancient wise It is also because of the teachings of our wise ancients, which many people now seek to experience "Enlightenment", this is truly being a condition in which you knowingly experience who you are. It is also a condition in which you physically experience that the Soul within "you" IS the real "you", this being that reality which is first witnessed when you begin to see the world through the silent bliss-filled spaces of the automatically and habitually repeating creeds and or mantra-like words and very often the time will come when you experience that you are your Soul. A condition which may first happen when you listen silently to your religious leaders' spoken sermons or your silent "disciplined" listening to the choirs singing – so sincerely our wise ancients, who did initiate all these practice's, were very wise.

So yes! There is truthfully an "Enlightening" experience that can only exist when the mind is empty, this being a condition which enables you to "Self-Experience" only the "Present Time". For in fact, truly the "Present Time" is our Heaven that exists only in our "Present Time" and which is a "Heaven" that can always "Self-Realised" by your Soul, but only when any entry into your mind, these being entries which are usually emanating for one of your five senses, is forbidden to enter via your "Freedom of Choice". Thus it is that the "Freedom of Choice" can be usefully supported by a disciplined sounding of a "habitual" creed based worshipping hymn, prayer or active physical service in which the practitioner can "Choose" to become still and "silent" via any or all of these this self-imposed" disciplines. For indeed this will eventually allow your Souls view of the world around you NOT to be blocked by a mind filling "I want" for me which is a constant ever-changing thought that creates within the mind of the thinker a non-existing Past or Future which genuinely does not exist and which is undoubtedly the place that which "The Book" calls Hell!

Why? Because truthfully, these are "I want" thoughts which are blocking the Souls view of the Creation through the mind via this misplaced stealing of the energy of consciousness, but which is stealing that cannot exist when a creed trained mind refuses to acknowledge any "I wants" that are targeting an entry into our mind – so creed worship is a habit that certainly needs pursuing.

Therefore, genuinely, the stating of this truth can now be acknowledged in a modern way. However, this is truly an ancient understanding, for did not the Prophet Muhammed say that the devil who spoke to God said: "I shall continue to lead your servants astray as long as their spirits are in their bodies" and God replied: "Then I shall continue to pardon them as long as they ask for my forgiveness." The "devil" of course is the animalistic five senses which are continually pursuing their animalistic "I Want" for ME! Also, the "spirit" is the Soul which exists within a person's body and then asking for "forgiveness" is genuinely the search for "Enlightenment" in which, when experienced, a person knows that they have immediately been forgiven of all past sins that they have committed. Again, this is an "Enlightening" experience which can only occur when the mind is silent. So the Soul can clearly see and so experience the outer world and therefore obey its duties to the Heaven which is in existence all around and within "everything"!

So yes! There is later established in "The Book", a modern "scientifically" proven way to achieve "Enlightenment", which is a modern way to achieve that which ALL our religions and philosophies seek and which is also a religious or philosophical experience that cannot be described even when experiencing it? For as previously mentioned, the Christian call it the *"peace that surpasses all understanding"* and in the Islamic religions *"a realm beyond the ability of words to properly convey."* Indeed, this correctly being a peace that comes to the individual when the mind rests in perfect "stillness", a condition which gives to the experiencer a full comprehension of any situation that exists in the "Present Time", for it allows the Soul one hundred per cent recognition of God's world a world that cannot be accurately described by any words for it the reality of the real world which surpasses all understanding.

So Yes! Indeed, it CAN be experienced but only by people, to be an excellent "Enlightening" experience and an experience which was also stated to be a "Godly" based experience by our wise ancients, this being many thousands of years ago. It was also, in those ancient times often stated to be a "Godly" experience but only when those ancient ones fully experience the "Present Time", which is genuinely Gods world or the world of Nature for the Non-Believer, this being that which can only exist in the "Present Time" for truthfully, all our ancient peoples' religions and philosophies agree that the "Present Time" is God's world. Therefore, is it not true that we exist in a world in which the needs of all life and non-life are harmoniously provided for and which is a life that is "Nature ally" agreed? Yet truly, is it not also a world that is negatively abused and pursued by deviating claims of many a personal individually desired "I Want" for ME! These being "I Want" for ME claims that are based upon an ignorance that creates selfish "I Want for Me" acting and a selfish "I Want for Me" thinking and YES! To overcome this ignorance is the purposeful creed based target of ALL our wise ancients who created our many religions and philosophical belief systems and who in earlier cultures, used their "Enlightening" words to explain different ways of experiencing this "Bliss that surpasses all Understanding", for indeed all those that our wise ancients spoke to they did also recognise to be themselves. So now is it not seen to be true that the endeavours of all our ancient wise were to stop people from being the enemy of God's harmony or Nature's Harmony for the Non-Believer, which included themselves? For really and truly, people can be plagued by an "I Want for Me" ignorance in which a simple creed practice can eliminate forever, and if you wish to know what this simple practice is – Read on.

56   THE STRANGE UNRELIGIOUS WARS WITHIN MANY CREEDS

Is it not true that great cultural-based religions and belief systems are instigated by our ancient wise, but then sadly upon their death and as the years roll by a negative *"I want this religion to be for ME and my way of control and my way of worship"*, this being that which is genuinely originating from the five senses. Does not this historical "I Want" for me not also factually hide the actual reality of our purposeful existence and the way of life that accurately and honestly emanates from a person's soul, this being that which is attached to "Everything" and can certainly be experienced to be so?

Therefore is it not certainly true that this ignoring of a correct "Heavenly" way of life, this being that which can exist only in the unthinking "Present Time", has disagreeably surfaced multiple times within the ages our many existing religions and their culturally-based religious belief systems? For is it not also true, as history shows, that some people or person arises who says *"I want control of this religion and it is to be preached and controlled by my way not your way,"* and also *"We should destroy that religion for it is not the way to Gods worlds for only our religion is the way to Gods world and God wants us to destroy that false religion"*. For truthfully this is a personal "I want" and a belief that went on to murder thousands of innocent men, women and children, yet sincerely and factually, has history shows, these disagreements were really about ownership of property and had nothing to do with religion.

Thus it was that people or their leaders, created a greed-based "I Want", this being a personal "I want" which gave birth too many inner religious conflicts, these being conflicts which indeed grew stronger after the originator of the religion died for it was then that "I Want" modifications became attached to the founder's religion. It was also this fact which went onto fracture many of the world's leading religions via the developing of their many personal "I Want" arguments stating, *"The leader of my way of worshipping within this religion, should be the true leader and the leader of your way of worshipping within this religion, is not"* and also *"My way of religious practices is the only true way to find God and not your way"*, these being disagreement that has nothing to do with God's world nor the religious practices that truly bring to a person an "Enlightenment" that certainly exists only within the "Present Time", which is God's created world or the created world of Nature for the Non-Believer. For truly Gods world is the "Heaven" which only exists in the "Present Time" and which is certainly not the "Hell" that indeed exists in a dreamed "Past" or a dreamed "Future", these being unreal worlds that do not exist and it also ignores the fact that the ME, is ALL people?

For indeed does not our history show that these religiously based inner separating "I Want" wars and conflicts are strictly indeed an "I Want" for ME, which is a personally based desire that conflictingly targets their wanted change to an existing way of worship, this also being within an existing religion. Yet is this not really and truly a personally dreamed "I Want" for ME activity? Therefore, is it not sadly true that this "I Want" is based upon an "I Want" my way of worship for this religion and not your way of worship for this religion?

Therefore, assuredly, does not our history show that these personal disagreements then splinter a religious truth? This truth is that God created all life and non-life which is the only child and a child in which only people were allowed the "Freedom of Choice", this being to "positively" support the benefits of the emerging creation that existed all around them, has it does within the singularity that exits within them. But over time, many people "animalistic-ally" forgot this truth and began to steal for themselves from the abundance that was all around them and so began to worship a personal "I Want" ownership of all things. Thus began the pursuit of conflicting wars which used dangerous savagery upon the killing of others as separating worshippers of various religions seek to place their own different "leader" and way of creed worship upon other religious ways of worship, these being "I Want" which pursued their way to a truth that was not shown to exist by the Creator of their religion, or is the truth not really " I Want for ME" your property and your riches.

So Yes! Does not history and our modern world not show this "I Want" for Me is a unique bullying culture which always leads to the stealing the riches and property of others, this being that which is also obtained by the killing of thousands of men women and children which is also an "I want" attempt that enables their own "instigating" leaders all power not only over their branch of the same-named region but over other many differently named religions and creeds. Yet honestly, does not our world's history always show that these "I Want only my religions way of life to be worshipped" are endeavours that "ALWAYS" fail! For genuinely, it should be known that these personal "I want" endeavours that are used to control others forcibly will always fail because God gave to people the "Freedom of Choice" and no person can take this fact from other people – they only "think" they can! For rightly, does not our history show those wars and other "I want" that which is yours, roughly being obtained from others by bullying – NEVER succeed. For assuredly, a group or a person's way of life which is based upon the "Freedom of Choice" will in time always return to be ruled by God's world or the world of Nature for the Non-Believer.

So yes! For certainly is it not also true that this animosity between religious leaders brought great wars and conflicts for many people and the history of our world shows how this religious "I Want" for ME, did bitterly cause considerable disagreements within the many ways of worshipping within the worlds Northern Hemispheres and so, as our history shows, a severe discord developed between the Christian religions "Catholic" worshippers and the Christian religions "Protesters", whose saviour and choice maker for both of them was the incarnate Jesus and later the same discord erupted between the leaders of the Islamic Sunni and Shia belief systems whose saviour and choice maker was Mohammed. For rightly, the entire world knows that the original teachers of these religions gave a tremendous natural truth to their followers, this being that which came directly via the "Holy Spirit" from the mouths of the Christian incarnate Jesus, the Creator of Christianity and the very wise ancient Muhammad who finalised the Islamic faith - Peace is upon them both.

Therefore is it not "scientifically" true that both paved a "creed" worshipping the way that worshipped the one, God? These revelation being a way in which they established personal "creeds" that brought to their followers an effective way of devotion in which they could fully experience the bliss of the One God and also a worshipping way which also included a direct path to "Enlightenment", this being a unity in which ALL people can knowingly experience Gods world.

For is it not true that "Enlightenment" is an actual reality and not a personal conjecture? Is it not also true that both these Northern Hemisphere religions contain the same personally directing truths that lead to "Enlightenment?" This being that which is Godly targeted by all our world's religions and philosophies, for indeed this is the target that rests within ALL the world's religions and philosophies, but which are stated and propagated in many ways because of a person's cultural need for an understanding?

Is it not also true that the "Mother of the Creation" supported the harmony seeking Christian leaders? They eventually ended this conflict between Catholic and Protestant has will soon end the conflict between Islamic Sunni and Shia belief systems, this being achieved by pursuing God's sincerity? For faithfully all "Enlightened" religious leaders will allow, within their religion, the Creation of different cultures but supporting ways of worship. For correctly and faithfully our God-given "Freedom of Choice" does factually ensure that this should be so, therefore a way of non-interrupting worship, this being that which harms no one should never be removed except by truthfulness and revelation.

So Yes! Does not the universal proof of this Godly reality stand all around us? For all people can now recognise that the Christian faith has around fourteen major different worshipping divisions, all guided by the chosen creeds of their religions creator. Is it not also seen that people who pursued their Godly given "Freedom of Choice" did choose leaders whose personnel authority defined different doctrinal issues?

These were issues that they "culturally" felt they could support for it brought to them the experiencing of Gods "Heaven" that rests upon our Earth. Theses all being Christian doctrinal issues such as the true nature of Jesus, the authority of apostolic succession, their Souls relationship to death, the existence of eternal judgment, to the existence of heaven or hell. Also of leadership such as papal supremacy and the accepting of different leaders and even within these "chosen" religious practices, there are at least twenty-two different "breakaway" groups of likened denominations all of which are endeavouring to find a way to achieve "Enlightenment". For indeed all people have the emotional feeling that there is something outside them that is also really within them and therefore many religions and philosophies wisely target the reality of this truth, this being to experience the reality that that which is outside you is also YOU!

Again God's gift to all people, this being the "Freedom of Choice" is now genuinely indeed being obeyed by the "Christian Faith". For this faith now culturally enables freedom in which smaller religious groups can be controlled by privatively appointed leaders who share similar cultural beliefs, practices, and historical ties which come under a category called "Branches of Christianity" or "Denominational Families".

For, in all honesty, all "Christians" are shadowing God's gift of all peoples "Freedom of Choice", this being as they follow their personally chosen leader's creeds, for it is their "Chosen" worshipping creed which contentedly pursues their own "understandable" way to experiencing Gods world. For indeed, many paths target the finding of "Heaven" that rests upon this Earth and also there are many ways of worship which people can genuinely establish for themselves and their families.

For is it not true that ALL the different religious and philosophical paths that are created throughout the world of people are created with only one purpose, this being to experience Gods world? Is it not also clearly seen to be true that their chosen religions purpose is culturally "created" to enable its followers, these being those within our worlds many different cultures, to instinctually "observe" and so become has one with God's world or the world of Nature for the Non-Believer. Is it not also acknowledged to be true that this can only be achieved by personally sacrificing their "I Want" for ME!

Thus, this "Freedom of Choice" is being a genuine commitment that is required by God of Nature for the Non-Believer, for a person to live in and also experience God's world. For justly, this is the world that can only exist in the "Present Time", which is the experiencing of a place that "I Want" thoughts cannot steal. For rightly this is a place in time that is arrived at by those who sincerely seek a mind silencing companion which allows them to experience God's world, which is a reality that is known to truly exists when their five senses mind filling "I Want for me" stops, this being a realty which allows their Soul to experience the "Creation" fully and so become "Self-Aware", a condition in which all that is experienced is known to be itself and then possibly onward to "Self-Realisation", this being the reality in which it experiences "Nothing", or more correctly put "No Thing" for it becomes "Everything" and so becomes has one with God or Nature for the Non-Believer. It also becomes a Soul that will never again return to "life" for it joins has one with God or Nature for the Non-Believer, which of course is the purpose of the life that exists in Gods only child.

So yes! Is it not correct that all the world's religions and philosophies are derived by culturally-different culturally-based creed systems? Is it not also true that all these religions and philosophies are always locally designed to attract people to "Join" in friendship the many ways of community worshipping in which all target a life lived within the unity of God's world? Therefore, is it not also genuine that all these different culturally-based creed systems and doctrines are all personally designed to knock on God's door and so endeavour to gain entry to God's Heaven that rests upon this Earth?

Yet is it not also strange that many people who develop religious ways to find God's home are often also responsible for creating holy wars, plus community and family conflicts which often bring years of discord, this being a fact in which many thousands of men women and children are innocently destroyed? Why is this? Therefore, is it not also strange that eventually, has history usually proves, that these disputes and personally created "I Want" wars and conflicts, which are usually created by different "culturally" designed creeds, are eventually realised to be just different ways of endeavouring to personally find a better economic outcome, i.e., an increase in personal wealth, this being an "I Want" mind-grabbing pursuit which has nothing to do with God's world that is genuinely based upon harmony?

For assuredly, without this greed, is it not true that we live in harmony, providing God's world or Natures world for the Non-Believer? A genuinely natural world which can bring, with practice, many culturally formed "I want" minds to concentrate on a mind filling silence in which they can experience the non-harmful bliss of being in the non-wanting peace of God's truth or Natures real world for the Non-Believer. Again, this being the realised silence that always exits in our "Present Time", this also being the blissful experience which all our worlds' religions and philosophies seek, this being that which the world and "The Book" calls "Enlightenment", the experiencing of being that which exists all around that which is known as "You".

So yes! Is it not now seen that the opposite of peacefully living in Heaven, which is God's world, is destroyed by your or another's "I Want" for ME, which always leads to arguing and then to brutal warring plus many continually conflicting actions that are readily and always supplied by those who live in a self-created Hell?

For certainly is not valid, as our history shows and also that which can show in our "Present Time", that there are people, who in their personal "Freedom of Choice", knowingly choose or unknowingly choose to live in a self-created "Hell". This condition is a Hell in which living and acknowledging people, those who may exist in politically and in hierarchical positions, do really condemn the religious and political based peacefully seeking "choice" of others and so forcibly endeavour to change the beliefs of the people with whom they live and do circulate. Can this disputing way of life not be likened be an arguing disagreement against a person who wishes to drink their own personally chosen wine peacefully or to eat their own personally chosen food? Do not those who live in this personally created "I Want" Hell, not tell them NO! You must drink this alcohol, and you must only eat this food and so forcibly cause around them many an "I Want for ME" conflicts and this being that which can occur in all the world's different cultures? Therefore, where is the God-Given "Freedom of Choice", this being a "Freedom of Choice" which cannot harm anything that exists within the creation that surrounds them – is this not true?

Therefore, is it not the real truth, this being for all our worlds people to understand, is the truth that the essential aspect of all religions and political systems is to find that *"Peace that surpasses all Understanding"* as stated in the targeting of the Christian belief system or as stated in words *"a realm beyond the ability of words to convey properly"*, which is the target of the Muslim belief system, for in truth, is this, not a personal target?

So yes! Is it not also undoubtedly true that this is experiencing the *"oneness with all that exists"* which is undoubtedly the target of ALL the world's religions and philosophies, these being those that exist throughout our world? For indeed, is not the "I Want" for ME, certainly against the teachings of the founders of two of our world's major religions?

Thus it is that the Christians incarnate Jesus who it is known would rather die than mistreat or kill another plus for the Muslims the Prophet Mohammed's "SAW" Quotes in which it is stated *"Be kind, for whenever kindness becomes part of something, it beautifies it"* and also *"The best among you is the one who doesn't harm others with his tongue and hands"* and also saying *"The dead are tortured in their graves to the point that animals can hear them"*, meaning religious and political leaders of the people whose self-applied personnel "I want" hurts or destroys their followers. Also, the word "kill" is never mentioned by the great Mohammed whose main philosophy states that people should defend themselves against being harmed by these destroyers of peace, primarily if they attack *"a realm beyond the ability of words to properly convey"*.

So yes! It is also a fact that in no words mentioned by the two creators of the Christian or Islamic teachings was a request to their followers in which they said: *"I want my current religious way to be the only religious way"*. For indeed this would be an infringement of Gods given "Freedom of Choice", therefore indeed a non-religious "I Want for ME" statement which could not possibly come from an "Enlightened" person. Therefore it must be an emanating "I Want" from others that have been responsible for the creating of many conflicts and wars and great discord within both these religions in which thousands were and in the Islamic religion are still being bullied, brutalised and killed simply because some people turn their "I Want" minds to an *"I want my creed to be the way of worship, not your creed"* which in truth they are seeking the property and wealth of others who they deem are weaker than themselves.

So Yes! This realty can also be likened to a profane person saying, *"You must eat potatoes, not rice"* and the conflicting answer being, *"No, we want to eat rice."* Thus creating a disagreeing fact which then leads to a conflict and a war that brings to people many years of a painful death, sorrow and ridicule simply because many people have forgotten the truth spoken by our worlds "Enlightened" teachers, this is that "forgetting" is always our worst enemy.

For indeed, God or Nature for the Non-Believer indeed created laws that gave people the "Freedom of Choice" even unto creating their death. For really, the "Freedom of Choice" is being because the choice of a "positive" personal act can support the emerging *"Peace that surpasses all understanding,"* and so sustain the Heaven that exists or is endeavouring to exist within our world. Yet, is it not also true, that this same act, under different circumstances, could be a "negative" act, which would destroy the emerging *"Peace that surpasses all understanding,"* this being an act that will lead to the ungodly world that is called Hell and so must be avoided.

Therefore, correctly, this "Freedom of Choice" law ensures that God or Nature or the Non-Believer could never lead to the punishing of people for *"ignorantly and mistakenly"* "choosing" to perform a contrary act. Still, woe to them who *"knowingly and wrongly"* choose to perform such acts, for the condition of Hell awaits them, this being that which negatively exist in the "Present Time".

Therefore is it not also true that God's existing laws and emerging laws cannot cease or stop existing and so can never be irreparably broken, although many unfortunate people ignorantly endeavour to do so and so pain is "educationally" reflected upon them. Therefore God or Nature for the Non-Believer does not punish people for their performing of a harmful act, so unwisely and maybe in ignorance, they severely punish themselves? For indeed the laws of God or Nature or the Non-Believer must negatively turn against them and so is it then that they then begin to live in Hell, which is undoubtedly not an afterlife place of residence but that world in which they have chosen to exist, for indeed their next birth will reflect these deeds. Therefore life can be likened to being a mirror, and those who inflict pain upon innocent others will receive their judgement in their next life- in which they may not be a person.

So yes! More simply and actively put is that people can decide by their "Freedom of Choice" to live in God's world or Natures world for the Non-Believer, this being that Heaven that truly, exists upon this Earth and which is the place in which many peoples culturally designed religions and philosophies reflect, or they can choose to live in Hell which is the most uncomfortable place upon this Earth but which is still a personal choice. Therefore, it not right that how to live your life is always a personal "choice", this being that which only people have and which God does never interfere.

So now the question is: "Which world do you want to live in?" and your answer should be "The world in which I have the freedom of choice." Therefore, sincerely, this is a heavenly choice in which you understand that no harm can be inflicted upon another. This being fact in which you fully understand that there is no "THEM", or "THEY" or "IT" is all realised to be "YOU!"

For was it not said by our incarnate Jesus, who knew and experienced this truth by His saying: *"You are the first in the queue and also the last".* For rightly, the choice is yours for you can live under God's laws or the laws of Nature for the Non-Believer or your own self-inflicted "I Want" for ME, this which is being a punishing law that governs a Hell which only people can falsely create by thoughts of a non-existing Past or Future. For did not the incarnate Jesus historically say *"But seek ye first the kingdom of God, and His righteousness, and all these things shall be added unto you for in this world to come the last shall be first and the first last."*

So honestly in our modern time, this ancient saying can now be known to mean, *"But seek ye first to understand your God's Kingdom of Heaven, which can exist only in the "Present Time",* this being the unified world which is all around you just has it is within you. For this "Present Time" indeed exists has the world that is called "Heaven", in which the last shall be first, and the first last for all people are has on an entity. For did not the incarnate Jesus also historically say to His followers *"Do not to worry about material things such as food or clothing, as God will provide all the needs of his followers",* for correctly if one pursues the needs of the unity of that which is all around them, then all that they need will be provided for them without a need for worry or anxiety.

Yes, this is not a lifeless act, but one that must be pursued with non-harming contentment. Therefore, indeed, the "Freedom of Choice" is yours. So you can "Choose" to live under "Heavenly laws" or live controlled by self-inflicted punishing laws that govern a Hell which only people can create, for it certainly is not "Hell", a self-created dream world, this being a non-existing Past or a Future "I Want" for ME world which is a personally created Hell that is founded upon an "I want for myself" false dream based existence? For surely, this is being truly is a false world that is very different from those who live in a "Heaven" which is a real personally supported peaceful system that that ALL our wise ancients target and which truly exists has God's Heaven or Natures Heaven for the Non-Believer.

Therefore, is it not seen to be true that the world of Hell is created by a person's false "I want" for me, this is usually being something that belongs under the care of other people? For indeed, does not the living in this self-created "I Want" Hell compel many followers of one religion to inflict torture and pain upon followers another religion or political system by their saying "I Want my religion and my political way of life to be best not your religion or your political way of life." Also an "I Want" self-created hell based upon the words, "My way to God is the best and only way to God for it is better than your way to God and I can prove that my God is stronger than your God and I can prove this by killing you and taking all your possessions which you deserve to lose by your believing in a false God!"

For strangely is it also not true that in our Earths Northern hemispheres, that the Christian and the Islamic religions "culturally" different religious teachings did have many hundreds of years of creed-based wars which were un-religiously fostered and grounded upon the above "I want" principles. Therefore, does not our Earths history also show that many punishing cruel wars did occur between the Christian religion and the Islamic religion, these being serious conflicts which lasted for around two hundred years?

Then is it not also physically known that around the year 1291 this middle eastern conflicts ended at the siege of Acre, for it was then that this last Christian occupied city was evacuated to allow Muslim rule, this being because it was found by the perpetrating ongoing leaders of these two religions that what was happening was that these wars were causing them to lose more than was being gained and so no "I want" was being achieved. It was indeed this that stopped this religious war that was based upon "I Want" more economic values.

What is also known to be sadly true is that when these two separate religions stopped warring upon in each other, the Christians leaders then turned their "I Want" upon the leadership of factions of their religion. Truthfully, his being an "I Want" in which one group stated that the "Christian Catholic" Pope should be the leader of all Christian worshippers and not someone who the challenging "Christian Protesters" stated should be democratically appointed by a local administration, which also should be allowed to pursue a different creed-based worshipping system.

Therefore, sadly, it was this dispute that is reputed to have caused over eighteen million Christian peoples deaths via war, famine and disease. Also, is it not true that Muslims became angered upon similar "leadership divisions" and also an imposed "creed" way of worship within their religion. This Muslim rift being caused because the Prophet Mohammed died without appointing a successor and those that became known as the "Islamic Sunni" believed that the new leader should be democratically elected while those that called themselves the "Islamic Shias" believed that their leader should be of the bloodline of Mohammed.

Therefore for the past 1400 years, this fracture within the Islamic religion, which was about who should be their leader and what method of creed worship should they follow, was the same has the fracture that occurred within the Christians religion. However, sadly this Islamic fracture is continuing, and it too has also killed and mistreated many millions and continues to do so. For again truly and religiously is it not very difficult to understand this internal "Islamic" war that is still killing and torturing thousands unto the present day? Yet is it not strangely similar with the past rift between the "Christian Catholics" and the "Christian Protestors" regarding their religions Christian leadership and the way of worshipping, also is it not true that the "Islamic Sunni's" and "Islamic Shias" have completely acceptable different creed worshipping systems both Sunni's and Shias are thoughtfully incorporating the teachings of Mohammed.

However, strangely they still demand the same "I want" my leaders and "I want" my creed to be used in worship and no other, why is this? Does the answer to this question not rest in who becomes the owner of the property and environmental values of that which used to belong to the vanquished or killed?

So Yes! Who or what creates these current "I Want" conflicts within our world? Is it a false religion, or is it false religious leaders, or is it the animalistic "I Want" what you have? For further and truthfully stated, it is only the followers of a non-harming way of life who experience *"the peace that surpasses all understanding"* and so reach *"a realm beyond the ability of words to properly convey"*, for accurately our ancient wise knew how to achieve this way of life. For correctly has it not been proven many times within our world, that all our differing religiously-based creeds systems can take their users to God's world and does not our history show that these strange "creed" based religious conflicts actually achieve nothing but death and persecution to millions of families and even worse to the perpetrators of these animalistic and un-religious acts.

For how can the physically punishing and killing of others be God originating? When honestly throughout our world there are many thousands of differing creeds, differing ways of worship, differing belief systems, differing religions and differing philosophical belief systems plus countless differing instigating leaders of these many ways to God's world or the world of Nature for the Non-Believer. For correctly ALL knowingly state *"Woe unto them who inflict punishment upon those who cannot defend themselves"*.

Therefore, is it not also known to be true that the great Mohammed was undoubtedly against the killing of others for any reason other than self-defence! For this was meaning that death could only be inflicted upon others when in an existing actual conflict, this being that which was taking place in the "Present Time" and which is an attack that is coming from others – and certainly not a killing of those who are undefended. For indeed, how can a religious person speak about killing others – especially why no harm to them is threatened, but care should be taken if the opposes being recent re-births from the animal kingdom who have forgotten that they are now a personal "Self", this being that which has a God give or Nature given for the Non-Believer, "Freedom of Choice"?

57 THE VARIATION OF THE CREEDS

So yes! Has not history proven that the goodness and support provided by "Mother of the Creation", who with her constant harmony seeking efforts has rightly maintained the goodness resting in God's "Present Time" or Nature "Present Time" for the Non-Believer – and especially in the showing of the harmony now existing within the Christian faith has revealed in the last chapter. Therefore genuinely is it not true, as previously stated, that the "Mother of the Creation" eventually and peacefully separated the warring Christian worshippers. They argued over an "I Want" my leader not your leader and "I Want" my way of creed worship and not your way of creed worship. Therefore is it not now true that there has been re-established the Godly provided "Freedom of Choice" within fourteen major culturally-based Christian belief systems plus their twenty-two culturally-based break away fringe groups, all of whom worship their own personal "chosen" culturally-based "creeds," and with their own personal "chosen" leaders. These all being religiously self-imposed creeds of worship that target, by their harmony seeking self-imposed instructions, the stopping of all personal "I Want" thoughts that are usually allowed to course through their minds and they are doing this in their own "chosen" way. For sincerely, is not the disciplinary stopping of these damaging "I Want" for myself thoughts being thoughts which take their viewer into the past or the future and away from the observing of God's world which can only exist in the "Present Time". For justly, these freely "privately chosen" and "self-selected" group worshipping creeds bring a disciplined outer concentration to the worshipping practitioner which opens the doorway to God's authority upon this

Earth, this being an authority which can only exist in the self "observing" and the self "experiencing" of God's world or the world of Nature for the Non-Believer. This real-world exists only in the mind binding silence that seems to be physically attached to the "Present Time", which is Gods world. For indeed, this God-filled observational experience of the "Present Time" can occur for it can even be self-experienced via the witnessing of Gods world through the spaces of a repetitive non-thought provoking praying discipline, this being an "experience" that can occur within the repeating of a personally chosen creed based prayer. This reality is a fact which is experienced by many religious followers and also none followers, to be an experience on "Enlightenment" which a sincere, disciplined worshipping of any creed can bring to the user, as it does within all religions and philosophies when carefully targeted to do so.

Thus praying is the first step towards an experience of "Enlightenment", this being a condition which the Christian religion calls being filled with the "Holy Spirit" or "Holy Ghost" in which a person's mind is filled by a *"Peace that Surpasses all Understanding."* The Islam religion describes it as *"being filled with the Angel Gabriel"* and also in this same religion, it is further described as *"a realm beyond the ability of words to properly convey."* In contrast, the Hindu religion calls it "Moksha" which loosely means *"Freedom from Ignorance."* Buddhists refer to it as "Bodhi" or "Nirvana". Which is undoubtedly being a personal experience described as *"awakening to the true nature of things"* and even the ancient Zoroastrianism religion of fifth Century BC, this is two thousand five hundred years ago, referred to it as *"Ushta"* meaning "liberation, salvation and emancipation of the Soul". It is also known by many other names that emanate from all our world's religions and philosophies such has previously mentioned, these being "Paradise", "Eden", "Heaven", "Nirvana", "Promised Land", "Moksha", "Shangri-la", "Kenshō ", "Bodhi", "Satori", "Kevala", "Jnana", "Svargamu", "Kā bāga", "Vāṭikā", "Kā jagaha", "Sukhabhavana", "Ushta", and all this can be described as the experiencing of "Enlightenment", and it is not the copyright of any religion or philosophy and it now awaits to welcome YOU! So strictly, it is via these many ways to "Enlightenment" that people realise that they can achieve the best and most beautiful experience in the world, this accurately is an experience in which they can become "Self-Aware" of the "Heaven" that exists all around them, which is similar to the unified "Heaven" that exist within them, but only in the "Present Time" and indeed a world that has been created for them to enjoy. Sincerely, this being the inwardly and outwardly experiencing an "observation" that they knowingly exist within the unity of all that exists outside them just has that which exist within them. So there can be no possible need of an "I Want" thought, For indeed, via meditation or prayer, you can become "aware" that you are everything and so you actually "experience" that you not only exist in God's world or the world of Nature for the Non-Believer but that you, have "The Book" modernly explains, can "knowingly" become "Self-Aware" that you are "viewing" from your soul in which you "realise" that you are indeed a part of "everything", which can lead to "Self-Realisation", this being a reality in which you experience that you are "everything", a condition within whose unity there is no observer, these being conditions which our worlds wise ancients have been preaching for thousands of years. But sadly, this factual reality is often forgotten when some people leave their place of worship with an example being the dispute between Shia and Sunni Islamic sects. For certainly both agree upon the teachings of Mohammed, (Peace be upon him), in which both agree on the essential details of their own personally chosen creed based acts of worship which wisely target the above mentioned "Peace that surpasses all understanding". Yet, sadly they are still tormented over an "I Want" my leadership choice, not your leadership choice to be obeyed and also an "I Want my way of creed worship not your way of creed worship to be obeyed", this being also the same disagreement that plagued the early Christians. Yet really, would not our Gods answer be, *"It is good that you worship in a way that brings you to ME! For did I not give to all my children the "Freedom of Choice", this being to be with ME and so weed my developing world and not kill or harm other gardeners!"*

So yes! How do you find and so become enabled to support these correct "weeding" actions, these being different actions which are privately chosen creeds of worship that can bring people to experience that which can be described as the "Peace that surpasses all understanding"? For indeed, do not all our wise ancients and all their taught religions and philosophies seek this personal way of weeding out the "I Want" for Me weeds that exist in a person self-created but false reality? For correctly these wise culturally-based teachings, which are the foundations of many of our world's religious and philosophical instructions, are all explained in different cultural ways just how to engage with and experience this "Peace that surpasses all understanding".

Is it not also true that this experiencing of "Enlightenment" is known to be the experiencing of the "bliss," that the reciting of creeds can bring to the disciplined and concentrating doer? Thus, it is known to be so, and it also a fact that cannot be contradicted. For again and anyone can experience the reality of this bliss, this being that which happens when they "disciplinary" concentrate physically upon a repetitive worshipping word, prayer or song, this being from a practically proven and personally chosen, religious creed way of worship.

This experience is that which births the reality of "Enlightenment", which can be birthed by any creed that is based upon the concentration of many words such has psalms or prayers or even one word that is disciplinary sounded in mind. These were well known real truths as long as they are words that are sounded and are not born by the willpower of the user and or the constant "I Want" for me demands that freely emanate from the five senses. In essence, these uncalled for demands should NOT be allowed to interfere with the growing stillness of the mind! For again is it not true that different religions and creeds can be likened to the many different ways of travelling to a place called "Enlightenment" – some travel on boats, cars, buses, bicycles, horseback, camels or they just walk. Still, the actual experiencing of unity with Gods world or the world of Nature for the Non-Believer is the same. No matter what religious or philosophical creed "transport" is taken, all "travellers" will eventually find that the "Mother of the Creation" loves all Her children and if unselfishly allowed, She will arrange a good "Enlightened" life for them in which they will find the reason why God gave to this part their only child, the "Freedom of Choice" – which was to support Her work, this being that activity which supports all Her family, for there are many different forms of worship which our wise ancients created for the worlds many varied cultures and these being forms of worship which also embodies the many different understandings of cultures that are also at different stages of spiritual development. But a significant question that can be asked is *"Why can there be such hatred between and among some religious sects? Why is this is being when actually all do worship the one God and so actually know that there is but one God?"* This fact can only be that such people must experience their religion has to be their property, which is likened to their saying "This is MY house, MY land, MY fruit", and so they forget that God or Nature for the Non-Believer, regularly provides all these things just has is provided with the sun above and the air we breathe?

So can it be true that a person can say to another person standing next to them that the sun that shines on me is better than the sun that shines on you and the air that I breathe is better than the air that you breathe, for such a person cannot be a believer in God who treats all His children the same like all good fathers do? But when such a person's mind is "Enlightened" by genuinely experiencing the knowledge of the creation, then all sectarian quarrels and beliefs disappear – for they become a true believer in Gods "lawful" world or the Natural laws of Nature for the Non-Believer, which is continuously governed by the *"Mother of the Creation"* who sincerely cares for Her only Child.

So Yes! Truly "Enlightenment" can only be experienced in the "Present Time", a real-time in which no past and no future thoughts can be experienced. Thus this "Enlightening" experience will and can occur firstly within the spaces of the words being sounded when a person "disciplinary" performs any of the religious creeds that are locked into the various Christian and Islamic and which also reside in the many hundreds of the world's religions plus philosophical teachings. For truthfully, as experience shows, those practising their culturally world based creeds will knowingly experience a feeling of "Enlightenment" this being that which can only be experienced only in the "Present Time".

So yes! It is then that they will honestly know God's world or the world of Nature for the Non-Believer. Therefore, this is the world in which exists a peace that certainly surpasses all understanding. For again, is it not "scientifically" true that all the wise ancients targeted within their followers, a creed based way to experience the "Present Time"? A time which is always being a creed based way which would activate for all genuine worshippers, the entry into God's world which exists only in the "Present Time"? Was this truth not also revealed to many of our worlds religious and philosophical followers, this being a knowledge that was targeted for them to experience by our many wise ancients'? These being wise ancients who introduced many "concentrated" and much disciplined self-imposed praying rituals, these being that which gave birth to

"Enlightenment"? This "Enlightenment" is that experience that became birthed within their serious follower's. For beyond doubt, "Enlightenment" is an experience that is quickly realised to be God's Heaven on Earth and clearly, it is a birthright that can be achieved by all people. But is it not also important to acknowledge a far greater truth? For this greater truth is a truth which should be known by all people in that another most crucial target would be that after their "ritual prayer," these worshipping "doers" should practice to stay in the "Present Time" and so not leave the harmony of the Heaven that exists upon this Earth when they stopped their prayers or when they left their place of worship. For sincerely people should continuously endeavour to "ALWAYS" stay in the "Heaven" that they have experienced during their worshipping mantras and chants, and so certainly not perform "I Want" only for myself actions, but to truly live within the harmony that can only exist within their "Present Time."

So yes! Can it not now also be "scientifically" understood, that all our religious and philosophical "prayer rituals", this being that which is contained within the worlds many religions and belief systems, do all seek the same goal, this being a goal which does genuinely bring the ***"Peace that surpasses all understanding",*** which is called "Enlightenment" and which can only exist in the "Present Time"; again it should be mentioned that forgetting is our worst enemy. For indeed, this is also something which all sincere worshippers can achieve when they are praying or participating in a group, or are individually active in solitary worship? For all our wise ancients knew that these "ritually imposed prayers" would eventually bring their worshippers to the "Heaven" that exists upon our Earth, but only in the "Present Time"; a time that exists without any "I Want" thoughts. Therefore, is it not also "scientifically" acceptable that these wisely introduced praying rituals would be "culturally" designed to show a home-based and so acceptable way for the worshiper of that country or region to acknowledge and so be enabled achieve and therefor experience the blissful experience of "Enlightenment", this being that which exists upon our Earth? For this is a well-known and also a blissful experience that these "prayer rituals" werc always designed to achieve, and which are prayers which would also be formatted by our wise ancients following the culture of those that lived around them. So cannot it easily be experienced to be accurate, that this is the "cultural" reason why there are so many different religiously worshipping ways within our world that "scientifically" endeavours to achieve the same target, justly being that which is the target of all religions, philosophies and which is usually based upon their culturally different beliefs? Therefore, is it not also a clear and presently known truth that ALL these many religions and ALL these many belief systems are seeking the same goal? This being that which ALL true worshippers can experience and which is the Heaven that can be physically experienced upon our Earth; for it rests in the "Present Time" this being that which always rests upon our Earth. For it is also good to be assured that "Enlightenment" can be experienced by ALL people and can be particularly experienced when they perform culturally and religiously based incantations, this being that activity which stops the "I want" for ME, which emanates from the "animalistic" and uncontrolled five senses, simply because people can believe that these five senses are them – they are not you, for you are the Soul, this being that which knows that it is also a part of everything that exists within Gods "Creation".

So yes! Can it not also be seen as real that it was overtime, that all these differing "prayer rituals" which were introduced by our wise ancients, became embedded within a culturally based worshipping system which developed in our many religions, and belief systems, these being that which religiously and philosophically dominated our world? Can it not also be said that this "group based need" was arrived at because of the instinct that was developed over millions of years, this life being when we existed as a group hunter or group gatherers. For was this not a much-needed survival group practice which existed within all tribal relationships. Is it not also seen in modern times that this belonging to a group is a need that also appears in spectator sports. For what is now spoken of here is the group needed the feeling that was also inherent in the current need to be attached to a group of twelve people has in the twelve disciples? Could this not also possibly be the same number of twelve families that left South Africa to populate the entire world with people? For indeed, we now know that they absorbed all other existing but different species who did not have this "group" tribal instinct, because of their past ice age environment, in which single families stood the best chance of survival. For was this "private" group not also based upon a minimum of twelve hunters, this being that which was needed to survive when hunting in the open plains of Africa. For truly would not single families who lived alone, find it difficult to survive in an area that was full of fast running open plane animals. This suggestion is being stated to show how people are a group based hunter of fast-moving animals. Is it not also true that a typical man has probably two close friends, this being within their group of twelve friends? For indeed, this suggestion being put forward to explain that we seem to have an influential tribally based group culture that is inherent within us, for is this not also the reason why we go to group-based places of togetherness? This grouping is a sought realty so we can gather together with likeminded people? For truly is this not an experience which satisfies the ancient personal need to belong to a "tribe" or a community of such people and so are churches being born as group places of worship, which then attach themselves to a like-minded "tribe" of people?

Yet sadly, we also know that inherent within people is that this tribal belief system and its "animalistic" knowledge, this being that which originates from our hunter-gathering days, is still felt to be a hunting system whose knowledge should be protected from all outsiders, these being those who are known to belong to other tribes, and so exist in another tribal "animalistic" system and its personal beliefs; Forgetting that this ancient and still pursued inner animosity was about the obtaining of food and the occupation of hunting lands in which survival needs were essential and not about concepts, ideas and particularly religious beliefs. But the most important factor to mention now is that belonging to a group may support and aid a person to live in God's world. Still, it is also essential to know that only has an individual can a person attach oneself to the experiencing of God's world, for this is an individual experience but one which can also be sought within a likeminded group but also importantly, when one is alone. Yet sadly and in the progress of time and with the loss of our wise ancient leaders, many have forgotten this exact purpose of their given "prayer rituals," that were established to bring them into the "Present Time", thus to live in the harmony of the Heaven that rests open this Earth and indeed, the actual "being" and the "realising" of God's silent existence, which rests upon this Earth.

So yes! Now it is essential to forget the "I Want" my religion to be the best, not your religion, which genuinely, contaminates the world. Therefore, is it not seen as accurate that in many parts of the world we see ancient tribal "hunting" beliefs stating there is only one God (our animal) and that He is a God (our animal) that recognises only our religion. (Way of hunting) It is then that people begin to try and destroy other belief systems (hunting grounds) and even fight amongst themselves,(This is mine, not yours) which means that they have lost God's gift of the "Present Time" and have begun to re-live in historically ancient hunting grounds or plan a personal future, where their "I Want" lives make them false believers and sadly many are trapped in this ignoring.

For example, now look at the historic "Four Horsemen of the Apocalypse", these being people who are more interested in hurting others than in doing well for themselves. Their names are:

The Stonewalled: - He who ignores the person that is talking to them and who it is said: "Starts an argument and waits until defensive excitement is aroused in another but then turns away and begins a being alone activity".

The Contempter: - Who disapproves, derides and scorns and who it is said "Shows a virulent mix of anger and disgust, for they always see a person as beneath them, rather than as an equal or a better person.

The Criticiser: -   Who blames scolds and condemns all others. For it turns an observed behaviour into a lousy statement about another person's character, this being done to ridicule a person negatively".

The Defensive: - Who justifies and accuses and resists differences. "It regularly plays at being a victim in all situations that surround it which it says it is NEVER its fault".

So yes! Sometimes doing any of the above can be constructive and healthy but it is when it is a habit, which is happening many times that these acts will destroy the user, but the question is "Can you recognise if one of them has to be YOU!?

58   THE TRUTH ABOUT THE   BROTHERHOOD
OF ALL RELIGIONS

So yes! Is it not also true that there is not only the Muslim and Christian way of worship within our world? For indeed, there are many hundreds of different religions and philosophies of worship throughout this world of ours? Is it not also and indeed well known that some worshipping desires are locally created to meet the needs of the community in which it exists and so is it not also true that these services are often personalised to meet their particular culture's needs. Is it not also well known to be a truthful fact that many people attend religious services just to attain the group company of others, and so seek the feeling of belonging and wellbeing that they receive from such like-minded companions, this being a very ancient and personal need? For rightly an individual within a religious group practice can fleetingly experience a personal "Enlightenment", this being a fact which is attained by a person when experiencing an outer group imposed agreeable worshipping system. This fact being enabled because a worshipper begins to concentrate on the imposed incantations of that which is occurring around them and so they "unknowingly" are requesting consciousness to energises will-power, to still the mind for the mind to "disciplinarily" and so fully accept that which is occurring all around it in the "Present Time", which is Gods existing world of "Heaven" and not the world of "Hell", this truly being the world of "Hell" which is falsely created by a mind filling Past or Future "I Want" for ME world. For again and faithfully this attending of a group based religious activity is an act which can factually stop the frequent "I Want" of the bodies five senses from filling the mind with their "I Want" demands, For genuinely it is this fact of silencing their demands from entering the mind which ensures that the "worshipper" will truly experiences "Enlightenment", even if momentarily. For it is a known fact that "Self-Awareness", this being the experiencing of "Enlightenment", can occur when attending well "disciplined" religious practices. For it is undoubtedly true that an empty mind rightfully ensures that a person's "Soul" can see and so experience Gods world, which is certainly an experience that cannot be "realised" through a mind which is blocked by many an "I Want" for ME thoughts, this being that which is a mind-filling "I Want" emanation from any one of the uncontrolled five senses.

For justly God created a world that can only exist in the "Present Time", and it is a world that can only be experienced when the soul is freed to see through the un-clouded mind that which we call the "Present Time", this being the only time in which a person can experience Gods world. This creation is the real world which is engendered by the sociability needs of the individual and it can also be experienced via the bonhomie and self-imposed discipline of the group, this being that condition in which this most sought need to achieve "Enlightenment", can best be satisfied.

Thus, this personal attending of a religious arrangement could also be because some people have mistaken the real purpose of the worshipping needs of the religion which they are attending; this being that the purpose of any religious worship is to achieve a very "individualistic" target, which is to achieve "Enlightenment". For knowingly, this target is indeed a religious and or philosophical target that is undoubtedly endeavouring to achieve the experiencing of "Enlightenment", genuinely being a condition in which the worshipper experiences the real facts of life. For indeed they can become "Self-Aware," this being the experiencing that they are "everything" that exists in Gods world which is the religious stage that occurs before the experiencing of "Self-Realisation" in which there is no observer for you become "Everything". For indeed a religions purposeful target is to stop all mind blocking "I Want" thoughts that are emanating from the five senses by imposing a group based mind silencing experience which is imposed by self-discipline, such as prayers, group incarnations and disciplined bodily action. For certainly praying is a self-disciplined way in which you can experience that you exist only at that moment, this being a moment that can "knowingly" exist only in the "Present Time".

For all our worlds worshipping creeds are ce genuinely initiated by our ancient wise whose target is to bring people to the experiencing of "Enlightenment", this being that which Christians state is to be filled with the "Holy Spirit" or "Holy Ghost". Genuinely, this is the experience that occurs when a person's Soul views through the empty mind that which we call the "Present Time". For again this is a reality that can only be achieved when the mind is not blocked by many a personal "I Want" thought, these being thoughts which are usually born from an imaginary "I Want" future or a disappointing past, in which a person "I Want" was not achieved. For indeed, there is no debate about this very ancient target that is to achieve "Enlightenment", whose purpose knowingly exists within ALL our world's religions and philosophies for it is truly a known to be factually achievable fact.

For truthfully all our Earthly religions and philosophies personally describe this illuminating experience of the mind, which "The Book" explains to be the experiencing of the stillness that can only exist in the "Present Time". This stillness always being a factual experience which is likened to the actual experiencing the freedom of eternal bliss created by a mind empty stillness which becomes all that exists in the "Present Time". For it is known that throughout the world all religions and philosophies have described their purposely sought target to be that which is stated to be an "Enlightening" experience which they say is being likened to living in *"Paradise", "Eden", "Heaven", "Nirvana", "Promised Land",* also with such names as *"Moksha", "Shangri-la", "Kenshō", "Bodhi", "Satori", "Kevala", "Jnana", "Svargamu", "Kā bāga", "Vāṭikā", "Kā jagaha", "Sukhabhavana",* and even the ancient Zoroastrianism religion of the fifth century BC referred to it as *"Ushta",* which was described by them to be the *"liberation, salvation and emancipation of the Soul"* and this was over 2500 years ago. All these names were born to describe "Enlightenment" which is quite an experience. All it is merely a mind without any "I Want" thoughts for how can you enlighten within the mind a personal "I Want", this being when you realise that you are factually living in God's world. It truly is just as it is described by the entire world's religions and philosophies, and it now awaits YOU!

So yes! It indeed is this experiencing of "Enlightenment", which all our wise ancients endeavoured to bring to their followers and it was a realty that was gained often by the disciplined chanting and also practising of various culturally worded creeds. It is also known to be a very personal experience and one which is realised when a person's silent mind allows the Soul, which is the real YOU! To experience the world of the ever silent "Present Time", this is God's world or the world of Nature for the Non-Believer. For indeed, this is the world in which no "I Want" changing thoughts occur for the mind contains no movement, and all is still as if frozen in time. But amazingly it changes, and it is also noticed to do so, for this is a world which is designed by God or Nature for the Non-Believer, and it can only be "wonderfully" experienced when the mind is empty and without thought. For sincerely this is an "Enlightened" condition which allows a person's Soul to see and also experience that which it is a unified part of, this being Gods creation, or Natures creation for the Non-Believer, which exits, but only in that which we call the "Present Time". It is this "Present Time" world of God or Nature for the Non-Believer, which exists without the need for any thought, particularly that many minds filling uncontrolled "I Want" for Me thoughts, these being that which takes a person into the non-existing Past or Future, this indeed being a non-existing world that we can call Hell. Therefore, is it not an absolute truth that this world of Hell is a non-existing dreamed world? For correctly is it not also true that this world of Hell it is created by the undisciplined "I Want" of the five senses? Thereof is it not also true that we have misplaced the world of "Heaven", this being that which genuinely and physically exists in the "Present Time" and so ignorantly live in a past or future world that "The Book" calls "Hell", this being a dream world which does not physically exist? For indeed this is a false world that is governed by five senses which animalistic-ally and so habitually cloud the mind with "I Want" desires which are "automatically" and "freely" allowed to be pursued by our "animalistic" five senses and therefore enabling them to fill the still mind with many "I Want" for ME, selfish desires – this being because we "think" that they are "US"! They are NOT US, for we are the only child of God or Nature for the Non-Believer and we are in truth – the reality of everything. It is undoubtedly this false "habit", which is genuinely based upon ignorance that creates a personal self-fabricated false world which is created by a never-ending pursuit of an "I Want" for ME world that is a constant request which is emanating from the five senses.

So yes! It is well to understand that our wise ancients developed creed based prayers for all their followers, these being that which were purposely designed to stop this "I Want" habit. For indeed, this is a false personally created world which is based upon the continued living via a past or a future "I Want", and it is truly a world that cannot and does not exist in the "Present Time". Therefore is it not true that any future or past "I Want", always takes people outside of God's or Natures grace, this being that which can only exist in the "Present Time". For truthfully, the target of our wise ancients and their purpose of introducing creed based practises which takes their followers to experience moments in which the "Present Time" is experienced and known to be God's world or the world of Nature for the Non-Believer. This fact is also unquestionably truthful because this world is experienced to exist in perfect harmony when observed by an inner Soul which is enabled to see through a "stilled" mind. For indeed the creation is also a blissfully still awareness that can be a reality which enables the Soul to move away from being the silent observer and so enable a person to become a "Self-Aware" or a "Self-Realised", thus becoming an active supporter of all Life and Non-Life. Thus being a realty which means that they can leave being an "observer" of God's world and so become like one entity with God's Creation, in which nothing else exists except the true "Self", which is the entirety of ALL the creation, which is truly God's world or the world of Nature for the Non-Believer.

So Yes! It is essential to understand that such a creed based worship is an "individual" task and not a group-based task and it is this very "individuality" that is required to do the "work" that achieves this *"Peace that surpasses all Understanding"* and so experience that which is known as "Enlightenment". For rightly said, "Enlightenment" is true "The Wages" that God, through the incarnate Jesus, spoke about in the parable of the vineyard. This realty is when Jesus said to those without a needful purpose and remembered this is God who was speaking through Jesus to people who were seeking real work. *"You go, and work* (support harmony) *in my vineyard,* (the Creation) *and I will pay you whatever is right"* (Sugar in the Water). *"So, they went to work in His vineyard. He then went out again about the sixth hour and the ninth hour and did the same thing and again at about the eleventh hour he went out and found still others standing around. He asked them, "Why have you been standing here all day long doing nothing?" "Because no one has hired us," they answered. He said to them, "You also go and work in my vineyard."* (This is being the Creation). *When evening came, the owner of the vineyard* (God*) said to his foreman, "Call the workers and pay them their wages, beginning with the last ones hired and going on to the first." The workers who were hired about the eleventh hour came, and each received the same money, but those came who were hired the first, they expected to receive more*. (This is being an "I Want" that separates people from the singularity of the Creation.) *But each one of them also received the same money. When they received it, they began to grumble against the landowner saying, "These men who were hired last worked only one hour," they said, "and you have made them equal to us who have borne the burden of the work and the heat of the day." But the owner answered one of them, "Friend, I am not unfair to you. Didn't you agree to work for this amount of money?* (This being Enlightenment) *Take your pay and go. I Want to give the man who was hired last the same as I gave you. Don't I have the right to do what I want with my own money? Or are you envious because I am generous?"* Indicating that in life, there is only one and also simply put you cannot receive more or less "Enlightenment" due to the amount of work you have done to achieve it. For it exists as a total entity and it is the same "amount" that you experience over many years or in a few minutes for it cannot be added to or reduced. Also, is it not true that then Jesus stated the most enlightening words: *"So the last will be first, and the first will be last?"* Thus accurately saying words which explained that not only is "Enlightenment," the same experience for all people, it also rightly meant that because Jesus was "Self-Realised", He could see only "ONE" person in the queue, which was also himself—thus stating a truth which means that all people are as one body and the vineyard story also has a distinct meaning. For it merely explains that it does not matter if your work towards "Enlightenment" takes you several days or many years to achieve, the rewarding wages are always the same.

This reward is the harmony of "Enlightenment", and this "Enlightenment" remains precisely the same reward for all people and you can only be rewarded once, and this can only be in the "Present Time".Now let us also clearly understand some of God's words that were knowingly spoken through Jesus, these being words in which God speaks about His world in which is experienced "Enlightenment", this is faithfully being said to be the world of people in which a personnel self-claiming "I Want" cannot exist and which God's "Present" to all people is the only world which exists. Therefore, is it not an agreed truth that Jesus did say: *"I am the gate; whoever enters through me will be saved. He will come in* (to the "Present Time") *and go out (*of the past and the future) *and find pasture* (The food of "harmony") - this being the only way to live correctly. Also stating *"Now let the dead bury their own dead"* (these being people who live in a world of "I Want" which can only exist in a dead past or the none-existing future), *but you go and proclaim the kingdom of God"* (which is the "Present Time"). Still, another said, *"I will follow you, Lord; but first let me go back and say goodbye to my family."* Jesus replied, *"No one who puts his hand to the plough and looks back* (lives in the past) *is not fit for service in the Kingdom of God"* (This Kingdom of God is that which can only exist in the "Present Time", the only place in which the natural supporting or the serving of God's harmony or Natures harmony for the Non-Believer, can take place).

So yes! It is good to hear more about the words of Jesus who knew He was God's only child which is the singularity of the Creation, for Jesus always speaks about this need to enter God's world that exists only in the "Present Time". For in His early days, did He not preach saying *"repent, for the Kingdom of Heaven is near?"* For again and indeed, is not the "Kingdom of Heaven" always that paradise which exists in the nearness "Present Time"? Which is that paradise which is only one unthinking step away? Therefore, is it not true that this reality of paradise is that which all people can experience when they leave their living in their self-created Past or Future, which is a self-created false world of "I Want" for ME! Also, did not Jesus state that when you begin to live in God's world, this being the world that can only exist in the "Present Time" and which cannot exists with any personal "I Want", that you may find that there is also much "harmony" assisting work that is being presented to you?

So yes! Is it not also true that Jesus often spoke about the work that is needed to maintain the harmony of the ever-developing "Present Time"? This maintaining of harmony is the real work of people? For did not Jesus say, *"When an evil spirit comes out of a man"* (This can be modernly said to be the five senses which always sound into the mind they're communicating "I Want". This being that which keeps the persons' mind locked into the false world of Hell) *"it goes through arid places seeking rest and does not find it.* (For the "I Want" of the five senses can never be satisfied with anything that exists in the world around it) *Then it says, 'I will return to the house it left.' When it arrives, it finds the house unoccupied, swept clean and put in order.* Is this not also a saying that is likened to the meaning being put forward by "The Book"? Naturally, this being a meaning which states that the uncontrolled five senses are the evil spirit that plague and so fill a person mind. But now with their being silenced and the mind is stilled, that person Soul can see through the mind and into "Present Time" and so experience the bliss that is their birthright. This realty being because the mind is empty and without thought and so the person experiences the *"Peace That Surpasses All Understanding"* so that even the Soul is stilled as the "choice" of the individual may see no need to complete any harmony seeking activity, for it will be certainly experiencing that which is in actual existence all around them. So with "House" – Gods world – on order, there is no need to engage in any activity that is needed to support any harmony that is taking place. Then Jesus continues His story by saying:- *"Then it* (this returning single "I Want" claim emanating from the "evil spirit" which "The Book" likens to be one of the five senses) *goes and takes with it seven other* ("I Want") *spirits more wicked than itself, and they go in and live there"* (These being the return of the bodies inner senses all claiming their personal "I Want" and so entering the mind of the now thinking person). *"And the final condition of that man is worse than it was at first. That is how it will be with this wicked generation."* For assuredly, this being a saying which "The Book" more modernly explains has been the bodies inner senses entering and so clouding the mind with their gabbling "I Want" words and pictures, for it is indeed it is their "I Want" that takes the person thoughts into the past or the future which is s self-created Hell. For beyond doubt, it is also this cloud of mind filling activity which stops the Soul from seeing through a clear and still mind, the ever actual world that exists only in the "Present Time. For truly this is the ever-busy "I Want" for Me thought-filled mind of those who do nothing to support the ever-growing harmony of that which exists in God's "Present Time" and which is all around them – this being a "Present Time" which is the only real world that can only arise from God. Simply put, do not be a hermit who lives in a cave and does nothing to support the harmony that is emerging all around you. For Jesus spoke to those who live in their self-created world of "I Want" by saying, *"Woe to you who are well fed now, for you will go hungry. Woe to you who laugh now, for you will mourn and weep."* Then Jesus at this time also stated these words to be helpful: *"If your right hand causes you to sin, cut it off and throw it away."* Thus Jesus's describes an "I Want" which traps people in the unreal world of Hell, this being that which is mind-fully self-created to exist in a non-existing past or future, for genuinely these are the worlds of a false creation and which traps people in a self-created past or a self-created future which is continually seeking an "I Want" for ME!. Then Jesus said, *"It is better for you to lose one part of your body than for your whole body to go into hell."* It can be said that the only part of a person body that Jesus speaks about losing must be the five senses. These being that which are always claiming and sounding and planning to obtain there many "I Want" which is often stolen from others.Then Jesus, who was indeed an incarnation, also speaks about the world of harmony which exists in the "Present Time" and which is true, God's heavenly world by saying, *"If someone forces* (needs) *you to go one mile, go with him two miles."* For correctly you need to be silently active as the "Present Time" calls to your Soul, this being that which positively identifies its needs. It is also then that Jesus says how to reach this world of harmony, which is continuously targeting the individual, for sure, it has nothing to do with group activities. *"But when you pray, go into your room, close the door and pray to your Father, who is unseen. Then your Father, who sees what is done in secret, will reward you!"* Indeed you will be rewarded with "Enlightenment". For correctly in time and with much practice of silencing the five senses from gabbling there "I Want" into the mind, you WILL experience the "peace that surpasses all understanding". Indeed, this is the "Enlightenment" that is often described by many names. Still, it is indeed the living in Gods Heaven or Natures Heaven for the Non-Believer, this being that which exists only within the "Present Time" upon this earth. It is undoubtedly true that it is this world that our wise ancients call Heaven, this being that which can be gained after much necessary "creed" practising. For it should be again said that this "praying" reward will be in the "wages" that can be likened to the bliss that exists in the "Present Times" world of heavenly harmony that is endeavouring to move through all that is outside of you just as it moves within all that is inside you and these "wages" can be yours at any time.

So yes! Is it not also true that Jesus often described God's world of harmony as existing in the "Present Time"? We also have the story of the adulterous woman. She, who upon touching the "Present Time" that existed within Jesus, was immediately able to experience "Enlightenment" and so join that "bliss" which existed within Him. Then did she not begin crying in bliss at the great feeling of relief that this true freedom of God's harmony had brought to her and is it not Biblically said by the observers around her, *"She began to wash His feet with her tears, and she dried them with her hair, kissing them many times and rubbing them with the perfume"* – for she identified immediately who Jesus was when she experienced the harmony of bliss that was emanating from Him, this being that which can only exist within "Present Time".

Yet when a Pharisee, who believed he was the inheritor of the traditions of Ezra and so was scrupulous in his obedience to the Torah law, which can be noted to be the laws stated in Christians Bibles Old Testament and in particular the ten Commandments which include instructions to worship only God, to honour one's parents, and to keep the Sabbath day holy, as well as prohibitions against idolatry, blasphemy, murder, adultery, theft, dishonesty, and desire", and who had invited Jesus to come to his home saw this, he then started a religious "I Want" to himself, saying, *"If Jesus were a prophet, he would know that the woman touching him is a sinner!"* So it was then that Jesus knowingly said to the Pharisee, *"Simon, I have something to say to you. Two men owed money to a certain moneylender. One owed him five hundred denarii, and the other fifty. Neither of them had the money to pay him back, so he cancelled the debts of both. Now which of them will love him more?" Simon replied, "I suppose the one who had the bigger debt cancelled." Jesus said, "You have judged correctly."* Jesus's "money lender" is God and this a statement which means that it does not matter what you have done in the past, as in the borrowing of much money that you cannot repay – for when you enter God's world which exists only in the "Present Time", you begin a new life and are "born again" which is the true meaning of being forgiven. Also, it is Biblically said: ***"Then Jesus turned toward the woman and said to Simon, 'Do you see this woman? When I came into your house, you gave me no water for my feet, but she washed my feet with her tears and dried them with her hair. You gave me no kiss of greeting, but she has been kissing my feet since I came in. You did not put oil on my head, but she poured perfume on my feet. I tell you that her many sins are forgiven as she showed great love'."*** Truthfully, is this not because she had entered the "Present Time" and saw the harmony that was needed. At the same time, Simon's Soul seemingly moved in and out of Gods "Present Time", this movement being when his mind became clouded with past and future thoughts of "I Want" which is truly the world of Hell. Therefore Simons Soul becomes unable to witness the "Present Time", and so it was said by Jesus. ***"But the person who is forgiven only a little will love only a little."*** Meaning that in the "Present Time" God's love is one hundred per cent and all-encompassing.

Then Jesus factually said to her, ***"Your sins are forgiven."*** Then the people sitting at the table began to say among themselves, ***"Who is this who even forgives sins?"*** Not knowing that Jesus could not forgive sins for they did not understand that Jesus was speaking about the actual world of God for only God alone can honour the laws that govern the "Present Time". For correctly this again that which can only exist in the "Present Time" and which is a world that immediately upon entering "automatically" forgives all sins and so then Jesus knowingly said to the woman – ***"Because you believed, (***and you have entered the "Present Time" were God's truth exists,) ***you are saved from your sins. Go in peace."*** Is it not also true God, speaking through Jesus declared, ***"I am the bread of life? He who comes to me will never go hungry, and he who believes in me will never be thirsty."*** For indeed, Jesus was quoting directly from God and again speaking about the "Present Time", a time in which only people can mind-feelingly create a non-factious Hell based "I Want" world which emanates from the past or is targeting an "I Want" only for ME future. For assuredly, this truly is a personally made Hell world which is a constant ongoing and physically created selfish world that is forgetting people have falsely created for themselves. For indeed, this is a false world that is emanating from personally created past or a personally chosen "I Want" for ME targeting future? These being painful factious worlds that can only exist in such greed-based falsely created "I Want" for my world, this being that world which takes that which belongs to others. For indeed this is a selfish attacking and so destroying of the real world, this being the world which truly exists and which cannot die for it is God's world or the world of Nature for the Non-Believer in which all life and non-life are targeted to be satisfied. This fact is truly being in the understanding that the "Present Time" is Gods world or the world of Nature for the Non-Believer and so must always be experienced to be the time which always exists and so cannot die, for again is it not said that this world of the "Present Time" is the real world in which only that which is in harmony with all life and non-life can peacefully exist. Is it not also recognised to be true that those leaders, who attack, steal, punish, control, and so destroy this world created by of God do again return to life within the animal kingdom? For factually, is it not also true that the growth in populations and the peaceful joining together of different language based countries, show this to be a fact in that these evil ones are always weeded out of the world of people? Therefore, indeed all of Life and Non-Life exists in harmony, and this is the harmony which only people can support, for again is it not true that only people have been given the "Freedom of Choice". This fact is also being a choice to be born again within their real life and so support the harmony that is around them – which is "NOT" for the people who, as Jesus said *"have let go of the commands of God and are holding on to the* ("I Want") *traditions of people."* Also, did not Jesus say very clearly how to leave the past or future hell that people have created for themselves by stating, *"Woe to the* ("I Want") *world because* ("it creates") *of the things that cause people to sin? Such things must come,* (when someone lives in a world of "I Want") *but woe to the man through whom they come!"* Therefore did not Jesus also speak about the need to control and so to remove the "I Want" for ME world that the power of the animalistic five senses always creates in the doers' mind, this being if they are allowed the freedom to steal from the world around them. For did not Jesus condemn any uncontrolled selfish maneuvers of the five senses by saying about:-

(1) "TOUCH" *"If your hand causes you to sin, cut it off. It is better for you to enter life maimed than with two hands to go into hell, where the fire never goes out and if your foot causes you to sin, cut it off. It is better for you to enter life crippled than to have two feet and be thrown into hell."* And also uncontrolled:-

(2) "HEARING": *"You have heard that it was said, 'Love your neighbour and hate your enemy'. But I tell you: Love your enemies and pray for those who persecute you."* About uncontrolled:-

(3) *"SIGHT"*: *"And if your eye causes you to sin, pluck it out. It is better for you to enter the Kingdom of God with one eye than to have two eyes and be thrown into hell".* A saying which correctly is explaining the "I Want" for me world of hell which is a life that is lived in the past or the future for Jesus then described this Hell as bearing the:-

(4) *SMELL* of rubbish, *"where 'the worm* – (this is the smell of the five senses being attracted to rubbish) – *does not die, and the fire –* (that burns and devours the individuals' Soul while one lives in an "I Want" world of rubbish) – *is not quenched'"* and so *"Everyone will be salted with fire."* This quotation is a definite assertion of a consuming never-ending punishment for all those who currently live in this false past or a future world of "I Want." Then about:-

(5) TASTE Jesus said, *"Salt is good, but if it loses its saltiness, how can you make it salty again? Have salt in yourselves, and be at peace* with each other – thus explaining the guaranteed condition of the Heaven that one lives in, but only in "Present Time" in which the past or the future cannot exist but be aware again that Jesus said, *"Again I tell you, it is easier for a camel to go through the eye of a needle than for a rich man to enter the Kingdom of God."* Let us now be very clear! Jesus is clearly saying that the "Kingdom of God" can be achieved

and so lived in by any person, this again is that which genuinely explains that the silent un-wanting "Present Time" is the Kingdom of God. It is a kingdom which is recognised by the experiencing of "Enlightenment". Therefore it is indeed also known that self-possessions and riches are a chain that hangs around the neck of many people who do not understand the right "Heavenly" reason or the real purpose as to why they have been given such control over such surplus wealth. Forgetting and this is all people's worst enemy, that they have been Godly appointed and so been Godly given these surplus riches to aid the development of others in their task to achieve "Enlightenment" plus wellbeing.

So yes! Many people go to religious ceremonies and join in prayer and other joint activities to be able to enjoy an ancient union that brings the safety and tribal pleasure of a group, which is an "I Want". It is also true that when they leave the pleasure of the group they also leave a group supporting the way to achieving "Enlightenment" which is an individually based exercise, but which can also be attained by group support. Yet honestly, in their happiness and contentment of being with a group or within the controlling of a group, they forget that it is ONLY their efforts and not the groups that are being rewarded. This being in their repeating or their personal reciting of a creed prayer, this being that act that can bring them a personal experience of "Enlightenment:- Which is again likened to being an experience which the Christians describe as experiencing the Holy Spirit or Holy Ghost within themselves and which the Islamic teaching describes as being filled by the Angel Gabriel and many other religions and philosophies call this the experiencing of *Paradise", "Eden", "Heaven", "Nirvana", "Promised Land", "Moksha", "Shangri-La", "Kenshō", "Svargamu", "Kā bāga", "Vātikā", "Kā jagaha", "Sukhabhavana"* and many other names.

So Yes! Indeed, these are the different names for this worldly known experiencing our heavenly reality, For it is via this silence in the mind that this "Enlightenment" does occur and in which experiencing people realise is the best and most beautiful experience that can occur in a world that cannot be seen or even touched, except by the totality of the whole body. For truly only people can inwardly and outwardly experience the unity within the totality of the Creation and so it is an experience that cannot be described. For assuredly, it is also within this experience that they remain without thought – for this is true, being God's world or the world of Nature for the Non-Believer and it is a world that cannot be described. It is an experience that exists, but only in the "Present Time".

Simply put it is only the individual's activity, this being that activity and personal performance that creates a life that truly enables them to live in God's world and so this cannot be a group achievement for it can only be a very personal experience. Yet truly, it is often misunderstood, for it is frequently thought to be a happy fleeting "experience" that is coming from the love and belonging of a chosen group. In essence, this is an incorrect viewpoint for it is a personal experience that arises only within the individual and it is an experience which can stay within the individual even when they are not with a group. Therefore this joy of "Enlightenment" is experienced in a non-thinking mind empty mode that will eventually become their new way of a life in which they will certainly and so positively experience the "Sugar in The Water" that truly exists, but only in the Present Time. For justly truly this is the real-life which is the direct opposite to a negative "I Want" life which is strangely full of "negative" events in which it should now be known that you are actually attacking and so punishing yourself. For there is no Godly punishment that can exist within the life of a person, for indeed any conflict between or within religions cannot be Godly created and therefore must be a personally based "I Want" my way to live within Gods Laws and NOT your way, which is undoubtedly an "I WANT" that genuinely emanates from those who do not believe in God world. Therefore, it not true that God has given to all people the "Freedom of Choice" which certainly does not apply to animal kind. Therefore can it not be "Scientifically" stated, that people who repeatedly self-choose to pursue separating physical "I Want" for ME needs, rather than unifying spiritual needs will be "Godly" reborn back into a life within the animal kingdom, and so live in a world that is without the "Freedom of Choice" which exists only the world of people. A Rebirth Yes and always necessary because it is true that the Soul or Consciousness for the Non-Believer, is an energy that is known to leave a person upon their death and is it not also a known fact that energy cannot be destroyed but must reappear somewhere else! Therefore is it not believable truth that a dying bodies energy will seek a life that is consistent with the need for life? Therefore can it not be factually correct that births of people, newly emanating from our animal kingdom, may have sadly failed to understand - stand under - how to live with Gods given "Freedom of Choice"? Rightly this being freedom of choice which is Godly provided to correct the clashing of natural laws such a clash being when reindeer's horns get caught in a tree or at helping people injured in a Road accident etc. Therefore is it not true that only people can correctly serve the Godly or Goodly birthing world that exists all around them but only if they do not live an "animalistic" I want for my life, this being a life which is self-targeted to benefit only them? Also may it not be true that those firstborn people, which are newly emanating from the animal kingdom, can inspire the animalistic tendencies that still rest within those people who have only been birthed a few times has people, and so quickly motivate these newcomers to greedily attack and steal from other people whose culturally born laws and religions they see as weaker than them? Yet, the real truth which our history easily recognises is that the singularities of all people's lives are supported by Gods non-contradicting laws which are birthed to act within our civilisations, just has the un-conflicting singularity laws act within our bodies. Thus all countries can be likened to seeking unification just has that which exists within our own body's unselfish unification? Genuinely this is being that "law" which "lawfully" binds together the trillions of interacting individual life forms that consistently and habitually supports the wellbeing of our own body. Yet truly, do not all our inner bodily parts also have a "Freedom of Choice". Therefore, is it not true that our body parts can "choose" incorrectly and so they can go wrong and ignorantly attack other parts of our body, this being a "selfish" choice which is also obedient to the laws that control the universal workings of the creation, these being natural laws which also exists within our own body? For rightly and truly all people know that the body can die and that it can undoubtedly become painful when another life, such as infectious diseases, brings a disorder which is caused by foreign organisms such as bacteria, viruses, fungi or parasites, which can, in ignorance, enter our bodies collective. Then is it not also known that under certain conditions this can cause death. This death being caused by those we can call "unbelievers" and which can be similarly likened to that life form which does not believe in the laws that govern not only the singularity of a person's body but in many cases the singularity based laws of a whole country and so they "animalistic ally" attack it like a virus. Because of this potential endeavour, many countries need to combine with a democratic based legal system in which 70% of the population agrees to the laws that surround them and yes! Like that goodness of the laws governing those trillion of individual entities that happily and contentedly exist within our bodies, it is a good cause for individuals to die to stop others from killing and destroying their countries innocents. For genuinely in your next life, you will be well rewarded. At the same time, these killers of a Godly given unity will return to the animal kingdom from whence they came, for indeed God cannot allow the deliberate killing of His Children for if someone deliberately killed your child – would you support them?

So yes! Truthfully God's laws or Natures laws for the Non-Believer are easy to understand for they also exist within us.

59. GOD'S WAYS OF WORSHIP IS NOT THIS WAY

What is known to be true is that always written in our many hundreds of creed-based religions and philosophies is that our wise ancients always state that it is crucial to object to violence towards others, this is because violence usually harms the instigator more that it harms their victim and this is especially true when such violence is targeted to force upon worshippers of one religion against another religion "Way to God" which is usually based upon the personal activity of their religious leaders "I want".

For it is undoubtedly their religious leaders' personnel "I want" which is seeking themselves to be more critical. So they encouragingly demand more followers to pursue these aggressive personally motivated violent acts against other religions or non-religious people. How can this be correct? Yet does not people history constantly show that acts of opposing religious violence against another way to God have only a temporary result?

What also can be seen to be true via history is that any act of religious violence against others is always regarded as being sinfully evil and always commonly felt by most of the world's people to be a real act of shame. Is it not also true that the world's greatest religious leaders agree that the damage that these violent acts do to the life of the doer of violence in their ongoing current life and especially in their next life is irreversible because they act outside the developing harmony of the Creation that is all around them.

For indeed, our many wise ancients, these being those who have taught across our world always teach that you cannot purchase by violent deeds the experience of "Enlightenment" which is the becoming aware that you are that which is all around you. Therefore, the truly living only in the "Present Time" and supporting the merging harmony of the Creation is in itself an "Enlightening" experience in which many people state is likened to being filled with the *"peace that surpasses all understanding"* as stated in the Christian belief system or as stated in the Muslim world *"a realm beyond the ability of words to convey properly"* or in the Hindu religion *"freedom from ignorance"* or Buddhist refer to it as *"awakening to the true nature of things."*

It is also true that even the ancient people of the Zoroastrianism religion, as stated two thousand five hundred years, ago described this personal experience as a *"liberation, salvation and emancipation of the Soul"* and also clearly explained in the many hundreds of other various describing names given by the world's religions and philosophies.

So Yes! "Enlightenment" does exist and it waits for you and if you feel the need to experience the above "Enlightenment" then read on for the small seed that rests within all the religions and philosophies that took their followers to "Enlightenment" is revealed later in "The Book" which also explains that you will NEVER experience "Enlightenment", by killing or torturing others. The world itself must feel a sense of great sadness for the people who do this. What is undoubtedly true is that when filled with the "Enlightening" experience gained by personal and practical creed worship, your body is always able to obey your Soul's request to support actively and so keep alive the harmony of the developing world around you.

For indeed, in "Enlightenment" in which rests true happiness and contentment, you will witness and if necessary support these harmonies needed and most beneficial acts that always assist the existing or emerging laws of God's world or the world of Nature for the non-believer and therefore cannot perform acts that support the violent clashing discording world of a personal "I want", this is being an "I want" which is imposed by an individual's pursuits for their own or their groups personal gain and are certainly not the "Mother of the Creation" pursuits which continually target harmony for all life and non-life and who can say that this is not true when it is continuously and peacefully emerging or trying to emerge all around them peacefully?

So Yes! Harmony truly exists in that world that endures all-around people or is waiting for people to assist and give it birth which is the real purpose of a person's soul. For rightly and indeed, God's given "Freedom of Choice" was so that people can "choose" the correct way of supporting harmony for all life and non-life. It is a "choice" that constantly exists within all people, and it always returns to freely exist even after some peoples have negatively chosen to displace it. Therefore, is it not a truth that God's laws have given people the "Freedom of Choice" in which they could even kill themselves if they so desired to do so?

So yes! This reality is God-given freedom of choice which always allows peoples to positively perform harmony supporting acts which release the evolving harmony of the Creation or to remain still, knowing that the same act can destroy the emerging or the existing harmony that is all around them. But forgetting is our worst enemy, and so in our forgetting the "why" of our given purpose of choice, people can and do perform harmful acts of violence against others or acts based upon personal greed because we sadly forget who we are. For really and honestly, we are from the seed of our Father who is named God which was given to grow within space, for space is the Mother who gave birth to the Creation and like the need and purpose of all Mothers, it is She who cares for Her only child.

So correctly and indeed their only child is called "Creation" and which upon our Earth the eldest part of this only child has been developed with the ability to support Her harmony seeking endeavours for indeed it is only people who know who they are that can always endeavour to support Her work which is to maintain the harmony within Her family which we call the Creation and in particular in our case, the emerging harmony within that which we call planet Earth.

Therefore, indeed does not Earths' natural harmony exist all around and within all life and non-life and is it not also silently beckoning to every people, especially those people who strangely believe that they are individuals. So they "think" that they separate from all that exists. Yet truly people always know by an inner feeling of an outer experience exactly just when we are within God's Heaven that rests upon this Earth. For the resting in the "Present Time" silently removes any "I want" personal claims which cannot occur when our minds become silent and without thought and so experiencers that which is itself – This being the Creation!

For indeed, this is also personal experience and an "Enlightened" condition which is a condition that allows the Soul to see through a mind when it is without and mind blocking "I Want for ME" thoughts and so can become "Self-Aware" or Self-Realised" of that which we call God's worlds or the world of Nature for the Non-Believer – which can only exist in that which we call "Present Time"."

So again truly, it is this "non-thinking" condition that is called "Enlightenment", and it is essential not to forget this fact for forgetting is our worst enemy. Yes, the animalistic five senses will do all within their power to mindfully cloud the mind and so stop this experience which prohibits them from controlling their outer world in which they obtain their greed-based "I Want" for ME!. For this is an Enlightenment experience that is always showing the truth that you are that which you also observe and which is a world that requests just what you should do to continue to aid or not need to aid the evolving harmony that is existing all around you but only in the "Present Time.

Is it not also true that all religious and philosophical "Creeds" born by our wise ancients are all generally based upon the seeking of a mind-emptying silence that is entered into before any prayer? Is not also true that this mind-empty silence is carried into the repetition or sounding of the prayer and continues until the ending of any group togetherness, such as the incanting of a faithful prayer or hymn. Does this not bring all serious worshippers the enjoyable feeling of being in the peace that can only exist in that which we call the "Present Time". A clear proof that this is the experiencing of only God's world or the world of nature for the Non-Believer, in which rests that *"peace that surpasses all understanding"* which sadly is an experience which ends when the praying ends has the prayer habitually and unknowingly goes back to an "I Want" for ME mind filling reality. It is also this much-appreciated peace occurring in praying, shown later in "The Book", which shows that an individual can ALWAYS experience "Enlightenment", this being *"a realm beyond the ability of words to properly convey"* for it is God's world or the world of nature for the Non-Believer, and a world that can be an achieved by a simple individual discipline – but first read on for motivation is often required and "The Book" seeks to obtain a very strong "I want" the experience of "Enlightenment", this being an "I Want" which stops when "Enlightenment" is achieved.

Therefore, is it not also true that when a new worshipper joins by their personal "choice" a nearby religion that is understood to be a religion or philosophy that will suit their needs, that they often find that when they begin to take part in that religions "chosen" active creed practices, that sometimes "Enlightenment" can be experienced fleetingly or maybe for more extended moments. This feeling of "Enlightenment" being the experiencing of the "existence", "knowledge" and "bliss" which is always silently around us and which is usually born within the explanations stated in many Eastern religions.

Also, in all of the world's religions and philosophies, there are moments in which followers explain an experience which describes the reality of "Enlightenment", which can be described in many culture-based names and sayings such as experiencing the *"freedom from ignorance".* For indeed, there are many religious and philosophical names for that experience which people encounter within the teachings of their attending religions and philosophies, this being that experience which "The Book" describes as "Enlightenment". For this fact of actually experiencing "Enlightenment" is a well-known truthful experience explained by countless religions and philosophies has an occurrence that happens when a people experiences the real "being" that rests within them. This "being" is their Soul which has been enabled to observe the "Present Time" through a still and un-clouded mind, this being God's world or the world of Nature for the Non-Believer.

So yes! Truly only people can experience "Enlightenment", this being that which is described by hundreds of different names within our many countless different religions and philosophical teachings that have emanated from our ancient wise. It is also noted that there are many hundreds of "creed" based incantations which did bring worshippers the experience of "Enlightenment".

This experience is undoubtedly based upon their religions or philosophies are culturally chosen "creed exercise". This being that which would have been born from any chosen religions or philosophical "creed" and this being chosen because it became experienced that if it's repeating is continuously pursued, then this activity can lead to a further experience which "The Book" calls becoming "Self-Aware" in which you become "aware" that you exist as a unified part of the creation which can then lead to that which is called "Self-Realisation" in which there is no observer for all that exists is YOU!

For genuinely this is an experience in which there is known to be no "observer" for the Soul joins with the unity of the Creation and becomes the only life force which rests within the Creation – For it was also anciently known and culturally described by 8th century great Adi Shankara in the "Advaita Vedanta", which states that the knowledge of one's true self is truly liberating. For this school of Hinduism teaches that there is no-dualism, also called non-duality, which states that you are not two but one undivided and without a second. This 1200-year-old school also stated to be "Non-dualistic", primarily refers to a developed state of consciousness in which the clash of being separate from that which is around you is cancelled. So you become "everything" and so "not-separate" from the creation whose totality is experienced has been YOU! "The Book" further states that this state of "consciousness" may appear spontaneous or fleeting, as when looking down a valley at a beautiful landscape, but justly all religions and philosophies' pursue continued meditative practices via the chanting of prayers which can also be likened to a repeating mantra.

For rightly and truly the target is to experience their explained "non-dualism" which they say is experienced by a "non-dual" consciousness, which can also be found within many of our world's religions and philosophies such as Hinduism (Turiya, Sahaja), Buddhism (emptiness, pariniṣpanna, rigpa), Islam (Wahdat al Wujud, Fanaa, and Haqiqah) and western Christian (Holy Ghost or Holy Spirit) and neo-Platonic traditions (enosis, mystical union). But it should also be known that this can also be a frightening experience for those who are unprepared. Still, an experience which is sought after by many of our world's ancient wise, particularly our wise from our ancient East, for it is said that there are no more rebirths when one becomes "Self-Realised".

So yes! "Enlightenment" is a beautiful experience but for the hesitating newcomer to the worlds many religious practices the full understanding of chosen religions creeds may be more baffling than rewarding, this being if they are surrounded by "I want" gossip. Such gossip being *"Only our religious creeds are true for only our religious leader's worship true creeds, and these other false religions follow creeds and leaders that are not obeying God's only true creed which we alone believe."* They may also say that *"Our leaders say that our religion is the only true way of worshipping and that only our religion knows the truth and what to pursue in this life."* Then sadly this gossip develops into, *"so to bring God's harmony to all we must stop these false creeds that will never find God's world",* a world which Christians describe as the **"peace that surpasses all understanding"** or as described in the Muslim world **"a realm beyond the ability of words to convey properly"** and which has previously stated is correctly described in countless religions and philosophies as a truth and a reality that can be attained by all people.

So yes! For the readers of "The Book" who are seriously searching for the contentment and happiness that always exists in God's world or the world of Nature for the Non-Believer, they may find it challenging to understand the history of the frightening wars which show that one creed-based religion did fearfully war with another similar creed-based religion, both of which have the same initiator of their faith and all believe in a solitary God? Or even more strangely, even in our "Present Time", these conflicts continue between similarly named religions whose leaders still falsely activate many individual worshippers by giving their particular and very personal interpretation of a religious truth, which is to attack another part of the same based religion.

For truthfully, cannot it be understood that there are "thousands" of different worshipping creeds within the worlds many hundreds of different religions and philosophies whose practical, but many different creeds successfully rest within our world? It is also strange that many newcomers to these warring ancient religious practices, even in our current time, also engage in a pursued killing of these others of a similar religious practice. These being newcomers who are unable to understand and so control the demanding "I want" emanating from their five senses, this being an animalistic ally based "I Want", which is an individual interpretation that brings forth thoughts stating that *"Only my religious practises are true, and they are the only way to God."* Yes, this is an "I want" that some religious leaders do make their many religious followers pursue and also violate those with a different religious worshipping system, even when their roots belong to the truthful sayings of the same wise ancient originator.

Yet is it not seen to be a truth that these fractures that occur within religions, must occur because of a simply selected different creed-based ways of worshipping the same God? For truly is it not reasonable that many people of the world say, *"Those who attack others can have no true belief in God for what Godly authority could allow such violence and hurt to happen between His people?"*

So yes! Is it not clearly understood by many newcomers, who search for God, that such violent conflicts that exist between the same followers of the religious teachings of one of our wise ancients can bring forward many puzzling questions? For indeed, these many newcomers to various religious pursuits and who are on their new journey to find God and God's world cannot understand as to why this fierce conflict exists amongst people who believe and who profess to live in a world of God. Their puzzling thoughts being *"Why do the people, recognised to be the followers of the same God and sometimes even within the same religion, argumentatively separate into different creed-based theological factors, and then these brothers and sisters go to war against themselves and so seriously kill and violate each other?"* For rightly it is known that the quarrelling between religions, this being that which often bring many killings and violations to occur between religious worshippers, do create many conflicts which are simply created because their religious leaders have developed and installed different creed-based worshipping systems. These being culturally different creed-based worshipping systems but which strangely arouse violent disagreements that then lead to imposing personal violence upon those who worship within these differing creed. It is also strange that we can attach such disagreement and the killings of others as the same attacks that people usually reserve for the stealing of land, property, riches and money all of which is the property of others. Sadly this can be some peoples most energetic "I want".

For really indeed, in the past did not these "I Want" conflicts always appear and even in our "Present Time" do not these "I Want" creed empowered past or future based disagreements lead to violently acting groups that wilfully begin attacking and harming unto death others that belong to a differing creed-based religious system? The question is "How can these attacks upon another people's way of finding God's world lead the attacker to "Enlightenment," the world in which an "I want" for ME cannot exist in the reality of an experience of a peace that brings them the individual realisation of God's world?"

What is also true, seen by all new seekers of the truth, is the historical example of the Christian religions ancient pasts in which warring disagreements created many conflicting wars and in which many millions of innocents were violently destroyed or cripplingly punished with the conflict being "I want my creed way of worship followed by everyone, not yours."

So indeed, the newcomer searching for God's world will find great difficulty in understanding why these "Godly based" conflicts brought so much death, pain and suffering to large populations. They were seeking only God's world. At this point for all Non-Believers, all newcomers, all past seekers and all established worshippers who are seeking an authentic "scientific" way to God's world that rests within all our ancient religions and philosophies can now have explained in a modern way that which will bring to them a "creed" that will establish them within a genuinely modern religious experiencing God's world, the world that truly, exists in the "Present Time". But first, it must be clearly understood that despite all this past religious strangeness, this being that which was created by interactive violence that begets violence, which is known to be always violence that is attached to a personal "I want" that is usually circling economic values, God's peace that always rests upon this Earth but only in the "Present Time", is worth attaining. It has nothing to do with economics.

So yes! It is suitable for the newcomer who is seeking God's real-world always to remember that wanting anything for yourself will always destroy the arrival of this real-world of "Enlightenment" for the truth is that you already have everything that you need to fully experience Gods world or the world of Nature for the Non-Believer. This world being that singularity of truth which exists only in the "Present Time" for indeed when you experience "Enlightenment" that is continuously resting in this "Truth" you realise that you have "EVERYTHING" and that the whole Creation is serving you! For it can be said from experience, that all the above and the following words will prove this to be so. For sadly it was not knowing this truth that there was born in some of our worlds creed-based ways of worshipping, a severe "I want my creed to be the only way to God and not yours", thus starting the many fierce conflicts between various religions even unto the current day. For indeed, did not the Christian conflict continue for many years until they were peacefully and agreeably settled around 1,648 years after the death of Jesus?

It was only after this time that the primary conflict between the Christian Catholics way of worship and its Christian Protesters way of worship did end. So they became two very "peaceful" and religiously "personal" creed based systems. They now truly, worship peacefully under the creeds of the Catholic Church and Protestantism, which is a later birthed system of worship in which Protestantism reformed into many different creeds worshipping systems and it was a new peace for the Christian religion which also included the Eastern Orthodox Church.

So yes! Now it is true that all the many differing "churches" of the Christian faith can peacefully worship as they find their accepted creed way to God's world. Indeed, in the current time that now exists in the Christian world, you can work next to or sit next to any person in any public place and not know which Christian creed they support or even if they support any creed, which is truly God's world of peaceful understanding - which means that all people should stand under the non-harming peaceful laws of God or Nature for the Non-Believer. Yet sadly, and honestly, our world's history shows that this previous Christian violence, which was based upon *"I want my creed way of worshipping not yours"*, is still creating conflicts within the Islamic religion similarly, this is when the great prophet Mohammed's 襟 died. The conflict arose because the Sunnis believed Mohammed's 襟 friend and advisor Abu Bakr was the rightful "caliph" of Muslims, while Shias thought that his cousin and son-in-law Ali was chosen by God to rule? So just as it was with the Christian divide who had the same conflict regarding who should be the leader of the Christian faith, this Islamic conflict is also bringing pain, torture and death to others of the Islamic faith, just as the Christian divide did with their leadership conflict and their different ways of worshipping of Jesus. It can only be hoped that it will not take one thousand 1,648 years after the death of Mohammed 襟 in 632, to settle this dispute this is being the pending year of 2280. For hopeful it will be realised, as it was within the worshippers of Christian faith, that it does not matter what is the religion of the person sitting next to you is as long as it does not interfere with your way of finding God's world and the "Enlightenment" which begets *"peace that surpasses all understanding"* or as stated in the Muslim world *"a realm beyond the ability of words to convey properly."* For indeed, when experiencing the result which is the "Enlightenment" of living in God's world, it does not matter which creed practice is used to bring you to experience Gods world, a world that can only exist in the "Present Time", this is a world in which the "I want" for myself cannot survive for they are just internal thoughts that come from the past or the future. They will always remove the experience of being in the "Present Time", This truly is God's world or the world of Nature for the non-believer.

60. A PEOPLES WAY TO A SUITABLE RELIGION

Of course, it is vital for the newcomer who is seeking the understanding of a way to experience "Enlightenment", whether to do this by their singularity approach or by the joining of a suitable religion and so attaché oneself to a group of likeminded people and so priorities a chosen religions or philosophies creed based worshipping systems. For rightly and honestly, within our world, there are many different systems of devotion which can satisfy any personal worshipping desire, and which is regularly practised within the worlds countless religions and philosophies.

One of the most important factors to understand is that any creed way of worshipping which has been created by our wise ancients will always endeavour to bring to any practising people individual "Enlightenment" the *"awakening to the true nature of things"*, which is their very own "personal" experience of "Enlightenment".

For strictly, it is not, as many creed worshippers believe, an experience that can only be achieved by them being in a group of likeminded others, this is an incorrect viewpoint for any creed emanating from the teachings of the ancient wise, is directed towards the individuals' inner abilities to realise and so experience Gods world that it all around them and therefore cannot be a group activity.

However, the group can certainly support the efforts of the individual. The reasoning why this is said is because a religious belief stating that only the worshipping in a group can a person reach the experience of "Enlightenment", will hinder the search for Gods "Present Time" because the activity then becomes an "I Want", this being an "I want" or "I need" the company of compatible others who worship the same creed and with whom I can experience this deep stillness of contentment". Again, this is truly an illusion, and it will hinder and always thwart the most beautiful experience that people can experience.

So yes! The search within all religious creeds is to achieve "Enlightenment personally", and it may also be fleetingly experienced by an individual who is "worshipping" within a group, or it may be for more extended periods, yet if it is believed to be a group based experience, then the experience of "Enlightenment" will leave the worshipper when the group dissipates.

For indeed if the individual believes that it is only a group-based experience, then the leaving of the group will also mean the leaving of Enlightenment, this is NOT a genuine concept! For the experience of the *"The Peace that surpasses all understanding"* and in the Islamic religions, *"a realm beyond the ability of words to properly convey,"* which is also described throughout the world's many religions and philosophies has *"Paradise", "Nirvana", "Moksha", "Kenshō", "Bodhi,", "Satori,", "Kevala", "Jnana", "Ushta"* and many more, which shows that ALL religions and philosophies seek and target via their creeds, – the truthful experience of "Enlightenment" or they may have found a way of life that never leaves the experience of who they really are and so continue the living in "Enlightenment". But one must first realise that "Enlightenment" is truly an individual experience and if the individual reader wishes to achieve this "Enlightenment", then "Read on".

So yes! Instead of understanding the real truth regarding the way to achieve "Enlightenment", this being an experience which is personally gained by a devout individual's disciplined creed worshipping, and which is truly an experience which brings the individual's consciousness away from their "Past" or "Future" mind filling I Want" and so into the experiencing of "Enlightenment", this being that which can only exist in the "Present Time". For many mistakenly believe that it is the bonhomie of the group, which brings the happy experience of "satisfaction" and "security." Still, honestly, this is an "I Want", and it is not "Enlightenment", for it is a pleasure-seeking "I Want" experience of being with a like-minded group. Therefore it must be clearly understood that group "satisfaction" and "security" is excellent and friendly, but searching for a group feeling, is not the way to achieve "Enlightenment," which is the real target of all personal and group, concentrated but individual, creed activities.

For indeed, the sincere repetition of a known group "creed" or an individual practising a known personal "creed", always discipline a person's consciousness to still the mind, and so block out the repeating "I Want" demands of the five senses; for indeed it is this fact which allows the Soul to observe and cleanly witness Gods world, this being that which can only exist in the "Present Time".

This truth is because the mind has been stilled and so silenced by the imposition of a well-known and religiously based disciplinary chanting of a prayer or hymn, and therefore the mind is without any interference emanating from an "I Want" activity emanating from one of the five senses; thus meaning that the five senses have been disciplined unto silence by a person who has "chosen" consciousness to activate their inner "willpower" to disciplinary repeat an outer body imposed request. For again it should be said that this is being an act which automatically stops "willpower" from habitually energising one of the five senses to sound into the mind their own personal "I Want".

This condition is also most useful when the chanting of a group prayer becomes habitually repeated mechanically. Therefore it may also be useful at this time of "automatically" incanting to continue habitually but slowly at the same time open your eyes, and while continuing to repeat the prayer, become mind-empty aware of all that is around you AND within you.

For what you will silently witness is the being of the stillness of Gods ever-present world and your mouth may open in amazement at the stillness of the experiencing of your "Self", this being that which is all around you as it is within you, but be aware, that if your own undisciplined "I Want" words begin to sound into the mind, these were words that are not attached to that which you are chanting, then go back to the outer "mechanical" and "unthinking" repetitive praying words, and so again return to that exercise which is a mind empty silent knocking upon the door to Gods world, which exists only in the "Present Time", this being the door which opens itself and so unselfishly draws you into Gods world a world in which you will always "know" that only "YOU" can open this door which upon entering you will become aware and also realise that there is no other world – for indeed there is only YOU!

So yes! Now you can be assured that all the historical teachings of our ancient wise certainly target that expansion of the silence that exists between the words of prayer so that eventually you will see even with eyes open, enter Gods world and by expanding the silent spaces between the words; you will without any internal thoughts enter and begin to live in Gods world, which is called the "Present Time". For, in reality, this is again a personal experience of your "Self" being a witness to that which is genuinely Gods world and this is the world in which rests the personal experience of "Enlightenment".

For rightly when there is no other mind clouding "I want" between the Soul and that which it can observe through a person's mind, all those who believe that they are individuals will see Gods world has a single unity of never moving, ever-developing interlocked Harmony, this is being a developing Harmony, in which the "Mother of the Creation" may also be seeking support, which upon being provided, will enable that supporting person to experience "Sugar in the Water", a definite proof that that the "Mother of the Creation" is smiling upon you, and that these bonhomie gifts WILL and CAN be experienced.

So yes! It is also true that if you believe that you're Soul, which can view the "Creation" through a silent mind and so be enabled to experience Gods world, can only be an experience that is accomplished when within a group based activity, then it will be an experience that will be ignorantly claimed and wrongly developed by the five senses. For correctly their request will endeavour, with mind clouding concepts, to seek out this newfound and pleasing group "bonhomie," has to imploring within your mind that this is an experience that can only be created within the fellowship of the group.

So you will always hear within the mind the "I Want" this group to be with". For indeed, it is then that the five senses will act within their habitual but wrongly given freedom to do so and so will solidly sound within the individuals' mind an "I Want" to be with this group! This demand then actually becomes an "I Want the love, I Want the wellbeing, I Want the safety, I Want the strength, I Want the comforts, and I Want the bonhomie of this like-minded group, for this is a group that can provide for me all that I need to gain in privileges and strength against all others!

Therefore, five senses, also in their search for pleasurable needs, will also see the leader of the group to be the provider of these "I Want" for ME needs, and woe to the group when the chosen leader seeks ways to "disciplinary" increase the power of the group that they lead. It is also sadly known that to enforce this leader's false "I Want a bigger group" belief system, is that a single member then becomes ganged with other members of the group who will willingly attack non-members, in a misplaced concept that these others are not showing loyalty to their group, this being done to forcibly expand the members of the group to please their leader. Thus this "I Want" is truthfully a false understanding of Gods world whose love bound unity is genuinely the only leader who should be "experienced". For the truth that exists in "Enlightenment" is that there is only one group, this "group" being all the life and non-life that truly exists all around us and which is a truth that knowingly exists upon our planet Earth but only on the "Present Time".

So yes! It also happens that when a person's belief becomes attached only to the bonhomie of a "group experience," which then manifest into a strong "I Want to belong within this like-minded group", that it then becomes the single paramount target of an "I Want," that the five senses enforcedly act upon within the individual and so when the group dissipates, so does the "Together with a group in unity" which is the negative to the experiencing of "Enlightenment", this being an "Enlightenment" which was explained 2,500 years ago in the Katha Upanishad has the ***"liberation, salvation and emancipation of the Soul"*** and also many hundreds of worshipping system throughout our world have given it ancestral names such has Moksha, Vi-moksha, Vi-Mukti and all Mukti terms which are used in Hinduism, Buddhism, Jainism, Sikhism. These words being that, which along with many others of our world's religions and philosophies, refer to various forms of emancipation, enlightenment, liberation, and release from bondage, this also is that which is described by Jesus has *the doctrine of salvation",* which is bound within the Christian teachings, especially the Christian doctrine of salvation through Jesus Christ and His religious principles concerning the human soul and its relationship to death, judgment, heaven, and hell.

For indeed it too refers to the anciently named freedom from "Samsara", this being the cycle of death and rebirth which is also clearly explained in "The Book". For sincerely, "The Book" endeavours to personally and simply reveal to all strata's of life, the meaning of our world's many culturally different religious and philosophical studies and in particular their targets and also to show a modern way to naturally free the Soul to become that which truly exists in Gods world or the World of Nature for the Non-Believer, in particular, its foundations, scope, and validity to gain freedom from ignorance which allows a person to become "Self-Aware", "Self-Realised" or self-Actualized" which is undoubtedly based upon and "Self-Knowledge", this being the knowledge and understanding that all that you experience is YOU!.

So yes, this is undoubtedly a personal experience and not a group-based experience, so the group is not a necessity for the way to achieve "Enlightenment" is individualistic. So it should be known that "Enlightenment" is an individual task, which can be accomplished alone. However, it may be useful when in the beginning phase, to pursue this way to "Enlightenment" with a likeminded group. For indeed it is the acknowledging that it is the automatic physical chanting and or the mentally performing of an individual or group chosen religious "Creed" word or words, this being that which could be based upon a song or phrase or a single worded prayer, that brings one to experience the harmony that rests within Gods world.

For truly although Gods world is the world that exists only in the "Present

Time", what may not be correctly understood is that in reality ALL the world's creeds within ALL the world's religions and ALL the worlds philosophies have been born and given by our wise ancients, to ALL their followers, to enable the individual to enter the "Present Time," which is Gods world or the world of Nature for the Non-Believer. So yes it is the knowledge and the only experiencing this world that exists all around us has it does within us, is called "Enlightenment", and so indeed this is the single target of ALL religions and philosophies.

So yes! It is this "Enlightenment" or the experiencing of the "Present Time" which enables the actual realisation of the peace that rests upon this Earth, which is an "Enlightenment" often found beginning in the chanting, singing or group activities of creed-based worship. It is also this brief glimpsing of "Enlightenment"; this "Out of the ordinary experience," that many religious worshippers interpret as being caused by the fellowship of the group, or gained by individually performing a repetitive prayer within sight of their leader.

It is also then that the individual worshiper can mistakenly believe that this peace that arises within them can only be created within their religious group, or in front of their religious leader. Therefore it is understood that the brief revelations of this beautiful experience are being caused by the presence of their group. So they mistakenly believe that it is a group-based experience which can only be shared and so experienced within a group. In essence, this is an incorrect viewpoint, for it is genuinely a personally achieved "individual" experience that once FULLY realised to be so, will never leave you.

It must, therefore, be severe and factually understood that experiencing the "Present Time", this being the only place that exists God's Heaven upon this Earth, is truly an individual experience that is created only by an individual's way of creed worshipping and that this experience has nothing to do with the group or its leader. For indeed the reality of creed worship is that it is the individuals' practical methodology and mind disciplined pursuit of the mantras, chants or physical activities that are attached by our ancient wise ancients to ALL creed worshipping activities.

It is this actual practice that brings the disciplined creed worshipper "personally" into Gods world, this is achieved because a creed based discipline eventually, in its on-going pursuit, stops the individual's mind from automatically being filled with a chattering "I want" that are specific demands emanating from the five senses for they cannot be you, who is the observer of these acts. For this is being the norm for a captured mind because the observer mistakenly believes that the words in one's mind are genuinely coming from them – when in reality, it again can be said that you cannot be that to which you observe or listen. For rightly, this is the noise of words and pictures that the five senses automatically bring flooding into the mind and which all are an emanating targeting from and a Past or a Future "I Want".

So yes, honestly, these many false creations within the mind are the "I Want" demands of the five senses and so ritual praying is therefore known by the wise ancients to be a way of developing a formal praying method, whose self-enforcement stops the mind -filling contamination of an "I Want." Again, this being an "I Want" that is coming from the five senses and which troublingly also uses up all conscious energy.

For indeed, this "creed praying" that exists within all our world's religions and philosophies are created to free "Enlightenment", and this is why they are based upon a systematic, unthinking uncontrolled disciplinary based chanting of words that eventually paves the way for the Soul to begin to see briefly the darkness of an empty mind, this being that which can now be seen through the more significant and more substantial spaces created within the stilling of the mind. These are being spaces that are occurring between the disciplinary installed and "automatic" and "unthinking" chanting of words that are "automatically" emanating within the disciples' mind and whose "Self" imposed target is to enable the viewer, which is the Soul, to see the real world that is outside the prayer's body.

For this is truly is the beginning which eventually brings a person the knowledge that only with a clear "empty" and "still" mind, can the Creation be seen by the viewer, which is the Soul that can now experience and so see the outer world that surrounds it and which it knows is "IT", and so physically via bodily actions, activate that which is needed to support the harmony of the "Creation" whose stillness is emerging according to the needs of Heaven and the will of the "Mother of the Creation", this being that which is genuinely seen and experienced when viewing God's Creation or the world of Nature for the Non-Believer.

So yes! It is this fact which then enables a constant unchangingly and known to aid the "Harmony" that exists in the "Heaven" that rests upon this Earth. It is also this unselfish but personal pursuit of one of the world's self-chosen creed that can bring a person to fully the experience "Enlightenment", this being the experiencing of God's "Present," which peoples call the "Present Time" a time in which rests the *"Peace that surpasses all understanding"*.

For strictly, it is this knowledge that is "personally" realised when one becomes "Enlightened", for certainly one "experiences" the real world, this being that which rests all around them; which is undoubtedly created by the automatic, unthinking chanting of a chosen creed. But strangely and sincerely, we must again realise that it is a fact that because "friendliness" can be an experience when sharing a "creed" activity within a group, that this experience is often mistaken as the harbinger of "Enlightenment," therefore it is good to understand that this is experiencing love, pleasure, bonhomie and the feeling of belonging to a group, is merely mimicking that which exists in Gods world of love.

For the real truth is that this experience of love for a group and the feeling of need for the group are NOT attached to or caused by the fellowship and wellbeing of the group which is a severe and incorrect viewpoint, for indeed it is all creation that is your "group". It is the "Creations" love for you that you are experiencing and which you should be reflecting the whole creation, which of course includes the group within whom you exist.

For loving creeds have become not only attached to different ways of religious worship and philosophies, of which our world contains many thousands; but also, to "group" cultures, which are a person's culturally-made way of worship and which have also been created via their own private "creeds" has in the worship of political parties and gangs. For all can see and understand the truth that when some different cultures meet, as within a differing or the same religions accepted creed way of worship, this can certainly bring the "Bonhomie" which of course is based upon the feeling of self-love and the peace that we speak about - but this friendship is not "Enlightenment", which is undoubtedly the experiencing of unity and security that exists in harmony.

So yes! This concept of creed worship is not only confined to religions and philosophies. Still, it can also be expanded to include spectator sports, schools, and universities, private and state organisation, political parties, nations, states, cities, districts, localities and even streets, homes and families for all have their own "personal" creeds of that which should be said and that which should not be said. For justly, history shows that people do know the feeling of "belonging", this being based upon their own group needs but honestly, this is only a poor copy of that which can be experienced when they join Gods world, this is being a true "Enlightenment" within which there is genuinely only one group, which is all life and non-life.

So yes! This "bonhomie" that can be experienced within a likeminded private group may not be "Enlightenment" for it is a view that can lead to a severe and incorrect viewpoint which can manifest itself has a group based "I Want" my group to be more potent than your group, This is undoubtedly a false belief that you are increasing Gods love for your group, and also your groups love for you. In essence, this is NOT true for God loves ALL His children equally and also because of the "Freedom of Choice" that God gave to all people, it is likened that He will just turn His back upon those who attack and hurt His creation. In essence, this world without God or the control of Nature for the Non-Believer is NOT a good world to live in for all goes sadly wrong when the Creation turns its back upon you. So serious woe comes to that person or group who, for whatever personnel reason, destroys Gods world.

For indeed, great sadness plus illness within a group becomes personally realised and also privately experienced as the group pursues that which belongs to others to support its agreeing members in contentment that falsely mimics Gods world, for actually, does not our worlds history constantly show this truth? For true "Enlightenment" cannot be based upon the loyalty and the supporting of a group which seeks to enlarge only the personal thinking of "I Want" for myself? This being that which is a never-ending "I want" which stops the Soul from seeing through the clear mind and stops it from viewing "Present Time" where a personal "I want" cannot exist. For indeed in Gods world, all people have everything that they need and non-believers "I Want for myself" should never be allowed stop the sharing of Harmony to ALL life and also all the non-life that is in existence all-around people.

So sadly, yes! The belief that supporting a group based "I Want" for me, bonhomie is the correct way to experience Gods "Enlightenment" is a very destruct full "I Want" for it is undoubtedly a group based "I Want" which can be originating from an experience which makes the individual believe that "Enlightenment" is caused by the needs of one's group, this is a dangerous illusion. For this belief often justifies likeminded "creed" groups attacking other groups who have "Creeds" which are different from their own. These personal gang based efforts are accruing because they want to prove that their creed is a more influential creed which makes their five senses feel kind and also because it brings in many "I Wants" and even whole countries can suffer from this problem. It is also that which is the cause of war.

So yes! Again this is also a false "Gang" based reality that gives birth to "Institutional Denial", these being government based denial statements and acts that are created by groups of likeminded people to protect their group's personal "creed" interests, this is because they believe that their "I Want" creed is the only pure creed. To confirm this belief, they actively or mischievously attack other creeds by the use of false opinions; this is usually achieved by giving birth, within their group, to many false opinions which they falsely give birth to combat another group's creed, this is done because they have an inherent fear, produced by their five senses, of losing their personal "groups" wealth and possible income. It is this fact that creates the many selfish "attacks" and even wars upon others, these being born by reflections from an "I Want" that they falsely believe their harbinger of the "peace that surpasses all understanding" - this is a false "Enlightenment" and indeed an incorrect viewpoint.

But sadly, this is often the usual way of group life that leads to group conflict and religious disagreement plus economic wars, and this is sadly true because what can also be so easily recognised is that these conflicts are based upon the individual and group fear of losing existing wealth or gaining assurances of obtaining more riches, this is a very "ignoring" way which will never obtain "Enlightenment for it is based upon an understanding that is born from satisfying the on-going greed of their five senses. Yet certainly, this is being a truly a false understanding which targets the joy of the five senses which are NEVER satisfied. But certainly, what would be good for all the "unbelieving" worlds people would be for them to understand that even in their world they could achieve a true "Enlightenment", this being that which surpasses – in great joy – all understanding.

For indeed, has all our wise ancients continuously say, this experiencing inner Joy can even be "Self-Experienced" by sitting alone in the middle of a dessert, for indeed this great joy wants for nothing, and it is a personal and not a group reflection of like minds and it is an "Enlightenment" that always "personally" targets the greater good of all life and non-life for this is an experience which belongs to all that is. It is also the "Self-Realizing" of this experience which took Jesus to the cross.

So yes! Simply put many creed based groups believe that the personal experience of "Enlightenment" emanates from a group experience of "togetherness", which is that security within the group emotion which they experience and which they believe to be achieved only within their recognised groups "Instructions". So, it is a known fact, just as the warring history of all our countries and all our nations show, that this false "Enlightenment" is an on-going condition that even many religious groups believe that what they experience is "Enlightenment" which is not valid for what they experience is group "Sociability". Accurately this is a condition which can only come from within their groups "Sociability", and they believe that their groups "Sociability" should be expanded to the rest of the world, which is simply a search for the security of their "I Want" which is coming from the desires of their five senses.

So yes! It is when a person experiences their own groups' falsely based reflection of "Enlightenment", this being a negative "Enlightenment," which is simply happiness based upon the satisfying of the "security" needs of their five senses when attached to the strength of the group. For indeed such a person experiences a personal "I Want" feeling in which there should be only one entity within the world around them, which in truth is not themselves but group-based contentment. It is then that this ideology becomes that groups' personal world and also world that they wish to enlarge. But sadly, this is not being the one correct entity within Gods or Nature's "Enlightenment" but within themselves and their group, for it is an "I Want" that they believe cannot be achieved when alone - - this is an incorrect viewpoint.

For it must now be fully understood that our Gods world is everywhere and can be recognisably experienced by all people for it is not privately set only for some chosen people. Still, ALL people, this is because "Enlightenment" is an absolute all-knowing and all-realising truth that is only experienced by attending to and obeying religious creeds which are certainly not the only way to finding Gods Heaven upon this Earth. For indeed, "Enlightenment" is that which is continuously shown to all peoples and so can be momentarily and individually self-experienced by any individual only by quietly listening to music which can also be likened to participating in a worshipping "creed" the listening to poetry can take you into the "Present Time" the world of Gods Heaven that rest upon this Earth.

So Yes! It is true that all around us we see "creeds" that are constantly reminding people of a way of entering the "Present Time" which is genuinely Gods world or the world of Nature for the Non-Believer and even when we listen to a simple music box we can also enter the "Heaven" that rests upon this Earth. For music and poetry are just two of the incidents that can stop "I Want" thoughts revolving through the mind and so can bring the listener into Gods world, this being that which exists only in the Present Time".

So yes! The need for the understanding of the Harmony created by Gods world or the world of Nature for the Non-believer is an "Enlightenment" that is experienced in the accepting of the many different creeds and beliefs of another group or other countries culture and religions all of which target the same Gods world of continuing "Enlightenment". For certainly is it not now known that all targets are designed to achieve the Godly given experience of "Enlightenment", this being the feeling of oneness and the need to support the Harmony that God always supports upon this Earth.

Is it not also seen as truly important to understand that our worlds difference in cultures, religions and philosophies are all targeting a way to Gods world and a countries culture explains why God summoned the wise ancients to make those particular countries creeds understandable and also in a certain very particular way, this indeed is a way that makes it agreeable that any person on the path to realising the "Enlightening" realisation that experiences Gods world, can quickly recognise an acceptable difference from their cultural creed based way and so explanations of other of our worlds various religions are not needed, for all target the same reality which is the harmony of "Enlightenment".

But sadly this gift from God is sometimes not recognised and the fear of the unknown - which is an illusion emanating from Hell - takes over. It is this which makes the unsatisfied "I Want" for ME people to attack that which is different from their groups' culture-based religion or philosophy. Again this is because they believe in an "I Want" group based creed which is a false group-based "Enlightenment" which is "Godly" understood to be a falsely emanating and a very personal "I want" for ME, this being that which has been self-created by such a group and which always emanates from the five senses, a system which is particularly rampant in politics.

61 THE WAY TO THE EXPERIENCING OF HEAVEN UPON THIS EARTH

What now should be understood by those who are seeking a purposeful meaning to life, whether currently attending the Earths many various religions or not attending any religious services, is to understand that the reciting and the performing of ALL religious creeds are targeting the religious and philosophical reality of that which "The Book" describes has "Enlightenment". Therefore it is good to remember that this is that which ALL religions and philosophies throughout our world are offering to their followers. It is an actual people experience which the Christians call being filled with the "Holy Spirit" or the "Holy Ghost" depending upon their sectional belief system and it is also described as being *"peace that surpasses all understanding"*.

In contrast, the Hindu religion calls it "Moksha" which loosely means *"freedom from ignorance."* Buddhists refer to it as "Bodhi" or "Nirvana", this is a people experience described as *"awakening to the true nature of things"*, and the Islam religion described it as *"being filled with the Angel Gabriel"* and it is described as *"a realm beyond the ability of words to properly convey."* So all our many Earths many religions and philosophies are designed to show the path to achieve this experience even back to the ancient Zoroastrianism religion of the fifth-Century BC who refer to this people experience "Enlightenment" as "Ushta" which they described as meaning *"liberation, salvation and emancipation of the Soul"*. So indeed this is that personnel "experience" which ALL our wise ancients target for their followers.

For yes, it is the experiencing of God's world or Natures world for the Non-Believer for actually truly this is the "Heaven" on Earth that only exists in the

"Present Time". Thus, the attending to any of the world's religious service is to enable the individual worshipper to be amongst people who are culturally likeminded and who are all pursuing a culturally accepted creed-based way of seeking "Enlightenment".

This "Enlightenment" is genuinely that condition in which any person can experience God's world or Natures world for the Non-Believer; for the method later being described in "The Book" shows just how to achieve and so experience "Enlightenment" this being the world of Heaven that rest only in the "Present Time" and which is targeted by ALL the religions and philosophies' that rest throughout our world.

For rightly, the seeker of this truth is or can be engaged in a praying group, or they can be solitary prayers, or regularly engaged in singing or in chanting or even to the listening to a leader's solitary spoken words, these being the many ways of taking personal thoughts away from the "I want" instructions emanating from the five senses which are automatically filling the mind and which are coming from the undisciplined five senses whose desires are always filling a person's mind. It is this fact which always takes the observers thoughts into past and or a future "I want" existence, these being thoughts that take them away from the real world which silently exists in the "Present Time".

Thus the birth of all these religious or philosophical incantations are all simply and culturally established by our wise ancients to achieve that which ALL religious and philosophical creeds seek, this being for the beholder and worshipper to achieve, and so realise the un-demanding stillness of God's' world or the world of Nature for the non-believer. Genuinely, this is that which we call "Heaven" which is truly the world that factually exists and so can be experienced. Still, only in the "Present Time", which these positive and mind-emptying outer "realised" pursuits take the doer and so away from the negative mind-filling inner trespassing "I Want for ME" world that is imposed by the animalistic five senses, this being the personally created non-existing world of Hell.

It should, therefore, be understood that ALL our religious creeds, these being that which have been established by our wise ancients, are "disciplinary" designed to remove an individual's constant mind blocking "I want for Me" thoughts, which seriously clouds and so stops the view of the thinkers' Soul, this being that entity which views through the still mind God's world, or the world of Nature for the Non-Believer, this genuinely being that physical world which can only exist in the "Present Time".

Therefore, is it not logically true that the "Present Time", which is God's world of Heaven or the world of Nature for the Non-believer, is the only place from where a person's wayward thoughts, these being that which are birthed by the "I Want" of the animalistic five senses which can "habitually" use the energy of consciousness'. For indeed this is a truth that exists because in childhood "consciousness" was instructed via our God-given "Freedom of Choice", to allow willpower to automatically fill the mind with the selfish "I want" desires that are continually emanating for our five senses. This fact is being because, in childhood, we understood that these emanations from the animalistic five senses were coming from ourselves. So eventually we accepted them as our true selves and so became with physical rather than spiritual needs.

So yes! These physical needs then began to dominate our personnel inner thoughts which can only emanate from a past or a future "I want" for ME thought, this being a false Hell made a world which these "I Want for ME" thoughts always "animalistic ally" create but which should not exist, for they do block an "I Want" thinkers Soul from seeing and so supporting the "Present Time" – which is truly God's world and so fulfil the task which was given only to people. Therefore the purpose of our wise ancients, who started our entire world's religions and philosophies', is to develop creeds based upon the culture of their followers, these being creeds that were culturally designed to impose a self-disciplined concentration that could eventually bring the incanting worshipper into the "Present Time", this being God's world or the world of Nature for the Non-Believer.

For our wise ancients knew that only when the mind was still and had no personal "I want" activity and so was not filled with an animalistic "I want", this being that which automatically supplies the energy that activates an animalistic "I Want for ME" inner thought, this being that which always blocks the Soul from seeing God's world that can only exist in the "Present Time". For again truly, it is this non-wanting which is born from any self-imposed inciting creed discipline that eventually stops the "I want" filling the mind and so enables the Soul to see that which exists in the "Present Time" and this firstly being experienced through the empty spaces between the words of the habitually imposed mind-controlling incanting creed until eventually, the habitual words cease and the empty mind remains.

It is this fact that allows the Soul to continue its "experience" of God's "Present Time", this is "Enlightenment", and it is indeed waiting for you! For genuinely, the reality is that the "Present Time" is God's world and a world of Heaven that can become a world that is no longer hidden by mind filling clouds of "I want", this is a fictitious world which ALL people "I Want for ME" thoughts target. Now it must be clearly understood that it is this "Enlightening" encounter with the "Present Time" that even if it is your first encounter, it is an encounter that will reveal an experience which is that which has been described above and by our many religions and philosophies as to be experiencing the *"peace that surpasses all understanding"*.

It is this peace this knowing of Heaven that exists upon our Earth that is called "Enlightenment", and it is an experience that does exist as is proven by the above. It is waiting for you, and you will never be able to describe it except maybe with the simple words "It just IS". So yes! the way ahead to attain this "Enlightenment" this inner peace within your mind, is created most quickly by a very simple creed which "The Book" puts forward has "Patient Meditation" which has been "scientifically" created by "The Book" to be successfully used by all known creeds. It is a very modern and unique form of meditation designed for Religious, Philosophical and Non-Religious people and designed to bring the modern "seeker of the truth" quickly to the "Present Time".

For it is undoubtedly true that meditation is a well-tried exercise which has been practised within all our world's religions and particularly in the East of our world for many thousands of years. It was also knowingly targeted to stop evil and violent activities and so attain a peaceful view of the world while the new 2020 target of "Patient Meditation" is to stop the mind of any person from actively living in the past or the future where it always manifests plans to obtain an "I want" that is truly understood by "The Book" to be a mind filling reality that is emanating from the greed of five senses, this being that activity which factually stops the view of the Soul from seeing the "Present Time".

So yes! Now certainly "Patient Meditation" is the simplest method which applies the necessary discipline that is needed to rest the mind in the "Present Time", which is the pure "Heaven" were only the ongoing peaceful world of God's harmony or Natures harmony for the non-believer truly exists and where no personal "I want" inner mind filling fabricated past or future exists. For indeed this world of a personally created world of Hell can be "accidentally" filled into the mind and so falsely create in mind an animalistic "I Want for ME" world which savages in greed that peace which exits all around it and so sadly creates the world of Hell and not the world of Heaven which people have been created to support and rightly if they harm others, they will not be born again.

So Yes! This creation is not for people to rest in as in a dreamed falsely created Hell, this being that world in which one creates a false past or targets an animalistic I want for ME false future. But it is a creation where all mortal bodies are filled with an energy that can be "Self-Disciplined" to "Choose" to support the Heaven that truly exists upon our Earth, but only in the "Present Time".

Indeed, this is being a Godly created way of life which disciplinary silences the inner mind so that the inner Soul can see through it and so become "Enlightened" to the fact that it exists within a life that is lived in the Heaven that truly exists upon our Earth, which is the only time that genuinely exists For it is undoubtedly not an ignorantly created world of Hell, which is a false animalistic world of greed that can be birthed by a person's animalistic five senses, thus self-creating an "I Want for ME" dreamed Past or Future world that does not exist but which is continuingly being sounded via our five senses, into what should be a quiet mind.

For indeed, what you have put into effect within you is the listening to yourself talking in your mind which is simply the craving words of an "I want" emanating from one of the five senses. But now, and scientifically "The Book" states that "Patient Meditation" is the simplest and quickest way to experiencing this "Enlightenment", this being that which is sought by all our worlds' religious and philosophical creeds that have been anciently established by ALL our wise ancients, this is truly being the way to realise the real harmony that rests in the peace of the "Present Time", and indeed, it is a life that is lived in a Heaven which truly exists upon this Earth.

So yes! The experiencing of "Enlightenment" is certainly not a world that allows the five senses to use a person's body to seek a past or a future "I want", which is well known to be rightly and truly a life that is living in Hell. For again the practice of "Patient Meditation" will eventually bring the "practiser" to understand the differences between the two worlds in which one is the living within God's laws or Nature's laws for the non-believer and the other in a self-made Hell. For indeed, the practice of "Meditation" will eventually and naturally bring the "practiser" to a life that is lived under God's laws in which the practiser will become an integral and useful part of the expanding harmony of the ever-non-moving stillness of "The Creation", this being an ever-evolving stillness which cannot be stopped and only temporarily changed.

Therefore, it is the living in the real world, which is the positive word of God's Heaven that truly exists upon this Earth. Therefore, successful "practiser" will never return to the false world of a personal "I want", this being the world which is likened to be living in a negative disharmony which can only lead a person away from God's' world and THIS is indeed living in Hell while on this Earth.

So yes! Is it not undoubtedly beneficial to know the difference between living in Heaven and living in Hell? Realy this being the living in a Heaven that will be easily realised via meditation which "The Book" suggests being the best way to find "Enlightenment". For indeed this activity will in due time and after many practices, enable the doer to live in and so to truly experience God's or Nature's Heaven that always rests in the "Present Time". Yes, this being the only world that genuinely exists without any need for a personal "I want". Why is this absolute truth? It is a certain truth because eventually, you realise that you have everything, for indeed with continued practice, you will realise that you ARE everything and almost certainly realise that you cannot die.

So yes, with right diligence and a twice-daily morning and evening exercise, the practitioner will eventually arrive at a thirty-minute meditational exercise consisting of a simple creed-based mantra sounding activity, this being a mind silencing activity which is conjoined in the early days with a few inner minds sounding words stating "not this", which are bringing to obedience the mind sounding "I Want" that is emanating from the animalistic five senses.

For indeed, in those early days, the constant inputs that are emanating from the five senses need a disciplinary command to be sounded into the mind to stop the unsolicited thoughts that come into the mind. For assuredly, this act is a disciplined practice that will eventually become a practice that will bring the meditational "practiser" to that target which all the creeds of all our world's religions and philosophies seek, and this is being "Enlightenment" the physical "Self-Aware" the first step that can lead to the "Self-Realization" of God's world or the world of Nature for the non-believer.

For indeed, it will then be found that "Heaven" really does exits upon this Earth and that it is the same existing unchanging "Heaven" that ALL our wise ancients endeavoured to show to their worshipping followers, this being just how to attain via prayer this Godly given, or Nature gave for the Non-Believer, a real reality. For it can be undoubtedly said that our wise ancients always targeted this reality by presenting many "concentrating" ways to self-discovering this heavenly based reality and they achieved this by creating many culturally based and variable creeds, songs, hymns and prayers which were in accordance to the acceptable culture of their worshippers' needs at that time.

So yes, this is rightly so, for is it not also known that many cultures of these ancient times, especially those in the Northern Hemisphere, would never have accepted such a simple yet very ancient exercise that "The Book" is now "scientifically" proposing. For indeed in our Northern Hemisphere was it not believed that you could only reach the experiencing of "Heaven" upon this earth, by believing and so pursing the "I Want" thoughts of a tribal leader? How strange this can be, for the simple reality is that you cannot be freed from an "I Want" by resting comfortably in the "I Want" of a self-chosen tribal leader, for truth is in not forgetting our worst enemy.

So yes, this is a self-disciplined exercise which is based upon stable and historical foundations which go back thousands of years and which all should now know is the decisive factor that will enable the practiser to enter and so live in God's world or the actual world of Nature for the Non-Believer. For how could our wise ancients have said to their followers that it is the space between the habitually sounding words of their chosen mantra or praying incantations, this being that which is necessary to stop the mind clouding "I want" that is contently filling their mind and which is emanating from one of their five senses and that it is this "disciplined" mantra sounding act which allows the Soul to see through these silent spaces occurring between the words of the "habitually" and "mechanically" sounding" mantra – and so experience the reality of God's world – this being the Heaven that rests upon our Earth

So yes! Only people have a way to become "Self-Aware" or to "Self-Realise" this Heaven that rests upon our Earth, for it is a Heaven that can always be realised to exist upon our earth for in its "stillness" it is quickly recognised as God's Heaven which is "realised" to continually support the harmony that truly exists alongside all life and non-life, this indeed is a "Heaven" that can be experienced and so lived while upon this Earth but only when it is lived in without the attachment to any personal "I want".

For even an "I want" thought of bringing harmony to the world is not for any person to pursue therefore truly the purpose of people is to support God's world of Harmony and so aid the work of the "Mother of the Creation" and it is essential not to forcibly attempt to self-create harmony by a personal "I want". For it is certainly seen to be real has in the "The Passion of Christ" this being that which is explained in the Christian Bible and which explains the betrayal of Jesus who was undoubtedly our God incarnate for indeed, He was a "Self-Realised" personification of God's Creation.

For it is certainly in "The Passion" that it explains that when Jesus was arrested, He never mentioned any "I want". Even when they mocked, insulted, spat, flogged and tortured Him until He was eventually nailed to a cross and left to die, He still never mentioned an "I want".

Is it not also true that He never attempted to harm or offend his punishers for is it not also true that He was silent until His last words which did arise from Him upon the cross when He experienced His oncoming death, in which He said, *"Forgive them for they know not what they do."* So indeed all people should now know what to do which is to simply support the harmony that is emerging all around you and not to attempt to retarget this emerging harmony or change the existing harmony for you personnel benefit, for this is an "I want" which certainly separates you from that which you are, which is "Everything".

So Yes! It is with the growing aid of a "Mantra Meditation" exercise, this being that which is undoubtedly an exercise that will eventually enable the Soul of any person to see through their empty and unblocked mind and so observe only the Present Time, this being that reality which our ancients did surrender themselves, which is genuinely the Heaven that also exists around all the life that lives upon our Earth. For it is undoubtedly true that this is a recognisable God based or Nature-based harmony for the Non-Believer and it is a harmony which seems to spring silently from this very Earth.

So Yes! All God's harmony seeking endeavours can eventually be quietly and personally realised and experienced via "The Books" chosen "Patient Meditation", this being that which is the quickest way to establish that of God's, or Nature's harmony is existing everywhere. Yet it is also wise to understand that only people can break this harmony by their "I want" claims upon others which mean that they are living in Hell.

For is not "Hell" the place that everyone can recognise as always being the endeavouring selfish-creation of only five kinds of "I Want" pursuits? These pursuits being based upon the pursuing of taste, smell, sound, seeing and touch? Are these pursuits also known to be supporting lust, anger, avarice, plus pride and envy, all of which are a criminal attachment to a person "I want?" Is this not the "I want" world that is called by our wise ancients "the great illusion? For again is it not also true that this is the false world that ALL our wise ancients speak about as being the world that gives rise to a personal "I want" and the statement "this is mine", this critically being a, "I Want for ME" world which even ensures that many people who worship and practice in our worlds many religions, to be still blindly chained to the world of Hell as they only seek company and the need to feel belonging to something when in a real reality they belong to everything.

Sadly, is it not also clearly proved to be true that those who live in this personally created Hell are always feeling that they are unfairly punished so that they then feel that they can jealously attack those who are contentedly and peacefully living in our Heaven upon this Earth? Therefore is it not also true, has our history does show, that many religious worshippers also attack worshippers of a different religion? These being worshippers who are practising a different personally chosen way of creed worship, this being a culturally-based way of worshipping that these people have found will keep them in God's world. So is it not true that these attackers do not fully understand that ALL creeds are targeting the same "Enlightenment", this being the unquestionable truth that they are seeking or have found their Gods world.

So yes! Is it not also true as history does show that these jealous different creed attackers and creed destroyers say, "Your creed way of worship is wrong, and my creed way of worshipping is right" and so wilfully attempt to terminate another's creed? What is also strange is that this attempt at destroying another worshipper's creed can continue for thousands of years which show that such punishing actions are wrong.

Therefore, is it also not clear for all people to see that the harmony of Godness "goodness" can only exist in God's world and that this can only occur and so be experienced in the "Present Time", which is genuinely Gods world or the world of Nature for the Non-Believer? This world is in a time in which an "I want" cannot exist for is it not seen to be true that the killing of others is undoubtedly based upon past or a future "I want", which cannot be a part of God's world. For assuredly, how can this killing and punishing of other lives be correct? Yet truly, what is also certainly known to be true is that all "I wants" can be stopped for as soon as living in Heaven begins all living in Hell is destroyed. Indeed, this is a task which is worth pursuing - so shall we now endeavour to start this task?

So yes, this is a task which is also historically realised to be a well-known method of removing the stress of living in a self-made Hell. This stress being caused by not achieving but trying to achieve that which is not ours to achieve and which is a condition which is said to "statistically" account for most visits to our Doctors. The reason for this fact is that living in Hell is also well known to be the cause of high blood pressure and cholesterol problems which all can lead to heart disease and stroke and an "I want" is also a well-known thought that certainly creates anxiety and stress along with worry, depression, insomnia all of which is to name but a few unfavourably conditions that plague people.

Of course, "parochialism" or "narrow-mindedness" is not a deliberate or sought way of life for it is usually and commonly based upon ignorance, especially in the ignoring that which used to exist in our educational system, but honestly, this ignorance is now more and more being avoided. It is now well known that various types of meditation are now moving into the curriculum of our schools. Indeed, it has now been stated by the knowing wise of that which is called the Western World that if only two per cent of a city's population meditated then that city would exist in a significant and enlightening "existence".

So yes! We now know that we can pursue this path to living in a real Heaven, this being that which our wise ancients did realise would be a good idea those thousands of year ago. For indeed this is a "coming-together" task now meaningfully being pursued in places where it was never pursued before, this genuinely being in regions now pursuing meditational practices that are being installed by the religions, philosophies and governments of this "Western World" that mainly exists in the Northern hemisphere of our world.

So indeed, we may find that the "North Atlantic Treaty Organisation" (NATO) will cease to exist and "Northern Hemisphere Treat Organisation" (NHTO) will replace it until; eventually, all our world becomes a communicating one existence and of course it is understood that it is a bit early for all our world to unite like this – but it will eventually, for this is the target of all our world's religions and philosophies', these being that which were created by our Ancient Wise. Therefore, by practising the explained exercise of "Mantra Meditation", we can leave this Hell on Earth, this being that which can exist as a personal way of life. Still, it is only a way of life because we allow ourselves, in our lack of knowledge, to ignorantly live in a non-existing world that always pursues a past and future "I want".

So yes and sincerely, this is being that false world which automatically controls us and which always leads to misery and derision, for we cannot self-own the Earth. However, many try to do so, but now we can truly begin the well-tried old way of living in the Heaven that rests upon our Earth. For actually, this is truly being the known harmony that can only be witnessed and experienced by people as the *"peace that surpasses all understanding"*, a statement described thousands of years ago and in many different languages by our wise ancients.

For indeed, this was the only way they found that could describe the living in Heaven while on this Earth, which is a "choice" that can be made only by people, because simply put, it is their birthright. So yes! "Mantra" Meditation, this being that which knowingly controls the bodies five senses, is a simple exercise which is VERY easy to achieve and like all exercises it will bring a person to a new way of life that is known to be historically achieved only by their practising of the reoccurring mantra.

Still, it must be remembered that it is a practice that is very "personal". It is also likened to all known exercises in that the building of this new way of life opens a new doorway and so allows a person to enter into to that which "The Book" calls "Enlightenment," it is also a door that will open in direct accordance to the number of times that the "Patient Meditation" exercise is performed. For again, like all exercises it is the repetitiveness that will "strengthen" the way ahead and so will definitely bring the exerciser into the understanding of a different way of life, particularly when it so disciplines' the five senses so that no sound from them will enter the mind unless requested to do so, This is the world of perfect stillness - God's world and the world that is knowing called "Enlightenment".

So yes! It is essential to understand the metaphor that the five senses can be likened to five untrained puppies that love you but do not obey because they have never been "house-trained". Therefore, is it not also true that the five senses like five untrained five puppies have always been allowed to run rampant in their animalistic claims for an "I want", this being that which within a person's such "I Want" inner mind creations blocks the mind and so contaminates the Souls view of the Creation and the knowing of the way of understanding its unfolding harmony?

For indeed this is because the undisciplined animalistic five sense always and consistently do automatically endeavouring to please themselves. But sadly, for some strange "animalistic" reason you historically believe that these five senses are you. Still, they are not you for you cannot be that which you observe or listen too, and these five senses can, therefore, be likened to five untrained puppies which are here to be trained and so must be trained into serving you and not you serving them.

So yes! The five senses are certainly just instruments for your use. For the truth is that you need to believe that you are NOT the five sense whose inner sounding "I want" keeps habitually sounding in mind. For assuredly, now is the time to truly understand that these five senses, these being that which you are habitually listening to and which are continually sounding and so blocking the mind are NOT you! For indeed you are the viewing Soul which at this stage of development cannot become "aware" or "realise" that it is also that which it observes and so cannot see the Heaven that truly exists upon our world, this being that which can only be seen through a still mind.

For sure, all our ancient wise endeavoured to bring to their listeners the experience that can only be realised when their listeners' willpower – via prayer - demanded the energy of consciousness to choose to disciplinary sound their prayer words verbally and also within their mind. For our wise ancients certainly knew that the activity of inner and outer compulsory praying did bring their followers to that *"Peace that surpasses all Understanding"* IE: "Enlightenment."

But what our ancient seekers of the truth did not know at that time, was that it was this newly activated self-imposed and self-disciplined outer and inner praying which, via the God-given "Freedom of Choice," cancelled the "chosen" in childhood energy of "Consciousness" to "automatically" allow "Willpower" to freely energise the "I want" mind filling demands that continually emanated from the five senses, this being because in child-hood it was thought that the five senses were them.

So yes! All our wise ancients certainly knew the definite benefits achieved within their followers who unquestionably pursued disciplinary imposed prayers plus inner and outer chants, these being that which certainly stops the mind filling "I Want" that was unknowingly freed in childhood to emanate from the five senses. Therefore indeed, again, it should be said that the five senses can be likened to five puppies which can be trained to come to "Heel" where their uncontrolled antics cannot be heard or seen. For now, it can be modernly said that this forbidding and controlling within the mind is caused by "Willpower" being restrained by "Consciousness", to continually refuse all unwanted words except only a "chosen" self-imposed disciplinary prayer into the mind.

This "self-imposed" prayer being that which "Consciously" compels the five senses to simply repeat a single worded mantra which eventually and seemingly becomes "habitually" free as these five "pups" are disciplinarily trained – via the God-Given or Nature given for the Non-Believer, *"Freedom of Choice"* to choose "Consciousness" to compel "Willpower" to sound repeatedly this single sounding word which allows the Soul to see God's world through the lengthening silent spaces that are occurring between the single sounding word of the chosen mantra.

But this takes time and many hours, days and maybe years of eye closed practice for you are now choosing "consciousness" to stop from habitually allowing the "I Want" of the five senses from filling the mind, for indeed this is automatic freedom is that which the five senses have had for a very long time. Then indeed, eventually with eyes closed the mantra also becomes free and automatically begins sounding just as the five senses used to "automatically" sound in mind. It is then and only then that a person can experience Soul looking into the silent mind, this being between the ever-lengthening spaces of the automatically sounding mantra. Indeed the Soul will eventually see that which our wise ancients called "The Clouds of Unknowing", which in reality is the still mind being viewed by the Soul, which is the real YOU! This "You" is being that which you will never see, never taste, never touch and never smell but everything that these bring to you – you will know to be your "Self", meaning that all you taste, see, smell, touch or hear – is not separate from the real YOU!. Thus it is that this still mind is no longer being entirely blocked and clouded by many sounding "I Want" images that used to be habitually perpetrated by the five senses which have now been stopped from entering the mind – but now you are fully aware of just what they are, and it is good to liken them to be your five grown pups who are now "silently" useful and trained to await your commands like good sheepdogs whose master tells them what to do

So yes! Eventually, with this still, silent and disciplined mind, the Soul within the body is now able to observe the world outside the body silently and therefore can regenerate its purpose which is to "choose" an ever "inner" silent way of life that supports the harmony of the world that God created, or Nature created for the Non-Believer. Yes, this is also an ongoing and efficient work which is genuinely and unselfishly "Godly" designed or Nature designed for the Non-Believer, to enable a person to support the work of the "Mother of the Creation" in Her constant efforts to maintain the harmony that exists within the Creation – which is their only child.

So yes! This "Mantra Meditation" exercise can again be likened to the training of five puppies so that they come to your heel and so now they rest in stillness behind you, and so you cannot see them, but you know that they are there. It is then that your Souls view of the Creation will become one hundred per cent and also that your five senses, likened to five well-trained puppies, will come forward only upon your silent request for any of them to "silently" and "unseen in mind" complete a task.

It also can be assured that when they are so trained, each solitary sense will give you one hundred per cent of that which is their duty to give to you. It is then, when in the Heaven that exists upon this Earth, that you will understand that you have never tasted, never touched, never smelt, never heard and never seen the world as it is except maybe that time when you silently looked down a fertile valley from a high point and with your mouth open, for a few seconds did see the world of harmony as it is. Yet! Yes, this is before hurriedly returning to the inner made world of "I want" and so again losing this enjoyable experience.

So yes! It is also essential to understand that the exercise of Patient

Meditation has nothing to do with group-based religious beliefs or any other group-based teachings system, for this is an exercise which is very personal to an individual and well beyond many a religious group prescribed belief systems. Of course, it is excellent also to practise such mediation within supporting groups. The genuine reason for this truth is that it can only be an individually based "self" fulfilling the task which "personally" and indeed reveals to you the Heaven that exists upon this Earth. For indeed this is being the Heaven in which all life and non-life rests and so exist within the harmony of an experience that is all around you. For naturally, it is "personally" your Heaven and your "personal" harmony and also your "personal" duty to support it for with the silencing of the five senses the Creation will be recognised as a world that you will be unable to claim for yourself. This being that "I Want" that previously was sung by anyone of the five senses which are NOT you, for you are the Soul the observer and harmonising assistant to all life and non-life.

So yes! It will also become factually known by you that the harmony that you experience and which you know genuinely resides within you and without you, is truly the "Heaven" that you now know exists upon this Earth. It will undoubtedly be a new world and a busy world which will silently reveal to you its silent request to seek or not to seek your aid. Undoubtedly, this is an aid to assist or not assist the development of a sought harmony or of an emerging harmony that is now knowingly being seen and "experienced" to be existing all around you and this is a harmony that can only exist in the "Present Time". Again, this being a "Present Time" in which "you know" you are the centre and in which "you know" that you are the silent observer, for now, "you know" that harmony means not to harm but to support that which you now know is YOU!

So yes! The exercise of "Patient Meditation" will undoubtedly bring you to this world which is the living in Heaven while on this Earth. For when the five senses are silent, the observer will actually but "silently" see eighty to one hundred per cent of the world that is around you, and it is in this world that the Soul can identify the uncontaminated view of all that is presented to it and so act or not act accordingly. Positively, this is the living in Heaven while on this Earth, and it is the Heaven that all incarnates, and wise ancients speak about, and it is the place in which you will genuinely; an experience that which our wise ancients state to be *"a peace that surpasses all understanding"* - *"The freedom from ignorance."* - *"The awakening to the true nature of things."* - *"Being filled with the Angel Gabriel."*- *"A realm beyond the ability of words to properly convey"* for indeed, all our many earth religions and philosophies know the reality of this experience. They remember our wise ancients taught this way to reality back to the ancient Zoroastrianism religion of the fifth-Century BC which was 2.500 years ago did refer this experience of "Enlightenment" as "Ushta" which they described as meaning *"liberation, salvation and emancipation of the Soul"* but their listeners did not have the knowledge of that which is now known in our modern world but knew well, you will not be able to describe it to others who live in a world of "I want" except by using the above "ancient" words ".

62. FINDING "ENLIGHTENMENT" WHICH IS OUR HEAVEN UPON THIS EARTH

The practice is of this simple creed exercise, which is based upon a single word, is the first step towards a life that can be lived in "Enlightenment". Without doubt, this is the experiencing of our Heaven that truly, exists upon our world. For this simple exercise will enable its doer to experience "Enlightenment" and then onto eventually being able to live in "Enlightenment", which is genuinely being the experiencing God's world or Natures world for the Non-Believer, this being that which all our wise ancients did endeavour to bring to their followers.

So yes! It is now right to be reminded of the world of Heaven in which the performing of this creed-based exercise will take you to, for indeed it is known that there are many worshipping creeds within our world's religions and philosophies. These being those ancient religious and philosophical creeds that still exist within our worlds many religions and philosophies, many of which have different cultural sayings, meanings, chants, songs, prayers and activities which are all based upon the many ancient cultural ways of the world's differing creeds.

For honestly all know that these religious and philosophical activities are still being personally worshipped and practised all around our world - but Yes! You can be assured that this "Scientifically Based" single worded meditational exercise that is released by "The Book", will take you quickly to realise the real purpose and the achieving of this target that all our worlds creed-based religions and philosophies pursue which of course is "Enlightenment", this being the actual experiencing Gods world or of Nature's world for the Non-Believer, for undoubtedly this meditational exercise that is stated in "The Book", is a simple exercise containing a single short word from an anciently established "creed" which has been "scientifically" found to be the most highly effective and quickest way to the realisation of "Enlightenment," a reality which will be brought to those who practise this mind disciplining creed based exercise, for naturally, it is known to be a simple practice that will bring the doer to God's world or the world of Nature for the Non-Believer.

It is also "physically" known that this twice a day 30-minute exercise, in which a person practises this creed based mind-silencing disciplinary based single word exercise, will reveal that God or Nature for the Non-Believer, has genuinely given only people the "Freedom of Choice". Naturally, this being freely given so those people can support the "Heavenly" emerging world that occurs only in the "Present Time" and that they are "truly," also the personal manager of the talkative "animalistic" five senses which are driven by physical appetites rather than spiritual needs and who have certainly NOT been given this "Heavenly" provided "Freedom of Choice", but did receive it when permitted by the child in the mistaken belief that the words in their mind, these being that which blocks the soul from seeing the world that can only exist in the "Present Time", were emanating from their own five senses. But now all readers of "The

Book" know that this is no longer true for you are the "Soul" and so you cannot be that which you observe or experience.

So yes! This forgetting who we are, which is undoubtedly our worst enemy, happened because people's "Consciousness", this being that which makes us aware of the "Heaven" that rests only in the "Present Time", gave to "Willpower" our heavenly given "Freedom of Choice", this being that which allows us to actively and purposely support the targeting goodness of our emerging world, for it is indeed well known that the same emerging act can create or destroy the established goodness that is residing in the "Present Time". But sadly in childhood, it should now be fully realised, that because of our holistically given "Freedom of Choice", we allowed "Consciousness" to automatically transfer to "Willpower", the ongoing ability accept or stop any behaviour emerging within our surroundings, but this was also an act that now "automatically" allows the birth of a personal "I Want" for ME activity that is positively emanating from one of the five senses, these being that in childhood we believed was US!.

So yes! Sadly our "Consciousness" did habitually give to "Willpower" a permission to allow the five senses to freely sound their demands and own choices continually into the mind and it should now certainly be known that "The Book" is designed to stop this activity, this being an activity which "mistakenly" creates much sorrow. Unquestionably, this being the sorrow and sadness that is always emanating from personnel "I Want" for ME greed-based "animalistic ally" pursued world for has a cognitive person they know that their real purpose is to support and follow the silent reasoning of their Soul in which a great sadness can develop for it is positively known that they are YOU!

The reason for this mistaken belief of many persecutors is because people can sadly believe that the "I Want for ME", these being the spoken words sounding in their minds, are coming from their true selves and so should be obeyed, but this is not true and can be proved to so! Therefore is it not commonly true that all our many millions of internal body parts live in a singularity which obeys the needs of all other body parts and is this not because they factually recognise each part of this singularly which we call "Our Self" has also been the singularly of themselves? Yet! Is it not also unquestionably an absolute truth that they are all "individually" created entities which live in a purposeful harmony that is called the unity "Life"? Therefore can the heart say to the lungs "I not like or want you for you are different from me?" Or blood says to water "Go away, for I want to live where you are living", which makes our forgetting who we are, our worst enemy.

Yet is it not also known to be true that you cannot be those inner produced "I Want" words which make "animalistic" demands that fill and clouds the mind with words and images that are merely emanating from the "I want for ME" demands to arise from one of the uncontrolled five senses, which means that you cannot be that which any of the five senses bring into your mind. It is this single worded "meditational" creed based exercise that will prove this fact to you. It is also a "meditational" creed based exercise that will also bring to the "practiser" the knowledge that when the Soul is released to do its work, this being works which is needed to support the harmony that is continually emerging in the "Present Time", it cannot speak. Still, it can silently achieve that which it needs to do – which is to support if needed, this emerging harmony of the Creation. Without doubt, this is truly God's world or the world of Nature for the Non-Believer.

For without doubt, indeed, the followers of this proposed single worded "creed" based exercise will eventually experience that it is only the silent and newly released Soul, that which rests within all people, that has the freedom of a truly correct choice, which is the actual reason why only people have been given the "Freedom of Choice". Naturally, this is a "Freedom of Choice" which automatically begins to act as the Soul "automatically" supports God's heaven that truly and now knowingly exists within the silent spaces residing between the now "habitual" single sounding word. For positively this silent space that exists between this "mantra" sounding word will begin to expand and thus allow the Soul to see the "Present Time", the only place in which exists God's Creation.

So Yes! It is a person's God-given consciousness that can command willpower to disciplinarily "choose" to chant a single repeating word into the mind. For unquestionably, it is only a person's God-given consciousness that, via our "Freedom of Choice", will freely command "Willpower" to repetitively sound this chosen single-worded mantra, spoken of later, into the mind of the meditator and so stop our historically allowed "Willpower" from regularly and habitually releasing into the mind blocking and mind clouding "I want" noise continually emanating from the five senses.

Then it can be genuinely said that later, depending upon the length and history of the *"Self-Disciplined"* meditational and mantra repeating times of the user, the space between the mantra habitually and automatically and "non-consciously" widens. It is then, via this habitual repeating and automatically based sounding of the inner mantra, that the Soul begins to see through the ever-widening spaces occurring between the sounding of this inner mantra, into the still mind which is described by our wise ancients as the soul seeing "the clouds of unknowing", but this should NEVER be an "I want". It is also a well and historically known the fact that you can rest assured that eventually "Enlightenment" will come to you, for positively honestly have not our wise ancients said for over two thousand five hundred years that it could be experienced and so be "Self-Realised"? Therefore eventually and after much practice and remembering that any "I want" that is filling the mind will undoubtedly stop you from experiencing "Enlightenment" especially when the five senses, which are not YOU, begin to tell you how silly it is.

So yes! It is also good to remember that with a silent and therefore a still and unclouded habitually "Self-Disciplined" mind, a person's "Soul" will truly and eventually, after much "training", knowingly experience that when the eyes are open, the "practiser" of this meditation will eventually "see" via the Soul and without any interference from the noise of the five senses, will experience God's world - which exists only in the "Present Time". Now excuse my smiling and excuse my laughter for it will be quite a "first" experience for you. For with no sound in mind you will truly "experience" and so understand (stand-under) the fact that you are in a world which words cannot explain and what you cannot explain is the knowledge that you are "everything" and also that you need "nothing", and you experience the "Peace that surpasses all understanding – which cannot be described – but is that which ALL our wise ancients targeted continuously.

So yes! God or Nature for the Non-Believer indeed gave only people a "consciousness" that could experience the real world which can only be experienced because of our allowed birthright; this being known as the "Freedom of Choice". For indeed this is a "Freedom of Choice" which automatically obeys the "FREE" will that is resting within all people and which is a free-will that has been created to support the emerging unity of that which we call "The Creation", this support of all that is around us can be likened to the same support provided by all internal body parts to all other inner body parts. Therefore the reality of this effortless eyes closed silent creed-based exercise is to repeat a solitary sounded word within the practitioner's mind. Unquestionably, this being a short exercise which is explained later in "The Book" and it is an exercise which shows an ancient creed-based method that will eventually silence that which was habitually allowed to occur in childhood, These being mind-blocking habits of the animalistic always sounding "I Want for ME", which is that noise that is persistently emanating from one or all the chattering five senses. For indeed our untrained five senses can be likened to being these five untrained pups, all of which can certainly be trained by the use of a person's "Willpower" to silently sound into the mind a disciplinary chosen single worded mantra, which forcibly and eventually stops their continual barking which in truth is an attention-seeking "I Want"!

For it is undoubtedly true that by using our God-given power of "Consciousness" and our God-given "Freedom of Choice", this being that energy which is resting within all people, that it is genuinely possible to silence thcsc mind filling "I want" emanations that are habitually and regularly originating from our five senses. For indeed, a mantras single inner sounding word can indeed be likened to the disciplinary training of five wild pups which, being untrained, are continually and habitually barking into the mind for attention. For eventually the inner self-disciplined repeating of the single sounding mantra will seemingly become "freed", via the "Freedom of Choice" to mechanically and quietly murmur on its own, this being the fact which then allows the viewing Soul to see through the enlarging's spaces of this single mechanically sounding mantra and so begin to "experience" Gods silent and ever still world, this being that which exists within and outside the mind.

So yes! Positively, this is a mind silencing experience which is disciplinarily aided by enlarging the silent spaces occurring between the repeating of the chosen mantra. Naturally, this being indeed the meditational purpose of ALL known religious and philosophical disciplinarily imposed prayers, hymns, mechanical actions and worded beliefs which are all, targeting the silence that can be self-realised to exist, but only in the "Present Time". For truly mantra meditation is an ancient and well-chosen "scientific" way to quickly experience Gods world or the world of Nature entirely for the Non-Believer and it is undoubtedly the quickest way that "The Book" identifies has to be the easiest way to achieve this fact. For truly and eventually this mechanically inner mind "sounding" single word mantra is undoubtedly being released by our "Freedom of Choice", this being to disciplinarily sound the only one repeating word into the mind. For definitely this is known to be an action that will eventually stop, via "The Books" offered "Patient Meditation, the entering into the mind of habitually allowed words and pictures that are constantly and freely emanating from the forever chattering "I want" of the five senses, which can be likened to being five untrained pups.

So yes! It is then that you will first begin to experience the mantra being consistently replaced by the freed in childhood "I Want" machinations and dreams that keep habitually filling the mind and which are genuinely emanating from the childhood freed animalistic five senses. But eventually and after much disciplinary practice, via the "Freedom of Choice," you will be able to cancel and so silence all "I Want" mind filling thoughts, which is achieved via the constant returning to the discipline imposed mantra. This task can be likened to the training of five wild pups, which are your five senses. For indeed the purpose of this "Patient Meditational" exercise, as explained by "The Book", can be likened to the training of five wild pups - your five senses - to come to your heel in which they are unseen but await your command regarding what to do!

So yes! Now we will truly begin to see, at first through the spaces of the disciplinary imposed mantra, which is undoubtedly the correct tool used to still the clamouring five senses which we now liken to being five obedient well-trained pups. For without doubt, undoubtedly, a "Patient Meditation" or any known historically based meditation practice will train them to stop from automatically, continually and freely passing into peoples mind their barking "I Want", which is also combined with their many ways of how to achieve their individual "I want for ME greedily". Then seemingly above this newly disciplined self-imposed single worded "mantra", which is now "habitually" passing below our Souls inner sight and which is being collectively sounded by our newly disciplined five senses, we witness that which our wise ancients call the *"Clouds of Unknowing",* this being the actual reality of that which exists within a still mind. Then after many mandatory "eyes closed" meditating times, which can be likened to training sessions, it can eventually become the time to open the eyes. By still automatically sounding the inner self-repeating mantra, this being that which controls the animalistic five senses, allow the Soul to view the stillness of the creation that lays before it but only in the "Present Time" and so be a witness to all that exists outside the body, this being "above" and "between" the habitually and "unthinkingly" slow-moving words of the of now freely sounding mantra, which can be likened to be emanating in chorus from the now thoroughly disciplined five previously uncontrolled senses who have now been "disciplinary" trained, like trained sheepdogs via the mantra, to stand at your heel awaiting instructions has to what to do next.

For indeed it should be now known that eventually and without any "I want" thoughts, these being that which need to be stopped from sounding in mind and which are emanating from one of the five senses, this being the condition which blocks the Soul from experiencing the real world that can only exist in the "Present Time", this being God's world or the world of Nature for the Non-Believer. For indeed it should be realised that it is your Soul that is the real "you" and so it is your Soul that is also the real observer and natural evaluator of all life and all Non-life that exists within the creation. Then eventually by the continuation of this short "creed based " meditational exercise, our five senses, which can be now be likened to five well-trained pups, will eventually stay out of sight until dutifully called for to perform a task for their owner which is the Soul, the faithful observer of God's "Present Time". Undoubtedly, this is being truly the "Heaven" that exists for all life and Non-life and which silently rests within and outside all people's bodies.

So yes! To continue with this meditational exercise it should be understood that it is born from the birthright of all people's freedom of choice, this being that which allows any person to automatically and determinedly "choose" with eyes closed, to use consciousness to apply the energy of willpower to sound a mantra in the mind that will stop all previous instructions that allow an "I want" for ME claim to be sounded in mind by any of the five senses. For positively and indeed, has our wise ancients knew, any person can choose to repeat a selected single sounding "mantra" word and so stop the five senses previously child-hood allowed "I want" from sounding in mind. For now, the controlled five senses are being disciplined to sound the single worded mantra into the mind dutifully, this being the disciplinary fact which also ensures that the five senses remain silent from their various and previously allowed emanations that seek a personal "I want", and so this silence is undoubtedly observed to continually remain within the empty and oft lengthening spaces that occur between this single repeating word.

So Yes! Indeed, it is this fact which is also allowed by a person's God-given or Natures given for the Non-Believer "Freedom of Choice", this is being that which enables a person to be able to choose their "Consciousness" to silently order the inner energy of "Willpower" to lengthen the spaces between this chanting "Mantra" word which is then allowed to become slower in it incantations and thus increase the non-thinking space that exists between these incanting words. It is this fact which then allows the Soul which is the real owner of a person body, to "observe" within the eyes closed darkness of the still mind, that which the wise ancients called *"The clouds of unknowing."* These being likened to dark, peaceful clouds which seem to be circulating and moving in front of what can only be the pure light of "Enlightenment," a light which seems to be continually moving behind the clouds of unknowing – glory be to them who eventually witness the fullness and without any obscuring clouds this pure light of that which we call "Enlightenment" especially when the eyes are open and in "Self-Awareness" the unity of all that exists with our world is seen and so onwards to "Self-Realisation" in which there is no observer for there is only YOU!

So yes! It is this "Self-Aware" reality is that which ALL our world's religions and philosophies do seek within the practice of their personally chosen culture-based creeds. For it is undoubtedly their self-imposed "creed" based culturally disciplined way of worship, this being that which is targeted to bring the doer of that culturally obedient person to the pure Heaven that exists but only in the "Present Time". For it is then when the mind is silent from the "I want" noise committed by the five senses, that the doer of this meditational exercise will then realise that all that exists is God's world or the world of Nature for the Non-Believer.

Undoubtedly, this is the world that can only exist in the "Present Time", for unquestionably, that which exists only in the "Present Time" is indeed known to be God's world. Of course, this being the world that is observed by the Soul due to the self-training and self-disciplined mantra exercise which first begins to be observed when the eyes are closed, and the viewing is resting within the silence of the dark spaces that are existing BETWEEN the creed-based sounding of a solitary word – this being that single repetitive word which is "sounding" within the silent mind. It is then and aided by this much-needed creeds' single worded prayer that the five senses are disciplined like five untrained pups that have never experienced discipline before, and so now they need to be trained. Unquestionably, this is not easy but has soon has anything except the mantra word enters the mind, it should be cancelled it immediately. What does this mean? Again, let it be clear that the purpose of this single worded creed based mantra sounding exercise is to echo a single chosen word until this single word replaces the constant habitual verbalising "I want" sounding into the mind, by the five senses, which is a habit that has been permitted for a very long time.

So Yes! To say again, with the application of consciousness, this being used to stop the previously given freedom of willpower from habitually and energizing these "I want" thoughts of the five senses, and so by this newly enforced "choice" re-direct the energy of consciousness by continually repeating the sounding of a single word into the mind, this is an action which stops any "I want" sound from entering the mind and which emanating from one or all of the five senses. It is also good to remember that this is not an overnight success story for your five senses which again can be likened to five active pups, these being five pups who have never in their lives experienced any discipline and so honestly, has previously stated it will take some time to train them to come behind your heel and remain there in silence until you call for them to obey your commands. Yes, this will take time and the length of time it takes is linked to your discipline, so it is wise to remember that the target is a peace that resides within you and it is also a peace that words cannot describe.

So yes! The way ahead is with the mind being still. The habit now to cultivate, is to "meditation ally" concentrate on the silence resting in the spaces between the single sounding word, until the word itself becomes automatic and the Soul looks through the spaces and into the darkness of the mind, now fully seeing the clouds of unknowing. For indeed, this silent space between the words exists in the "Present Time", and it is space which will eventually be personally "realised," and so experienced in the silence occurring between the "automatically" repeating word, which your power that exists in the "Freedom of Choice" is seeking.

So Yes! The problem is that the untrained five senses, has previously said and which is a fact that cannot be repeated often enough, can be likened to the five untrained puppies, which keep leaping-up, with their "I want" needs, into this silent space which is an activity that has not being created by the observing Soul but by re-energizing of past "I Want for Me" allowed habits. Again, it should be said that this practical exercise of the repetitive single sounding word is to stop the five senses from the habitually claiming all the conscious energy which they have been allowed to use, via the constant sounding of their own "I Want" into an unaware person mind. So always remember that it is this allowed jungle of an "I want" for me habit that is continuously being sounded by one the five senses, which blocks the Soul from seeing God's world, this being through a still mind.

So yes! Naturally, this proposed and controlled "meditational" exercise is based upon using a person "Consciousness" to engage "Will-Power" to silence the "I Want" chattering of the five senses. Unquestionably, this is a task which can take some time to achieve fully. Still, you can be assured that with this practice, every time the power of your personal choice looks at these plaguing incoming "I want" thoughts, they can, again and again, be stopped from emanating into thought. Like our proverbial five well-trained puppies, they will return to your heel, in which they cannot be seen or heard – until they are called to achieve a chosen task.

So Yes! By persevering with this meditation for months or years, you will achieve this peace that cannot be described. In essence, it is guaranteed by ALL our wise ancients to rest within you and guaranteed by ALL our wise ancients to be the most effective way of increasing your happiness, wellbeing and health. For now, you have received the gift of knowing that all the thousands of culturally-based creeds and worshipping systems that exist upon our Earth, were all designed to discipline the mind, to stop the five senses from their ever repeating "I Want," and so bring the doer into the "Present Time" – God's world or the world of nature for the Non-Believer. And now simply put, out of the many highly effective creed-based repeating of prayers and hymns, this being that which the basis of most of our worlds many religions incantations ALL of which were personally designed by our ancient to still the mind from pursuing "I Want for ME" personal thoughts.

So yes! Single worded meditations are by far the easiest and speediest way to learn, practice and so achieve "Enlightenment", and so experiencing the "Peace that surpasses ALL understanding" which is the target of all our religious and philosophical creeds. For indeed it can be said and so realised, that it is essential is to find the peace resting between the words of the mantra until the mantra is no longer needed.

For sure and genuinely, the motivation and the target of this simple creed based "Meditational" exercise proposed by "The Book" are to achieve "Enlightenment", this being that which ALL our wise ancients targeted for their followers. Now let us listen again for purely motivational purposes, to a few sayings of our wise ancients, plus two incarnates, these being Jesus of the Christian teachings and Krishna, who was the Hindu incarnate, for they both speak about this experience of "Enlightenment" which is truly the reality of when the mind is without an "I want" thought.

For all our wise ancients knew that without any "I Want for ME" thoughts, these being that which takes the thinker into the Past or Future, this being the real Hell in which this "I Want for Me" persons lives and which unquestionably does not exist. For indeed a person's mind should rest in the "Present Time" and therefore truly experience God's world or the world of Nature for the Non-Believer, which ALWAYS exists in the "Present Time", for again it can be said that this is the world of "Enlightenment" which our dictionaries refer to as having a *"full comprehension of a situation"*. Naturally, this is the target for all people and for which ALL our wise ancients established many religions and philosophical creeds.

So yes! "Enlightenment" is sought by all religions. It is that which the Christians call being filled with the *"Holy Spirit"* or the *"Holy Ghost,"* depending upon their local belief system. It is also stated by Christians as being an experience in which the mind is filled by ***"peace that surpasses all understanding,"*** while the Hindu religion calls it ***"Moksha,"*** which loosely means *"freedom from ignorance."* The Buddhists refer to it as ***"Bodhi"*** *or* ***"Nirvana".*** Therefore, indeed, this is being personal experience often described by our ancients to be an *"awakening to the true nature of things."*

Even in the ancient Zoroastrianism religion of the fifth-Century BC, they refer to this experience of "Enlightenment" as *"Ushta"* meaning ***"liberation, salvation and emancipation of the Soul"*** and the Islam religion described it as ***"being filled with the Angel Gabriel",*** and it is described as ***"a realm beyond the ability of words to properly convey."*** Of course, there are many hundreds of religions and so many names to describe this personal experience of the mind being without thought, which makes it firmly established and existing only in the "Present Time". It is also a much sought-after experience which is described throughout the world's religions and philosophies as "Paradise", "Eden", "Heaven", "Nirvana", "Promised Land", "Moksha", "Shangri-la", "Kenshō", "Bodhi", "Satori", "Kevala", "Jnana", "Svargamu", "Kā bāga", "Vāṭikā", "Kā jagaha", "Sukhabhavana", "Ushta" and many more, for ALL religions and philosophies seek, via their cultural creeds, this same target of "Enlightenment". So genuinely, if the reader wishes to achieve that which all these religions and philosophies described, and which the entire world's religious and philosophical followers seek, although many have forgotten what they seek. – Read on.

However, let us first hear some motivating philosophical words about this subject, that were stated by our many wise ancients and from which our many creeds-born ancient religions and philosophical systems were first established, for they were anciently established as being practical ways to make the praying follower find "Enlightenment" within their current time, although in our modern times many have forgotten that this was the purpose of our ancients' religions pursuits, this being that which was held within our ancients various culture-based creeds, for indeed, forgetting is our worst enemy. This forgetting is that creed practices can undoubtedly lead to "Enlightenment" this being that which was described by our wise ancients as experiencing within oneself a complete serenity of peace, tranquility, freedom and the joy of a reality, which is personally experienced when the Soul becomes free and supports the harmony that exists or is trying to emerge all around you.

So yes! God's world is the positive Heaven that exists only in the "Present Time", and it is an empty still, silent and heavenly world that cannot exist when disturbed by any personal "I want for ME" which can enter the mind and so takes the thinker to the world of Hell that can be said to be the unreal world exists in the past or the Future. Unquestionably, this is being a time in which forgetting people allow to fill and so control their mind; thus live in the Hell about that which our wise ancients speak. For indeed this stillness of the empty mind can be likened to the waters of a tranquil lake which reflect the real world of all the "Present Time" that is around them. Still, it is a reality which is destroyed when "I want" thoughts intrude, these being thoughts which likened to rocks and stones being thrown into a lake's still waters.

So the question is "who are you"? For indeed what we are speaking about here is the real "you", this being the you that is observing all this? Unquestionably, this being the real "you" who can continuously look at that which is before "you" and all-around "you" as if looking into this calm lake that we are now likening to be the "Present Time" that exists all around you, this being the time that truly, reflects God's entire world. Therefore is it not true that the Creation can only exist in the "Present Time" and is this not then truly a "Present Time" which is always placed before "you" and which is truthfully the "Heaven" that exits upon our Earth. For honestly and clearly, the "Present Time" is the Heavenly world that is without any personal "I want"? Undoubtedly, this being an "I want" that forgetting people can liken to that of throwing "I want" into their mind like that of rocks being thrown into a still lake.

So Yes! Is it not a "scientific" fact that it is only people who disturb the heaven that rest all around them? Unquestionably, this is being factually done by throwing these "I want" disturbing rocks into the mind, a fact which certainly disturbs the real silence which disrupts the mind, just as these thrown rocks would disturb the stillness of a great lake?

For indeed, with a still and unthinking mind, the real "you" will see a world that is without intellect, or ego, or any "I Want" demands from the five senses, for without doubt "you," are a person who can "choose" to move beyond all that. "You" will also know that the real "You" is not the air, nor the Earth, nor water nor fire, nor the wind. For it is undoubtedly true that you will also know that

"You" are not only the conscious energy that rests within "you" nor are "you" anything that exists or works within "your" body. Neither is it "you" that is the thought in mind, or that which thinks or speaks nor is it "you" that which uses hands or feet, nor any part of the body that moves, for these are all just tools that are all for "your" use.

For "you" also know that "you" indeed, contain no hatred or dislike, neither have "you" any different relationships for "you" exists within all things. "You" also have no liking and no greed, delusion, pride or arrogance nor do "you" have any feelings of envy or jealousy. "You" also have no known future duty, nor any desire, or need to seek freedom, for "you" are a part of all that exists and so "you" are filled with such a knowing that nothing else needs to be known, for all knowledge that "you" need to know is given to "you" in the "Present Time". Unquestionably, this is the time of the "Now," for "you" know that "you" cannot live, experience or exist in the Past or the Future. Neither do "you" experience or appreciate or depreciate any value or devalue anything that is attached to "you," nor can any happiness, sorrow, pain nor pleasure be attached to "you" for "you" understand and fully know that "you" are beyond all these things. "You" no longer need memories or experiences of creeds, holy places, scriptures, rituals or sacrifices of time and leisure.

These are because "you" are genuinely the observer and so exist within a person who simply experiences the process of observing and of "being" and all within a self-knowing that that which "you" observe is always likened to be realised as "yourself. For "you" know that "you" are a life force that knowingly contains the realisation of all life and Non-life and "you" know that "you" are responsible for everything that genuinely, exists round "you" and also within you in this ever-moving world that unknowingly moves from perfect stillness. "You" also do not have any fear of death for "you" know that "you" cannot die and "you" never have any fear of being separated from that which "you" know is the real "you." "You" also do not have any doubt about "your" existence nor the reason why "you" exist, nor have "you" any judgement on the place and conditions of "your" birth, for "you" know that no Earthly father or mother created "you" or gave "you" birth. "You" also have no relatives or friends nor have "you" a teacher, nor are "you" that which is taught.

For "you" know and understand that "you" are all that can be and that "you" are all-pervading, without any attributes and any form. "You" also know that "you" cannot be attached to the world and neither can "you" be freed from it nor do you need to wish for anything because "you" are everything that is everywhere and "you" also feel that "you" exist in all time zones within which "you" are always in perfect balance. "You" also cannot be an individual "Server" who is instinctively accommodating, caring, nurturing, hospitable and charitable. Nor can "you" be an "artisan" who is undoubtedly creative, inventive, imaginative, playful, and dexterous. Nor can "you" be a "warrior" who is instinctively forceful, loyal, protective, determined, and steadfast or are "you" a "scholar" who is logically curious, attentive, academic, analytical, and neutral. Nor can "you" be an engaging "sage" who is, unpretentiously articulate, charming, entertaining plus expressive nor a "priest" who is undoubtedly inspirational, uplifting, motivating, energising, visionary and lastly "you" cannot be a king or a queen who is spontaneously commanding, assured, powerful, authoritative and decisive.

Yet "you" know" that "you" are a real a life force that knowingly contains the reality of all the life, for "you" know" that "you" are responsible for everything that truly exists in this ever-moving ever still world. For "you" are knowingly attached to all life and Non-life and automatically serve to bring goodness to all that is around "you" for "you" Know that "you" are a personal life force, that knowingly contains and is part of all life and Non-life and "you" know that "you" have a responsibility for everything that genuinely, exists around "you" and within "you" in this ever-moving ever still world. Naturally, this is a world which "you" know is filled with a blissful harmony that is based upon a love that has no neighbour and "you" know that "you" are also an entity with total awareness of that which is "No-Thing" (Nothing) which is God and "you" indeed, know that God's highest bliss is when the male and the female become as one – but "you" may have forgotten all this – for forgetting is our worst enemy; and what the above is endeavouring to explain is the experience of Self-Realisation which can be realised after "Enlightenment," which cannot be described. So, who are "you?" "You" are the Soul, this being that which cannot die and whose only purpose is to support the emerging harmony of the Creation which can only be accomplished in the "Present Time".

63. THE FIRST TWO-MINUTE STEP TOWARDS A LIFE LIVED IN HEAVEN

This first step to the living in our Heaven is based upon a simple exercise that will introduce us to a life that exists only in the "Present Time", this indeed is God's world which is cared for by the "Mother of the Creation" or the world of Nature for the Non-Believer, for this is a simple two-minute twice-a-day creed based exercise which is best done at sun-up and sundown. Still, it can also be completed at any convenient morning or evening time, and of course, you can do it more often if time allows, especially if stress is moving upon you. It is also the first uncomplicated step towards a life that can be lived in our "Heaven", this being that which always exists but only in the definite "Present Time" and it will certainly take you away from the negative "Hell" that we can self-create in a non-existing "Past" or "Future". Without doubt, this is, therefore, the simplest way to experience the "Heaven" that exists upon our world and which all our wise ancients targeted their religions' and their philosophies 'to accomplish.

So Yes! The following exercise introduces the "first" creed exercise that is a "scientifically" proven to be a first step exercise that will take the doer towards eventually achieving the living in a world of Heaven that has no "I Want" for Me negative thoughts; these being the imposing "I Want" thoughts that continually paint over the real world this being that which can only exist in the real world of the "Present Time" – thus obstructing the reality of experiencing God's world or the world of Nature for the Non-Believer.

The first step is to sit on a hard-backed chair only; these being the typical upright type of chair that you sit upon at a table for eating a meal. Then tuck in your seat and "feel" the bottom of your back on the back support of the chair. Then sit up with you back has straight as is possible, firmly push your head towards the sky and then forget that thinking– this is very important. Now simply rest your hands upon your knees which can be palms facing up or palms facing down but knowing that palms facing upwards are the favoured position.

Then with both feet firmly on the ground and then feeling and so "knowing" of the pressure of your weight upon the seat of the chair also the touch of your feet resting upon the ground and "feel" the back of the thighs and your rump "heavily" pressing upon the seat of the chair. Then in this position of experiencing the "Present Time" and if necessary ignoring any noise sounding around you, imagine a piece of the strong cord being tied to the base of your spine then weightily plunging deep into the Earth and then feel it silently and firmly being stationery held there by the love of gravity, thus feeling it pulls the full weight of your body upon the chair and then forget this cord but keep the experience of your weight upon the chair. Now relax and FEEL the weight of your body upon the chair and keep your mind filled with just this experience of your weight pressing upon the seat of the chair and now know that as soon as you no longer feel the weight of your body upon the chair that you have left the Heaven that exists only in "Present Time" and have gone into an unreal self-created world of Hell that does not exist, except in your mind.

Now being fully aware of the above experience in which you are resting only in the "Present", imagine that this cord, that is now unthinkingly tied to a weight called gravity, is continuing to go up through the straight has is a possible spine and further up through a very straight neck and out through the top of your head and into the sky above. Now experience and therefore silently know that the end of this upward targeting cord is hooked tightly to something unknown but high in the sky and that this something is attempting, on its own, to lift you into the sky. Then "Self-Realise" with chin gently tucked in and with a straight back, that this imaginary cord is trying to lift you out of the chair but cannot because the love of gravity, this being that which can only exist in the "Present Time" is holding you firmly in its loving and all-embracing grip. So you are suspended from this cord by the feeling of the weight of your body upon this chair.

So Yes! Now the cord is pulling your spine as straight as it can be physically straightened, but you know that deep within you and without any need for thinking, that the love of gravity will never stop loving and so will always keep you in its loving embrace. Now forget these cords that are attached to the "Present Time" but never leave or forget the feeling of that loving embrace which you knowingly and silently experience has is being your weight upon the chair. It is then that the body fully relaxes.

So you experience within this straight sitting position, the love that gravity holds you with and so always and importantly feel this love has your weight upon the chair. Then with head high and your back pulled straight, and your head carefully and lovingly balanced, keep this position from which you cannot fall or tilt. Now close both eyes and with eyes closed endeavour to "look" into the darkness of the silent mind, this being that which seemingly rests in front of your viewing. The task is now to create a silent mind which is without any "I want" words or really ANY words, pictures or indeed any thoughts that can be "observed" to appear and so experienced to be created in mind.

So yes! The question can now be "What is it that is automatically creating these thoughts that appear within the mind and what is it that keeps cancelling them has not wanted? The answer, of course, is that which has been previously stated. This being that only people where God-given or Nature-given for the Non-Believer the "Freedom of Choice". Indubitably, this was only given to people so that they can support the emerging activity of the creation, which can create or destroy depending upon developing circumstances. But in childhood, we mistakenly believed that the five senses were the real "us" and so we "freed" them to become "us automatically"! Sadly it was this choice that enabled the five senses too continually, and animalistic ally block and so cloud the mind with their continually sounding and verbal machinations of their "I Want for ME", this being that which fills a person's mind and which also actually creates the world we call "Hell". It is also this which factually stops the Soul from seeing the emerging creation. Therefore it is also this fact which stops our Soul from performing the duties that it was created to perform. Unquestionably, this is being the supporting of the emerging creation that is continuously emerging from existing in the "Heaven" that is all around us, but only existing in that which we call the "Present Time"! Therefore if thoughts of any type or any nature do appear in mind during this exercise, this being that which we now know to be emanating from the animalistic five senses, simply "choose" to say the words "Not this", then physically return to the silent darkness that the Soul is viewing within the mind. Therefore "Again" experience the silence that you are now observing in the still mind as you "again" return to the weight of your body that you "again" experience upon the chair, this being that which "again" keeps you attached to the Godly created Heaven that can "again" only exist in the "Present Time" and away from the falsely created "I Want for Me" Hell. For truly, this being that which "again" binds a person to live "again" in their self-created Hell and away from the Heaven that exists all around. Naturally, this being that world which exists without thought, and I can assure you that you will get MANY emotional arguments about how silly you are, but always remember who or what it is that is calling you silly and most importantly who or what is that listening to this complaint?

So yes! It is not easy to attain this "Peace that surpasses all understanding", and so you do need a regular "meditational" practice that will continually bring you back to constantly re-entering the "Present Time", which indeed means that you have left Hell which can be said to be devilry created. So you will have re-entered Heaven which all know is Godly created or the real world of Nature for the Non-Believer, and it is a heaven that can only exist in the "Present Time".

So Yes! Indeed it is good to endeavour physically, this being when you feel the weight of yourself seated upon your chair, to hold steady to the un-thinking silence that you are endeavouring to create within the mind. But I can indeed estimate that once you have attained the beginning of this weight-feeling exercise and so have established the above explained good posture for experiencing the silence of the "Present Time", this being that which occurs within the mind, your mind will be "quiet" for about two seconds before words will again be sounded within your mind.

Don't be concerned about this, for it is now god to remember that your five senses are like those five pups that have never been trained but have always been allowed to do freely whatever they want to do, but also remember that these five senses are wiser than any pup. They should also be loved as such. For indeed, and, yes, they will also complain and tell you how silly you are and how this exercise of keeping them quiet and not listening to them is ridiculous and not necessary. But do not be concerned and just say "Not this" to them each time that they sound their "I Want" or any words into your mind. They will become silent as you return to feeling your weight upon the chair, which will probably last for another two seconds before they again sound in your silent mind. But then with further experience, you will be able to say "Not This," as soon as any words appear, which can be liked to saying to those untrained five pups "heel" and all know this training system to be a fact that eventually, they will always stay behind your heel until called to do a duty – ask any shepherd, but always silently remember that you five senses have a great deal more "experience" than those five pups.

So yes! Now you can fully experience the love of gravity that is holding you in place, and you need to give no more thoughts to the keeping of this seated posture, once it is physically attained. It is also good to remember that without any words or thoughts entering the mind and so indeed experiencing your weight upon the chair means that you are in God's world or the world of Nature for the Non-Believer. Unquestionably, this is the world of the "Present Time", for the mind is without any sounding words of "I want", and the experience that you feel can ONLY be your weight upon the chair, this being that which can only be experienced in the "Present Time", and what is indeed looking into and experiencing the darkness within the calm mind – is your Soul, which is the REAL you for you are certainly not the five senses that are ever chattering into the mind.

So yes! This introduction to meditation is only a two-minute first-time exercise, and the target is to do this twice a day exercise is an endeavour to "consciously" feel your bodies' weight upon the chair, which is a feeling that can only exist in the "Present Time". Indeed an exercise that will target the "desire" to stop ANY words or "pictures" entering the mind via the commands of the five senses. It is this stopping and "choosing" of your consciousness to redirect willpower to the experiencing of your weight upon the chair, that takes you out of the false world of the past or the future, which the previously allowed "I want" of the five senses keeps taking you. For indeed, it is these-mind entering words and pictures that have been allowed to emanate from the five senses that "you" in your very young days, and with God's gift of pure consciousness, did "choose" to habitually command willpower to allow and so manifest their wishes and their desires to enter into the mind. This act was then transferred into a habit whereby the five senses no longer needed a God-given or Nature given for the Non-Believer permission to enter the mind. This activity MUST be stopped, and a new habit introduced, and it will take time and a serious effort to achieve this much-needed task.

So yes! It is God's allowed "Freedom of Choice" which was given only to people via their "consciousness", this being that same "Freedom of Choice" which permits the childhood allowed "I Want" claims of the five senses to "habitually" and freely begin to fill the mind. For indeed it is this accepted habit which stops the Soul from seeing through a clear mind and into the needs of the "Present Time". So again and indeed, this is now known to have been based upon a God-given or Nature-given for the Non-Believer, "Freedom of Choice", which was given to all people. Therefore it is true that people can now "choose" consciousness to stop willpower from habitually sounding the "I want" needs of the five senses into an empty mind. It is also well known that once this task has become satisfyingly and habitually accomplished, then a person's mind will become "silent" and without thought and so the "habitual" use of "willpower" that is energising the "I wants" of the five senses is no longer activated by this child based "I want" and so the adult person is no longer controlled by this childhood desire.

So yes! It is this fact which stops the five senses from "automatically" filling the mind with their personal "I want", which many peoples believe is the true "them". Therefore, it is the purpose of this two-minute-exercise to begin to correct this bad habit, for sure, it is the beginning of a "meditational" training system that is "choosing" the individual's consciousness to stop willpower from feeding its energy into allowing any of the five senses to voice their "I want" straight into the mind of the "practitioner" – and YES! It can be achieved. Therefore, this simple exercise targets the bringing of the real "you" to God's world or the world of Nature for the Non-Believer, which exists only in the "Present Time".

For this two-minute first exercise is that which will begin to re-establish the correct way of a person's life. For it is a physical effort to "choose" to re-target the energy of consciousness, to stop its currently allowed habit of energising any "I Want" of the five senses so that they can freely. Without hindrance sound, this "I want" into the cognitive mind of themselves. For this two-minute exercise should be used at the beginning of this journey, to live in God's world or the real world of Nature for the Non-Believer.

So yes! it is a "scientific" truth that any people can use their freedom of choice to request "consciousness" to stop the energy of "willpower" from automatically releasing into the mind the "I want" of the five senses. It is this first step exercise which begins the physical "choosing" of people "consciousness" to stop the energy of willpower" from its past allowed "chosen" habit of automatically allowing any of the five senses from filling the mind with a gabble of "I want", this being a constantly released gabble which clouds the mind with their demanding past or future "I want" machinations. Indeed, this is the "scientific" fact that removes the ability of the Soul to see through the mind the right harmony of the world which exists only in the "Present Time".

So yes! It can be "scientifically" proven by anyone that our wise ancients introduced these creed based "meditational" exercises to their followers to discipline their "consciousness" to re-direct "willpower" by the repeating of an imposed creed – this being an act which automatically replaces the machinations of the five senses. For indeed our wise ancients were wise enough to know that the imposed repeating of a creed word or prayer did "physically" change the behaviour patterns of their followers, for it brought them to their God's world for indeed, all understood that the "Present Time" was an act of God – which it is. Still, now in "The Book", it can also be described as an act of Nature for our Non-Believers'. For indeed, our wise ancients knew that they could use the Godly gift of "choice" to request their followers to physically bring their mind to silence or, which is explained later in "The Book", repeat their chosen culture-based creed sound, which knowingly did stop the habit of willpower' from habitually releasing into the mind the "I want" of the five senses. For indeed, their imposed silence or disciplined chanting would often lead to the emptying of the mind empty, so that their Soul would begin to see the outer world which brings to the doer "Enlightenment", this being the much sought *"Peace that surpasses ALL Understanding"* and as our world history shows it certainly does succeed in establishing happiness and contentment in a world that cannot be described!

So yes! this is the purpose for the beginning of this two-minute exercise which is ALWAYS to choose" your "consciousness to empower "willpower" to concentrate upon the "Present Time", and so stop your consciousness from freely and automatically releasing the "I want" that is habitually and continuously being released into the mind via the five senses. Indeed, this can be simply done by consistently and mindfully experiencing and so "feeling" the weight of you upon the chair.

For assuredly, this is a simple exercise which will stop or reveal all the frequent "I want" sounds entering the mind as all aspects of your body are feeling the body's weight upon the chair - and so the habit becomes to empower "consciousness" to focus "willpower" only upon the weight of your body pressing upon the chair, which can only be experienced in the "Present Time". You will also find that it is not an easy task. Still, it does in a modern way; begin to develop a discipline that will lead to the use of a "Meditational" creed based exercise which our wise ancients creatively installed within their disciplined recitals, hymns, and prayers. But back to our exercise and to note that it is okay not be too concerned if you realise that you "always" keep leaving the "Present Time".

This being as thought words and pictures etc. keep entering your mind for they will occur when you leave the "Present Time" and so no longer feel the weight of your body upon the chair and so have entered Hell, this being a personally created Past or Future. Therefore, always KNOW that you are merely doing a two- minute training exercise in which the task is to keep returning to feeling the weight of yourself upon the chair, this being an exercise which is bringing your mind into the experiencing of only the "Present Time".

Thus with eyes being closed the "experience" is to achieve is to consistently "choose" to experience the feeling of your weight upon the chair and the looking of your Soul, which is the real you, into the still darkness of the silent mind, this is the purpose of this exercise. Also, it is important not to worry about being rude to the five senses, whose words or pictures WILL keep entering your mind and so clouding mind. Therefore when you realise that you have entered the Hell of the non-existing Past or Future, just repeat "Not This," when this fact happens and return to the silence within the mind or wisely just "automatically" choose your consciousness to energise willpower to cancel them and return to viewing your empty mind. Also, whenever you know you are "talking" to yourself in mind, then you know you have left the existence of God's world and entered the world of Hell, this being a world that does not exist, and surely it will regularly happen.

Still, the exercise is to stop it from happening regularly. Subsequently, you will consciously experience silence in the mind as you return to feeling the weight of your body upon the chair. Rightly this is because you will quickly realise and always begin to know that your freeing of "willpower" is now being re-programmed by consciousness to focus upon the silence in mind, which is stopping it's old allowed in childhood habit of allowing the five senses to control and so bring to your mind their constant "I want".

For it is also indeed well known by our wise ancients that when you are silently concentrating upon religious or philosophical "creeds," you will experience the nothingness in mind. So our wise ancients knew that you WILL eventually enter God's world or the world of Nature for the Non-Believer. But now, the modern and quickest way of experiencing this *"realm beyond the ability of words to properly convey"* is to always return to feeling your weight upon the chair, again this is a simple beginning whose target is to be able to achieve silence within the mind and so realise the "Present Time", which is God's world or the world of Nature for the Non-Believer.

So yes! Do not become disheartened for at the beginning of this exercise, and you will fully experience your weight upon the chair, this will be for about three seconds; for words will habitually enter the mind which again takes you out of God's world. But the task is to keep continuing this first two-minute exercise, twice a day for a period four weeks and yes, the five senses will continuously keep telling you how useless and not-wanted this exercise is, but always remembers that they are not you, for you cannot be that to which you observe or listen.

So yes! In this exercise, your five senses will become VERY argumentative and very noisy, and they will keep telling this. So it is good to understand that this exercise will lead you to a greater discipline, which will allow you to enter the next exercise which is being a more purposeful exercise which will seriously reverse the past "unknown" habit of your willpower from being "automatically" allowed to serve the five senses; for in the real world, your body will learn to serve the Soul which can only see the outer world when the mind is still, again this is an experience that is called "Enlightenment", which is indeed a world without desire. For in God's world or the world of Nature for the Non-Believer– you have everything that you need, and you also will begin to know indeed that this is undoubtedly a very factual truth.

For indeed that which is religiously known to be the second coming is the experiencing of "Enlightenment", this being the kingdom of God which rests within you and a truth that is known to set you free. For interestingly this "Enlightened" realty was anciently said to be caused by the bite of the anciently known Kundalini snake. For positively this very ancient description of attaining Enlightenment emanates from around 4000 years ago, and it was stated in the ancient Sanskrit language, named to be "God's language, that the term "Kundalini Shakti", which translates as "Serpent Power", did originate. It was also physically described in the Sanskrit to be energy released within an individual and which was created by using specific meditation technique and was always symbolically described as a serpent coiled at the base of the spine.

So again, this upright position with a "stretched" straight back is needed, because a straight spine or a straight has possible spine is essential, again this is because in this straight spine rests a truth, which was culturally explained by our wise ancients who stated that the spine is the keeper of energy which they called "the coiled one," and which was also named the "Kundalini" in our ancient Sanskrit language. It was also stated that there were many creed ways to teach a method that would awaken this "Kundalini" this being the "energy" which they said brought to the people full spiritual enlightenment and a range of supernormal powers in the form of primal energy (or **_Shakti_**), and this "coiled one" is said to be located at the base of the spine – ancient words indeed, and actual strong beliefs based upon reality and described culturally for the acceptance the ancient need to understand. Of course, what their "creed" teachings brought to their followers was "Enlightenment". Therefore simply put, this "coiled one" is culturally described by our wise ancients as the energy that unblocks and so releases power for people to experience "Enlightenment". It can now be said in our modern time, that this silent energy which brings "Enlightenment", also supports the explanation that people need to clear the mind of all thoughts, which can be likened to the cleaning of a window of all unneeded properties so that the viewer can see the outside world.

Our wise ancients also stated that when the "coiled one" is released; which can be explained in our modern time as being by the power of a person "choice," this being that which engages consciousness to compel willpower to hold still the mind so that the Soul can see the outer world and thus experience "Enlightenment". The wise ancients also say that only people can experience "Enlightenment", this being self-realised when the inner-mind "Snake Bite" occurs. For assuredly when this "Enlightenment", this "release" happens, it is like a sudden burst of energy that can be likened to a force that physically "splits" the brain from the point where the spine enters the brain at the top of the back neck and then flashes over the top of the head to arrive at the centre of the forehead quickly, it is a split second occurrence. Still, you will certainly know when it happens.

There is nothing magical in Indeed this, but it is said that when the "coiled one" strikes it is a step towards the release of a person's behaviour patterns that are following the order that makes a heavenly lived life within our universe an absolute reality, again this is because it brings an experience in which the observing person knowingly and automatically understands the correct duties, rights, laws, conduct, virtues and the ''right way of living'', these facts enter into the very being of those who experience this strike of "Enlightenment".

So Yes! Indeed, the "coiled one" can be described as primal energy resting at the base of all peoples spine and which is an energy that can be activated by the constant use of a person's "choice", this being to direct "consciousness" to enable "willpower" to hold still the mind; an act that is pursued by all creed worshippers when reciting their creeds, again this is because the reciting of an imposed creed blocks a person's "I want" from entering the mind. Indeed, our wise ancients knew this and that the most attractive part of the creed is the silence between the chanting words.

So yes! This is sitting in silence for two minutes upon a chair, which is explained above, is the beginning of a modern way to explain how to enter God's world or the world of Nature for the Non-Believer, this being that which exists only in the "Present Time". Therefore indeed it should be said that there are many different "cultural" based ways to achieve "Enlightenment", this being that which all our wise ancients targeted, but which was described differently within our worlds many different cultures, this being those many years ago and for this way to "Enlightenment" was indeed explained in accordance to the culture of their followers.

Also, this truth about the "coiled one" can be recognised in stories from our ancients' understanding of the many worshipping ways of culturally different people, has in the horned God called Pan, whose horns are seen as a particular connection to the secrets of the serpent – the horned snake – which represented the now known "Kundalini". For it was also Pan who our ancients said, showed a way to release the serpent that rests within all people. It was even said that the Greek God Zeus knowingly transformed himself into a snake with horns, to bring his son Dionysus back to life.

These ancient snake horns known to be attachments to the head of the "Kundalini" snake, were also described as being able to bring new life-giving aspects known as a gift from God, this being the "Enlightenment" that is still said to be a gift from God. Thus this Godly gift of "Enlightenment", which was only given to people, was then depicted by these ancient ones by the showing of these snake horns to be protruding from the head of an "Enlightened" person. It is also understood that this was the reason why some of our ancient "religious" belief systems used the bull as a significant part of their ancient cult based religion because the bull showed a more meaningful set of horns which were more potent than the snake.

For it is certainly interesting that in our ancient times, the horned image of the "Kundalini" snake also transformed into the horns of the bull, which in turn, also transformed into the horns of the goat – all to depict that the "horned one" represented a person that was "Enlightened". Therefore, it is interesting to understand that it was initially the very ancient worshipping of the snake depicted by the snake's head and particularly its horns, which became an ancient religious symbol of an "Enlightened" person, this indeed is a person who obediently pursued Gods laws or the Laws of Nature for the Non-Believer. For all recognised the amazing change within an "Enlightened" worshipper, which showed that the worshipper was said to live in a new world that was said to contain all the knowledge of God, this being the world we all call "Heaven"– which was recognised by the "light" (calmness) that emanated from their being.

So yes! "Enlightenment" is shown in many of our ancient world's historical pictures and models to be symbolised by horns, haloes or crowns, upon the heads of many of our wise ancients, even unto modern times, again this is understood to show that the horned or crowned one is "Enlightened". Then in ancient times, it was also shown that these horns became changed into a halo of light which replaced the shining of the horns. Thus this emanated in our ancient times to show that these developing religious and holy developments originated from a knowledge that was gained by the striking of the "Kundalini" snake. It was also known, within our history, that these snake horns became a "shining", halo of light as if from a light within the person, this all being related to the actual experiencing "Enlightenment", which was original and still is, to be acclaimed to be created by the bite of a snake that is resting within the spine of all people. It was undoubtedly this ancient named snake that was deemed to be resting in all people which was given the name "Kundalini" by many of our ancient wise.

Therefore, the "strike" of the snake into the mind, was recognised by our ancient ones to be the symbolic reason for the releasing of "Enlightenment" within the individual. The reason for this is that due to the continuing practice ordained by our many religious and philosophical practices, that a bolt of energy likened to an electric current suddenly leaves the top of the spine, moves up and over the top of the head and ends at the centre of the brow like the striking of a snake. "The Book" explains that this is the energy of the Soul, now being enabled to see through an empty mind. For it is undoubtedly this realty that brings "Enlightenment", which is the experiencing of the peace within the "Enlightened" one that surpasses all, understanding and this is that which all our religions and philosophies describe in different ways. Still, ALL seriously are describing the same experience.

So yes! Many of our wise ancients indeed used different historical creed-based traditions to teach methods of awakening the "Coiled One", this being in the purpose of their teachings towards "Enlightenment" and their revealing of God's world or the world of Nature for the Non-Believer. Thus the "coiled one" known in the ancient Sanskrit world as "Kundalini" is frequently described as being unused and so sleepily "coiled" at the base of the spine and is often said by our wise ancients to represent either a goddess or sleeping serpent that is always waiting to be awakened. Also in modern explanations, the "coiled one" or the anciently named "Kundalini," depending upon a person's place of birth, has been described as unconscious energy, or mechanical energy. In our current world, it is described as being primal energy, which is an unconscious, instinctive or libidinal force. This strike of energy from the top of the spine and over the top of the head to knowingly end at the centre of the brow is a release of energy into the mind has even been described as being "The Mother of Energy" or an "Intelligence of Complete Maturation". It is also certainly known that the awakening of this energy is said to result from regular meditation, this being that which brings "Enlightenment", also meaning the bliss that surpasses all understanding.

So yes! Indeed, this is likewise described by our wise ancients who honourably state these realities which "The Book" now actually and modernly explains can be experienced by the exercising of a "mantra" or "creed" repeating act that will still and so empty the mind of all thoughts which "scientifically" enables a vacuum condition that will then arouse energy within a person that which when awakened, is historically known, has previously mentioned, to be an energy that is physically felt to move up the body's spine and then seemingly smash through a blockage at the top of the spine and continue like the feeling of lightening over the top of the head and ends by biting the centre of the forehead, which is a place that is said, by many of our wise ancients, to be the centre of all people spiritual power. It immediately results in a beautiful experience as you see the real world that exists all around you and which you now physically know that you are a part of all that exists.

So yes! It's real, and here is what a layman once said about this experience. *"Before my Kundalini awakening, I did not know what Kundalini energy was. Like a bolt out of the blue, one unsuspecting evening while meditating, I was taken by complete surprise by this life-changing phenomenon. My story is a testimony to the fact that while walking the path of spiritual evolution, there comes an understanding, after the awakening of the Kundalini, that there is a time, place and natural order for everything."* To this statement, I agree! For YES, this is being that world which we all call the "Present Time", this being God's world or the world of Nature for the Non-Believer.

A further interpretation of this striking force is that it is "freed" within people by choosing "Consciousness" to energise "Willpower" so that a person can continually apply a sustained force that is exerted to do something or restrain impulses, and because people have a "Freedom of Choice" in the application of this force, this means that they can "Choose" to either habitually empower consciousness to give energy to the "I wants" of the five senses that fill the mind and which stops the Soul from seeing the outside world, or they can choose to habitually stop all these "I wants" from entering the mind, this being that fact that would then allow the Soul to see through the mind and into the real world that surrounds them! Again, this is known as "Enlightenment", and an excellent thought emanating from "The Book" is that the release of the "Kundalini" snake could really be "Soul" becoming free.

It is also this captured "Energy" that is culturally described by our wise ancients as becoming an imprisoned "Energy" within people's backbone through lack of use, again this is a fact that it was also probably strongly impounded by economic developments such as the freedom of the hunter-gatherer changing to the "I want" land enclosures of capitalism, again this is being that which led to the many wars of capitalism which are continuing. These being economical "I Want" warring systems which are factually understood to be the competing doctrine or practice of giving to the tribal strong the freedom to invade other cultures and so impose more trade and therefore more profit, which is outside the government of the tribal majority and thus also, of all people. For assuredly, this is currently being a newly developing economically worshipped world that is actively controlled by an "I want" more profit; this being that which is a surplus to needed requirements, which can be likened to the "Kundalini" energy being trapped as a deposit in the bank, this being at the base of the spine – so YES! It needs to be freed.

Indeed, this is said because it is a well-known fact that when this energy is released by the seeker of Nature's truth, all greed and also the newly enlightened one's separation from life and non-life disappears into a singularity to which they knowingly belong and in which there is no me and no them, but only contentment in the knowledge that we all are part of God's world or the world of nature for the Non-Believer. It was also historically understood by our ancient wise, that this static coiled energy that exists within all people, can be freed by "creed" worship; especially the ancient but now modern "Scientifically" understood "hammer and chisel," repetitive method of worship, again this is being that "meditation" habitually becomes automatic, thus allowing the unseen energy of concentration to focus upon the enlarging and observed silent space which naturally exists between the repeating creed words.

This silent space between the mantra then factually becomes a reality that automatically allows a person's "consciousness" to choose "willpower" to deepen and slowly enlarge the sense of stillness that is existing within that space, this being that space which is occurring between the solitary praying "mantra, this being that which is being sounded within the mind.

For eventually, it is within this space that suddenly is freed the Kundalini, which is likened to the Soul now being enabled to see through the mind and into the "Present Time". This experience of the releasing Kundalini is described as being - *Like a bolt out from the blue.* Still, now it is good to remember that you may never experience the striking of the Kundalini, for our wise ancients' say that it could already have happened to you in childhood, this being because of your past lives.

So yes! This freeing of the Kundalini or the natural occurring of "Enlightenment" because of past lives, is certainly achievable because our wise ancients knew that this meditational combination of sounding a creed-based chant, this being a prayer which is empowered by "consciousness" and maintained by "willpower", is a prayer that becomes mechanically and so if habitually repeated creates the ability for the Soul to see through an empty mind which is free from of all thoughts which "The Book" states are emanating from the five senses. For it was undoubtedly our wise ancients who introduced this method of "praying" via a repetitive creed sounding word, which when it became automatic, enabled a person's consciousness to allow willpower to expand the silence existing between the spaces of this creed chanting mantra. For indeed, it is this automatic and so disciplined mind chanting exercise which can break the past allowed habit of allowing words emanating from the desires of the five senses, from filling the mind with their constant "I want" requests, which are all past or future "I want", this certainly is that which they have allowed continuously to fill the mind and so block the view of the Soul from seeing God's world or the world of Nature for the Non-Believer.

So yes! Beyond doubt, this is the way to empty the mind from all "I want" thoughts, stories and pictures that continually emanate from the greed of the animalistic five senses. Thus again it can be said that this can be achieved via mantra-based worship which is purposely targeted to stop a person's willpower from habitually allowing the "I want" images and words emanating from the five senses, to enter the mind. For indeed, these "I Want" thoughts can be stopped by consciously applying willpower, which will "eventually," via the God-given or Nature has given for the Non-Believer "Freedom of Choice", this being to refuse to allow ANY thoughts to enter the mind.

Therefore, it is this simple creed based exercise that enables the mind to be filled with "No-Thing", and it is this that will eventually allow the Soul to see all the truth that exists. Still, only in God's world – the world of the "Present Time", again this is god's or Nature's "Present Time", and it is a time which was simply brought into knowledge by our wise ancients, who introduced the need to consciously allow people to use willpower to enable and target the silent space between the habitually introduced creed based mantra that would eventually stop all the "I want" thoughts that have habitually been allowed to emanate from the five senses.

Now you have a target and the beginning of the above "Progressive" Meditational way ahead, is to begin to feel without any thought and for two minutes, the weight of your body upon the chair which is the first step to a way of achieving the above "realisation" which will eventually be slowly expanded via knowledge later produced within "The Book", to a 30-minute exercise performed twice a day and with a purposely given mantra.

64. PEOPLES CONSCIOUSNESS THAT EMPOWERS PEOPLES WILLPOWER

So yes! It is well known that all people have a God-given or Nature given for our Non-Believers, the "Freedom of Choice". This being to pursue or not to pursue a desire of their animalistic five senses. So yes it is because of this freedom of choice that it is only people can freely use their consciousness to empower the energy of willpower to control the mind, this being how people have desired and controlled their behavioural habits and desires throughout a millennium which is signified by their ability to choose their death or even when or where to die. But what is also true is that this fact also allows people too accidentally or purposely and maybe unknowingly "choose" to pursue a false world, which they have first personally created within their mind, again this is an "I Want" for ME world is usually generated by the greed and fear of the animalistic five senses, this also being that fact which stops them from pursuing and realising the harmony of the real Creation. Yet indeed! Should not that which exists outside peoples bodies be recognised to be the same as that which certainly and "Heavenly" exists within their "Enlightened" inner body in which all parts are different but comfortably and naturally serve each other no matter how different they are- is this not ordinarily true, this being very different from people who believe that they are separate from everything and so fearfully want "everything".

Beyond doubt, this again is being a situation, has our history consistently shows, is a situation that can be rectified and so corrected by a very ancient tried and tested method of a controlled concentration that is well known and so well targeted by all our wise ancient's. Therefore is it not known to be true that all our wise ancients did regularly show that "Enlightenment", this being a condition in which people know that they are a whole part "everything" and so indeed have "everything", which is an experience that can be self-realised only by a "creed" based worshipping system in which an individual's "consciousness" simply disciplines "willpower," to create an empty mind that is free from any "I Want" for ME thinking that is emanating from the five senses, this being that "thinking" which was mistakenly allowed in childhood because the child thought that the "I Want" words emanating from five sense were them. "I Want" for ME thinking that is emanating from the five senses, this being that "thinking" which was mistakenly allowed in childhood because the child thought that the "I Want" words emanating from five sense were them. For indeed is not this more clearly put by Jesus of the Christian faith which, after disciplinary fasting, an ancient method to silence and so control the "I Want", did give an answer to a statement from one of Peters five senses in which Jesus declared the words *"Get thee behind me Satan"* and so rebuked Peters "tempter", for Jesus certainly had no problem with the five senses and does not His going to the cross indeed prove this fact.

So yes! It is now possible to achieve this that was known to exist within Jesus and all our wise ancients who did establish many ways of disciplinary praying, singing, inner-canting and physical movement exercises, all of which is a state of disciplined mediation that blocks the "I Want" from entering the mind, again this is an endeavour to protect the people from the all empowering "I want" for ME, this being that which is habitually allowed into the mind and is also that which emanates from one or all of our animalistic enlivened five senses.

So yes! It is now essential to understand that in ALL religions and philosophies our wise ancients have carefully introduced various creeds, by the culture and behavioural patterns of their followers; this being so that their followers can and often without knowing it, correct this false "I Want" world that falsely exist within people. But what should now be indeed understood is that it is not the saying of repetitive creed words that brings "Enlightenment" to the individual but rather the "Nothing" that indeed exists between the words being incanted by people seeking God's world or the world of Nature for the Non-Believer, again this is what exists within the silent space between the incanting words.

So yes! Now in "The Book" is a proclamation in which ALL Readers have been given the most straightforward and best scientific target whereby they can choose to concentrate using their "willpower" upon this first exercise, which is merely endeavouring to sit quietly without thought for two-minutes, again this is a scientifically-based creed act described in "The Book" as a preparation for the next step; which is the creed worship of the sounding of a single word – this will be explained later. It is this carefully prepared creed-based single worded exercise which then "scientifically" allows the "Nothing" (No-Thing) that rests between the spaces of this single mentally-sounding word to repetitively and unknowingly act as a silent attraction for inner energy that rests within the people spine. This silent exercise of the repeating of a single word exercise continues for an unknown amount of time, depending upon the will of the "practiser," until eventually "bang" this energy "physically" breaks through this blockage of past self-inflicted barriers, suddenly reaching the point where the spine enters the brain and the energy so released, surges through as if splitting the top of the head and then stops and remains silent at the top centre of the forehead, again this is the experience called by our wise ancients the awakening of the coiled one – anciently named as the "Kundalini." It is also known to be silently achieved for you only feel the certainty of the "stillness" of God's Creation envelope within and without you.

It is, without doubt, real experience and it is felt like a "stillness" that seems to "scientifically," clean out the centre of the brain, again this is the valley between the left and the right side of the brain. It is also an experience which you will be aware of happening, for it is like a bolt of electricity or a silent awareness as this energy moves from the base of the neck to the centre of the forehead, thus allowing the spine and both sides of the brain to be linked by what appears to be a very "ancient" energy - and indeed, you will be aware of this "incident," for the "stillness" of the "Present Time" does envelop you, and I apologise for my smiling now. Yet the most important thing to remember is not to make it an "I want," of this experience, so it is best just to neglect that thought and quietly establish it in "Nothing".

So yes! it is after this experience whereby your mouth will open as you look at a very different world; and again, I apologise for my laughter; as you now "briefly," experience maybe for seconds or minutes "Enlightenment" or "liberation, salvation and emancipation of the Soul." What must be understood now is that this "release of coiled energy" experience will not be achieved quickly? Still, with perseverance, it can indeed be released, but NEVER think of it as an "I want", again this is an experience achieved because the mind has stopped containing the false "I want" world that was previously and personally created. You have briefly allowed the Soul to see the world that is in front of you, which is God's world or the world of Nature for the Non-Believer.

So yes! Just to re-iterate, "Enlightenment" is a well-known experience which occurs when the mind has become empty of all thoughts which allows a person's Soul to see clearly into the "Present Time", this indeed is that which occurs when seemingly a very person existence enters the "Present Time"; for it is then and only upon this first occasion, that that which some of our wise ancients call "Kundalini Energy", can be experienced to pour into the mind like a lightning bolt which seems to join together vigorously and so "Enlighten" the previously split mind, this strike being experienced to happen from where the spine enters the brain and continues over the top of the head to the centre of the forehead, or it could be experienced simply as energy moving from the base of the neck to the forehead. It is quite an experience.

Now please do not desire, wish or think about this topic again if you do, it will become an "I want" that the five senses now wish to experience, for indeed they can be likened to be similar to five wild pups, again this is also an "I Want for Me" claim! For indeed this is a claiming thought which will forbid this experiencing of "Enlightenment" from happening. What is also important is that when you "THINK" you are experiencing "Enlightenment", just say "Not this" to these thoughts and go back to the "mechanical" chanting of the single word – later to be explained – this being during mediation and while always "looking" through the space between "automatically" the mantra repeating a word, which actually forbids and so cancels this "I Want" which we now know is emanating from one of the five senses and so the real you. Who is the observer of all, can say "Not This", which will remove its claim upon you so that it cannot happen, but it is easy to forget Indeed this, and forgetting is our worst enemy? But of course, that is not an energy that you will experience, but a silent "realisation" and an awareness of the stillness and beauty of God's world or the world of Nature, for the Non-Believer. Now, let us look again at this first exercise of sitting for two-minutes upon a chair in a quiet room.

Now, when newly sitting upon the chair and whist aiming for a target of sitting for two-minutes, close your eyes and say nothing and think of nothing - which you will find VERY difficult. It is then that you will experience your five senses freely talking to you and telling you to stop this nonsense and to stop this silliness etc. They will also take you into the false past or future world of "I want" but your meditational practice is to "choose" your consciousness to engender willpower to stop listening to them for you will now know just why peoples have a choice, again this is a "choice" to pursue a task that ends with "Enlightenment". For certainly your five senses will try to please you and be very strong in an attempt to stop your attack upon them. So it is good ALWAYS to remember that they are not "YOU" for you cannot be that to which you listen! It is also true that they will continuously state within the mind the need for their personal "I want" and they also will show you how you can achieve this personal "I want"; meaning that they are keeping saying into your mind that "You" need to plan to achieve the "Future" that they are creating and they will also fill your mind with a "Past" thriving "I want" or not successful machinations that failed to achieve their "I want", but now you should be beginning to realise and to know that this "Past" or "Future" world in mind is the cynical non-existing world that people call Hell.

So Yes! Indeed, the task is to quietly silence these that we have likened to be five wild pups who now seriously need work and house training, for now, you know that they are NOT you. For you are the Soul that is hearing their words and so you longer "think" that they are YOU! For "YOU" now indeed and "scientifically" know that "YOU" are the Soul, whose sight of Heaven which always exists in the "Present" time" is blocked by these five pups ever demanding "I want" that is continuously clouding the mind and to which YOU are listening. Still, now you realise the truth of the above words while sitting on this chair. For indeed, this is being because YOU can stop their habitual freed talking and barking, from sounding into the mind which is disciplinarily achieved by "knowingly" bringing them all to a respectful silence. This respectful silence being a respectful silence from which they were mistakenly freed in childhood, via our "Freedom of Choice" that is invested within all people by God or Nature for the Non-Believer. This act indeed being because in childhood you "thought" that these inner thoughts were you when simply all thoughts could be likened to exist in a filing cabinet for the "personal" use of your Soul who may seek knowledge from the experiencing of one or all of the five senses regarding past activities.

So yes! It is genuine that "You" are really the Soul and so by sitting in silence and undoubtedly straight-backed upon a chair, "YOU" will begin again to "Self-Realise" by feeling your weight upon the chair and without any thoughts in mind, that which we call the "Present Time". It is also then while sitting silently upon this chair that you will become aware that indeed these mind filling and mind blocking thoughts are more and more intruding within your mind, but always remember that your mind is now in training because in childhood you transferred, via your God-given "Freedom of Choice", this gift to the five senses. This act indeed being because you "thought" that they were you when simply they are just past experiences that have been placed into a filing cabinet for the use of your Soul and so when any though habitually enters the mind, just knowingly say "Not This", and they will immediately stop. Your mind will then become silent, for maybe a few seconds. Now develop the habit to discipline unto silence all thoughts that are habitually emanating from these wild pups and so welcome a silence within the mind and so again and again, turn your attention inwardly and so enable the Soul to stare into the mind's cloud of unknowing that the Souls is looking at, and whose sight it is continually viewing. This silent endeavour is to always and eventually enable the Soul to look into and then through the mind, without any distractions and so experience all that which exist in the "Present Time"; especially without the "I Want" pictures or words emanating from the five senses, which are still habitually endeavouring to make you believe that they are you. They are not you, for you cannot be that which you observe for indeed you will begin to "Self-Realise" that you are indeed the observer of all that exists in the "Present Time" and also you will "Know" that this observer is indeed your Soul, this being that which exists within your body and which is also that which observes everything that is outside your body, this being that which you will eventually begin to "Self-Realise" is also a part of YOU! Therefor continue this two-minute practice which to always to return to feeling the weight of your body upon the chair, this being that experience which can only be "Self-Realised" in the "Present Time". Therefore, it is a self-disciplining exercise which is to always return to the "experience" of knowing that you indeed are the "viewer, this being the silent, all-seeing Soul and so allow your Soul, which is the real you, to stare into the darkness born within your non-imaging non-reflecting mind.

So yes! It is also good to "always" understand that if the senses begin to chatter their "I want" into your mind, just "choose" your God-given "Freedom of Choice" to consciously take your past allowing of "willpower" away from them, and so return to the "Present Time". For assuredly, this can be done again and again by silently feeling the pressure of your weight upon the chair, which you can "experience" as the loving embrace that gravity always holds you firmly and lovingly within its awareness. For indeed, this experience you seek can only be experienced in the "Present Time", which the five senses cannot enter or contaminate by their ever-demanding "I Want" for ME!

So yes! It is the all-embracing love of gravity that you should now recognise to be that which indeed and always exists, again this is because this first exercise is to repeatedly and disciplinarily sit for two-minutes, silently and with no reflections or thoughts of any "I wants" that habitually emanate from the outside world or from the five senses that you have freely been allowed to enter your mind. For indeed, the task of silently sitting upon your chair is to "choose" to habitually apply your consciousness to instruct willpower to enable yourself to target the realty of you very "being," meaning to just sit silently in the stillness that is all around you and within you, this being that which can only exist in the "Present Time", which is indeed Gods world o the world of Nature for the Non-Believer.

So again, it is also good to be reminded continuously, via your mind filled filing system, that within this concept you should always remember that when you find yourself observing, via the listening to the sound of words or pictures coming into the mind, that you are indeed creating a false "I Want" for ME world that is emanating from the Past or the Future and so is a false world that is falsely and dreamingly being created by an "I Want" that is undoubtedly emanating from one of the animalistic five senses. Now the task is to cancel them by saying "Not This" and then immediately return to your consciousness by the feeling of your weight upon the chair, which can be quickly achieved by experiencing the feeling of the pressure of your weight upon the chair; for when you feel your weight upon the chair - you are in the "Present Time", where gravity and Heaven lives and not the past or the future which indeed can be likened to a self-created Hell, again this is the non-existing past or a non-existing future which is personally created Hell, this indeed is a non-real world which can only exist via your mind painted "I want" for ME thoughts. These thoughts being that which always takes you to live in a self-made Hell and no matter what the word is that is entering the mind; it is always emanating from an "I Want" of the animalistic the five senses which again is always a personally developed "I want" for ME! For surely now it is time to continually rest in the silence of the reality that exists within the "Creation", again this is indeed that which exists all around you and without any thought in mind simply seek to rest in Gods world or the world of Nature for the Nonbeliever.

So yes! It is now while sitting alone in a room and upon this chair, that you have a single target. This target is to sit quietly alone simply and if thoughts do emerge into the mind, which they habitually will cancel them, just switch them off and silently return to feeling your weight upon the chair and then endeavour to rest in the silence of experiencing this constant feeling of "love" by which gravity holds you in its embrace. So you are attempting to do this for "two-minutes". You will then quickly realise that the words entering your mind are not from "you," because they are quickly being "chosen" to be cancelled by the REAL you, which is the Soul. For it is within this first two-minute exercise that you will indeed realise that logically, your essence and that which is experienced to be the real you is certainly your inner Soul, again this is that which sees through the mind and into the outside world, which is Gods world or the world of Nature for the Non-Believer, this being that world which your soul should knowingly report to; this being that which activates and energises it and within which it knows that it cannot die. It is also within this first two-minute exercise that you will understand and KNOW that you have the certainly have a freedom of choice, this being that which enables you to always return to the experiencing of the love of gravity, as it holds you in its embrace upon the chair. But it is also true that you can "choose" to leave this "love embrace" that can exist only in the "Present Time" and instead listen to the demanding sounds in your head which indeed takes you into a non-existing Past or Future which those unruly "puppies" create – these being that which you call your five senses. For it is certainly true that within this simple two-minute exercise you will begin to have a glimmering of an understanding that you have an observing non-sounding Soul that with eyes closed and no thoughts in mind, is recognised to be the real you who quietly observing a still mind, for indeed you will become aware that this is the real "YOU." For you are the Soul, the real observer who with your bodies eyes closed, your Soul will look into the darkness of the mind for it is then that you begin to understand that there is only one actual "reality fully", again this is the Soul that rests within your body and which is "looking" into the "clouds of unknowing" which is the empty awaiting mind that rests as if knowingly before it.

So Yes! Simply put, you cannot observe your Soul or smell it. Nor can you can touch it or hear it or taste it, for you cannot be that which "realises" all these experiences which are reporting only to YOU! Therefore YOU are indeed your un-claiming Soul, this being that which eventually with eyes open and after

MUCH practice, YOU will self realise that within this "Present Time" stillness you are living in God's world or the world of Nature for the Non-Believer; but you will also "realise" that there are many habits to stop and many Soul-seeking exercises to be done before you leave the world that can only exist in a false "I want for Me" world, this being that world that can only exist in a self-made world of Hell. For indeed this is an "I Want for Me" non-existing world that we call the Past or the Future. These being false worlds that do not exist and so can never be holistic worlds in which a person can become indeed "Self-Aware" or "Self-Realised" of the totality of Gods or Natures well established and fully caring creation, which of course also means that it is not good to stand upon a volcano when it is beginning to erupt. For indeed, it is then, when factually and unselfishly but disciplinary working towards experiencing one of these two factors, this being "Self-Awareness" or "Self-Realisation", that you indeed begin to understand that living in "Heaven" while on this Earth is the only actual reality and that it is a reality that can only exist in the "Present Time" a world in which a dream based "I Want" cannot exist, this being a fact which is undoubtedly acclaimed by ALL our wise ancients. While the other "non-reality" is the "individualistically" living in an "I want" dreamed past or a future world of living in "Hell", this being that which does not exist but is being targeted to exist by mind filling verbalizations that are indeed being created by our animal-based five senses, this being that which you think is the real You! They are not YOU! For you cannot be that which you observe or listen too! For believing that these noises and or pictures arising in mind are you, is indeed being a decision that ties you to a non-existing world which is the living in an "I Want for ME" animal-based dream, which can also be a personally created "Nightmare". For indeed this kind of life is that which is targeted to exists around an animal-based "I Want" thought, which can lead to a selfishly created world that revolves around these mind filling dreams of "I Want for ME" judgments. For indeed all mind filling thoughts create the world of "Hell", this being that world which is created by a "Past" or a "Future" dreamed "I Want" for ME, which brings forward an activity that creates "Hell", this being that world which is hurtfully and selfishly brought to exist in our "Present" time, this being the real "Heaven" that is known to exist all around us and which is always realised, but only when the Soul is enabled to see through a still mind, the "Present Time". For assuredly, this being the world that ALL our wise ancients targeted and it is a world that they created to remove this personally made Hell that is often inflicted upon others by its selfish targeting. Therefore this simple chair sitting exercise, which is beginning with only two minutes of sitting on a chair, will bring you into "being", and so you will begin to "realise" that which you indeed are and therefore personally understand who you are. For indeed this is a beginning in which you will certainly "scientifically" begin to also "realise" that you are indeed that which cannot die.

So Yes! During this two-minute straight-backed comfortably seated exercise, your target is to simply feel the gravity that is lovingly holding you with constant love and so the fact is that you are simply very still and quiet and with the sole purpose to target a mind that is without any thoughts which are seeming "automatically" arising within your mind which you "think" is emanating from the real you. Still, now you know that you cannot be that which you experience. For it is during this two-minute silent, solitary exercise, that you will personally endeavour to continue "always" to experience the loving hug of gravity, this being that which you can only "feelingly" experience when you are in the "Present Time". For indeed you will find that gravity "always" gently and safely holds you lovingly close to itself. But indeed, this is a love that is forgotten when your five senses cloudily play within your mind. Still, this exercise is to "disciplinary" cancel these thoughts, and this happens when you return to the feeling the weight of yourself upon the chair   Eventually you will also begin to fully and personally love this experience of gravity whose love can never leave you, for in truth it is attached to Gods world or the world of Nature for the Non-Believer and so it will never leave you.

So yes! At the beginning of this chair sitting exercise, you will quickly find that your self-realising of the real world, in which the loving hug of gravity exists, will quickly leave you when an "I Want for Me", this being that which is emanating from one of your five senses, is verbally sounded into your mind. For it is undoubtedly true that these "I Want" thoughts, these being that which emanate from a personally created Past or Future "Hell", have "physically" and "habitually" plagued you most of your life but now they should be stopped. For now, is the time to say quietly "Not This" and so always return to "Heaven" where the loving hug of gravity always exists, for as soon as you no longer feel the pressure of your weight upon the chair. You have left the "Present Time" and go into the past or a future self-created Hell, which is animated by many self-claiming constant "I want" thoughts.

So yes! It is upon the realisations of the right knowledge activated by this two-minute sitting on a chair exercise that will eventually lead you, after two weeks, to another exercise. This being that which "The Book" created and calls "Patient Meditation" which starts with an exercise of five minutes at sun up and sundown or any convent time which has close has is possible to these two events, this also being a meditational aspect but which is now based upon the sounding within the mind of a single creed based "holistic" word that will eventually bring to you an "Enlightenment" that can eventually lead to you becoming "Self-Aware" or "Self-Realised", again this is being that existence which ALL our ancients spoke about; and which ALL our philosophical and religious plus non-religious creeds do target. But now, has "The Book" explains, it is undoubtedly not the mantra sounding word that brings to the worshipper the real world of God, or the world of Nature for the Non-Beleive, but the silent spaces between these mind stilling words, again this is being that which allows our inner Soul to silently witness the "Present Time", which can only be achieved when looking through a still mind.

Now, as an interesting aside, this is that when you are seated and have so trained yourself to leave all thoughts that enter the mind, this being done by returning to the feeling of gravity described by "The Book" as being the love that hugs you, but only in the "Present Time"; that whenever you are walking or standing, you can feel that same love that holds you but which is now felt like a "hugging" pressure under your feet! Indeed it is good to stop, if possible to do so, and staying with the "feeling" of experiencing that love of gravity now known to be holding you at your feet and then look at the world around you, while doing so. Fascinating world - isn't it? But yes! There is a long way to go with those five pups, meaning that your five senses have been free for a long time - and which also means that for a long time you have always believed they are YOU! They are not YOU, for you cannot be that which you observe or experience, for indeed you are the undying Soul, the observer of all things and indeed, the supporter, seeker and maintainer of the harmony that exists and is endeavouring to exist in God's or Nature world for the Non-Believer, this being the ever-evolving world that can only exist in the "Present Time".

For God's or Natures world for the Non-Believer, is that "Creation" which can only exist in the "Present Time" and it is also a world in which our supporting Soul exists and also it is indeed a world that is without any "I want," for it is a world that provides everything and all needs. Still, it is often corrupted by the "I Want" for ME claims in which forgetting people steal that which belongs to others. It is also indeed a created world that is without selfish ego, or the ever-demanding "I Want" that is continuously emanating from a person's five senses, for indeed the Soul of people has been created to move beyond all that. For it can be said that the Soul is also not the ether, nor the Earth, nor water or fire, for the Soul is "YOU"! This "YOU" is being undoubtedly a "YOU" which cannot be touched, smelled, seen, tasted or heard, for within the experience of "Enlightenment" "YOU" are indeed really the observer of all these things. The Soul is also not the energy that rests within the body, nor can you Soul be that which works within your body. Nor is your Soul that thought in mind, which thinks or speaks, nor is the Soul that which holds another's hands nor is the Soul any part of the body that moves, for indeed the Soul is that life force that knowingly contains the realisation of all life and non-life. For the Soul knows and understands that it is a part of everything that exists, in Gods or Natures world for the Non-Believer, this being that which is our ever-moving ever-still world. Also, a world that consists of the blissful harmony of a love that has no neighbour and your Soul is an entity with total awareness of that which is "No-Thing", this being God or Nature for the Non-Believer, for indeed, your Soul is an observer and commander of that which should be done to support all that exists with this creation. For indeed the Soul contains no hatred or dislike, neither has the Soul any relationships with others because it knows that it is "others", for indeed the Soul has no greed, nor delusion, pride or arrogance nor does the Soul have any feelings of envy or jealousy. The Soul also has no desires, nor does it have any need to seek freedom for the Soul knows that it is much loved, and that "IT" also loves all things. For the Soul within the people is filled with the knowledge that nothing needs to be known; for all knowledge rests within the Soul and so the Soul only needs to acknowledge the need for that act that brings harmony to the "Present Time". For the Soul is a life force that knowingly contains the realisation and belonging togetherness of all life and non-life, for the Soul understands that it is part of everything that exists in this ever-moving ever-still world, a world which consists of living in the blissful harmony of a love that has no neighbour. The Soul, which exists only within people, is also an entity with total awareness of that which is "No Thing" which is our God or Nature for the Non-Believer, for the Soul who is everything sincerely believes in "No Thing". Neither does the Soul experience any value or devalue attached to it. Nor can any happiness, sorrow, pain nor pleasure be attached to the Soul, for the Soul is beyond all these things. The Soul does not need creeds, holy places, scriptures, rituals or sacrifices of time and leisure; again, this is because the Soul is indeed the eternal observer that exists within all people. So that the people who indeed, and silently experiences, via "Enlightenment" the process of observing, will know that that which he or she observes is always known to being a part of themselves. For the Soul is that life force that knowingly contains the realisation of all life and non-life; for the Soul also understands that it is part of everything that exists in this ever-moving, ever still world, consisting of a blissful harmony of a love that has no neighbour and in which the Soul is an entity with total awareness of that which is "No Thing" (GOD), the Father of the Creation.

For assuredly, the Soul does not have any fear of death, for the Soul knows that it cannot die, and the Soul has no fear of being separated from that which the Soul knows is the real combined Soul of all people. The Soul does not doubt its existence and the reason why it exists nor does the Soul have any judgement on the place and conditions in which it was born, for the Soul, also knows that it did not have an Earthly father or a mother who gave birth to the body in which it exists. The Soul also knows that it has no relatives or friends nor has it a teacher, nor is it that which is taught. For the Soul is that life force that knowingly contains the realisation that it is joined to all life that exists within all living families and also all non-life, for the Soul understands that it is part of everything that exists in this ever-moving, ever still world, consisting of the blissful harmony of a love that has no neighbour and the Soul of people is also an entity with total and attached awareness of that which is "No Thing" (GOD).

For the Soul "knows" and understand that it is all-pervading, that it is also without any attributes and any form. The Soul also cannot be attached to the world, nor can the Soul be freed from it. The Soul need not wish for anything because the Soul is everything that is everywhere, and the Soul exists in all people and in all time zones, within which the Soul is always in perfect balance. For the Soul is that life force that knowingly contains the realisation of all life and non-life; for the Soul understands that it is part of everything that exists in this ever-moving, ever still world, consisting of the blissful harmony of a love that has no neighbour; and the Soul of people is also an entity with total awareness of that which is "No Thing" (GOD). The Soul also cannot be a person that has just been born or a "server" who is naturally accommodating, caring, nurturing, hospitable and charitable. Nor can the Soul be an "artisan" who is naturally creative, inventive, imaginative, playful, and dexterous. Nor can the

Soul be a "warrior" who is naturally forceful, loyal, protective, determined, and steadfast, nor is the Soul a "scholar" who is naturally curious, attentive, academic, analytical, and neutral. Also, the Soul cannot be a naturally engaging "sage," who is articulate, charming, entertaining plus expressive. Nor can the Soul be a "priest" who is a naturally inspirational, uplifting, motivating, energising, and visionary. Lastly, the Soul cannot be a king or a queen who is naturally commanding, assured, powerful, authoritative and decisive. For the Soul is that life force that has no "I want," for it knowingly contains the realisation of all life and non-life, for the Soul understands that it is part of everything that exists in this ever-moving, ever still world. This world is consisting of the blissful harmony of a love that has no neighbour and that it is also living in a bodily entity, with total awareness of that which is "No Thing" (GOD). Who are you? You are the Soul that which cannot die and whose purpose is to support the emerging harmony of the Creation - if such acts are needed, so indeed you now know who you are.

65. YES! YOU HAVE THE ABILITY TO CHOOSE?

That above simple two-minute exercise is the easiest way to show to all people that they have a choice to either live in the real world of Heaven, where gravity lives, or to live in Hell where the unreal world of your "I Want" lives - but always be aware, that it could be that before this exercise you had forgotten or had no memory that these two "Creations" existed; one being created by God or Nature for the Non-Believer, and the other being created by the ever demanding "I Want" of your five senses.

But now you factually know that one Creation that you can live in is undoubtedly created by God or Nature for the Non-Believer, and the other Creation that you can live in is created by people, and they're "I Want". For indeed it is now known that it the forgetting of this fact that is always our worst enemy. For constantly at the beginning of this two-minute exercise it is essential to simply understand that if you lose the feeling of your weight upon the chair, then you do know that you have left the real world via the experiencing the "Present Time" in which rests "Gravity" and you are now indeed joined, via listening, to the many "I Want" words now arising in mind. Strictly this is being that sound which is filling the mind and which is an "I Want" that is emanating from one of the "animalistic" five senses, and thus they are creating their world, this being there "I Want" world that they are creating within YOU.

But now you TRULY know, by returning to experiencing your weight upon the chair that those mind-clouding words can always be cancelled and silenced by the willpower of your God-given "Freedom of Choice". Also, this two-minute exercise that you are now pursuing will show to you that these thoughts that enter your head are not coming from "you," but are coming from an "I Want," is created by your animalistic five senses because they can be cancelled by YOU, and so trained to stop and become quiet.

For now, you fully comprehend and understand – stand under – the fact that they are not you, for you cannot be that to which you observe or listen. So truly you are now beginning to learn that you are the Soul, this being that which is gazing into the still and dark silent mind, which strangely seems to have a light behind it, but genuinely knowing that this darkness now being observed within the mind, can only exist in the "Present Time".

For indeed your Soul is a harmony seeking "being" that cannot act in the past or the future but can undoubtedly recognise that which can be genuinely experienced but only in the "Present Time" – God's world or the world of Nature for the non-believer. Now the question is, do you want to live in agreed filled "I Want" never fully obtainable sad world in which the five senses are the insatiable dictator? Or to continue with this first simple "Two Minute" exercise which will be the start of bringing you to a world of love and understanding (standing-under) of a life that wants for nothing, (No-Thing) because you will eventually realise that in God's Creation or Nature world for the non-believer, you have "everything", but sadly much can be taken from you by another's persons "I Want".

So yes! Now with this first two-minute exercise, you are beginning to stand under the "scientific" truth, this being the truth that in the obeying and so pursuing of these "I Wants" that are originating from your five senses and which you are allowing to enter your mind, you are living in a self-made world of "Hell", which can only exist in the past or the future. For this certainly shows that your "mind" has left the "Present Time" in which the harmony of God's Creation or Natures Creation for the Non-Believer does reside and has gone back into the "animalistic" mind-filling unreal "I Want" personally created world that imaginary exists in an unreal past or an unreal future. Falsely, this being a personally created world that is in direct pursuit of a conniving "I Want" machination that is based upon a personal and usually greed-based "I Want for ME."

This is actually the "I Want" that keeps one living in a Hell that they self-create and so bring to exist in the "Present Time". The fact is also knowing that even if you attain your "I Want", is it not also well known that this will not bring the "Peace that surpasses all understanding," but instead, will always bring to you another "I Want"; this being a continuation of another self-created personal world of misery and dissatisfaction and also a world that you can be inflicted upon those around you. For does not your past life and also your present life not show that your uncontrolled five senses, these being that which you have "self-chosen" to control you, are NEVER satisfied and that you are living in an unsatisfactory Hell while on this Earth and also a self-created Hell that you inflict upon others and which in turn, they then inflict their "I Want" Hell upon YOU! Rightly, this is NOT an authentic life! For this is an "I Want;" a personally created living in HELL that you bring to this Earth and your life and the lives of others?

So yes! Now it is an excellent time to continually remember that any thoughts within your mind, "always" target an "I Want" for ME future or a self-altered past in which you only "thoughtfully" exist, this is being because you simply think that your five senses are the real you, they are NOT you, they are just instrument for your use. But now you know and so "realise" that by performing this simple two-minute exercise, you will quickly be able to "realise" that they are NOT you, they are merely God-given, or Nature allowed for the Non-Believer, instruments for your use, for they are specific thoughts that are NOT emanating from the real you. For indeed the real you is the Soul who is "observing" these entire mind blocking entanglements and so beginning with this two-minute exercise, YOU are now truly enabled, via wisdom, to cancel these "I Want" thoughts, that are habitually being "chosen", via the God-given or Nature allowed for the Non-Believer "Freedom of Choice", to fill the mind.

For it is truly and certainly these "I Want" mind filling words that are emanating from one or all of the five senses. It is this historically allowed and self-chosen "I Want" act which is blocking the Soul's needed view of the "Present Time". For indeed this needed view is necessary to allow you to see and so support the harmony that is continually evolving and so growing from the "Present Time", and it is undoubtedly "ignorance" if the people so captured, chooses to "ignore" this truth.

So yes! Now all practising "doers", this being in the very early days of this two-minute exercise, will fully understand that during this simple exercise; when an "I Want" or any thought begins to appear in mind, then your "willpower", which is energised by your "consciousness", can now become immediately aware of the true meaning of the words pronounced by the incarnate Jesus, This was when He turned and said to Peter: ***"Get behind me. Satan! You are a stumbling block to me; you do not have in mind the things of God, but the*** (I Want) ***things of men."*** Thus Peter's thoughts can be likened to any of the five senses that are seeking their own a personal "I Want;" but during this two-minute exercise, all that the doer needs to do is to return to feeling the weight of their body upon the chair, which will still the mind and so allow the Soul to observe the darkness of the still mind.

This condition is being darkness which can be likened to the dark cloud that appears to have a light shining behind it but ignores this light seeing fact. For rightly, there is no need to say all those words spoken by Jesus because in those ancient times, these "I Want" thoughts were culturally explained as being from the Devil. Still, in our modern age, "The Book" reveals "thoughts" to be coming from your personally animated five senses, which are continually pursuing an "I Want." For indeed "The Book" reveals that the "Devil" does not exist but the ever-existing and glaring "I Want" for Me thought undoubtedly does, and this is based upon the certainty that you cannot be that which sounds words, or which creates mind filling pictures for in truth, you cannot be that to which your eyes see or ears listen. Nor can you be that which the mouth tastes or the nose smells, or that which you touch or which touches you, for you are that which all these gifts silently report to; for assuredly, you cannot be that which you experience for you is a pure Soul, the experiencer who observes all life and non-life and can observe all things, and whose real task is to assist and support the growing and evolving harmony which can only exist in the "Present Time". For rightly, this is also the reason why God or Nature for the Non-Believer gave people the freedom of "any" choice because the same act can create or destroy our emerging future, depending upon circumstances.

Therefore this is undoubtedly a much-needed exercise, and it is genuinely assisting in recognising and also stopping the "I Want" only for me world, or any thinking activity which takes the observer into viewing the unreal non-existing past or future worlds that are simply created by an "I Want" thought that is genuinely emanating from one of the five senses. It is also a simple exercise in which you only need to experience your weight upon the chair, which immediately brings you back into God's word for it stops the "I Want" thoughts, these being that takes you into the non-existing past or the non-existing future.

So yes! It is with this exercise that we can return to the concept of house training our unruly five puppies, who have been allowed to run wild all their lives. For strictly, at the first instant of any interrupting "thought" entering the still mind, you can "scientifically" say or silently "feel" the true meaning of the word "Heel". For justly, this is a well-known command and its beneficially sought result will mentally "silence" all interrupting and complaining thoughts that consistently appear; primarily this is being so when kindly treat these seeming undisciplined self-occurring thoughts as if they are your five well-loved but untrained puppies, who you are now "kindly" training to obey your loving command immediately.

Thus, an internally-sounded "heel" or better still, its unsounded mind squeezed expectation, will immediately stop any thoughts that come into your mind. For accurately, it can be perfectively likened to the training of five puppies that are now being trained to obey your commands, for it is good to remember that the five senses are not your enemy but are certainly like untrained puppies which constantly barking excitedly at you for their animalistic ally based "I Want" – so they need training. This two-minute exercise is the beginning of this training, and this is a good metaphor, for most people will know that untrained and undisciplined puppies can tear a room to shreds, also attack innocent life and all other non-life forms and they do this by continually seeking their uncontrolled and very personal "I Want," which certainly creates disharmony in all the places that exist around them.

Therefore, is it not also an actual and common knowledge that only people have been given the "Freedom of Choice", meaning that they are the only life form that can self-create disharmony or self-create harmony upon this Earth? For indeed all those floods, earthquakes and droughts is simply Nature easing its growing muscles as it grows and expands or shrinks into the future. A difficult or impossible world to control, but truly nearly all people know that there is a popular way to train a dog to be obedient, this being obedience in which they will obey their master's wishes, which is a well-known condition that is achieved by a training system which simply commands untrained pups to stop their mischievous and uncontrolled nature, until, eventually well trained, they silently come to rest unseen and unheard behind the heel of their master, that is until called to pursue an action which is needed by their master.

For correctly, this is also a similar situation in which many "I Want" for me thoughts, these being that which are continually emanating from the untrained "animalistic" five senses, do block the seeing of the reality that exists in the "Present Time", and they are like our five wild pups, not needed to be heard or seen in the mind.

So yes! Accurately, this is also the way to train those noisy untrained five senses so that they silently obey the "thought" command of "heel", or more realistically the inner mind thought to the command of "Not This", an input which immediately silences the intruders but always knows, has in the "Shepherd" training of his sheepdog, our habitually five wild pups will need this command to be silently sounded via inner mind sounding and MANY times, but be diligent, like any shepherd who is training his sheepdog.

Yet eventually it can become a silencing command that does not need to be sounded or realised, for it could just take a habitual but conscious mind "squeeze", likened to a silent un-sounding "Not this", a realty being born from silent disciplinary energy within the mind, which knowingly removes the energy of willpower which has been "habitually" freed to act within people by their consciousness.

Honestly, in those early days of "training", you could say "Not this," to any sudden thought that enters the mind, even when merely practising when walking to a destination. For now, you will accurately know that it is these mind filling "thoughts" that are really and simply "I Want" noises emanating from your untrained five senses, these being that which is genuinely blocking your Soul from seeing the real world, this being that world which truly and only exists in the Present Time.

It is this fact that stops your Soul, which is the real you, from fully experiencing the harmony that is birthed by nature and which is that which truly exists all around you has also does the harmony that lovingly exists within you. For again and honestly it can be said, that in this first two-minute exercise you will "fleetingly" experience this fact, particularly when feeling your weight upon the chair, which you can only experience in the "Present Time".

It is, therefore, useful to understand that this ancient and silent but well-practised re-direction of consciousness, to newly support willpower, with a newly "modernised" will, to stop any attempt of "thought" from entering the mind, this being that which always blocks the view of the Soul from seeing the real world that we call "The Creation". So the task is to stop these untrained "I Want" thoughts from entering the mind, this being so they can no longer be inwardly "seen" or "heard" but can always be "stilled" by inner contentment, especially until there is work to be done. This certainty being just as a sheepdog will silently obey its master even if not seen or heard, for, in reality, these "inner" pups now becoming trained dogs, which you have never tried to control - until now.

For indeed you are NOT them you are the Soul which we are likening to be the Shepherd who cares for Gods world or the world of Nature for the Non-Believer for truly the most relevant task to Shepherd is the "Present Time", in which I shall not want. For the reality of life can be likened to the Soul being the Shepard and the five senses being the sheep-dog that quickly looks after the herd of sheep has their task is to be constantly aware that all that around them is safe and will not be harmed.

So yes! it is an unusual first exercise which, once started can be performed anywhere and wherever you can peacefully sit alone and undisturbed, such as on a bus or a train, for the barking of the five senses will be seen to be very obtrusive within the mind. It is an exercise that will reveal the work that is needed to be done to slow down, dismiss eventually and then stop the five senses from "barking" their "I Wants", for indeed; this is a "work" which will be quickly recognised as leading the doer to a new reality. Simply put each time these five senses sound a "bark" it is a beginning, middle or end of an "I Want". Eventually, they can be stopped from sounding in mind. For correctly it is then that the doers' Soul can "see" clearly through the mind and so experience God's world or the world of Nature for the Non-Believer, for rightly, this is the world that should be lived in via a constant "harmony" with all that is around you. Now again, it can be said that the barking of the five senses into the mind can indeed be stopped. It is the acknowledging of these new skills that will move you to a further stage of development that will take you to "Enlightenment" and thereby unobtrusively live in the harmony that exists all around you has it does within you. You can be assured that you WILL eventually experience the "Full comprehension of any Situation".

So yes! Again let us reiterate that at the very beginning of this two-minute exercise and while sitting on a chair and knowingly being loved by the hug of gravity, this being that which you are witnessing to occur within you, there is a need to immediately "squeeze" your mind and so awaken a way to silently stop the active "arising" of any thought within the mind, or, upon suddenly realising that your mind is engaged in an "I Want" conversation, just simply say "Not This," and immediately return to the stillness that is resting within you. For assuredly, after some training this makes the sounding of words within your mind, disappear out of sight as if they have gone behind you for they longer exist, for indeed, this is also an expression which can be usefully tried when doing the two-minute exercise or even when walking.

For indeed, this "two-minute" exercise can be done at any time, and for much longer than two minutes, which can be later explained when you choose to do so, For indeed the "Freedom of Choice" is always yours. Positively, this exercise clearly shows that you are not the five senses for you are unquestionably that which controls them. Therefore, correctly the "choice" to experience "Enlightenment" starts to grow from these simple first attempts at this two-minute exercise. For assuredly, this is his being the first disciplinary applied "Freedom of Choice", this being to do this meditational practice and so fully understand "Stand-Under", that when performing this first two-minute exercises that you are the observing Soul who, with the "Freedom of Choice" is your Soul "choosing" to discover a way of life that is needed to search for the silent harmony that always rests in the "Present Time".

Therefore, indeed, is this not always being that unified time which is truly all around you, just has it also is unified within you? And is this not that which our many wise ancients have spoken continuously about for thousands of years. The second choice is to now grow this "Meditational" pattern into a simple five-minute exercise and still to practice twice a day and has close to sun up and sundown has is possible, while also always remembering that practising during Sun up and Sundown is an excellent time. It is also useful to know that you can also practise this "experiencing" of "Self-Realising" the "Present Time" between these two exercises and wherever you are, and sometimes even without the need for sitting, for the love of gravity will never leave you. It is also good to know that "The Present Time", which is Gods world or the world of Nature for the Non-Believer is always there and so will never leave you, but you can leave it, this being when you enter the mind blocking "I Want for Me" world which self-created by many a mind filling "I Want" noises.

But now, with this first two-minute exercise, you will begin to realise that the five senses are controlling you and that in their ever irrational "I Want," they are commonly acting like new birthed wild pups that are barking and attacking or wanting to attack and who pursue an "I Want" everything that exists around them – which you think is you! They are NOT you for you are the Soul, this being that which a part of the Creation. This first revisionary two-minute exercise is the first step towards "Enlightenment," and it is necessary because many people often do not realise that they already have "Enlightenment" within them, but that it is being blocked from being experienced by a simple forgetting, which many of our wise ancients say is our worst enemy. Thus, the condition that exists at the start of this two-minute exercise has it will with the five minutes, is that the doer will "faintly" begin to understand that these five senses can be stopped from talking in the head for a few seconds.

Still, the necessary understanding is to realise that it can be done and they can and eventually, via mediation, be stopped forever until called to release their knowledge into the reality of another beholder silently. Therefore, it is upon this "realisation" that the next stage after a month or three of practising this two-minute exercise is that you can then start a creed based mantra sounding meditation, in which a single word is repeatedly sounded in mind, which we can discuss later. Rightly, this is now explained in "The Book" as a well-known fact, for it is a perfect creed way to bring these five senses entirely under the control of the practiser, so that they will stay silent until the Soul silently instructs them to do something, as with the master of our well-trained pups.

For it is then that the five senses will become like well-trained dogs for your five senses will recognise that you are their master, and only when asked to do something will they joyfully and without noise silently follow your wordless instructions? I say silent because these non-sounding directions to your five senses come from your non-speaking Soul, this is being a Soul that automatically and silently instructs them to do that which is necessary to be done, which is to support or starting acts that are not needed to support the emerging harmony that is developing around you.

The Soul also quietly does this without producing any thought that will take you from the "Present Time" in which the Soul lives for it cannot exist in the past or the future for it "lives" only in the Preset Time. For it is now certainly known by you that your current "thoughts" do genuinely originate from a non-real world that is akin to demands emanating from the five-sense, this is truly being a self-created world, which can only be in a self-dreamed future or past, which indeed, does not exist. For certainly this is being an unreal and selfish world that can only be created by our ancient animalistic ally based five senses and which only exists in the head of the "thinker". It is these thoughts which automatically corrupt and so destroys the correct view of the "Present Time" – the world of Heaven, which is God's world or the world of Nature for the non-believer.

So yes! Scientifically and eventually, via mediation, this will enable your Soul to "seemingly" take you to live with a tranquil none thinking inner life that can only exist in the "Present Time", a time that can be achieved via "Patient Meditation" to become that which you are, this being your Soul, which can also soundlessly and via no expectation silently command your taste sense to "taste this". Or to your hearing request without any inner sound to "hear this" and to your touch "feel this," and to your sight "see this," and also to your smell "smell this".

Then rightly truly, you will be staggered with the experience that these five senses in their non-clamouring silence within "Present Time" can bodily experience for you and all without any sound in mind. Then really, it will be a "Present Time" in which you will genuinely and by experience know to be God's world or the world of Nature for the Non-Believer. For do remember the view down that green valley or a view from that mountain top, or that viewed painting or that listened to music? How silently your mouth opened at the experiencing of this realisation as your mind became still at the sheer wonder at what your "Soul" was experiencing, this being was the "being" that entirely existed in the "Present Time" and this "being" was your Soul, joining with the "Preset Time".

For these wonders can "always" be fully appreciated and achieved but only in the "Present Time", and this is the world that all our wise ancients spoke about, which is the "Heaven" that exists upon our Earth. It is also a Heaven that is always recognisably known to be experienced within you, for did not the wise incarnate Jesus say: *"nor will people say, 'Here it is', or 'There it is', because the kingdom of God is within you,"* and did He not say this to people who unknowingly were living in their self-created Hell, this being that which they purposely created within their "I Want for ME" world?

Also, did not Jesus, who was our God incarnate, also state that this "unknowing" of who you are, will leave you? For all people have a God-given "Freedom of Choice" and because of our now known new modern understanding and a simple two-minute exercise, expanding to a five-minute exercise, which will quickly now grow to a thirty-minute twice a day exercise, the doer will begin to understand truly, that the world of Heaven that truly exists upon our Earth, will no longer be without them.

Therefore these people will never say "Here it is" or "There it is" for indeed "Heaven" is within you and can never be without you unless you personally "choose" it to be so, for you are a genuine person who has been created by God or Nature for the Non-Believer, to support the emerging of the creation.

So Yes! Again, we can now fully understand the words of Jesus when He said: *"Repent, for the kingdom of heaven is near,"* because Yes! It is within you and this controlling and silencing of the five senses is also the bread of Heaven that Jesus spoke about when He said: *"This is the bread -* (this is the "Present Time") *- that came down from heaven and he who feeds on this bread will live forever."* This feeding can only be achieved in the "Present Time" for rightly, this means that Heaven is for those who live in the harmony of the "Present Time", without thought for any past or a future "I Want". Then again, this is the spoken truth from Jesus when he said: *"I tell you the truth unless you change and become like little children, you will never enter the kingdom of heaven,"* for do not little children, particular below the age of two, live in the "Kingdom of Heaven" which is the "Present Time", without thought of any past or future "I Want?" For assuredly, this is correctly being the most precise advice from God, given through Jesus to all people when He said, *"Therefore, whoever humbles himself like this child, is the greatest in the kingdom of heaven."* For really does not "humble" mean modest and unassuming in attitude and behaviour? Does this not also mean feeling and also showing respect and deference, plus meaning to be obliging towards other people? Does this not personal "humbling" simply support and give birth to the greater good of harmony, that the Creation is continually endeavouring to develop all-around "YOU"?

So Yes! If you wish to enter this Kingdom of Heaven that sincerely loves you, while living on this Earth - Read on, for it is waiting for you.

66.   THE WAY TO LIVE IN HEAVEN AND NOT IN HELL

So yes! It is true that with this first two-minute exercise you are targeting a way to attain "Enlightenment," which is that bodily experience brings within you and without you, that which our ancients describe has *"The Peace that surpasses all understanding"*. It should be further understood that this is a very subjective experience which rests only within people. It is this experience which our entire world's religions and philosophies all do seek, for indeed, this is being a devotedly based system that is locked into our entire world's many ancient ways of worship and devotion. Therefore is it not strange that one religion can fight to destroy another religion, and is it not even stranger when the same religion causes an internal war of conflict because they want to change to a differing Creed based worshipping system? For undoubtedly such religious conflicts cannot be based upon the search for "Enlightenment", this being the experience of being has one with the Creation, which is genuinely Gods world, the world that ALL religions seek to experience. Therefore is it not known, which makes it even more puzzling, that ALL religions profess to have the same target, which is to live in and so experience God's world? Yet sadly, is it not also true that some people who profess to be religious and a lover of God, cause harm to others for not believing in "their" God? What Father would allow this amongst his children? Also, what father would punish a child to whom he has given the "Freedom of Choice"?

So yes! Is this not strange that people can act like animals that have no soul? Genuinely, this being that entity which has the "Freedom of Choice", a known "scientific" reality which God gave only to people so that they could support His ever-developing ever still creation. How is it possible that a person with a Soul can claim an animalistic "I want", and so hunt others by acclaiming "Our way to God is better than your way to God, so you should follow our way and not your way." Then, with this ungodly statement they animalistic ally hunt and then kill, destroy and maim worshipers from other religions or even in the same religion, this being in a strange belief that God is supporting and blessing them for doing so. How strange is this, for is it not true that God gave to all people "The Freedom of Choice" to support His work and not to destroy it. Therefore the only explanation that can be "scientifically" stated and which "The Book" puts forward, is that these attacking and destroying people can only be new rebirths from our animal kingdom and so are habitually behaving as they did in their "I Want" past life, so surely they should be cared for as such needs are. For certainly is it not true that all around our world we see the continual growth of people being from solitary caves to the modern days conjoining, absorbing and a "frictionally" coming together of all people from many languages and many nations who are being led by their language-based leaders who have had many lives and who are recognised by their observing silence.

For rightly, can it not also be said that God's harmony seeking laws have been in force for millions of years and that no person, or culturally based religion or philosophy, can change the target of these continually evolving laws; so is it not Godly true that all people have the same task, which is to support these harmony seeking laws as they emerge only within the "Present Time" – this being that which can only be God's world or the world of Nature for the Non-Believer. Therefore, it not also very accurate that we observe throughout our world, that our wise ancients created many personal and cultural ways in which their followers could achieve enlightenment and thus support the way of God or Nature for the Non-Believer. For indeed it can be said that all our world's religions and philosophies have been constructed and taught by our wise ancients in such an orderly way as always to support the knowledge of "Enlightenment", this being that which is all around us and also to support the emerging "Enlightenment" which can also be identified has grown all around us, and this being not only for themselves but for others also? So is it not real that the target of our wise ancients was to obtain for their followers, a life that could be lived in the "Kingdom of Heaven", which can factually be realised only by people who endeavour to live in the "Present Time", this being a time which has no past and no future.

Therefore, Can it not also be said to be true that none of our many wise ancients stated that a person should attack and or kill another for worshipping with a different creed or even for having no creed to worship? For knowingly is not this Earthly creation God's world or the world of Nature for the Non-Believer? For certainly is not the "Present Time" Gods world or the world of nature for the Non-believer. This "Present Time" is a place in which the mind is without any thoughts which are demanding a selfish Future or a Past "I want". For assuredly, is it not true that God or Nature for the Non-Believer did provide everything that exists within the world that we live this also being likened to that which includes the "Heaven" that exists within our bodies, in which trillions of different entities willing support and care for each other? Also, is it not true that the ever-still "Present Time" is the real world of that which we call "The Creation"? For is not this "Creation" VERY accurately called by all our wise ancients and in their ancient terminology "The Kingdom of Heaven", this being that which is genuinely named by our wise ancients to be OUR "Heavenly Kingdom", this "OUR" being that terminology which ALL our wise ancients do speak. For the Heathen upon our world does genuinely exists, and it is currently all around you has it is within you and YES! The "Patient Meditation" exercise revealed in "The Book" will take you to truly live in this heaven that wants nothing but your love and support and which exists all around you. The question now being is that does ANY of our wise ancients, these being those Enlightened" ones who created ALL our worlds' religions and philosophies, say that you must kill to enter "Kingdom of Heaven?" NO! They do not, for you can never even experience "Enlightenment" if you inflict any pain upon others which you are genuinely inflicting upon yourself.

So yes! Now it should be fully understood that the harmony of the "Present Time", this being that which is all around the body, should also be likened to that harmony which regularly and quietly works within the body. For do not these trillions of separate entities that lovingly exist in our bodies, not commonly work in perfect harmony within the body, all working together for the greater whole and also indeed are all these "separate" entities not healthily and regularly living without any hate and also without creating any conflict within themselves. Therefore, cannot a person's body experienced as a deep all-satisfying harmonised wonder, which gives one a personal understanding of how all that is outside the body should also, behave?

So Yes! Is it not this early emerging from the animal kingdom the reason why some people can inflict upon others this painfully punishing cross of life? This being that which is imposed by the animalistic "I want" of those many separately, and individually existing "others" who are often called religious "freethinkers" and who are often supported by mob oriented false religious leaders? It must be stated that the problem that creates this punishing way of life must come from many confused "I want" thinkers who want others to believe only that which they believe, this is animalistic "pack" behaviour in which people are driven by physical appetites rather than spiritual needs. Strictly, this being a simple act of disharmony which is caused by a selfish "animalistic" and persecuting "I want," which is undoubtedly created by these ignoring people who "animalistic ally" target the world in which they want to live – which is not God's world. Also sadly, it is known that the cries and activities of many of these "I want" for myself doers, always inflict pain upon others, which are not of their creed, by saying, "I want my creed to be the right creed, not your creed." Thus again it should be said, that this is genuinely being the "not knowing" which is caused by "animalism" and so they do not "Realise" in their ignorance, that in God's world, they are severely punishing themselves as they act outside God laws, these being laws that ALWAYS purposely create harmony within this world and in preparation of the next.

Again, simply put, those who "unknowingly" live in this self-inflicted pain of Hell, this being that which they create for themselves and into which they often drag others, see the quiet discipline of a "controlled" and "blissful" non-thinker as being an obstacle to achieving their constant "I want" desires. For did not the "Mother of the Creation", speaking through Jesus say to the disciples: *"Woe to the world because of the things that cause people to sin! Such things must come, but woe to the person through whom they come!"*

So yes! Is it not the greatest sin to wilfully attack to maim and kill others just for their property? Is this not also a personal "I want", this being that which targets and so causes these attacking people to "sin"? Also, did not Jesus state: *"Things that cause people to sin are bound to come, but woe to that person through whom they come."* Therefore truly this is certainly not an idle conversation, but a great gift to those who can hear and so understand these words. For, as previously stated before, God does not and cannot punish people to whom He has purposely given "Freedom of Choice". For God made legal any "choice", this being for people to do what they think is correct; therefore people cannot break God's law and so cannot be punished by God, but He could turn his back upon them and so they will find that they will begin life in a very different world.

So Yes! It is also intimated by many of our wise ancients, that those who commit these evil crimes against others will not be born again as people, but will return to the animal kingdom in which they will be born again, but without a Soul and beyond doubt certainly into a life that has no "Freedom of Choices". For again, as previously stated, those who live in their self-created Hell upon this Earth, can be likened to the driver of a car motoring through a city who disobeys the "Highway Code" and so ignores which side of the road he or she should drive upon and even ignores the harmonious law of traffic lights, thus willfully disobeying the harmony of the "Highway Code". Therefore, who is punishing this driver when their actions in life bring to them much pain and confusion has they painfully clash with the harmony that always exists within "Highway Code" of the road has it does within the Creation? These greed-based animalistic "drivers" should now know that it is their five senses and not their true "Self" which is actively driving them into many problems with their life, but honestly now "The Book" says that such ignorance is no longer an excuse?

So yes! What should now be clear to all readers is that which causes people to sin against the Creation's "Present Time" can be compared to the "purity" of those people who obey the "Highway Code" of life, for justly and indeed they can go through their life being fully supported by the "High Way Code" of other drivers. But for sure, these "High Way Code" sinners "I want for myself" thoughts and actions always lead their outward behaviour patterns. But what is now clearly understood is that the "woe" which comes to these "High Way Code" transgressors does not come from the positive creation of God, but this woe is coming from the negative "reflections" of their own "I Want" for ME activities. It is undoubtedly these "I want" for myself activities, which positively create a selfish based life of a punishing and very disagreeable Hell, in which these sad people live. For indeed you cannot break the harmony of God's laws or Nature laws for the Non-Believer, for you only think you can and any "punishment" you receive is being inflicted by your own "chosen" actions; for God's harmony will always correct itself, for it is indeed "lawfully" well-supported by the "Mother of the Creation".

So yes! You will undoubtedly find it to be a fact that by pursuing the "Patient Meditation" exercise, which explained in "The Book"; this being an exercise which will take you to live within the SELF of the harmony of the world that surrounds you, which will be a similar experience has to that of the life which exists within you and so "Naturally" you will become an existing part of the harmony that exists in the "Kingdom of Heaven, this being that "Heaven" which can only exist in the "Present Time". For eventually, with this creed based "Patient Meditational" practice, you will find that you can never again be a person of woe, for you will truly understand and experience that the harmony of the "Present Time" is not only that which exists "inside you" but it is also certainly an existence that you will identify as being "outside you" because you will "Realise" that you are an integral part of the Creation's harmony which is God's world or the world of Nature for the Non-Believer. For appropriately, did not our holy living great incarnates, prophets and wise ancients show to their followers' many ways to find how to experience the "Present Time", which is the Heaven that exists upon this Earth and did they not also wisely use, for identification purposes, the current understandable culture of their believers to achieve this fact? Therefore, is it not also "scientifically" valid that many of our wise ancients achieved this way of how to enter into God's world by introducing to their followers a culturally-based disciplinary self-imposed "ritual" of praying, these being creed-based chanting's, choruses or silent "meditational" prayers which ensured that their followers brought their mind away from an "I want" personal world and into the experiencing of the "Present Time", which is God's world. Therefore, is it not certainly true that our wise ancients knew the need for these voluntary and personally disciplined praying activities! These being "religiously" imposed group or individual based activities that with constant and regular perseverance do stop a person's mind from being filled by an "I Want," this being that which selfishly emanates from their past or future desired personally-created mind-filling "I Want" thoughts, which "The Book" clearly explains to be the world of Hell. For in the reality of our present-day understanding and our specific knowledge now of the different cultural ways that our world's diverse religions and philosophies do worship, they can still understandably follow the creeds that have been culturally introduced by their wise ancient founders. These being our ancient wise who used the home-based culture of their listeners to target God's world, the world that genuinely persists in the "Present Time", this being the only time in which Gods "Heaven" can actually and so genuinely exist. So all our ancient wises religious guidance would be in direct accordance with the shared cultural wisdom of the time and place of the actual "Creation" of that countries or districts religion or philosophy.

So Yes! As previously stated, it is undoubtedly a "scientific" truth to say that all our worlds many culturally-based religions did commonly originate through variably different creed-based worshipping cultures, all of which were "culturally" created by our wise ancients to be based upon obligatory imposed religious prayers and obligatory chants, these to be a group or individually imposed and which were all used to target within the worshipper the experiencing of the "Present Time". For indeed these "praying" disciplines were imposed to stop the worshippers' mind from always thinking about a past or a future very private "I want for ME", these being attention filling emanations that are being created by one or all of the five senses, for indeed all our wise ancients knew that you could not be that which you observe for you are the soul, that which observes everything but which cannot see the "Creation", this being that which it knows it is a part of, through a mind that is blocked by a past or a future "I "Want", this being that which is mind cloudily emanating from one of the five senses. Therefore, All knowledge of the world's past certainly shows this fact to be exact! This being that ALL the various religions and philosophies were "culturally" introduced by our wise ancients, who knowingly brought the doer to target the *"Peace that surpasses all Understanding"* this is the encountering with "Enlightenment" that always rests in the "Present Time"?

Is it not also "scientifically" correct that these many different religious practices, born by our wise ancients within the many cultures that existed in the world of their believers, are now known and also modernly recognised to have very different "worded" hymns and prayers and other different praying activities? These are being within all our worlds culturally introduced and so different "creed" and culturally based worshipping systems and rituals. For faithfully truly, these enlightened ones were bringing to their followers a "taste" of the beyond doubt realisation of God's world. Accurately, this is being the real world that only exists only within the "Present Time". Simply put, this was also the reason why our wise ancients personally introduced the many very variable "ritual" praying systems to their followers; for their target was to take all worshipping "doers" towards this *"Peace that surpasses all Understanding"?* Yet sadly, is it not also "scientifically" known to be accurate, that over a long time, that many followers of these ancient belief systems have simply forgotten the real target of our wise ancients, this target being that which exists only in the reality of the "Present Time." Sincerely, this being a forgotten but always existing target being replaced when the worshippers left the weekly worshipping of their religions personally pursued creed-based ritual praying activities plus incantations and other culturally based private praying actions. For is this, not a truth that enabled them to weekly experience the "Kingdom of God" which truly exists but only in the "Present Time," this also being a mind-empty time in which an "I want" thought cannot exist. For indeed this is a God based existence of a ***"Peace that surpasses all Understanding"*** which their religious attendance will have brought to them and which also enabled them to reflect this wellbeing of Gods world into the community to which they belonged. Yet sadly again, this truly establishes the fact that forgetting is our worst enemy; for now, when some worshippers leave their place of worship, in which they have experienced "Enlightenment", they deem it "animalistic ally", this being that which emanates a preoccupation with physical rather than spiritual needs, that it is necessary to protect their "culturally" based religious belief system in which they have fully experienced Gods love, which sadly is a "personal protection" that is just another "I Want". For genuinely truly this mind clouding "I Want", this being that which is cunningly emanating from their five senses, also makes them attack other "culturally" based religious worshipping system has to be a way to defend their personally experienced feeling of "Enlightenment seemingly". Therefore and correctly, this is being an attacking activity which is acclaimed as being in defence of their religion and also their personal defending of their experiencing of "Enlightenment". Or is it merely some religious leader requesting their controlled worshippers to obtain the goods and property that is the property of other worshipping cultures? Then truly their followers will undoubtedly leave their experiencing of the "Kingdom of God" and quickly enter the "Kingdom of Hell" to which they may become more "habitually" familiar and sadly may even believe that their sadness is Gods punishment for allowing other religions a different way to experience Gods Heaven that can only exist in the "Present Time" when it is a personal sadness self-created by an "I Want for ME" activity that is dominating their life.

So Yes! Again and indeed, with the following explained "Patient Meditation" exercise, a religious, philosophical and even a Non-Believer can and so will, find their way to God's world or the world of Nature for the Non-Believer and so fully experience the real world that can only exist in the "Present Time". For it is undoubtedly and anciently known to be true that all people can establish this attainable self-knowledge, this being that "pursued" exercise which is based upon the realisation of all that exists in the "Present Time". For indeed this is being a self-planned "individual" exercise in which a person will experience that which will correct this contradiction of really forgetting who we are, and so allow the meditational doer to follow a well-known and historically trusted way that teaches them how to live "contentedly" within the "Kingdom of God", this being that which can only exist in the "Present Time". It is also very accurate that many established creed worshippers, who exist within our world's many and various religions and philosophies, will also be able to use this quickest and most straightforward way to "Enlightenment" in which a person can continually live in the Kingdom of God. Strictly, this is truly being the

"Present Time" and a time when a constant "I Want" cannot exist.

So yes! It is, therefore, a well-known "scientific" truth that our wise ancients established many varied and different culturally-based religious practices into which many various management systems developed to support their many different creeds based "praying rituals", all of which were founded upon their accepted culture's way of worshipping within their culture based regions and communities. But rightly indeed, the world now acknowledges that our world's religious and philosophical management systems are well-known to be "naturally" very "culturally" different in the way that they administer their control of the many different creed-based ways to worship, even within the same religion. So truly they need to be to control individual culture-based variances, that shine out from all our local and worldly cultural ways of worship. For now, in Gods "Present Time" and with the all-knowing and all-interacting web-based communication system, we all can now recognise and understand that our world correctly truly contains many different religions and philosophies all of which "scientifically" and so honestly, target God's world or the world of Nature for the Non-Believer. So is it not now also understood as previously stated, that all our religious belief systems have been taught, by our wise ancients to practice different ritual praying and preaching approaches, all of which are personally used to target a reality that is designed to bring their praying members away from thoughts that are concerned only with past and or a future "I want" Hell, this is certainly being the well-known legendary world of Hell? The Book" also states that there is certainly a need for a cultural and therefore a personal understanding of Gods world or the world of Nature for the Non-Believer, this being to stand under the one God whose world can only exist in the "Present Time", and it is a factual truth that the way to bring a worshipper to the world of "I Want Nothing", is legendary and very culturally based. Therefore, is it not also true that all worshippers were served to bring their very existence into the knowledge of the "Present Time", this truly is God's world? For again, is this not truly the ever sought experience of being in the "Heaven" that we call the "Present Time," this being that place which indeed rests upon our Earth and which is far away from the worshippers' constant desire to obtain a personal "I want", this being an "I Want for ME" that ALWAYS confine the "I Want" thinker to the negative Hell that they "falsely" create to exist upon our Earth, for truly God gave or Nature gave for the Non-Believer to all people the "Freedom of Choice – which also means that only people can "choose" to live in Heaven or they can "choose" to live in Hell.

So now it can be easily and modernly seen by all to be accurate, that our wise ancients introduced so many different praying and worshipping rituals, which were culturally designed to bring their worshippers to the heavenly harmony of the "Present Time", this truly, being the Heaven that always rests upon our Earth? Therefore can it not also be easily seen to be accurate, that even when practised in our modern times, that any follower who truly, commits themselves to their cultures religious practices, would always realise and so experience "Enlightenment". Thus bringing into their lives what the Christians call being filled with the "Holy Spirit" or the "Holy Ghost," in which a person's mind becomes satisfied by a "Peace that surpasses all understanding"? Yet is it not also seen to be true that many forget this God based experience, mainly when they leave their place of worship? Is this because they "think" that their chanting group based creeds can only bring them to God's world when surrounded by likeminded others; or is this because they also believe that God's world exists only within the walls of their place of worship?

So yes! Now indeed this is the time to realise and so acknowledge an understanding that soon will be an excellent time to introduce to your "Self", the individually based and personally explained short creed exercise that will be introduced later in "The Book". This being that short "exercise" which shows the most natural way that sincerely, and "scientifically" will take you, the "practiser" to "Enlightenment"; that which the Hindu religion calls "Moksha," which loosely means *freedom from ignorance,*" a real pathway to "Enlightenment." For truly, this is indeed being the same "Enlightenment" that can be found by a believer in God and also for a Non-Believer in God. For indeed, there is undoubtedly a wise ancient very condensed way to experience the Heaven that rests upon our Earth entirely. It is also an old way that is based upon a straightforward activity which has become the fastest known way to reach the "Kingdom of Heaven", this being that which always rests up this Earth, but only in the "Present Time". For assuredly, this being a "Heaven" that can be reached by a single word which is an exercise of mindfully repeating a single word that is anciently known to be called a "Mantra". For genuinely this is a very ancient exercise whose proof is in the doing and not the thinking and this is indeed a well-known reality in that it is the space between this single sounding "prayer" word in which indeed rests the "Kingdom of Heaven". For certainly this "Patient Meditational" practice being offered by "The Book", is the actual sounding into the mind a single word, this being that which is called a "mantra". This exercise is targeted to discipline, and so silences the constant words that are emanating from the five senses by training these "pups", your five senses, to obey your command to sound this single word obediently and no other. For indeed, this is being a very ancient exercise which will eventually, after some "training", allow your Soul to see through the spaces of what will eventually become the automatically "single" sounding word of your carefully chosen mantra, for indeed your "pups", which are genuinely your five senses, will become obedient to the request of your all-seeing Soul. Sincerely, this being a factual activity which is known by our wise ancients to enable the doer, which "The Book" knowingly explains to be the Soul, does first observe the "Clouds of Unknowing", which is explained by our ancients, has that activity which can be seen in a still mind, this only being when the eyes are closed. For undoubtedly and "scientifically" it is now stated to be true that ALL modern "True Believers" and all modern "Non-Believers" can, with this meditational exercise, experience "Enlightenment", this being an experience which the Buddhist refer to as *"Bodhi"* or *"Nirvana"* which can eventually be achieved by reciting this single worded oration. Sincerely, this is being a personal experience which our wise ancients described as *"an awakening to the true nature of things,"* which can be knowingly and certainly achieved by reciting this single word oration? This actuality being based upon a simply worded recitation that can and will bring the doer and experiencer to reside only in the "Present Time", which is a time that can be realised by those with the discipline or the need to find this "scientific" truth. Therefore, indeed, it can be said that establishing the realisation of this "experience" was the target of ALL our religious and philosophical belief systems? For genuinely it will be found that once the "Present Time" is "experienced", the experiencer will find that they could NEVER willingly leave this place that can be realised, but only in the "Preset Time", this being that which they have found and so "realised" by this unique exercise. Beyond doubt, this is being an exercise which brings to them that which the Islam religion describes as *"being filled with the Angel Gabriel"* and which is known by the worshipping Muslims to be *"a realm beyond the ability of words to properly convey,"* an absolute reality that if pursued and once "realised" will eventually never leave the finder. For correctly, and "scientifically," you will find that eventually, after much practice, you will find that you can never leave that which this simplest of all creed praying methods, this being that will bring to you the experience which ALL religions and philosophies seek, this being that which "The Book" calls "Enlightenment" and which the ancient Zoroastrianism religion of the fifth-Century BC referred to as *"Ushta"* meaning *"liberation, salvation and emancipation of the Soul".* Therefore correctly, this is being that experience which only exists in God's world and is indeed that which is also attainable to the Non-Believer. But yes, this experiencing of "Enlightenment" is not easy to attain for the rogue "I want" of the five senses will have been with you for most of your life. Therefore, is it not undoubtedly also true that the experiencing of "Enlightenment" is also known to be the place in which no leader or any religious manager can tell you what to do. For only God's harmony seeking laws or the law of Nature for the Non-Believer can fulfil this task.

So Yes! Rightly and truthfully, the "Practiser" who is seeking God's world or Natures world for the Non-Believer, will eventually understand that after experiencing "Enlightenment", this being that which will eventually be experienced by this simple one-worded meditation, will truly make it impossible to attack other religious creeds. Strictly, this is because it is silently experienced within "Enlightenment" that no "Godly" or "Natural" harmony can be achieved by a task that seeks to penalize others. So it is known to be a physical impossibility to practise such acts or any "punishing" act and woe to those who do commit this sin, for indeed God's laws automatically turn their back upon such sinners who break life's ongoing harmony. For faithfully, all religions seek the same goal, this being that which "ALWAYS" rests in the "Present Time"; for truly ALL people can experience "Enlightenment," this being a time in which the "I want for myself" cannot occur. For undoubtedly such "I want" exist only within a falsely created Hell, this being that which we call the past or future; for justly these are worlds that cannot exist in the Heaven that is ALWAYS resting upon our Earth but can rightly exist in the self-created world that ALL people call Hell.

67. HOW TO KNOW WHAT IS YOU

So Yes! The question that now emerges is how do you personally choose, with your God-given or Nature has given for the Non-Believer "Freedom of Choice", in the world that you wish to live? How do you choose a personally made discipline that ensures an inner peace which allows you to live in an environment of goodness that is a definite benefit to all and which is knowingly resting in that which we call "Heaven" upon this Earth, this being that which can only exist in our "Present Time"? Or do you live in a self-made Hell; this being that selfishly-created world which can only exist in the Past or the Future, this being a world in which you target self-made benefits that only you want? So how do you choose to realise and so manufacture the inner discipline which can stop the energy of "consciousness" from allowing "willpower" to automatically support the "I want" needs of the chattering five senses, for indeed, it is these five senses which always and cloudily fill your mind with their "I want" demands? Therefore can it not be accurate and "scientifically," said that the stopping of all thoughts from clouding the mind, will allow the Soul to see through your clear mind and into God's Creation, this being that which exists, but only in the "Present Time". This being that Godly of Nature created a reality which is all around the observer, which is genuinely YOUR soul. It is also this fact which enables the Soul to pursue its only purpose, which is to care and support the "Mother of the Creation" and Her constant development of the emerging harmony, which can only be achieved in the "Present Time". Of course, this is being the only time that can be "Self-Experienced" for it is the only time that truly exists. So the only time which can be "factually" lived in, but only when YOU are without an "I want" thought or any thoughts of any Past or Future desired machinations, for the task now is to use your given power of the "Freedom of Choice again" to still and so empty the mind until it is again without any thought. Therefore, unquestionably, this is genuinely being that fact which then allows your Soul to see, and so "experience" the "Present Time", this indeed being Gods world or the world of Nature for the Non-Believer.

So yes! Now it is time to know well that the "first step" necessary to achieve this is to use your God-given or Nature given for the Non-Believer, your personal "Consciousness" to authorise the energy of "Willpower" to energise a silencing activity, which is a disciplined way, will stop your willpower from automatically and habitually energising the release into the mind of the machinations of the desiring "I want" demands that are always emanating from your "individualistic" five senses. The most common tool used by our wise ancients, this being to engender the above self-imposed disciplinary activity, was to introduce disciplinary prayers and personal culturally-based movements, mantras and many other self-disciplined culturally based activities. This introduction to self-imposed disciplinary religious and philosophical activities was known by our wise ancients to bring their worshipper to stillness and silent contentment of that which can only be experienced in the "Present Time", this being that which they knowingly called Gods World. For indeed it was unknown by our ancients that it was, has the "The Book" now reveals, the mind filling "I want" that was continually emanating from the five senses that was being "disciplinary" silenced by their religious and philosophically imposed prayers, chants and physical praying activities, this being that which was brought to their followers *"The peace that surpasses all understanding"*.

So yes! These imposed and disciplinary based "worshipping" activities that were introduced by our ancient wise was factually known to still the mind and so engendered a "Godly" silence within the worshipper as they entered the "Present Time". Without a doubt, this is truly being an outer imposed worshipping discipline which stopped the mind from displaying any "I Want" for ME activity. For indeed it can be stated that these "I Want" for Me targets would have been greedily known to be pursued by their followers before they met with our ancient wise, which "The Book" now modernly explains to be the "I Want" chatter which is always originating from the undisciplined five senses, these being that which always cloud the mind with a past or a future "I want" desire. For our wise ancients would not have known that it was the undisciplined activities of our personally imbibed five senses that were always shouting into a person's mind their "I Want". This being that mind-filling noise that stopped the Soul from seeing through their clouded mind, for again it is said that it was this fact which stopped a person from "self-experiencing" the reality of God's world or the real world of Nature for the Non-Believer. For the absolute truth is that God's world can only be "self-experienced" in a time that actually and physically exists. Unquestionably, this is being a world which exists only in the "Present Time". If there is any doubt about this task, it is good always to remember that you can NEVER be that which you observe, touch, smell, taste or hear, so the only entity that you are is the all-seeing Soul, for you can never observe, touch, smell, taste or hear, the all-seeing Soul.

So yes! The constant correction of peoples selfish "I want" habit was the target of our wise ancients who always endeavoured to show to people how to perform a "personally" imposed meditational tasks such as a song, a prayer or an activity which was accurately designed so that it chose a person consciousness to redirect willpower to stop the mind habitually being clouded by past and future "I want" thoughts. For indeed, it should now be realised that our many wise ancients always attempted to stop people's thoughts from creating past or future machinations, these being that which are being fed by a constant "I want" for ME, which is now stated in "The Book" to be always emanating from the five senses. Without doubt, this is being a self-created activity which is continually streaming into the mind "I want" thoughts that also plan how to achieve such outcomes. For it can now be stated that it is these constant negatively undisciplined "I Want" thoughts which are clouding the mind simply because they were accidentally "chosen" via the God-given "Freedom of Choice" to inform consciousness to allow "willpower" to do so, this "choice" being made when they were children. But now let us understand some of the positive disciplines introduced by our wise ancients, these being disciplines that are targeted to stop these selfish and mercenary "I want" mind blocking thoughts, which are as follows:

1 THE BENEFIT OF PRAYING:

Now it should be understood that our wise ancients showed that the observing and experiencing God's world could be achieved by a positively introduced praying discipline. These being imposed disciplines that can be based not only upon the confession of a person's believed sins but also achieved by the chanting of an outer imposed prayer which is also disciplined by others. These prayers are being sacred words which the beholder has to compulsory listens and so chooses by their willpower, acquiring a conscious experience of the "Present Time", which can be achieved by outer "disciplinary" imposed group singing or chanting. There are many types of these outer imposed prayer-based "hymns" and "chants" which also include the introduction of pronouncing good wishes for another's health; all of which are performed under a positive discipline that is imposed by another person. These meetings are chosen by others to be at a particular time of each day or week, and within groups or as even has a personal mantra which can be personally chosen take place at various times during the day.

2   THE BENEFIT OF FASTING:

Also introduced by many of our wise ancients, again in an endeavour for people to personally witness the glory of God's world, this being that which can only exist in the "Present Time" is Fasting; such as not eating meat on a Friday or fasting without food for a given period; again designed to enforce "The Freedom of Choice" to choose consciousness to empower willpower to discipline the mind. For indeed this act is being performed to bring the doer into the "Heaven" that exists only in the "Present Time" and away from the "Hell," in which the mind is clouded with a Past or Future "I want".

3 THE BENEFIT OF PILGRIMAGES TO HOLY PLACES:

Without doubt, this is usually an uncomfortable travelling experience, which is known to impose a positive discipline and the bringing of the traveller into experiencing "Present Time", which is Gods world. It is also a journey which is usually unwillingly undertaken by the traveller, who will also perform HOLY RITES (Sacraments), these being that which are contained in many different religious practices. For indeed, all these self-imposed religious disciplines point towards the same trend, which is that no person who has faith in God's world should give preference to their own privately claimed world or to their personally mind-filling created selfish worlds or pursue their self-interested laws and to put these "I Want" laws above those that their wise ancients tell them truly exist in God's world. For undoubtedly all the wise sayings and suggested deeds of our wise ancients always honour and show a way to achieve a living only in God's world, this is being a world without thought and a world that exists only in the "Present Time".

But now is the time for the reader to know that in the beginning, you can silence the mind for a few seconds and look at the world that is all around you, this being the Heaven that rests in the "Present Time". For it is now also necessary to be constantly aware that the dark cloud of "I want" anticipations that are emanating from the "I Want" will of the five senses, will undoubtedly stop the Soul from seeing through a needed empty mind, and into God's world; the world of "Heaven" that genuinely, rests in the "Present Time"–and so to target the experiencing of "Enlightenment".

4 THE BENEFIT OF GIVING ALMS TO CHARITIES

These being charitable contributions to those in need but what we should now understand is that all prayers, all methods of worship, all times of fasting, all pilgrimages, all the performing of Holy Rites plus the giving of all Alms are all designed, in a disciplined way, to stop the five senses from activating an "I want", and so all the above actions are attempting to bring the doer into God's world that can only exist in the "Present Time", for this is being the world that can only exist in the "Present Time", which is Gods world. For indeed, the above are all "outer imposed" thinking practices which engage "consciousness" to redirect "willpower" from its previously allowed in childhood habit of "automatically" allowing the energy of a person's "willpower" previously released by "consciousness" to habitually obey the greed-filled "I want" needs of the "animalistic" five senses; which always fill the people mind with their never-ending "I want".

Therefore, it should now be known that the endeavours of all the above are various introductions to worship that have been installed by our wise ancients, to end and eventually stop the animalistic "I want" desires that have habitually been allowed to fill and so cloud the mind. This fact stops that person's Soul from witnessing the "Present Time", this without a doubt being Gods world.

5 THE BENEFIT OF MANTRA MEDITATION:

So Yes! Now it should again be known that the quickest and most secure way to find "Enlightenment", that which ALL our Earth religions and philosophies always seek for their followers, is to now, in modern-day terminology, mentally "choose" to discipline our "consciousness" to stop the energy of "willpower" from freely and "automatically" energising into the mind the "I Want" demands of our "animalistic" five senses. The reason for this much-needed correction is because in childhood we "habitually" informed our "consciousness" to accept immediately and so, via the "Freedom of Choice" we "Chose" to free our five senses to enter our minds, this truly being because in our childhood we thought they were "US", but they are NOT us, for our five senses are merely instruments for our bodies use. For truly we are the Soul whose job, via the God-given or Nature has given for the Non-Believer "Freedom of Choice," is to support the emerging Creation that is developing all around us but only in our "Present Time" that which "The Book" calls the real "Heaven" that we are all here to support.

So yes! It was in childhood that we mistakenly allowed our "Freedom of Choice" to free the "I Want" of the five senses to fully enter our mind with the totality of their never-ending "I Want" desires and honestly this was because we thought that they were US! But indeed, they are NOT us, for you cannot be that which you observe for we are truly the Soul, this being that which cannot die and which has everything and so needs nothing for it lives in a "Heaven" that truly exists, but only in the reality of the "Present Time". For is it not a well-known truth that only people have been given the "Freedom of Choice", this being because the same act can support or destroy the Godly emerging or Natures emerging "Heaven" for the Non-Believer, this being a "Heaven" that can only exist in the "Present Time", a time which people have been truly created to support. But this "Freedom of Choice" truth also factually means that people can "choose" to support a world of "Hell"? Therefore, is it not true that this is being a false world which is personally created by the mind-filling "I Want for ME" world, this being a world that is being created by the animalistic five senses and which is truly a Non-Existing Past or Future, which "The Book" calls a personally made Hell. For truly it can be said that these mind blocking "Hell" creating thoughts are blocking a person's Soul from seeing the "Present Time", this being the "Heaven" that truly exists upon our Earth? For sadly is not this "I Want for ME" a personally created world of Hell? For indeed this is being a self-created but non-existing "I Want" for me world that that in animals is usually a worldly need that can be created to only occur in the "Present Time", which is their "Heaven" that exists upon our earth. But in people does not this animalistic and mind filling "I Want for ME" world, this being that which is originating from our animalistic five senses, always fully cloud a person's mind, this being that fact which stops a person's Soul for seeing the world of the heavenly creation in which all life exists, this truly existing in that which we call the "Present Time", this truly being our "Heaven" that exists upon our earth. For now, it should be known that the purpose of mantra mediation, this being a mind-emptying exercise, is to return us to be enabled to view, via the Soul and so actively support the solidarity and unity of the heavenly creation which truly and steadily exist all around us, just has it does within us! For again and truly, is not our "Present Time" the "Heaven" in which we were birthed to live truly?

So yes! "Patient Meditation" will disciplinary correct this incorrect "I Want" behaviour, simply because the five senses are truly very "animalistic" in nature and so can to be trained into understanding, like our five wild pups previously mentioned, that they are fully protected under the care of the Soul, which "knowingly" understands that they used to possess us and did actually "animalistic-ally" guide us before we were given the "Freedom of Choice". For truly the "Freedom of Choice" was God-given or Nature gave for the Non-Believer, and this gift is that which indeed enables us to command our "consciousness" to engage "willpower" to "habitually" repeat, via "mediation", the sounding of a single word into the mind. For indeed, this is being an act that commands these "pups" to sound this single word and so be trained to stop their mind-filling " I Want" barking machinations, so truly, this is that which is "habitually" emanating from their undisciplined condition. So this act will eventually stop there uncontrolled "I Want for ME" demands and how to pursuits from filling the mind and a so allowing the Soul to see through the mind all that exists in the "Present Time".

For without a doubt this is a personal experience which firmly develops a mind empty condition which has been achieved via a "SOUL" imposed discipline which, via the "Freedom of Choice", can now silence the five senses, this being that which is a condition in which you will know that that which is observing all that can be observed is your "SOUL" in which you will positively know to be the real "YOU"!

So yes! Again it should be said, that this actual condition of the five senses controlling you, was because in your childhood you unknowingly, via this same "Freedom of Choice", did command "Consciousness" to allow your "Willpower" to energise into the mind all their "I Want" for ME thoughts, these being that sound which was genuinely emanating from the five senses. For again and it can be factually said that this occurred because we automatically allowed this to happen in our infancy when we "thought" that the noise in our minds was emanating from ourselves. But "scientifically", these thoughts cannot be us, for we are the Soul, the observer of these mind clouding thoughts and so the self-controlling and repetitive slow "sounding" of a single word into our mind will eventually and "disciplinary" stop and so eventually silence these "I want" desires emanating from our animalistic five senses.

So Yes! Eventually, after some disciplined time, the habitually allowed mind-filling words that were sounding from the five senses via the "automatic" permission willpower will fall away. The single worded mantra becomes "purposely" chosen by "consciousness" to direct "willpower" to sound in mind, just as it previously and automatically been chosen to "habitually" release into the mind the "I want" of the five senses? Now honestly, it must be said that this "Patient Meditation" endeavour can be likened to being as a war against the five senses and the single sounding word of the chosen mantra should ALWAYS be returned to immediately when other words "habitually" enter the mind, which they will. For indeed, when the single sounding word of the mantra becomes habitually automatic, this is when a person's Soul will be able to see through the spaces of the automatically sounding mantra, and so viewing that which our wise ancients called the "clouds of unknowing". These swirling clouds will eventually be seen to be a fact when "Consciousness" energises "Willpower" to sound into the mind the repeating mantra automatically. For undoubtedly this is an ancient act which "physically" begins to stop "willpower" from activating the "I want" that had historically and habitually, been previously allowed to flow into the mind the "I Want" that is continually emanating from the five senses; a fact which filled the mind and so blocked the Soul from seeing God's world – therefore this meditating target is to stop this false existence.

So yes! Then definitely indeed, the time will come when the "meditational practiser" recognises that the sounding of the mantra, by the five senses, has become "habitual" and "mechanically" repetitive and that the "meditator" now spends much of their meditational time seemingly staring with the eyes of their Soul into *"the clouds of unknowing"* which is simply the moving energy that exists in their still and empty mind, this being that which is seen between the space of the sounding mantra which the now disciplined five senses are obediently sounding.

For naturally, it is then that after many months of meditational repetition that the "practiser" of this meditation can open their eyes and by still automatically sounding their mantra can then experience their true self which is the observing Soul and this maybe for the first time. For surely, it is then that your Soul will see and also fully experiencing the wonders of the unmoving ever still "Present Time", this being that "Heaven" which is always all around you and evermore shall be so.

So yes! You can then eventually let the mantra fall away and so be stopped only to be called for when needed to be sounded, thus experiencing the real YOU, this being that which knowingly exists, but only in the "Present Time". For it is then that with this entirely still mind that you will truly experience God's world or the world of Nature for the Non-Believer, this being the actual world which only exists in the "Present Time", but be prepared, for it is then that you will also fully experience the real feeling of love and the existence of belonging to all that exists – this is indeed being "Enlightenment" but always understand that in these early days forgetting is our worst enemy.

So Yes! Now your continuing and practical efforts at stilling the mind has enabled your Soul to see through the empty mind and into the "Present Time", this is God's world and the world in which no personal "I want" can exist. For this are the target of ALL religious and philosophical songs, prayers, incantations, chants, mantras, conversations, doings, and also journeys, giving, eating, caring, loving and belonging. For truly, this is the sought-after "Enlightening" experience, which ALL our wise ancients have targeted in all the world's religions and philosophies. For it is indeed an illuminating experience, which can only happen to a "non-thinker" for "thinking" is ALWAYS the creation of a personal "I want," even if it is a want for others. Then eventually you will enter the stage where the only thing that can enter the mind may be the flash of a picture or of a useful memory which can be sent into the mind by the now dutiful and obedient five senses, this being that which will indicate to you a possible short-cut or a past flash of a memory of something useful for you to realise, in your current "Present Time" activities. For truly, it is known that many of our world's religions have endeavoured to describe this non-thinking experience in their cultural way but mostly by describing it as an experience that cannot be described, for it is the experience of being filled with God's world; a world that has been presented to all of the people and so it is certainly worth achieving; and also rest assured – it can be achieved for all people have a Soul which, because of God's gift of choice, needs to be "chosen" to be released because it is usually in prison surrounded by the "chosen" prison bars of an ever sounding "I want", this being that which is emanating from one or all of the five senses. Therefore the task is to still the mind with the surest way to accomplish this being via a Patient meditational practice, this being an advanced into modern times, ancient act that is known to change peoples allowed childhood habit, this being that childhood act which enabled consciousness to command willpower to automatically energise the animalistic "I want" to enter the mind from any or all of the five senses.

So yes! The best way to stop living in this false world of Hell is to engage in a single worded meditational based exercise in which consciousness is chosen to disciplinary command willpower to energise a single word into the mind, this being an exercise which blocks a previously freed willpower from habitually energising the release of an "I want," that is emanating from the greed of the animalistic five senses. This Patient meditational exercise is that which so stills the mind that the Soul is then enabled to "see" through the mind eighty or ninety per cent or eventually one hundred per cent of God's Heaven upon this world or the world of Nature for the Non-Believer, this being that which truly exists upon this world, but only in the "Present Time". For indeed, this is genuinely a significant fact; for it enables a person's Soul to obey the harmony seeking needs of the Creation, just as do the trillions of cells residing within the body do unselfishly obey the instructions of the inner body's needs and whose organizer of these inner deeds within our bodies is the Soul.

Therefore, let it be repeated that it is the singularity of the above Patient meditational "choice," which truly, brings the knowledge of "Enlightenment", this being that which is sought by all our world's religions and philosophies. For truly, it is a meditational practise that brings the enlightenment that was always targeted by our wise ancients, this being that act which allows a person's Soul to see through the still mind and so by this simple act also "sees" and experience the "Heaven" which rests upon this Earth, for truly this is a fact which also reveals God's "Present" to all people. It is also an "Enlightened" reality which allows a person to automatically behave in the "Present Time" like an enlarged "worldly" body part, this being that which automatically and without thinking, supports the harmony seeking needs of the Creation that also similarly exists within the singularity of a person's body. It is also with this new freedom that the Soul can fulfil its purpose which is to support God's laws or Natures laws of harmony and so aid this same loving pursuit of that which we call "The Creation". For truly, this is the way which ensures that as an "Enlightened" person, you will live in God's Heaven or Nature's world for the Non-Believer, this being an existence that truly rests upon this Heavenly Earth. It is a Heaven that has been blissfully created to be lived in- by YOU!

So yes! This "Enlightened" experience is often religiously and philosophically called *"the light within one's self"*, or it is also further been attempted to be explained by our wise ancients as the "sixth sense". For indeed this is a supposed intuitive faculty, said to give an awareness not explicable in terms of ordinary perception, but which has often described as "some sixth sense told him he was not alone," for, in Heaven, it is impossible to feel alone, for the pressure of love that is all around you is likened to a "being" within one's self.

So Yes! Now, let this following modern explanation be obvious: the explanation is that when the Soul looks through a still mind and into the world, it knows it to be Gods world or the world of Nature for the None-Believer, this being the Heaven that exists but on in in the "Present Time". It is then that the individual Soul sees that which needs to be done to support and help maintain the evolving harmony that exists in God's world. This insight is LOVE, and so you know that you cannot harm or be harmed by that which aids peopled and also that which you love, and which you know loves you.

So yes! It is also no secret that many peoples must have often experienced flashes of God's world or the world of Nature for the None-Believer, this is truly being the Heaven that rests in the "Present Time", and many people have achieved this entry into the "Present Time" and this also being many thousands of years ago. For indeed, our hunter-gatherers must have stared into fires or investigated the vastness of space and then seen, silently descending upon them, the experience of "Enlightenment" which ensued for them the *"Peace that surpasses all understanding"*. For assuredly, is it not true that many people who are currently living upon our Earth, have also experienced this brief glimpse of "Enlightenment," for example when looking into a fire made to keep them warm. But the most significant inaccuracy is when "Enlightenment" is categorised as a "Trance-Like State", which – it is certainly NOT. For such a state can only be imprisonment! Therefore, is it not also known to be true that it is possible to encounter this reality when staring into a fire or down a valley or across a lake and so experienced this sudden blissful, peaceful silence, which exists in the love that is God's world; a world that even our hunter-gatherers must have experienced?

So yes! It is to reach this world permanently and to also consistently live in this real world that "The Book" endeavours to engender within all people. For definitely, when going back in time to that period when worshipping of any religion or philosophy first started, you will find data which will show that even during prehistoric times, older civilizations used repetitive and rhythmic chants during the many offerings to their personally made Gods. It is also true that you will often most likely become aware of the religious context in which praying was first known to be practised – all of which were religious and philosophical exercises that targeted "Enlightenment". For unquestionably and honestly, many people have had the experience of being only aware of the "Present Time", a time which contains no Past or Future and which is truly God's world or the world of Nature for the Non-Believer. For the reality is that this is the "Heaven" which is the reality that rests upon our Earth, and it is a task that is worth achieving for it certainly takes you out of Hell, this being that which can only exist in a thought created Past or Future.

68. ONLY LIVES LIVED IN THE "PRESENT TIME" CAN ACHIEVE "ENLIGHTENMENT"

Where is the "Present Time" and where do you find IT? Did not the "Mother of the Creation" inform everyone with her words when she spoke through Jesus saying in Luke 18:2-5 "The Parable of the Persistent Widow", this being the parable which was to show all people how to reach the "Present Time" where God's Justice or Natures Justice for the Non-Believer does reside, and also this is the only place where a person can experience "Enlightenment", For indeed this message was revealed when She spoke to Her only Child through Her only child saying "Once upon a time, there was a magistrate in a town who had neither fear of God nor respect for his fellow-men. There was a widow in the town that kept coming to him, saying, 'Please protect me from the man who is trying to ruin me.' And for a long time, he refused. But later he said to himself, 'Although I don't fear God and have no respect for men, yet this woman is such a nuisance that I shall give judgment in her favour, or else her continual visits will be the death of me'!" To which the "Mother of the Creation", speaking through Jesus also said: Luke 18:6-8 – "Notice how this dishonest magistrate behaved. Do you suppose God, patient as He is, will not see justice done for His chosen, (Children) who appeal to him day and night? I assure you he will not delay in seeing justice done." Therefore, it is clearly shown that it is very wise for a person to pray and so meditate in a regular effort which "The Book" explains has been likened to a person saying, "Please protect me from desires emanating from a past and a future which is a "Self-Created" Hell, and so allow me to live only in the "Present Time" – God's world of a "Self-Realised" Heaven." Therefore, is it not also useful to understand the correct "creed" that will accomplish this task? Also is it not persistently correct that ALL our wise ancients introduced many different creeds, based upon the known culture of their followers, which are now established in many of our world's culturally different religions and philosophies.

So yes! To pray is to meditate, this being that which factually stops the mind, via a "Soul-Imposed" discipline, from creating a false "I Want" for me world which truly is self-created perjury that is believed to be correct, but which is not valid. So the purpose of "Patient Meditation" has with all meditations and prayers, is to quickly bring the "seeker" to exist only in the "Present Time", where all God's laws or the laws of Nature for the Non-Believer are truly realised and so really experienced.

So yes! There are many different "meditational" based creeds for they are as numerous as our many different religions, but "scientifically," it can now be clearly and sincerely stated that our wise ancients introduced their culturally creed-based chants, hymns and prayers to make their believers perform a task that would take their minds away from many a past or future "I Want", and so they targeted a way to bring their followers minds into the "Present Time", for this is undoubted, God's world or the world of Nature for the Non-Believer. For unquestionably, many did achieve this for was it not said that the disciples of Jesus appeared as if a light was shining inside them, as many prayers and worshippers throughout our world also described those who had become "Enlightened" – so how was this achieved? For assuredly, many of the cultures of our world have changed. So there is now a modern way to "Enlightenment" that can easily be explained, for this is undoubted because of our modern understanding of the ways people and also the world that exists around us. For "scientifically," it can now be stated that it was not the words that existed in the world's many hundreds of culturally based chants, hymns and prayers that created within many of our creed based worshippers that which is known as "Enlightenment". For factually it was called "Enlightenment"   because it seemingly brings light to shine within a person who pursues religious or philosophically imposed disciplines based upon right wordings and or right actions, for definitely, there is knowing light that seems to shine within them.

What is now being put forward by "The Book" is that "Enlightenment" can be eventually achieved by "habitually" and "automatically" repeating the chanting of any disciplinary imposed and so "accepted" words or repetitive acts which have no applied internal "thought" filling creative "I Want" for ME energy attached to them – especially when they are silently and disciplinary performed and so become automatically habitual to the doer? It is this automatically imposed "praying" or "chanting" which enables the Soul to see within the still mind, especially when the eyes are closed, the "clouds of unknowing," which is the experiencing of the Soul seeing into the energy of an empty and still mind. For truly, this is happening because the five senses are being self-disciplined via consciousness empowering willpower to "automatically" perform a chosen religion or a philosophical outer imposed discipline. For indeed this is being the fact which seemingly becomes a "habitual" non-thinking incantation or action, thus "eventually" enabling the soul to "automatically" see into the silent mind, this being the fact which occurs when the mechanically imposed religious or philosophical incantations take place, for indeed these "Five Pups", likened to be the five senses, can be trained. Therefore it is also factually accurate that when the eyes were opened - the Soul would then see through the empty mind and so directly into God's world which is truly that which can only exist in the "Present Time" and this is an experience called "Enlightenment," for there is no past and no future; only God's world or the world of Nature for the Non-Believer. But sadly, many would unknowingly leave this experience, as they moved back into the mind clouding "I Want" for ME world, this being that which was all around them.

So yes! With this knowledge, it can now be understood why some of our wise ancients reduced all creeds to a simple Mantra Meditation, which is based upon a single word and which is, therefore, the most useful way to "automatically" empty the mind of all thoughts, this being to accept just this one chanting word, which quickly becomes habitual, and so requires no "I Want" energy to repetitively sustain it in mind. Therefore, yes, this is, without doubt, the most successful way of "praying," which is a popular creed way to aid mental and spiritual development. Therefore, yes, it is known that this "habitual" method needs no mind-filling energy to sustain it, and it is also the most well-known proven task to bring about "Enlightenment" eventually. For truly, this an empty state of mind which brings to people the experience of only that which "Just is", which is a gifted creation that was seeded by God. For you will eventually reach a stage in which you do not habitually sound the mantra, and the mind remains still, and silent and so observes with eyes closed the clouds of unknowing – which is the empty mind. Then, with eyes open, you will also FULLY experience that which "Just is," this being the "Present Time", which is called "Enlightenment" for no thoughts of an "I Want" future, exists to cloud your vision of Gods world which can only exist in the "Present Time".

So yes! Indeed, this is also the surest way to experience "justice;" for justice is that which "Just is," and what "Just is" can only be experienced in the "Present Time", and therefore it should also be known that the entity within people that witnesses this "Just is," is that which is known to be the Soul. Unquestionably, this is certainly the only entity that can truly, say *"I am who I am"* - which makes the famous words *"I think therefore I am"* as being incorrect. For the truth is that that which observes the "Present Time" can never attach an "I Want" thought to that which it observes because this changes the truth of the observation. For the truth is that which silently observes the "Present Time", cannot pursue an "I Want" thought, this being that which comes from the past or the future. For the reality of the Soul is that it "knows" that it already has everything that exists within the Creation for the Soul also knows that it must care for all the life and non-life that surrounds it, which is the "Creation".

So Yes! To truly, understand these words one should listen to the words that the "Mother of the Creation" spoke through Jesus, whose body was certainly beyond "Enlightenment" for indeed He was certainly "self-realised" for He knew that He was the unified Soul of all life and non-life. So it was His Soul now knowingly personified as the Creation, who spoke these words: *"I am the bread of life. He who comes to me will never go hungry, and he who believes in me will never be thirsty."* For indeed, this is the Soul which is unified with the Creation of all that exists speaking, and which says through Jesus: *"I am the bread of life"* and also *"I am the living bread that came down from heaven. If anyone eats of this bread, he will live forever. This bread is my flesh, which I will give for the life of the world."* Jesus is talking about the Soul being the "Bread of Life", which is undoubtedly the "God's Creation" which rests within and without ALL people, and especially when you hear His words saying: *"I am the light of the world. Whoever follows me will never walk in darkness but will have the light of life."* This light is the universal Soul speaking to people and the bread being spoken of is the Creation which is "Everything", so the Soul is clearly explained as being has one with the Creation that exists upon this Earth, this being that which includes all life and non-life.

So yes! Indeed, the Soul of people can never attach any "I Want" values, based upon past or future thoughts; for the Soul can only experience and so "live" in the "Present Time". Without doubt, this is the "Present Time" time in which can only exist "Justice," meaning "Just is". For truly, any personally thought "I Want" for ME is that which creates an individually based personality that this is not "justice," for it is stated by our wise ancients to be personal stealing and so changing the harmony which is all around you and which is also continually endeavouring to emerge all around you. Therefore, is it not also true that these "I Want" mind filled personally claiming thoughts are truly emanating from the past and which are thoughts that always physically target the future and so constantly endeavours to corrupt that which exists in the "Present Time". Therefore, is it not true that a person, in ignorance, is painting within their mind, the thoughts of how to steal the harmony of that which exists in the "Present Time", this truly being Gods world or the world of Nature for the Non-Believer.

So Yes! Can it not also clearly be seen that with all this paint that people can cover over the existence of the "Present Time", a person will never understand nor truly, see the "Heavenly" justice that exists unchangingly all around them? Sadly, could it not be said that they will never experience the real world in which they live, and which is genuinely a world which will bring to them the *"peace that surpasses all understanding"*, this being the happiness and contentment that is their birthright. Again is it not also clearly seen as being true that no "I Want" personal thought can be attached to the "Present Time", without a desire to change it, thus making the "Present Time" fake and not real?

So Yes! Is it not well to understand that the "Present Time" is when God or Nature for the Non-Believer is also beginning to create the future; for truthfully the stillness of the "Present Time" cannot be changed by anyone? For unquestionably truly this is being that "Nature" which is all-around a person, and evermore shall be so. For indeed God's eventual target will not be changed by one jot, for it will always return to its ongoing purpose – so be warned those who inflict punishment upon others to acquire their own "I Want", this is because the purpose of God's creation can do strange things to those who knowingly disobey it.

So yes! Justice or "Just is" is the "Present Time". The time of a pure Heaven that rests upon this Earth. For certainly is it not also true that even in the justice system, this being that which is created by people, that any stealing is known to be based upon an "I Want" and this is regarded as "illegally" breaking the harmony of a community that is made by people? For naturally, do not all our wise ancients say that the "I Want" being pursued by many people, is not the "justice" that exists within the Creation, for the justice spoken of by Jesus can only be experienced when one attaches themselves to the "Present Time", this being the "Present Time" which is the Kingdom of God or Nature for Non-Believers. For certainly is it not true that all people "scientifically" recognise that it is within this unmoving "Present Time" that all God's plans or Nature's plans for the Non-Believer can come to pass. Undoubtedly, this is also why our wise ancients always explained that living in the "Present Time" is "Enlightenment," which is truly an experience that can be realised, for it does exist. It is also an exactness of that which happens when a person truly understands that they are living in harmony, with all that exists around them, This is the same harmony that is activated for all life and non-life; thus making "Enlightenment" a "scientific" truth which can be experienced and it is forever waiting for those who endeavour to attain it!

So yes! The stillness of mind is the real experiencing "Enlightenment", and this can be attained by a mantra or any prayer or hymn, this being that which all our religions and philosophies target to be done, this being when you endeavour to experience the world of God or Nature for the Non-Believer. Without any doubt, this is the "Present Time", which is VERY beautiful and VERY peaceful for you can undoubtedly experience the *"peace that surpasses all understanding"*, this being an actual realisation, for when you are in the "Present Time", you can be assured that you will "experience" this

"Enlightenment", which again must be said is the *"peace that surpasses all understanding,"* and which you will also realise that you are in the company of God when experiencing you being the only child, which is the Creation and also that which is in knowing called the Holy Ghost, which is the "Present Time", this being factually "Self-Realised" when becoming the only child, which is the "Creation". It is then that you will physically realise that you are has one with the trinity, this being that which supports the Soul. Therefore, let this feeling of peace be your sought treasure, for eventually, your heart will also be there, and this can be described as the "Bread of Life," this being that which that Jesus often spoke.

So yes! The reason for experiencing this *"peace that surpasses all understanding,"* is because the problems of the past and the future do not exist in the "Present Time"; for it is your constant thinking, and you're self-creating of a personal "I Want" that takes you into isolation and away from God's "Present Time". Simply put, when experiencing the "Present Time," the thinking of an "I Want," becomes none existing for these "I Want" thoughts cannot exist in the "Present Time", for if they do, it is then you are not truly experiencing the "Present Time".

So Yes! Now *"those who have ears to hear"* will fully understand just which Jesus was explaining when He said: *"Martha, my dear, you are worried and bothered about providing so many things. Only a few things are needed, perhaps only one. Mary has chosen the best part, and you must not take it away from her!"* Jesus was explaining that Mary was in the "Present Time", this is a time without thoughts of the past or the future, which also means that the expensive oil that she washed Jesus's feet with, had no value to her, for the "Present Time" has no values, for there can be no additional added value to God's "Present" and Mary was living in the present, which is genuinely our Heaven upon Earth. So indeed can this not now be said to be "scientifically" valid?

So YES! The living in God's "Present Time" can be likened to living your life in Heaven? An example being likened to playing in a great orchestra, in which you are a player and tunefully playing your part in the harmony that exists all around you? Could it not also be said that all people are players in this orchestra and that many people can play magnificently together and mostly in harmony – for they certainly have "chosen" to do so. Could it not also be said that only one person is listening in the audience, this is our God or "No Thing", which is God's name given by the Non-Believer, who believes in "Nothing". Would it not also be correct to say that God is the producer of the orchestra, but that God is a producer who never interferes with the rehearsing of music or the music that is played to an audience? The reason for this is that He knows that every player has been given comprehensive training, and also has perfect musical knowledge and that in rehearsals they can even choose the instrument they are best suited to play in the current "freestyle" method which can be likened to various groups playing in harmony together - especially the "Enlightened" ones.

Of course, the conductor is the "Mother of the Creation", who sees and knows that all the people within the orchestra are a single unified life form which is also Her only child, just as non-Enlightened people see, within each person, a single individual life form, even though it consists of many different, unified parts that also work in true supporting harmony, like any orchestra; for genuinely the "Mother of the Creation" does care for this only child, which also includes all the people who exist upon planet Earth. For it is undoubtedly true that it is the "Mother of the Creation" who is the actual conductor of all life and non-life and it is She who controls the various harmonies of all the large and small groups and is even "She" who is responsible for that which everyone is playing. It is also Her baton that can be likened to that which supports and expands the harmony of the music coming from the various sections of the orchestra, who make their music louder, and the individual groups become more considerable. Again truly, it is she who makes the music quieter or louder and the groups smaller or larger, while always encouraging valuable new inputs of trending harmony seeking music players with her "Sugar in the Water".

Under these conditions, it could also be described that sometimes, within the group in which you are "playing", a group player hits a wrong note which sounds a discord. The question now do you stop playing, and scream at them, telling them that they are doing wrong or do you smile to yourself and keep playing in harmony with the rest of the group, knowing that the positive example of harmony which is all around you and within you, will bring this discordant player back to understanding the harmony now being played successfully and tunefully by the group.

But now imagine that you and your entire group is playing music created by Mozart when suddenly a member of the group starts to play free-style-Jazz? Do you scream at them? Chastise them? Tell them that they are wrong? Tell them to go away? Or do you just become angry with them and shout at them to "get in line" and so willfully organise others to replace them thus throwing them out of the group, particularly if you understand that the "conductor" of the orchestra was simply ignoring them? Or do you remember that it is a known truth that the Divine Mother, or the "composer" in this epistle, cannot punish or chastise anyone because ALL have been given the "Freedom of Choice" and our Divine Mother will never contradict Her Husbands plans for the "Future" for, in contrast, She has controlling care of the "Present" a unifying fact which God will never contradict? But indeed, this fact also rests within people who also have the same individually based "Freedom of Choice", a fact which can make it difficult for people to be faithful all the time. For certainly life can throw at people many needed commitments yet love is always a unified experiencing the "Present" and "Future" needs - for indeed it should be understood that "Love" is the experiencing of a unified existence that can exist only in the "Present Time". Therefore, is it not also seen to be true in our "Present Time," that in the life of people a man and wife singularity can be troubled when this "Nature" is forgotten, and forgetting is our worst enemy? This troublesome forgetting being that man is motivated by "Future" needs and that a woman is motivated by

"Present Time" needs and of course, the word "woman" is the shortened version of "Whole-Man". For assuredly, it can be naturally realised that woman cares for the needs of the "Present Time", which is the only time that truly exists and it is only in the "Present Time" that man can bring "Future" needs; this unity is a critical practice, for indeed that which "We Need" is very different from a personal "I Want"? For indeed these "I Want" problems will arise if the woman says to the man *"This window needs painting"* for it would be wiser to say *"Do you think that this window needs painting?"* To which natures answer emanating from the man, would be *"Yes! Which colour would you like?"* For God or Nature for the Non-Believer did give to all people "The Freedom of Choice," which is the negative or positive variable that is needed to support the ever-changing harmony of the emerging and ever-developing Creation?

Now, regarding our emerging free-style Jazz player who has started playing Jazz while you and all around are playing music created by Mozart? How would you feel if you saw the "conductor", who is likened to be the Divine "Mother of the Creation", is then seen to point Her baton at the energetic jazz player and waved for him or her to play their freestyle Jazz music much louder, even while still sitting amongst all the Mozart players? Also, how would you begin to feel if many others in the group dropped Mozart and began playing free-style-Jazz alongside you and other existing Mozart players? Beware of "Institutional Denial" which attacks those who "unofficially" go against a developing group's personally seeking harmony, for surely it is more purposeful to find the reason why this change is happening!

There is also an interesting question to ask here: "Where does the "Mother of the Creation", who is also in this example the conductor of the orchestra, see what is needed to continue the harmony which exists within this orchestra of life?" Is it the music being played or the player that needs Her endeavouring support? Of course, it is the player, for what player can bring harmony to a Creation that is always existing or constantly endeavouring to exist in harmony all around them, especially if they cannot bring it to themselves.

Is it not also an excellent example that the orchestral "music" being played, this being that which Jesus silently suffered at the end of His teaching, which was terrible torture which also included a nailed crucifixion all about which He never complained and whose last words were: ***"Forgive them, for they know not what they do!"*** Are these words not stunningly accurate! For was not Jesus endeavouring to persuade all people to acknowledge the harmony that was struggling to emerge all around them! Was this not also a truth because Jesus certainly knew, as did all our wise ancients, that the direction of the Creation cannot be stopped?

So Yes! All people had come a long way from an emerging time when cave family loved or fought another cave family, for now, it is also being seen to be coming true that ALL the countries of the North of the Northern Hemisphere are struggling to become sufficiently "harmonised," by countries that are all seeking their majority rule. For, without doubt, all these different language based countries are currently seeking a way to overcome a problem created by a country, such as the UK which has so many variable and different parties for which to vote. It is this strangeness which enables the successful ruling party to be supported only by a small minority of voting people. So yes, this is a sure way to encourage discord and strife within these countries. So yes! Beware of "institutional denial," this being that which attacks those who "unofficially" or "officially" go against a minority ruling party's "I Want".

69. HOW PATIENT MEDITATION FREES THE SOUL

Consciousness is that the part of the human being that is capable of transcending animal instincts, this being that which exists in all life but indeed it is only to people that God or Nature for the Non-Believer, gave the "Freedom of Choice!" For assuredly, it is not the same simple choice given to all our Earthborn life forms, whose only choice is mainly to care for their loved ones and the obtaining of food and of course for procreation. It should also be known that it is only a person's Soul that also has the job to decisively "Choose" to get your body to act in supporting the continuing evolving of harmony which is developing in the "Present Time", this being a "Present Time" which your Soul can only "realise" and so evaluate when seeing through a silent mind.

This silent mind means that your Soul never has any past or future needs and so can only perform harmonising acts in support of God's world, or the world of Nature for the Non-believer, this being that which can only exist in the "Present Time" and whose ongoing ever-developing harmony is also controlled and birthed by the "Mother of the Creation". For it is "She" who actively and spiritually controls the ever-developing harmony of Her only child; which is the ever-growing and never still, that which we call "The Creation". For it is only "She" who also seeks to be knowingly aided by the "Freedom of Choice", that God gave to all people. But it should be understood that the "Mother of the Creation" cannot control or demand harmony seeking actions from her children, for all people have been given freedom of "choice," a fact in which forgetting is our worst enemy.

So Yes! The known way of remembering is to acknowledge that an individual's Soul, this being that which rests only within people, needs the occupied bodies mind to be without thoughts. Therefore it is essential to "choose" to make the mind still and so it is essential to be without any "I Want" thoughts which clouds the mind and so stops the Souls view of the "Present Time". For it is certainly true that only people have been Godly given or Nature has given for Non-Believer "The freedom of choice", which is an activity used by people to consciously and actively support the work of the "Mother of the Creation", for all know that one act can support the merging Creation. Still, in other circumstances, the same act can destroy it, which also explains the reason as to why only people have been gifted with the "Freedom of Choice".

This freedom of "choosing" is also needed to accept the directions given by the occupying Souls "knowing", this being a knowing which silently develops, via a person's consciousness, to be a much-needed condition. For it is a condition that will support and so allow the Soul to see through the unclouded mind harmoniously, all there is to see in God's evolving heaven, this being that which exists only in the "Present Time". Thus bringing into existence the personal reason why only people have the "Freedom of choice", this being to act or not to act, even unto their death, as we saw in Jesus of the Christian faith, this being when He went to the cross and said *"Forgive them for they know not what they do"* but now all readers of "The Book" know what to do, this being to still the mind so that no "I Want for ME, can exist.

So yes! It is this stilling the mind fact which also enables the all-knowing unifying Soul, this being that which your body carries has also does the bodies of all people, to silently evaluate and so decisively "Choose" the best way to support the on-going needs of our ever-developing ever-growing world. Unquestionably, this being that world which truly and physically exists all around our Soul and so just as your Soul "automatically" performs the needed harmony that exists within your own body; it also endeavours to support the same harmony to that which exists in the world around you. For indeed only the harmony that holds together the whole of the "Creation" can and should exist in the "Present Time", this being that world that exists outside you which is also intended to exist with the same harmony has the world that exists within you. Naturally, this truly is the purpose of your all-knowing soul, and it certainly lives connected to the world that "The Book" calls "Heaven", this being that which rests upon our Earth, but only in the "Present Time". For it can again be said that it is this "stillness", this being that which rest within all peoples never wanting Soul, this being that which can certainly be experienced with an un-clouded and unthinking mind. For this is first being that "Self-Aware" experience which can be eventually created by any individual meditational "choosing" consciousness to "re-program" and therefore "re-discipline" our ancient animal-based willpower from automatically allowing "I Want" thoughts from entering the mind. For it is this animalistic mind-filling clamouring which "fills" and "clouds" the mind which stops the Soul from seeing and so experiencing the creation that can only exist in the "Present Time". Therefore, certainly indeed the "Soul" cannot see the "Creation" that exists all around it through such an emotionally cloud-filled "I Want" for ME clouded mind. These being the "I Want" anciently based animalistic thoughts that are emanating from the five senses but which can now be disciplinarily stopped, via mediation, from habitually clouding the mind. For it should now be known that this factual clouding of the mind is created by a continually emanating very personal "I

Want" that is born from our animalistic five senses, which "The Book" explains to be the living in an animalistic "personally" created "I Want for ME" Hell, which can be falsely created by people. For this self-made Hell is an individually based "I Want" which stops their holistically based Soul, this being that which is controlled by the same discipline has that which exists within all parts of our body, from seeing through the mind and out into the world of the "Present Time", which must be accepted in its totality rather than just its parts. For assuredly, it is these "I want" mind filling thoughts which are coming from the five senses that are enabled to arise from our ancient "animalistic" nature, this being when we were driven by physical appetites rather than spiritual needs. It is this ancient based "animalism" which enables people to "choose" to be hurt from a past un-obtainable "I Want", and so they leave the harmony that only people can create because factually people always have the "Freedom of choice" resting within them, for God has given, or Nature has given for the Non-believer the ability to control our actions just as we control our hands and our legs.

So Yes! Is it not true that sad thoughts, emanating from the five senses, do seek to automatically explode their "I want" needs into the minds of people? So, therefore, is it not beneficial to understand that an "individual" person's task is to establish a clear "silent" mind, which allows the Soul to see God's world or the world of Nature for the Non-Believer. For certainly is it not also seen that in this actual holistic world, this being the world in which people have been Godly or Nature has given for the Non-Believer, a "Freedom of choice", this being so that they can simply live to support the many variable needs of the ever-evolving ever stillness of a "Creation" that can only exist in the "Present Time"? Therefore, is it not our heavenly given "Freedom of choice", this truly being that which enables only people to naturally and unthinkingly perform any activity that will "Heavenly" support the harmony evolving tasks that are required to endorse the originating needs of "Mother of the Creation"; these being Her freely birthed needs that can only be performed in the Heaven that exists in Earths "Present Time", with Hell being the past or a future personally created "I want" for myself illusionary world. For indeed, this is a false illusionary world which can only be created by people, for sure, they are free to use their God-given which enables only people to be able to create or destroy the world that exists around them, but only in the "Present Time". But where is the purpose of a heavenly given "Freedom of Choice" going if it is not being chosen to make still a person's mind, this being an act which is factually needed to allow the Soul to support the needs of the harmony that is earthly emerging or trying to emerge, all around it, just as it activates, and so controls the harmony seeking needs within the body to which is it attached? Sadly, it seems that people have forgotten that they have been "Heavenly" given the "Freedom of choice" so has to enable them to purposely assist the harmony creating work of the "Mother of the Creation" and so live in the Heaven that truly exists within the "Present Time" upon our Earth; Yet sadly, is it not true that this God-given or Nature has given for the Non-Believer, freedom of choice, has also been used by some people to allow the energy of "willpower" within their body to be falsely, totally and greedily used by their animalistic five senses? Is it not this fact which allows their animalistic nature to be habitually and painfully energised to chase the many mind-filling "I want" activities that the five senses are always craving for, just as they do for all creatures that live in the animal world? For indeed this seems factual because many peoples seem to have misplaced their real purpose and so now "choose" to live in a self-created mind thinking "Hell", this being because, just as previously stated, they have chosen to allow the freed willpower to allow the five senses to dominate and fill their mind. After all, they think, like our lower animals, that the five senses are themselves.

So Yes! It is again useful to repeat that the Soul cannot direct or manage consciousness nor enforce, direct or change any activity that is taking place outside the people body for God or Nature for the Non-Believer truly, gave people the freedom of choice and no energy that exists within the Creation can take that away from people. It is this "forgotten" fact which allows the five senses to fill the people mind with their constant planning of a way to achieve their own personal greedily but never satisfied "I want" desires, usually to be taken from others or stolen from God's Nature. Therefore, it is this constant planning of an "I want" which keeps the five senses filling the mind with wished-for past or future events, which absorbs all the energy of peoples "consciousness," so that the people cannot use this energy to still the mind. Indeed, this is the only act that allows the Soul to see the outer world so that it can silently activate any support needed by the harmony that is continuously endeavouring to evolve within the Creation. For indeed, this must is the reality of the "Freedom of choice" given by God to all people, which is also acknowledged by the "Mother of the Creation" who cannot request any person to support Her harmony seeking actions for all the Creation must obey God's laws which have purposely given to all people the "Freedom of Choice". For again can it not be said that this truly is the fact which enables people to choose their actions or inactions and nothing that exists within the "Creation" can take that "Freedom of Choice" from them and even torture, inflicted by people who are newly emerged from the animal kingdom, can take away that "Freedom of Choice" from them. For was this, not factually proved by the Christian religions Jesus when He was forced to the cross and of course also many of our wise ancients who would not be stopped from speaking this truth, even unto death. Indeed, this is also being the reason why people cannot be punished by God's law or Natures law for the Non-Believer, for is it not clearly stated in many religions and philosophies that any selfish "I want" act that creates disharmony is immediately forgiven by God or the "Mother of the Creation"? Because truly is it not a saying by our wise ancients that these punishers, ***They know not what they do",*** but they do now, for sure, this is a historical truth. Still, it is certainly not now genuinely known by the reader of "The Book", for sure "The Book" clearly and carefully explains that the purpose of a person's life is to support the God based or Nature-based "Heaven" that can only exist in the "Present Time". For truly it can no longer be "unknown" or be "ignored" by the reader, this being that which many people can and do has they "inharmoniously" support themselves in a personally created "I Want" for ME world, this being a self-satisfying area of an often enforced continuing personal activity, which tends to think that violence against violence will control violence. In essence, it does not, for it ALWAYS creates it, but more of this later in "The Book".

So yes! Has it is revealed by "The Book" that instead of personally living-in and also supporting a Heaven-based harmony that exists or is continually striving to exist upon this Earth, many people live in the Hell of a personal self-inflicted "disharmony," which is indeed living in Hell while in their current existence upon this Earth. For this is a known condition that is self-created by all people who break God's laws or the laws of Nature for the Non-Believer, for indeed, this is also an activity which can be likened to a driver who ignores all "highway code" trafficking laws. So when ignoring these and while passing through a traffic control red light, which results in them, having a severe accident, they then say, "Why am I being punished like this?" The real question now is "Who is punishing who?"

So Yes! Indeed, it can be understood (stood-under) that a person's "Freedom of Choice" is Godley gave, or Nature has given for the Non-Believer. It is not a freedom of choice which is given by a person's Soul, this being that part of us that enables us to be aware of ourselves. For indeed, our Soul is an essence of life which is eternal, and its' spirit lies outside and also inside the physical parameters of the Creation or Nature for Non-Believer. Moreover, that which is most important to understand is that the Soul, this being that which manages the unity of all that which is within the body, has also been created to manage directly, via the use of its inhabited body, the unification of the world around it. For indeed, this is done by using "consciousness" to view through the empty mind the activities that are emerging in the static, unmoving "Present Time", a time in which the Future and the Past do not exist.

Yet sadly, this "Freedom of Choice" can now be mistakenly energised into our minds by our animal-based "Willpower" who's anciently based "animalistic" target is to want everything for itself. For indeed this is that which factually happened in our childhood when the Godly given, or Nature has given for the Non-Believer "Freedom of Choice" is being used to allow "Willpower" the ability to habitually bypass "Consciousness" with the many

"I Want for Me" demands, all of which are animalistic based. For truly, this was because that which spoke to us in our mind we "thought" was the real US, but yes, it is known that you cannot be separate from that to which you listen. For truly it is "Self-Experienced" that the Soul is that which "factually" knows, via its inhabited bodies "consciousness", that all people are "Non-dualistic" and so exist in unity, this is being a truth in which our wise ancients primarily referred to has been a personally developed state of consciousness in which the clash of "thinking" that you are separate from that which is around you, can be cancelled via mediation. Therefore in an actual "Self-Reality", you become "everything". For faithfully in the "Now Time" your consciousness knows that you are not a separate entity from the creation that exists all around you, just as you are not separate from that which is also within you and whose unified totality truly exists. Therefore all life and none-life can be self-experienced to be the real and only YOU!

So yes! It was in childhood that we mistakenly used our God-given or Nature given for the Non-Believer "Freedom of Choice". This being to free our ancient animalistic "I Want" and so enabled it to commandingly emanate from the animalistic "Willpower" that is controlled by our five senses and not our Soul controlled "Consciousness". This being that "scientific" decision which now commits many people to habitually and personally target the mind-filling thoughts of our always demanding animalistic five senses, this being self-created to personally seek out and so obtain their own animalistic "I Want for ME". Or we can again "Choose" via our "Freedom of choice", to similarly empower the need to hold the mind empty and still, which is an act that allows the Soul to clearly see through the still unclouded mind and into the harmonising needs of the outer world that exists all around it but only in the "Present Time", this being the Heaven that exists upon our earth.

So yes! It is also after this accomplished "meditational" mind-emptying act, which can take some time, that a person's "Freedom of choice" will stop their "Willpower" from pursuing their childhood allowed "mind-filling" five senses from habitually filling their mind with an "I want" that is continually emanating from one or all the five senses, who in childhood they believed was them; They are not "Them" for you cannot be that which you observe in mind, this is truly being a mind clouding "I want" world called "Hell" which imaginary exists in a non-existing Past or Future. For it is a dreamed non-real world that is continuously being created by one or all of the animalistic five senses and it is this which stops a person's Soul from seeing and participating in the world of Heaven, this being that which can only exist in the "Present Time".

So yes! A meditational exercise is that which again uses the "Freedom of Choice" to directly command "consciousness" to re-direct "willpower" to stop its previously allowed sounding into the mind their ever-demanding "I

Want for ME", this is being that activity which is continuously and "mind-cloudily" emanating from the bodies ancient animalistic five senses. For indeed this meditational exercise is to automatically assist the Soul's honest abilities to see into the Present Time and so support God's Creation or Nature's Creation for the Non-Believer and, if necessary, redirect an emerging evolving natural law into a direction that would enhance and so free it to act in accordance to Gods emerging laws or Nature's emerging laws for the Non-Believer, this is being that which can only be genuinely "realised" in the "Present Time".

For indeed this is the fact as to why only people have been given the "Freedom of Choice" so that the Soul can observe and if necessary "choose" actions which will silently assist the evolving laws of God's Creation or natures Creation for the Non-Believer. For rightly, the Souls only purpose is to automatically support the harmony seeking needs of "Present Times" evolving Creation. However, for these chosen acts to develop, a still unclouded mind is required to see and so support the harmony that is Godly or naturally endeavouring to emerge all-around people.

So Yes! Why did God or Nature for the Non-Believer, give only to people the "Freedom of Choice? Is this not because the same personally chosen act that once assisted the emerging harmony of the Creation could, on another occasion, be an act that could destroy the emerging harmony. Maybe this "personal choice" has also been given by God because God, like all Fathers, wants to be loved by His children as does the "Mother of the Creation" who I believe is that which is called Nature by the Non-Believer.

70 THE WAY TO MEDITATE INTO GOD'S KINGDOM ON THIS EARTH

Before we start this disciplined, repetitive, inner-mind-sounding, single worded, self-created, and "un-thinking" exercise, this being the next needed advancement which follows the aforementioned two-minute exercise in which you have sat and experienced your weight upon the chair and thus targeted the reality of having no thoughts in mind. It is well to know that this creed based exercise is the repeating of a single word being sounded in mind. This sounding is being an activity which knowingly targets that which our entire creed based religions and philosophies target and it is to target a reality that will bring the doer to the experience of "Enlightenment," or being known by many religions and philosophies as living in the "Kingdom of Heaven" or the "World of Nature" for the Non-Believer.

It should be further understood that this personal "Enlightenment" seeking activity is an activity in which only "one word" is, therefore, being repeated in mind, and it is not a group activity. For the bonhomie of others is not sought or desired to be experienced, as it can be in churches or during meetings and sermons, etc., these being active seeking congregational meetings which are founded upon the seeking of love and friendship that can emanate from an excellent religious gathering with others, for certainly all religious and philosophical meetings are only to remind you who and what you are.

So yes! This solitary and silent inner mind repeating exercise is best performed in isolation. Still, of course, it can be practised within a group of like-minded people, which can be welcoming support in the early days. It may also be useful to understand that this secret sounding creed-based word is called a "mantra" by our Hindu and Buddhist cousins, and it means a repeating song. It is also known to be the quickest way to "personally" experience a life lived in a constant state of harmony with that which is all that is around you in the world that is called the "Present Time" in which no Past or Future can exist. For sincerely the "meditational practiser" eventually becomes "lovingly" as one with creation, this being that which exists all around them just has it exists within them and which seemingly returns this love - for the Heaven that exists upon our Earth exists only in the "Present Time," the only real existence in which all life and all non-life do exist. The single "mantra" word that "The Book" has chosen is a Sanskrit word, which is a religious and philosophical language from the ancient religious times of over three thousand five hundred years ago, but which was a parochial word denied by the management of the religions of the Northern Hemisphere up until modern times.

This single word which "The Book" has chosen is the word "AUM," which is seemingly pronounced as OM. It may also be interesting to know that the ancient Sanskrit language, which is reputed to be over 5,000 years old, is often described as the oldest language known on our Earth, and it is also the root language of all the European languages which also includes the Hindu language. The other reason why this Sanskrit word was chosen, is because Sanskritians regarded the physical world as having been created by the "sound" of a person's voice and that it was this sound which created the physical world that people now live in – which also clarifies these words from the Christian Bible, that was also written by our wise ancients not so long ago.

Here is a modernized saying from John 1:1-14 in the King James Version who wrote about the power of a single "Word" :

1. "In the beginning was the Word, and the Word was with God, and the Word was God" (this is the pronunciation of a single word).

2. "The same was in the beginning with God" (in the beginning was the time when God did say this single word that created all life and non-life).

3. "All things were made by Him, and without Him was not anything made that was made" (the Creation was brought forth by the sound of this single word).

4. "In Him was life, and the life was the light of people" (life in which that only one word removed all darkness).

5. "And the light shines in the darkness, and the darkness comprehended it not" (the "light" as in this single word that removes the falseness and the falseness cannot stop it).

So Yes! A single word targeted to bring "The light that shines and removes all darkness" and was chosen by "The Book" to be the most straightforward and most powerful word that can be repeated in mind, this being the word "AUM," seemingly pronounced "OM." The reason for this chosen word is because the correct pronouncing of this is a single word that contains ALL the sound that can be made by the voice of ALL people. Of course, it is also imperative to sound this one word correctly, and the learning of the correct way to sound this word is that before repeating this word silently within the mind, it is to physically open the mouth as wide as you can, as in a big yawn. Then, with the jaw as low as is possible, gently and "continuously" slowly breathe out, and while continuously breathing out, fixedly listen to that single sound you are making in the "Present Time." Then, just slowly begin to close your lips until they meet then again return to mouth wide open - you have then sounded "truly" the word "AUM" as it should be sounded.

It is undoubtedly true, which many thousands of years have proven. However, some religions have banned this individually based way to "Self-Realising" Gods world, for it certainly takes the controlling power away from religious leaders who say that the realizing of the Heaven that exists upon our earth can only be realized through them and their teachings – which of course is not valid. For what can again be "Self-Realised" to be true is that this single sounding word contains every sound that can be "created" by a person's voice. The ancient translation is that it is also this sound that created the universe, which is likened to the first original "vibration" that creates the birth, death and re-birth process of all life and non-life. Interesting isn't it, and it is also known to be an ancient word, and so you can be assured that it is well known and so tested to bring "personally" to you - a Godly made or Nature made for the Non-Believer "truth" that you are everything that exists within this creation, and so you need "Nothing" (No-Thing)

So yes! Now to become practical for there are things to do and so silently while upon your chair and with a little self-listening in process, sound this word "AUM" out loud a few times, until you are happy with it and feel that the sound is "balanced equally." Then stop it from being released into the world and with your eyes closed to take it silently to be repeated gently and freely into your mind. For naturally when you are happy with this equally balanced sound, it is then time to "meditation ally" take this repeating sound into the mind and so with eyes gently closed and sitting balanced and upright on your silent chair, continue repeating and so "disciplinary" knowing that your "unthinking" Soul is "viewing" and "listening" to the sound of this word that is being released into your mind for two minutes twice daily – morning and evening. This exercise can be targeted for a week, and knowing that Sun up and Sun down are good times but always "know" that any time with a reasonable space between these exercises is excellent. It is also good to again remember that rope which is seemingly attached to your head and which is pulling you gently into heaven and also that rope which is fastened to the base of your spine and which is pulling you into the Earths centre and why is this? You cannot be informed for all thoughts take you into the world of Hell, this being that which exists in a non-existing Past or Future. The silent experiencing the weight of your body upon the chair – is truly an experienced "realization" which keeps you in the "Present Time," and who or what is it that is being controlled to sound this mantra into your mind? Well, your five senses, of course, for now, what you are beginning to "seemingly" bring to stand behind your "Heel" is those previously explained five wild "pups." It is also good to remember that your five senses will undoubtedly try to stop you for even while "observing" them, they will tell you that THEY are YOU! It is also useful to remember that you do not have to stop the thoughts during mediation physically, but harmoniously just replace them with the mantra, this being that which is being sounded by your now controlled five senses which are likened to being just five untrained pups.

Then it is good to increase this mantra sounding mediation by five minutes twice a day for a week, then repeat this procedure to ten, then fifteen, then twenty minutes until you quickly after five weeks arrive at thirty minutes, twice a day. For as with your first two-minute chair exercise, this inner sounding of a one-word exercise needs to be performed twice a day, preferably fifteen minutes before and fifteen minutes after sun up or sun down - but of course, any convenient time, is useful, especially in the Northern Hemisphere.

So yes! Now this well-tried and very ancient creed-based inner sounding single worded hymn will bring you to an actively growing new recognizable contented life that arises within you and which you know is also outside you, for you cannot be that which your Soul observes. For depending upon your character and perseverance and with self-discipline, YOU will begin, via this meditational eyes closed exercise, to truly recognize that YOU are the observing Soul that is factually observing the space that exists between the now repeated "mantra" sounding single word being sounded into the mind and that YOU, the observing Soul, is also genuinely observing the space around this single habitually sounding word. This disciplined "Meditational" exercise will eventually end your previously imprisoned Soul's incarceration. This being imprisonment, which was factually caused by many a mind filled blocking words and pictures that have continuously been allowed in childhood, to be birthed by one or all of your animalistic five senses to cloud the mind vigorously.

So yes! This silencing of the mind will allow the Soul to become aware of all that exists in the "Present Time," that which is always before you and for so long has been without you. For now, you have begun with this single worded "Mantra" hymn, to control and so silence the five senses, this being achieved by removing the past child-hood habit of a God-given or Nature-given "Freedom of Choice" which was used to choose "Willpower" to bypass "Consciousness" and so freely energise the constant "I want" that can only be emanating from our animalistic five senses.

So yes! Now you are beginning to stop this habit by now "Choosing" consciousness to energize willpower to only repeat a solitary word into your mind. Of course, you can use any chosen word that does not have an emotional history, but never change it and never tell anybody what your mantra is, but the word "AUM" (OM) you will find most useful.

So yes! It is now essential to remember that "consciousness" is that which keeps the body alive and that "willpower" is that which provides the energy for the body to achieve its tasks. For naturally truly, it should be understood that the Soul cannot direct or change any activity that is taking place outside a person's body or manage "consciousness" or "willpower" unless it is "Chosen," to do so. For it is undoubtedly right to understand that your body is that which is needed to do those tasks which God or Nature for the Non-Believer, needs people to support and yes the "Freedom of choice" is needed because the same task can create or destroy the emerging creation, depending upon circumstances. These being task which can only be performed in the "Present Time" and nothing within the Creation can take that away from people.

So yes! you will fight with your hands, and therefore it is also consistently good to remember that performing this task will not be easy; for the five senses past habits – likened to be our five wild pups - will continually endeavour to stop the reciting of this internal hymn by whining or moping and so your five senses will sound into your mind many good reasons why you should stop this practice, for indeed they can whine and mope. It is this which you must persistently reject by returning only to the inner sounding mantra, and this is not an easy task, especially in the beginning for the problem is in your past childhood "habit" of "choosing" your personal "willpower" to be enabled to bypass "consciousness," to release its energy to support and so give mental birth to the "I want" demands of the five senses.

This developed habit is because, in the past, you have always thought that these five senses were YOU! They are NOT you! For you are the Soul, and the five senses are NOT your employer. Therefore it is always good to remember this when you sense their "none-allowed" words entering into your mind. For positively truly any of their words entering your mind can be "disciplinary" and immediately stopped by the returning to the single repeating mantra, this being that act which obediently stops any words emanating from the five senses which in turn, allows your Soul to eventually and inwardly "see" clearly past the "mantra" word now being mechanically and so disciplinarily repeated by your five senses and so seemingly bringing those wild pups to heel. Now it is most important "realize" that it is your observing Soul, which is the real "YOU", that is gazing into the empty dark with the light behind space that is silently resting in front of your viewing Soul. Then eventually, after much practice, and with eyes open and the mind still, the inner Soul will view the real world that is "non-judgingly" resting all around you. For indeed, this is the "Present Time," and it will be quite a surprise as you discover the real world, for unquestionably truly this is the "Heaven" of the "Present Time," which always rests all around you.

So yes! It is an old and ignorantly established "deep-rooted" habit that this repeating mantra is now endeavouring to stop and also replace; for now, you are creating a new "choice." Undoubtedly, this being a new choice which will allow the silent Soul to view itself, which seemingly is that which is all around you, and it is a choice which will replace the old "choice" of habitually believing that

526

you are separate from everything. For now, you are developing a habit that forbids the five senses from entering the mind in which they have always been allowed to control you by sounding their greed-based habitually and always enticing "I Want," this being that which takes the mind into the past or into targeting the future – un-naturally the self-fabricated world of Hell. Yet, and this can be guaranteed, you will, by persevering with this "mantra hymn," succeed in stopping this misbehaving "I want" from appearing in mind. Then you will fully encounter "Enlightenment," and so realise and experience God's world or the world of Nature for the Non-Believer, and this is also a very ancient and very well-proven historical fact which has been continuously revealed by our ancient wise.

So Yes! Now it must be understood that this old habit of allowing uncontrolled words to enter the mind will take some stopping and your five senses, which "The Book" calls pups, WILL complain, particularly, in verbally and individually telling you how silly you are but how can you be that which you listen to and which you can immediately "disciplinarily" turn off like a radio or a music player? Therefore, is it not now also known that Jesus of the Christian faith did say in Mathew 16:23, *"Get behind Me, Satan! You are an offence to Me, for you are not mindful of the things of God, but the things of people."* These *"things of people"* truly being the desires of the uncontrolled five senses and the "things" of God can only exist in the "Present Time."

For naturally truly, you will undoubtedly begin to "realise" that eventually, with such "meditational" dedication, you will succeed in stopping this "I Want" habit that is mind-cloudily filling the mind from one or all of your animalistic five senses and then. However, fleetingly at first, you will begin to enter the "Present Time", and so become mindful of the things of God or the things of Nature for the Non-Believer, for indeed, your mind will become empty and silent. So the more you meditation ally "discipline" these five senses, likened to be five wild pups, to stop from habitually and regularly to sound their "I Want" into your mind. The lengthier will be this disciplinary imposed "space" that naturally rests between the now "automatically" repeating mantra.

So yes! The spaces between this disciplinary and singularly imposed inner-sounding "mantra" word, that "consciousness", via the "Freedom of choice", is now imposing upon "willpower", to sound into the mind, will "Enlighten" this space to naturally expand, with eyes open, into the revealing to your all-seeing Soul the "Present Time", which is the actual world and a world that exists without any mind clouding animal-based "I want". For again and of course right, this is the experiencing of the "Present Time", the real world of "Heaven" that is genuinely Gods world or the world of Nature for the Non-Believer.

So yes, this is truly experiencing the world called "Heaven" which is the genuine unifying factor of existence that exists all around us, just has it is the real unifying factor that exits within us. It is a factor that will begin to appear more and more, until eventually and with perseverance, eighty per cent, ninety per cent of one hundred per cent of living under the existence and care of the "Present Time", will be accomplished. Positively, this is true "Enlightenment", a reality which factually occurs when the mind is silent, has it should be. But it should also be clearly understood that at the beginning of this exercise, these "snapped" occurrences of your Souls viewing of the "Present Time" will be brief at first. Still, as the months or years pass, you will be able to achieve an extended silence within the mind, which will rest truly upon an "Enlightened" life, this being that which can only exist in God's world or the world of Nature for the Non-Believer.

So yes! This "Present Time" existence is the only actual reality which is created via the use of the above "meditational" exercise. It is a reality in which you truly know that there is nothing that you want – for you realise that you already HAVE everything you need for even if your body has problems your Soul, who is the "driver" of the body and in which the body can rest, is 100% perfect. For as you daily progress through this single worded creed-based hymn and into peacefully modifying and changing of old habits, you will begin to find that within the "Present Time" there is a stillness that can be "self-realised" only when you have quieted and so stopped all the "I Want" for Me noise that is always emanating from your animalistic five senses. For indeed this will happen when you have trained them, like our proverbial five wild pups, to stop from continually barking into the mind their persistent "I Want" for ME! For now, you can "Scientifically" understand that they are the cause of ALL the thoughts that continually enters into the mind. It is this mind filling noise which fills the mind and so blocks the view of the Soul, which is the real you, from witnessing the outside world? Therefore, is it not also "Scientifically" right that you cannot be that which you observe?

Thus, it is therefore undoubtedly true, that this single short word based practising of a "Mantra Meditation", this exercise that which is now being "Scientifically" and "Disciplinary" performed by a God-given or Nature allowed for the Non-Believer, "Freedom of Choice", this that is being a "choice" to immediately activate "Consciousness" to instruct "Willpower" to stop the five senses from individually and automatically sounding into the mind they're demanding "I Want" for ME! For assuredly, They were given permission and so "chosen" to do so in childhood because we thought that the five senses were the US! They are NOT us! For it was anciently proven to be accurate, that the five senses can be "chosen" to "disciplinary" sound into the mind only this one single worded mantra. For indeed it is then that our five senses, which can be likened to five wild pups, are then disciplined to repetitively sound only this single word into the mind, which can be likened to eventually "training" those pups to stay behind your heel and so out of sight and therefore certainly removing their "I Want" barking from out of your mind. For unquestionably and yes, this meditational exercise is an anciently known "meditational" fact which "empties" the mind. So our wise ancients knew that with the mind unclouded and without any "I Want" thoughts, the Soul could see clearly through the mind and into the "Present Time", which our ancient wise called "Enlightenment", this being the full experiencing Gods world or the world of Nature for the Non-Believer.

So yes! Your "Soul", which is the real you! Can, via the continuing practice of meditation, be enabled to "realise" 100% of the "Present Time", which is very anciently known experience called "Enlightenment", this being that experience which was sought by ALL our wise ancients and which is factually obtainable but only when the mind is silent and so resting in the "Present Time", which "The Book" calls the experiencing of "Heaven". For unquestionably it should be known that the "I Want" mind clouding images of a non-existing Future or Past, which "The Book" calls the world of a personally created "Hell", which genuinely does not physically exist but this is the fact which creates all our world's problems.

So yes! It is also the practising of this meditational exercise which will undoubtedly and eventually lead to an "Enlightened" condition in which you will firstly become "Self-Aware", this being that you are aware that all that exists is you and therefore "Know" that you are a unified part of all that exists in the "Present Time" and then, eventually, with continuing practice this experience can lead to becoming "Self-Aware". For indeed, it can again be said that it is within this "Awareness" that you become the observer of everything that exists in Gods world or the world of Nature for the Non-Believer. You also become "Aware" that everything that observably exists around you is "YOU" for assuredly; you will be aware that this is a highly "Enlightened" world in which you exist. It is also a condition which can lead to becoming "Self-Realised", this being an "Enlightened" state which "The Book" reveals, via ancient revelations, to be a condition in which you do not exist for long. Therefore, definitely and undoubtedly many of our worlds hermits sought this fact, and also many of our ancient aged men did go to the forest to seek this oneness of all nature. This fact proved very difficult to be achieved by our newcomers from the animal kingdom.

Therefore it should be known that upon such a death, your Soul does become has one with the "Creator", which is God or Nature for the Non-Believer. For "The Book" explains that it should be certainly be known that the real purpose of the Creation is so that God can experience the love of His only child or that Nature for the Non-Believer can experience ITS SELF. Therefore has a separate entity you no longer exist nor are you re-born again because you have become and so stay as one with your Creator.

These two realisations, now being modernly explained by "The Book" to becoming "Self-Aware or of being "Self-Realised", is also a well-known ancient reality and it was a reality that was factually taught by our wise ancients to be that which is experienced when one is bitten by the Kundalini "snake", which "The Book" modernly describes as being when the heart courses with a just freed, via the hammering of mediation energy and then courses up a person's spine or backbone and knowingly breaks open the blockage at the base of the neck and strikingly courses over the top of the head in which "The Book" states that this act then joins the left and the right side of the brain to become has one entity and then stops, with force, has it "bites" at the centre of the forehead.

For naturally and yes, this truly is quite an "Enlightening" experience and it is known to be an experience that was known even before our written history and even before the beginning of our ancient Egypt and certainly before the construction of the pyramids. For positively, it is well-known that the Pharaohs of ancient Egypt wore the snake has a crown to show they were "Self-Aware," thus meaning that they had all-knowing wisdom of being unified with all that existed around them, just as does the singularity of that which exists within them. For indeed our history shows the this being a "Self-Aware" or "Self-Realised" realty was shown by wearing of a head-worn snake display which then did gradually and historically change during Greek emergence and then eventually, the snake slowly evolved into the modern-day crown that now rests upon the heads of our kings and queens. Naturally, this being that reality which eventually and probably led to a group belief of a leader who had the snake to crown power to give to their follower's many physical benefits. These are being that which usually belonged to others rather than under the care of their Soul, who knew that in truth it was unified with "everything".

So yes! In ancient truth, individually and historically, the freeing of the Kundalini "snake" also awakens an "existence" that rest only within you which seemingly and firstly empowers your "consciousness" to become knowingly "Self-Aware"; this being the awareness that you are an integral part of and a singularity of "everything". For without doubt and honestly, as is often stated by our wise ancients, the striking of the Kundalini is a powerful experience occurring via Consciousness', this being that experience which also brings a "Spiritual Awakening" as if your "Consciousness" is awakening to experience itself, which is "everything" and so your "Consciousness" is there for feeling its true Identity. Positively, this is again genuinely being a "Self" identifying experience in which you feel that you really are "everything" and so you will experience everyone (and everything) as being "Yourself".

So yes! You will also, in genuine behavioural kindness, serve and support the goodness emanating from others who you knowingly experience as being yourself, which is actually "you" realising that they are simply parts of your real yourself. You will also be very quietly positive in your actions plus knowingly unreserved and also generous in your endeavours to avoid negativity any kind of harm for you are now experiencing that you "self-exist" only in the light of consciousness, this being that which can only exist in the "Present Time".

So yes! It is also true that you will certainly and automatically avoid any "I Want" personal temptation that can develop around you for you know that it does not separately exist. For it is also sure that you will always experience a decisive "Yes" as you embrace and accept every situation being knowingly and unknowingly being presented to you. You will also be known, by those who believe that they are separate, to be silently composed but energetically favourable in everything you do. For absolutely, this "self-born" consciousness is also a Spiritual awakening in which you become aware of your true "Self". It is also well to understand that you may have already "unknowingly" experienced the freedom-seeking Kundalini snake bite, which could factually have been in your childhood in which you "unknowingly" returned to that which our wise ancients called a "Self-Awakened Sleep", which explains the experience of your being "uncomfortable" with that which you are currently evaluating.

So Yes! Thus becoming "Self-Aware", meaning that we have become aware that we are actually "everything", this being that which is factually stated by our wise ancients as being an experience which can be achieved by the practising of a meditation-based ritual, which has been known to bring this actual reality over many thousands of years. For assuredly, it is based upon an ancient known exercise in which, via our independent God-given or Nature gave for the Non-Believer "Freedom of Choice", this being that which is acclaimed by our Soul, we can "choose" to redirect our "consciousness" to regain its control over "willpower", which was freed in childhood, and so stop its energy from habitually and ignorantly supporting the five senses. These being that which are always sounding their "I want" into the mind and which is an "I Want for ME" that continually fills the mind and so blocks the view of the Soul from seeing through the mind and into the "Present Time", this is being that simple fact which keeps a person living in Hell which is also a false world which does not physically exist.

So yes! It is now honestly stated that it is this "I want" noisy inner mind activity emanating from the five senses that indeed block the Soul from seeing through the mind and into the real world. For sure certainly, this is also the reason why many people live in a self-created "Hell" and not in the "Heaven" that naturally truly exists upon this Earth. For now, it must be clearly understood and again stated, that only by creed exercises, this being that which was knowingly brought into existence by our many wise ancients, can people truly self-discipline themselves to enter the Heaven that rests in the "Present Time" and so leave the Hell of their own-made imaginary "I want" for Me world.

So yes! Again, it is stated that this single worded internal "mantra" sounding hymn is the best "scientifically" chosen way to re-direct a person's willpower, to change its habit, which was previously and mistakenly allowed in childhood, to be freed from the control if their personal "consciousness". Unquestionably, this is a difficult task to achieve, for again it should be said that this fact is because previously, when in childhood, many people did silently "choose" to enable their "consciousness", this being that which is used to activate or restrain impulses, to automatically release energy to their "willpower" so that it could freely support the "I want" of the five senses because these young people thought that these five senses were them. They are not "YOU", for they are simply instruments for your use. For, of course, these culturally creed-based worshipping systems were released by our wise ancients to stop people from habitually supporting the "I Want" noise being created by the five senses. For it is only then that "Enlightenment" will be achieved, this being the actual realisation of God's world or the world of Nature for the Non-Believer.

So yes! Again, the work of this one worded mantra-based hymn is to habitually target and so use the God-given or Nature given "Freedom of

Choice", to redirect "consciousness" to enforce "willpower," to stop it from automatically and habitually supporting the releasing into the mind the "I want" that is emanating from one or all the animalistic five senses. For this is a mantra-based hymn that will eventually widen the silent spaces between the mechanically repeating word of the mantra; for this is a space that contains the true "self-reality" that is developing in mind, and it is this emptiness which will eventually allow the Soul to fully see through the empty mind the real Creation that exists in the "Present Time".

So yes, this is indeed the first step towards "Enlightenment," and so again let us hear that our target is towards an "Enlightenment," which again should be mentioned, was named by many of our world's religions and who called *it* *"Paradise", "Eden", "Heaven", "Nirvana", "Promised Land", "Moksha", "Shangri-la", "Kenshō", "Bodhi", "Satori", "Kevala", "Jnana", "Svargamu", "Kā bāga", "Vāṭikā", "Kā jagaha", "Sukhabhavana", "Ushta"* and many more and all these worldly language-based religious words can be described as meaning "Enlightenment" and it now also awaits YOU!

It is also good to remember again the metaphor that the training of the five senses can be likened to seeing them as five untrained puppies that have never been house trained, and so they run rampant and annoyingly all over the house, but you still love them. For indeed, the five senses can be likened to being these five puppies that fight, bark, and chew furniture, and are always taking your attention away from that which you wish to achieve. It is also good to remember a well-known puppy training system again. This training being when you say to the unruly animal "Heel," this being a sound which automatically trains the pup to stop what it is doing and to come immediately to your heel, and so it remains behind you and quietly out of sight. For eventually, this leads to the fact that you cannot experience any unruliness' from "them", although you know well that with proper training they can be called to perform any task that you direct them to perform.

It is also a known fact that at the beginning of this mind training exercise, it will also be found that the silent thought of the results of a similar training word such as "not this", which can be sounded into the mind and which stops any emerging uncontrolled thought, this being very useful when not meditating. For again, like the world "Heel", the words "Not This" will factually bring the noise emanating from any of your five senses, to also silently disappear which allows your mind to returns to the silence that is the target of all these exercises, for truly even during meditation you are merely targeting to increase the silent space of that single word that you are now automatically and habitually repeating into the mind. For figuratively speaking, this control during and towards a meditational success will also allow your Soul, which is the real you, to "knowingly" stare with your eyes closed, into the spaces between the repeating mantra and this "space" is knowingly recognised to be filled by that which our wise ancients called "the clouds of unknowing". For truly, these mind filling "I Want" sounds that are emanating from the five senses, will eventually and habitually begin to remain silent and so will not be sounded into your mind even when you are not meditating. For truly and factually they will always remain unheard throughout all the tasks that you physically support, instigate or do simply witness within the emerging Creation's harmony which is all around you, this being that which can only exist in the "Present Time". For indeed, this harmony does exist or is endeavouring to exist, for it is always around you or endeavouring to emerge around you.

So yes! Indeed the "Creation" is all "YOU", and this is a "YOU" that upon factually realizing the reality of the "Present Time", this real "YOU" will be enabled and maybe unto death, to support, in silence if that is necessary, the unfolding "Present Time" target, which is all around you has it within you. For absolutely, this is an inner and outer unity which is now silently being achieved by a mind that is without any "I Want" thought and it is also a supporting activity which will be found to be very harmonious to that which is all around you as it is also within you. For indeed and again, figuratively speaking, your five senses which have been likened to five untrained pups will eventually end their need for training. So you will find it very useful when not meditating, that if any noise appears in mind, to simply sound the controlling thought "Not this". For then quickly, your mind will return to a silence in which your Soul will never forget any knowledge that it is observing in front of it. In these early days, this is how you are enabled to control any words that spring into your mind, these being words which are ALWAYS emanating from one or all of the five senses.

So yes! It is correct that your five senses should be trained as you would kindly train five puppies to obey your silent commands. For this "mantra" training method of blocking the five senses from chattering and sounding in mind, does eventually succeed in silencing the mind. In the beginning, it can take some time to expand this silence within you. Of course, time and the repeating of this chosen "Mantra" single worded exercise is undoubtedly needed, just as with all our physical and mental exercises in which we seek to reach an understanding. But then slowly and finally, all sounds in the head will come to "heel," and all chattering in mind will knowingly stop, and so remain out of your mind and therefore freeing your Souls sight of your bodies outer world. For it is truly only then, that you will know that you are moving towards that which Christians describe as the "peace that surpasses all understanding", and it is then that that which the Christian religion identifies as the "Holy Spirit" or "Holy Ghost" will seemingly settle upon you and within you. Also, and it must be understood that in the very beginning, the "stilling" and "silencing" of the mind is not an easy task. For truly has with all beneficial exercises, some we perform willingly and some very unwillingly, and you can be assured that those fives will tell you how silly you are and so always acknowledge that you cannot be that which you observe or listen too – so just persevere for the real world awaits "You".

So Yes! Of course, the most important thing to remember, this being when meditating has previously stated, is that when thoughts come into the mind, just "disciplinarily" return to allowing the Soul to view the space between these now mechanically chanting single words. For really those "puppies" will eventually become trained, and so seeming to go out of sight has if behind you, and they will truly remain silent and so no longer block the Souls view through the mind of the "Creation" that "Observingly" rests in front of it. For truly you will find that although this is a simple single-worded "Creed" like a hymn, it can reveal to the practitioner the experiencing of "Enlightenment" which is the target of ALL the worlds' religions and philosophies which all use the chanting of mind silencing outer imposed words, that which we call "prayers" or "mantras", this being their own "Cultural" way of achieving or working towards "Enlightenment". It can, therefore, be said that those praying will experience being filled by what the wise ancients of the Northern world called the Holy Ghost, or the Holy Spirit, or the Angel Gabriel; for it is then that you will see the world as it is - and yes as often stated by all our wise ancients - it is beautiful!

So again, it is good to remember to continually target that which is being sought by this simple mantra which is being used to stop any other sound from entering the mind which is endeavouring to replace this chosen "Mantra" word. For truly you cannot "think" of two things at the same time and only the chosen and imposed "Mantra" is taking you "unattached" to experience God's Harmony or Natures Harmony for the Non-Believer, this being that which exists only in the "Present Time". For truly only in the "Present Time" can exist the real Heaven upon this Earth and so mind filling thoughts is that which takes you into the non-existing past or a non-existing future, which is the world of a self-created Hell upon this Earth. Therefore it is essential to understand that when you become aware that your chosen "mantra" word has stopped. You are listening to an internal thought that is sounding in your mind, just quickly and silently instruct the silent willpower to inform consciousness with the single order "Not this," or just silently remove the energy that is feeding these unwanted words. It is then that the non-requested chattering in mind will stop, this also being when you return to your ever repeating mantra which will again be the only sound in your mind and so it will silently stop the chattering "I want" from entering the mind, this being that which takes you to live in Hell.

71 THE WAY AHEAD VIA PATIENT MEDITATION

So yes! Indeed, Non-Believers can also reach "Enlightenment," for this door to living in God's Heaven or the world of Nature for the Non-Believer truly does exist, but only in the reality of the "Present Time." For truly, both these beliefs that rest upon our Earth are beliefs that cannot hinder the way to achieve "Enlightenment," for truly this is achievable by all who seek to experience it. For truly, it is then upon this entry in which one experiences the "Present Time," that the "Enlightened" one will fully understand that God or Nature for the Non-Believer, does not need to do anything in this world, for all the laws that are needed to maintain a "Heaven" upon this Earth have already been installed. For again, let us understand that all that is life and all that is non-life exists in God's world or the world of Nature for the Non-Believer. It was this "Originator" that first brought forth space, which in these modern writings "The Book" calls the "Mother of the Creation" in whom God planted the seed that brought forth their only child named "The Creation." For certainly is it not also "scientifically" known by all life that it does take a male to provide the seed and a female to grow and also bring forth care and support for her child? Also is it not truly known by all, that upon a child's birth it is naturally the "Mother" who cares and looks after her child; for truly, it is the "Mother" who ensures that her child grows up in harmony, wisdom, and balance and it is the "Mother" who will see that the child grows according to the parent's needs; so it is the same with the "Mother of the Creation" and especially regarding our planet Earth. It is also the "Mother of the Creation" who likened to all mothers, knows all that is needed to be known in the caring of her child. Therefore, it is naturally true that it is the Mother who supports and advises that which she has given birth to, even those children who believe that they are non-attached individuals. For assuredly, is it not also true that their creating Father, who cares for the on-coming future, gave to that part of their only child, which is known on Earth as people, the "Freedom of Choice." This gift being so that they can physically support their celestial Mother, who cares for the "Present Time" and therefore help Her to maintain the harmony that exists within their only ever-growing child, this being that which is unfolding within God's or Nature for the Non-Believers, ever-growing plan; and YES! Those who have ears to listen – let them listen for this is the reason why only people have been given the "Freedom of Choice." There again and truly is this not because within the ever-evolving Creation, which exists only in the "Present Time," the changing ever-growing reality of this only child's ageing can sometimes need positive on-going "physical" assistance or a negative declining ending, this being that which establishes the need for "choosing" a supporting or non-supporting act within the growing child. Therefore, that which is truly needed from people is the correct choice, this being to choose an act which establishes a healthy continuation in the supporting of the "Heaven" that rests upon this Earth but knowledgeably knowing that the same act can create and support evolving goodness (Godness) or remove regressing badness. This reality is the only real truth, and it is a truth that is found in the peace of true meditation, in which the mind rests without any mind filling "I Want" inputs from the five senses. Admittedly, this is that known experience which is called "Enlightenment" and which is an experience of "being" has one entity with that which we call the "Present Time." Naturally, this being God's gift or Natures gift for the Non-Believer which has been given to all people and which is the root seeking an experience of that which is sought in all our world's religious and philosophical belief systems. For the real "scientific" truth, which can now be modernly understood, is that if you can hear "speaking" in mind, it is one of the five senses that you are listening to for you cannot be that which you can listen to and yes! How they always like to argue and Yes! They truly cannot be "you"; for you are the listening Soul, this being that which should be experiencing all life and nonlife but only through a still "unclouded" mind, for your Soul cannot observe the creation through the ever on-going words that fill and so plague the mind. Of course, your unruly five senses will fearfully tell you that this is not true, and then seemingly argue noisily within your mind just how to prove it. Still, with the discipline of this simply worded "mantra" based meditation, previously introduced, you can now discipline to silence the antics of these five senses. This mind empty silence, which allows your soul to see your body's outer world, is a fact which occurs because your previously forgotten Soul has become your body's leader. Whose one solitary disciplinary "look" does now make quite the babbling of these inner children, who previously and before obeying the creed mantra-based discipline, were all mind-filling with the selfish clamouring for their own "I Want?" Therefore, always now be aware of this discipline that if you hear talking in mind know that it is the five senses which should be treated as previously explained like five unruly pups that should be trained, via the previously introduced Mantra Meditation, to come silently to your "heel" automatically and so out of sight and therefore stopping their mind filling noise which has been blocking the Soul from seeing the outer world. For indeed, this is an activity and realisation which means that your five senses will seemingly come behind you and will be unobserved and without noise until they are required to perform the task which they are best suited to "quietly" do. For truly with your five senses disciplined to be silent, it is then that if listening to music, you can sit in peace and "feel" the silent command to your listening sense to arise within you, as if you are silently commanding "listen to this music." Then the listening sense, with all other senses silent, will hear the right harmony of music that you have never heard so well before. Also, you could sit down for a meal and, with a silent mind, experience the taste sense, which is now 100% physically tasting this food that you are now eating, for truly, you will taste food as you have never tasted food before, and it will be the same with touch, sight, and smell. Yes, these now silenced senses will reveal to you ninety to one hundred per cent of their abilities and not ten or fifteen per cent, as they did before. For indeed this is because you are in the "Present Time," and these five senses now have to obey you for you no longer obey them, this being because you thought they were the real you – they are NOT you for they are simply an instrument for your use. So you WILL indeed find the reality of this truth. You will also acknowledge that by using the "Freedom of Choice," your Soul will be enabled to manage these unruly five senses which previously spent more than sixty per cent of the "Present Time" frivolously "time-travelling" into the Past or the Future which "The Book" calls Hell. Therefore, is it not true that these are sense-created imaginary worlds that do not exist in the "Present Time," which "The Book" calls Heaven because it is truly God's world or the world of Nature for the Non-Believer? Again, is it not also true that usually eighty-five to ninety per cent of their "Time-Travelling" is uncontrollably being loaded into the mind to create an "I Want" future need and which are also bringing supporting thoughts from the past, this being that activity which continually takes your observations away from the "Present Time" and into experiencing a mind filled viewing of all that which does not exist.

Is it not also a "scientifically" proven truth known to all drivers, that when driving you can sometimes cover miles and not remember any of them or in conversation, you suddenly awaken and ask a friend to repeat what has just been said? Is it not also "scientifically" correct that you are continually listening to these activities in the mind because you believe that they are you? Indubitably, this is the "you" that relentlessly endeavours to satisfy an "I Want," which usually breaks the Creations on-going harmony, which is always developing or striving to exist all around you? Is it not also "scientifically" valid that these "I Want" for Me actions do usually bring chaos and disharmony to all that exists in the "Present Time?" Therefore would it not be useful to now start, if not already done so, to "scientifically begin the meditational repeating of a single word within your mind and so show to your five senses that which is really in charge of your thoughts and that you can "Choose" to start this ASAP. Especially now that you know that you can do this activity when you are alone, which is the best way unless you are with known others of like mind? For if you do not, then the humour or fear coming from the others around you may distress you, for you will have enough problems dealing with the complaints from your own five senses without having to deal with the fearing five senses that will come from the minds of others. Also, it may be well to know that the first step that you will experience when you are approaching "Enlightenment," via your Mantra Meditation, is that you may feel fear. For it is truly a real feeling of a personal fear of loss that your five senses will bring to you when you begin your Mantra Meditation. For truly it is as if they have tears in their eyes as they explain that this exercise is a "silliness'" and it is an excellent experience when eventually who "you" think is "you" is now really known to be fearing words coming from the five senses, which will habitually begin to weaken. You will know it by their "explaining" words to you. For truly "you" will then hear that which you have always believed to be "yourself," calling this Mantra Meditation useless, silly, and unworkable plus without any meaning plus boring. But do not worry, for this "you" that you hear is not "you." For real, you can hear and observe these words, and you cannot be that which you listen to or observe. For "you" is your Soul, who is the real you and who is also a Soul that which cannot interfere with a person's God-given right to the "Freedom of Choice" which in Childhood was a "Freedom of Choice" that was accidentally used to "Choose" the five senses to be accepted as the real you.

So yes! Now is the time to remember that they are NOT you for they are merely mortal instruments for your personal use and has "The Book" states, that your "Freedom of Choice," this being has to what actions or non-actions to perform, was self-chosen in childhood to be given to the animalistic five senses who seek only their enjoyment and who do not know that which should be done or that which should not be done, this being that which their Soul is designated to do to support the harmony of God's Creation or Nature's on-going development for the Non-Believer.

So yes! It is your inner creation supporting Soul, this being that which can truly observe the outer world, but only through an empty un-clouded mind, the needed support that is required to maintain the developing harmony of a Creation that is emerging all around it. For definitely this is being a fact which is only "realized" when these "Present Time" harmonizing needs are seen through an empty and unclouded mind. For indeed this is a God-given task or Nature has given for the Non-Believer. It is that fact which a person cannot be "aware" of or "realise" when the mind is blocked by a many demanding "I Want" that is continually emanating from the five senses; for truly it will be quickly known, via mediation, that your five senses will seemingly experience great fear. For certainly is it not a non-meditating truth that the "I Want" continually emanating from your five senses has un-knowingly ruled you for many years, this being because you believed that these thoughts were the real "you." But you now know that they are NOT YOU! For "YOU" are certainly and truly your Soul, this being the messenger, the first in line supporter of the emerging "Creation," which is developing all around you. Still, only in the "Present Time" this is the only time that genuinely exits upon our Earth.

So yes! Is it not now known to be true that "Meditation" was also "unscientifically" used by our ancient wise many thousands of years ago? Admittedly, this reality being, without doubt, to unknowingly but effectively stop the greed-based animalistic machination that was continually emanating from the five senses? For certainly or ancients historically knew that this exercise would silence their mind and bring to them *"The Peace that surpasses all understanding".* But what can now be known is that mediation disciplinary stops this mind clouding "I Wants" which are continually blocking the Souls view through the mind of the "Present Time." Without doubt, this being a fact which our wise ancients did not fully realize but "The Book" now modernly states, quite clearly, that it is these mind blocking thoughts emanating from the bodies "animalistic" five senses, which keep the real you, which is your Soul, from seeing through a still mind God's "Present Time," which "The Book" and all history calls the pure "Heaven" that is known to rest upon our Earth. Therefore, is it not now known to be true that it is this previously unknown habit that takes you into a mind-filled "I Want" life that is continually pursuing a non-existing past or a non-existing future, which "The Book" calls the real world of "Hell"! For again, these five senses should be likened to five wild pups that will begin to annoy you at the beginning of your mantra sounding "mind" stilling exercise, and like untrained pups, these five senses will constantly clamour for their way. For truly at the beginning of your silent straight-backed chair sitting mantra sounding mediation, you will continuously find yourself habitually "viewing" and "listening" to their chattering "I Want" for ME. Undoubtedly, this being a mind filling noise, which is now known to be habitually and freely originating from the five senses, which in the past, you thought was the real you. But now you know that the real "you" cannot be that which you observe or listen to, for YOU is your SOUL, this being that which is truly the observer and listener for again indeed, this meditational act is to free your soul by enabling it to see, through a mind that must be without any thought, the actual reality of that which we call the "Present Time," this being Gods world or the world of Nature for the Non-Believer. This very ancient "Meditational" task, this being that which enables the mind to become still, is an act which factually allows the Soul to see and so "realize" only the existence of the "Present Time." Unquestionably, this is undoubtedly being that fact which was unknowingly pursued by our wise ancients in their endeavour to silence their mind by continually returning to making their five senses "disciplinarily" chant a mind-filling single worded mantra or many worded hymn. Indeed an energizing act that was actually but unknowingly used to disciplinary silence the five senses. A fact which was achieved by making them, via a self-imposed discipline, to jointly sound this single worded Mantra or many worded hymn, into their mind. For indeed this is an activity that will eventually silence their "I Want" as you personally and habitually begin to silence them by continually returning to the mantra or prayer, which truly trains these five senses which "The Book" likens to the task required to train five wild pups to silence their mind-filling barking.

So yes! It may be the first time that you are attempting to train them. So they will eventually and quietly "realize," again and again, your meditational command "Not this," this being when you become aware that they are not sounding the "Mantra" or you can simply return to the enforced sounding of the "Mantra" which removes their unwanted "barking," and this genuinely having you "realize" these entries into the mind are NOT YOU! For YOU are the "SOUL," this being that which is the observer and master of all that is within you and eventually you will become "Self-Aware" or become "Self-Realised" to know and experience that "YOU" are everything that exists in this never changing ever still "Present Time."

So yes! It is necessary for the beginning of meditation, to seemingly instruct your five senses, via the disciplining of your Soul, to chant the enforced and commanded mantra, this being likened to five wild pups silently and disciplinarily coming behind your heel and so enabling the Soul to see the still mind. Again, this is being a mindful training and well-proven way of establishing a truth in which meditators will begin to become aware of that which can only rest in the "Present Time,"; this being the world of "Heaven," which indeed rests within the real "physical" world. This persevering mantra will eventually subdue and silence the noisy five senses and so enable the meditator to experience "Enlightenment", this eventually being when the mind is silent, and the Soul is "observingly" resting in God's world or the world of Nature for the Non-Believer. Naturally, this is simply because the five senses have been disciplinarily stopped from sounding into the mind their constant mind filled clamouring and arguing, plus their constant ongoing and individual demands for a selfish "I Want for ME!" Now, it is because you now know that this noise in the head is not the true you, that they have been forced to become silent and to now automatically react to the inners Souls silent request to satisfy the harmony seeking needs of the outside world, just as its silent controls all the body's internal organs, these being naturally controlled to obey God's laws of harmony that obediently exist outside the body as they do within the body of the meditator. Therefore, without doubt, this is positively truly the way and path to achieve the experience that history calls "Enlightenment," that which was always the target of our wise ancients and which is the realisation all life and Non-Life that can only exist in the "Present Time," which is all around you and within you and evermore shall be so.

So yes! It is then when being "Enlightened" that you will also experience no more personal "I Want" for ME, for what you are experiencing within and outside you is the "Present Time," God's Heaven upon this Earth. For indeed, you will then experience, within the "Present Time" a self-reality which automatically decides on all needed harmony seeking actions that will genuinely emanate from you. This emanation genuinely being a personal condition that our wise ancients called "bliss," this being a constant experiencing "Enlightened." It is also this self-reality that has also been self-created, and it indeed occurs when the clamouring five senses are stopped from filling the mind with their ever-demanding "I Want." For it is truly only then that you will undoubtedly encounter the real world, this being that "Heaven" which can only exist in the "Present Time and which God or Nature for the Non-Believer has given to you and which is monitored by the "Mother of the Creation" who in truth, is the Nature of the Non-Believer. Thus "Enlightenment" is genuinely the always sought condition, which is the only target pursued by all our Earth's religions and philosophies; this is indeed the purpose of ALL religions and philosophies.

72   HOW ACHIEVE "ENLIGHTENMENT?"

Again it can be said that the reason why our wise ancients put forward the exercise of mediation to their followers was to stop their minds from being filled by an invasion of past and future mind filling "I Want" thoughts. These being that which are emanating from their animalistic five senses and which stops their Soul from seeing through their mind the real existence of the "Present Time," which can only be the being of God's world or the World of Nature for the Non-Believer. For indeed our wise ancients also knew that this experiencing of the "Present Time" can undoubtedly be achieved by this exercise called "Mantra Meditation," which is also now again becoming a popular modern way of establishing an "Enlightened" way of life in which a person supports Gods world or the world of Nature for the Non-Believer and not the "I Want" for Me world which is regularly sought by the animalistic five senses of themselves or in the destructing animalistic pursuits of a dominant leader.

So yes! Mantra meditation is also well known to be an exercise which "prejudicially" has not been commonly allowed or used in the Northern Hemisphere because of ancient religious conflicts in which a person's pursuing activities were based upon leaders "I Want" and not upon the individuals "Enlightened" way of life, a reality in which Jesus and many other of our world religious leaders gave credence too. For it is an inevitable truth that "Enlightenment" and the pursuit of "Enlightenment" is a very personal activity and also a very silent activity that genuinely targets the individual's way to a fact that knows *"The Peace that surpasses all understanding,"* which our ancients say exists in Heaven and which all successful mind empty mediators will undoubtedly find that this "Heaven" really does exist upon our Earth, but only in the current time. For this is a single worded creed "prayer," now being practised, is an activity which replaces and also firmly opposes and then stops any "I Want" or other sounds from entering into the mind. It is also now known to be a simple act that is based upon the mind filling concentration of a single word, for again and naturally, this is an exercise which will eventually bring to the "practitioner" a state of existence which our ancients called "Enlightenment." For indeed, this is a condition which is genuinely a historical and very anciently known experience which enables the experiencers Soul to view through their empty mind the world that rests in front of them. For indeed this condition is experienced when there is no evaluating and personal "I WANT" sounding in the silent mind that is emanating from one or all of the five senses, except when you read, of course, this being when the Soul can hear and lovingly appreciate the words that are entering your mind which is being sounded by one or more of the disciplined five senses. What is being witnessed by the observing Soul is the perfect stillness that can only exist in the "Present Time" and which can only be experienced in that condition, which is called "Enlightenment."

So yes! It is this "Enlightenment," which brings to the realisation and understanding of a person that which the Christians call *"The Peace that Surpasses all Understanding"* and to Muslims *"a realm beyond the ability of words to convey properly."* It is also known as being *"filled by the Holy Ghost,"* or *"filled by Holy Spirit,"* and the Muslim faith as the experiencing of *"The Angel Gabriel"* and what many other of our world's religions and philosophies' call it the experiencing of *"Paradise," "Eden," "Heaven," "Nirvana," "Promised Land," "Moksha," "Shangri-La," "Kenshō," "Bodhi," "Satori," "Kevala," "Jnana," "Svargamu," "Kā bāga," "Vāṭikā," "Kā jagaha," "Sukhabhavana," "Ushta"* and of course many other names, for indeed, this is God's world or the world of Nature for the Non-Believer which can only exist in the *"Present Time."* For without doubt, indeed all the world's culturally differing philosophies pursue a known and similar but variable way to bring this "Enlightenment" to their followers yet sadly many people attached to various religions state that only their religion knows the correct way to God world and that all other religions are wrong. But knowingly "The Book" accepts this, for it knows that such attacking people are newly birthed people emanating from the animal kingdom and who are merely showing great love for their pack leader. For definitely and honestly, it is known that eventually, their love will be for all the family of the One God who truly exists in a singularity, but only in the "Present Time" or the world of Nature for the None-Believer which "The Book" identifies as the "Mother *of the Creation*" ." This experiencing of "Enlightenment" is achieved by the practising of the previously mentioned and scientifically understood, mantra-based meditational exercise. Unquestionably, this is being that experience which can only exist within an individual when they stop the arousing into the mind of any past or future thoughts, which are usually based upon a simple "I Want" which separates them from the real world in which they know that they have "Everything" that they need in their life. Therefore historically and knowingly but simply put, it is this repetitive sounding of a single word that brings a physical reality in which the mind entering five senses, become fully "trained" and so eventually disciplined to become still and therefore their "I Want" demands are firmly stopped by the God-given or Nature-given for the Non-Believer "Freedom of Choice" which now stops their always emanating "I Want" demands. This "Freedom" is achieved by these five senses being internally disciplined to continually repeat the chosen inner mind sounding mantra, which is certainly not an easy task to achieve, especially in the beginning. For assuredly, your five senses will attack you in many ways, and in particular, they will tell you how silly you are to believe in such nonsense that they are not you or that they are just instruments for your use? Yet truly! Who is listening to these words, and who is enforcing them to only have the sounding of the single worded mantra into the mind? It is good to just ignore their distracting attempts by always "disciplinarily" returning them to sound the mantra; for sincerely their many "worded" interference will always endeavour to make you stop this controlling activity have they actively endeavour to take you away from the "Present Time" and this will also occur MANY times in the beginning. But truly whenever you "awaken" and so "realize" to their being any other words than the mantra that is being sounded in mind, you now know that you need to return to the quietly repeating mantra. For you now know that "you" are your soul, this being that which "scientifically" cannot be that which it listens or that which it observes, for positively and undoubtedly, this is a "meditational" exercise, which can actively take a long while to understand fully. Still, you will succeed, and then your five senses will become like experienced sheepdogs that will stay behind your heel and in silence until you need them to experience something for you. Then, after some years, or earlier, depending upon your sincerity, you will undoubtedly become "Self-Aware." Unquestionably, this being an experience in which you need nothing because you will become "aware" that you are "everything" that you observe, this being an "Enlightenment" that can only occur when the mind is silent and so allows the inner Soul to see the creation and so experience itself with that which exists all around it just has it experiences the singularity of the world within the body which contains it. For it is undoubtedly true that you will "silently" experience the reality of the "Present Time," this being an experience which ALL our ancient creators of all our world's religions and philosophies seek, this unquestionably being the awareness of an experience that can only be obtained with a silent "unthinking" mind. Positively, this will be a truth that can be "scientifically" experienced, and it is a "Self-Aware" reality of experiencing that which you will never have experienced before or ever been previously "aware" off.

So yes! It is also then and after much perseverance with this simple meditational exercise; that the Soul is enabled to witness and also be aware that it is a part of all that exists in the "Present Time," which is the same unified "Heaven" that exists within you has, it does all around you. For indeed it is then, when you experience this awareness "Enlightenment," that you will fully understand the existence of the real world, this being that which all our "Self-Aware" and "Self-Realised" wise ancients' did speak. For, without a doubt, you will become "Aware" and or "Realise" that this is being a world that has always existed, but again should be said, only in the "Present Time." For it is only then, in the experiencing of "Enlightenment" that you will fully recognise and also be very clearly aware of that which all people call the "Present Time," which is God's world or the world of Nature for the Non-Believer. For undeniably true, it is then that you will personally and privately know that this is also an experience of reality which has continuously been spoken of by all our wise ancients, this being that which truly goes beyond all understanding and so cannot be described. For, in reality, this is also an experience in which none have ever been enabled to explain, this being when your very existence experiences the singularity of "Enlightenment." For indeed, you will also "understand" within this experience that many people have never fully realised the actual reality of the "Present Time," this being that which rests upon this Earth and which is the powerful singularity of that which exists all around you has it does within you. Therefore, indeed it is the same singularity that exists within you that also exists outside you for all life and non-life are but one entity. Therefore it is good to remember this last saying by the "Enlightened" and "Self-Realised" Jesus upon his death for when being nailed to die when upon that cross he said *"forgive them for they know not what they do,"* so said honestly in the knowledge that His persecutors were obeying the "I Want" of their animalistic five senses.

It can also be said to be true that when experiencing and so becoming "Self-Aware" of this reality of "Enlightenment," this being described as the *"peace that surpasses all understanding,"* which is genuinely experienced when the eternal Soul is enabled to encounter the reality of the "Present Time fully," this being a time in which you may have fleetingly experienced many times before. Therefore, it is genuinely sure that knowingly within this experience, you will understand the target which all our religions and philosophies seek. For positively, this is undoubtedly the experiencing of "self-awareness" in which you will silently recognize this experience to be God's existing or Natures existing "Present Time." A time which exists only in the real world and which is genuinely a world which is called "Heaven" by our ancient wise, for it is undoubtedly NOT a personally created "I Want" for Me world! Yes, this is being a mind-filling imaginary world, which is indeed now known to be a non-existing mind-dreamed Past or Future world which "The Book" calls a personally created "Hell." For God's world or Natures world for the Non-Believer exists only in the "Present Time," and which is a time that targets an unknown future, and it has undoubtedly been targeting this future for many millions of years. It will continue to do so for many millions more. Therefore, it is as well to remember that for the few years that you live in each reborn life, you will not change God's will or, in any way, change God's movements towards His unknown target – but if wise? You will find ways to support it and not just take from it.

So yes! How wonderful and peaceful it is when you can observe and so are

"Self-Aware" of only the reality of the "Present Time" and so acknowledging the supporting of this has your real way of life, this being a time in which no past or future "I Want" thought can exist, for indeed this is how you will eventually be able to readily, silently and continuously "observe" the real world in which no "I Want" for Me can exist. For it is true that the practising of "Mantra Meditation" can be likened to developing a "muscle" in mind. Undeniably, this being a muscle that will stop the five senses from sounding their "I Want" into the mind, for indeed this is how they habitually cloud the Soul's view of the need to see the reality of that which is genuinely happening in Gods world or the world of Nature for the Non-Believer, this being the "Present Time." Now, let us allow "The Book" to mention again just how the silent mind allows the Soul to see just how it needs to react to that which is being presented to it by the Creation and therefore enabling it to support God's harmony or Natures harmony for the Non-Believer, this being a harmony which can only exist in the "Present Time." Thus this following metaphor is truly to explain the experiencing of the real supporting and the real living in Heaven while on this Earth and which is that "target" about which all our wise ancients speak. It also explains why the Soul, this being that which currently exists behind a cloud-filled "I Want" mind, is unable to do its Godly supporting work, and indeed why a person often does the opposite, which is living in a personally created self-made made Hell.

So yes, to understand this reality more correctly, it is good to use this following exercise has a metaphor; this is an exercise that requires you to act as if you are in a darkened room that is without any light. Now just stretch out your left arm and with the tips of your fingers and thumb, which are likened to be your five senses, being fully stretched apart and while pointing forward and opened outwards? Now right angle your wrist for your palm to become upright and you palm facing away from you but also keep your fingers and thumb well-spaced and pointing forward? Now just "concentrate" upon looking at the back of your hand as if looking through a large glass window. Now, imagine that at the tip of each finger there is a light like a torch which is shining away from you and which you can individually move and so shine on and so evaluate, according to the skills of that particular sense, anything that is "Enlightened" to appear in front of you within this darkened room. Then, as you move your hand around, imagine that you are your Soul which is viewing the world through the back of your hand, which is likened to be your mind and whose fingers are likened to be the five senses with each emanating an evaluating light that is shining forward into this darkened room. Now you understand that your Soul can see 100% of the world that is in front of you while also knowing that hand is powered by the light of "consciousness," which is the battery that is empowering the beam of light which is likened to a torchlight that is shining from the tip each finger. Now imagine that this hand is uncontrolled and that each finger is free shining upon whatever it "personally" wants to shine upon again like five arguing wild pups. Now imagine that your hand has been disciplined to go behind your mind and now each light "disciplinary" and silently shines through the empty mind upon that at which your Soul commands it to look. For indeed, this is that "Enlightened" world that our inner light of consciences shines upon, and it is this world which can only exist in the "Present Time, which is God's world or the world of Nature for the Non-Believer.

So yes! This practical darkroom exercise is to allow us to experience and to acknowledge that the fingers upon the hand are being likened to the assisting five senses of sight, hearing, smell, taste and touch and that each has been liked to radiate an individual and evaluating light that shines upon the "Present Time" which is that time that is always being supported by the Soul. Of course, this is being a silent evaluation for the Soul has not been purposely given the "Freedom of Choice." Still, it has undoubtedly been geared to support the "Enlightenment" which is continuously unfolding all around it, but only in the "Present Time." For indeed, this is a world that can only exist in the "Present Time," and it is a time that unquestionably emits a light that enables the Soul to evaluate and so support that which it is witnessing. For what it a witness is a real and personal situation which is ethically being described by our wise ancients to be living in Heaven. For definitely this living in Heaven while upon this Earth is an observed awareness which is factually realised by the Soul that rests within you and seemingly without you. But it is only through a silent "mind" that the inner Soul is enabled to observe all that is happening within the "Present Time", a time which can only be fully witnessed when the mind is without thought. For definitely this witnessing by the undying and internal Soul that rests within you is further realised via the five senses when, in their disciplined silence, the Soul can experience an actual one hundred per cent of the world that exists all around you.

It is in this way and the only way, that the Soul can support the emerging creation in which it can, when the five senses are silenced, automatically react to any required needs that are required to maintain the harmony of the "Present Time"; just as it automatically reacts to the inner harmony, wisdom and balance required within our bodies. Therefore, it is undoubtedly true that it is a person's Soul that also supports and so automatically maintains the needed harmony of the inner workings of our bodies. It is also this inner body harmony maintaining law, which the inner Soul also reflects in the outer harmony of its current environment. For definitely, the Souls purpose is also to maintain that which supports all the life and Non-Life that currently exists in God's Heaven, or Natures purpose for the Non-Believer, this being that which exists upon our Earth. For definitely and naturally, this is also an outer body harmony seeking activity which can be correctly likened to its inner body's harmony seeking activity, this being that which supports the needs of the heart and lungs and the trillions of other individual life forms that live in the Heaven being "automatically" maintained within a person body which also like nature can attempt the impossible. For assuredly, it is also agreed that the inner workings of a person's body can go wrong, just as they can within the harmony of the clashing parts of the emerging Creation that rests upon our Earth. But is it not also clearly seen to be true that the "Mother of the Creation" always corrects and so restores the harmony, wisdom and balance of the Creation, and often with the needed physical support of people; which is why only people have a free will that is called "Freedom of Choice" because, in truth, the same very personal act can be beneficial or detrimental, according to the conditions of the ever-evolving creation. Still, it is also good to remember that the Soul of a person cannot die, but the supporting body can. But now let us continue with the previously mentioned left-hand five-finger exercise in which we have likened the five fingers to be the five senses silently "pointing" behind and through our empty mind to that which can be observed, an act which was anciently called "Enlightenment". This being that which "The Book" says occurred when a person was genuinely experiencing only the "Present Time". "The Book" is also now modernly enabled to explain that this ancient termed "Enlightenment" is an experience which can only occur when the mind is without thought and "The Book" further explains that this "awareness" is only "realised" when the five senses are silenced, thus factually allowing the light from our "consciousness" to shine into the "Present Time", this being that reality which allows the Soul to see, via the light of consciousness, all the harmonising needs of the emerging creation, that is if there exist such needs – but which are also needs that can only be obvious through a clear and empty mind.

For assuredly, it can be said that these observations of the Soul, which we have likened to be seeing the created world via the light of "Consciousness", does enable the Soul to evaluate silently, through the unthinking mind, 100% of all that upon which the bodies silenced senses "Enlighten". For undoubtedly, the embodied Soul, this being with the creation that exists around it, does silently enable it to identify any remedial needs, which can be identified to be occurring in the "Present Time", just has it identifies and completes the needs of the body's internal workings. For correctly with this example of the finger-pointing exercise, the Souls sightings through a still mind are that which can only exist in the "Present Time", therefore the Soul is enabled to silently acknowledge the "automatic" evaluations, which "The Book" modernly states to be naturally and silently emanating from the supported teachings of the "Mother of the Creation". These silent evaluations, which are occurring within the "Mother of the Creation" well-trained child, are certainly needed to support the needs of the developing "Creation". Indubitably, this is being that silently arrived at need which factually allows the Soul to support, if required, the ever still ever-moving world that we call the "Creation". Now to continue with our hand exercise and also under the same condition, this being in which we likened it to be an upright hand that was facing the world in front of it but with crooked and pointing fingers tips emitting the same shining light. Now take the back of this left hand and place it in front of the face and resting fully upon the nose. Now using the same five fingers, which we have likened to be your five senses, eagerly start to tap all the fingers together, this can be likened to be outwardly pointing and also inwardly pointing their light upon their own and each other's "I Want", plus also fist opening and clasping all fingers together in despair at "Past" recollection and also in the new eagerness of "Future" possibilities. Now again imagine your

Soul is silently looking at the back of your hand and its constant finger tapping, touching and clasping of all fingers, which we have likened to be an activity which is undoubtedly clouding and filling of your mind? What is now being seen by the Soul is an unreal "Past" or non-existing "Future", for the "Present Time" is blocked by unknown uncontrollable and not existing Past or a Future Time "I Want" thoughts. These being thoughts which the left hand, whose light emanating fingers have been likened to be "I Want" emanations from the five senses, are actively filling and clouding the mind, this being that which is blocking the view of the Soul from seeing the needs of the "Present Time. For indeed the job of the Soul is to support the emerging "Present Time", this being a "Present Time" which it can no longer fully see.

So yes! Now, where is the dirt in the room that we are targeting to be cleaned? Where is the broken chair that needs mending, and where is the out of place furniture and the lost spectacles? This bombardment of the five fingers is likened to the five senses making inner requests, to shine in mind. It is this continuing bombardment that makes it impossible to see the needs required supporting the harmony that is being reflected by the "Present Time", this is being that which truly exists is all around you.

So yes! Is not the Soul unable to view the outer world because of the inner hammering and clasping of the many "I Want" that is a mind-filling noise that is emanating from the five senses? So again, which condition can be likened to be trying to reflect the real "Present Time" back to the viewer? For this example certainly shows why the Soul is unable to see the needs of the "Present Time", this being because the mind is blocked by the "I Want" claiming demands of the five senses within it. So factually, this is undoubtedly the living in a self-created Hell upon our Earth, and it is certainly a life that will continue, unless the constant "I Want" that is emanating from the five senses, is stopped from filling the mind with their "I Want" for Me, selfish claims. It is the constancy of this false world of Hell that caused our ancient wise to create our worlds many religions and philosophies, this being to take their followers from this personally created "Hell" and bring them to live in Gods or Nature for the Non-Believer, world of "Heaven", this being that world which can only exist in the "Present Time".

So yes! Praised be to this, for this was a reality which was factually achieved by their introducing to their followers the task of self-disciplined prayers, songs, chant, movements and even the food to eat and the food not to eat, all to discipline unto silence the demands of their five senses. But in those ancient days, how could it be explained that the sound entering their minds was not being genuinely sounded by them, but that they were emanating from the animalistic "I Want" of their five senses. For "absolutely" all the disciplines suggested by our ancient wise, which still exist within our current religions and philosophies, were instigated by our ancient wise to bring their followers into the "Present Time," in which exists the word of God or Nature for the Non-Believer.

So yes! All our worlds differently "Self-Named" religions and philosophes still currently pursue the "Self-Disciplined" tasks initiated by their culturally

"Self-Aware" and "Self-Realised" wise ones; these being "Self-Imposed" solitary or group performed religious and philosophical exercises which have all been disciplinary "Self-Created" within their followers who were guided to use "Self-Discipline" to maintain these "Self-Performed" tasks. But now in 2020, it can be "Self Stated" that the "Self" is the individual Soul. Therefore it can now also be modernly "Self-Said" that our Earths wise initiated all our "Earthborn" religions and philosophies to stop, via a "Self-Initiated" introduction to the "Self-Levied" performing of a "Self-Discipline", this being that which our wise ancients did "Self-Knowingly" target the removal of the mind filling demands emanating from our ancient animal-based five senses. For knowledgeably and undoubtedly our ancient wise knew, via their personal experience, that that which they called God did also rest within all people and that all people could "Self-Experience" this fact with "Self-Imposed" disciplines such as "Self-Based" inner and outer "Self-Chanting" of prayers and other disciplinary "Self-Activated" pursuits, all of which were culturally based upon a God-given or Nature gave for the Non-Believer "Freedom of choice".

So yes! Our wise ancients knew that this God-given or Nature gave for the Non-Believer, "Freedom of choice" was the birthright of the "Self" that rested within all people and that it could, therefore, be positively used to become "Self-Aware" or "Self-Realised" with a "Self-Unity" with all that exists within the creation, or it could be a negative "I Want for ME", a world in which nothing exists except YOU! For assuredly, what our wise ancients did not know, as many of our to-days people can recognize, is that it is the ancient animalistic five senses, this being that which was anciently encased in all people, that did continually and animalistic-ally fill the mind with many an "I Want" for Me, this being a continuing target of the unwise beholder. But now "The Book" clearly states that the Soul of ALL people is NOT animalistic, but that it is an integral and joined part of that which we call the "Creation", this being the reality which was birthed by God or Nature for the Non-Believer and that any person can become "Self-Aware" or "Self-Realise" that this truth is exceptionally factual. For assuredly, the most straightforward exercise to achieve this being that exercise which our ancient wise and also "The Book" has chosen, this being the activity which our ancients called "Mantra Meditation" which is a very personal discipline. For indeed, it is historically known that this "Self-Imposed" and disciplinary activated mantra-meditation, is the most serious and quickest way to eventually and disciplinary stop the animalistic-ally based soundings into the mind of the five senses. For assuredly, it is then that you will then live in a world that incarnates and ALL our wise ancients call "Enlightenment". For faithfully, "Enlightenment" is a word that describes illumination, clarification, information, insight, instruction and education plus the removing of ignorance, meaning to see a light which will take you from absolute darkness, for unquestionably it is this "light" naturally conjoined with the Soul that is seeing the "Present Time", and it is undoubtedly an "Enlightened" experience which surpasses all understanding.

Now let us hear what the "Mother of the Creation" said in the Christian

Bible about this light that takes away "darkness," which is genuinely the ignoring of Gods world or the world of Nature for the Non-Believer. She said these words when She spoke through an "Enlightened" one: *"In the beginning was the Word, and the Word was with God, and the Word was God. Through Him, all things were made; without Him, nothing was made that has been made. In Him was life, and that life was the light of people. The light shines in the darkness, but the darkness has not understood it."* Which "The Book" explains to be a "Word" which can only be heard when living in the "Present Time". A time which rests within God's presence and which is also a time in which past or a future personally created "I Want" world, this being that false world that is being "mind-filling" created by the five senses, will never understand unless it is disciplinarily trained to do so. Without doubt, this being an exercise which can be liked to our training the five senses which can be regarded to be like five untrained wild pups who always destroy the home in which they live. Now we clearly and honestly know that even a one-worded meditation will bring a silencing well-trained discipline to the mind of the meditator, this being that which will eventually remove all the "darkness" spoken of above. For sure, the mind will become still because our five senses, likened to be our five wild pups, are trained to become silent and so are likened to be behind our heel like sheepdogs, which are often called to perform a duty by the instructions of their master, which is YOU! Therefore, a mediation practiser will fully begin to understand about the "Enlightenment" that is spoken of here. Now listen to these other ongoing words about "Enlightenment," spoken of by the Divine Mother through the Incarnate Jesus: *"He was in the world, and though the world was made through Him, the world did not recognize Him. He came to that which was His own, but His own did not receive Him."* Yes, this was because they were not "Enlightened" and so lived in the selfish world of "I Want". Also, it was further stated *"Yet to all who received Him, to those who believed in His name",* (these being those who became "Enlightened") *"He gave the right to become children of God, for certainly Children are not born of natural descent, or of personal decision or a husband's will, but born of God."* When you are enlightened, you know that this is true; for you are therefore indeed, "born again" and become has one with everything. For was it not also wisely said that *"The Word became flesh and made His dwelling among us."* Again, this being the same for all people who become "Enlightened" and so become unified with the needs of all flesh. Also *"We have seen His glory, the glory of the only who came from the Father, full of grace and truth. From the fullness of His grace, we have all received one blessing after another."* Yes, this is true, but it is only when a person is enlightened that one can "see" and so "understand" (stand-under) the reality of the unified Creation; but sadly for those who live in a world of "I Want," they will find it difficult to find this "reality" and so will never understand the following: *"For the law was given through Moses; but grace and truth came through Jesus Christ,"* this being that truth which "Enlightenment" brings and which is mentioned above. Also*: The Father who sent me also speaks for me, but you* *have never heard his voice or seen him face to face.* The Divine Mother, speaking through Jesus, made it known to unenlightened ones that Jesus was talking about the "Present Time" in which Gods world is continuously speaking to people who cannot hear it because they live in the Past or the Future, this being the un-real "I Want" for Me world that the animalistic five senses take them. Therefore, is it not also an absolute truth that ALL our wise ancients speak of this certain truth? For definitely the "Mother of the Creation" has indeed spoken through all our ancient wise to bring to the world of Her children the world of "Enlightenment." in which all can see grace and truth, which is the harmony, wisdom and the balance that exists within all life and nonlife, but only in the "Present Time", for was it not also honestly said that *"People do not live on bread alone, but on every word that comes from the mouth of God."* Consequently is it not an inevitable truth that God can only sound His world creating a voice in the "Present Time and certainly NOT in the past or the future can these words be spoken so that ALL can hear and also in answer to the following: *"Do not put the Lord your God to the test."* – Which means that you cannot break the Heaven that always rests, but only within the "Present Time".

So Yes! Did not the "Mother of the Creation" say through Her "Self-Realised" Son Jesus, *"Away from me, Satan!"* for undoubtedly, Satan is likened to be the five uncontrolled senses? Then the truthful saying about the "Preset Time", *"Worship the Lord your God and serve him only."* For is it not a truth that this factual physically based "worship" can only be achieved while living in the "Present Time?" and also being obedient to the needs of the harmony that is all around you. Plus and finally did not Jesus say: *"I tell you the truth, no one can see the kingdom of God unless he is born again."* Yes! Being born again is bringing the mind from living in the unreal past or future and entering fully into the needs of the "Present Time"; this truly being Gods world or the world of Nature for the Non-Believer, in other words, becoming "Enlightened" as described in the words of the above, for indeed was it not also said at this time: *"Flesh gives birth to flesh, but the Spirit gives birth to spirit."* For naturally and indeed these are ageless directions which are continually emanating from our ancient wise whose Godly target is to bring "Enlightenment" to all people and so enable them as if to join has one with the "Holy Spirit," and so support the on-going harmony that always gives birth to the work of the "spirit". It is indeed known that to achieve entry into this actual world of reality, is to practice Mantra Meditation which "The Book" identifies has the quickest and surest way to enter and so become as one with Gods world or the world of Nature for the Non-Believer.

So YES! When you finally stop the demanding "I Want" that is continuously emanating from the five senses, these being that which are always talking and cloudily claiming an "I Want" in the mind of the beholder, you will enter the "Present Time" which is that reality which is described as "Enlightenment". Yet naturally, you may have already glimpsed, or momentary realised the "Present Time", which could have been the time when you looked down a fertile green valley or from the top of a mountain or just looked at the sea or any outstanding view of Nature which took your breath away. For again is it not an inevitable truth that at this point you became silent and "still" in mouth-opening amazement at such a beautiful unthinking "Enlightening", which gave you a clear view of Nature, and this is as if you see the world as it is and for the first time. For sure, is this not a Self-Realising experience which could last for some seconds, this being that which is known as "Enlightenment". Therefore this is certainly an experience that can be with you all the time, but without any amazement, because experiencing "Enlightenment" becomes VERY "natural" and VERY "wonderful" – but it is also an experience that cannot be described. For assuredly, I remember once walking through a large grassy park in which there were trees with one of my students during a break in our philosophical discussions. She had just started regular meditation, and so she asked me the question: "Where is this Mantra Meditation taking me and what will be the results?" I answered, "Only Time and practice can show you because it is a personal experience, just keep working towards the stillness of the "Present Time". We continued our walk, and suddenly I realised that because of our environment and togetherness her mind had seemingly joined with my silence and so had reached the personal experience of the stillness that I had just spoken of, for sure, this is as if recognizable light shines from a person when their mind becomes still. I stopped our walking, and in this still silence pointed to a tree, and I said to her: "Look at that tree and tell me what you see!" Then in her "stillness," she looked at the tree and slowly these first words came from her; saying, "I can see the tree; I can see the tree," and I knew that for the first time in her life, she had encountered the "Present Time," and had experienced the *"peace that surpasses all understanding"*, this being for the first time. It is an "Enlightening" experience and very enjoyable, and so now it is good to know well that there is a harmony in our Heaven that exists upon our Earth, and it is always resting here – and it is there for you!

So yes! The "Present Time" is God's world which has been given to you, and when you see and enter this "light" that God shines within the "Present Time", you will have great difficulty in disobeying its presence and the needs for its growth. Therefore it is because of this "realisation" that you will always see and understand (standing under) the pure truth of all of that you witness and experience. For never again will your life be controlled by a false chattering and therefore a false existence within your inner mind, this being that sound which is continuously emanating from your five senses and of other peoples similar propaganda, this being that which creates an "I Want" which is being always sounded within you by the five senses.

So Yes! To those who have ears to hear, let them hear? For definitely, this is an ancient saying; therefore it is good to ponder it well, for all our wise incarnates, and all our wise ancients speak of it, but in an ancient language which many have forgotten how to understand. But now it is in modern terminology these words are given to you so that you can "modernly" understand the path that our wise ancients explained in their ancient wisdom, the path to "Enlightenment". It is also confident that the new practitioner will also realise that in this meditational task towards "Enlightenment", it is no good asking God to give you something or to do something for you because He has already done everything needed regarding that task. For indubitably, this means that all the self-seeking beneficial "I Want" prayers that are requested in the entire world will not change by one jot God's world; for sure all that exists in the "Present Time" is undoubtedly God's world or Nature's world for the understanding of a Non-Believer who can also achieve "Enlightenment".

73 THE CLOUDS OF UNKNOWING

So yes! It is with eyes closed and without any "I Want" words or pictures always filling the mind, these being that which is emanating from the five senses, that the Soul is now enabled to see into the mind the silent dark movement of that which our wise ancients call "The Clouds of Unknowing", this only being the Soul looking into an empty mind. For indeed this is the targeted situation which is eventually and habitually arrived at via the disciplining of the five senses to consistently and repetitively repeat into the mind this single word, which is called a "mantra". For positively and certainly this stillness, this being that which is seen to exist between the "automatic" sounding words of the mantra, is undoubtedly the target of all our world's religions and philosophies. For indeed ALL our Earths ways of worshipping are "disciplinary" targeting the stillness that always exists, but only in the "Present Time", which is genuinely Gods world of Heaven or the world of Nature for the Non-Believer. For again all should now know that the Past and the Future is the non-exiting world of Hell, which is an "I want" fabricated world being created in mind by the fives sense and it is a world that unquestionably does not exist.

So yes! The targeting of all religions and philosophies is to enable a person to experience the living of life only in Gods world or the world of Nature for the Non-Believer, this being that "Heaven" which can only exist in the "Present Time" and this is the target of meditation, and yet, it may take some time to achieve this reality. For it is undoubtedly a well-known truth that the silencing of the mind is not an easy task for these "Pups" have been wild, undisciplined and for a long time has been free to seek their pleasures and all simply because you thought that they were YOU! They are NOT you, for indeed your five senses and all your body is simply an instrument for your use. But certainly now is the time to understand (Stand-Under) and so appreciate the current need to correct their wild behaviour and especially to "seemingly" teach them that they can trust their new master, which is the Soul, this being that entity which now needs permission to stop their behavioural seeking pursuits - by quietly commanding "Not This" to any thought, which they will eventually begin to obey. For now is a good time to remember that it was in childhood that we mistakenly via the "Freedom of Choice", permitted the five senses to become "US", they are NOT us, they are only instruments for our use.

For it is indeed genuine that your mind will not become habitually silent and or habitually still very quickly, therefore it is good to remember that these five "Pups" can talk into your mind. They know the words that you like to hear and also that which you do not like to hear. Therefore it is inevitable that during the early days of mediation they will bark at you such words has "Don't be silly" and "This is all nonsense" plus "Let's eat" or "I want to go and watch TV" and especially "Why are you doing this nonsenses?" etc. But eventually, via your inner mantra "disciplined" sounding observations, you will experience a feeling as if the real "YOU", who is unquestionably your Soul, is knowingly flying silently forward into the darkness of the silent inner mind which our wise ancients called "The Clouds of Unknowing".

Undoubtedly, this is being after some considerable "meditational" practises, in which you have redirected via your "Freedom of Choice" to allow the Soul to disciplinary instruct the five senses to sound only the repeating single worded mantra into your mind. For undoubtedly this is a training system which is being imposed to stop their past habit of being allowed to sound any "I Want" into the mind, this being allowed because in childhood you thought that they were the real you! They are NOT you! For you are the Soul and your body and its animalistic five senses are simply instruments for your use. For indeed and again it can be said, that this simple "Mediation" exercise is really your redirected "Consciousness" becoming "Self-Aware" and so enabled to "Choose" to power into the mind, a solitary "Mantra" based word that is being "Repetitively" imposed by your ever observing Soul, this being that which is needed to "Disciplinary" silence the "I Want" chattering of your animalistic five-senses. For again it can be said that this "Meditational" activity is certainly being enabled, via an order to your inner five senses, which are now being instructed by your Soul, via a God-given or Nature has given "Freedom of Choice", to "disciplinary" sound this single world into the mind, which again is said to be a simple activity which ALL our world religions and philosophies' purse via their culturally based hymns, psalms, prayers, and praying procedure. Still, the repeating of a single world is all that is necessary to empty the mind and so allow the Soul to "Silently" and "Automatically" evaluate the "Singularity" of the world in which you live for indeed you will become aware that everything that you witness is really "You" or has our wise ancients say Your-Self".

So Yes, this is a simple internal mind training exercise which is being imposed by your God-given or Nature given for the Non-Believer "Freedom of Choice"! Without doubt, this being for you to "Choose" for a single word to be sounded into the mind by a now collectively disciplined five senses. Again, this can be said to be a mantra chanting inner mind activity that enables, via the "Freedom of Choice", for any person to impose a training discipline upon their chattering five senses silently. For, without doubt, this singularity of "being" and so living in mind silent existence, is a reality which occurs when the senses have finally stopped their "I Want" mind filling distractions, these being "I Want" for ME distractions which fill the mind and so factually block the Soul's view, through a needed clear mind, of the real world. For indeed it is this animalistic mind filling "I Want" claiming of the five senses, which you think is the real you, is that condition which condemns a person to animalistic ally pursue their "I Want" which is that "I Want" for ME, which only the five senses can create?

Admittedly, this is again being a never-ending greed-based "I Want" for ME world, which is a world that continually fills the mind. It is this which factually stops the Soul from seeing and so "Holistically" supporting the real emerging world, this being that which can only exist in the "Present Time".

So yes! It is undoubtedly within any person's "Freedom of Choice", this being that which enables any person to "Choose" their "Consciousness" to re-direct the energy of their "Willpower" to stop a childhood "Choice". For this was that which was an "I Want" that allowed the animalistic five senses to enter the mind freely –because it was thought has a child that they were you! They are not you for you are the SOUL, this being that which is unified to "Everything".

Therefore if this meditational exercise is stopped by "re-thinking" of the past habit of allowing the chattering animalistic five senses to have free unrestricted entry to the mind, this meditational activity will stop this habit by continually "choosing" to return to the repeating of this single mantra; it is then by this simple exercise that the five senses will become habitually trained and so controlled unto silence by the mechanically empowered and disciplined chanting of this single worded "Mantra". For indeed this is a creed based exercise that will use your God-given or Nature given "Freedom of Choice" to newly request "consciousness" to activate the energy of "willpower" to sound this single worded mantra into their mind. Without doubt, this being a meditational act that will factually and disciplinary stop the past habitual uncontrolled freedom that was "chosen" to be given in childhood, to the "I Want" demands of your bodies five senses.

Yet indeed, this is also a meditational training exercise that will continue for some time – but now the question remains? Who will you "choose" to win? Will your God-given or Nature has given "Freedom of Choice" be to live in the real world of Heaven, this being that which can only exist the present times" "Peace that surpasses all Understanding" or the world of "I Want" for me, which is a direct connection to the world of Hell. Without a doubt, this is being that which our ancients describe as being a life subjective to constant punitive suffering and often likened to torture which is often felt like an unwanted punishment? Therefore, is it not also true that Jesus of the Christian faith and also many others did decide to die rather than join the "I Want" Hell that existed all around them? For undoubtedly many would become "Self-Aware" and so would be born again into a better world, or they could be "Self-Realised", has was Jesus, and so would not be born again as he would become as one with God, for cannot it be said to be true that the purpose of the creation is so that God can experience "Himself"?

So yes! This single word-based "Mantra Meditation" is undoubtedly a self-chosen and "disciplinary" based training exercise, this being a Self-imposed exercise which is targeted to train unto a respectful silence those inner five senses, which "The Book" likens to be animalistic "pups". It is also true that they will undoubtedly become trained and also habitually controlled. This being that which begets a "Present Time" situation that is very different mind filling differing words created by the "I Want" demands that used to come from these previously freed five senses. That honestly, did fully cloud the mind, this being that which stopped their Soul from engaging in the outer world. So the exercise is to distract and therefore re-direct your puppy, use these meditational time outs effectively and endeavour to stop your puppy from barking - does this not sound familiar?

So yes! Therefore, after some "considerable" practice of meditational exercises, this being because your pups will not like being silenced and they will also certainly bark within you many words telling you just how silly you are being. But then it will eventually plus logically be "Realised", by the meditator, that their silent Soul is now peacefully viewing within the mind the "clouds of unknowing", these being clouds which are seeming "seen" to be moving in front of powerful light. This peaceful and seemingly "un-energised" viewing of your Soul into your mind, will undoubtedly occur after a considerable "training" time, for it is good to remember that these "Pups" have been un-disciplined for many years. At first this "viewing", this being through the spaces that eventually occur between the now automatically repeating via the "pups" of the "single" worded mantra, for it is simply known to be that this act stops their mind filling and thought to create an "I Want", this being that act which for many years has been emanating from the five senses, which we are likening to be five untrained pups. For positively this a mind viewing reality accomplished by the Soul, that many of our wise ancients described as the Soul viewing the "clouds of unknowing". Without doubt, this is an experience that silently becomes stronger and longer, as the space between the freed one word sounding and repeating mantra becomes wider and wider and then automatic so that it can be ignored. For indeed, you then begin to "experience" and so feel that you are silently "flying" through these "clouds of unknowing" that now exist within your silent mind as if you are on a silent journey towards an "unknown" reality. For naturally, within this silent mind, there is no other sound of that you are aware. There is just the feeling that your viewing is being powered by an unknown force, that has brought life to that who viewed the single repeating creed word, which can now be likened to a silent experience of you "riding" as if empowered by this single word through that which our wise ancients naturally called the "clouds of unknowing".

It is also known that within the early days of seeking the silence of this ride through these "clouds of unknowing", that when an "I Want" replaces the single chanting word and so enters the mind, it is immediately stopped – which is a hard task, especially in the early days. For it was this past that habitually allowed into the mind the demands of the five senses; which is a sound which can no longer be allowed to enter the mind for if any do, you must immediately, automatically and habitually, become aware that the old habit of "consciousness" to reject them, by stating "Not this" or directly by "consciously" with one glance of the Soul – refuse and so cancel their existence.

So yes! Eventually and within this single worded meditational practice, you will automatically stop all "I Want" from sounding within your mind. Of course, it can be said that the Soul is not moving towards the light that can be seen as if resting behind the "clouds of unknowing". For indeed, it is the vital and natural energy that is moving within the empty mind that is being seen by the Soul, for the Soul is the observer of all that truly is. For when the soul sees through a silent mind, a mind that is having no interference, then it sees how to support God's Creation that exists only in the "Present Time", which when observed without thought, is experiencing "Enlightenment" – that which ALL the creeds of ALL our wise ancients' religions and philosophies sought. So yes! you will find that listening to this one-word creed exercise, which the five senses have been trained to repeat automatically, is the way to allow your Soul to ride into the "clouds of unknowing seemingly", this is being that which is naturally seen by the Soul when the mind rests in silence.

Unquestionably, this is not an easy task, and it may not be easy for many. Still, it is essential to endeavour to succeed in this, for people does have the ability to triumph, and this is simply the reason why people have been given a "choice." So for thirty minutes in the morning and thirty minutes in the evening with your eyes closed and with your back straight plus your seat pulled into the power of the chair and head pulled into the sky and with the freedom of a God-given choice, allow the mantra to "freely" sound its single word into the mind all of which to be silently experienced and observed by your Soul – for truly Enlightenment awaits you.

For indeed, it is this ability to freely "choose" that enables people to establish and so fix our consciousness to exist only within the domain we call the "Present Time". For it is only in this way, that we can experience the world of Heaven in which we all live. It is also a Heaven that is indeed a beautiful place to live, and of course, it also depends upon past lives as to just how quickly this moving into the "present" is achieved – but its "rightfulness" can be achieved over time, and that is a personal guarantee.

So yes! There are many ancient sayings about the "clouds of unknowing" through which you will actively experience the fact that you will feel that you are silently flying through them. Undoubtedly, this is an all "seeing" experience as if you are in a flight that is mechanically powered by the single word of the mantra. It is also then that you appear to be flying like "Superman" through these twirling dark clouds, that you recognise that they seem to be unfolding in front of your flight. It also seems as if these dark clouds are moving in front of a powerful light, which you seem to be approaching. Of course, it is not you that is moving into these "clouds of unknowing"; for "seeing" the movement within the still mind is just the observing of your Soul, which is the real you, for the body is NOT you, it is an instrument for your use. So now we can "realise" that this meditational exercise is to stop the five senses from automatically and continually filling the mind with their "I Want", for sure, this is a meditational exercise that will stop their animalistic demands for your body to pursue their never-ending "I Want automatically". For indeed; we are not of the lower animals, for we are indeed a life form that has been given the "Freedom of Choice" and so with a silent and still mind, our Soul can see the needs or non-needs of the emerging Creation, this being that which in stillness emerging all around us.

So yes! It is with this personal meditation that we become free from the demands of the five senses, and with eyes open and a calm mind, we will then experience "Enlightenment", this being that which all the creed scriptures of the entire world's religions and ALL our philosophies seek. Naturally, this being the stopping of a personal "I Want" from filling the mind, which then allows the Soul to experience the stillness within the beauty of the world around you. Again, this is being the real world and not a world desiring to be created by the mind blocking five senses which are always pursuing an "I Want" false world that cannot exist and so it cannot be fully observed within the "Present Time". For indeed the "Present Time" is God's world or the world of Nature for the Non-Believer. So again it should be said that it is the experiencing of this "Realisation", this being of the real world of "Enlightenment", which is that which all our wise ancients endeavour to bring to ALL people. It may be worthwhile also to mention here that my personal experience of going beyond the above and so entering the "white light" which is beyond the dark "clouds of unknowing" was that all my "observations" of the Creation stopped. For my experience of "being" within this white light was that there is no longer an "Observer," which can be likened to the Soul viewing the outside world as if in the reflection of a still mirror. I now understand it to be "Self-Realisation", which is an existence in which you become a part of the unified Soul, has one with the Creation, and so you become the "Creation". It is an experience which enables you to know that you are everything that exists within the Creation, and there is no us, no them and no that – there is only YOU!

So absolutely it can now be understood that in the becoming of "everything", this being that which our wise ancients call "Self-Realisation" you experience that there is no observer, for you then genuinely become as one with the Creation. Without doubt, this is indeed a singularity in which there is no experience of a separate reality, only an all-encompassing unity. It is an experience in which there is no other separated understanding of any life or non-life, for indeed, you become only has one existence and so "experience" that there is no observer and this is the experience which our wise ancients called "Self-Realisation" because you realise that the true Self is "Everything". Unquestionably, this is certainly an experience which is beyond being "Self-Aware" which is also a condition called "Enlightenment". Naturally, this is being an "Enlightenment" in which you are "Self-Aware" that the Soul is the observing part of that which is "everything" and that "Self-Realisation" is undoubtedly an experience in which you realise that you "ARE" everything and that there is undoubtedly no observer. But at this occurrence, I must have loved the observing of the singularity to which I was knowingly a part of, this being the experiencing that which existed in my current life, for strangely. I understand that it was because of this love that I returned to the "Present Time", this again is as being an observer of the Creation in of which I knowingly existed to be a part. But I also certainly know that this return was physically achieved by the repetitive sounding of a new mantra, which and only upon returning to be an observer of the "Present Time", I recognised to be the repeating of my surname. I was glad for I love life and being a part of "everything", which is knowingly called "The Creation".

So yes! Regarding mantra meditation, it is good to understand that it is mainly by disciplining the animalistic five senses and achieving this by having them repeat this single creed based word within the mind, that you will eventually become "Self-Aware" and so become "aware", via knowledge that you are the observing Soul, which is the all-seeing all-knowing "observer" of all life and Non-Life. You will also become aware that your Soul is without any distortions and also that it wants nothing, for the Soul knows that it has all that exists within the Creation, which is truly God's world or the world of Nature for the Non-Believer, which is just another name for the *"Mother of the Creation"*.

So now truly, with this simple exercise, you will also begin to understand, and maybe for the first time, that you have been given the "Freedom of Choice" to support or not support the harmony that exists or is emerging from existing around you. For it is also useful to remember that when the incarnate "Self-Realised" Jesus was arrested in the garden of Gethsemane, this being by people who worshipped through their leaders and their leaders desired image God - for crucifixion, He was then tortured, beaten, humiliated and painfully nailed to a cross. Still, He said nothing to the people who did this to Him but accepted the forcefully controlled harmony that was all around Him. Without doubt, this was his full acceptance up until His painful death, at which His last words were ***"Forgive them for they know not what they are doing."*** For it is a well-known fact that Jesus gave no support, even by denial, to the false personal "worshipping" harmony that was around Him and your Soul will always behave in the same way.

So yes! This single worded recitation is the first activity which all our wise ancients pursued via their prayers and chants, this being a controlled disciplinary exercise of revealing and realising that you are the Soul, which is a knowing part of "everything", for sure, it is good to know that the Soul is that entity which is undoubtedly within you and also that entity which is outside you. It is also meditational activities that will disciplinarily stop all the "I Want" disfigurement that can cloud the "mind," which is now known to be caused by a staggering number of a personal "I Want" for ME thoughts which emanates from our past existence within the animal kingdom. It is this mind filling noise which is perpetrated continuously by the five senses, all of which can now be personally recognised to be not the real you, for you cannot be that which you observe in the mind just as you cannot be that which you observe on television, for both you can turn off. For now, you will certainly understand that the uncontrolled five senses will certainly perform acts which can be likened to the throwing of coloured paint onto a beautiful picture, which is truly the "Present Time". For it is undoubtedly this inner mind painting and then it's seemingly compulsory targeting activity that changes your personal view of the real world into a personally created unreal and self-imagined non-existing past or future world, which is the world of Hell. For honestly and factually, this is being a life lived in a non-existing false world in which the mind was being filled by an "I Want" dream, for indeed, this is being that which stops the Soul from seeing the real world which is now clearly understood to exist only in the "Present Time".

So yes! The past or the future is a place in which the Soul has no jurisdiction, for its task is to support God's harmony that can only exist in "Present" time or Nature harmony for the Non-Believer. For indeed, is it not here in the "Present Time" that rests the *"peace that surpasses all understanding"* and the world of the Holy Spirit, the Holy Ghost or the Angel Gabriel. It is also the sought to experience the "Present Time" which is the same targeting reality of all our worlds culturally varying religions and philosophies. For is it not true that ALL our worlds ancient wise created religions and philosophies that targeted the same goal, this being to bring the worshipper into experiencing the beauty and harmony of Gods world. Unquestionably, this being a world can only be experienced when a person's mind rest only in the "Present Time". But to achieve this actual reality our ancient wise had first to establish beneficial ways to remove each person "I Want" for ME", this being that which kept their targeted followers living in a personally created Past or Future, which "The Book" calls the non-existing world of Hell. Therefore, is it not easily recognised to be true that all our many religions and philosophies have all been initiated by our ancient wise? For assuredly, these are originators who created all our worlds culturally varied religions and philosophies? Is it not certainly known to be true that our wise ancients also introduced self-disciplined methods of praying which were based upon "Soul" controlled incantation praying, this being when unified within a group or has an individual. For indeed all our wise ancients were targeting this "Soul" creating exercise which was targeted to bring the doer out of their self-created world of an "I Want" Hell and into the "Present Time". This being that which our wise ancients knew to be Gods unified world, a world in which the Soul was created to support and which is also a world that can only be experienced in the "Present Time". For indeed, this is the targeting of "Enlightenment" which many people "feelingly" encounter during these outer-imposed prayers and or group-based and solitary incantations – but only fleetingly if this "awareness" of the "Present Time" is an unknown target.

But now this "Heavenly" target is known to exist, but only in the "Present Time". For "The Book" now "scientifically" explains that the "Practitioner" of a meditational short single worded mind stilling exercise, will now be able to realise that the Hell which they can now leave, was caused by their "Mind-Fully" living in a non-existing Past or Future. For only in the past or the future can exist the unreal world which is created and lived in by the five-senses, these being that animalistic entity which continually creates an unrealistic mind filling "I Want", a fact which keeps the observer locked into a world knowingly described as "Hell", this being because it does not exist but which can be imposed upon Gods world or the world of Nature for the Non-Believer. For indeed, this is a world in which the uncontrolled five senses chain people to their "I Want" for ME, targeting tasks, this being that activity which our entire wise ancient's imposed creeds did endeavour to silence. Without a doubt, this truly is being the only factual exercise which can remove those chains that tie a person into a non-existing "I Want" Past or Future. It is also good to remember that this newly imposed "disciplinary" chanting of a single world into the mind, via the now controlled five senses, is now a consciously imposed exercise which gives a "scientific" way to eventually reveal the factual evidence that is needed for any person to accomplish a life in the real world, a "Heavenly" reality that exists only in God's world or the world of Nature for the Non-Believer and known by both believers to be only enabled to exist in the "Present Time", for the Past and the Future is the non-existing world of a greedily imposed Hell.

For definitely, as all doers of this simple meditational exercise will find, that this simple exercise is a reasoning way to a truth which people in our ancient times would never have fully understood but still targeted to accomplish. It is also an exercise that will show all doers a "Scientific" way to this truth in which they will personally experience "Enlightenment". For it is truly only then and only in the experiencing of the "Present Time", that all people can realise and fully know and experience the "Enlightenment" which all our wise ancients spoke, for knowledgeably, this is undoubtedly an "Enlightening" truth that can be certainly experienced. But yes, if you do not experience this, then your five senses are controlling you, for your misunderstanding is based upon a simple "I Want" which is blocking your mind and so barring the view of your Soul, through the mind, of witnessing the "Present Time". Now let us hear the words of a pure incarnate that we know to be named as Jesus, also known to be called the Son of God and now definitely known to be "Self-Realised". The following is that which Jesus said about the real world, this being the world that the praying, as mentioned earlier, will take a people to. For certainly now all can fully understand His meaning and with added modern additions for Jesus said: 4:13-*14 "Everyone who drinks this water will be thirsty again."* He meant those who live in the past or the future. *"But whoever drinks the water I will give to him will never be thirsty again. For my gift will become a spring in the man himself, welling up into eternal life."* It was in this way that Jesus described the life of those who lived in the "Present Time", which is Gods world, this being the world of true harmony which is obtained through meditation. Also: 4:32 – To which Jesus replied, *"I have food to eat that you know nothing about."* - This food is the living with the understanding of a harmony that truly exists for all people in the world, but only in the "Present Time", for indeed, this is about the food that Jesus spoke.

Also: Jesus said 4:34-38. *"My food is doing the will of him who sent me, and in finishing the work, He has given me,"* for assuredly, this is the upkeep and explaining the need to support the harmony that exists only in the "Present Time". Also, Jesus said in 4.35 *"Don't you say, 'Four months more and then comes the harvest'?"* These being words that can be explained has an "I Want", for it does not exist in the "Present Time". Then Jesus says *"But I tell you to open your eyes"* – via creed worship – *"and look to the field"* – which is the "Present Time" – *"they are gleaming white, all ready for the harvest."* – The harvest is the harmony of the real way of life that can only be reaped or sown in the "Present Time". Also, Jesus stated *"The reaper is already being rewarded and getting in a harvest for eternal life"* – The reaper being those people who live only in the "Present Time" which is Gods world– *"so that both sower"* who is God *"and reaper"* who is an enlightened person – *"may be glad together."* For in these wise sayings is born the real truth, for one person can sow a harmony that is reaped by another person, for this is indeed the same harmony that inner bodily exists within ALL life and ALL non-life', for is it not true that we are all only one body?

For did not Jesus add: *"I have sent you"* – meaning all people – *"to reap a harvest for which you never laboured;* this being the Creation which exists all around us and within us: Then saying *other people* – These being our wise ancients – *have worked hard, and you have reaped the results of their labour,"* for definitely, this is living in the harmony that always exists and which is also continually endeavouring to be created around you.

Also, here are some perfect sayings from Jesus, which also explains the food that creed worship will bring to a person for did Jesus say within the bibles 6:27-29 *"Believe me,"* replied Jesus. *"You are looking for me now, and this is the reason why you wish to pray, not because you saw my signs but because you ate that food and had all you wanted"* – this being a food that can be likened to feeding on past or a future "I Want". *"You should not work for the food which does not last."* – These being the "I Want" thoughts based upon the past or the future – *"but for the food which lasts on into eternal life,"* – that which exists in the "Present Time", this is indeed the world in which the food of life exists, but only in the "Present Time" – *"that the Son of Man will give you, and he is the one who bears the stamp of God the Father."* It is a food that is presented to all who have ears to hear and is given to all people by creed worship, for unquestionably you, the reader, now have ears that can hear.

6:35-40 – (35) Then Jesus said to them*, "I am the bread of life"*, which is the "Present Time*". "The man who comes to me* (The "Present Time"*) will never be hungry, and the man who believes in me will never again be thirsty",* this being to live only within and for the needs of the "Present Time", the only world in which life and non-life exist.

(36)"Yet I have told you that you have seen me and do not believe," this is a belief being in the right harmony of all life that can only exist in the "Present Time". (37) *"Everything that my Father gives me will come to me* (In the Present Time), *and I will never refuse anyone who comes to me."* – Meaning that all can people can live in the "Present Time" and away from any past or future "I Want" which is the personally created world of Hell. For did not Jesus say in (38) *"I have come down from Heaven, not to do what I want, but to do the will of him who sent me,"* this is the living of a life that exists in the harmony of the current Creation which can exist only in the "Present Time". For was this not honestly said in the psalm (39) *"The will of him who sent me is that I should not lose anything of what he has given me but should raise it up when the last day comes*." – This "I" could be "You", the reader, on your "last day" of living has a selfish person and who is now deciding to leave their

personally invented past or future "I Want" for me world. Unquestionably, this being a never satisfying world in which they did claim all things for themselves.

So upon deciding to leave this untrue sadly dreamed "I Want" Past or Future world, they then enter the "Present Time", the word of God's harmony in which everything is provided for them and even more so after death. (40) *"And this is the will of the one who sent me, that everyone who sees the Son,"* who in this "Present Time" is the personification of the Creation "and trusts in him" He who is the personification of the "Present Time*", "should have eternal life, and I will raise him up when the last day comes."* This passage clearly explains that Jesus knew that He WAS a "Self-Realised" singularity of the "Present Time" and God's true Son; truly, someone who knew He was the child of God, the embodiment of the Creation and so was enabled to teach all people that they are "ALL" only one child. Still, many have forgotten this fact and forgetting is our worst enemy. Therefore, is it not also indeed stated in John (1) *"In the beginning was the Word, and the Word was with God, and the Word was God".* Meaning is that you can hear and so experience any sound – but only in the "Present Time". Also (3) *"All things were made by him, and without him was not anything made that was made".* Meaning that you can experience all things made, but only in the "Present Time", and (4) *in him was life, and the life was the light within all people.* This light is the unified "consciousness", which shines on all things, but again, only in the "Present Time."

Now honestly, an essential concept to remember is that you will not achieve immediately, via this meditational repetitive single worded creed based prayer, the realisation and or experience of the "Present Time". Unquestionably, this is being the only time in which the mind dwells without any entering thought. You will also not "realize" immediately or quickly that there is only one blissful form of that of which you are indeed a part. But you will eventually realise, with steady perseverance, this truth that you will ultimately begin to live in, and so achieve the "Enlightenment" spoken of by ALL our wise ancients. For this "Enlightenment" experience is that which was known even before the written word and it is that which ALL our worlds' faiths, religions and philosophical creeds seek.

For indeed, *"In the beginning was the Word".* The word is the now inner sounding mantra which "The Book" explains to be a faith-based practical and straightforward exercise, this being that which will bring your Soul, which is the real you, to a life that is lived only has an existing part of the "Present Time". For indeed it is historically well known that the more you silently repeat this single mantra, the quicker will be the time when you will live in God's "Present Time" or Nature's "Present" for the Non-Believer. Unquestionably, this is until eventually, this single silently worded creed based exercise is no longer necessary, for once "habitually" experienced, you can never leave this truth which is true, YOU!

For did not Jesus, who knew who He was, say: *"I am the bread of life; whoever comes to me shall not hunger, and whoever believes in me shall never thirst."* And also: *"I am the living bread that came down from Heaven. If anyone eats of this bread, he will live forever. And the bread that I will give for the life of the world is my flesh,"* this "flesh" that exists only in the "Present Time" is also the body that carries the Soul. Therefore, for is not also true that Jesus, speaking as the unified Soul, also said: *"I Am the Light of the World. Whoever follows me will not walk in darkness but will have the light of life. For as long as I am in the world*, (The Soul within a person body) *I am the light of the world,"* this is undoubtedly a clear direction for all people to follow, for your Soul is that which never wants anything for itself and it is genuinely an entity which rests within you. Again; Jesus explained the way of the Soul, by saying, *"Truly, I say to you, I am the door of the sheep and if anyone enters by me, they will be saved and will go in and out and find pastures."* He is speaking about a person's Soul that never seeks an "I Want" for it knows that everything that it needs is already availed to it. Then the Enlightened and Self-Realised Jesus describes the Soul as the good shepherd, by saying, *"I am the good shepherd who lays down his life for the sheep for I know my own and my own know me."* Meaning that the soul within us is the true shepherd and which is also the true singularity which rests within ALL of the people. Then again; Jesus described the Soul as in the first person, by saying: *"I am the resurrection and the life. Whoever believes in me, though they die,* (Leaving the thoughts of an "I Want" gainful Past or Future*) yet shall they live, and everyone who lives and believes in me* (this being the Soul within) *shall never die".*

How clear these words are explaining that which you are. Then again, these wise words from Jesus speaking directly as the Soul, by saying: *"I am the way and the truth and the life and no one comes to the Father (God) except through me"* (The Soul). Adding: *"If you had known me* (The Universal Soul), *you would have known my Father* (God) *also."* Then adding: *"From now on, you know Him and have seen Him."* This "knowing" is the now knowing of your Soul which can be silently experienced when you "silently" read these words, for did not Jesus when speaking as a "Self-Realised" Soul, say: *"I am the true vine, and my Father is the vinedresser. Every branch in me that does not bear fruit He takes away, and every branch that does bear fruit He prunes, that it may bear more fruit."* This pruning is that which is now taking place in YOU! For indeed, does this not also explain why there is "Sugar in the Water". Honestly, it is undoubtedly realised that Jesus is not speaking about His body, but that which the body carries – The is being the universal Soul? Also at this time, in the garden of Gethsemane, Jesus now realised that His "gardening and pruning work" was now ending. So it should be understood that the unknowing Judas was selected by Jesus to betray Him, this being because their hands touched in their search for food at the last supper, for Jesus knew that His persecution and death were imminent. He also knew that He could not allow His condemners to attack and hurt His many followers in their search to punish Him

74 THE WAY TO GODS WORLD OR THE WORLD OF NATURE FOR THE NON-BELIEVER

It can again be said to be possible that our cave-dwelling ancient relatives realised a meditational silence that brought to them the experiencing of "Enlightenment," this is being after a long day of the male hunting and the female gathering, as in an occupying silence they sat down and silently stared at the fire and so arrive at a condition in which they would enter an "Enlightened" like state. It can also be believed that "Enlightenment" would have happened when spending time in the unthinking loneliness associated with living in dark caves, which led to the inhabitants slipping into an altered state of consciousness in which all past and future thoughts did not exist therefore all that they could experience the "Present Time".

For indeed, our wise ancients need for creating cave drawings explains that people can undoubtedly bypass their many worded and creed based group sayings or creed based group songs, which factually enabled our cave dwellers to confirm a personal drawing, this being based upon a well-established individual concentration. These old pictures even being such as the personal image of their hand, which even thirty thousand years ago was made by blowing some kind of pigment upon it while holding it against a wall and it is interesting that in a past life this personal "signature" may have been created by you! This artistry was often being performed deep inside a cave; an exercise which must have had great solitary significance for them; just as would have been the sounding of a song or a chant which eventually led to the need for a constant repeating of only one word; a word that is purposely sounded by the group or within the individual's silent mind.

So yes! Chanting with a silent mind that is "inwardly observed" to be silent was also a ritual system which was written about, this also being explained when writing first came into the world of people. This writing is about an exercise which was written about three thousand years ago, and it was called "Mantra Meditation. It was ancient writing that had no serious explanation. Still, it was knowingly stated to eventually take the doer into God's world, a world that can only exist in the "Present Time". But now, thanks to modern understanding, "The Book" scientifically explains it to be an exercise which commands a person's consciousness to discipline their willpower to obey only the sounding and repeating of a single word into their mind, this is being a single word that is then "disciplinary" released, via the God-given "Freedom of Choice" into the individual's accepting mind and nothing else is requested except the sounding into the mind of this one repeating word. An act which would eventually "disciplinary" stop a person's animalistic five senses from "wordily" and always sounding their

"I Want" into the mind, this being a habit which was established in childhood via the same God-given "Freedom of Choice" because in childhood we mistakenly thought that the words emanating from the five senses were really "US". They are not "US", for indeed you are your Soul and the Soul cannot be that which it listens to or sees, or tastes, or touches or smells and your personal "Freedom of Choice" was individually given by God. This gift being factually given so that you could support the harmony seeking work of the "Mother of the Creation", for sometimes the same act can create harmony, or it can destroy it, and the purpose of the Soul is to support this work which can only occur in the "Present Time."

So yes! "Scientifically", this creed-based and very ancient praying system called "Mantra Meditation" is that which factually targets "Enlightenment". It is this "prayer" that is being put forward as an act that will enable you, via your personal "Freedom of Choice", to "choose" a single word and then also importantly "choose" to inform your "consciousness" to empower "willpower" to disciplinary repeat and so sound this single word into the silent mind. It is now right to also remember that only in people did God or Nature for the unbeliever give their "consciousness" the need to disciplinary obey the God-given "Freedom of Choice", for this is certainly required if you wish to support Gods world or the world of Nature for the Non-Believer.

So yes! Just as a cigarette smoker, at the beginning of their smoking, did purposely "choose" via their "consciousness" to enforce their "willpower" to overcome their coughing and so smoke cigarettes until their smoking became cough free, and then later it was needed to again "choose" their "consciousness" to enforce "willpower" to break the "habit" of smoking. For indeed there is also a similar need to "forcefully" stop the habitually allowed energy of "consciousness" from automatically allowing "willpower" from powering and releasing into the mind, the pictures and words based upon the "I want" desires that are always filling the mind, this being that which is undoubtedly emanating from the animalistic five senses. It should now be known and understood that "willpower" has habitually been allowed to claim many an "I want," because the "thinker" has mistakenly believed that the five senses are really "themselves".

They are NOT you, for sure; they are genuinely the animalistic tools of the ancient body, which is a real truth. For indeed and firstly in those early "meditational" days you cannot experience to be yourself that which your Soul observes. For, in the beginning, this meditational "disciplinary" exercise is to silence the mind of all thoughts successfully. For this, you need great patience AND perseverance for your five senses, which "The Book" likens to be five untrained pups, have for a long time been thought of as being the real YOU! For now, it is good to understand that this is not true that you cannot be that which you listen to – in mind, but you will succeed.

Those five senses will become silent and entirely obedient to your requests which factually enables your Soul, which is the true you, or your consciousness for the none-believer, to experience the real world and so fear and worry no longer exists as you become "Self-Aware" that all that the five senses experience, this being that which the Soul witnesses, is the totality of YOU! For when becoming "Self-Aware" you experience the "I am the I am" of everything and so your observing soul, which is you, has no feelings of selfishness, and also no feelings like jealousy of others, or materialistic greed for money nor a desire for name and fame which can no longer exist within you.

These were the factors which always keep a person trapped in the vicious circle of a never-ending "I Want" for me race, this being for material properties. For indeed becoming "Self-Aware" ensures that an "I Want for Me" life has no meaning anymore. For truly then life's purpose becomes the supporting of a "Heaven" for all people which continuously and oft unknowingly do consistently reflects the message of love which also continually targets freedom from all sufferings, this being for all that exists. For unquestionably being "Self-Aware" ensures that there is no fear of losing anything even our own lives for our own body is experienced to be just a medium to carry your soul, this being that which you know cannot die and whose ultimate goal is the spreading love, happiness and also the togetherness of good preaching's.

It is then of course that eventually will come to the final stage of life, this being that which called "Self-Realization", whose ultimate goal is the spreading of love, happiness and also good advisory preaching's. For certainly following a "Self-Aware" existence and dedication, this being in the constant supporting of the emerging creation, that such an "Enlightened" person will move away from the silent needs of the emerging creation, in which all five senses are quietly controlled until called into use and so will eventually become "Self-Realized". Undoubtedly, this being an experience in which there is no observer for only the existence of a unified singularity which is "you" exits. This reality is being when you become everything in Gods world or the world of Nature for the Non-Believer. It can also be knowledgeable stated that from this "Self-Realised" existence you are never born again, for you eventually become one with God, which "The Book" states are the purpose of the Creation in which God wishes to experience the totality of the love that emanates from Himself.

So yes! Now indeed, all people should understand that the purpose of ALL our worlds religious and philosophically creed-based rhythmical hymns, prayers, songs, chants and actions are all self-imposed disciplines and actions that are used, via our God or Nature gave "Freedom of Choice", to command a person's "consciousness," to engage the energy of "willpower," to perform only those religious and philosophical activities that are requested by others within their culturally accepted way of worshipping. Without doubt, this is being a worshipping system in which people acknowledge that there is undoubtedly something more significant than them. These are wisely, and usually, groups supported but are certainly self-imposed disciplinary praying and worshipping exercises that actually re-places and so stops the habit of their inner "consciousness" from habitually allowing their "willpower" to energising into their mind a previously and automatically allowed "I Want", this being an "I Want" that is emanating from any one of the five senses. These automatic "I Want" emissions are usually commands emanating from the five senses. So it is they who are the instigator and creator of the false "I want" dream world, which can only exist in the unreal world of the past or the future which "The Book" calls Hell. For indeed our wise ancients who created our many variable world religions and philosophies knew that during these creed-based self-disciplined exercises, God's world, this being that which can only exist in the Heaven that we call the "Present Time" – can and will be realised, and so actually and personally experienced by their followers, which is an experience that is never forgotten nor is it an experience that can be forced upon others.

So yes! It was well known by all our wise ancients, who originated all our world's religions and philosophies, that during their followers performing of any actively outer-imposed creed-based rhythmical and group disciplined performing of a hymn, prayer, song, chant or action, that the doer of these acts can and will leave their dream based "I Want for ME" world of their personally created "Hell", and so experience the "Present Time", which is the "Heaven" filled bliss of God's world or the world of Nature for the Non-Believer. For indeed, this is the real world, and it begins with the momentary feeling of a "bliss" that is without thought. It is happening that can sometimes be experienced at or during a creed imposed exercise. Still, it can indeed be an experience that can eventually lead to "Enlightenment" which once experienced, can be pursued fully and never again will it be lost.

So yes! It is because people have been created with the "Freedom to Choice", that they can "choose" to guide their inner "consciousness" towards directing the energy of "willpower" towards refraining from automatically supporting the mind-entering words of the "I want," that is automatically emanating from the five senses. As you would expect, this is not an easy task, because, for many years, believers and non-believers have understood that these mind filling "I want" are really emanating from themselves and so are thoughts that are needed to full-fill their existence, not realising that they are acts that also stop the Soul from viewing through a clear mind, the "needs" required to support the emerging harmony of the Creation actively, this is being a "creation" supporting which can exist only in the "Present Time". For indeed, this is being that which is existing all around us has it does unselfishly exist within us. For as expected, the supporting of this harmony seeking target can only occur in the "Present Time", this being the real purpose of our existence and also the purpose of our God-given or Nature has given "Freedom of Choice". Therefore, it is well to understand that the purpose of ALL our world's religions and philosophies, which were established by our Earths ancient wise, was to purposely install many culturally-based types of self-disciplined praying and chanting, which is a meditational exercise in which our wise ancients intentionally used the energy from our "consciousness" to redirect our "willpower" purposely, to resist short-term gratification and so be "holistically" re-trained by "consciousness" NOT habitually to obey the demands of the five senses.

So yes! It is agreed that during the meditational exercise proclaimed by "The Book", you will undoubtedly be distracted from this mantra imposed activity by the habitual words of the five senses entering your mind. Still, it is wise that when upon recognising this false world, to "immediately" and willfully enforce your "consciousness" to redirect "willpower" to energise "ONLY" the mind-filling sound of the repeating mantra. For assuredly, in the beginning, you will find that this exercise needs severe discipline, for the five senses will instinctively put up a fight to stop this exercise, for these "five pups" are unbelievably cunning and they will twist you into thinking that they are the real you! They are NOT you, for you are genuinely the inner observing ever-living never-dying Soul and "scientific" proof of this is that in your current lost state you now understand that you cannot be that which you observe or listen to, or smell, or touch, or see, for you are the observer of all these things, for again. Again and truly, you are the all-seeing, all-knowing SOUL, this being that which can never see its self but which knows that it is an integral part of the singularity of a "Heaven" that truly exists, but only in the "Present Time".

So Yes! The real purpose of re-choosing consciousness to re-direct willpower to repeat a single word within the mind can replace ALL our worlds' religious and philosophically introduced creeds, but not the bonhomie of such communal practices. This common practice being the bonhomie of a togetherness which is "culturally" disciplined and thereof supporting ally useful and certainly an excellent way to experience the togetherness of that which is attached to many a religion culturally based ways of praying and worshipping, all of which were initiated by our wise ancients to support a group-based activity that developed a unity of oneness within it, worshippers. Yet, sadly, is it not also known that this friendliness, this being that which is experienced when praying or worshipping with others within a culturally chosen way of worshipping, that this peaceful act can develop into a sinful "I Want" others to experience the happiness and bonhomie of my religion – and some people will even kill those who say "NO, I am happy with my religion". Of course, this is NOT Gods world nor the supporting world sought by the "Mother of the Creation", who will both turn their backs upon such people who do not support the emerging creation but use their God-given "Freedom of Choice" to try to destroy it. But is it not exciting to know just where they will be born again in their next life?

So yes! All self-imposed chanting, worshipping, singing and praying, this being culturally established within all our world's religions and philosophies, was a personally targeted effort which our wise ancients knew would bring their worshippers into the "Present Time". For assuredly, these religious and philosophical targets were designed to replace their followers personal "I Want", this being that which are mind-filling emanations that are born from the five senses. For it is undoubtedly true that this is that which usually fills the mind with a Past or a Future "I Want", which is the world of "Hell". Indeed, this is being that which factually stops the inner Soul from "realising" the actual outer world, a world that can only exist in the "Present Time", which is the world "The Book" calls "Heaven". For all self-imposed chanting, worshipping, singing and praying were certainly designed by our wise ancients to bring their followers into the "Present Time", this being that which is genuinely Gods world or the world of Nature for the Non-Believer.

So yes! Now it is explained by "The Book", that all self-imposed chanting, worshipping, singing and praying can be reduced to a single word. It is this disciplined mantra-sounding single world that can be used replace the childhood "choice", which was to obey the selfish "I want" needs of the five senses because in childhood they thought that the words in the mind were indeed emanating from the needs of themselves. They are NOT the needs of themselves but the "I Want" needs of their five senses.

Therefore the REAL secret hiding behind this repetitive mind filling sounding single worded "mantra", this being that which is also a secret word that should not be revealed to others, is that it should be "scientifically" known that the meditator is using a God or Nature given for the Non-Believer "Freedom of Choice". Unquestionably, this is being that which is used to choose "Consciousness", to automate "Willpower" to automatically and repetitively sound within the mind this single worded mantra. For indeed, this will eventually begin to act like a closed door to all other thoughts these being that which have habitually been allowed, in childhood, to emanate from the animalistic five senses. For definitely the mantra is a mind-controlling fact because this single inner sounding word will eventually become habitual and unthinkingly "Soul-Disciplined" or "Self-Disciplined" for the Non-Believer. For positively it is undoubtedly a purposeful single worded mind filling activity that does "automatically", and "disciplinary" refuse entry of all other "words" or "thoughts" that have been allowed – in childhood - to emanate from the animalistic five senses. Without doubt, this being their individually desired "I Want for ME", truly a constant mind filling noise which has been allowed to fill and cloud the mind for many years. Simply put, these five senses can be likened to be similar to five wild pups that have never been trained to come to heel, meaning to be disciplined and so rest silently behind your heel until called to do an action – also like a sheepdog.

It is then, during this mind silencing mantra-based exercise, that the meditator will eventually become eyes closed aware that within the spaces of this now automatically sounding mantra, this being a mantra-based single word that was previously and forcibly created but is now a word that is being automatically sounded by the newly disciplined five senses. Therefore, indeed, the mind is now being "observed" to be truly empty. Without any thought, this is undoubtedly being a mind stillness which now allows the Soul, for the first time, to begin to see that which our ancients called "The clouds of unknowing", this being the ever still and seemingly ever cloudy movements that can only occur in a silent mind.

To explain this meditation task further – look at your left hand and with eyes open and looking forward mechanically move it out of sight behind your left ear and then move it rightwards until out of sight, behind your right ear – now mechanically repeat this left-hand movement from left ear to right ear and in front of your eyes for a few minutes. Also, do this without thought while looking at a picture of the room in front of you! It is then that you will begin to understand that you can see all that is in front of you and seemingly without any hindrance, this being as the hand mechanically passes back and forth for this is the same experience that is happing when with eyes closed you are seemingly inwardly "viewing" beyond the mechanical-sounding mantra the slow movements of the silent mind – this being that which our ancients called the "clouds of unknowing". For assuredly, this viewing will undoubtedly be after many weeks of hearing and cancelling many words and conversations taking place in your mind and often saying how silly you are and also how you should stop this silliness of an imposed mantra – but the real question is "Who is saying these inner sounding words and more important who is listening to them? For truly you will find when this happens that you cannot sound the mantra, this being that which disciplinary brings you and keeps you within the existence of the "Present Time", which is Gods world of Heaven, or the World of Nature for the Non-Believer and also you cannot at the same time mentally talk to yourself, this being an exercise which takes you into a make-believe non-existing Past or Future, which is the world of an "I Want for ME" Hell.

So yes! The real target of meditation is to use the God-given or Nature Given for the Non-Believer "Freedom of Choice" to stop the five senses from continually sounding their "I Want for ME" into the mind, this being a fact which was "habitually" allowed to happen in childhood because it was thought that these sounds in the head were emanating you. Still, now it is well to understand that these words in the mind are not you, for you cannot be that which you observe or to that which you listen. For truly "YOU" are the Soul, this being that entity which also cannot interfere with your God-given or Nature has given for the Non-Believer "Freedom of Choice. For truly this again being said is a supporting of the "Freedom of Choice" that is Godly or Nature gave to support the emerging creation that can only occur in the "Present Time". For certainly meditations purpose is to make still the mind so that a person's Soul can see and evaluate the outer world and if necessary silently energise one's consciousness to employ their willpower to support the emerging creation correctly, via the God-given or Nature gave for the Non-Believer "Freedom of Choice". For truly, it is then, after much practice of meditation and with no longer any personal "I Want for me" ideas filling the now empty mind, that with eyes open, the Soul will then see through the clear mind and into the outside of the body's world, this is being the world of the "Present Time", which is God's world or the world of Nature for the Non-believer.

So yes! The starting of the above meditation exercise, this being that which is designed to free your Soul or your Consciousness for the Non-Believer; this being the freeing of that Soul which is resting within you and it is certainly an exercise in which you can personally begin at any time? For certainly what is needed is a personal set aside time, this being that which can be targeted to achieve the practising of mediation twice a day. It is also good to begin this acute meditational exercise after the sitting straight-backed on chair exercise spoken of earlier, this being that which begins with a two-minute developing to 15 minutes silent seeking mind emptying exercise as you regularly target the experiencing of feeling only your weight upon the chair which can only be experienced in the Present Time, but over time, and when you feel peaceful and relaxingly ready, you can then introduce the use of the single worded mantra has previously stated, *this being that which certainly keeps you in the "Present Time"* and then, ensure that over-time this mantra's silently sounding duration will disciplinarily build from fifteen minutes to a maximum of thirty minutes duration and to be performed twice a day.

Do not think about how well or how quickly you are progressing, for these are just "I want" ideas, entering the mind. But you can be assured that the mind will eventually become still like the space between the inner sounding mantra appears even when you not sounding the mantra, for sure the outer world will become still as is the silence within the mind. It is then, with this silence in mind, that you will witness "Enlightenment", which is God's world or the real world of Nature for the Non-Believer, this is the real world, and it is a world that can only exist in the "Present Time", and it is certainly a world that your Soul has been given life to witness and also to support. For only in the "Present Time" can your Soul silently see the world outside your body and so to naturally perform its tasks which is to support the harmony that exists or is emerging from existing, all around you – which is also the real you! For it is then and only then, with the mind silently empowered and habitually stilled by your bodies "consciousness" via its controlling "meditational" management. For indeed this is a factual and physical activity that is now reprogramming your God-given "Freedom of Choice", this being a gift which your "instinct" claimed in childhood and so allowed the "I Want for ME" demands of your five senses to fill your mind and so block the viewing and understanding of the real world and the Nature of the Creation. For indeed, as can be physically witnessed, your Soul, after much meditational training, is now "silently" able to see through a still mind the evolving needs of the Creation, and so can unselfishly support the harmony that truly, exists within the "Present Time". Unquestionably, this is being the real work of the observing Soul, which is to aid the emerging work of God's Creation or of Nature for the Non-Believer, which of course is the "Mother of the Creation". Again, this truly is the only natural activity of your Soul, for its purpose is to support the harmony that exists or is seeking to exist within the "Present Time", and which factually can only be performed when the Soul sees through the still mind and into the pure observing of the "Present Time".

So Yes! In those early days of "Meditation towards Enlightenment", this being when first sitting on that chair with your back being straight and your head pushed high towards the sky. For in some people, there can occur panic attacks which are the fear emanating from your five senses, which have nothing to do with the real you, which is your Soul, this being that which you now know is the observer of everything, even the observing of the panic attack.   But usually in the beginning not much happens. Still, you will certainly begin to become aware of thoughts – which you habitually think is you – these being that which, via ingrained habit, continually enter the mind. These thoughts usually being about your "I Want" from life or just merely attacking your attempts to silence them for you are genuinely endeavouring to stop them from entering your mind. Still, eventually, the stillness within the mind will grow these five senses, likened to be five wild pups, learn to be controlled and silenced by their master, which is your Soul.

For indeed the stillness required in mind will undoubtedly develop and you will begin to fully understand just who the witness is to all that is around you?   Your meditation will also automatically ease anxiety, and mental stress plus cure depression has this emptiness clears the mind, this being a fact that is experienced by the true you, which is the "Soul", for sure, your Soul is the silent observer to this mind filling "I Want" emanation from your five senses. For in truth, you are that which is the Soul within your body, this is being that which is the indeed the observer of all these things. Therefore it is essential to remember that it is "Mind Emptiness" or "Mind Fullness" which you are experiencing. For certainly "Mind Emptiness" can be simply achieved by sitting on a chair, as described above. For it is achieved by quietly just sitting and experience your weight upon a chair and listen to your breathing for two minutes, then later four, then later six until you reach 30 minutes. For indeed "Patient Meditation" and the use of a mantra is the best target for reconciliation with all life and none-life, for sure, it is the best reunion with the existence of all life and none life of which you are indeed a part.

So yes! Again, it must be stated that in mind there can be no thinking of any "I want" thoughts; for these are thoughts that take a person into the past or the future and are also thoughts which block the Soul from seeing through the mind, that task which is needed or not needed, to support the harmony of the emerging "Present Time". For indeed, it is now understood and recognised, that the Soul is only enabled to see the "Present Time" through a silent mind, this being that condition which is certainly required to perform any harmony seeking acts, these being acts which are supporting the evolving harmony which is continuously arising within the developing Creation, and it is this silent mind reality which is anciently called "Enlightenment".

So yes! It will become known by all meditational practising people, that these harmony seeking acts can only be evaluated and "automatically" performed when the mind is silent, for indeed within "Enlightenment" you become has one with the Creation, thus experiencing all that is around you is the same as that which is within you. For indeed, has "Enlightened" experience will show, it is only when the mind is silent that the Soul can see through the mind and into the "Present Time", this being that condition in which a person will be enabled to support the harmony that exists within all life and none-life; which is also actually supporting the harmony seeking endeavours of the "Mother of the Creation". It is then, and it can be repeated forever, that your mind and all that your silent five senses have been created to support, will become "Enlighteningly" exist, but only within the "Present Time".

So yes! Naturally, this is the place where the Soul within you will silently view all that God, supported by the "Mother of the Creation", has provided for YOU, who are also the singularity of all the people of the world. For positively, only people can knowingly live in Heaven, while on this Earth and this is that existence which all our wise ancients spoke about, and it is also why our wise ancients always endeavoured to create praying, singing or chanting creeds for their flowers to pursue. Undoubtedly, this being that which is needed by ALL people who are seeking that which is called "Enlightenment" and so to become "Self-Aware" that all that you're five sense reveal is YOU! A condition which could lead eventually to "Self-Realisation" in which there is no observer, only YOU! A condition in which you will not be born again for life is for God to experience "Himself", which is YOU!

For indeed, "Enlightenment" is a personal experience and it is that condition which is targeted by all our world's religions and philosophies, these being the religions and philosophies which have been revealed to all the worlds people by our many wise ancients. It is certainly an experience that is much sought after by those who care about the world. Again it may be stated that it is this condition which the Christian religion calls being filled with the "Holy Spirit" or the "Holy Ghost", depending upon their sectional belief system and it is also stated as an experience in which a person's mind is filled by a *"Peace that surpasses all understanding"*. While the Hindu religion calls this "Enlightenment" *"Moksha"* which loosely means *"freedom from ignorance"* and the Buddhists refer to it as *"Bodhi"* or *"Nirvana"*. Indeed, this being an experience which is described as *"awakening to the true nature of things"*. Also, the Islam religion speaks of it as *"Being filled with the Angel Gabriel"* and describes it as *"a realm beyond the ability of words to properly convey."* For indeed, all the religions and philosophies started by our worlds wise ancients target this "Enlightenment", this being that which goes all the way through all our worlds known history. Even going back to the time of in the ancient *Zoroastrianism* religion of the fifth-Century BC, this refers to this people experience "Enlightenment" as *"Ushta"* which they anciently describe as meaning *"liberation, salvation and emancipation of the Soul"*.

So yes! It certainly exists and is worth achieving and all you need to do to experience the above world of "Enlightenment", this being that is sought to be given to you by all our wise ancients, is to repeat a single worded mantra, this being sounded silently in mind. For indeed this historically known fact will bring to you, during these meditational practices and eventually after these practices, the experience of being in the harmony that truly exists all around you, but only in the "Present Time", for is it not also true that Jesus, of the Christian religion, experienced harmony, even when being nailed to a cross? This being has he said, *"Forgive them for they know not what they do"*, for His condemners lived in their own personally created "I Want for ME!" world, and not the world of God in which they had been provided with everything that they needed - which is God's world or the world of Nature for the Non-Believer. Unquestionably, this is being a world that truly exists and a world which can only be truly experienced when the mind is silenced by the truth of "Enlightenment".

Also, this is a truth that is clearly shown by the words of the Incarnate Jesus who said: *"When you are brought before synagogues, rulers and authorities do not worry about how you will defend yourselves or what you will say, for the Holy Spirit will teach you at that time, what you should say?"* Meaning that "Enlightened" people will be within an unthinking "Present Time", in which a personal "I want" cannot exist, and so will produce from the silence within their mind, the words that will reveal the direction towards the harmony for all. For undeniably, this is being that which is continually endeavouring to emerge all around you and will eventually emerge, even when denied its emergence by a mistaken "I Want for ME" people. Therefore, is it not also true that the "Enlightened" incarnate Jesus also added: *"but anyone who speaks against the Holy Spirit will not be forgiven, either in this age or in the age to come,"* meaning in these simple words that those who "knowingly" go against the "Mother of the Creation" work of supporting the creations emerging harmony and also all who read these words of "The Book", will now know the real truth. Indeed, this being that they will not only be living in the Hell of disharmony, as does the ignorant sinner, but in their next life to come, they will not be forgiven, this truly is *"in the age to come"*. For unquestionably, ALL religions and philosophies indeed state this truth and now you, dear reader, also, fortunately, know this absolute "Freedom of Choice" truth.

So yes! That tremendous experience of "Enlightenment" gained by Mantra Meditation, this being that which again can be stated, brings to the mind of a true worshiper the *"peace that surpasses all understanding,"* as explained in the Christian worship. It is also described as *"a realm beyond the ability of words to convey" as explained by the Muslim worshipper adequately*. For indeed, this mind empty "Enlightenment" is a beneficial and peaceful realisation which cannot be explained in words. For obviously certainly the "Present Time" cannot be brought to exist has a thought in one's head, for it is a reality that exists outside of thought, for evidently and only the images of the past or future Hell can be brought to an "I want" thought within the mind.

So yes, this "Enlightenment" is an experience that can happen to ANY mantra meditating person. Still, it is an experience that can only exist when the mind enters the "Present Time", and so is genuinely empty of all thoughts. For again it must be said that "Enlightenment" can only be experienced when the mind is without any personal "I want" thoughts, which are usually claims emanating from the five senses; these being "I want" personal claims which are conjectured within the mind as a claim for a past or a future dreamed existence, an existence which often projects actions that usually bring discord to the world around those who are seeking only to achieve their own personal "I want".

So yes! Now let us again take a look at an example of how the Soul works "silently" supporting the emerging harmony, which exists or is endeavouring to emerge within the Creation. For indeed the Soul works "silently," as when harmonising the activity that is taking place within a person's body, for without doubt the Soul also appears to perform similar actions "automatically" when acting within the body of that which we call the "Present Time". Of course, this also is the same activity that is required to fulfil the emerging and evolving activities that are needed to support God's harmony, this being that which is endeavouring to emerge outside a person body, just as it sustains the harmony that exists within a person's body, for definitely, the work of the Soul is to support God's laws continually and also to become a good child of the "Mother of the Creation".

Of course, again, it must be said that this is only possible when the mind has been so disciplined by the creed-born exercising of a Mantra Meditation, that it becomes silent and no longer tolerates the many "I want" that can continuously be emanating from the five senses, for indeed they can be stopped by this simple "meditation" exercise, this being from their wanting the whole of the Creation to be theirs. For within "Enlightenment" they can no longer block the reality of God's world or the world of Nature for the Non-Believer. For unquestionably, the Soul works in silence, this being while it is supporting the harmony seeking actions that exist in the bodies outer world and again it is good to repeat; just as it works in the same silence has when it is supporting the inner workings of a person's body.

So Yes! Now is undoubtedly the time via this meditational exercise, for all readers to allow their Soul to see through the empty mind and into the "silent" world of the Creation. This being that activity which then enables the Soul to accomplish the needed harmony performing tasks and duties that it has been truly created to complete. For now, as a practical example of that which the above speaks, let us look at a parable which is akin to a truth that can beneficially give to all people a clear understanding of the silence that can be established within them. Undoubtedly, this also is a fact which allows the Soul to work in the harmony that exists within the Creation's expanding endeavours, for indeed, this is undoubtedly a simple exercise which will reveal the real knowledge of a practical reality that releases the Soul to see only the "Present Time".

The following exercise will also show you in the world that you currently live. So now the exercise is to take both your hands and place the palms over your eyes, and you can see nothing of the outer world. Now create a space in front of your eyes by moving both hands side by side to become two or three inches in front of your eyes. Now vigorously wriggle your fingers and palms together and sometimes allow fingers and palms to collide with your face and your fingers also to keep staring forward at the fingers and palms that are vigorously moving back and forth in front of your face and so motivating ally colliding in front of your viewing eyes and face. This effect can be likened to a similar view to that which your Soul sees when looking through your active "I Want" mind; for these can be likened to "I want" images from the past or the future, that are filling the mind, and which are true "I want" that are uncontrollably and freely emanating from the five senses. Now keep staring at your hands and, while keeping your head still and your eyes staring ahead, now very slowly fold your arms and so trap your fingers and hand under your armpits. You are now looking at that, which can be likened to the "Present Time", and this is the difference that your Soul sees, when looking through an empty the mind and not a busy "I Want for ME", which is a clouded false mind filling the world. Amazing is it not?

As a further motivating awakener, this being towards the achieving of the meditational task now being presented to you, you may be further strengthened to know that the psychological benefits of an applied meditation are "modernly" said to be: reduced stress and anxiety, increased creativity and intelligence, reduced depression, increased learning ability, moral reasoning, reduced irritability and moodiness, plus feelings of vitality and rejuvenation. Also, an increased emotional control, increased self-awareness, good self-esteem, increased alertness, improved relationships and improved concentration and an eye-opening "wow", when coming together as one entity.

There are also some physiological benefits, such as it can help to lower blood pressure, and prevent or slow down or control the pain of chronic diseases. It is also known to boost the immune system, lower cholesterol levels, and improve airflow especially in those with asthma; plus ensuring a younger biological age – all which are known facts that cannot be disproved.

75 THE TARGET OF ALL RELIGIONS
AND ALL PHILOSOPHIES

So yes! God's harmony seeking plan of developing towards His Godly unknown target, which "The Book" believes is to experience Himself, or Nature's plan for the Non-Believer, is working and cannot be stopped; for indeed, all can still see the constant developing time-honoured removal of the warring tribalism that tends to exist within the growing and emerging cultures and also the different religions of our world.

Without doubt, this is tribalism which was once confined to single-family plus relative based group, who hid in caves and protected their valleys and which now appears to be continuing warring tribalism which is now confined to the borders of different countries, these being borders which are now allowing people to break out of their private cage, this being that which in the past encased them in different cultures and languages. For all know and history also proves, that this fear of other cultures and languages does pass, as "we" enter their world and "they" enter our world. Indeed, as history shows, all are the better for it, but yes, there are still some who live in fear and point fingers saying, "they are different, stay away from them" and how many people choose the honour of their tribe before Gods way or Nature's way for the Non-Believer? – But in truth only the "I want for ME", that rests within that complaining person is different,

Yet, is it not strange that some of our world religions and their "domesticated" and "disciplinary" residing laws still pursue an *"I want the laws of my religious creeds to be believed as the only way to God, and not the creeds of you or your religion,"* – and even the selfish *"I want my religious way to be the only way, for your religious way is not a true way".* But is it not true that these factions, has our world history shows, are eventually Godly driven to come together in their search for God's harmony, in which good "humour" appears to be the primary binding factor in this development, as it usually does at the end of many disputes. For indeed, as the Christians religion eventually found, this being that it does not matter what creed a person pursues as long as they are seeking the harmony and peace that exists only in God's world; a world in which all people can peacefully sit next to any other person and not even know or care what religion they pursue; therefore is it not correct to say that it is not essential to know which religion a person is attached to or not attached, to has long as they obey the harmony that exists in Gods world and so supports the work of the "Mother *of the Creation" .*"

So yes! Is it not truly very important to "always" remember; has our history shows, that no matter what religion a person painfully attacks or painfully tries to stop, God's plan or Nature's plan for the Non-Believer will always be accomplished? Therefore, is it not true that Gods plan or Nature plan for the Non-Believer, will always come back to pursue that which it seeks, and that which it is, which is always pure harmony? Therefore, it is undoubtedly an excellent proposal to live a life which pursues and aids the natural harmony of God's developing plan or Nature's on-going plan for the Non-Believer. For certainly has our Earths history consistently shows, there is only one correct way in which ALL religions, ALL philosophies, ALL Non-Religions and also ALL Non-Believers can pursue; no matter what their creeds or common law beliefs are.

For indeed all are here to truly support God's or Nature's constant on-going silent "harmonious" plan of development; this being a real way of life, which is undoubtedly for the benefit of ALL life and ALL non-life. Therefore, is it not certainly seen to be true that the "Creation", this being that which is supported by the ever-watchful, ever caring, ever harmonising work of the "Mother of the Creation", She being that entity which always ensures that "Goodness" or "Godness" will always surround all people. For surely is this not also a world which is called "Nature" by the Non-Believer? Unquestionably, this being a world that is within all people and also existing around each person and which is automatically and continuingly being always created to support everybody. Therefore no person can say to another, "My God is better than your God" or "My way of worship is better than your way of worship" or even purposely destroy God's harmony seeking ways, by punishing or killing others, these being those who see a different way to claim for themselves God's world; for there are only one God and one harmony that exists in the "Present Time", which is undoubtedly the world of a single creator.

So yes! Would it not be interesting if everyone stopped complaining about the lack of harmony around them or needling about the actions of others, mainly when their complaint is targeting their personal "I want" for ME! If you feel that you cannot stop your selfish ungodly "I want" acts, then do endeavour to do nothing, for indeed God's Creation or Natures Creation for the Non-Believer, cannot punish you. However, the "Mother of the Creation" will ignore you, and in truth, as our world history shows, this is NOT in a good position to be, for emerging events can harm you, like crossing a busy road with your eyes closed – who is punishing you? Therefore, is it not true that God's laws can be again likened to a people law of the "highway code". For unquestionably, as has previously been said, if you break these people-made laws by driving through red lights, or on the wrong side of the road, or drive down a one-way street the wrong way, then driving in such a way will bring many problems to exist for you. So it will be when you act against the laws of harmony that is all around and also emerging all around you.

Therefore, it is much better to "behave" and so supportive and so please the "Mother of the Creation" and therefore experience the sweetness of the harmony that exists or is emerging from existing, all around you. Yet sadly, many will break God's laws and inflict their sadness upon others, therefor in the harnessing to pursue their own "I want" they may "animalistic ally" attack you. Therefore it is always good to remember that the disobeying of the harmony that God or Nature for the Non-believer does create to exist around you, is like disobeying the rules of the High way code. For harmonies, the real purpose will keep crashing into the negative you.

Therefore, it is much better to support the harmony that is around you. If it is God's harmony and not a people-based harmony, then indeed, you will taste the "Sugar in the Water," which is the tasting of God's harmony that is always endeavouring to support you and not smash into you. Yet truly, this obedience to harmony can lead to you choosing death, as it did to Jesus who silently allowed the false harmony around Him to painfully destroy Him and even His words: *"Forgive them for they know not what they do"* as history shows, was a killing that was of no advantage to His persecutors, as can also be seen in many of the wars of our world. Again, is it not also true that according to our current "scientific" belief system, that there was "No-thing" (Nothing) before the "Big Bang"? Is this because a person's mind cannot grasp the reality of a "Godly" creator, this being that "something" which must have existed before the "Big Bang"? Also is it not "scientifically" understood that this "God" which is often deemed to be "No-Thing" (Nothing), did seed the reality of something that must have been in existence, this something being that which we knowingly call "Space"? Therefore "Scientifically" this "Space" must be the "Mother of the Creation"? For unquestionably is it not known to be true that it is the "Mother" who, when "seeded" by a father does gestate and later will give birth to a child, which is knowingly called "The Creation"? For the "scientific" fact remains that no one can prove this naturally based occurrence to be wrong? For indeed this fact makes all of life and non-life to be a singularity of existence and the only child of the "Father of the Creation" called "God"–AND– the "Mother of the Creation" who "The Book" calls "Space".

For unquestionably is it not a "scientific" truth that to begin a new life a "Father" is needed to seed a "Mother", who like all good Mothers is the one who continually cares for the growth of an only child. For often a person's thoughts cannot grasp the singularity of an existing God, therefore in accordance to the current "scientific" and factual belief system, "Space" can be the only "reality" of that which was before the "Big Bang". Therefore it must also be that entity which was seeded to give birth to an only child that was "Motherly" created and also birthed by this "Space", which "The Book" calls the "Mother of the Creation". The most critical reality regarding this fact is that everything you touch, see, hear, taste or smell, is really "YOU", a truth which is experienced within "Enlightenment." For you really cannot die, for your Soul usually chooses the next body before birth which can be likened to the choosing of a car to drive in, but only if the moving Soul had not previously existed in a body that had animalistic ally inflicted pain upon others! In that case, God would choose under what conditions it will next be birthed in and if you wish to know the reason for this – read on.

So Yes! With this truth based realty, is it not now factually known to be correct that you dear reader, are personally an integral part of this only child, for indeed, it can be said that if you are alive you must be part of this unified singularity; this energy which makes up that which is the "Creation" or that which is also be called the "Universe," by our non-believers. Yet is it not very accurate, for all to know, that God or that which can be called "Nothing" (No-Thing) by our Non-Believers, did seed the "Mother of the Creation". Therefore, did She not gestate and then birthed the unified energy of all life and non-life, this being that which exists all around us and within us. Is it not also "scientifically" known to true that this created energy can neither be duplicated nor destroyed; but can exist in a variety of forms, such as electrical, mechanical, chemical, thermal, or nuclear, and also that this energy can be transformed from one form into another, which confirms reincarnation. Is not this energy also known and experienced to be all-around people and also within all life? Therefore, can it not be said that this single "Unity of Energy", this being that which rests within and also outside of all people, is also "consciously" and so "knowingly" be that which also exists within all people?

So yes! Is this not a singularity, which we call "The Creation", a perfect unity in which "Self-Awareness" or "Self-Realisation" can be "scientifically" experienced has is being the unity of an only child? Again, this being an only child who is cared for and looked after by its Mother, who is stated by "The Book" to be the "Mother of the Creation", this being that single entity whose Motherly "love" holds the family (the Creation) together, as it does in all families? Even though in our thinking heads we are dominated by the knowledge that many separating thoughts in the heads of many people can bring the machinations of a personal "I want"; this is a false "reality," which causes peoples to believe that they are individuals, when in reality, we are therefore indeed, of only one body.

The question now is what would happen if all people supported all the harmony seeking ways of the Creation which is all around us, just as all is supported in harmony seeking ways of all our "personal" body parts? Could we imagine our body stopping the blood supply to the eyes because they did not like their colour? A fact which can be likened to a body part killing or punishing another body part, because that body part did not believe in there "God" or worshipped in their own culturally and creed based way or had some items within their possession which these "others" wanted, or even worse, that this observed body part looked different, even though it is well said that all people are of the one body and also did originate from the same South African mother. At the same time, indeed, it is agreed that the weather did change some of our outer parts, but the inner body did not change.

For agnostics, who are interested in the words of our wise ancients, it may be useful to understand or "imagine", depending upon your wisdom, that the Christian incarnate Jesus was speaking to all people, this being as the voice of the "Creation, and especially as the voice of our planet called Earth. For cannot all people truly recognise these words of Jesus to be always very loving words, which can also be likened to the loving energy of the Earth, and also the unselfish energy of that which is contained within the bodies of all life and non-life. Therefore, can it not also said that this is the same energy which "harmonises" our inner bodies many millions of separate parts, these being that which interact purely for the benefit of all the different functional parts of our own body. Or do our inner parts behave like some people do this being to continually endeavour to take that which does not belong to them? Indeed, our inner bodily parts do not break this natural law, for they usually do only their duty, as if understanding and remembering the words of the great Hindu Krishna, who said, *"To do the duty of another is fraught with danger."*

So Yes! Again, it is good to be reminded of that target which our wise ancients gave within our entire world's major religions and philosophies, this being that absolute truth which they gave to their followers. We're not ALL their truthful messages telling us to be un-selfishly supportive, especially in the control of the world around us, as is the supportive world that rests within us? Where we not also taught to stop claiming the "I want", that which is now known to be regularly emanating from our animalistic five senses? Therefore, is it not now truly known to be a factual reality which will lead all practitioners to useful life, this being a life which our wise ancients knew would be achieved by any individual who pursued the maintaining of all goodly endeavours and this also being within other willing supportive and practising groups. Was this reality not also achieved by the individual chanting of group-based creeds, which also brought the chanter into the "Present Time"? Until eventually a "Self-Aware" time would come, this being that time when everything you look at you will treat as yourself.

Therefore, with this understanding, there cannot be any personal "I want" desire arising within you or for you to acknowledge. For honestly now you know that you are a part of God's world, or the world of Nature for the Non-Believer, thus making you the only child of all that is within and all that which is without the harmony of the Creation, which is that which is there to be supported by your Soul. So yes! A person's life needs to arrive at a silent judgement that pays no heed to births circumstances but recognises all life and non-life as being "themselves". Therefore, is not true that all our worlds people are of the same unified entity, but that their uncontrolled "I want" thoughts, this being that which they think is them, makes them very different from those around them. Also does not this truth often make them enemies who attempt to destroy the social world in which they live? For did not the "Self-Realised" Jesus truthfully say: *"For those who have ears to hear let them listen"*.

76   THE KINGDOM OF GOD OR OF NATURE FOR THE NON-BELIEVER IS WITHIN YOU

Now as an expansion of these above words and also regarding many of the targets of our world's religions, let us hear a song from one of our wise ancients who was also a developer and supporter of many Eastern religions and philosophies. This creed based song or prayer is described as an Eastern prayer which is about our only real world, this being that which is God's world or Natures world for the Non-Believers and it is that which we call "Present Time". This revealing song is called *"The Song of The Self"*, and it was written by the wise ancient *"Adi Shankara"* in the years between 788-820 CE.

Its specific purpose is to describe that which is recognised by any person who is experiencing "Enlightenment", for it is undoubtedly a "song" that explains the understanding of the pure "awareness" of being "Enlightenment". This "awareness" is that which is known to exist within an "Enlightened" person for this song also explains how a person becomes as an existing and seemingly "static" part of the ever-still yet ever-moving Creation, this being the "Present Time" that exists all around them and also within them. It is undoubtedly a "song" which gives an excellent "understanding" and an "acknowledging" of a person Soul or Consciousness for the Non-believer, this being that which can truly experience the fullness of that which the ancients named to be "Enlightenment".

We should also note that this Eastern "song" knowingly describes the "Soul" as an entity that aids, creates, protects and transforms the ever still ever moving harmony of the still but ever-growing Creation or that which is named Universe by the Non-Believer. For this song correctly explains the Souls impartiality towards all of that which we call "activity", this being that activity which is ever still but ever-growing in the "Present Time", the only time in which exists the life of this only child. For is it not known to be true that all people have been given the "Freedom of Choice"?

Thus being enabled to choose to do or choose not to do any personal activity or non-activity, all of which has been purposely and wisely "chosen" to activate and support the love of the "Mother of the Creation", whose caring consistently supports the growth of Her only Child, whose named the "Creation". Therefore, undoubtedly, the truth is that God does nothing within the existing Creation, for He has already done all that is needed to be done, and He has the future to create. However, He certainly aids the "Mother of the Creation", and so creates a future that supports Her work, which is to maintain forever the harmony that can only exist in the "Present Time".

So yes! Now here is the wise ancient Shankara's *"The Song of The Self"*. Written over a thousand years ago during 788 to 820 CE and which is a song that identifies his Soul, this also being that which does not judge the work of the "Mother of the Creation", and he wrote this slightly modernised version as follows:

1/ I am not mind, nor intellect, nor ego, nor the reflections of the inner self. I am not the five senses. I am beyond that. I am also not the ether, nor the Earth, nor the fire, nor the wind (the five elements).

I am indeed, That eternal knowing and bliss, I am the Soul, the supporter of harmony, love and pure consciousness.

2/ neither can I be termed as energy, nor five types of breath, nor the five coverings. Neither am I the five instruments of elimination, procreation, motion, grasping, or speaking.

I am indeed, That eternal knowing and bliss, I am the Soul, the supporter of harmony, love and pure consciousness.

3/ I have no hatred or dislike, nor affiliation or liking, nor greed, nor delusion, nor pride or arrogance, nor feelings of envy or jealousy. I have no duty, nor own any money, nor any desire, nor even liberation. *I am indeed, That eternal knowing and bliss, I am the Soul, the supporter of harmony, love and pure consciousness.*

4/ I have neither merit nor demerit. I do not commit sins or good deeds, nor do I have happiness or sorrow, pain or pleasure. I do not need mantras, holy places, scriptures, rituals or sacrifices. I am none of the harmonies of the observer or one who experiences the process of observing or experiencing, or any object being observed or experienced. *I am indeed, That eternal knowing and bliss, I am the Soul, the supporter of harmony, love and pure consciousness.*

5/ I do not have a fear of death, as I cannot die. I have no separation from my true self and have no doubt about my existence, nor have I discrimination based on birth. I have no father or mother, nor did I have a birth. I am not a relative, nor the friend, nor the authority, nor the disciple. *I am indeed, That eternal knowing and eternal bliss. I am the Soul, the supporter of harmony, love and pure consciousness.*

6/ I are all-pervasive. I am without any attributes and any form. I have neither attachment to the world or liberation. I have no wishes for anything because I am everything, everywhere, every time, always in equilibrium. *I am indeed, That eternal knowing and bliss. I am the Soul, the supporter of harmony, love and pure consciousness.*

(To which "The Book" adds: *"I am the lover of life, and I cannot hurt my Divine Mother for all love is for the Divine "Mother of the Creation" ".*)

Now let us move from the ancient East and read these ancient Western words of Jesus. It may also be interesting to know that sixty years ago, the Christian Bible was forsaken by me to be entirely meaningless, contradictory and not understandable, but I was wrong. This understanding of the actual Christian teaching came some thirty years later after I had studied many other religions and philosophies, particular Shankaracharya, a philosopher and theologian, who specialised in teaching the way to Enlightenment and Self-Realisation, which was eventually experienced. At this later date, the Christian Bible was picked up once more and then began the read the new testaments mysteries and strange explanations again. Still, this Bible had the words emanating from Jesus printed in red, and so suddenly I began to read-only these words that were written in red. It was then that my jaw dropped, and my mind expanded into nothingness as it was realised that this was not a man speaking to me but God Himself was understandably known to be speaking to me through this man called Jesus.

So Yes! Now it is KNOWN and fully understood, that by removing all explanations, additions and stories surrounding the words emanating from Jesus, that by reading only the words being spoken by Jesus, it will be quickly recognised and understood that it is God, on behalf the *"Mother of the Creation"* that is speaking directly to all people. They are words that need no interpretation or support.

So Yes! It is also with this truth of reading only the words of Jesus that are in red that the reader will realise that all past ancient or modern interpretations or spoken additions are not needed and also can be misleading.

Therefore it is undoubtedly reasonable to listen again and to understand, via a modern interpretation, that these are the words of God as He spoke through Jesus with such words saying, *"The kingdom of Heaven is within you, nor will people say, 'Here it is', or 'there it is' because the Kingdom of God is within you."* God is speaking through Jesus about the Soul which "The Book" is also freeing. Yes, this experience of "Enlightenment" brings a clear recognition of the Soul that is resting within you and which is that which is "knowingly" attached to all that is outside you, for indeed, it is "Heaven" that exists within you and all around you. It is a "Heaven" that can only exist in the "Present Time". Rightly, this is the world that people's thoughts cannot reach but which can be bodily and silently experienced.

77   THE ONLY CHILD OF GOD OR OF NATURE FOR THE UNBELIEVER

What is also clearly seen is that the Christians Ten Commandments will also guide you with the prime commandments being:

1. "I am the Lord your God; you shall have no other God's before me."

2. "You shall not make any graven images of God."

3. "You shall not use the Lord your God's Name in vain."

And it is also understood that the most important commandment is:

4. "You shall not commit adultery."

Sincerely, this is an immoral act that breaks the unifying law, which is stated in the first three commandments, and it has nothing to do with male or female activity.

So Yes! Isn't it strange how people eventually changed this commandment on adultery to be interpreted mainly as a crime against man, rather than a sin against the above three commandments? It is, therefore, understandable to think that this imposed interpretation of adultery came into being when people left their hunting and gathering way of life and entered farming.

So defiantly, male farmers wanted to be sure that their offspring was their child and not that of another man. The remaining six commandments of the Christian religion are laws for community living, which we should all try to obey. These being the consensual laws that are accepted by the majority of people, yet we must always remember that the Creation was not built upon laws made by people or their "thinking" of what is a truth, but rather by a God based "scientifically" known unchanging fact.

These being facts which are governed by God's unchanging natural laws, which are laws that were made at the very beginning of time and will still be progressively working until the end of time. The task of life is to enjoy the Godly legality of all life and non-life and to fulfil its purpose plus also to tell all about your enjoyment and never to commit adultery against God's laws, for you will undoubtedly disappoint the "Teacher" who cares for all the Creation, this being the "Mother of the Creation" who "The Book" says is named Nature by the Non-Believer.

For indeed, if you recognise that your life's purpose can be likened to unifying the emerging strings of Nature together, these being two developing harmony seeking realities that will be emerging all around you, the *"Mother of the Creation"* will never turn Her face away from the caring of you. Also, if you control by silencing the demanding "I Want" which is being shouted into the mind by your body's five senses, then you will also find your life will joyfully surpass all your expectations, for you will have reached the ***"peace that surpasses all understanding"***, this being that which is called "Enlightenment". For then you will be living in a world without any personal "I Want," for you will fully know that you have everything and, if you have doubts about what to do when your peaceful activities are thwarted, just remember the peace of mind that was shown by the many Christians who faced lions in a Roman arena; what a piece of string that was, but they will be born again into a world of greater understanding.

However, now we know the truth and this truth being that the Creation is the only child of God, then there must be some final questions that we need to answer! These are simple questions which ask: "Who is Jesus?" "Who is Krishna and Buddha, or Muhammad plus who is Baha'u'llah, Confucius, Tao, Plato, Laozi, Vivekananda, Sri Shankara and Sri Ramakrishna, plus many more of the world's wise ancients who all spoke and explained in different cultural ways and languages the same truth? But the final question should no longer be "Who are YOU?" or "Who am I?" For these wise ancients, all put forward elementary religious and philosophical messages that stated to all people that WE are closer than the concept of brother, sister, mother and father.

Therefore the real question is: "Who are WE?" For certainly is it not a "scientific" fact that ALL our scientists state that each person originated from the same mother and that we all came from the same African valley that we then when birthed, all called "home". For undoubtedly truly, is not the "current" difference in appearances of our bodies caused by the *"Mother of the Creation"*, who is called Nature by the Non-Believer, who did carefully re-harmonise our body's for it to comfortably accept all the new environmental conditions that existed in the new places of our re-births, these being the new places we began to call "home"? It is also interesting to understand the silent reality of the why of our changed bodies, particular the reason why men grew beards, this being when they moved into colder countries in which their bodies need to be fully clothed, and therefore the beards purpose was to attract the ladies as opposed to hot countries where the body is not fully clothed, and so a beard is not necessary.

Also, another similar wonder of nature being the ladies cleavage, this being that which was created when we began to stand on two legs and which was especially enlarged when the need arose to be fully clothed as was needed in colder countries, for the cleavage was to continue to attract the men, for childbirth, is a constant necessity and the *"Mother of the Creation"* knows well these needs of an attraction. For the truth is that which we call you, and I are genuinely the singularity of the one life-force called people, and we also live in the one body called Earth, so should we not behave as our heart and lungs behave towards each other?

For the truth is that we only "think" we are separate entities, but the Creation cannot lie for did not the Creation, through this man called Jesus to say, ***"You shall love your neighbour as yourself"***, meaning that your neighbour is truly your "self". For when the "Enlightened" and "Self-Realised" Jesus speaks it can be likened to God or Nature for the Non-believer speaking directly to you. This theological meaning of the Christian and also of our worlds many Gospels gives the correct meaning to the following words of Jesus, when He said as in Mathew 19:30: ***"But many first shall be last, and the last first"*** because, the actual meaning of this is that there is only one person in the queue, so why do many in the queue think they are separate, for in real truth when the one at the front is being served, so is the one at the back and all religions and philosophies call this "unity". It has nothing to do with wealth.

It can also be agreed that much of what Jesus was saying in that ancient time was too difficult for people to fully understand, especially the fact that His teaching explained that they were not individuals – but were of one body consolidated within the single energy of the Creation – especially planet Earth. Thus, we have the reason why it was stated that we must *"turn the other cheek,"* for those who strikes another is striking themself. Don't just take our wise ancients written word for it, just read ONLY the words of Jesus spoken in the Bible, which are also shown at the end of "The Book", then attempt to bring things together by following the above stated "reasonable" way of unity that encases all people, and so find the real "Good Life". For indubitably it can now be "scientifically" understood that the theological meaning of the Christian Gospels, this being that which was born through a man called Jesus, who was the personification of the Creation but was known to a motherly born and who certainly walked the Earth as a man within whom positively spoke the "Mother of the Creation".

Also, a known fact is that whenever you actively support God's harmony that is developing all around you, you will also encounter that "gush" of pleasurable fulfilment for yes, it can be experienced. Yes, this is the taste of the "Sugar in the Water," so just enjoy this excellent taste when it is given to you, for it certainly quenches all thirsts. It is also a taste which emanates from that which is called "The True Way of Life" for, as previously stated, it is now essential to support attempts to re-develop the European Union, this being to remove tribalism and become unified into a genuine European Union, which encases all tribes of both the East and the West of Europe and by ending tribalism move onto the union of the whole of the Northern Hemisphere, and so onto a world union – for all know that it will come but only by the majority will of the people, and not by the will of a small minority who fear to lose their individual tribal "political" power or of those tribally rich who fear losing money, which is currently happening.

If you find this unity challenging to believe, then look in a mirror and ask yourself, "Who is this? Or "Who am I" plus "Who made me"? And also "Why am I here?" And then ask yourself, "How else is it possible for a single "Earthbound Creation" like me to communicate with the world of people." The answer being is just to support the non-personal emerging harmony that is currently developing or is endeavouring to develop all around you and as pursued within our entire world's religions and philosophies; this will always give you a good indication of the way of truth, for it is undoubtedly always endeavouring to emerge right next to you just has it also does within you.

For it is true that no one can dispute the ancient authority of our righteously and positive "Present Time" Godly targeting religions and philosophies unless they worship that which is called the "Devil", this being that force which falsely lives in the past or the future, for sure, they use these false worlds to target greed and inflict pain upon others. For indeed did not our wise ancients state *"Do not judge, or you too will be judged, for in the same way you judge others, you will be judged, and with the measure you use, it will be measured to you"*. Also, they advised, *"Why do you look at the speck of sawdust in your brother's eye and pay no attention to the plank in your eye and how can you say to your brother, let me take the speck out of your eye,' when all the time there is a plank in your eye? You hypocrite, first take the plank out of your eye, and then you will see clearly to remove the speck from your brother's eye.*

For indeed, this "speck" that our ancients speak about is an "I Want" that is stolen from the harmony that is attempting to exist everywhere. For assuredly did not our wise ancients also say those thousands of year ago *"Beware of false prophets for they come to you in sheep's clothing, but inwardly they are ravenous wolves, but by their fruit, you will recognize them"* and again *"Are grapes gathered from thornbushes, or figs from thistles, for every good tree bears good fruit, but a bad tree bears bad fruit"* for positively these "I Want" for me, trees can be readily identified but woe to them and to those that support them.

For did not our wise ancients explain that we have to be careful with people who steal the power of religious culture and to use it personally for their benefit? For indeed they are not God who can harm no one and who loves all, but it is also known, even within the nature of people, that a father will turn his face away from those in his family who transgress his true love. For definitely God, or Nature for the Non-Believer, cannot physically harm or anyone but will silently turn His back upon those who break His natural laws, these being laws that seek unity within His only child, this only child is that which we call "The Creation".

78 REAL LOVE SEARCHES FOR REASON

All people should fully understand that all religions and all philosophies do continually state that God's laws or the Laws of Nature for the Non-Believer are continually searching for harmony within the Creation. It is also true that we should fully understand that it is only people who have this God-given or Nature given for the Non-Believer "Freedom of Choice". For indeed, this is why it is only a person who can "choose" to break these ever-unfolding "Laws" that can only be created to exist in the "Present Time". Indeed, this is why our entire world's religions and philosophies preach that it is a "sin" to destroy any harmony seeking act for really this activity opposes God's unifying laws, these being those laws that govern the Earth's emerging harmony, which exits around and within the all-life and non-life. Thus it is also a fact that within the breaking of these harmony seeking laws that people will surely lose the current "Present Times" beneficial "wages", these being the "wages" which also contain the harmony seeking acts controlled by the *"Mother of the Creation"*, who is called Nature by the Non-Believer.

It should also be understood that this is an absolute truth which all religions and philosophies state, this being that there can be no righteousness in the destruction of God's harmony and woe to those who willingly kill another person for own personal rewards or even at the request of others – for what parent could install laws that favour their child for killing a brother or a sister or destroying their home or their well-being. For is this not a sad truth which can be seen throughout the history of all people? Sincerely, this being sadly being exampled by those who crucified Jesus, and by so doing lost their God-given "wages" when they destroyed the embodied incarnate that walked amongst them, for it was certainly not God or the *"Mother of the Creation"* called Nature by the Non-Believer, who destroyed them. For indeed, was not everything taken from them as their own personally targeted disharmony replaced God's on-going and constantly emerging harmony.

Therefore we should "always" remember that once any person performs a unifying of harmony act, they will not only immediately begin to obtain their on-going "wages," which "The Book" calls "Sugar in the Water," but they will also become activated by this thirst-quenching joy of happiness and contentment as all their past sins – in which they broke the existing harmony of that which was around them– are immediately forgiven, for they will again be set free to play on the level playing field of their life's progress, this genuinely indeed being a judgement made or not by the *"Mother of the Creation"*, this being depending upon the thoughts of the individual. For did not Jesus explain this upon the entering of His bodily death, *"Forgive them for they know not what they do,"* for real, it was God who spoke through Him. So yes, sorrowful acting people will be forgiven and yo-yo sinners will always "experience" Gods humour. For correctly it can be indeed stated, that the "Mother of the Creation" provides the same quality of Godly controlled harmony which is imposed upon to ALL people. Rightly, this is correctly being a way of living that is in direct accordance to that group's variable culture and language and which is also factually known to have created many different forms of our worlds "creed" and "culturally" based worshipping religions and also philosophies'; all of which freely targets a spiritual development that is undoubtedly based upon their God-given "Freedom of Choice".

Yet, strangely, is it not also true that this Godly given "Freedom of Choice" fact can also bring much antagonism from greed-based "bullying" that can occur between religions, this fact emanating from those who state that our God and our way of worship is better than your God and your way of worship. Genuinely, this is being a strange fact which can occur amongst our worlds various religious, even though all worship the one, God. Of course, the real false belief that is originating from these lost souls is the belief that *"this is my land"* and *"this is my house,"* and *"this is my property"* and *"this is my family". It is also* factually accurate that many worshippers have been told by mistaken religious leaders also to add the claim *"this is my religion"* thus recognising that their religion is their private property which they indeed fear losing, for yes, people can experience that all personal belongings to be themselves.

So they protect and support the words of their religion and glorify it as they do their personal belongings which are steadfastly and need fully claimed to be better than any other way of life. Is this not the reality as to from where this is attacking and religious persecution coming? Is this being the persecution of others? This being that is used to glorify their religion, which can be likened, has an endeavour to partition and claim a part of the sky?

So yes! What is the real motivational target in a religious or sectarian war in which none can truthfully succeed? For how can a world which is fathered by the one God and a world which is also monitored by the Mother of all that physically exists, this being that which is called Nature by the Non-Believer, be supportive of a world which continually targets the killing and maiming of their children, which is ALL people? Thus they sadly and truly view a selfish group's "I Want" what you have, this is being persecution against weaker people. The latter have been identified by these "I Want for me" ungodly transgressors, has not being attached to their religion? For truthfully, how can a God obeying religion include the destruction of whole families that worship God differently?

So yes! How can this be of benefit to these cruel attackers own culturally based and personally chosen religions worshipping ways? Can it not be said that this destruct full maiming, killing and stealing from whole families is truly a pursuit that is emanating from some mistaken religious leader who is pursuing an "I want" my God to be worshipped by more people and this to be done in my way for God speaks only to me. Still, honestly, is this not an attempt to bring more wealth and power to themselves? For truly is it not the religious and philosophical target of all people to live within and so support the emerging harmony that exists and is emerging from existing in our entire world, this being that which thrives around everything?

So Yes! What is it that seeks conflict and so attacks other countries and other religious and other creed-based targets that are differently created to find God's world or the real world of Nature for the Non-Believer? Can it be because the leaders and instigators plus originators of these conflicts are people who knowingly pursue that which are known to stimulate much of the targeting motivational actions emanating from many people? Strictly, this is action is that which is economically known to be targeting monetary profit, this being that which is the surplus money that is attached to a needed expenditure, for indeed, this is the language of capitalism, which now also rules the North of the Northern hemisphere. But of course, regarding economics, individual countries personally-established monetary value will always lose its value has profit-seeking printed money loaned and so created by banks always deflates its value. The future way of overcoming this problem seems to be coming from the modern way of communication in which the people of the world can immediately achieve access to everything and everybody – if permitted to do so!

From this fact there is currently emerging a world accepted currency whose purchase value is being established by a "Market Economy" in which its "Internet" purchases are being evaluated by many of our world's different countries' currencies, these being different currencies which have been released to the world's people by their countries banking systems. For indeed this is a new world system that has nothing to do with any countries currency controlling banks for it is undoubtedly controlled by the "Market Economy", this being that which feeds the people.

So yes! Strangely, can it not be said that usually separate sides of a conflict which are targeting to destroy each other, are both making a financial profit for the providers of a war's needs. Justly, this need being that which beggars the question *"is also some political leaders obtaining a share of this armament seeking profit?"* For assuredly, this expenditure from taxation is being used to continue armament manufacturing and also the purchasing of the needed very variable equipment that is needed to kill those families who culturally do economically live and worship differently.

Yet indeed, when the mind is "Enlightened" by truth, all these creed disagreements that create conflict disappear, as faith becomes the purpose of life, and the peculiarities of other creeds and sects become as No-Thing (nothing) which can be likened to all our Earths life and non-life is as one entity within Gods world or the world of Nature for the Non-Believer, this being that which exists within the singularity of our planet Earth.

So yes! Everyone should pursue the faith that rests within the devotional exercises of their own cultures accepted creed based religions, and this is a personal understanding of that which culturally enables them to relax in the actual knowledge that ALL creeds rest upon a faith in the true one God or the world of Nature for the Non-Believer. For accurately, it is only supported by the fear of narrow-minded people who fear their thoughts or those leaders who are "animalistic-ally" trapped in fear of the future, a future in which they cannot see a greed-based surplus. For sadly, this "I need surplus" indeed leads to the abuse of other religions or philosophies – for how can a personal and cultural belief in the non-harming truth of the one God be better than some other beliefs in God?

But, certainly culturally and historical based religions can bring a Godly unity to their attenders. From the year 2020, it will be seen that ALL Religions will seek a unity of "togetherness" in the belief of the one God and His one Child, the Creation. For again, you can never say that you do not have a choice! You always have a choice, and there are many ways of worshipping a loving God but can it be correct to say *"My way of worshipping God is the only correct way and your way of worshipping God is the wrong way"*, which can be likened to a disagreement in the way we breathe air. For indeed, the purpose of people is to support others just has their inner body supports them.

But again, as all religions and philosophies honestly state, if you continue sinning and breaking harmony via personnel selfishness, then you will continue to receive your negative wages, this being that which helps your life spiral downwards into misery, grot and depression, despite the falsely claimed richness of a people created world, this being a world that you gather around you. For example: If a person willfully fires a bullet from a gun at a child, then the gun's mechanisms, the flying bullet and the child's body, all obey God's natural laws of harmony. Therefore is it not further understood that if the child dies, then it too is obeying God's laws, which are based upon harmony and the "Freedom of Choice", this being that which is given only to people.

Is it not also understood "scientifically", that a breaker of this natural harmony will "always" become isolated from all the good life which exists around them – for it can also be certainly expected that the willful shooter will receive the "wages" of countless years of grot and derision, plus loneliness and upon death will naturally and "harmoniously" be reborn into the animal kingdom where the "Freedom of Choice", which they have betrayed – does no longer exist for them. But it should be further understood that the dead child's Soul, to fulfil its truthful purpose, will naturally and quickly go on to seek another life within its kin, for "scientifically" there can be no wasteful, or magically congregating myth existing outside of God's Creation, this being a creation which can only exist in the "Present Time".

Simply put there is no mystical everlasting "Heaven" or a separate "Hell", which is classed as being different places to go to when we die, for this is a story told to children. It is also often used to comfort people into seeking a pleasurable afterlife, but "scientifically", the physical reality of God's created energy, this being that which can only exist within the "Present Time", cannot be destroyed or changed by any person. Still, many people falsely endeavour to claim it for themselves.

So yes! All the Creation is but only one child, and positively, all the activity of each person is forever judged by the ever-existing, ever seeking harmony-based laws of that which is called God or Nothing by the Unbeliever. Therefore, is this personal life not similar to a well-known common understanding, this being that just as the prime number "nothing" judges and activates all prime numbers in our personally-made world, it also without changing always remains has "nothing"? For assuredly, science cannot go against this belief in God or the unbelievers "Nothing," for this absolute proof of what this number "nothing" self-creates in our world, is all around us and can any person change this law?

So Yes! You may now ask again, "What is sin"? Well, it is good to realise that just as there is only one child whom we call the Creation, there is only one sin. For justly, this is the sin of attempting to separate the one harmonising life force that exists all around us and so destroy the harmony that surrounds all things, this being that which can be liked to that unity which exists within our bodies, truthfully does the heart attack the lungs or the blood refuses to serve the eyes? Simply put, this way of existence can be realised "scientifically" in the understanding that all life and that which we call "Non-Life" is indeed unified, for truly it is this self-supporting unification which enables the laws of God to work correctly but only within the affirmative supporting act that is emanating from people, these being acts which are certainly sustained by "Space" which "The Book" calls the "Mother of the Creation" or that which is named "Nature" by the Non-Believer.

For certainly attempting the opposite is unquestionably a harmful activity which can be likened to driving through red traffic lights. For both acts, you will naturally receive your rewards, and if you are not sure which reward you are receiving, look at your environment and the life around you? Are you content with this life that exists around you? Are you endeavouring to unselfishly live and support the harmonising laws that exist or are attempting to exist all around you? Who are the people responsible for creating this unified harmony and who are the people who are endeavouring to destroy it?

For indeed, this "it" is your only home and just as all your many millions of body parts usually work in a unified harmony, this being that which unhesitatingly supports all that which is within you, then your freed Soul will do the same to all that which is around you. Then rightly you will find "Sugar in the Water" even if it is after death, for you will undoubtedly be born again.

So yes! Reach out now and touch something and indeed, that which you touch is God's Creation, a Creation that is being harmonised continuously by the "Mother of the Creation" who became as a person and spoke through the man we call Jesus. Listen now to the world around you, and you will hear "Mother of the Creation" speaking. Look, and you will see Her. Smell, and it is She that you smell. Taste and it is Her body that you taste. Touch and it is "Mother of the Creation" that you touch and behind all these things is the one God whose loved singularity is the "Mother of the Creation" and Her only child, for it is She who is the real hidden energy that brings love, justice (just is) and healing to Her only child, this being that which is supported by the "Free Will" of that which is a part of their only child and which is called "People". Therefore it is correct to believe in the one God who is the Father that cares for the "Future" and to also believe in the one Mother, who cares for the "Present Time" and certainly believe in their only Child and that part of the one-child called "People" who have been given the "Freedom of Choice" to support the wellness of this one Child which is the Creation that exists within you and all around you, a factor which is without a doubt supported by the constant caring and judgement of "Mother of the Creation".

So Yes! Believe and now KNOW that "YOU", dear reader, are an integral part of these sacred three, this being that you are an integral part of all that exists around you and also within you. For now, you know that the only child of God, this being that which is called the Creation, necessary includes people who are the only life force within the Creation who have been parentally allowed the "Freedom of Choice". Of course, this being a "Freedom of Choice" which is physically needed to support and care for the rest of the growing child and correctly the "Mother of the Creation" forever seeks within all people a fellowship which continually endeavours to serve and so support the wellbeing of their only child. A fact which is genuinely based upon a real communion within the Creation and it is undoubtedly a fact which is based upon the caring for all life and non- life, which is why this God-given "Freedom of Choice" was importantly given to all people- at birth. Is this not true? Can any person – "scientifically" prove that this is not a truth in that all people should be caring for a creation that personally exists all around them?

For in the previous pages of "The Book" are exercises that show, via personal meditation, how to remove any individualistic "I want" for ME! An "I Want for ME" which is based upon "negative" developing aspects which target a re-directing of the Creations emerging development. This personal "I Want for Me" activity is indeed NOT based upon the "positive" caring of the emerging

Creation, for this "I Want" is a severe misuse of a Godly provided "Freedom of Choice", this is being a God-given activity that when misused, can bring to reality a whole new world of negative discontentment which is then thrown into the face of all those seeking the correct way of life. Genuinely, this is rightly being a life which positively supports the goodness of ALL the life that is around it and which is endeavouring to emerge around it. Therefore from now until this current life's ends, the reader should never be encased in loneliness, for their smile will always be in harmony with God, the "Mother of the Creation" and also with the obedience to the Creation's search for "harmonised unity".

So yes! At this point, it is well for all people to acknowledge that only the "Teacher", this truly is being the "Mother of the Creation", will and can reward any persons unifying activities. So it can now be said that it can only be "YOU" dear reader, who can personally bring about the ending of any loneliness and or the experiencing of isolation. For indeed this experiencing of loneliness could be based upon a personal refusal to tie the bits of unifying string together that the "Mother of the Creation" hands to you, therefore maybe you should now be thinking of the word "redemption"? For unjustly the pursuer of God obedience to the Creation's search for "harmonised unity", who we named as Jesus, did painful die on the cross when an agreement to support His prosecutors would have stopped it?

For indeed, this was a crucifying painful act in which Jesus, as an incarnation of God, steadfastly refused to condemn those who crucified Him, which would have been a sin, because it would be harmfully against the current and prevailing discord of that which was around Him, for all harmony must be seen as a step towards the harmony of the greater good and such discord will "ALWAYS" be heavenly and therefore naturally corrected. Therefore, is it not also clearly known that Jesus had already revealed the truth to all that could hear His words? Therefore the quest now is to just read His words in the Gospels, these also being in the next chapter, and so accept no other interpretation of these words except your own. For genuinely in the Christian's "New Testament" the incarnate Jesus revealed many of the teachings that exist in God's laws, and He also revealed all the truths that were held within them.

So Yes! It is undoubtedly true that our incarnate called Jesus revealed all the truths that are certainly bound within the Creation, but yet He still is unwisely and incorrectly interpreted, this being because He was just seen as a man who lived in a world made by people and not a God-made world, for definitely, this was a mistake that has lasted for many years. Yet, Jesus certainly knew that His end was near. For absolutely, this would be when people, at that ancient time, began to unrealistically see Jesus as a leader who would lead them to destroy the foreign Roman occupiers, but, Jesus knew that this was a selfishness-based non-harmony-seeking act and not one of unification.

For indeed this pursuit of conflict had a different and isolated purpose, for it wanted the destruction of their Roman controllers, not knowing that the Creation cannot destroy its emerging self, and it is also interesting that the "Mother of the Creation" cannot activate judgement against those who attempt to destroy the harmonic laws that bind the Creation together, for, without doubt, She acknowledges the God-given "Freedom of Choice". (Interesting that the Soviet people of the USSR also moved away and so put aside and therefore removed their past controllers – agreeably and peacefully via the majority of its people.).

For as Jesus said in His sermons: *"Judge not, that ye may not be judged."* Yet those acting illegally against Nature's harmony pursued Jesus to the cross, and what a false piece of string that was! So it was time for Jesus to have an Earthly death and an honourable one, for Christ's Soul did not dies when His body was nailed to a cross which also showed the actual truth that you cannot die and that you must be born again as He was, and yes, the "Mother of the Creation" will continuously show that there is always harmonising work to be done; just as was the need revealed in the bottle of clouded water at the Russian Birobidzhan presentation which began my journey to this truth, for they realised that clarity could be clouded.

So yes! The real teacher, which is the "Mother of the Creation", will through the passage of time, destiny and serendipity, always allow peoples "Freedom of Choice", this being that which should be wisely targeted to support Her harmonising work and so support the cleansing of any soiling that appears has "Sugar in the Water". This "Freedom of Choice" activity is that which can be likened to be a cleansing need that is required to support all life and all non-life, this being that which was acknowledged by the needs seen in this clouded bottle of water. Therefore, without doubt, if you wish to be presented with the sweetness of "sugar" during your swim through life – then assist in the development of "harmony", and you will find that the "Mother of the Creation" will give to you a sugar which will be recognised as an excellent sweetener within your current life.

For indeed this will be given to you to when you purposely assist in Her work, for again and definitely, when you support God's laws of harmony it is a reality which can be likened to travelling by car through a city and all the traffic lights turn to green when you approach them. For positively, this is because God's harmony will "automatically" support your harmony pursuing endeavours, and this is genuinely the tasting of the "Sugar in the Water", this taste is likened to a red traffic light when being approached turns to green, and so allowing your journey to continue without stopping. Finally, these actual words from the incarnate Jesus of the Christian religion which many will understand after reading "The Book":

2-3-17-21 *"Nor will people say, 'Here it is', or 'there it is' because the Kingdom of God is within you."* ... and truly exists in the "Present Time" which is within you and without you. Amen

79   THE MODERN INTERPRETATION OF GODS WORDS
SPOKEN THROUGH JESUS

The following words are for those who wish to hear, in modern terminology, to truly understand those ancient words of God who spoke through the incarnate Jesus and explained about the laws of His "Heaven" that reigned upon this Earth, but only in the "Present Time". Indubitably, this being that which exists has a loving and caring reality that endures all around you and within your plus everything that knowingly exists upon this planet. Therefore, it is now wise to understand that when you read only the words of Jesus, that there is an absolute need to be fully aware that it is God that is speaking directly to you and who is naturally explaining the never-changing path to experience the truth. So, hear again that which God said through Jesus this being numbered in the Christian Bible under the following truths which **Jesus said** when speaking to his disciples:- **Mathew 12-25** *"Jesus knew their thoughts and said to them: 'Every kingdom divided against itself will be ruined, and every city or household divided against itself will not stand'."* He is speaking to those people who live upon our Earth as if they are separate from it. They are not! For the kingdom in which they live should be likened to be their own body whose inner parts serve unification with each other for unquestionably all our bodies internal and also separate entities serve each other, it is this supporting fact which Jesus is implying should also be applied to the "kingdom" that is all around a person's body. For it is undoubtedly true that Godly harmony cannot be divided but that it should serve all people, and all nature has it serves the inner body. Now let us hear more of the words that Jesus spoke to His disciples and which Mathew repeats.

Jesus said in Mathew 12-26 *"If Satan drives out Satan, he is divided against himself, how then cans his kingdom can stand?* Simply put; that if an individual's five senses seek only their own "I Want". How can the unity of the heavenly body that exists in the "Present Time" be possible?

Jesus said in Mathew 12-27 *"And if I drive out demons by Beelzebub, by whom do your people drive them out? So then, they will be your judges."* It can be understood that "Beelzebub" is a right way of describing the uncontrolled five senses, for indeed it is their "I want" that becomes your judge and so now know well that they cannot judge themselves. So who is best to serve and so to be obedient? Should your obedience be to your five senses or your Soul?

Jesus said in Mathew 12-28 *"But if I drive out demons by the Spirit of God, then the kingdom of God has come upon you."* The Spirit of God is the Soul which can give directions to the energy of people's consciousness; this is the greatest of people's strengths for with Gods "Freedom of Choice", their "Soul" can empower "consciousness" to energise "Willpower" to control the five senses and bring the "observer" this being the Soul, into the reality of God's world. This world serves "Present Time".

Jesus said in Mathew 5-3 *"Blessed are the poor in spirit, for theirs is the Kingdom of Heaven*." Of course, the poor in the spirit described here are those people who controlled by five senses but truly blessed are those whose senses have become silent and so serve the Soul. For they have no "I want" for they know that they have "Everything" and so live in the Kingdom of Heaven which can only exist in the "Present Time".

Jesus said in Mathew 5-10 *"Blessed are those who are persecuted because of righteousness, for theirs is the Kingdom of Heaven."* For indeed God's righteousness is the living in a God supporting world which is the "non-thinking" and "non-wanting" for myself world that can only exist in the "Present Time", this being the only time in which can exist the Kingdom of Heaven. For it is undoubtedly true that all that exists is truly God's world, and this is a world that is ruled by the laws of "His Heaven" which exists all around us as it does within us. Therefore it is true that it is only in the "Present Time" that the meditational practitioner will begin to fully observe and so realise, via the viewing of their Soul through a still mind, that this above-quoted "persecution" not only refers to the "I Want for Me" demands of their bodies "animalistic" five senses but also the "I Want for ME" demands of other peoples persecutions that are emanating from their animalistic five senses. But honestly, when the meditational practitioner eventually reaches, via meditation, this mind silent God's world, it is then that their understanding will be that any further unrighteous persecution from any source can gain no energy from them. For unrighteous based greed has no meaning to them, and so cannot exist in the silence that indeed rests within them for they know that they are the non-judging harmony seeking Soul that is observing all worldly life and this is a mortal life which cannot be persecuted even unto death – for positively the Soul cannot die for it will be knowingly re-born into a world in of which it will consciously be a part. Indeed it can choose this world and place in which it feels a need to serve.

Jesus said in Mathew (NIV) 5:19 *"Therefore anyone who sets aside one of the least of these commands and teaches others accordingly will be called least in the kingdom of heaven, but whoever practices and teaches these commands will be called great in the kingdom of heaven".* These commands allied to the "Kingdom of Heaven" are the commands of God's or Nature's harmony for the Non-Believer. These being the harmony seeking God based or Nature-based for the Non-Believer, "Natural Laws" that without doubt, exist and which are all-knowing laws that have emerged or are silently endeavouring to emerge all around people – but only in the "Present Time".

Therefore, when people via meditation, "choose" to enter the harmony that exists in the "Present Time", this being the world that exists without thought, they eventually stop living in the non-existing thought-filled world of the Past or Future in which an "I Want for ME" thought fills their mind, and so blocks the view of the Soul from seeing the "Present Time". These continuing never-ending thoughts are being that which do emanate from the five senses never-ending "I want" demands. Always, this being an "I Want for ME" thought which is continually chattering and animalistic ally stealing or planning to steal from the harmony that exists all around them. Thus ensuring that people with such animalistic thoughts cannot enter the world of Heaven, this being that which can only exist in the "Present Time". For assuredly, it is only through a silent mind that a person can join and so evaluate, that which only an un-blocked silent mind can reveal to their Soul. For indeed and again it should be continuously said that all people have a God-given or Nature given for the Non-Believer, a "Freedom of Choice" and so truly your doings upon this Earth are controlled by YOU! So yes! You can "choose" the animalistic five senses NOT to control you.

Jesus said in Matthew 5-20 (NIV) *"For I tell you that unless your righteousness surpasses that of the Pharisees and the teachers of the law, you will certainly not enter the Kingdom of Heaven."* These Pharisees and these teachers of the law live in the Hell of the Past time or a Future mind filling "I want for ME," not knowing that an unthinking and un-wanting mind is all that is needed for their Soul to enter the Kingdom of Heaven, this being that which can only exist in the "Present Time", the only world which God has created.

Jesus said in Mathew 6-10 (NIV) *"Your kingdom come, you will be done on Earth as it is in Heaven."* Earth exists in the here and the now, this being an existence that occurs only within "Present Time". So honestly, it is good to understand the words *"on Earth as it is in Heaven,"* for this "Heaven" is Gods world that exists within the observable oneness that rests only in the "Present Time", this being that in of which a person Soul is an old part.

Jesus said in Mathew 6-33 (NIV) *"But seek first his kingdom and his righteousness, and all these things will be given to you as well".* Seek a silent mind and not a self-claiming "I want" noisy mind that is being "I Want" hounded by the animalistic five senses. For undoubtedly, God's Kingdom and God's righteousness is all around you and is genuinely always serving you or waiting to be served by your Soul, this being when you leave the mind-controlling thoughts that can be continually emanating from your animalistic anciently based five senses.

Jesus said in Mathew 7-21 (NIV) *"Not everyone who says to me, 'Lord, Lord,' will enter the kingdom of heaven, but only the one who does the will of my Father who is in heaven.* This "Will of my Father" can only be experienced by a silent mind whose real purpose is to serve and so support the harmony-seeking needs of the developing Creation. For indeed, those who unselfishly serve the emanating needs of those acts which are occurring in the "Present Times", will fully experience the bliss of God.

Yet naturally, this can only happen when they no longer serve the "I Want for Me" animalistic demands that are always emanating from the five senses in which only this greed-based "I Want for ME" exists. For in an innocent ignorance many people falsely believe that the animalistic "I Want" needs of their five senses are the needs of the real "them". Now, after the reading of "The Book" this ignorance no longer exists. For surely, in meditation, you will gain the knowledge that your heavenly Father is God or Nature for the Non-Believer. So truly you will also experience the ever-evolving bliss that is emanating from your heavenly Mother, which "The Book" identifies to be "Space", this being that which is within and also without you and who also gave birth to YOU, Her only child, this being that ever-growing child which we call "The Creation".

Jesus said in Mathew 13-11 (NIV) *Jesus replied, "The knowledge of the secrets of the Kingdom of Heaven has been given to you, but not to them."*

So Yes! This knowledge contained in "The Book" has also been given so that all readers can go and do the will of God or Nature for the Non-Believer, and not to "them." These "them" being the five senses which wilfully and animalistically claim all that is emerging around them. Therefore it is now wise to remember to support the oneness silently and so aid the emerging harmony of that which is all around you.

Jesus said in Mathew 13-12 (NIV) it is stated: *Whoever has will be given more, and they will have an abundance. Whoever does not have, even what they have will be taken from them.*

These are the words of Jesus who is undoubtedly speaking to those who only live in the abundance of the "Present Time", a time in which a personally thought "I Want for ME" cannot exist.

Jesus said in Mark 4:26-29 *(NIV)* **The Parable of the Growing Seed:-** *"This is what the kingdom of God is like. A man scatters seed on the ground. Night and day, whether he sleeps or gets up, the seed sprouts and grows, though he does not know-how. All by itself, the soil produces grain— first the stalk, then the head, then the full kernel in the head. As soon as the grain is ripe, he puts the sickle to it, because the harvest has come."*

For indeed, this is explaining the harmony of the "Heaven" existing in the "Present Time" and not the living in "Hell" of the mind filling "I want" inner birthing weeds of the five senses, thus creating an "I Want only for Me" self-dreamed Past or Future, which is a world that does not exist. For certainly now all readers of "The Book" know that God's world can only exist in the "Present Time". Without doubt, this being a time in which all supporting harmony is provided for and which the most advanced seed is that which is known as "People". For indeed all life is being purposely and constantly re-planted and re-harvested to grow and evolve within the harmony of the Creation until eventually, after many rebirths a or by the "Self-Disciplinary" practice of mediation, a person can become fully ripened and so become "Self-Realised", meaning to become as one with our Creator, thus allowing God to experience "Himself" and no person has ever returned to explain the truth that is resting within this accomplished experience.

Jesus said in Mathew 13-31.32 (NIV) He told them another parable: *"The kingdom of heaven is like a mustard seed, which a man took and planted in his field. [32] Though it is the smallest of all seeds, yet when it grows, it is the largest of garden plants and becomes a tree, so that the birds come and perch in its branches"* **The Kingdom of Heaven exists only in the "Present Time"** This mustard seed story is used to describe an ever-growing unselfish Godly based emerging harmony that only people can choose to support growingly. Positively, this being an act of the unselfish supporting of God's emerging harmony, that can aid Gods harmony to grow and so expand within the community, in which, when fully grown, will be that state in which all people can peacefully rest.

Jesus said in Mathew 13-33 (NIV) *He told them still another parable: "The kingdom of heaven is like yeast that a woman took and mixed into a large amount of flour until it worked all through the dough.* This parable is also clearly describing how any person can choose to unthinkingly and so naturally support the harmony of Heaven that constantly exists within the "Present Time", this being a time which is naturally without any selfish thought. For it is those people who definitely and "unselfishly" do actively work supporting ally within their community and also within other communities' as a Godly provided yeast, this being that which is being "mixed" within the activities "Present Time".

For it is essential to follow the Golden Rule which is to treat others as you would like them to treat you, for it is wise to think and actually to know, that they are genuinely YOU! Yet we honestly do know that the harmony of "Heaven", this being that which can only exist in the "Present Time", can and is continually being broken by people who choose, via the God-given "Freedom of Choice", to pursue their personal "I Want for ME actively". Again, this is undoubtedly being that activity which always takes that which belongs to others and which is based upon a thought which is originating from an imagined past or an imagined "I Want for ME" future. Yet this parable also says that an unselfish "Godly" harmonizing act can "expanding ally", and Godly work all through a mixed community of people to which these following many parables are now given to explain:-.

Jesus said in Mathew 13-38 (NIV) *"The field is the world, and the good seed stands for the sons of the kingdom. The weeds are the sons of the evil one."* The sons of the kingdom are those who support the needs of God's harmony that growingly exists within the "Present Time", and the weeds are those people who pursue a personal future emanating from a past based "I want." So they ignore or invariably destroy the Godly harmony or Natures harmony for the non-believer, this being that which is all around them as they attack and kill all others of all breeds, races and ages.

Jesus said in Mathew 13-39 (NIV) *", and the enemy who sows them is the devil. The harvest is the end of the age, and the harvesters are angels."* Although the Devil does not exist in modern "Holistic" understanding, these words can be used to show that people who target a personal "I Want" for myself are the real destroyers of the harmony that exists or is endeavouring to exist in that farm which can only exist in the "Present Time". So undeniably, the consequences (harvest) of this "I Want for Me", which is likened in this epistle to be not only an energizing destroyer of goodness but also an un-eatable weed growing activity, will eventually and certainly bring inadequate and unsatisfactory experience to the doer.

Yet what is clearly stated here is that those "angels," these being those pursuers of God's truth who are without any personnel "I Want" only for myself, are in this saying the earthly farmers who are steadily growing and cultivating the goodness or God-ness of that which can only be harvested in the "Present Time". This fact is undeniably being because these farmers certainly live without any personal "I want only for me", which is likened to be the growing of goodness for indeed they are people who act as "guardians" of God's world, this is being the world that can only exist in the "Present Time".

Jesus said in Mathew 13-40 (NIV) "As the *weeds are pulled up and burned in the fire so that it will be at the end of the age."* For it is certainly known that this "I want" only for myself activity is the growth of an un-edible weed, this also being that which factually leads to the destroying of a growing "Godness", for it is not a part of nor does it support the harmony that exists in God's world. Therefore it will eventually and always destroy the evildoer. For assuredly, this reality will continue until the end of their time – unless they change and does not our Earths history always prove this?

Jesus said in *Mathew 13-41 (NIV) "The Son of Man will send out His angels, and they will weed out of His kingdom, everything that causes sin and all who do evil."* This epistle is explaining that the "Son of Man", which in this epistle is Jesus, will develop within His followers many "angels" who will develop into supporters of the harmony that exists in God's world; this is being that world which can only exist in the "Present Time". It is these unselfish ones who, without any personal thinking "I want for ME" thoughts will throughout our world always endeavour to save these mistaken ones, who "The Book" says maybe new rebirths from the animal kingdom who have never had the "Freedom of Choice" before and so are being habitually empowered by their greed to prey upon all other life.

Jesus said in Mathew 13-42 (NIV) *"They will throw them into the fiery furnace, where there will be weeping and gnashing of teeth."* The fiery furnace being the "Present Time", this being that in which only people have the "Freedom of Choice" to "burn out" all that is destroying the harmony of that which emerges in the "Present Time" and so live in the harmonious Heaven which certainly does "fiery" exists all around them. For assuredly, this being a personal existence in which a disciplined consciousness has stopped all the animalistic targeting fired by the intuitive animalistic thinking that *"This world is only for me"*, these being their previous life's animalistic and constant thoughts which are still entering the mind of their newly born life as a "Person", this being a life that is now genuinely owned by the Soul, in which "animalistic" forgetting of this fact is their worst enemy.

Thus the task of the angels is to remove the *"I want for me"* mind-filling animalistic thoughts which are continually being birthed by one of the five senses, this being that condition which is still emanating from their past lives activities. It is undoubtedly this past constant activity that is still filling their mind and so stops their Soul from seeing the "Present Time" which is God's world or the world of Nature for the Non-Believer. For indeed it is this "ignoring" of the "Present Time" which keeps the "animalistic" thinker in the world of sin, now known by all to be the world called Hell, this being that which only people who live in the past or "I Want for Me" future, can personally create upon this world.

Jesus said in Mathew 13-43 (NIV) *"Then the righteous will shine like the sun in the kingdom of their Father, they who have ears, let them hear."* It is then that those who accomplish this task of silencing the mind will undoubtedly be those who will naturally enter God's heaven upon this Earth, this being that which can only exist in the "Present Time". For indeed they will shine as a light upon this earth and unquestionably that person who understands this need for stillness within the mind will undoubtedly accomplish this inner light that glows within all who experience and so to live in Gods world.

Jesus said in Mathew 13-44 (NIV) *"The Kingdom of Heaven is like a treasure hidden in a field. When a man found it, he hid it again, and then in his joy went and sold all he had and bought that field."* Yes! Once a person has glimpses of the harmony and bliss of the "Enlightenment", this being that which can only exist in the "Present Time", they will find that leaving the world of "I want for ME" is the required purchase price for a life to be lived within the harmony of "Enlightenment".

Jesus said in Mathew 13-45 (NIV) *"Again, the Kingdom of Heaven is like a merchant looking for fine pearls. When he found one of great value, he went away and sold everything he had and bought it."* Yes! When you realise the joy and bliss that you bodily experience when in the unthinking "Enlightenment" of the "Present Time", you will realise that there is nothing else that you require, for God or Nature for the Non-Believer has already given to you everything that you need in the Heaven which rests upon that which we call Earth.

Jesus said in Mathew 13-47 (NIV) *"Once again, the Kingdom of Heaven is like a net that was let down into the lake and caught all kinds of fish."* The fish being likened to every kind of happiness which exists but only in the "Enlightenment" of the "Present Time"– So you do not need to investigate the Past or the Future for the net and the lake can only exist in the "Present Time".

Jesus said in Mathew 10-7 (NIV) *"As you go, preach this message: 'The Kingdom of Heaven is near'."* This parable is indeed very real for it is not only a world that is all around you but is also the same world that is within you, for it does exist, but again it should be said to exist only in the "Present Time", this being the time which is ALWAYS there to fully experience, for it is undoubtedly God's world or the world of Nature for the Non-Believer and so is a world that can be genuinely experienced by that which our ancients called "Enlightenment." Again, this is being the experience which is achieved when one leaves the mind filled thought that the world is a personally created "I Want only for Me" Hell and so enters the world of the unthinking Heaven, this being the world that has no "I Want" for it is a world in which you truly know that you have and are "Everything".

Jesus said in Mathew 18-3 (NIV) *"I tell you the truth unless you change and become like little children, you will never enter the Kingdom of Heaven."* Naturally, this is an absolute saying for it clearly shows that the "Kingdom of Heaven" is in the "Present Time", and it can certainly be experienced by an enlightened one. For indeed it can be said that a child before the age of two is naturally "Enlightened," but sadly loses this as the child's environment compels them to forget and so to forget is our worst enemy.

Jesus said in Mathew 18-4 (NIV) *"Therefore, whoever humbles himself like this child is the greatest in the Kingdom of Heaven."* An "Enlightened" person is naturally humble, for they want for nothing and if you see a child of two eating a biscuit, ask the child for the biscuit – and it will immediately be given to you, for the child around the age of two or three, lives in the perfect harmony of the heavenly world it has just left in which all that exists is really "Them".

Jesus said in *Mark 9-47 (NIV)* *"And if your eye causes you to sin, pluck it out. It is better for you to enter the Kingdom of God with one eye than to have two eyes and be thrown into hell."*** The Eye is the most significant harbinger of an "I want for me." So this Godly advice is to stop this plaguing "I Want" for myself habit and immediately you will enter the Kingdom of God, this being that which always exists, but only in the "Present Time" – this being the time that cannot contain a selfish "I want" thought.

Jesus said in Mathew 18-4 (NIV) Therefore*, whoever humbles himself like this child is the greatest in the Kingdom of Heaven."*

And: **In Mathew** 23-12 (NIV) *"For those who exalt themselves will be humbled, and those who humble themselves will be exalted.* A child up to the age of two or three experiences this condition called "Enlightenment", this being their birthright into which they were born. Undeniably, this is being the natural "Enlightenment" that rests within all people. For a child "automatically" experiences that they live in the Heaven in which greed-based "I want" cannot exist.

Jesus said in Luke 11-9 (NIV) *"So I say to you: 'Ask, and it will be given to you; seek and you will find; knock and the door will be opened to you'."* This door within all peoples mind is the way to "Enlightenment". Again, this is truly God's world; this being that which exists all around you has it certainly does within you, this being a world that is usually blocked from being seen or realised by the mind filling energy of an "I want" desire - which now can indeed be stopped by meditation. This fact goes back many thousands of years.

Jesus said in Luke 11-10 (NIV) *"For everyone who asks receives; he who seeks finds; and to him who knocks, the door will be opened."* So yes! Via meditation, you will realize your true self and so find within yourself that which releases the vision of your Soul, this being that which rests within you. For the still and unclouded by thinking mind, definitely allows the Soul to see through the unclouded mind and so be enabled a witness God's world or the world of Nature for the Non-Believer. For sure, this is "Enlightenment", an actual realization in which your silent mind becomes has a door opening to God's world, this being that which exists and which can only be seen and experienced when the Soul is enabled to view through a still mind, God's world, this being the world called Heaven that can only exist in the "Present Time".

Jesus said in Luke 11-11 (NIV). *"Which of you fathers, if your son asks for a fish, will give him a snake instead?"* When you work towards "Enlightenment" and then achieve it with a still mind – God's world will not and cannot betray or harm you.

Jesus said in Luke 11-12 (NIV) *"Or if he asks for an egg, will give him a scorpion?"* Teach your child to work towards "Enlightenment", and you and they will experience that "Peace *that surpasses all Understanding",* this being that which gives an actual birth to all life and non-life, and which cannot possibly harm you.

Jesus said in *Luke 11-13 (NIV) "If you then, though you are evil, know how to give good gifts to your children, how much more will your Father in Heaven give the Holy Spirit to those who ask him?"* The experiencing of the Holy Spirit IS certainly "Enlightenment", for the experiencing of "Enlightenment" is to experience the Holy Spirit within you, and this is truly a Holy Spirit that wants for nothing, for it has found God–which is "No-Thing" or "Nothing", yet indeed is everything.

Jesus said in Luke 11-17 *"Jesus knew their thoughts and said to them: Any kingdom divided against itself will be ruined, and a house divided against itself will fall."* You cannot live in God's world, which is in the "Present Time" and also live in the Past or the Future was a Hell based "I want" for myself always and in many ways does take you. Neither can you be forced to live in a divided kingdom for certainly your "Freedom of Choice" can take you to live in self-made Hell or to live in the natural world of Heaven, even unto the cross?

Jesus said in Luke 11-18 (NIV) *"If Satan is divided against himself, how his kingdom can stand? I say this because you claim that I drive out demons by Beelzebub."* In this saying, Beelzebub can be likened to the five senses which are constantly chattering their animalistic "I want" into the beholder's mind, which keeps the beholder in Hell. If you can hear it in mind, then it can be anciently likened to the chattering of Beelzebub or Satan, taking you away from God's world, this being the Heaven that can only exist in the "Present Time". Thus "Enlightenment" can only be experienced when a person is without thought, this being that which is called "Enlightenment", thus being filled by the Holy Spirit. Then Jesus said, after being accused of driving out demons, did state*:*

Jesus said in Luke 11-19 (NIV) *"Now if I drive out demons by Beelzebub (The Devil), by whom do your followers drive them out? So then, they will be your judges."* "The Book" explains that the five senses are simply organs that are attached to a person's ancient animalistic "parietal lobes" and so have been created to allow all life forms to evaluate that which is emerging in the world around them. But forgetting and forgetting is our worst enemy, many people experience the five senses as to be their authentic selves, and it is this which explains why the actions of some people become likened to that entity which is called the Devil. This likening is being when they pursue the animalistic "I want" of their own personal or pack targeting thoughts, this indeed being that which targets a Past time or a Future "I Want for ME", and it is undoubtedly this which can create the Hell lived-in by people and also a Hell which they impose upon others.

So clearly, the five senses are bodily and therefore a separate entity from a person Soul, this being that which obeys the needs of the "Present Time". For indeed "The Book" describes these "I Want for ME" thoughts to be as "Demons" that are filling the mind with this allowed chatter, thus stopping Soul from seeing and so experiencing through the clear mind the Heaven that truly exists, but only within the "Present Time", a time which is without thought.

For positively, it is this "I Want" mind filling activity which blocks the Soul from seeing and activating the individuals need to do God's work, this being that which is to support the emerging harmony that exists all around them which is a truly, God's world or the world of Nature for the non-believer. For did not Jesus honestly answer the Devil, which "The Book" modernly explains to be the animalistic five senses, when they inwardly said to Jesus who was stood upon a very high mountain, this being in **Mathew 4:9** *"All this I will give you, if you will bow down and worship me."* For then indeed came the smiling answer as in **Mathew 4:10** (NIV) in which Jesus said *"Away from me, Satan!"* which "The Book" says that Satan was an ancient fictitious name which can now be modernity known to be your animalistic five senses and also:

Jesus said in Mathew 4:7 "*For it is written: 'Worship the Lord your God and serve Him only'."* Unquestionably, this is being a worshipping which "factually" can only be done in the "Present Time", this being when the five senses have been silenced and are no longer dominating and clouding the mind, for again it should be said that this is that which stops the Soul from seeing the harmonizing needs of the "Present Time", which can only be witnessed through a still mind.

Jesus said in Luke 11-20 (NIV) *"But if I drive out demons by the finger of God, then the Kingdom of God has come to you."* The demons that Jesus can instantly drive out by His touch, this being that which can only be experienced in the "Present Time" are again said by "The Book" to be the mind-filling five senses, this being that which factually keeps the "I want for ME" thinker living in a self-made Hell and not the righteousness' of the Heaven that truly, exists all around them, but only in the "Present Time".

Jesus also said in Luke 12-31 (NIV) *"But seek His Kingdom, and these things will be given to you as well."* Again, simply put "His Kingdom" is the world of Heaven which again is said to exist only in the "Present Time", for indeed this is a world which cannot exist in a thought created "Past" or non-existing "Future", which is a personally created world of Hell. This "Hell" again is called by "The Book" to be the world of "I want for myself", without a doubt the reality of the world of Hell that "The Book" says is continually being created by the body's animalistic five senses.

Jesus also said in Luke (NIV) 12-32 *"Do not be afraid, little flock, for your Father has been pleased to give you the kingdom."* Yes! A life that can be lived in Heaven is waiting for all of the people, but positively truly, only for those who have endeavoured to silence the mind filling "I want" of the five senses; and if this process of silencing the five senses is bringing fear to you, do not be afraid, but be brave and continue this real disciplined work of silencing them by inwardly saying "Not this" and then undoubtedly you WILL enter the Kingdom of Heaven – this being that which truly exists within you and also all around you.

Jesus also said in Luke 9-60 (NIV) Jesus said, *'Let the dead bury their own dead, but you go and proclaim the Kingdom of God'."* Yes! The past and the future are dead, and the death of the five senses means that they are no longer dominating and filling your mind nor are they stopping your view of Gods Present, which is undoubtedly the experiencing of the "Kingdom of God" this being that exists within you and also all around you.

Jesus said in Luke 9-61 (NIV) Still another said, *"I will follow you, Lord; but first let me go back and say good-bye to my family."* Jesus replied, *"No one who puts his hand to the plough and looks back is fit for service in the kingdom of God."* Yes! Truly meditation stills the mind for it "disciplinary" stops any "I Want for Me" words emanating from the five senses from dominating or even entering the mind, for it stops all "looking back" to "thoughts" of the Past or the Future – for it is only in the "Present Time", when the mind is without thought, that God's world can be experienced. All that is needed to be cared for should be genuinely cared for. For unquestionably, any thought in mind is only creating a world that does not exist – and is anciently called "Satan's" world. Indubitably, this is being sincerely the Hell that continually emanates from a personal "I want for Me" and not the Heaven of God's world, in which all that you need is provided for you. Also, all that you observe to be the needs of others are provided to you.

Jesus said in Mathew 19-23 (NIV). *Then Jesus said to His disciples, "I tell you the truth; it is hard for a rich man to enter the Kingdom of Heaven."* The rich have many treasures, resources, materials, possessions and assets to think about continually, and great pain can be experienced when the responsibilities of these false claims and their imposed distress upon the world begin to shrink.

Jesus said in Mark 10-24 (NIV) The disciples were amazed at His words. But Jesus said, *"Again I tell you, it is easier for a camel to go through the eye of a needle than for a rich man to enter the kingdom of God."* Again, these certain truths within simple words, these being that which state that it is easier for a well-loaded camel to enter city's gates than for a "well-loaded" rich person with much cared for surplus riches, to enter the "Present Time" – The Kingdom of God.

Jesus said in Luke 18-17 (NIV) *"I tell you the truth; anyone who will not receive the Kingdom of God as a little child will never enter it."* Always remain without any "I Want". This being has you were before the age of three! So YES! Like a small child, you should want for nothing, for sure, the Creation is here to serve you, just as you "knew" at this young age, which you are being loved and cared for by the singularity of your celestial parents which is truly God and the *"Mother of the Creation"*. And now finally, these valid words from the incarnate Jesus of the Christian religion which many will understand, after reading "The Book".

Jesus said in Luke 17-21 (NIV) *"Nor will people say, 'Here it is', or 'there it is' because the Kingdom of God is within you."* For indeed, you will experience this Heaven upon our Earth when you begin to live in the "Present Time", this being an "Enlightened" time in which an "I want for myself" cannot exist. So yes! Is it not also true that we should be careful of some religious teachers? Their personnel "I want" can be religiously forced upon others by compulsory telling them precisely what to do and what not to do. For truly only a person's Soul has this silent position of authority for definitely the universal Soul within each person knows exactly what is a right action and what is not a right action and all know this to be true. For indeed the Soul can harm no one, especially when "one" realise that what "one" is observing is also the real YOU!

80. THE FACTUAL WORDS OF GOD SPOKEN THROUGH THE PROPHET MOHAMMED

Mohammed, (Blessed be His name), was undoubtedly an "Enlightened" person who is also identified to be the last of the prophets and so "The Book" recognizes the need to explain to all non-followers of Mohammed the about "knowledge" that the blessed Mohammed did speak. Without doubt, this being Mohammed's experiencing the "Present Time", the time that holds no "Past" and no "Future" or any "I Want for ME" thoughts. Unquestionably, this is again positively being Gods world or the world of Nature for the Non-Believer. Hence, now hear again that which God said through Mohammed and in a modern understanding hear the wisdom of their meaning: For Mohammed – said: – *"Go in the quest of knowledge even unto China, even unto 'edge of the earth'.* (This being the quest to absorb only the experience that rests in the "Present Time".)

'Seek knowledge from the cradle to the grave'. (Seek the experiencing that can only exist in the "Present Time".)

'Excessive knowledge is better than excessive praying, and the bedrock of religion is abstinence'. (Meaning there is a need to abstain from awakening any Past or Future "I Want" thoughts. Therefore, is it not positively true that to obtain this "Excessive Knowledge" it is essential to target a silence in the mind which can only exist when the mind experiences only the unthinking "Present Time". Indeed this being a time which contains no mind filling thoughts of any Past or any Future "I Want" prayer, a condition which "The Book" also states does block the Soul from seeing Gods world which can only exist in the "Present Time". For certainly Mohammed knew that such thinking or "I Want" praying encases people in mind filled world of Hell although it is certainly good to be aware that unselfish praying does discipline the mind.

'He, who knoweth his own self, knoweth God'. (The "Present Time" is within you and outside you; this is Gods world in which there is only one "self", for naturally, you are "everything").

'To listen to the words of the learned and to instil into others the lessons of science, are better than religious exercises'. (It is a scientific fact that all that "scientifically" exists can only exist in the "Present Time", which is Gods world or the world of Nature for the Non-Believer and the purpose of all religious exercises is to become as one with this realty).

'The ink of the scholar is more holy than the blood of a martyr'. (This being the written word that shows and guides you to a life lived only in the Present Time – Gods world).

'He, who leaveth home in search of knowledge, walketh in the path of God'. (The path of God can only exist in the Present Time for this is indeed the home created by God and not by the thoughts of the people who believe that their body is their only home).

'The acquisition of knowledge is a duty incumbent on every Muslim, male or female'. (This acquired knowledge is the silent "Self-Realizing" experiencing that which can only exist within the harmony of the "Present Time", this being the totality of Gods world). For sure it is this experiencing of the unthinking "Present Time" that Mohammed says should be acquired and not the Past or a Future "I Want" thought, this being the Hell which is "Selfishly" created in the minds of people who pursue their personnel "I Want for ME".

And finally, Mohammed's words that give specific proof that the "knowledge", which is the experiencing Gods harmony, can only exist in the "Present Time" and not in personal thoughts which do consistently create a Past or a Future "I Want". These being the machinations that can dictate a person's life, for has Mohammed explained: – *'Acquire knowledge?'* (Which is the experiencing the knowledge of the "Present Time", this being Gods world for indeed) *It enabled its possessor to distinguish right from wrong; it lighteth the way to heaven; it is our friend in the desert, our society in solitude, our companion when friendless; it guideth us to happiness; it sustained us in misery; it is an ornament amongst friends, and armour against enemies: – 'With this knowledge people riseth to the heights of goodness and to a noble position associateth with sovereigns in this world and attaineth to the perfection of happiness in the next'.*

What Mohammed, blessed be his name, is speaking about is the living only in the "Present Time", a time that cannot exist within a thought based "I Want" – for all thoughts takes the thinking person away from the "Present Time" which is Gods world of Harmony or the world of Nature for the Non-Believer and into a personally created world of "I Want for ME" Hell.

Therefore it is good to remember that Mohammed's "Jihad", is a personal struggle to free the Soul. This fact always leads to "Enlightenment", this being when one knowingly becomes "Everything", which is the world of the "Present Time" and there is neither Past nor any Future, these being the worlds of a self-made Hell.

For Mohammed, Blessed be His Name, was the last of the prophets to explain this to the world. For Mohammed after becoming "Enlightened" in 610, knew that the only purpose of his life was to remind people that they should live in a supporting unity, as does the space that is within them and which is also all around them. Naturally, this is being a space which "The Book" knows to be the "Mother of the Creation", a power that exists to care for the "Present Time", and a time that is also evolving towards Gods targeted future or a future being targeted by Nature for the Non-Believer. For indeed it was the experiencing of

"Enlightenment" in the year 610 which caused Mohammed to know that Gods world cannot be seen or experienced within a mind filled with any "I Want for ME" thoughts. For all thoughts takes the thinker away from observing and from actually experiencing the harmony seeking needs of the "Present Time", which is the stillness of Gods emerging world or the growing world of Nature for the Non-Believer. Therefore it is always good to remember that *Mohammed's* "Jihad", clearly written in the Holy Qur'an, was a struggle to free a person's Soul, this being a freeing which always leads to the experiencing of "Enlightenment". For honestly Mohammed did know that in "Enlightenment" a person does factually experience the knowledge of "Unity", this being with all that which can only be experienced in the "Present Time". Indeed this being the time which is knowingly understood by "The Book", to be cared for by the "Mother of the Creation" and also a "Present Time" which is comfortably understood to be moving into Gods or Nature for the Non-Believer, carefully planned future. For unquestionably the "Enlightened" Mohammed knew that the only enemy of his teaching of a unified "Togetherness", this being "Togetherness" in which a person truly experiences the unity of "Enlightenment", was a person's constant mind filling thoughts of an "I Want for ME", this being because Mohammed knew that this was a selfish sin which always did mind floutingly blocks the Soul from seeing the world of the "Present Time. For truly this "mind floutingly" fact can now be modernly explained to be experienced by a person who "sinfully" misuses their God-given "Freedom of Choice". Naturally, this is being that "Freedom of Choice" which was factually given by God to all people so that they could support the work of the *"Mother of the Creation"."* For indeed all people know that the same act can support or destroy that which is occurring all around them, so the "Choice" of the Soul must be a deciding factor. Of course, this is being a "scientific" factor which is undoubtedly destroyed by a mind clouding "I Want for ME", which is a mind filling and clouding demand that is being created by the ancient animalistic five senses. For certainly now in modern times it can be genuinely understood that *Mohammed's* declared *"jihad against the infidels"* was undoubtedly that which began a spiritual struggle within oneself! This "Jihad" being against the sins being selfishly perpetrated by the "I Want for ME" mind clouding demands that were being created by one or all of the animalistic ally based five senses, this being that which "The Book" says is the real "Jihad."

For it is also undoubtedly true that Mohammed could not accept the surrounding belief systems in which many worshipped more than one God, these being likened to gods of touch, taste, smell, sound or enticing things to hear, for is it not true that *Mohammed,* the last of the ancient prophets, was entering the modern world? For definitely all *Mohammed's* endeavours within his life were devoted to leading humanity back to the pure worshipping of the one God.

For it is undoubtedly true that Mohammed led a sober life based on the most heavenly values, which indeed initiated tremendous changes in Arabia and beyond. For truly it was the condition of "Enlightenment" which authorized *Mohammed* actually to call upon his fellow Meccans, these being those who lived in the most holists of cities, to cease their worship of idols and to affirm the Oneness of a signal God and also to live a life of righteousness and piety, according to that which supporting existed all around them, this being that which can only exist in the "Present Time", which *Mohammed* always emphasised contained equality and justice. Also, is it not known that *Mohammed* warned his listeners of a life that would arise after death, this being an existence in which they would be held accountable for their earthly deeds. And is it not also true that *Mohammed* gave joyful news of a paradise to those who believed and lived a God-conscious life. Which in modern times "The Book" explains to be a re-birth into Gods "Present Time", for indeed is it not now modernly and scientifically understood that the energy unfolding in the "Present Time" cannot be destroyed.

It is also known that *Mohammed's "Freedom for the entire world's religions"* was instituted in Medina; this freedom is that all people were equal under the eyes of God and that woman where to be honoured and respected as equals; racial discrimination was practically eliminated; tribal warfare was replaced with uniting ties of brotherhood; usury and alcohol the harbingers of evil were forbidden entirely. Also, the history around this "Enlightened" one naturally reflected *Mohammed's* readiness to undergo many persecutions for his beliefs, these being belief's that were based upon *Mohammed's* "Self-Aware" experiencing the singularity of the "Creation", thus meaning that which was all around him would be considered to be producing the same support as all that which was within him. For indeed within the life of his private dealings *Mohammed* treated friends and strangers, the rich and poor, the powerful and weak, with equity that was beloved by the ordinary people and which was undoubtedly based upon the warmth with which he received them even when he listened to their complaints.

So yes! Is it not true that in the time of his most significant power *Mohammed* maintained the same simplicity of manners and appearance as he did in the days of his persecution and was uncomfortable when, upon entering a room, if many testimonials of respect were shown to him, these being that which separated him from the unity of that which he knowingly experienced to be always all around him as being the same unity of that which was within him. For certainly does not history show *Mohammed's* readiness to silently undergo persecutions for his belief that all things are unified? Also, is it not true that Mohammed generated a high and personal moral character within the people who believed in him and who also looked up to him as a leader? All of which was based upon fundamental integrity in which Mohammed is now modernly understood to have been "Self-Aware", meaning that he knew that all that he experienced was really himself and so could not put himself forward for destruction as did the "Self-Realised" Jesus who could not disagree with a "Self-Realisation" in which there is no observer but only existence, knowledge and bliss.

Now listen to these words emanating from a "Self-Aware" *Mohammed* who experienced the same unity of all that which was around him to be the same as the unity of that which was within him. For did not Mohammed put forward a covenant to all the people of the newly created Muslim world saying *"Those who adopt Christianity, these being people who are near or far from us, we are with them".* Also stating *"Verily it should, therefore, be known by all people that I, my servants and my helpers, and also all my followers WILL defend them because Christians are also my citizens; and by God, I will hold out against anything that displeases them. So no compulsion is to be placed upon them to change their religion. Neither are their judges to be removed from their jobs nor their monks from their monasteries. No one is to destroy a house of their religion or to damage it, or to carry anything from it to be given to Muslims' houses. Should anyone forcibly take any of these, they would spoil God's covenant and also disobey His Prophet.*

Verily I say unto you, that they are my allies and so have my secure charter against all that they hate. Not one of my followers is to force them to travel or to oblige them to fight, for Muslims are to fight for them and not against them. If a female Christian is to be married to a Muslim, this act is not to take place without her approval. She is also not to be prevented from visiting her church nor told how to pray. These Christian churches that are upon our land are declared to be protected. They are neither to be prevented from repairing them neither is the sacredness of their covenants to be challenged. No one of our nation (All Muslims) *is to disobey this covenant till the Last Day* (end of the world). For truly are these not the faithful words of an "Enlightened" one who died 1,388 years ago? Therefore, is it not undoubtedly true that **Mohammed** was an "Enlightened" person who was "Self-Aware" of the spiritual struggle that can occur within oneself against sin? Which "The Book" explains in the year 2020 language to be an internal "jihad" struggle against the "I Want for ME" world that takes a person to live in the Past or the Future, which "The Book" knows to be Hell? For truly is not Heaven, that which can only exist in the "Present Time", a time which exists without thought and a time which is naturally opposed to any attack originating via an "I Want for ME", this being that which is "animalistic ally" be taken from others!

Thus in the years 610 AD, spoke **Mohammed** the last of the Prophets. Therefore is it not an inevitable truth that understanding this "Knowledge", emanating from all our religions and philosophies, this being an understanding – standing under -   that which leads to "Enlightenment", which is the experiencing of that which can only exist in the "Present Time" and thus experiencing a real-life lived in Gods world of harmony. Naturally, this being an existence which is certainly not a life that is steadily based upon capturing personal "I Want" thoughts, these being that which fill the mind with so many ways of dreamily pursuing and or gaining a personal "I Want" for ME! For indeed, this separating and truly individualized thinking can rule and therefore ruin a person's life. Again it can be said that this is being a life that is ignorantly forced to exist in a personally-made and personally-created world of an "I WANT FOR ME", truly a personally created Hell. Indeed, this is again that particular way of chasing a "false truth", this being that which ALL our wise ancients did explain in so many different ways how to stop and or avoid. For sincerely, this finalizing of "The Book" is not "The End." For "The Book" is to show the way to the beginning of a true-life lived within the Kingdom of God or Nature for the Non-Believer and so steadily support this world that is truly being cared for by the "Mother of the Creation".

So yes! Any purposeful religion or philosophy is factually targeting a way for the one child, this being the creation which exits within us and all around us, to accept the evolving experience of the planned world of it parents who "The Book" names to be the one God who plans the future and the *"Mother of the Creation"* who cares for the "Present Time" – both called Nature by the Non-Believer. For truly within this only child, all life and non-life do simply and obediently exist under the natural and caring laws of its parents, whose parental target, "The Book" says, is to experience the love of their only child. This target is undoubtedly the purpose of all our worlds' religions and philosophies, and it is a target that is continually laid before the highest life force that exists within the one child – this being separately named as people, which is finalized in the entity called "YOU! For certainly the Soul, being that which certainly exists within a person's body, is not your ally for it is YOU! For undoubtedly the above Muslim religion, the last of our many ancient religions are based upon the same truth that supports, via different cultural understandings, ALL the world's religions and philosophies, for certainly all religions and philosophies explain how a person can experience only the "Present Time", this being the "Enlightened" world of the "Heaven" created by the one God and the *"Mother of the Creation"* – both called Nature by the Non-Believer – and not the world of Hell which is an unreal Past or Future, this being a "Hell" that is being personally created by many "animalistic" "I WANT for ME" separating thoughts, which "The Book" says is a sin, this being because it is committed when you think you are separate from all things. For truly a person soul cannot hurt the creation or harm anyone for the Souls purpose is to support the creations "Godness" just has the heart and all bodily parts support the bodies "Goodness".

So Yes! "The Book" is a beginning and so also achieve indeed not an ending, and it is written for those people who seek the experiencing of a life which about ALL our wise ancients spoke. For "The Book" now modernly explains all that needs to be explained. For in faith, is it not said to be accurate, that we often find that it is that which instead of giving advice, solutions, or cures, does choose to share our discomforts and wounds? This being that which is naturally being done with a warm and tender heart which shows a God-filled future life that is experiencing abundance, optimism, and that which we often call luck, this being that which is created by the *"Mother of the Creation"*. For real-life is the un-selfish effort of finalizing towards an unknown end and so the reading the "The Book" to the end, means that you are one of those people who feel happy when they can help people who are in need because there is no "Them or Us" there is only YOU! So YES! For sure the "NOW" time will never end for it is always your *"BEGINNING"* therefore let a real-life now begin for you dear reader has you join with your real "Self" – which is "Everything

."Well, "The Book" is now finished, and I now understand that this is probably the work I was commanded to do when I nearly died in that road accident those 58 years ago. For now, I identify that my life's pursuits had nothing to do with the development of a fair and just economic payment to others? For indeed it seems I misunderstood those words I received when I was "worriedly" going down that white tunnel in which I was earnestly commanded to *"Go Back you have work to do"*.

So maybe now, after the completion of "The Book", I should happily prepare where next to be born for I seek a country which is preparing to unite the world's "Golden Age" culture into one economic market place, this also being a market place that appreciates the natural beliefs, religions and philosophies of all purchasers? But inwardly I believe that the "Mother of the Creation" has already smilingly decided which country and in which area this should be and maybe even who will be my new father and mother – interesting, isn't it? For I assure you, dear reader, that you cannot die but will be born again – for energy cannot end, so choose well when that white tunnel comes to you and do this with a smile for your "Soul" will soon be with a new body.

So YES! Sincerely reading "The Book" is not "The End" for indeed the "NOW" time is never the ending: Therefor let a real-life based upon the now time begin for you dear reader has you activate and so join with your real "Self", which is "everything" you experience in:

NOW IS THE BEGINNING
Which is always the
PRESENT TIME

ABOUT THE AUTHOR

William spent twenty years training UK business executives on how to achieve targets and prosper, he also established several new UK manufacturing sites for PLC companies and 11 years he owned and managed a successful Bradford UK clothing manufacturing company in which he paid all his workers wage born tax stating that all taxes should be paid from the profits of the company and not taken from the wages of is workers. In 1988 the UK economy was in recession, the burgeoning forces of globalization resulted in the loss of his clothing manufacturing factory and his business. With every crisis comes opportunity, William had always been religiously interested in Russia a country that had no religion, and through losing his factory, he was able to accept the invitation from the British Chamber of Commerce to attend a Moscow Joint venture conference. On arrival, he was shaken to see such poverty amongst its starving people and quickly realised that Communism had failed. After a Moscow TV interview in which he stated the many ways needed for economic development in Russia, he was invited back by the Moscow USSR Chamber of Commerce. It was during this second visit that he was asked to give a presentation to a team selected by President Gorbachev to find ways out of the USSR's stagnation and deficit. He presented a lecture in which he persuasively demonstrated that collectivism offered no prosperity to the market place but could only develop further stagnation and ever-larger deficits. The relationships and deep friendships William built with politically correcting and business seeking leaders in Russia lasted over 20 years both in the run-up to and after 1991's "Three days that shook the world". He was invited over 100 times to visit Russia in which he gave presentations which showed scientific ways to free the people to target market value, this being to Russia's regional and city governments in which he suggested that these newly freed "Private" entrepreneurs should be feeding the needs of all people in a new "Market Economy", and also that they should receive 45% of value-added profits engendered by their enterprise, with 55% being claimed has tax to be distributed to the current owners who were the central, regional and local governments, this being that which would always be publically audited – – especially the market developed of all wage payments which are naturally based upon a market evaluation of work which is completed and most importantly to avoid religious or political people who attack or ridicule another religion or government. For this means that they are seeking an animalistic "I Want" a predatory authority over others which does not include the groups' environmental well-being.

Printed in Great Britain
by Amazon

44633610R00348